Handbooks on the History of Religions

THE RELIGIONS OF INDIA

Handbooks on the History of Religions

THE RELIGIONS OF INDIA

BY

EDWARD WASHBURN HOPKINS

PH.D. (LEIPSIC)

GYAN

Published by

GYAN

Gyan Publishing House
5, Ansari Road
Daryaganj, New Delhi-110002
Phone: 011-47034999, 9811692060
E-mail: books@gyanbooks.com

Distribution Network
gyanbooks.com
India, USA, Canada, UK, Australia, France

ISBN : 978-81-212-1262-5 (PB)
First Published, 1895

2nd Impression 2021

Printed at: Gyan Press, Delhi.

The Religions of India
Author: Edward Washburn Hopkins

Handbooks on the History of Religions

THE RELIGIONS OF INDIA

BY

EDWARD WASHBURN HOPKINS
PH.D. (LEIPSIC)

PROFESSOR OF SANSKRIT AND COMPARATIVE PHILOLOGY IN
BRYN MAWR COLLEGE

"This holy mystery I declare unto you:
There is nothing nobler than humanity."

THE MAHĀBHĀRATA.

BOSTON, U.S.A., AND LONDON
GINN & COMPANY, PUBLISHERS
1895

TO THE MEMORY OF

William Dwight Whitney

THIS VOLUME

IS AFFECTIONATELY DEDICATED

BY THE AUTHOR

PREFATORY NOTE

BY THE EDITOR.

THE growing interest both in this country and abroad in the historical study of religions is one of the noticeable features in the intellectual phases of the past decades. The more general indications of this interest may be seen in such foundations as the Hibbert and Gifford Lectureships in England, and the recent organization of an American committee to arrange in various cities for lectures on the history of religions, in the establishment of a special department for the subject at the University of Paris, in the organization of the Musée Guimet at Paris, in the publication of a journal — the *Revue de l'Histoire des Religions* — under the auspices of this Museum, and in the creation of chairs at the Collège de France, at the Universities of Holland, and in this country at Cornell University and the University of Chicago,[1] with the prospect of others to follow in the near future. For the more special indications we must turn to the splendid labors of a large array of scholars toiling in the various departments of ancient culture — India, Babylonia, Assyria, Egypt, Palestine, Arabia, Phoenicia, China, Greece, and Rome — with the result of securing a firm basis for the study of the religions flourishing in those countries —

[1] In an article by the writer published in the *Biblical World* (University of Chicago Press) for January, 1893, there will be found an account of the present status of the Historical Study of Religions in this country.

a result due mainly to the discovery of fresh sources and to the increase of the latter brought about by exploration and incessant research. The detailed study of the facts of religion everywhere, both in primitive society and in advancing civilization, and the emphasis laid upon gathering and understanding these facts prior to making one's deductions, has succeeded in setting aside the speculations and generalizations that until the beginning of this century paraded under the name of "Philosophy of Religion."

Such has been the scholarly activity displayed and the fertility resulting, that it seems both desirable and timely to focus, as it were, the array of facts connected with the religions of the ancient world in such a manner that the summary resulting may serve as the point of departure for further investigations.

This has been the leading thought which has suggested the series of Handbooks on the History of Religions. The treatment of the religions included in the series differs from previous attempts in the aim to bring together the ascertained results of scholarship rather than to make an additional contribution, though the character of the scholars whose coöperation has been secured justifies the hope that their productions will also mark an advance in the interpretation of the subject assigned to each. In accord with this general aim, mere discussion has been limited to a minimum, while the chief stress has been laid upon the clear and full presentation of the data connected with each religion.

A uniform plan has been drawn up by the editor for the order of treatment in the various volumes, by following which it is hoped that the continuous character of the series will be secured. In this plan the needs of the general reader, as well as those of the student, for whom, in the first place, the series is designed, have been kept in view. After the introduction, which in the case of each volume is to be devoted to a setting forth of the sources and the method of study, a chapter follows on the land and the people, presenting those ethnographical and geographical considerations, together with a brief historical sketch of the people in question, so essential to an understanding of intellectual and religious life everywhere.

In the third section, which may be denominated the kernel of the book, the subdivisions and order of presentation necessarily vary, the division into periods being best adapted to one religion, the geographical order for another, the grouping of themes in a logical sequence for a third; but in every case, the range covered will be the same, namely, the beliefs, including the pantheon, the relation to the gods, views of life and death, the rites — both the official ones and the popular customs — the religious literature and architecture. A fourth section will furnish a general estimate of the religion, its history, and the relation it bears to others. Each volume will conclude with a full bibliography, index, and necessary maps, with illustrations introduced into the text as called for. The Editor has been fortunate in securing the services of distinguished specialists whose past labors and thorough understanding of the plan and purpose of the series furnish a guarantee for the successful execution of their task.

It is the hope of the Editor to produce in this way a series of manuals that may serve as text-books for the historical study of religions in our universities and seminaries. In addition to supplying this want, the arrangement of the manuals will, it is expected, meet the requirements of reliable reference-books for ascertaining the present status of our knowledge of the religions of antiquity, while the popular manner of presentation, which it will be the aim of the writers to carry out, justifies the hope that the general reader will find the volumes no less attractive and interesting.

UNIVERSITY OF PENNSYLVANIA.

PREFACE.

IT has been said somewhere by Lowell that "an illustration is worth more than any amount of discourse," and, if we were asked to specify in which regard we thought that this manual, when compared with the only other book that covers the same ground, was likely to be useful, we should reply that, whereas Barth in his admirable handbook (the outgrowth of an article in the *Encyclopédie des Sciences Religieuses*) aimed at making his reader know all about the religions of India, we have sought to make our reader know those religions. We have tried to show the lines on which developed the various theological and moral conceptions of the Hindus, not only by furnishing, from the point of view of a foreign critic, an annotated narrative of the growth of these conceptions, but also and chiefly by taking the reader step by step through the literature that contains the records of India's dogmas. The scheme of Barth's Religions excludes all illustrative matter. His reader must take as authoritative the word of some modern scholar, or he must look up for himself the texts to which occasional reference is made. By omitting all quotations the author was enabled, in the compass of a small volume, to give an account, extraordinarily compact and complete, of every ramification of Hindu belief, and his book deserves all the praise that it has won. It is invaluable as exegesis. But it presents the religions of India as Bernhardy exhibits the literature of Greece, or as the daylight lecturer describes invisible stars. If one desire to orient himself in respect of any point of the Hindu creeds, if he wish a reliable sketch of those creeds, he will obtain from Barth the information he is seeking, and find a survey not only traced in detail, but at the same time discussed in so masterly a way as to make superfluous for long any new *résumé* of the sort, withal despite the fact that in some regards Barth's views have become obnoxious to later criticism. But it is not to criticise Barth that this book was written. It is to reveal the religions of India by causing them to reveal themselves, and to elucidate them by commenting on them as they appear before the reader, traverse his field of vision, and finally leave his sight. We admit that it behooves whoever writes under the same title with that of the French savant, to show cause why he does so; but we think that to open up the religions of India from within, and in orderly succession to explain them as they display themselves, will not be otiose if there be any students ignorant of Sanskrit who yet desire independently to examine and to make their own the very words of the Hindu sages.

In accordance with this plan of teaching Hindu religions we have been more prone to ignore than to collect such results of modern scholarship as tend to blur the picture we would show. For a first view of Greek theology Homer is more useful than Preller, and the same is true elsewhere. Above all, as we have said in the Introduction, in regard to many a recent 'interpretation' of Hindu deities, we are content to be conservative. We doubt the historical value of most of these expositions, and, since we are not of those scholars that try to keep abreast of the times by swallowing every new idea, we have not been inclined to broach unsatisfactory theories without a good deal of provocation, which existed for us only in the case of one or two Vedic divinities, where the religious significance of new interpretations compelled attention.

In regard to the great length at which we have reviewed the gods of the earlier period, we have not forgotten what difference exists between mythology and religion, but we believe that the reader will see, before he gets to the end of the book, that such amplitude of treatment as we have permitted ourselves was not alien to our proper subject-matter.

We scarcely can hope that the professional Indologian will see much that is valuable to him in this work, which is intended only for students, although we think that our view of the relation of Vedic belief to that of the 'primitive Aryans' is one that some scholars of the day might substitute with advantage for their own. But our more especial field of investigation has lain along the lines marked by the two chapters on Hinduism, and these such Sanskrit scholars as have not made particular study of the Hindu epic perhaps may find to be readable.

Although we have quoted Hindu works more often than we have referred to those of European scholars, yet have we endeavored to make the notes sufficiently copious to put the reader *au courant* with the most important studies of the present time.

As to the method of writing Sanskrit words, being unable to adopt the unpleasant characters of the Sacred Books, and knowing no other system that is satisfactory both to English eye and to linguistic sense, we have employed the simplest transcription, ignoring, in fact, all linguals save the sibilant, which alone can be rendered by English letters, and which usage has long made familiar.

E. W. H.

BRYN MAWR, PENNA., *July, 1894.*

CONTENTS.

Chapter		Page
I.	Introduction	1
II.	People and Land	26
III.	The Rig Veda.—The Upper Gods	37
IV.	The Rig Veda (continued).—The Middle Gods	87
V.	The Rig Veda (continued).—The Lower Gods	105
VI.	The Rig Veda (concluded).—Yama and Other Gods, Vedic Pantheism, Eschatology	127
VII.	The Religion of the Atharva Veda	151
VIII.	Early Hindu Divinities Compared with Those of Other Aryans	161
IX.	Brahmanism	176
X.	Brahmanic Pantheism.—The Upanishads	216
XI.	The Popular Brahmanic Faith	242
XII.	Jainism	280
XIII.	Buddhism	298
XIV.	Early Hinduism	348
XV.	Hinduism (continued).—Vishnu and Çiva	388
XVI.	The Purānas.—Early Sects, Festivals, the Trinity	434
XVII.	Modern Hindu Sects	472
XVIII.	Religious Traits of the Wild Tribes	524
XIX.	India and the West	542
	Addenda	572
	Bibliography	573

ABBREVIATIONS.

AIL.	Zimmer's Altindisches Leben.
AMG.	Annales du Musée Guimet.
AJP.	American Journal of Philology.
AR.	Asiatick Researches.
ASL.	Müller's Ancient Sanskrit Literature.
BB.	Bezzenberger's Beiträge.
BOR.	Babylonian and Oriental Record.
IA.	Indian Antiquary.
IF.	Indogermanische Forschungen.
IS.	Weber's Indische Studien.
JA.	Journal Asiatique.
JAOS.	Journal of the American Oriental Society.
JRAS. . . .	Journal of the Royal Asiatic Society.
KZ.	Kuhn's Zeitschrift für vergleichende Sprachforschung.
OLS.	Whitney's Oriental and Linguistic Studies.
OO.	Benfey's Orient und Occident.
OST.	Muir's Original Sanskrit Texts.
PAOS. . . .	Proceedings of the American Oriental Society.
SBE.	Sacred Books of the East.
WZKM. . . .	Wiener Zeitschrift für die Kunde des Morgenlandes.
VS.	Pischel's and Geldner's Vedische Studien.
ZDA.	Haupt's Zeitschrift für Deutsches Alterthum.
ZDMG. . . .	Zeitschrift der Deutschen Morgenländischen Gesellschaft.

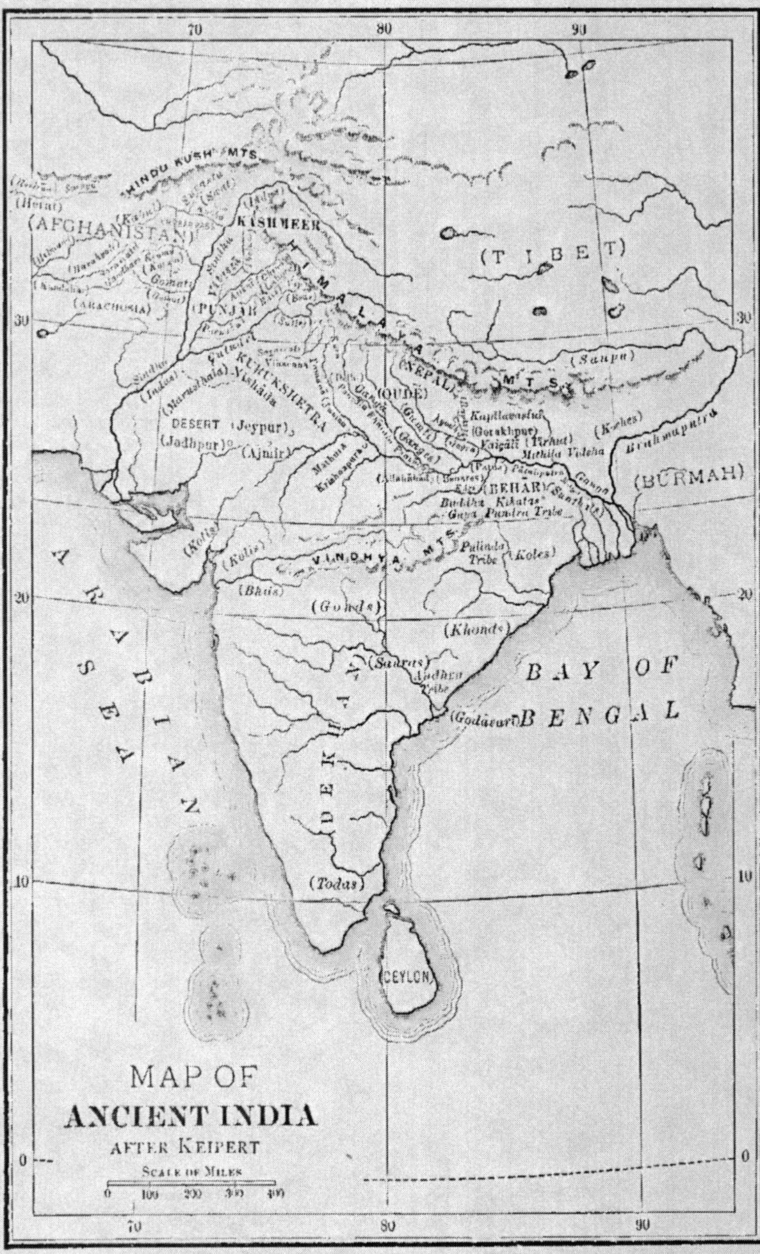

MAP OF
ANCIENT INDIA
AFTER KEIPERT

THE RELIGIONS OF INDIA.

CHAPTER I.—INTRODUCTION.

SOURCES.—DATES.—METHODS OF INTERPRETATION.—DIVISIONS OF SUBJECT.

SOURCES.

INDIA always has been a land of religions. In the earliest Vedic literature are found not only hymns in praise of the accepted gods, but also doubts in regard to the worth of these gods; the beginnings of a new religion incorporated into the earliest records of the old. And later, when, about 300 B.C., Megasthenes was in India, the descendants of those first theosophists are still discussing, albeit in more modern fashion, the questions that lie at the root of all religion. "Of the philosophers, those that are most estimable he terms Brahmans (*βραχμᾶνας*). These discuss with many words concerning death. For they regard death as being, for the wise, a birth into real life—into the happy life. And in many things they hold the same opinions with the Greeks: saying that the universe was begotten and will be destroyed, and that the world is a sphere, which the god who made and owns it pervades throughout; that there are different beginnings of all things, but water is the beginning of world-making, while, in addition to the four elements, there is, as fifth, a kind of nature, whence came the sky and the stars. . . . And concerning the seed of things and the soul they have much to say also, whereby they weave in myths, just as does Plato, in regard to the soul's immortality, judgment in hell, and such things."[1]

And as India conspicuously is a country of creeds, so is its literature preëminently priestly and religious. From the first Veda to the last Purāna, religion forms either the subject-matter of the most important works, or, as in the case of the epics,[2] the basis of didactic excursions and sectarian interpolations, which impart to worldly themes a tone peculiarly theological. History and oratory are unknown in Indian literature. The early poetry consists of hymns and religious poems; the early prose, of liturgies, linguistics, "law," theology, sacred legends and other works, all of which are intended to supplement the knowledge of the Veda, to explain ceremonies, or to inculcate religious principles. At a later date, formal grammar and systems of philosophy, fables and commentaries are added to the prose; epics, secular lyric, drama, the Purānas and such writings to the poetry. But in all this great mass, till that time which Müller has called the Renaissance—that is to say, till after the Hindus were come into close contact with foreign nations, notably the Greek, from which has been borrowed, perhaps, the classical Hindu drama,[3]—there is no real literature that was not religious originally, or, at least, so apt for priestly use as to become chiefly moral and theosophic; while the most popular works of modern times are sectarian tracts, Purānas, Tantras and remodelled worldly poetry. The sources, then, from which is to be drawn the knowledge of Hindu religions are the best possible—the original texts. The infor-

[1] Megasthenes, Fr. XLI, ed. Schwanbeck.

[2] Epic literature springs from lower castes than that of the priest, but it has been worked over by sacerdotal revisers till there is more theology than epic poetry in it.

[3] See Weber, *Sanskrit Literature*, p. 224; Windisch, *Greek Influence on Indian Drama:* and Lévi, *Le théâtre indien*. The date of the Renaissance is given as "from the first century B.C. to at least the third century A.D." (*India*, p. 281). Extant Hindu drama dates only from the fifth century A.D. We exclude, of course, from "real literature" all technical hand-books and commentaries.

mation furnished by foreigners, from the times of Ktesias and Megasthenes to that of Mandelslo, is considerable; but one is warranted in assuming that what little in it is novel is inaccurate, since otherwise the information would have been furnished by the Hindus themselves; and that, conversely, an outsider's statements, although presumably correct, often may give an inexact impression through lack of completeness; as when—to take an example that one can control—Ktesias tells half the truth in regard to ordeals. His account is true, but he gives no notion of the number or elaborate character of these interesting ceremonies.

The sources to which we shall have occasion to refer will be, then, the two most important collections of Vedic hymns—the Rig Veda and the Atharva Veda; the Brahmanic literature, with the supplementary Upanishads, and the Sūtras or mnemonic abridgments of religious and ceremonial rules; the legal texts, and the religious and theological portions of the epic: and the later sectarian writings, called Purānas. The great heresies, again, have their own special writings. Thus far we shall draw on the native literature. Only for some of the modern sects, and for the religions of the wild tribes which have no literature, shall we have to depend on the accounts of European writers.

DATES.

For none of the native religious works has one a certain date. Nor is there for any one of the earlier compositions the certainty that it belongs, as a whole, to any one time. The Rig Veda was composed by successive generations; the Atharvan represents different ages; each Brāhmana appears to belong in part to one era, in part to another; the earliest Sūtras (manuals of law, etc.) have been interpolated; the earliest metrical code is a composite; the great epic is the work of centuries; and not only do the Upanishads and Purānas represent collectively many different periods, but exactly to which period each individually is to be assigned remains always doubtful. Only in the case of the Buddhistic writings is there a satisfactorily approximate terminus a quo, and even here approximate means merely within the limit of centuries.

Nevertheless, criteria fortunately are not lacking to enable one to assign the general bulk of any one work to a certain period in the literary development; and as these periods are, if not sharply, yet plainly distinguishable, one is not in so desperate a case as he might have expected to be, considering that it is impossible to date with certainty any Hindu book or writer before the Christian era. For, first, there exists a difference in language, demarcating the most important periods; and, secondly, the development of the literature has been upon such lines that it is easy to say, from content and method of treatment, whether a given class of writings is a product of the Vedic, early Brahmanic, or late Brahmanic epochs. Usually, indeed, one is unable to tell whether a later Upanishad was made first in the early or late Brahmanic period, but it is known that the Upanishads, as a whole, *i.e.*, the literary form and philosophical material which characterize Upanishads, were earlier than the latest Brahmanic period and subsequent to the early Brahmanic period; that they arose at the close of the latter and before the rise of the former. So the Brāhmanas, as a whole, are subsequent to the Vedic age, although some of the Vedic hymns appear to have been made up in the same period with that of the early Brāhmanas. Again, the Purānas can be placed with safety after the late Brahmanic age; and, consequently, subsequent to the Upanishads, although it is probable that many Upanishads were written after the first Purānas. The general compass of this enormous literature is from an indefinite antiquity to about 1500 A.D. A liberal margin of possible error must be allowed in the assumption of any specific dates. The received opinion is that the Rig Veda goes back to about 2000 B.C., yet are some scholars inclined rather to accept 3000 B.C. as the time that represents this era. Weber, in his *Lectures on Sanskrit Literature* (p. 7), rightly says that to seek for an exact date is fruitless labor; while Whitney compares Hindu dates to ninepins—set up only to be bowled down again. Schroeder, in his *Indiens Literatur und Cultur*, suggests that the prior limit may be "a few centuries earlier than 1500," agreeing with Weber's preferred reckoning; but Whitney, Grassmann, and Benfey provisionally assume 2000 B.C. as the starting point of Hindu literature. The lowest possible limit for this event Müller now places at about 1500, which is recognized as a very cautious view; most scholars thinking that Müller's estimate gives too little time for the development of the literary periods, which, in their opinion, require, linguistically and otherwise, a greater number of years. Brunnhofer more recently has suggested 2800 B.C. as the terminus; while the last writers on the subject (Tilak and Jacobi) claim to have discovered that the period from 3500 to 2500 represents the Vedic age. Their conclusions, however, are not very convincing, and have been disputed vigorously.[1] Without the hope of persuading such scholars as are wedded to a terminus of three or four thousand years ago that we are right, we add, in all deference to others, our own opinion on this vexed question. Buddhism gives the first semblance of a date in Hindu literature. Buddha lived in the sixth century, and died probably about 480, possibly (Westergaard's extreme opinion) as late as 368.[2] Before this time arise the Sūtras, back of which lie the earliest Upanishads, the bulk of the Brāhmanas, and all the Vedic poems. Now it is probable that the Brahmanic literature itself extends to the

1 Jacobi, in Roth's *Festgruss*, pp. 72, 73 (1893); Whitney, *Proceed. A. O. S.*, 1894, p. lxxxii; Perry, *Pūshan*, in the *Drisler Memorial;* Weber, *Vedische Beiträge*.

2 Westergaard, *Ueber Buddha's Todesjahr.* The prevalent opinion is that Buddha died in 477 or 480 B.C.

time of Buddha and perhaps beyond it. For the rest of pre-Buddhistic literature it seems to us incredible that it is necessary to require, either from the point of view of linguistic or of social and religious development, the enormous period of two thousand years. There are no other grounds on which to base a reckoning except those of Jacobi and his Hindu rival, who build on Vedic data results that hardly support the superstructure they have erected. Jacobi's starting-point is from a mock-serious hymn, which appears to be late and does not establish, to whatever date it be assigned, the point of departure from which proceeds his whole argument, as Whitney has shown very well. One is driven back to the needs of a literature in-respect of time sufficient for it to mature. What changes take place in language, even with a written literature, in the space of a few centuries, may be seen in Persian, Greek, Latin, and German. No two thousand years are required to bridge the linguistic extremes of the Vedic and classical Sanskrit language.[1] But in content it will be seen that the flower of the later literature is budding already in the Vedic age. We are unable to admit that either in language or social development, or in literary or religious growth, more than a few centuries are necessary to account for the whole development of Hindu literature (meaning thereby compositions, whether written or not) up to the time of Buddha. Moreover, if one compare the period at which arise the earliest forms of literature among other Aryan peoples, it will seem very strange that, whereas in the case of the Romans, Greeks, and Persians, one thousand years B.C. is the extreme limit of such literary activity as has produced durable works, the Hindus two or three thousand years B.C. were creating

[1] It must not be forgotten in estimating the *broad* mass of Brāhmanas and Sūtras that each as a school represents almost the whole length of its period, and hence one school alone should measure the time from end to end, which reduces to very moderate dimensions the literature to be accounted for in time.

poetry so finished, so refined, and, from a metaphysical point of view, so advanced as is that of the Rig Veda. If, as is generally assumed, the (prospective) Hindus and Persians were last to leave the common Aryan habitat, and came together to the south-east, the difficulty is increased; especially in the light of modern opinion in regard to the fictitious antiquity of Persian (Iranian) literature. For if Darmesteter be correct in holding the time of the latter to be at most a century before our era, the incongruity between that oldest date of Persian literature and the "two or three thousand years before Christ," which are claimed in the case of the Rig Veda, becomes so great as to make the latter assumption more dubious than ever.

We think in a word, without wishing to be dogmatic, that the date of the Rig Veda is about on a par, historically, with that of 'Homer,' that is to say, the Collection[1] represents a long period, which was completed perhaps two hundred years after 1000 B.C., while again its earliest beginnings precede that date possibly by five centuries; but we would assign the bulk of the Rig Veda to about 1000 B.C. With conscious imitation of older speech a good deal of archaic linguistic effect doubtless was produced by the latest poets, who really belong to the Brahmanic age. The Brahmanic age in turn ends, as we opine, about 500 B.C., overlapping the Sūtra period as well as that of the first Upanishads. The former class of writings (after 500 B.C. one may talk of writings) is represented by dates that reach from circa 600–500 B.C. nearly to our era. Buddhism's *floruit* is from 500 B.C. to 500 A.D., and epic Hinduism covers nearly the same centuries. From 500 to 1000 Buddhism is in a state of decadence; and through this time extend the dramatic and older Puranic writings; while other

[1] '*Rig Veda Collection*' is the native name for that which in the Occident is called Rig Veda, the latter term embracing, to the Hindu, all the works (Brāhmanas, Sūtras, etc.) that go to explain the 'Collection' (of hymns).

Purānas are as late as 1500, at which time arises the great modern reforming sect of the Sikhs. In the matter of the earlier termini a century may be added or subtracted here and there, but these convenient divisions of five hundreds will be found on the whole to be sufficiently accurate.[1]

METHODS OF INTERPRETATION.

At the outset of his undertaking a double problem presents itself to one that would give, even in compact form, a view of Hindu religions. This problem consists in explaining, and, in so far as is possible, reconciling opposed opinions in regard not only to the nature of these religions but also to the method of interpreting the Vedic hymns.

That the Vedic religion was naturalistic and mytho-poetic is doubted by few. The Vedic hymns laud the powers of nature and natural phenomena as personified gods, or even as impersonal phenomena. They praise also as distinct powers the departed fathers. In the Rig Vedâ I. 168, occur some verses in honor of the storm-gods called Maruts: "Self-yoked are they come lightly from the sky. The immortals urge themselves on with the goad. Dustless, born of power, with shining spears the Maruts overthrow the strongholds. Who is it, O Maruts, ye that have lightning-spears, that impels you within? . . . The streams roar from the tires, when they send out their cloud-voices," etc. Nothing would seem more justifiable, in view of this hymn and of many like it, than to assume with Müller and other Indologians, that the Marut-gods are personifications of natural phenomena. As clearly do Indra and the Dawn appear to be natural phenomena. But no less an authority than Herbert Spencer has attacked this view: "Facts imply that

[1] Schroeder, *Indiens Literatur und Cultur*, p. 291, gives: Rig-Veda, 2000–1000 B.C.; older Brāhmanas, 1000–800; later Brāhmanas and Upanishads, 800–600; Sūtras, 600–400 or 300.

the conception of the dawn as a person results from the giving of dawn as a birth-name." [1] And again: "If, then, Dawn [in New Zealand and elsewhere] is an actual name for a person, if where there prevails this mode of distinguishing children, it has probably often been given to those born early in the morning; the traditions concerning one of such who became noted, would, in the mind of the uncritical savage . . . lead to identification with the dawn." [2] In another passage: "The primitive god is the superior man . . . propitiated during his life and still more after his death." [3] Summing up, Spencer thus concludes: "Instead of seeing in the common character of so-called myths, that they describe combats of beings using weapons, evidence that they arose out of human transactions; mythologists assume that the order of Nature presents itself to the undeveloped mind in terms of victories and defeats." [4] Moreover (*a posteriori*), "It is not true that the primitive man looks at the powers of Nature with awe. It is not true that he speculates about their characters and causes." [5] If Spencer had not included in his criticism the mythologists that have written on Vedic religion, there would be no occasion to take his opinion into consideration. But since he claims by the light of his comparative studies to have shown that in the Rig Veda the "so-called nature gods," [6] were not the oldest, and explains Dawn here exactly as he does in New Zealand, it becomes necessary to point out, that apart from the question of the origin of religions in general, Spencer has made a fatal error in assuming that he is dealing in the Rig Veda with primitive religion, uncritical savages, and undeveloped minds. And furthermore, as the poet of the Rig Veda is not primitive, or savage, or undeveloped, so when he worships *Dyaus pitar* (Ζεὺς πατήρ) as the 'sky-father,' he not only makes it evident

[1] *Principles of Sociology*, I. p. 448 (Appleton, 1882).
[2] Ib. p. 398. [3] Ib. p. 427. [4] Ib. p. 824.
[5] Ib. [6] Ib. p. 821.

to every reader that he really is worshipping the visible sky above; but in his descriptions of gods such as Indra, the Dawn, and some other new gods he invents from time to time, long after he has passed the savage, primitive, and undeveloped state, he makes it no less clear that he worships phenomena as they stand before him (rain, cloud, lightning, etc.), so that by analogy with what is apparent in the case of later divinities, one is led inevitably to predicate the same origin as theirs in the case of the older gods.

But it is unnecessary to spend time on this point. It is impossible for any sober scholar to read the Rig Veda and believe that the Vedic poets are not worshipping natural phenomena; or that the phenomena so worshipped were not the original forms of these gods. Whether at a more remote time there was ever a period when the pre-historic Hindu, or his pre-Indic ancestor, worshipped the Manes exclusively is another question, and one with which at present we have nothing to do. The history of Hindu religions begins with the Rig Veda, and in this period the worship of Manes and that of natural phenomena were distinct, nor are there any indications that the latter was ever developed from the former. It is not denied that the Hindus made gods of departed men. They did this long after the Vedic period. But there is no proof that all the Vedic gods, as claims Spencer, were the worshipped souls of the dead. No *argumentum a fcro* can show in a Vedic dawn-hymn anything other than a hymn to personified Dawn, or make it probable that this dawn was ever a mortal's name.

In respect of that which precedes all tradition we, whose task is not to speculate in regard to primitive religious conceptions, but to give the history of one people's religious progress, may be pardoned for expressing no opinion. But without abandoning history (*i.e.*, tradition) we would revert for a moment to the pre-Indian period and point out that Zarathustra's rejection of the *daevas*, which must be the same *devas* that are worshipped in India, proves that *deva*-worship is the immediate predecessor of the Hindu religion. As far back as one can scrutinize the Aryan past he finds, as the earliest known objects of reverence, 'sun' and 'sky,' besides and beside the blessed Manes. A word here regarding the priority of monotheism or of polytheism. The tradition is in favor of the latter, while on *a priori* grounds whoever thinks that the more primitive the race the more apt it is for monotheism will postulate, with some of the older scholars, an assumed monotheism as the pre-historic religion of the Hindus; while whosoever opines that man has gradually risen from a less intellectual stage will see in the early gods of the Hindus only another illustration of one universal fact, and posit even Aryan polytheism as an advance on the religion which it is probable that the remoter ancestors of the Aryans once acknowledged.

A word perhaps should be said, also, in order to a better understanding between the ethnologists as represented by Andrew Lang, and the unfortunate philologists whom it delights him to pommel. Lang's clever attacks on the mythmakers, whom he persistently describes as the philologists — and they do indeed form part of that camp — have had the effect of bringing 'philological theories' into sad disrepute with sciolists and 'common-sense' people. But the sun-myths and dawn-myths that the myth-makers discover in Cinderella and Red Riding Hood, ought not to be fathered upon all philologists. On the other hand. who will deny that in India certain mythological figures are eoian or solar in origin? Can any one question that Vivasvant the 'wide gleaming' is sun or bright sky, as he is represented in the Avesta and Rig Veda? Yet is a very anthropomorphic, nay, earthly figure, made out of this god. Or is Mr. Lang ignorant that the god Yima became Jemshid, and that Feridun is only the god Trita? It undoubtedly is correct to illuminate the past with other light than that of sun or dawn, yet that these lights have shone and have been quenched in certain personalities may be granted without doing violence to scientific principles. All purely etymological mythology is precarious, but one may recognize sun-myths without building a system on the basis of a Dawn-Helen, and without referring Ilium to the Vedic *bila*. Again, myths about gods, heroes, and fairies are to be segregated. Even in India, which teems with it, there is little, if any, folk-lore that can be traced to solar or dawn-born myths. Mr. Lang represents a healthy reaction against too much sun-myth, but we think that there are sun-myths still, and that despite his protests all religion is not grown from one seed.

There remains the consideration of the second part of the double problem which was formulated above — the method of interpretation. The native method is to believe the scholiasts' explanations, which often are fanciful and, in all important points, totally unreliable; since the Hindu commentators lived so long after the period of the literature they expound that the tradition they follow is useful only in petty details. From a modern point of view the question of interpretation depends mainly on whether one regard the Rig Veda as but an Indic growth, the product of the Hindu mind alone, or as a work that still retains from an older age ideas which, having once been common to Hindu and Iranian, should be compared with those in the Persian Avesta and be illustrated by them. Again, if this latter hypothesis be correct, how is one to interpret an apparent likeness, here and there, between Indic and foreign notions, — is it possible that the hymns were composed, in part, before the advent of the authors into India, and is it for this reason that in the Rig Veda are contained certain names, ideas, and legends, which do not seem to be native to India? On the other hand, if one adopt the theory that the Rig Veda is wholly a native work, in how far is he to suppose that it is separable from Brahmanic formalism? Were the hymns made independently of any ritual, as their own excuse for being, or were they composed expressly for the sacrifice, as part of a formal cult?

Here are views diverse enough, but each has its advocate or advocates. According to the earlier European writers the Vedic poets are fountains of primitive thought, streams unsullied by any tributaries, and in reading them one quaffs a fresh draught, the gush of unsophisticated herdsmen, in whose religion there is to be seen a childlike belief in natural phenomena as divine forces, over which forces stands the Heaven-god as the highest power. So in 1869 Pfleiderer speaks of the "primeval childlike naïve prayer" of Rig Veda vi. 51. 5 ("Father sky, mother earth," etc.);[1] while Pictet, in his work *Les Origines Indo-Européennes*, maintains that the Aryans had a primitive monotheism, although it was vague and rudimentary; for he regards both Iranian dualism and Hindu polytheism as being developments of one earlier monism (claiming that Iranian dualism is really monotheistic). Pictet's argument is that the human mind must have advanced from the simple to the complex! Even Roth believes in an originally "supreme deity" of the Aryans.[2] Opposed to this, the 'naïve' school of such older scholars as Roth, Müller,[3] and Grassmann, who see in the Rig Veda an ingenuous expression of 'primitive' ideas, stand the theories of Bergaigne, who interprets everything allegorically; and of Pischel and Geldner, realists, whose general opinions may thus be formulated: The poets of the Rig Veda are not childlike and naïve; they represent a comparatively late period of culture, a society not only civilized, but even sophisticated; a mode of thought philosophical and scep-

1 Compare Muir, *Original Sanskrit Texts*, V. p. 412 ff., where are given the opinions of Pfleiderer, Pictet, Roth, Scherer, and others.

2 ZDMG., vi. 77: "Ein alter gemeinsam arischer [indo-iranic], ja vielleicht gemeinsam indo-germanischer oberster Gott, Varuna-Ormuzd-Uranos."

3 In his *Science of Language*, Müller speaks of the early poets who "strove in their childish way to pierce beyond the limits of this finite world." Approvingly cited, SBE. xxxii. p. 243 (1891).

tical; a religion not only ceremonious but absolutely stereotyped. In regard to the Aryanhood of the hymns, the stand taken by these latter critics, who renounce even Bergaigne's slight hold on mythology, is that the Rig Veda is thoroughly Indic. It is to be explained by the light of the formal Hindu ritualism, and even by epic worldliness, its fresh factors being lewd gods, harlots, and race-horses. Bloomfield, who does not go so far as this, claims that the 'Vedic' age really is a Brahmanic age; that Vedic religion is saturated with Brahmanic ideas and Brahmanic formalism, so that the Rig Veda ought to be looked upon as made for the ritual, not the ritual regarded as ancillary to the Rig Veda.[1] This scholar maintains that there is scarcely any chronological distinction between the hymns of the Rig Veda and the Brāhmana, both forms having probably existed together "from earliest times"; and that not a single Vedic hymn "was ever composed without reference to ritual application"; nay, all the hymns were "liturgical from the very start."[2] This is a plain advance even on Bergaigne's opinion, who finally regarded all the family-books of the Rig Veda as composed to subserve the *soma*-cult.[3]

In the Rig Veda occur hymns of an entirely worldly character, the lament of a gambler, a humorous description of frogs croaking like priests, a funny picture of contemporary morals (describing how every one lusts after wealth), and so forth. From these alone it becomes evident that the ritualistic view must be regarded as one somewhat exaggerated. But if the liturgical extremist appears to have stepped a little beyond the boundary of probability, he yet in daring remains far

[1] The older view may be seen in Müller's *Lecture on the Vedas* (Chips, I. p. 9): "A collection made for its own sake, and not for the sake of any sacrificial performance." For Pischel's view, compare *Vedische Studien*, I. Preface.

[2] Bloomfield, JAOS., xv. p. 144.

[3] Compare Barth (Preface): "A literature preëminently sacerdotal.... The poetry ... of a singularly refined character, ... full of ... pretensions to mysticism," etc.

behind Bergaigne's disciple Regnaud, who has a mystical 'system,' which is, indeed, the outcome of Bergaigne's great work, though it is very improbable that the latter would have looked with favor upon his follower's results. In *Le Rig Veda* (Paris, 1892) Paul Regnaud, emphasizing again the connection between the liturgy and the hymns, refers every word of the Rig Veda to the sacrifice in its simplest form, the oblation. According to this author the Hindus had forgotten the meaning of their commonest words, or consistently employed them in their hymns in a meaning different to that in ordinary use. The very word for god, *deva* (deus), no longer means the 'shining one' (the god), but the 'burning oblation'; the common word for mountain, *giri*, also means oblation, and so on. This is Bergaigne's allegorical mysticism run mad.

At such perversion of reasonable criticism is the exegesis of the Veda arrived in one direction. But in another it is gone astray no less, as misdirected by its clever German leader. In three volumes[1] Brunnhofer has endeavored to prove that far from being a Brahmanic product, the Rig Veda is not even the work of Hindus; that it was composed near the Caspian Sea long before the Aryans descended into India. Brunnhofer's books are a mine of ingenious conjectures, as suggestive in detail as on the whole they are unconvincing. His fundamental error is the fancy that names and ideas which might be Iranian or Turanian would prove, if such they really could be shown to be, that the work in which they are contained must be Iranian or Turanian. He relies in great measure on passages that always have been thought to be late, either whole late hymns or tags added to old hymns, and on the most daring changes in the text, changes which he makes in order to prove his hypothesis, although there is no necessity for making them. The truth that underlies Brunnhofer's extrava-

[1] *Iran und Turan*, 1889; *Vom Pontus bis zum Indus*, 1890; *Vom Aral bis zur Gangā*, 1892.

gance is that there are foreign names in the Rig Veda, and this is all that he has proved thus far.

In regard to the relation between the Veda and the Avesta the difference of views is too individual to have formed systems of interpretation on that basis alone. Every competent scholar recognizes a close affinity between the Iranian Yima and the Hindu Yama, between the *soma*-cult and the *haoma*-cult, but in how far the thoughts and forms that have clustered about one development are to be compared with those of the other there is no general agreement and there can be none. The usual practice, however, is to call the Iranian *Yima*, *haoma*, etc., to one's aid if they subserve one's own view of *Yama*, *soma*, and other Hindu parallels, and to discard analogous features as an independent growth if they do not. This procedure is based as well on the conditions of the problem as on the conditions of human judgment, and must not be criticized too severely; for in fact the two religions here and there touch each other so nearly that to deny a relation between them is impossible, while in detail they diverge so widely that it is always questionable whether a coincidence of ritual or belief be accidental or imply historical connection.

It is scarcely advisable in a concise review of several religions to enter upon detailed criticism of the methods of interpretation that affect for the most part only the earliest of them. But on one point, the reciprocal relations between the Vedic and Brahmanic periods, it is necessary to say a few words. Why is it that well-informed Vedic scholars differ so widely in regard to the ritualistic share in the making of the Veda? Because the extremists on either side in formulating the principles of their system forget a fact that probably no one of them if questioned would fail to acknowledge. The Rig Veda is not a homogeneous whole. It is a work which successive generations have produced, and in which are represented different views, of local or sectarian origin; while the hymns from a literary point of view are of varying value. The latter is a fact which has been ignored frequently, but it is more important than any other. For one has almost no criteria, with which to discover whether the hymns precede or follow the ritual, other than the linguistic posteriority of the ritualistic literature, and the knowledge that there were priests with a ritual when some of the hymns were composed. The bare fact that hymns are found rubricated in the later literature is surely no reason for believing that such hymns were made for the ritual. Now while it can be shown that a large number of hymns are formal, conventional, and mechanical in expression, and while it may be argued with plausibility that these were composed to serve the purpose of an established cult, this is very far from being the case with many which, on other grounds, may be supposed to belong severally to the older and later part of the Rig Veda. Yet does the new school, in estimating the hymns, never admit this. The poems always are spoken of as 'sacerdotal,' 'ritualistic,' without the slightest attempt to see whether this be true of all or of some alone. We claim that it is not historical, it is not judicious from a literary point of view, to fling indiscriminately together the hymns that are evidently ritualistic and those of other value; for, finally, it is a sober literary judgment that is the court of appeals in regard to whether poetry be poetry or not. Now let one take a hymn containing, to make it an unexceptionable example, nothing very profound or very beautiful. It is this well-known

HYMN TO THE SUN (*Rig Veda*, I. 50).

Aloft this all-wise[1] shining god
His beams of light are bearing now,
That every one the sun may see.

[1] Or "all-possessing" (Whitney). The metre of the translation retains the number of feet in the original. Four (later added) stanzas are here omitted.

Apart, as were they thieves, yon stars,
Together with the night,[1] withdraw
Before the sun, who seeth all.

His beams of light have been beheld
Afar, among (all) creatures; rays
Splendid as were they (blazing) fires.

Impetuous-swift, beheld of all,
Of light the maker, thou, O Sun,
Thou all the gleaming (sky) illum'st.

Before the folk of shining gods
Thou risest up, and men before,
'Fore all — to be as light beheld;

(To be) thine eye, O pure bright Heaven,
Wherewith amid (all) creatures born
Thou gazest down on busy (man).

Thou goest across the sky's broad place,
Meting with rays, O Sun, the days,
And watching generations pass.

The steeds are seven that at thy car
Bear up the god whose hair is flame
O shining god, O Sun far-seen!

Yoked hath he now his seven fair steeds,
The daughters of the sun-god's car,
Yoked but by him;[2] with these he comes.

For some thousands of years these verses have been the daily prayer of the Hindu. They have been incorporated into the ritual in this form. They are rubricated, and the nine stanzas form part of a prescribed service. But, surely, it were a literary hysteron-proteron to conclude for this reason that they were made only to fill a part in an established ceremony.

[1] So P.W. Possibly "by reason of (the sun's) rays"; *i.e.*, the stars fear the sun as thieves fear light. For 'Heaven,' here and below, see the third chapter.

[2] Yoked only by him; literally, "self-yoked." Seven is used in the Rig Veda in the general sense of "many," as in Shakespeare's "a vile thief this seven years."

The praise is neither perfunctory nor lacking in a really religious tone. It has a directness and a simplicity, without affectation, which would incline one to believe that it was not made mechanically, but composed with a devotional spirit that gave voice to genuine feeling.

We will now translate another poem (carefully preserving all the tautological phraseology), a hymn

TO DAWN (*Rig Veda*, VI. 64).

Aloft the lights of Dawn, for beauty gleaming,
Have risen resplendent, like to waves of water;
She makes fair paths, (makes) all accessible;
And good is she, munificent and kindly.

Thou lovely lookest, through wide spaces shin'st thou,
Up fly thy fiery shining beams to heaven;
Thy bosom thou reveals't, thyself adorning,
Aurora, goddess gleaming bright in greatness.

The ruddy kine (the clouds) resplendent bear her,
The Blessed One, who far and wide extendeth.
As routs his foes a hero armed with arrows,
As driver swift, so she compels the darkness.

Thy ways are fair; thy paths, upon the mountains;
In calm, self-shining one, thou cross'st the waters.
O thou whose paths are wide, to us, thou lofty
Daughter of Heaven, bring wealth for our subsistence.

Bring (wealth), thou Dawn, who, with the kine, untroubled
Dost bring us good commensurate with pleasure,
Daughter of Heaven, who, though thou art a goddess,
Didst aye at morning-call come bright and early.

Aloft the birds fly ever from their dwelling,
And men, who seek for food, at thy clear dawning.
E'en though a mortal stay at home and serve thee,
Much joy to him, Dawn, goddess (bright), thou bringest.

The "morning call" might, indeed, suggest the ritual, but it proves only a morning prayer or offering. Is this poem of a "singularly refined character," or "preëminently sacerdotal" in appearance? One other example (in still a different metre) may be examined, to see if it bear on its face evidence of having been made with "reference to ritual application," or of being "liturgical from the very start."

To Indra (*Rig Veda*, I. 11).

'Tis Indra all (our) songs extol,
Him huge as ocean in extent;
Of warriors chiefest warrior he,
Lord, truest lord for booty's gain.

In friendship, Indra, strong as thine
Naught will we fear, O lord of strength;
To thee we our laudations sing,
The conqueror unconquerèd.[1]

The gifts of Indra many are,
And inexhaustible his help
Whene'er to them that praise he gives
The gift of booty rich in kine.

A fortress-render, youthful, wise,
Immeasurably strong was born
Indra, the doer of every deed,
The lightning-holder, far renowned.

'Twas thou, Bolt-holder, rent'st the cave
Of Val, who held the (heavenly) kine;[2]
Thee helped the (shining) gods, when roused
(To courage) by the fearless one.[3]

[1] *jétāram áparājitam.*

[2] The rain, see next note.

[3] After this stanza two interpolated stanzas are here omitted. Grassman and Ludwig give the epithet "fearless" to the gods and to Vala, respectively. But compare I. 6. 7, where the same word is used of Indra. For the oft-mentioned act of cleaving the cave, where the dragon Val or Vritra (the restrainer or envelopper) had coralled the kine (*i.e.*, without metaphor, for the act of freeing the clouds and letting loose the rain), compare I. 32. 2, where of Indra it is said: "He slew the snake that lay upon the mountains . . . like bellowing kine the waters, swiftly flowing, descended to the sea"; and verse 11: "Watched by the snake the waters stood . . . the waters' covered cave he opened wide, what time he Vritra slew."

Indra, who lords it by his strength,
Our praises now have loud proclaimed;
His generous gifts a thousand are,
Aye, even more than this are they.

This is poetry. Not great poetry perhaps, but certainly not ground out to order, as some of the hymns appear to have been. Yet, it may be said, why could not a poetic hymn have been written in a ritualistic environment? But it is on the hymns themselves that one is forced to depend for the belief in the existence of ritualism, and we claim that such hymns as these, which we have translated as literally as possible, show rather that they were composed without reference to ritual application. It must not be forgotten that the ritual, as it is known in the Brāhmanas, without the slightest doubt, from the point of view of language, social conditions, and theology, represents an age that is very different to that illustrated by the mass of the hymns. Such hymns, therefore, and only such as can be proved to have a ritualistic setting can be referred to a ritualistic age. There is no convincing reason why one should not take the fully justified view that some of the hymns represent a freer and more natural (less priest-bound) age, as they represent a spirit freer and less mechanical than that of other hymns. As to the question which hymns, early or late, be due to poetic feeling, and which to ritualistic mechanism or servile imitation, this can indeed be decided by a judgment based only on the literary quality, never on the accident of subsequent rubrication.

We hold, therefore, in this regard, that the new school, valuable and suggestive as its work has been, is gone already farther than is judicious. The Rig Veda in part is synchronous with an advanced ritualism, subjected to it, and in some cases derived from it; but in part the hymns are "made for their own sake and not for the sake of any sacrificial performance," as said Müller of the whole; going in this too far, but not into greater error than are gone they that confuse the natural with the artificial, the poetical with the mechanical, gold with dross. It may be true that the books of the Rig Veda are chiefly family-books for the *soma*-cult, but even were it true it would in no wise impugn the poetic character of some of the hymns contained in these books. The drag-net has scooped up old and new, good and bad, together. The Rig Veda is not of one period or of one sort. It is a 'Collection,' as says its name. It is essentially impossible that any sweeping statement in regard to its character should be true if that character be regarded as uniform. To say that the Rig Veda represents an age of childlike thought, a period before the priestly ritual began its spiritual blight, is incorrect. But no less incorrect is it to assert that the Rig Veda represents a period when hymns are made only for rubrication by priests that sing only for baksheesh. Scholars are too prone to-day to speak of the Rig Veda in the same way as the Greeks spoke of Homer. It is to be hoped that the time may soon come when critics will no longer talk about the Collection as if it were all made in the same circumstances and at the same time ; above all is it desirable that the literary quality of the hymns may receive due attention, and that there may be less of those universal asseverations which treat the productions of generations of poets as if they were the work of a single author.

In respect of the method of reading into the Rig Veda what is found in parallel passages in the Atharva Veda and Brāhmanas, a practice much favored by Ludwig and others, the results of its application have been singularly futile in passages of importance. Often a varied reading will make clearer a doubtful verse, but it by no means follows that the better reading is the truer. There always remains the lurking suspicion that the reason the variant is more intelligible is that its inventor did not understand the original. As to real elucidation of other sort by the later texts, in the minutiae of the outer world, in details of priestcraft, one may trust early tradition tentatively, just as one does late commentators, but in respect of ideas tradition is as apt to mislead as to lead well. The cleft between the theology of the Rig Veda and that of the Brāhmanas, even from the point of view of the mass of hymns that comprise the former, is too great to allow us with any content to explain the conceptions of the one by those of the other. A tradition always is useful when nothing else offers itself, but traditional beliefs are so apt to take the color of new eras that they should be employed only in the last emergency, and then with the understanding that they are of very hypothetical value.

In conclusion a practical question remains to be answered. In the few cases where the physical basis of a Rig Vedic deity is matter of doubt, is it advisable to present such a deity in the form in which he stands in the text or to endeavor historically to elucidate the figure by searching for his physical prototype? We have chosen the former alternative, partly because we think the latter method unsuitable to a handbook, since it involves many critical discussions of theories of doubtful value. But this is not the chief reason. Granted that the object of study is simply to know the Rig Veda, rightly to grasp the views held by the poets, and so to place oneself upon their plane of thought, it becomes obvious that the farther the student gets from their point of view the less he understands them. Nay, more, every bit of information, real as well as fancied, which in regard to the poets' own divinities furnishes, one with more than the poets themselves knew or imagined, is prejudicial to a true knowledge of Vedic beliefs. Here if anywhere is applicable that test of desirable knowledge formulated as *das Erkennen des Erkannten.* To set oneself in the mental sphere of the Vedic seers, as far as possible to think their thoughts, to love, fear, and admire with them — this is the necessary beginning of intimacy, which precedes the appreciation that gives understanding.

DIVISIONS OF THE SUBJECT.

After the next chapter, which deals with the people and land, we shall begin the examination of Hindu religions with the study of the beliefs and religious notions to be found in the Rig Veda. Next to the Rig Veda in time stands the Atharva Veda, which represents a growing demonology in contrast with *soma*-worship and theology; sufficiently so at least to deserve a special chapter. These two Vedic Collections naturally form the first period of Hindu religion.

The Vedic period is followed by what is usually termed Brahmanism, the religion that is inculcated in the rituals called Brāhmana and its later development in the Upanishads. These two classes of works, together with the Yajur Veda, will make the next divisions of the whole subject. The formal religion of Brahmanism, as laid down for popular use and instruction in the law-books, is a side of Brahmanic religion that scarcely has been noticed, but it seems to deserve all the space allotted to it in the chapter on 'The Popular Brahmanic Faith.' We shall then review Jainism and Buddhism, the two chief heresies. Brahmanism penetrates the great epic poem which, however, in its present form is sectarian in tendency, and should be separated as a growth of Hinduism from the literature of pure Brahmanism. Nevertheless, so intricate and perplexing would be the task of unraveling the theologic threads that together make the yarn of the epic, and in many cases it would be so doubtful whether any one thread led to Brahmanism or to the wider and more catholic religion called Hinduism, that we should have preferred to give up the latter name altogether, as one that was for the most part idle, and in some degree misleading. Feeling, however, that a mere manual should not take the initiative in coining titles, we have admitted this unsatisfactory word 'Hinduism' as the title of a chapter which undertakes to give a comprehensive view of the religions endorsed by the many-centuried epic, and to explain their mutual relations. As in the case of the 'Popular Faith,' we have had here no models to go upon, and the mass of matter which it was necessary to handle — the great epic is about eight times as long as the Iliad and Odyssey put together — must be our excuse for many imperfections of treatment in this part of the work. The reader will gain at least a view of the religious development as it is exhibited in the literature, and therefore, as far as possible, in chronological order. The modern sects and the religions of the hill tribes of India form almost a necessary supplement to these nobler religions of the classical literature; the former because they are the logical as well as historical continuation of the great Hindu sectarian schisms, the latter because they give the solution of some problems connected with Çivaism, and, on the other hand, offer useful un-Aryan parallels to a few traits which have been preserved in the earliest period of the Aryans.[1]

[1] Aryan, Sanskrit *aryà*, *ā́rya*, Avestan *airya*, appears to mean the loyal or the good, and may be the original national designation, just as the Medes were long called Ἄριοι. In late Sanskrit *ārya* is simply 'noble.' The word survives, perhaps, in ἄριστος, and is found in proper names, Persian Ariobarzanes, Teutonic Ariovistus; as well as in the names of people and countries, Vedic Āryas, Īran, Iranian; (doubtful) Airem, Erin, Ireland. Compare Zimmer, BB. iii. p. 137; Kaegi, *Der Rig Veda*, p. 144 (Arrowsmith's translation, p. 109). In the Rig Veda there is a god Aryaman, 'the true,' who forms with Mitra and Varuna a triad (see below). Windisch questions the propriety of identifying Īran with Erin, and Schrader (p. 584[2]) doubts whether the Indo-Europeans as a body ever called themselves Aryans. We employ the latter name because it is short.

CHAPTER II.

PEOPLE AND LAND.

THE Aryan Hindus, whose religions we describe in this volume,[1] formed one of the Aryan or so-called Indo-European peoples. To the other peoples of this stock, Persians, Armenians, Greeks, Italians, Kelts, Teutons, Slavs, the Hindus were related closely by language, but very remotely from the point of view of their primitive religion. Into India the Aryans brought little that was retained in their religious systems. A few waning gods, the worship of ancestors, and some simple rites are common to them and their western relations; but with the exception of the Iranians (Persians), their religious connection with cis-Indic peoples is of the slightest. With the Iranians, the Hindus (that were to be) appear to have lived longest in common after the other members of the Aryan host were dispersed to west and south.[2] They stand in closer religious touch with these, their nearest neighbors, and in the time of the Rig Veda (the Hindus' earliest literature) there are traces of a connection comparatively recent between the pantheons of the two nations.

According to their own, rather uncertain, testimony, the Aryans of the Rig Veda appear to have consisted of five tribal groups.[3] These groups, *janas*, Latin gens, are subdivided into

[1] We take this opportunity of stating that by the religions of the Aryan Hindus we mean the religions of a people who, undoubtedly, were full-blooded Aryans at first, however much their blood may have been diluted later by un-Aryan admixture. Till the time of Buddhism the religious literature is fairly Aryan. In the period of "Hinduism" neither people nor religion can claim to be quite Aryan.

[2] If, as thinks Schrader, the Aryans' original seat was on the Volga, then one must imagine the Indo-Iranians to have kept together in a south-eastern emigration.

[3] That is to say, frequent reference is made to 'five tribes.' Some scholars deny that the tribes are Aryan alone, and claim that 'five,' like seven, means 'many.'

viças, Latin vicus, and these, again, into *grāmas*. The names, however, are not employed with strictness, and *jana*, etymologically gens but politically tribus, sometimes is used as a synonym of *grāma*.[1] Of the ten books of the Rig-Veda seven are ascribed to various priestly families. In the main, these books are rituals of song as inculcated for the same rites by different family priests and their descendants. Besides these there are books which are ascribed to no family, and consist, in part, of more general material. The distinction of priestly family-books was one, possibly, coextensive with political demarcation. Each of the family-books represents a priestly family, but it may represent, also, a political family. In at least one case it represents a political body.[2]

These great political groups, which, perhaps, are represented by family rituals, were essentially alike in language, custom and religion (although minor ritualistic differences probably obtained, as well as tribal preference for particular cults); while in all these respects, as well as in color and other racial peculiarities, the Aryans were distinguished from the dark-skinned aborigines, with whom, until the end of the Rig Vedic period, they were perpetually at war. At the close of this period the immigrant Aryans had reduced to slavery many of their unbelieving and barbarian enemies, and formally incorporated them into the state organization, where, as captives, slaves, or sons of slaves, the latter formed the "fourth caste." But while admitting these slaves into the body politic, the priestly Aryans debarred them from the religious congregation. Between the Aryans themselves there is in this period a loosely defined distinction of classes, but no system of caste is known before the close of the first Vedic Collection. Nevertheless, the emphasis in this statement lies strongly upon system, and

1 RV. III. 33. 11; 53. 12. Zimmer, *Altindisches Leben*, p. 160, incorrectly identifies *viç* with tribus (Leist, *Rechtsgeschichte*, p. 105).

2 Viçvāmitra. A few of the hymns are not ascribed to priests at all (some were made by women; some by 'royal-seers,' *i.e.*, kings, or, at least, not priests).

it may not be quite idle to say at the outset that the general caste-distinctions not only are as old as the Indo-Iranian unity (among the Persians the same division of priest, warrior and husbandman obtains), but, in all probability, they are much older. For so long as there is a cult, even if it be of spirits and devils, there are priests; and if there are chieftains there is a nobility, such as one finds among the Teutons, nay, even among the American Indians, where also is known the inevitable division into priests, chiefs and commons, sometimes hereditary, sometimes not. There must have been, then, from the beginning of kingship and religious service, a division among the Aryans into royalty, priests, and people, *i.e.*, whoever were not acting as priests or chieftains. When the people becomes agricultural, the difference tends to become permanent, and a caste system begins. Now, the Vedic Aryans appear in history at just the period when they are on the move southwards into India; but they are no irrupting host. The battles led the warriors on, but the folk, as a folk, moved slowly, not all abandoning the country which they had gained, but settling there, and sending onwards only a part of the people. There was no fixed line of demarcation between the classes. The king or another might act as his own priest—yet were there priestly families. The cow-boys might fight—yet were there those of the people that were especially 'kingsmen,' *rājanyas*, and these were, already, practically a class, if not a caste.[1] These natural and necessary social divisions, which in early times were anything but rigid, soon formed inviolable groups, and then the caste system was complete. In the perfected legal scheme what was usage becomes duty. The warrior may

[1] Caste, at first, means 'pure,' and signifies that there is a moral barrier between the caste and outcast. The word now practically means class, even impure class. The native word means 'color,' and the first formal distinction was national, (white) Aryan and 'black-man.' The precedent class-distinctions among the Aryans themselves became fixed in course of time, and the lines between Aryans, in some regards, were drawn almost as sharply as between Aryan and slave.

not be a public priest; the priest may not serve as warrior or husbandman. The farmer 'people' were the result of eliminating first the priestly, and then the fighting factors from the whole body politic. But these castes were all Aryans, and as such distinguished most sharply, from a religious point of view, from the "fourth caste"; whereas among themselves they were, in religion, equals. But they were practically divided by interests that strongly affected the development of their original litanies. For both priest and warrior looked down on the 'people,' but priest and warrior feared and respected each other. To these the third estate was necessary as a base of supplies, and together they guarded it from foes divine and mortal. But to each other they were necessary for wealth and glory, respectively. So it was that even in the earliest period the religious litany, to a great extent, is the book of worship of a warrior-class as prepared for it by the priest. Priest and king—these are the main factors in the making of the hymns of the Rig Veda, and the gods lauded are chiefly the gods patronized by these classes. The third estate had its favorite gods, but these were little regarded, and were in a state of decadence. The slaves, too, may have had their own gods, but of these nothing is known, and one can only surmise that here and there in certain traits, which seem to be un-Aryan, may lie an unacknowledged loan from the aborigines.

Between the Rig Veda and the formation or completion of the next Veda, called the Atharvan, the interval appears to have been considerable, and the inherent value of the religion inculcated in the latter can be estimated aright only when this is weighed together with the fact, that, as is learned from the Atharvan's own statements, the Aryans were now advanced further southwards and eastwards, had discovered a new land, made new gods, and were now more permanently established, the last a factor of some moment in the religious development. Indications of the difference in time may be seen in the geographical and physical limitations of the older period as compared with those of the later Atharvan. When first the Aryans are found in India, at the time of the Rig Veda, they are located, for the most part, near the upper Indus (Sindhu). The Ganges, mentioned but twice, is barely known. On the west the Aryans lingered in East Kabulistan (possibly in Kashmeer in the north); and even Kandahar appears, at least, to be known as Aryan. That is to say, the 'Hindus' were still in Afghanistan, although the greater mass of the people had already crossed the Indus and were progressed some distance to the east of the Punjāb. That the race was still migrating may be seen from the hymns of the Rig Veda itself.[1] Their journey was to the south-east, and both before and after they reached the Indus they left settlements, chiefly about the Indus and in the Punjāb (a post-Vedic group), not in the southern but in the northern part of this district.[2]

The Vedic Aryans of this first period were acquainted with the Indus, Sutlej (Çutudrī), Beas (Vipāç, Ὕφασις), Ravi (Parushnī or Irāvatī); the pair of rivers that unite and flow into the Indus, viz.: Jhelum (Vitastā, Behat), and Chināb (Asiknī,[3] Akesines); and knew the remoter Kubhā (Κωφήν, Kabul) and the northern Suvāstu (Swat); while they appear to have had a legendary remembrance of the Rasā, Avestan Rañha (Rangha), supposed by some to be identical with the Araxes or Yaxartes, but probably (see below) only a vague 'stream,' the old name travelling with them on their wanderings; for one would err if he regarded similarity or even identity of appellation as a proof of real identity.[4] West of the Indus the Kurum and Gomal appear to be known also. Many rivers are mentioned of which

[1] Compare RV. iii. 33, and in I. 131. 5, the words: 'God Indra, thou didst help thy suppliants; one river after another they gained who pursued glory.'

[2] Thomas, *Rivers of the Vedas* (JRAS. xv. 357 ff.; Zimmer, *loc. cit.* cap. 1).

[3] Later called the Candrabhāga. For the Jumna and Sarayu see below.

[4] This is the error into which falls Brunnhofer, whose theory that the Vedic Aryans were still settled near the Caspian has been criticised above (p. 15).

the names are given, but their location is not established. It is from the district west of the Indus that the most famous Sanskrit grammarian comes, and long after the Vedas an Indic people are known in the Kandahar district, while Kashmeer was a late home of culture. The Sarasvatī river, the name of which is transferred at least once in historical times, may have been originally one with the Arghandāb (on which is Kandahar), for the Persian name of this river (*s* becomes *h*) is Harahvati (Arachotos, Arachosia), and it is possible that it was really this river, and not the Indus which was first lauded as the Sarasvatī. In that case there would be a perfect parallel to what has probably happened in the case of the Rasā, the name — in both cases meaning only 'the stream' (like Rhine, Arno, etc.) — being transferred to a new river. But since the Iranian Harahvati fixes the first river of this name, there is here a stronger proof of Indo-Iranian community than is furnished by other examples.[1]

These facts or suggestive parallels of names are of exceeding importance. They indicate between the Vedic Aryans and the Iranians a connection much closer than usually has been assumed. The bearings of such a connection on the religious ideas of the two peoples are self-evident, and will often have to be touched upon in the course of this history. It is of less importance, from the present point of view, to say how the Aryans entered India, but since this question is also connected with that of the religious environment of the first Hindu poets, it will be well to state that, although, as some scholars maintain, and as we believe, the Hindus may have come with the Iranians through the open pass of Herat (Haraiva, Haroyu), it is possible that they parted from the latter south of the Hindukush[2] (descending through the Kohistan passes from the north), and that the two peoples thence diverged south-east

[1] Compare Geiger, *Ostiranische Cultur*, p. 81. See also Muir, OST. ii. p. 355.

[2] Lassen, I. p. 616, decided in favor of the western passes of the Hindukush.

and south-west respectively. Neither assumption would prevent the country lying between the Harahvati and Vitastā [1] from being, for generations, a common camping-ground for both peoples, who were united still, but gradually diverging. This seems, at least, to be the most reasonable explanation of the fact that these two rivers are to each people their farthest known western and eastern limits respectively. With the exception of the vague and uncertain Rasā, the Vedic Hindu's geographical knowledge is limited by Kandahar in the west, as is the Iranian's in the east by the Vitastā.[2] North of the Vitastā Mount Tricota (Trikakud, 'three peaks') is venerated, and this together with a Mount Mūjavat, of which the situation is probably in the north, is the extent of modern knowledge in respect of the natural boundaries of the Vedic people. One hears, to be sure, at a later time, of 'northern Kurus,' whose felicity is proverbial; and it is very tempting to find in this name a connection with the Iranian Kur, but the Kurus, like the Rasā and Sarasvatī, are re-located once (near Delhi), and no similarity of name can assure one of a true connection. If not coincidences, such likenesses are too vague to be valuable historically.[3]

Another much disputed point must be spoken of in connection with this subject. In the Veda and in the Avesta there is mentioned the land of the 'seven rivers.' Now seven rivers are often spoken of in the Rig Veda, but only once does this term mean the country, while in the 'Hymn to the Rivers' no

1 From Kandahar in Afghanistan to a point a little west of Lahore. In the former district, according to the Avesta, the dead are buried (an early Indian custom, not Iranian).

2 Geiger identifies the Vītaĝuhaiti or Vitanghvati with the Oxus, but this is improbable. It lies in the extreme east and forms the boundary between the true believers and the 'demon-worshippers' (Yasht, 5, 77; Geiger. *loc. cit.* p. 131, note 5). The Persian name is the same with Vitastā, which is located in the Punjāb.

3 On the Kurus compare Zimmer (*loc. cit.*), who thinks Kashmeer is meant, and Geiger, *loc. cit.* p. 39. Other geographical reminiscences may lie in Vedic and Brahmanic allusions to Bactria, Balkh (AV.); to the Derbiker (around Merv? RV.), and to Manu's mountain, whence he descended after the flood (Naubandhana): *Çatapatha Brāhmana*, 1. 8. 1, 6, 'Manu's descent').

less than twenty-one streams are enumerated (RV. X. 75). In order to make out the 'seven rivers' scholars have made different combinations, that most in favor being Müller's, the five rivers of the Punjāb together with the Kabul and (Swat or) Sarasvatī. But in point of fact 'seven' quite as often means many, as it does an exact number, and this, the older use, may well be applied here. It is quite impossible to identify the seven, and it is probable that no Vedic poet ever imagined them to be a group of this precise number. It would be far easier to select a group of seven conspicuous rivers, if anywhere, on the west of the Indus. A very natural group from the Iranian side would be the Herīrūd, Hilmund, Arghandāb, Kurum, Kabul, Indus, and Vitastā. Against this, however, can be urged that the term 'seven rivers' may be Bactrian, older than the Vedic period; and that, in particular, the Avesta distinguishes Vaikerta, Urva, and other districts from the 'seven rivers.' It is best to remain uncertain in so doubtful a matter, bearing in mind that even Kurukshetra, the 'holy land,' is said to-day to be watered by 'seven streams,' although some say nine; apropos of which fact Cunningham remarks, giving modern examples, that "the Hindus invariably assign seven branches to all their rivers."[1]

Within the Punjāb, the Vedic Aryans, now at last really 'Hindus,' having extended themselves to the Çutudrī (Çatadru, Sutlej), a formidable barrier, and eventually having crossed even this, the last tributary of the Indus, descended to the Jumna (Yamunā), over the little stream called 'the Rocky' (Drishadvatī) and the lesser Sarasvatī, southeast from Lahore and near Delhi, in the region Kurukshetra, afterwards famed as the seat of the great epic war, and always regarded as holy in the highest degree.

Not till the time of the Atharva Veda do the Aryans appear as far east as Benares (Vārānasī, on the 'Varanāvatī'?), though

[1] *Arch. Survey*, xiv. p. 89; Thomas, *loc. cit.* p. 363.

the Sarayu is mentioned in the Rik. But this scarcely is the tributary of the Ganges, Gogra, for the name seems to refer to a more western stream, since it is associated with the Gomatī (Gomal). One may surmise that in the time of the Rig Veda the Aryans knew only by name the country east of Lucknow. It is in the Punjāb and a little to the west and east of it (how far it is impossible to state with accuracy) where lies the real theatre of activity of the Rig Vedic people.

Some scholars believe that this people had already heard of the two oceans. This point again is doubtful in the extreme. No descriptions imply a knowledge of ocean, and the word for ocean means merely a 'confluence' of waters, or in general a great oceanic body of water like the air. As the Indus is too wide to be seen across, the name may apply in most cases to this river. An allusion to 'eastern and western floods,'[1] which is held by some to be conclusive evidence for a knowledge of the two seas, is taken by others to apply to the air-oceans. The expression may apply simply to rivers, for it is said that the Vipāç and Çutudrī empty into the 'ocean', *i.e.*, the Indus or the Çutudrī's continuation.[2] One late verse alone speaks of the Sarasvatī pouring into the ocean, and this would indicate the Arabian Sea.[3] Whether the Bay of Bengal was known, even by hearsay and in the latest time of this period, remains uncertain. As a body the Aryans of the Rig Veda were certainly not acquainted with either ocean. Some straggling adventurers probably pushed down the Indus, but Zimmer doubtless is correct in asserting that the popular emigration did not extend further south than the junction of the Indus and the Pañcanada (the united five rivers).[4] The extreme south-eastern geographical limit of the Rig Vedic people may

[1] RV. x. 136. 5. [2] RV. iii. 33. 2.

[3] RV. vii. 95. 2. Here the Sarasvatī can be only the Indus.

[4] Pañca-nada, Punjnud, Persian 'Punjāb,' the five streams, Vitastā, Asiknī, Irāvatī, Vipāç, Çutudrī. The Punjnud point is slowly moving up stream; Vyse, JRAS. x. 323. The Sarayu may be the Herirūd, Geiger, *loc. cit.* p. 72.

be reckoned (not, however, in Oldenberg's opinion, with any great certainty) as being in Northern Behār (Māgadha). The great desert, Marusthala, formed an impassable southern obstacle for the first immigrants.[1]

On the other hand, the two oceans are well known to the Atharva Veda, while the geographical (and hence chronological) difference between the Rik and the Atharvan is furthermore illustrated by the following facts: in the Rig Veda wolf and lion are the most formidable beasts; the tiger is unknown and the elephant seldom alluded to; while in the Atharvan the tiger has taken the lion's place and the elephant is a more familiar figure. Now the tiger has his domicile in the swampy land about Benares, to which point is come the Atharvan Aryan, but not the Rig Vedic people. Here too, in the Atharvan, the panther is first mentioned, and for the first time silver and iron are certainly referred to. In the Rig Veda the metals are bronze and gold, silver and iron being unknown.[2] Not less significant are the trees. The ficus religiosa, the tree later called the 'tree of the gods' (*deva-sadana*, *açvattha*), under which are fabled to sit the divinities in heaven, is scarcely known in the Rig Veda, but is well known in the Atharvan; while India's grandest tree, the *nyagrodha*, ficus indica, is known to the Atharvan and Brahmanic period, but is utterly foreign to the Rig Veda. Zimmer deems it no less significant that fishes are spoken of in the Atharvan and are mentioned only once in the Rig Veda, but this may indicate a geographical difference less than one of custom. In only one doubtful passage is the north-east monsoon alluded to. The storm so vividly described in the Rig Veda is the south-west monsoon which is felt in the northern Punjāb. The north-east monsoon is felt to the south-

[1] Muir, OST. ii. 351; Zimmer, *loc. cit.* p. 31 identifies the *Kīkaṭas* of RV. iii. 53. 14 with the inhabitants of Northern Behār. Marusthala is called simply 'the desert.'

[2] The earlier *áyas*, Latin *aes*, means bronze not iron, as Zimmer has shown, *loc. cit.* p. 51. Pischel, *Vedische Studien*, I, shows that elephants are mentioned more often than was supposed (but rarely in family-books).

east of the Punjāb, possibly another indication of geographical extension, withal within the limits of the Rig Veda itself.

The seat of culture shifts in the Brahmanic period, which follows that of the Vedic poems, and is found partly in the 'holy land' of the west, and partly in the east (Behār, Tirhut).[1] The literature of this period comes from Aryans that have passed out of the Punjāb. Probably, as we have said, settlements were left all along the line of progress. Even before the wider knowledge of the post-Alexandrine imperial age (at which time there was a north-western military retrogression), and, from the Vedic point of view, as late as the end of the Brahmanic period, in the time of the Upanishads, the north-west seems still to have been familiarly known.[2]

1 Weber, *Indische Studien*, I. p. 228; Oldenberg, *Buddha*, pp. 399 ff., 410.

2 Very lately (1893) Franke has sought to show that the Pāli dialect of India is in part referable to the western districts (Kandahar), and has made out an interesting case for his novel theory (ZDMG. xlvii. p. 595).

CHAPTER III.

THE RIG VEDA. THE UPPER GODS.

THE hymns of the Rig Veda may be divided into three classes, those in which are especially lauded the older divinities, those in which appear as most prominent the sacrificial gods, and those in which a long-weakened polytheism is giving place to the light of a clearer pantheism. In each category there are hymns of different age and quality, for neither did the more ancient with the growth of new divinities cease to be revered, nor did pantheism inhibit the formal acknowledgment of the primitive pantheon. The cult once established persisted, and even when, at a later time, all the gods had been reduced to nominal fractions of the All-god, their ritualistic individuality still was preserved. The chief reason for this lies in the nature of these gods and in the attitude of the worshipper. No matter how much the cult of later gods might prevail, the other gods, who represented the daily phenomena of nature, were still visible, awe-inspiring, divine. The firmest pantheist questioned not the advisability of propitiating the sun-god, however much he might regard this god as but a part of one that was greater. Belief in India was never so philosophical that the believer did not dread the lightning, and seek to avert it by praying to the special god that wielded it. But active veneration in later times was extended in fact only to the strong Powers, while the more passive divinities, although they were kept as a matter of form in the ceremonial, yet had in reality only tongue-worshippers.

With some few exceptions, however, it will be found impossible to say whether any one deity belonged to the first pantheon.

The best one can do is to separate the mass of gods from those that become the popular gods, and endeavor to learn what was the character of each, and what were the conceptions of the poets in regard both to his nature, and to his relations with man. A different grouping of the gods (that indicated below) will be followed, therefore, in our exposition.

After what has been said in the introductory chapter concerning the necessity of distinguishing between good and bad poetry, it may be regarded as incumbent upon us to seek to make such a division of the hymns as shall illustrate our words. But we shall not attempt to do this here, because the distinction between late mechanical and poetic hymns is either very evident, and it would be superfluous to burden the pages with the trash contained in the former,[1] or the distinction is one liable to reversion at the hands of those critics whose judgment differs from ours, for there are of course some hymns that to one may seem poetical and to another, artificial. Moreover, we admit that hymns of true feeling may be composed late as well as early, while as to beauty of style the chances are that the best literary production will be found among the latest rather than among the earliest hymns.

It would, indeed, be admissible, if one had any certainty in regard to the age of the different parts of the Rig Veda, simply to divide the hymns into early, middle, and late, as they are sometimes divided in philological works, but here one rests on the weakest of all supports for historical judgment, a linguistic and metrical basis, when one is ignorant alike of what may have been accomplished by imitation, and of the work of those later priests who remade the poems of their ancestors.

Best then, because least hazardous, appears to be the method which we have followed, namely, to take up group by group

[1] Such for instance as the hymn tọ the Açvins, RV. ii. 39. Compare verses 3-4: 'Come (ye pair of Açvins) like two horns; like two hoofs; like two geese; like two wheels; like two ships; like two spans'; etc. This is the content of the whole hymn.

the most important deities arranged in the order of their relative importance, and by studying each to arrive at a fair understanding of the pantheon as a whole. The Hindus themselves divided their gods into highest, middle, and lowest, or those of the upper sky, the atmosphere, and the earth. This division, from the point of view of one who would enter into the spirit of the seers and at the same time keep in mind the changes to which that spirit gradually was subjected, is an excellent one. For, as will be seen, although the earlier order of regard may have been from below upwards, this order does not apply to the literary monuments. These show on the contrary a worship which steadily tends from above earthwards; and the three periods into which may be divided all Vedic theology are first that of the special worship of sky-gods, when less attention is paid to others; then that of the atmospheric and meteorological divinities; and finally that of terrestrial powers, each later group absorbing, so to speak, the earlier, and therewith preparing the developing Hindu intelligence for the reception of the universal god with whom closes the series.

Other factors than those of an inward development undoubtedly were at work in the formation of this growth. Especially prominent is the amalgamation of the gods of the lower classes with those of the priest-hood. Climatic environment, too, conditioned theological evolution, if not spiritual advance. The cult of the mid-sphere god, Indra, was partly the result of the changing atmospheric surroundings of the Hindus as they advanced into India. The storms and the sun were not those of old. The tempests were more terrific, the display of divine power was more concentrated in the rage of the elements; while appreciation of the goodness of the sun became tinged with apprehension of evil, and he became a deadly power as well as one beneficent. Then the relief of rain after drought gave to Indra the character of a benign god as well as of a fearful one. Nor were lacking in the social condition certain alterations which worked together with climatic changes. The segregated mass of the original people, the braves that hung about the king, a warrior-class rapidly becoming a caste, and politically the most important caste, took the god of thunder and lightning for their god of battle. The fighting race naturally exalted to the highest the fighting god. Then came into prominence the priestly caste, which gradually taught the warrior that mind was stronger than muscle. But this caste was one of thinkers. Their divinity was the product of reflection. Indra remained, but yielded to a higher power, and the god thought out by the priests became God. Yet it must not be supposed that the cogitative energy of the Brahman descended upon the people's gods and suddenly produced a religious revolution. In India no intellectual advance is made suddenly. The older divinities show one by one the transformation that they suffered at the hands of theosophic thinkers. Before the establishment of a general Father-god, and long before that of the pantheistic All-god, the philosophical leaven was actively at work. It will be seen operative at once in the case of the sun-god, and, indeed, there were few of the older divinities that were untouched by it. It worked silently and at first esoterically. One reads of the gods' 'secret names,' of secrets in theology, which 'are not to be revealed,' till at last the disguise is withdrawn, and it is discovered that all the mystery of former generations has been leading up to the declaration now made public: 'all these gods are but names of the One.'

THE SUN-GOD.

The hymn which was translated in the first chapter gives an epitome of the simpler conceptions voiced in the few whole hymns to the sun. But there is a lower and a higher view of this god. He is the shining god *par excellence*, the *deva*, *sūrya*,[1]

[1] *Deva* is 'shining' (deus), and *Sūrya* (sol, ἥλιος) means the same.

the red ball in the sky. But he is also an active force, the power that wakens, rouses, enlivens, and as such it is he that gives all good things to mortals and to gods. As the god that gives life he (with others)[1] is the author of birth, and is prayed to for children. From above he looks down upon earth, and as with his one or many steeds he drives over the firmament he observes all that is passing below. He has these, the physical side and the spiritual side, under two names, the glowing one, Sūrya, and the enlivener, Savitar;[2] but he is also the good god who bestows benefits, and as such he was known, probably locally, by the name of Bhaga. Again, as a herdsman's god, possibly at first also a local deity, he is Pūshan (the meaning is almost the same with that of Savitar). As the 'mighty one' he is Vishnu, who measures heaven in three strides. In general, the conception of the sun as a physical phenomenon will be found voiced chiefly in the family-books: "The sightly form rises on the slope of the sky as the swift-going steed carries him . . . seven sister steeds carry him."[3] This is the prevailing utterance. Sometimes the sun is depicted under a medley of metaphors: "A bull, a flood, a red bird, he has entered his father's place; a variegated stone he is set in the midst of the sky; he has advanced and guards the two ends of space."[4] One after the other the god appears to the poets as a bull, a bird,[5] a steed, a stone, a jewel, a flood, a torch-holder,[6] or as a gleaming car set in heaven. Nor is the sun independent. As in the last image of a chariot,[7] so, without symbolism, the poet speaks of the sun as made to rise by Varuna and Mitra: "On their wonted path go Varuna and Mitra when in

[1] Let the reader note at the outset that there is scarcely an activity considered as divine which does not belong to several gods (see below).

[2] From *su*, *sav*, enliven, beget, etc. In RV. iv. 53. 6 and vii. 63. 2, *pra-savitar*.

[3] RV. VII. 66. 14–15; compare X. 178. 1. In the notes immediately following the numbers all refer to the Rig Veda.

[4] V. 47. 3; compare vs. 7, and X. 189. 1–2.

[5] Compare X. 177. 1.

[6] X. 37. 9.

[7] V. 63. 7. Varuna and Mitra set the sun's car in heaven.

the sky they cause to rise Sûrya, whom they made to avert darkness"; where, also, the sun, under another image, is the "support of the sky."[1] Nay, in this simpler view, the sun is no more than the "eye of Mitra Varuna,"[2] a conception formally retained even when the sun in the same breath is spoken of as pursuing Dawn like a lover, and as being the 'soul of the universe' (I. 115. 1–2). In the older passages the later moral element is almost lacking, nor is there maintained the same physical relation between Sun and Dawn. In the earlier hymns the Dawn is the Sun's mother, from whom he proceeds.[3] It is the "Dawns produced the Sun," in still more natural language;[4] whereas, the idea of the lover-Sun following the Dawn scarcely occurs in the family-books.[5] Distinctly late, also, is the identification of the sun with the all-spirit (*ātmā*, I. 115. 1), and the following prayer: "Remove, O sun, all weakness, illness, and bad dreams." In this hymn, X. 37. 14, Sûrya is the son of the sky, but he is evidently one with Savitar, who in V. 82. 4, removes bad dreams, as in X. 100. 8, he removes sickness. Men are rendered 'sinless' by the sun (IV. 54. 3; X. 37. 9) exactly as they are by the other gods, Indra, Varuna, etc. In a passage that refers to the important triad of sun, wind and fire, X. 158. 1 ff., the sun is invoked to 'save from the sky,' *i.e.*, from all evils that may come from the upper regions; while in the same book the sun, like Indra, is represented as the slayer of demons (*asuras*) and dragons; as the slayer, also, of the poet's rivals; as giving long life to the worshipper, and as himself drinking sweet *soma*. This is one of the poems that seem to be at once late and of a forced and artificial character (X. 170).

[1] IV. 13. 2–5; X. 37. 4; 85, 1. But *ib.* 149. 1 Savitar holds the sky 'without support.'

[2] VII. 63. 1; I. 115. 1; X. 37. 1.

[3] III. 61. 4; VII. 63. 3.

[4] VII. 78. 3.

[5] I. 56. 4; IX. 84. 2; Compare I. 92. 11; 115, 2; 123. 10–12. V. 44. 7, and perhaps 47. 6, are late. VII. 75. 5, is an exception (or late).

Although Sūrya is differentiated explicitly from Savitar (V. 81. 4, "Savitar, thou joyest in Sūrya's rays"), yet do many of the hymns make no distinction between them. The Enlivener is naturally extolled in fitting phrase, to tally with his title: "The shining-god, the Enlivener, is ascended to enliven the world"; "He gives protection, wealth and children" (II. 38. 1; IV. 53. 6–7). The later hymns seem, as one might expect, to show greater confusion between the attributes of the physical and spiritual sun. But what higher power under either name is ascribed to the sun in the later hymns is not due to a higher or more developed homage of the sun as such. On the contrary, as with many other deities, the more the praise the less the individual worship. It is as something more than the sun that the god later receives more fulsome devotion. And, in fact, paradoxical as it seems, it is a decline in sun-worship proper that is here registered. The altar-fire becomes more important, and is revered in the sun, whose hymns, at most, are few, and in part mechanical.

Bergaigne in his great work, *La Religion Védique*, has laid much stress on sexual antithesis as an element in Vedic worship. It seems to us that this has been much exaggerated. The sun is masculine; the dawn, feminine. But there is no indication of a primitive antithesis of male and female in their relations. What occurs appears to be of adventitious character. For though sun and dawn are often connected, the latter is represented first as his mother and afterwards as his 'wife' or mistress. Even in the later hymns, where the marital relation is recognized, it is not insisted upon. But Bergaigne[1] is right in saying that in the Rig Veda the sun does not play the part of an evil power, and it is a good illustration of the difference between Rik and Atharvan, when Ehni cites, to prove that the sun is like death, only passages from the Atharvan and the later Brahmanic literature.[2]

[1] *La Religion Védique*, I. 6; II. 2. [2] Ehni, *Yama*, p. 134.

When, later, the Hindus got into a region where the sun was deadly, they said, "Yon burning sun-god is death," but in the Rig Veda they said, "Yon sun is the source of life,"[1] and no other conception of the sun is to be found in the Rig Veda.

There are about a dozen hymns to Sūrya, and as many to Savitar, in the Rig Veda.[2] It is noteworthy that in the family-books the hymns to Savitar largely prevail, while those to Sūrya are chiefly late in position or content. Thus, in the family-books, where are found eight or nine of the dozen hymns to Savitar, there are to Sūrya but three or four, and of these the first is really to Savitar and the Açvins; the second is an imitation of the first; the third appears to be late; and the fourth is a fragment of somewhat doubtful antiquity. The first runs as follows: "The altar-fire has seen well-pleased the dawns' beginning and the offering to the gleaming ones; come, O ye horsemen (Açvins), to the house of the pious man; the sun (Sūrya), the shining-god, rises with light. The shining-god Savitar has elevated his beams, swinging his banner like a good (hero) raiding for cattle. According to rule go Varuna and Mitra when they make rise in the sky the sun (Sūrya) whom they have created to dissipate darkness, being (gods) sure of their habitation and unswerving in intent. Seven yellow swift-steeds bear this Sūrya, the seer of all that moves. Thou comest with swiftest steeds unspinning the web, separating, O shining-god, the black robe. The rays of Sūrya swinging (his banner) have laid darkness like a skin in the waters. Unconnected, unsupported, downward extending, why does not this (god) fall down? With what nature goes he, who knows (literally, 'who has seen')? As a support he touches and guards the vault of the sky" (IV. 13).

There is here, no more than in the early hymn from the first book, translated in the first chapter, any worship of material

[1] RV., IV. 54. 2. Here the sun gives life even to the gods.

[2] Ten hundred and twenty-eight hymns are contained in the 'Rig Veda Collection.'

phenomena. Sūrya is worshipped as Savitar, either expressly so called, or with all the attributes of the spiritual. The hymn that follows this[1] is a bald imitation. In V. 47 there are more or less certain signs of lateness, *e.g.*, in the fourth stanza ("four carry him, . . . and ten give the child to drink that he may go," etc.) there is the juggling with unexplained numbers, which is the delight of the later priesthood. Moreover, this hymn is addressed formally to Mitra-Varuna and Agni, and not to the sun-god, who is mentioned only in metaphor; while the final words *námo divé*, 'obeisance to heaven,' show that the sun is only indirectly addressed. One cannot regard hymns addressed to Mitra-Varuna and Sūrya (with other gods) as primarily intended for Sūrya, who in these hymns is looked upon as the subject of Mitra and Varuna, as in vii. 62; or as the "eye" of the two other gods, and 'like Savitar' in vii. 63. So in vii. 66. 14–16, a mere fragment of a hymn is devoted exclusively to Sūrya as "lord of all that stands and goes." But in these hymns there are some very interesting touches. Thus in vii. 60. 1, the sun does not make sinless, but he announces to Mitra and Varuna that the mortal is sinless. There are no other hymns than these addressed to Sūrya, save those in the first and tenth books, of which nine stanzas of I. 50 (see above) may be reckoned early, while I. 115, where the sun is the soul of the universe, and at the same time the eye of Mitra-Varuna, is probably late; and I. 163 is certainly so, wherein the sun is identified with Yama, Trita, etc.; is 'like Varuna'; and is himself a steed, described as having three connections in the sky, three in the waters, three in the sea. In one of the hymns in the tenth book, also a mystical song, the sun is the 'bird' of the sky, a metaphor which soon gives another figure to the pantheon in the form of Garutman, the sun-bird, of whose exploits are told strange tales in the epic, where he survives as Garuda. In other hymns Sūrya averts

[1] iv. 14.

carelessness at the sacrifice, guards the worshipper, and slays demons. A mechanical little hymn describes him as measuring the 'thirty stations.' Not one of these hymns has literary freshness or beauty of any kind. They all belong to the class of stereotyped productions, which differ in origin and content from the hymns first mentioned.[1]

SAVITAR.

Turning to Savitar one finds, of course, many of the same descriptive traits as in the praise of Sūrya, his more material self. But with the increased spirituality come new features. Savitar is not alone the sun that rises; he is also the sun that sets; and is extolled as such. There are other indications that most of the hymns composed for him are to accompany the sacrifice, either of the morning or of the evening. In II. 38, an evening song to Savitar, there are inner signs that the hymn was made for rubrication, but here some fine verses occur: "The god extends his vast hand, his arms above there —and all here obeys him; to his command the waters move, and even the winds' blowing ceases on all sides." Again: "Neither Indra, Varuna, Mitra, Aryaman, Rudra, nor the demons, impair his law." We call attention here to the fact that the Rig Veda contains a stong current of demonology, much stronger than has been pointed out by scholars intent on proving the primitive loftiness of the Vedic religion.

In III. 62. 7–9 there are some verses to Pūshan, following which is the most holy couplet of the Rig Veda, to repeat which is essentially to repeat the Veda. It is the famous Gāyatrī or Sāvitrī hymnlet (10–12):

> Of Savitar, the heavenly, that longed-for glory may we win,
> And may himself inspire our prayers.[2]

[1] X. 37; 158; 170; 177; 189. Each has its own mark of lateness. In 37, the dream; in 158, the triad; in 170, the sun as *asurahā́*; in 177, the mystic tone and the bird-sun (compare Garutman, I. 164; X. 149); in 189, the thirty stations.

[2] See Whitney in *Colebrooke's Essays*, revised edition, ii. p. 111.

Whitney (*loc. cit.*) says of this hymn that it is not remarkable in any way and that no good reason has ever been given for its fame. The good reason for this fame, in our opinion, is that the longed-for glory was interpreted later as a revealed indication of primitive pantheism, and the verses were understood to express the desire of absorption into the sun, which, as will be seen, was one of the first divine bodies to be accepted as the type of the All-god. This is also the intent of the stanzas added to I. 50 (above, p. 17), where Sūrya is "the highest light, the god among gods," mystic words, taken by later philosophers, and quite rightly, to be an expression of pantheism. The esoteric meaning of the Gāyatrī presumably made it popular among the enlightened. Exoterically the sun was only the goal of the soul, or, in pure pantheism, of the sight. In the following [1] the sin-forgiving side of Savitar is developed, whereby he comes into connection with Varuna:

> God Savitar deserveth now a song from us;
> To-dây, with guiding word, let men direct him here.
> He who distributes gifts unto the sons of men,
> Shall here on us bestow whatever thing is best;
> For thou, O Savitar, dost first upon the gods
> Who sacrifice deserve, lay immortality,
> The highest gift, and then to mortals dost extend
> As their apportionment a long enduring life.
> Whatever thoughtless thing against the race of gods
> We do in foolishness and human insolence,
> Do thou from that, O Savitar, mid gods and men
> Make us here sinless, etc.

But if this song smacks of the sacrifice, still more so does V. 81, where Savitar is the 'priest's priest,' the 'arranger of sacrifice,' and is one with Pūshan. He is here the swift horse (see above) and more famous as the divider of time than anything else. In fact this was the first ritualistic glory of Savitar, that he divides the time for sacrifice. But he receives more in

[1] iv. 54.

the light of being the type of other luminous divinities. In the next hymn, another late effort (v. 82; see the dream in vs. 4), there may be an imitation of the Gāyatrī. Savitar is here the All-god and true lord, and frees from sin. There is nothing new or striking in the hymns vi. 71; vii. 38 and 45. The same golden hands, and references to the sacrifice occur here. Allusions to the Dragon of the Deep, who is called upon with Savitar (vii. 38. 5), and the identification of Savitar with Bhaga (ib. 6) are the most important items to be gleaned from these rather stupid hymns. In other hymns not in the family-books (ii.–viii.), there is a fragment, X. 139. 1–3, and another, I. 22. 5–8. In the latter, Agni's (Fire's) title, 'son of waters,' is given to Savitar, who is virtually identified with Agni in the last part of the Rig Veda; and in the former hymn there is an interesting discrimination made between Savitar and Pūshan, who obeys him. The last hymn in the collection to Savitar, X. 149, although late and plainly intended for the sacrifice (vs. 5), is interesting as showing how the philosophical speculation worked about Savitar as a centre. 'He alone, he the son of the waters, knows the origin of water, whence arose the world.' This is one of the early speculations which recur so frequently in the Brahmanic period, wherein the origin of 'all this' (the universe) is referred to water. A hymn to Savitar in the first book contains as excellent a song as is given to the sun under this name. It is neither a morning nor an evening song in its original state, but mentions all the god's functions, without the later moral traits so prominent elsewhere, and with the old threefold division instead of thrice-three heavens.

TO SAVITAR (I. 35).

I call on Agni first (the god of fire) for weal;
I call on Mitra-Varuna to aid me here;
I call upon the Night, who quiets all that moves;
On Savitar, the shining god, I call for help.

After this introductory invocation begins the real song in a different metre.

Through space of darkness wending comes he hither,
Who puts to rest th' immortal and the mortal,
On golden car existent things beholding,
The god that rouses, Savitar, the shining;
Comes he, the shining one, comes forward, upward,
Comes with two yellow steeds, the god reverèd,
Comes shining Savitar from out the distance,
All difficulties far away compelling.
His pearl-adorned, high, variegated chariot,
Of which the pole is golden, he, reverèd,
Hath mounted, Savitar, whose beams are brilliant,
Against the darksome spaces strength assuming.
Among the people gaze the brown white-footed
(Steeds) that the chariot drag whose pole is golden.
All peoples stand, and all things made forever,
Within the lap of Savitar, the heavenly.

[There are three heavens of Savitar, two low ones,[1]
One, men-restraining, in the realm of Yama.
As on (his) chariot-pole[2] stand all immortals,
Let him declare it who has understood it !]

Across air-spaces gazes he, the eagle,
Who moves in secret, th' Asura,[3] well-guiding,
Where is (bright) Sūrya now? who understands it?
And through which sky is now his ray extending?

He looks across the earth's eight elevations,[4]
The desert stations three, and the seven rivers,
The gold-eyed shining god is come, th' Arouser,
To him that worships giving wealth and blessings.

[1] Two 'laps' below, besides that above, the word meaning 'middle' but also 'under-place.' The explanation of this much-disputed passage will be found by comparing i. 154. 5 and vii. 99. 1. The sun's three places are where he appears on both horizons and in the zenith. The last is the abode of the dead where Yama reigns. Compare iv. 53. The bracketed verses are probably a late puzzle attached to the word 'lap' of the preceding verse.

[2] Doubtful.

[3] The Spirit, later of evil spirits, demons (as above, the *asurahá*). Compare Ahura.

[4] A numerical conception not paralleled in the Rig Veda, though mountains are called protuberances ('elevations') in other places.

The golden-handed Savitar, the active one,
Goes earth and heaven between, compels demoniac powers,
To Sūrya gives assistance, and through darksome space
Extends to heaven, etc.[1]

PŪSHAN AND BHAGA AS SUN-GODS.

With Pūshan, the 'bestower of prosperity,' appears an ancient side of sun-worship. While under his other names the sun has lost, to a great extent, the attributes of a bucolic solar deity, in the case of Pūshan he appears still as a god whose characteristics are bucolic, war-like, and priestly, that is to say, even as he is venerated by the three masses of the folk. It will not do, of course, to distinguish too sharply between the first two divisions, but one can very well compare Pūshan in these rôles with Helios guiding his herds, and Apollo swaying armed hosts. It is customary to regard Pūshan as too bucolic a deity, but this is only one side of him. He apparently is the sun, as herdsmen look upon him, and in this figure is the object of ridicule with the warrior-class who, especially in one family or tribe, take a more exalted view of him. Consequently, as in the case of Varuna, one need not read into the hymns more than they offer to see that, not to speak of the priestly view, there are at least two Pūshans, in the Rig Veda itself.[2]

As the god 'with braided hair,' and as the 'guardian of cattle,' Pūshan offers, perhaps, in these particulars, the original of Rudra's characteristics, who, in the Vedic period, and later as Rudra-Çiva, is also a 'guardian of cattle' and has the 'braided hair.'

Bergaigne identifies Pūshan with Soma, with whom the poets were apt to identify many other deities, but there seems to be little similarity originally.[3] It is only in the wider circles of

1 The last stanza is in the metre of the first; two more follow without significant additions.

2 The texts are translated by Muir, OST, v. p. 171 ff.

3 *La Religion Védique*, ii. p. 428. Compare Hillebrandt, *Soma*, p. 456.

each god's activity that the two approach each other. Both gods, it is true, wed Sūryā (the female sun-power), and Soma, like Pūshan, finds lost cattle. But it must be recognized once for all that identical attributes are not enough to identify Vedic gods. Who gives wealth? Indra, Soma, Agni, Heaven and Earth, Wind, Sun, the Maruts, etc. Who forgives sins? Agni, Varuna, Indra, the Sun, etc. Who helps in war? Agni, Pūshan, Indra, Soma, etc. Who sends rain? Indra, Parjanya, Soma, the Maruts, Pūshan, etc. Who weds Dawn? The Açvins, the Sun, etc. The attributes must be functional or the identification is left incomplete.

The great disparity in descriptions of Pūshan may be illustrated by setting vi. 48. 19 beside x. 92. 13. The former passage merely declares that Pūshan is a war-leader "over mortals, and like the gods in glory"; the latter, that he is "distinguished by all divine attributes"; that is to say, what has happened in the case of Savitar has happened here also. The individuality of Pūshan dies out, but the vaguer he becomes the more grandiloquently is he praised and associated with other powers; while for lack of definite laudation general glory is ascribed to him. The true position of Pūshan in the eyes of the warrior is given unintentionally by one who says,[1] "I do not scorn thee, O Pūshan," *i.e.*, as do most people, on account of thy ridiculous attributes. For Pūshan does not drink *soma* like Indra, but eats mush. So another devout believer says: "Pūshan is not described by them that call him an eater of mush."[2] The fact that he was so called speaks louder than the pious protest. Again, Pūshan is simply bucolic. He uses the goad, which, however, according to Bergaigne, is the thunderbolt! So, too, the cows that Pūshan is described as guiding have been interpreted as clouds or 'dawns.' But they may be taken without 'interpretation' as

[1] i. 138. 4.
[2] vi. 56. 1.

real cows.[1] Pūshan drives the cows, he is armed with a goad, and eats mush; bucolic throughout, yet a sun-god. It is on these lines that his finding-qualities are to be interpreted. He finds lost cattle,[2] a proper business for such a god; but Bergaigne will see in this a transfer from Pūshan's finding of rain and of *soma*.[3] Pūshan, too, directs the furrow.[4]

Together with Vishnu and Bhaga this god is invoked at sacrifices, (a fact that says little against or for his original sunship),[5] and he is intimately connected with Indra. His sister is his mistress, and his mother is his wife (Dawn and Night?) according to the meagre accounts given in vi. 55. 4–5.[6] As a god of increase he is invoked in the marriage-rite, X. 85. 37.

As Savitar and all sun-gods are at once luminous and dark, so Pūshan has a clear and again a revered (terrible) appearance; he is like day and night, like Dyaus (the sky); at one time bright, at another, plunged in darkness, vi. 58. 1. Quite like Savitar he is the shining god who "looks upon all beings and sees them all together"; he is the "lord of the path," the god of travellers; he is invoked to drive away evil spirits, thieves, footpads, and all workers of evil; he makes paths for the winning of wealth; he herds the stars and directs all with *soma*. He carries a golden axe or sword, and is borne through air and water on golden ships; and it is he that lets down the sun's golden wheel. These simpler attributes appear for the most part in the early hymns. In what seem to be later hymns, he is the mighty one who "carries the thoughts of all"; he is

1 In i. 23. 13–15 Pūshan is said to bring king (*soma*), "whom he found like a lost herd of cattle." The fragment is late if, as is probable, the 'six' of vs. 15 are the six seasons. Compare vi. 54. 5, "may Pūshan go after our kine."

2 Compare vi. 54.

3 He is the 'son of freeing,' from darkness? vi. 55. 1.

4 iv. 57. 7.

5 vi. 17. 11; 48. 11 ff.; iv. 30. 24 ff. He is called like a war-god with the Maruts in vi. 48.

6 So, too, Bhaga is Dawn's brother, I. 123. 5. Pūshan is Indra's brother in vi. 55. 5. Gubernatis interprets Pūshan as 'the setting sun.'

like *soma* (the drink), and attends to the filter; he is "lord of the pure"; the "one born of old," and is especially called upon to help the poets' hymns.[1] It is here, in the last part of the Rig Veda, that he appears as ψυχοπομπός, who "goes and returns," escorting the souls of the dead to heaven. He is the sun's messenger, and is differentiated from Savitar in X. 139. 1.[2] Apparently he was a god affected most by the Bharadvāja family (to which is ascribed the sixth book of the Rig Veda) where his worship was extended more broadly. He seems to have become the special war-god of this family, and is consequently invoked with Indra and the Maruts (though this may have been merely in his rôle as sun). The goats, his steeds, are also an attribute of the Scandinavian war-god Thor (Kaegi, *Rig Veda*, note 210), so that his bucolic character rests more in his goad, food, and plough.

Bhaga is recognized as an Ādityá (luminous deity) and was perhaps a sun-god of some class, possibly of all, as the name in Slavic is still kept in the meaning 'god,' literally 'giver.' In the Rig Veda the word means, also, simply god, as in *bhágabhakta*, 'given by gods'; but as a name it is well known, and when thus called Bhaga is still the giver, 'the bestower' (*vidhartā́*). As *bhaga* is also an epithet of Savitar, the name may not stand for an originally distinct personality. Bhaga has but one hymn.[3] There is in fact no reason why Bhaga should be regarded as a sun-god, except for the formal identifi-

1 Contrast I. 42, and X. 26 (with 1. 138. 1). In the first hymn Pūshan leads the way and drives away danger, wolves, thieves, and helps to booty and pasturage. In the last he is a war-god, who helps in battle, a 'far-ruler,' embracing the thoughts of all (as in III. 62. 9).

2 For the traits just cited compare iv. 57. 7; vi. 17. 11; 48. 15; 53; 55; 56. 1–3; 57. 3–4; 58. 2–4; II. 40; X. 17. 3 ff.; 26. 3–8; I. 23. 14; all of I. 42, and 138; viii. 4. 15–18: III. 57. 2. In X. 17. 4, Savitar, too, guides the souls of the dead.

3 That is to say, one hymn is addressed to Bhaga with various other gods, vii. 41. Here he seems to be personified good-luck ("of whom even the king says, 'I would have thee,'" vs. 2). In the Brāhmanas 'Bhaga is blind,' which applies better to Fortune than to the Sun.

cation of him as an Ādityá, that is as the son of Aditi (Boundlessness, see below); but neither Sūrya nor Savitar is originally an Ādityá, and in Iranic *bagha* is only an epithet of Ormuzd.

HYMNS TO PŪSHAN AND BHAGA.

To Pūshan (vi. 56).

The man who Pūshan designates
With words like these, 'mush-eater he,'
By him the god is not described.

With Pūshan joined in unison
That best of warriors, truest lord,
Indra, the evil demons slays.

'T is he, the best of warriors, drives
The golden chariot of the sun
Among the speckled kine (the clouds).

Whate'er we ask of thee to-day,
O wonder-worker, praised and wise,
Accomplish thou for us that prayer.

And this our band, which hunts for kine,[1]
Successful make for booty's gain;
Afar, O Pūshan, art thou praised.

We seek of thee success, which far
From ill, and near to wealth shall be;
For full prosperity to-day;
And full prosperity the morn.[2]

To Bhaga (vii. 41).

Early on Agni call we, early Indra call;
Early call Mitra, Varuna, the Horsemen twain;
Early, too, Bhaga, Pūshan, and the Lord of Strength;
And early Soma will we call, and Rudra too.

[1] The hymn is sung before setting out on a forray for cattle. Let one observe how unsupported is the assumption of the ritualists as applied to this hymn, that it must have been "composed for rubrication."

[2] After Muir, V. p. 178. The clouds and cattle are both called *gâs*, 'wanderers,' which helped in the poetic identification of the two.

This stanza has been prefixed to the hymn by virtue of the catch-word 'early' (in the morning), with which really begins this prosaic poem (in different metre):

> The early-conquering mighty Bhaga call we,
> The son of Boundlessness, the gift-bestower,[1]
> Whom weak and strong, and e'en the king, regarding,
> Cry *bhágam bhakshi*, 'give to me the giver.'[2]
>
> O Bhaga, leader Bhaga, true bestower,
> O Bhaga, help this prayer, to us give (riches),
> O Bhaga, make us grow in kine and horses,
> O Bhaga, eke in men, men-wealthy be we!
>
> And now may we be rich, be *bhaga*-holders,[3]
> Both at the (day's) approach, and eke at midday,
> And at the sun's departure, generous giver.
> The favor of the gods may we abide in.
>
> O gods, (to us) be Bhaga really *bhaga*,[4]
> By means of him may we be *bhaga*-holders.
> As such an one do all, O Bhaga, call thee,
> As such, O Bhaga, be to-day our leader.
>
> May dawns approach the sacrifice, the holy
> Place, like to Dadhikrā,[5] like horses active,
> Which bring a chariot near; so, leading Bhaga,
> Who finds good things, may they approach, and bring him.

As this is the only hymn addressed to Bhaga, and as it proves itself to have been made for altar service (in style as well as in special mention of the ceremony), it is evident that Bhaga, although called Aditi's son, is but a god of wealth and (like Ança, the Apportioner) very remotely connected with

[1] Compare ix. 97. 55, "Thou art Bhaga, giver of gifts."

[2] *Bhágam bhakshi!* Compare baksheesh. The word as 'god' is both Avestan, *bagha*, and Slavic, *bogu* (also meaning 'rich'). It may be an epithet of other gods also, and here it means only luck.

[3] Literally 'possessed of *bhaga*,' *i.e.*, wealth.

[4] May Bhaga be *bhágavān*, *i.e.*, a true *bhaga*-holder. Here and below a pun on the name (as above).

[5] Mythical being, possibly the sun-horse. According to Pischel a real earthly racer.

physical functions. But the hymn appears to be so late that it cannot throw much light on the original conception of the deity. We rather incline to doubt whether Bhaga was ever, strictly speaking, a sun-god, and think that he was made so merely because the sun (Savitar) was called *bhaga*. A (Ζεύς) Bagaios was worshipped by the Phrygians, while in the Avesta and as a Slavic god Bhaga has no especial connection with the sun. It must be acknowledged, however, that every form of the sun-god is especially lauded for generosity.

VISHNU.

In the person of Vishnu the sun is extolled under another name, which in the period of the Rig Veda was still in the dawn of its glory. The hymns to Vishnu are few; his fame rests chiefly on the three strides with which he crosses heaven, on his making fast the earth, and on his munificence.[1] He, too, leads in battle and is revered under the title Çipivishta,[2] of unknown significance, but meaning literally 'bald.' Like Savitar he has three spaces, two called earthly, and one, the highest, known only to himself. His greatness is inconceivable, and he is especially praised with Indra, the two being looked upon as masters of the world.[3] His highest place is the realm of the departed spirits.[4] The hymns to him appear to be late (thus I. 155. 6, where, as the year, he has four seasons of ninety days each). Like Pūshan (his neighbor in many lauds) he is associated in a late hymn with the Maruts (V. 87). His later popularity lies in the importance of his 'highest place' (or step) being the home of the departed spirits, where he himself dwells, inscrutable. This led to the spirit's union with the sun, which, as we have said, is one of

[1] I. 22. 17, etc.; 154 ff.; vii. 100.

[2] vii. 100. 5–6. Vishnu (may be the epithet of Indra in I. 61. 7) means winner (?).

[3] vi. 69; vii. 99. But Vishnu is ordered about by Indra (iv. 18. 11; viii. 89. 12).

[4] I. 154. 5. In II. 1. 3, Vishnu is one with Fire (Agni).

the first phases of the pantheistic doctrine. In the family-books Vishnu gets but two hymns, both in the same collection, and shares one more with Indra (vii. 99–100; vi. 69). In some of the family-collections, notably in that of the Viçvāmitras, he is, if not unknown, almost ignored. As Indra's friend he is most popular with the Kanva family, but even here he has no special hymn.

> None born, God Vishnu, and none born hereafter
> E'er reaches to the limit of thy greatness;
> 'Twas thou establish'st yon high vault of heaven,
> Thou madest fast the earth's extremest mountain. (vii. 99. 2.)
>
> Three steps he made, the herdsman sure,
> Vishnu, and stepped across (the world). (I. 22. 18.)
>
> The mighty deeds will I proclaim of Vishnu,
> Who measured out the earth's extremest spaces,
> And fastened firm the highest habitation,
> Thrice stepping out with step all-powerful.
>
> O would that I might reach his path belovèd,
> Where joy the men who hold the gods in honor. (I. 154. 1, 5.)

Under all these names and images the sun is worshipped. And it is necessary to review them all to see how deeply the worship is ingrained. The sun is one of the most venerable as he is the most enduring of India's nature-gods.[1] In no early passage is the sun a malignant god. He comes "as kine to the village, as a hero to his steed, as a calf to the cow, as a husband to his wife."[2] He is the 'giver,' the 'generous one,' and as such he is Mitra, 'the friend,' who with Varuna, the encompassing heaven, is, indeed, in the Rig Veda, a personality subordinated to his greater comrade; yet is this, perhaps, the sun's oldest name of those that are not descriptive of purely physical characteristics. For Mithra in Persian keeps the

[1] Thus, for example, Vishnu in the Hindu trinity, the separate worship of the sun in modern sects, and in the cult of the hill-men.

[2] X. 149.

proof that this title was given to the Indo-Iranic god before the separation of the two peoples. It is therefore (perhaps with Bhaga?) one of the most ancient personal designations of the sun, — one, perhaps, developed from a mere name into a separate deity.

HEAVEN AND EARTH.

Not only as identical with the chief god of the Greeks, but also from a native Indic point of view, it might have been expected that Dyaus (Zeus), the 'shining sky,' would play an important rôle in the Hindu pantheon. But such is not the case. There is not a single hymn addressed independently to Dyaus, nor is there any hint of especial preëminence of Dyaus in the half-dozen hymns that are sung to Heaven and Earth together. The word *dyaus* is used hundreds of times, but generally in the meaning sky (without personification). There is, to be sure, a formal acknowledgment of the fatherhood of Dyaus (among gods he is father particularly of Dawn, the Açvins, and Indra), as there is of the motherhood of Earth, but there is no further exaltation. No exaggeration — the sign of Hindu enthusiasm — is displayed in the laudation, and the epithet 'father' is given to half a dozen Vedic gods, as in Rome Ma(r)spiter stands beside Jup(p)iter. Certain functions are ascribed to Heaven and Earth, but they are of secondary origin. Thus they bring to the gods the sacrifice,[1] as does Agni, and one whole hymn may thus be epitomized: 'By the ordinance of Varuna made firm, O Heaven and Earth, give us blessings. Blest with children and wealth is he that adores you twain. Give us sweet food, glory and strength of heroes, ye who are our father and mother.'[2]

The praise is vague and the benevolence is the usual 'bestowal of blessings' expected of all the gods in return for

[1] II. 41. 20. [2] vi. 70.

praise. Other hymns add to this something, from which one sees that these deities are not regarded as self-created; for the seers of old, or, according to one poet, some wonderful divine artisan, "most wondrous worker of the wonder-working gods," created them. Their chief office is to exercise benign protection and bestow wealth. Once they are invited to come to the sacrifice "with the gods," but this, of course, is not meant to exclude them from the list of gods.[1]

The antithesis of male and female, to Bergaigne's insistence on which reference was made above (p. 43), even here in this most obvious of forms, common to so many religions, shows itself so faintly that it fails utterly to support that basis of sexual dualism on which the French scholar lays so much stress. Dyaus does, indeed, occasionally take the place of Indra, and as a bellowing bull impregnate earth, but this is wholly incidental and not found at all in the hymns directly lauding Heaven and Earth. Moreover, instead of "father and mother" Heaven and Earth often are spoken of as "the two mothers," the significance of which cannot be nullified by the explanation that to the Hindu 'two mothers' meant two parents, and of two parents one must be male, — Bergaigne's explanation. For not only is Dyaus one of the 'two mothers,' but when independently used the word Dyaus is male or female indifferently. Thus in X. 93. 1: "O Heaven and Earth be wide outstretched for us, (be) like two young women." The position of Heaven and Earth in relation to other divinities varies with the fancy of the poet that extols them. They are either created, or they create gods, as well as create men. In accordance with the physical reach of these deities they are exhorted to give strength whereby the worshipper shall "overreach all peoples"; and, as parents, to be the "nearest of the gods," to be "like father and mother in kindness." (I. 159; 160. 2, 5.)

1 I. 160. 4; iv. 56. 1–3; vii. 53. 2.

One more attribute remains to be noticed, which connects Dyaus morally as well as physically with Savitar and Varuna. The verse in which this attribute is spoken of is also not without interest from a sociological point of view: "Whatsoever sin we have committed against the gods, or against a friend, or against the chief of the clan (family)[1] may this hymn to Heaven and Earth avert it." It was shown above that Savitar removes sin. Here, as in later times, it is the hymn that does this. The mystery of these gods' origin puzzles the seer: "Which was first and which came later, how were they begotten, who knows, O ye wise seers? Whatever exists, that they carry."[2] But all that they do they do under the command of Mitra.[3]

The most significant fact in connection with the hymns to Heaven and Earth is that most of them are expressly for sacrificial intent. "With sacrifices I praise Heaven and Earth" (I. 159. 1); "For the sake of the sacrifice are ye come down (to us)" (iv. 56. 7). In vi. 70 they are addressed in sacrificial metaphors; in vii. 53. 1 the poet says: "I invoke Heaven and Earth with sacrifices," etc. The passivity of the two gods makes them yield in importance to their son, the active Savitar, who goes between the two parents. None of these hymns bears the impress of active religious feeling or has poetic value. They all seem to be reflective, studied, more or less mechanical, and to belong to a period of theological philosophy. To Earth alone without Heaven are addressed one uninspired hymn and a fragment of the same character: "O Earth be kindly to us, full of dwellings and painless, and give us protection."[4] In the burial service the dead are exhorted to "go into kindly mother earth" who will be "wool-soft, like a maiden."[5] The one hymn to Earth should perhaps be placed

[1] I. 185. 8 (*jāspati*). The expiatory power of the hymn occurs again in I. 159.
[2] I. 185. 1. [3] iv. 56. 7. [4] I. 22. 15.
[5] X. 18. 10 (or: "like a wool-soft maiden").

parallel with similar meditative and perfunctory laudations in the Homeric hymns:

To Earth (v. 84).

In truth, O broad extended earth,
Thou bear'st the render of the hills,[1]
Thou who, O mighty mountainous one,
Quickenest created things with might.
Thee praise, O thou that wander'st far,
The hymns which light accompany,
Thee who, O shining one, dost send
Like eager steeds the gushing rain.
Thou mighty art, who holdest up
With strength on earth the forest trees,
When rain the rains that from thy clouds
And Dyaus' far-gleaming lightning come.[1]

On the bearing of these facts, especially in regard to the secondary greatness of Dyaus, we shall touch below. He is a god exalted more by modern writers than by the Hindus!

VARUNA.

Varuna has been referred to already in connection with the sun-god and with Heaven and Earth. It is by Varuna's power that they stand firm. He has established the sun 'like a tree,' *i.e.*, like a support, and 'made a path for it.'[2] He has a thousand remedies for ills; to his realm not even the birds can ascend, nor wind or swift waters attain. It is in accordance with the changeless order[3] of Varuna that the stars and the moon go their regular course; he gives long life and releases from harm, from wrong, and from sin.[4]

[1] The lightning. In I. 31. 4, 10 "(Father) Fire makes Dyaus bellow" like "a bull" (v. 36. 5). Dyaus "roars" in vi. 72. 3. Nowhere else is he a thunderer.

[2] I. 24. 7–8. The change in metaphor is not unusual.

[3] This word means either order or orders (law); literally the 'way' or 'course.'

[4] I. 24 (epitomized).

Varuna is the most exalted of those gods whose origin is physical. His realm is all above us; the sun and stars are his eyes; he sits above upon his golden throne and sees all that passes below, even the thoughts of men. He is, above all, the moral controller of the universe.

To Varuna (i. 25).

Howe'er we, who thy people are,
O Varuna, thou shining god,
Thy order injure, day by day,
Yet give us over nor to death,
Nor to the blow of angry (foe),
Nor to the wrath of (foe) incensed.[1]
Thy mind for mercy we release —
As charioteer, a fast-bound steed —
By means of song, O Varuna.
. . . .
('T is Varuna) who knows the track
Of birds that fly within the air,
And knows the ships upon the flood;[2]
Knows, too, the (god) of order firm,
The twelve months with their progeny,
And e'en which month is later born;[3]
Knows, too, the pathway of the wind,
The wide, the high, the mighty (wind),
And knows who sit above (the wind).

(God) of firm order, Varuna
His place hath ta'en within (his) home
For lordship, he, the very strong.[4]
Thence all the things that are concealed
He looks upon, considering
Whate'er is done and to be done.
May he, the Son of Boundlessness,
The very strong, through every day
Make good our paths, prolong our life.

[1] Perhaps better with Ludwig "of (thee) in anger, of (thee) incensed."
[2] Or: "Being (himself) in the (heavenly) flood he knows the ships." (Ludwig.)
[3] An intercalated month is meant (not the primitive 'twelve days').
[4] Or 'very wise,' of mental strength.

Bearing a garment all of gold,
In jewels clothed, is Varuna,
And round about him sit his spies;
A god whom injurers injure not,
Nor cheaters cheat among the folk,
Nor any plotters plot against;
Who for himself 'mid (other) men
Glory unequalled gained, and gains
(Such glory) also 'mid ourselves.

Far go my thoughts (to him), as go
The eager cows that meadows seek,
Desiring (him), the wide-eyed (god).
Together let us talk again,
Since now the offering sweet I bring,
By thee beloved, and like a priest
Thou eat'st.
I see the wide-eyed (god)!
I see his chariot on the earth,
My song with joy hath he received.

Hear this my call, O Varuna,
Be merciful to me today,
For thee, desiring help, I yearn.

Thou, wise one, art of everything,
The sky and earth alike, the king;
As such upon thy way give ear,
And loose from us the (threefold) bond;
The upper bond, the middle, break,
The lower, too, that we may live.

In the portrait of such a god as this one comes very near to monotheism. The conception of an almost solitary deity, recognized as watcher of wrong, guardian of right, and primitive creator, approaches more closely to unitarianism than does the idea of any physical power in the Rig Veda.

To the poet of the Rig Veda Varuna is the enveloping heaven;[1] that is, in distinction from Dyaus, from whom he

[1] viii. 41. 7; vii. 82. 6 (Bergaigne); X. 132. 4.

differs *toto caelo*, so to speak, the invisible world, which embraces the visible sky. His home is there where lives the Unborn, whose place is unique, above the highest heaven.[1]

But it is exactly this loftiness of character that should make one shy of interpreting Varuna as being originally the god that is presented here. Can this god, 'most august of Vedic deities,' as Bergaigne and others have called him, have belonged as such to the earliest stratum of Aryan belief?

There are some twelve hymns in the Rig Veda in Varuna's honor. Of these, one in the tenth book celebrates Indra as opposed to Varuna, and generally it is considered late, in virtue of its content. Of the hymns in the eighth book the second appears to be a later imitation of the first, and the first appears, from several indications, to be of comparatively recent origin.[2] In the seventh book (vii. 86–89) the short final hymn contains a distinctly late trait in invoking Varuna to cure dropsy; the one preceding this is *in majorem gloriam* of the poet Vasistha, fitly following the one that appears to be as new, where not only the mysticism but the juggling with "thrice-seven," shows the character of the hymn to be recent.[3] In the first hymn of this book the late doctrine of inherited sin stands prominently forth (vii. 86. 5) as an indication of the time in which it was composed. The fourth and sixth books have no separate hymns to Varuna. In the fifth book the position of the one hymn to Varuna is one favorable to spurious additions, but the hymn is not otherwise obnoxious to the criticism of lateness. Of the two hymns in the second book, the first is addressed only indirectly to Varuna, nor is he here very prominent; the second (ii. 28) is the only song which stands on a par with the hymn already

1 Compare Bergaigne, *La Religion Védique*, iii. pp. 116–118.

2 The insistence on the holy seven, the 'secret names' of dawn, the confusion of Varuna with Trita. Compare, also, the refrain, viii. 39–42. For X. 124, see below.

3 Compare Hillebrandt's Varuna and Mitra, p. 5; and see our essay on the Holy Numbers of the Rig Veda (in the *Oriental Studies*).

translated. There remain the hymns cited above from the first, not a family-book. It is, moreover, noteworthy that in ii. 28, apart from the ascription of general greatness, almost all that is said of Varuna is that he is a priest, that he causes rivers to flow, and loosens the bond of sin.[1] The finest hymn to Varuna, from a literary point of view, is the one translated above, and it is mainly on the basis of this hymn that the lofty character of Varuna has been interpreted by occidental writers. To our mind this hymn belongs to the close of the first epoch of the three which the hymns represent. That it cannot be very early is evident from the mention of the intercalated month, not to speak of the image of Varuna eating the sweet oblation 'like a priest.' Its elevated language is in sharp contrast to that of almost all the other Varuna hymns. As these are all the hymns where Varuna is praised alone by himself, it becomes of chief importance to study him here, and not where, as in iii. 62, iv. 41, vi. 51, 67, 68, and elsewhere, he is lauded as part of a combination of gods (Mitra or Indra united with Varuna). In the last book of the Rig Veda there is no hymn to Varuna,[2] a time when pantheistic monotheism was changing into pantheism, so that, in the last stage of the Rig Veda, Varuna is descended from the height. Thereafter he is god and husband of waters, and punisher of secret sin (as in ii. 28). Important in contrast to the hymn translated above is v. 85.

To Varuna.

"I will sing forth unto the universal king a high deep prayer, dear to renowned Varuna, who, as a butcher a hide, has struck earth apart (from the sky) for the sun. Varuna has

1 Varuna's forgiving of sins may be explained as a washing out of sin, just as fire burns it out, and so loosens therewith the imagined bond. V. 2. 7. Thus, quite apart from Varuna in a hymn addressed to the 'Waters,' is found the prayer, "O waters, carry off whatever sin is in me . . . and untruth." I. 23. 22.

2 But as in iv. 42, so in x. 124 he shares glory with Indra.

extended air in trees, strength in horses, milk in cows, and has laid wisdom in hearts; fire in water; the sun in the sky; *soma* in the stone. Varuna has inverted his water-barrel and let the two worlds with the space between flow (with rain). With this (heavenly water-barrel) he, the king of every created thing, wets the whole world, as a rain does a meadow. He wets the world, both earth and heaven, when he, Varuna, chooses to milk out (rain) — and then do the mountains clothe themselves with cloud, and even the strongest men grow weak. Yet another great and marvellous power of the renowned spirit (Asura) will I proclaim, this, that standing in mid-air he has measured earth with the sun, as if with a measuring rod. (It is due to) the marvellous power of the wisest god, which none ever resisted, that into the one confluence run the rivers, and pour into it, and fill it not. O Varuna, loosen whatever sin we have committed to bosom-friend, comrade, or brother; to our own house, or to the stranger; what (we) have sinned like gamblers at play, real (sin), or what we have not known. Make loose, as it were, all these things, O god Varuna, and may we be dear to thee hereafter."

In this hymn Varuna is a water-god, who stands in mid-air and directs the rain; who, after the rain, reinstates the sun; who releases from sin (as water does from dirt?). According to this conception it would seem that Varuna were the 'coverer' rather than the 'encompasser.' It might seem probable even that Varuna first stood to Dyaus as cloud and rain and night to shining day, and that his counterpart, Οὐρανός, stood in the same relation to Ζεύς; that Οὐρανός were connected with οὐρέω and Varuna with *varī*, river, *vāri*, water.[1]

[1] Later, Varuna's water-office is his only physical side. Compare Āit. Ār. ii. 1. 7. 7, 'water and Varuna, children of mind.' Compare with *vāri*, οὐρά = *vāra*, and *varī*, an old word for rivers, *varṣ* (= *var* + *s*), 'rain.' The etymology is very doubtful on account of the number of *var*-roots. Perhaps dew (ἕρσα) and rain first as 'coverer.' Even *var* = *vas* 'shine,' has been suggested (ZDMG. xxii. 603).

It is possible, but it is not provable. But no interpretation of Varuna that ignores his rainy side can be correct. And this is fully recognized by Hillebrandt. On account of his "thousand spies," *i.e.*, eyes, he has been looked upon by some as exclusively a night-god. But this is too one-sided an interpretation, and passes over the all-important fact that it is only in conjunction with the sun (Mitra), where there is a strong antithesis, that the night-side of the god is exclusively displayed. Wholly a day-god he cannot be, because he rules night and rain. He is *par excellence* the Asura, and, like Ahura Mazdao, has the sun for an eye, *i.e.*, he is heaven. But there is no Varuna in Iranian worship and Ahura is a sectarian specialization. Without this name may one ascribe to India what is found in Iran?[1] It has been suggested by Bergaigne that Varuna and Vritra, the rain-holding demon, were developments from the same idea, one revered as a god, the other, a demon; and that the word means 'restrainer,' rather than 'encompasser.'

From all this it will be evident that to claim an original monotheism as still surviving in the person of Varuna, is impossible; and this is the one point we would make. Every one must admire the fine hymn in which he is praised, but what there is in it does not make it seem very old, and the intercalated month is decisive evidence, for here alone in the Rig Veda is mentioned this month, which implies the five-year cyclus, but this belongs to the Brahmanic period (Weber, *Vedische Beiträge*, p. 38). Every explanation of the original nature of Varuna must take into consideration that he is a rain-god, a day-god, and a night-god in turn, and that where he is praised in the most elevated language the rain-side disappears, although it was fundamental, as may be seen by comparing many passages, where Varuna is exhorted to give rain, where his title is 'lord of streams,' his position that of 'lord

[1] The old comparison of *Varena cathrugaosha* turns out to be "the town of Varna with four gates"!

of waters.' The decrease of Varuna worship in favor of Indra results partly from the more peaceful god of rain appearing less admirable than the monsoon-god, who overpowers with storm and lightning, as well as 'wets the earth.'

The most valuable contribution to the study of Varuna is Hillebrandt's 'Varuna and Mitra.' This author has succeeded in completely overthrowing the old error that Varuna is exclusively a night-god.[1] Quite as definitively he proves that Varuna is not exclusively a day-god.

Bergaigne, on the other hand, claims an especially tenebrous character for Varuna.[2] Much has been written on luminous deities by scholars that fail to recognize the fact that the Hindus regard the night both as light and as dark. But to the Vedic poet the night, star-illumined, was bright. Even Hillebrandt speaks of "the bright heaven" of day as "opposed to the dark night-heaven in which Varuna also shows himself."[3]

In the Rig Veda, as it stands, with all the different views of Varuna side by side, Varuna is a universal encompasser, moral as well as physical. As such his physical side is almost gone. But the conception of him as a moral watcher and sole lord of the universe is in so sharp contrast to the figure of the rain-god, who, like Parjanya, stands in mid-air and upsets a water-barrel, that one must discriminate even between the Vedic views in regard to him.[4]

It is Varuna who lets rivers flow; with Indra he is besought not to let his weapons fall on the sinner; wind is his breath.[5]

[1] In *India: What Can it Teach us*, pp. 197, 200, Müller tacitly recognizes in the physical Varuna only the 'starry' night-side.

[2] *Loc. cit.* III. 119. Bergaigne admits Varuna as god of waters, but sees in him identity with Vritra a 'restrainer of waters.' He thinks the 'luminous side' of Varuna to be antique also (III. 117–119). Varuna's cord, according to Bergaigne, comes from 'tying up' the waters; 'night's fetters,' according to Hillebrandt.

[3] *Loc. cit.* p. 13.

[4] One of the chief objections to Bergaigne's conception of Varuna as water-restrainer is that it does not explain the antique union with Mitra.

[5] II. 28. 4, 7; vii. 82. 1, 2; 87. 2.

On the other hand he is practically identified with the sun.[1] How ill this last agrees with the image of a god who 'lives by the spring of rivers,' 'covers earth as with a garment,' and 'rises like a secret sea (in fog) to heaven'![2] Even when invoked with the sun, Mitra, Varuna still gives rain: "To whomsoever ye two are kindly disposed comes sweet rain from heaven; we beseech you for rain . . . you, the thunderers who go through earth and heaven" (v. 63), — a strange prayer to be addressed to a monotheistic god of light! "Ye make the lightning flash, ye send the rain; ye hide the sky in cloud and rain" (*ib.*). In the hymn preceding we read: "Ye make firm heaven and earth, ye give growth to plants, milk to cows; O ye that give rain, pour down rain!" In the same group another short hymn declares: "They are universal kings, who have *ghee* (rain) in their laps; they are lords of the rain" (v. 68). In the next hymn: "Your clouds (cows) give nourishment, your streams are sweet." Thus the twain keep the order of the seasons (i. 2. 7–8) and protect men by the regular return of the rainy season. Their weapons are always lightning (above, i. 152. 2, and elsewhere). A short invocation in a family-book gives this prayer: "O Mitra-Varuna, wet our meadows with *ghee*; wet all places with the sweet drink" (iii. 62. 16).

The interpretation given above of the office of Varuna as regards the sun's path, is supported by a verse where is made an allusion to the time "when they release the sun's horses," *i.e.*, when after two or three months of rain the sun shines again (v. 62. 1). In another verse one reads: "Ye direct the waters, sustenance of earth and heaven, richly let come your rains" (viii. 25. 6).

Now there is nothing startling in this view. In opposition to the unsatisfactory attempts of modern scholars, it is the

[1] vii. 87. 6; 88. 2.

[2] viii. 41. 2, 7, 8. So Varuna gives *soma*, rain. As a rain-god he surpasses Dyaus, who, ultimately, is also a rain-god (above), as in Greece.

traditional interpretation of Mitra and Varuna that Mitra is the god of day (*i.e.*, the sun), and Varuna the god of night (*i.e.*, covering),[1] while native belief regularly attributes to him the lordship of water.[2] The 'thousand eyes' of Varuna are the result of this view. The other light-side of Varuna as special lord of day (excluding the all-heaven idea with the sun as his 'eye') is elsewhere scarcely referred to, save in late hymns and viii. 41.[3] In conjunction with the storm-god, Indra, the wrath-side of Varuna is further developed. The prayer for release is from 'long darkness,' *i.e.*, from death; in other words, may the light of life be restored (ii. 27. 14–15; ii. 28. 7). Grassmann, who believes that in Varuna there is an early monotheistic deity, enumerates all his offices and omits the giving of rain from the list;[4] while Ludwig derives his name from *var* (= velle) and defines him as the lofty god who wills!

Varuna's highest development ushers in the middle period of the Rig Veda; before the rise of the later All-father, and even before the great elevation of Indra. But when Sūrya and Dawn were chief, then Varuna was chiefest. There is no monotheism in the worship of a god who is regularly associated as one of a pair with another god. Nor is there in Varuna any religious grandeur which, so far as it exceeds that of other divinities, is not evolved from his old physical side. One cannot personify heaven and write a descriptive poem about him without becoming elevated in style, as compared with the tone of one that praises a rain-cloud or even the more confined personality of the sun. There is a stylistic but not a metaphysical descent from this earlier period in the 'lords of the atmosphere,' for, as we shall show, the elevation of Indra

1 Compare Çat. Br. v. 2. 5. 17, "whatever is dark is Varuna's."

2 In ii. 38. 8 *varuṇa* means 'fish,' and 'water' in i. 184. 3.

3 v. 62. 1, 8; 64. 7: 64. 5; 65. 2; 67. 2; 69. 1; vi. 51. 1; 67. 5. In viii. 47. 11 the Ādityas are themselves spies.

4 Introduction to Grassmann, ii. 27; iv. 42. Lex. s. v.

and Agni denotes a philosophical conception yet more advanced than the almost monotheistic greatness attained by Varuna. But one must find the background to this earlier period; and in it Varuna is not monotheistic. He is the covering sky united with the sun, or he whose covering is rain and dew. Indra treats Varuna as Savitar treats Mitra, supplants him; and for the same reason, because each represents the same priestly philosophy.

In the one extant hymn to Mitra (who is Indo-Iranian) it is Mitra that 'watches men,' and 'bears earth and heaven.' He is here (iii. 59) the kindly sun, his name (Mitra, 'friend') being frequently punned upon.

The point of view taken by Barth deserves comment. He says:[1] "It has sometimes been maintained that the Varuna of the hymns is a god in a state of decadence. In this view we can by no means concur; . . . an appeal to these few hymns is enough to prove that in the consciousness of their authors the divinity of Varuna stood still intact." If, instead of 'still intact,' the author had said, 'on the increase, till undermined by still later philosophical speculation,' the true position, in our opinion, would have been given. But a distinction must be made between decadence of greatness and decadence of popularity. It has happened in the case of some of the Vedic inherited gods that exactly in proportion as their popularity decreased their greatness increased; that is to say, as they became more vague and less individual to the folk they were expanded into wider circles of relationship by the theosophist, and absorbed other gods' majesty. Varuna is no longer a popular god in the Rig Veda. He is already a god of speculation, only the speculation did not go far enough to suit the later seers of Indra-Savitar-hood. Most certainly his worship, when compared in popularity with that of Agni and Indra, is unequal. But this is because he is too remote to be popular.

1 *Religions of India*, p. 17.

What made the popular gods was a union of near physical force to please the vulgar, with philosophical mysticism to please the priest, and Indra and Agni fulfilled the conditions, while awful, but distant, Varuna did not.

In stating that the great hymn to Varuna is not typical of the earliest stage of religious belief among the Vedic Aryans, we should add one word in explanation. Varuna's traits, as shown in other parts of the Rig Veda, are so persistent that they must be characteristic of his original function. It does not follow, however, that any one hymn in which he is lauded is necessarily older than the hymn cited from the first book. The earliest stage of religious development precedes the entrance into the Punjāb. It may even be admitted that at the time when the Vedic Aryans became Hindus, that is, when they settled about the Indus, Varuna was the great god we see him in the great hymn to his honor. But while the relation of the Ādityas to the spirits of Ahura in Zoroaster's system points to this, yet it is absurd to assume this epoch as the starting point of Vedic belief. Back of this period lies one in which Varuna was by no means a monotheistic deity, nor even the greatest divinity among the gods. The fact, noticed by Hillebrandt, that the Vasishtha family are the chief praisers of Varuna, may also indicate that his special elevation was due to the theological conceptions of one clan, rather than of the whole people, since in the other family books he is worshipped more as one of a pair, Varuna and Mitra, heaven and sun.

ADITI.

The mother of Varuna and the luminous gods is the 'mother of kings,' Boundlessness (*aditi*),[1] a product of priestly theosophy. Aditi makes, perhaps, the first approach to formal pan-

[1] The Rik knows, also, a Diti, but merely as antithesis to Aditi — the 'confined and unconfined.' Aditi is prayed to (for protection and to remove sin) in sporadic verses of several hymns addressed to other gods, but she has no hymn.

theism in India, for all gods, men, and things are identified with her (i. 89. 10). Seven children of Aditi are mentioned, to whom is added an eighth (in one hymn).[1] The chief of these, who is *par excellence* the Āditya (son of Aditi), is Varuna. Most of the others are divinities of the sun (x. 72). With Varuna stands Mitra, and besides this pair are found 'the true friend' Aryaman, Savitar, Bhaga, and, later, Indra, as sun (?). Daksha and Ança are also reckoned as Ādityas, and Sūrya is enumerated among them as a divinity distinct from Savitar. But the word *aditi*, 'unbound,' is often a mere epithet, of Fire, Sky, etc. Moreover, in one passage, at least, *aditi* simply means 'freedom' (i. 24. 1), less boundlessness than 'un-bondage'; so, probably, in i. 185. 3, 'the gift of freedom.' Ança seems to have much the same meaning with Bhaga, *viz.*, the sharer, giver. Daksha may, perhaps, be the 'clever,' 'strong' one (δεξιός), abstract Strength; as another name of the sun (?). Aditi herself (according to Müller, Infinity; according to Hillebrandt, Eternity) is an abstraction that is born later than her chief sons, Sun and Varuna.[2] Zarathustra (Zoroaster, not earlier than the close of the first Vedic period) took the seven Ādityas and reformed them into one monotheistic (dualistic) Spirit (Ahura), with a circle of six moral attendants, thereby dynamically destroying every physical conception of them.

DAWN.

We have devoted considerable space to Varuna because of the theological importance with which is invested his personality. If one admit that a monotheistic Varuna is the *ur*-Varuna, if one see in him a sign that the Hindus originally worshipped one universally great superior god, whose image effaced that

[1] Müller (*loc. cit*, below) thinks that the 'sons of Aditi' were first eight and were then reduced to seven, in which opinion as in his whole interpretation of Aditi as a primitive dawn-infinity we regret that we cannot agree with him.

[2] See Hillebrandt, *Die Göttin Aditi;* and Müller, SBE., xxxii., p. 241, 252.

of all the others,[1] then the attempt to trace any orderly development in Hindu theology may as well be renounced; and one must imagine that this peculiar people, starting with monotheism descended to polytheism, and then leapt again into the conception of that Father-god whose form, in the end of the Rig Vedic period, out-varunas Varuna as encompasser and lord of all. If, on the other hand, one see in Varuna a god who, from the 'covering,' heaven and cloud and rain, from earliest time has been associated with the sun as a pair, and recognize in Varuna's loftier form the product of that gradual elevation to which were liable all the gods at the hands of the Hindu priests; if one see in him at this stage the highest god which a theology, based on the worship of natural phenomena, was able to evolve; then, for the reception of those gods who overthrew him from his supremacy, because of their greater freedom from physical restraints, there is opened a logical and historical path — until that god comes who in turn follows these half-embodied ones, and stands as the first immaterial author of the universe — and so one may walk straight from the physical beginning of the Rig Vedic religion to its spiritual Brahmanic end.

We turn now to one or two phenomena-deities that were never much tampered with by priestly speculation; their forms being still as bright and clear as when the first Vedic worshipper, waiting to salute the rising sun, beheld in all her beauty, and thus praised

The Dawn.[2]

As comes a bride hath she approached us, gleaming;
All things that live she rouses now to action.
A fire is born that shines for human beings;
Light hath she made, and driven away the darkness.

[1] That is to say, if one believe that the 'primitive Aryans' were innoculated with Zoroaster's teaching. This is the sort of Varuna that Roth believes to have existed among the aboriginal Aryan tribes (above, p. 13, note 2).

[2] vii. 77.

Wide-reaching hath she risen, to all approaching,
And shone forth clothed in garments white and glistening,
Of gold her color, fair to see her look is,
Mother of kine,[1] leader of days she gleameth.

Bearing the gods' eye, she, the gracious maiden,
— Leading along the white and sightly charger[2] —
Aurora, now is seen, revealed in glory,
With shining guerdons unto all appearing.

O near and dear one, light far off our foes, and
Make safe to us our kines' wide pasture-places.
Keep from us hatred; what is good, that bring us,
And send the singer wealth, O generous maiden.

With thy best beams for us do thou beam widely,
Aurora, goddess bright, our life extending;
And food bestow, O thou all goods possessing,
Wealth, too, bestowing, kine and steeds and war-cars

Thou whom Vasistha's[3] sons extol with praises,
Fair-born Aurora, daughter of Dyaus, the bright one,
On us bestow thou riches high and mighty,
— O all ye gods with weal forever guard us.

In the laudation of Varuna the fancy of the poet exhausts itself in lofty imagery, and reaches the topmost height of Vedic religious lyric. In the praise of Dawn it descends not lower than to interweave beauty with dignity of utterance. Nothing in religious poetry more graceful or delicate than the Vedic Dawn-hymns has ever been written. In the daily vision of Dawn following her sister Night the poet sees his fairest goddess, and in his worship of her there is love and admiration, such as is evoked by the sight of no other deity. "She comes like a fair young maiden, awakening all to labor, with an hundred chariots comes she, and brings the shining light; gleam forth, O Dawn, and give us thy blessing this day; for in thee is the life of every living creature. Even as thou hast rewarded the singers of old, so now reward our song" (i. 48).

[1] Clouds. [2] The sun.

[3] The priest to whom, and to whose family, is ascribed the seventh book.

The kine of Dawn are the bright clouds that, like red cattle, wander in droves upon the horizon. Sometimes the rays of light, which stretch across the heaven, are intended by this image, for the cattle-herding poets employed their flocks as figures for various ends.

The inevitable selfish pessimism of unripe reflection is also woven into the later Dawn-hymns: "How long will it be ere this Dawn, too, shall join the Dawns departed? Vanished are now the men that saw the Dawns of old; we here see her now; there will follow others who will see her hereafter; but, O Dawn, beam here thy fairest; rich in blessings, true art thou to friend and right. Bring hither (to the morning sacrifice) the gods" (i. 113).

Since the metre (here ignored) of the following hymn is not all of one model, it is probable that after the fourth verse a new hymn began, which was distinct from the first; but the argument from metre is unconvincing, and in any event both songs are worth citing, since they show how varied were the images and fancies of the poets: "The Dawns are like heroes with golden weapons; like red kine of the morning on the field of heaven; shining they weave their webs of light, like women active at work; food they bring to the pious worshipper. Like a dancing girl is the Dawn adorned, and opens freely her bosom; as a cow gives milk, as a cow comes forth from its stall, so opens she her breast, so comes she out of the darkness (verses 1–4) . . . She is the ever new, born again and again, adorned always with the same color. As a player conceals the dice, so keeps she concealed the days of a man; daughter of Heaven she wakes and drives away her sister (Night). Like kine, like the waves of a flood, with sunbeams she appears. O rich Dawn, bring us wealth; harness thy red horses, and bring to us success" (i. 92). The homage to Dawn is naturally divided at times with that to the sun: "Fair shines the light of morning; the sun awakens us to toil; along the path of order goes Dawn arrayed in light. She extendeth herself in the east, and gleameth till she fills the sky and earth"; and again: "Dawn is the great work of Varuna and Mitra; through the sun is she awakened" (i. 124; iii. 61. 6–7). In the ritualistic period Dawn is still mechanically lauded, and her beams "rise in the east like pillars of sacrifice" (iv. 51. 2); but otherwise the imagery of the selections given above is that which is usually employed. The 'three dawns' occasionally referred to are, as we have shown elsewhere,[1] the three dawn-lights, white, red, and yellow, as they are seen by both the Vedic poet and the Florentine.

Dawn becomes common and trite after awhile, as do all the gods, and is invoked more to give than to please. 'Wake us,' cries a later poet, 'Wake us to wealth, O Dawn; give to us, give to us; wake up, lest the sun burn thee with his light'—a passage (v. 79) which has caused much learned nonsense to be written on the inimical relations of Sun and Dawn as portrayed here. The dull idea is that Dawn is lazy, and had better get up before Sūrya catches her asleep. The poet is not in the least worried because his image does not express a suitable relationship between the dawn and the sun, nor need others be disturbed at it. The hymn is late, and only important in showing the new carelessness as regards the old gods.[2] Some other traits appear in vii. 75. 1 ff., where Dawn is 'queen of the world,' and banishes the *druhs*, or evil spirit. She here is daughter of Heaven, and wife of the sun (4, 5); *ib.* 76. 1, she is the eye of the world; and *ib.* 81. 4, she is invoked as 'mother.'

There is, at times, so close a resemblance between Dawn-hymns and Sun-hymns that the imagery employed in one is

[1] JAOS., xv. 270.

[2] Much theosophy, and even history (!), has been read into ii. 15, and iv. 30, where poets speak of Indra slaying Dawn; but there is nothing remarkable in these passages. Poetry is not creed. The monsoon (here Indra) does away with dawns for a time, and that is what the poet says in his own way.

used in the other. Thus the hymn vi. 64 begins: "The beams of Dawn have arisen, shining as shine the waters' gleaming waves. She makes good paths, . . . she banishes darkness as a warrior drives away a foe (so of the sun, iv. 13. 2; x. 37. 4; 170. 2). Beautiful are thy paths upon the mountains, and across the waters thou shinest, self-gleaming" (also of the sun). With the last expression may be compared that in vi. 65. 5: "Dawn, whose seat is upon the hills."

Dawn is intimately connected not only with Agni but with the Twin Horsemen, the Açvins (equites)—if not so intimately connected as is Helen with the Dioskouroi, who, *pace* Pischel, are the Açvins of Hellas. This relationship is more emphasized in the hymns to the latter gods, but occasionally occurs in Dawn-hymns, of which another is here translated in full.

To Dawn (iv. 52).

The Daughter of Heaven, this beauteous maid,
Resplendent leaves her sister (Night),
And now before (our sight) appears.

Red glows she like a shining mare,
Mother of kine, who timely comes—
The Horsemen's friend Aurora is.

Both friend art thou of the Horsemen twain,
And mother art thou of the kine,
And thou, Aurora, rulest wealth.

We wake thee with our praise as one
Who foes removes; such thought is ours,
O thou that art possesst of joy.

Thy radiant beams beneficent
Like herds of cattle now appear;
Aurora fills the wide expanse.

With light hast thou the dark removed,
Filling (the world), O brilliant one.
Aurora, help us as thou us'st.

With rays thou stretchest through the heaven
And through the fair wide space between,
O Dawn, with thy refulgent light.

It was seen that Savitar (Pūshan) is the rising and setting sun. So, antithetic to Dawn, stands the Abendroth with her sister, Night. This last, generally, as in the hymn just translated, is lauded only in connection with Dawn, and for herself alone gets but one hymn, and that is not in a family-book. She is to be regarded, therefore, less as a goddess of the pantheon than as a quasi-goddess, the result of a poet's meditative imagination, rather than one of the folk's primitive objects of adoration; somewhat as the English poets personify "Ye clouds, that far above me float and pause, ye ocean-waves . . . ye woods, that listen to the night-bird's singing, O ye loud waves, and O ye forests high, and O ye clouds that far above me soared; thou rising sun, thou blue rejoicing sky!"—and as in Greek poetry, that which before has been conceived of vaguely as divine suddenly is invested with a divine personality. The later poet exalts these aspects of nature, and endows those that were before only half recognized with a little special praise. So, whereas Night was divine at first merely as the sister of divine Dawn, in the tenth book one poet thus gives her praise:

Hymn to Night (x. 127).

Night, shining goddess, comes, who now
Looks out afar with many eyes,
And putteth all her beauties on.

Immortal shining goddess, she
The depths and heights alike hath filled,
And drives with light the dark away.

To me she comes, adornèd well,
A darkness black now sightly made;
Pay then thy debt, O Dawn, and go.[1]

[1] Transferred by Roth from the penultimate position where it stands in the original. Dawn here pays Night for the latter's matutinal withdrawing by withdrawing herself. Strictly speaking, the Dawn is, of course, the sunset light conceived of as identical with that preceding the sunrise (*ushás*, ἠώς, 'east' as 'glow').

The bright one coming put aside
Her sister Dawn (the sunset light),
And lo! the darkness hastes away.

So (kind art thou) to us; at whose
Appearing we retire to rest,
As birds fly homeward to the tree.

To rest are come the throngs of men;
To rest, the beasts; to rest, the birds;
And e'en the greedy eagles rest.

Keep off the she-wolf and the wolf,
Keep off the thief, O billowy Night,
Be thou to us a saviour now.

To thee, O Night, as 'twere an herd,
To a conqueror (brought), bring I an hymn
Daughter of Heaven, accept (the gift).[1]

THE AÇVINS.

The Açvins who are, as was said above, the 'Horsemen,' parallel to the Greek Dioskouroi, are twins, sons of Dyaus, husbands, perhaps brothers of the Dawn. They have been variously 'interpreted,' yet in point of fact one knows no more now what was the original conception of the twain than was known before Occidental scholars began to study them.[2] Even the ancients made mere guesses: the Açvins came before the Dawn, and are so-called because they ride on horses (*açva*, *equos*); they represent either Heaven and Earth, or Day and

[1] Late as seems this hymn to be, it is interesting in revealing the fact that wolves (not tigers or panthers) are the poet's most dreaded foes of night. It must, therefore have been composed in the northlands, where wolves are the herdsman's worst enemies.

[2] Myriantheus, *Die Açvins;* Muir, OST. v. p. 234; Bergaigne, *Religion Védique*, ii. p. 431; Müller, *Lectures*, 2d series, p. 508; Weber, *Ind. St.* v. p. 234. Sāyana on i. 180. 2, interprets the 'sister of the Açvins' as Dawn.

Night, or Sun and Moon, or two earthly kings—such is the unsatisfactory information given by the Hindus themselves.[1]

Much the same language with that in the Dawn-hymns is naturally employed in praising the Twin Brothers. They, like the Dioskouroi, are said to have been incorporated gradually into the pantheon, on an equality with the other gods,[2] not because they were at first human beings, but because they, like Night, were adjuncts of Dawn, and got their divinity through her as leader.[3] In the last book of the Rig Veda they are the sons of Saranyū and Vivasvant, but it is not certain whether Saranyū means dawn or not; in the first book they are born of the flood (in the sky).[4] They are sons of Dyaus, but this, too, only in the last and first books, while in the latter they are separated once, so that only one is called the Son of the Sky.[5] They follow Dawn 'like men' (viii. 5. 2) and are in Brahmanic literature the 'youngest of the gods.'[6]

The twin gods are the physicians of heaven, while to men they bring all medicines and help in times of danger. They were apparently at first only 'wonder-workers,' for the original legends seem to have been few. Yet the striking similarity in these aspects with the brothers of Helen must offset the fact that so much in connection with them seems to have been added in books one and ten. They restore the blind and decrepit, impart strength and speed, and give the power and seed of life; even causing waters to flow, fire to burn, and trees to grow. As such they assist lovers and aid in producing offspring.

The Açvins are brilliantly described. Their bird-drawn chariot and all its appurtenances are of gold; they are swift

[1] Muir, *loc. cit.* Weber regards them as the (stars) Gemini.

[2] Weber, however, thinks that Dawn and Açvins are equally old divinities, the oldest Hindu divinities in his estimation.

[3] In the Epic (see below) they are called the lowest caste of gods (Çūdras).

[4] x. 17. 2; i. 46. 2.

[5] i. 181. 4 (Roth, ZDMG. iv. 425).

[6] Taitt. S. vii. 2. 7. 2; Muir. *loc. cit.* p. 235.

as thought, agile, young, and beautiful. Thrice they come to the sacrifice, morning, noon, and eve; at the yoking of their car, the dawn is born. When the 'banner before dawn' appears, the invocation to the Açvins begins; they 'accompany dawn.' Some variation of fancy is naturally to be looked for. Thus, though, as said above, Dawn is born at the Açvins yoking, yet Dawn is herself invoked to wake the Açvins; while again the sun starts their chariot before Dawn; and as sons of Zeus they are invoked "when darkness still stands among the shining clouds (cows)."[1]

Husbands or brothers or children of Dawn, the Horsemen are also Sūryā's husbands, and she is the sun's daughter (Dawn?) or the sun as female. But this myth is not without contradictions, for Sūryā elsewhere weds Soma, and the Açvins are the bridegroom's friends; whom Pūshan chose on this occasion as his parents; he who (unless one with Soma) was the prior bridegroom of the same much-married damsel.[2]

The current explanation of the Açvins is that they represent two periods between darkness and dawn, the darker period being nearer night, the other nearer day. But they probably, as inseparable twins, are the twinlights or twilight, before dawn, half dark and half bright. In this light it may well be said of them that one alone is the son of bright Dyaus, that both wed Dawn, or are her brothers. They always come together. Their duality represents, then, not successive stages but one stage in day's approach, when light is dark and dark is light. In comparing the Açvins to other pairs[3] this dual nature is frequently referred to; but no less is there a triality in connection with them which often in describing them has been ignored. This is that threefold light which opens day; and, as in many cases they join with Dawn, so their color is

[1] vii. 67. 2; viii. 5. 2; x. 39. 12; viii. 9. 17; i. 34. 10; x. 61. 4. Muir, *loc. cit.* 238–9. Compare *ib.* 234, 256.

[2] Muir, *loc. cit.* p. 237. RV. vi. 58. 4; x. 85. 9 ff.

[3] They are compared to two ships, two birds, etc.

inseparable. Strictly speaking, the break of red is the dawn and the white and yellow lights precede this.[1] Thus in v. 73. 5: "Red birds flew round you as Sūryā stepped upon your chariot"; so that it is quite impossible, in accordance with the poets themselves, to limit the Açvins to the twilight. They are a variegated growth from a black and white seed. The chief function of the Açvins, as originally conceived, was the finding and restoring of vanished light. Hence they are invoked as finders and aid-gods in general (the myths are given in Myriantheus).

Some very amusing and some silly legends have been collected and told by the Vedic poets in regard to the preservation and resuscitating power of the Açvins — how an old man was rejuvenated by them (this is also done by the three Ribhus, master-workmen of the gods); how brides are provided by them; how they rescued Bhujyu and others from the dangers of the deep (as in the classical legends); how they replaced a woman's leg with an iron one; restored a saint's eye-sight; drew a seer out of a well, etc., etc. Many scholars follow Bergaigne in imagining all these miracles to be anthropomorphized forms of solar phenomena, the healing of the blind representing the bringing out of the sun from darkness, etc. To us such interpretation often seems fatuous. No less unconvincing is the claim that one of the Açvins represents the fire of heaven and the other the fire of the altar. The Twins are called *nāsatyā*, the 'savers' (or 'not untrue ones');[2] explained by some as meaning 'gods with good noses.'[3]

[1] In *Çat. Br.* v. 5. 4. 1, to the Açvins a red-white goat is sacrificed, because 'Açvins are red-white.'

[2] Perhaps best with Brunnhofer, 'the savers' from *nas* as in *nasjan* (AG. p. 99).

[3] *La Religion Védique*, ii. p. 434. That *nāsatya* means 'with good noses' is an epic notion, *nāsatyadasrāu sunasāu*, Mbhā. i. 3. 58, and for this reason, if for no other (though idea is older), the etymology is probably false! The epithet is also Iranian. Twinned and especially paired gods are characteristic of the Rig Veda. Thus Yama and Yamī are twins; and of pairs Indra-Agni, Indra-Vāyu, besides the older Mitra-Varuna, Heaven-Earth, are common.

Hymn to the Horsemen.

Whether ye rest on far-extended earth, or on the sea in house upon it made, come hither thence, O ye that ride the steeds. If ever for man ye mix the sacrifice, then notice now the Kanva [poet who sings]. I call upon the gods [Indra, Vishnu][1] and the swift-going Horsemen.[2] These Horsemen I call now that they work wonders, to seize the works (of sacrifice), whose friendship is preëminently ours, and relationship among all the gods; in reference to whom arise sacrifices . . . If, to-day, O Horsemen, West or East ye stand, ye of good steeds, whether at Druhyu's, Anu's, Turvaça's, or Yadu's, I call ye; come to me. If ye fly in the air, O givers of great joy; or if through the two worlds; or if, according to your pleasure, ye mount the car, — thence come hither, O Horsemen.

From the hymn preceding this, the following verses:[3]

Whatever manliness is in the aether, in the sky, and among the five peoples, grant us that, O Horsemen . . . this hot *soma*-drink of yours with laudation is poured out; this *soma* sweet through which ye discovered Vritra . . . Ascend the swift-rolling chariot, O Horsemen; hither let these my praises bring ye, like a cloud . . . Come as guardians of homes; guardians of our bodies. Come to the house for (to give) children and offspring. Whether ye ride on the same car with Indra, or be in the same house with the Wind; whether united with the Sons of Boundlessness or the Ribhus, or stand on Vishnu's wide steps (come to us). This is the best help of the horsemen, if to-day I should entice them to get booty, or call them as my strength to conquer in battle. . . . Whatever medicine (ye have) far or near, with this now, O wise ones, grant protection. . . . Awake, O Dawn, the Horsemen, goddess, kind and great. . . . When, O Dawn, thou goest in light and shinest with the Sun, then hither comes the Horsemen's chariot, to the house men have to protect. When the swollen *soma*-stalks are milked like cows with udders, and when the choric songs are sung, then they that adore the Horsemen are preëminent. . . .

Here the Açvins are associated with Indra, and even find the evil demon; but, probably, at this stage Indra is more than god of storms.

[1] Perhaps to be omitted.

[2] *Pischel*, Ved. St. i. p. 48. As swift-going gods they are called 'Indra-like.'

[3] viii. 9 and 10.

Some of the expanded myths and legends of the Açvins may be found in i. 118, 119, 158; x. 40. Here follows one with legends in moderate number (vii. 71):

Before the Dawn her sister, Night, withdraweth;
The black one leaves the ruddy one a pathway.
Ye that have kine and horses, you invoke we;
By day, at night, keep far from us your arrow.

Come hither, now, and meet the pious mortal,
And on your car, O Horsemen, bring him good things;
Keep off from us the dry destroying sickness,
By day, at night, O sweetest pair, protect us.

Your chariot may the joy-desiring chargers,
The virile stallions, bring at Dawn's first coming;
That car whose reins are rays, and wealth upon it;
Come with the steeds that keep the season's order.

Upon the car, three-seated, full of riches,
The helping car, that has a path all golden,
On this approach, O lords of heroes, true ones,
Let this food-bringing car of yours approach us.

Ye freed from his old age the man Cyavāna;
Ye brought and gave the charger swift to Pedu;
Ye two from darkness' anguish rescued Atri;
Ye set Jāhusha down, released from fetters.[1]

This prayer, O Horsemen, and this song is uttered;
Accept the skilful poem, manly heroes.
These prayers, to you belonging, have ascended,
O all ye gods protect us aye with blessings![2]

The sweets which the Açvins bring are either on their chariot, or, as is often related, in a bag; or they burst forth from the hoof of their steed. Pegasus' spring in Helicon has been compared with this. Their vehicles are variously pictured

[1] Doubtful.

[2] The last verse is not peculiar to this hymn, but is the sign of the book (family) in which it was composed.

as birds, horses, ships, etc. It is to be noticed that in no one of their attributes are the Açvins unique. Other gods bring sweets, help, protect, give offspring, give healing medicines, and, in short, do all that the Açvins do. But, as Bergaigne points out, they do all this pacifically, while Indra, who performs some of their wonders, does so by storm. He protects by not injuring, and helps by destroying foes. Yet is this again true only in general, and the lines between warlike, peaceful, and 'sovereign' gods are often crossed.

CHAPTER IV.

THE RIG VEDA (CONTINUED).—THE MIDDLE GODS.

ONLY one of the great atmospheric deities, the gods that preëminently govern the middle sphere between sky and earth, can claim an Aryan lineage. One of the minor gods of the same sphere, the ancient rain-god, also has this antique dignity, but in his case the dignity already is impaired by the strength of a new and greater rival. In the case of the wind-god, on the other hand, there is preserved a deity who was one of the primitive pantheon, belonging, perhaps, not only to the Iranians, but to the Teutons, for Vāta, Wind, may be the Scandinavian Woden. The later mythologists on Indian soil make a distinction between Vāta, wind, and Vāyu (from the same root; as in German *wehen*), and in this distinction one discovers that the old Vāta, who must have been once *the* wind-god, is now reduced to physical (though sentient) wind, while the newer name represents the higher side of wind as a power lying back of phenomena; and it is this latter conception alone that is utilized in the formation of the Vedic triad of wind, fire, and sun. In short, in the use and application of the two names, there is an exact parallel to the double terminology employed to designate the sun as Sūrya and Savitar. Just as Sūrya is the older ἥλιος and sol (acknowledged as a god, yet palpably the physical red body in the sky) contrasted with the interpretation which, by a newer name (Savitar), seeks to differentiate the (sentient) physical from the spiritual, so is Vāta, Woden, replaced and lowered by the loftier conception of Vāyu. But, again, just as, when the conception of Savitar is formed, the spiritualizing tendency reverts to Sūrya, and makes of him, too, a figure reclothed in the more modern garb of speech, which is invented for Savitar alone; so the retroactive theosophic fancy, after creating Vāyu as a divine power underlying phenomenal Vāta, reinvests Vāta also with the garments of Vāyu. Thus, finally, the two, who are the result of intellectual differentiation, are again united from a new point of view, and Sūrya or Savitar, Vāyu or Vāta, are indifferently used to express respectively the whole completed interpretation of the divinity, which is now visible and invisible, sun and sun-god, wind and wind-god. In these pairs there is, as it were, a perspective of Hindu theosophy, and one can trace the god, as a spiritual entity including the physical, back to the physical prototype that once was worshipped as such alone.

In the Rig Veda there are three complete hymns to Wind, none of these being in the family books. In x. 186, the poet calls on Wind to bring health to the worshipper, and to prolong his life. He addresses Wind as 'father and brother and friend,' asking the power that blows to bring him ambrosia, of which Wind has a store. These are rather pretty verses without special theological intent, addressed more to Wind as such than to a spiritual power. The other hymn from the same book is directed to Vāta also, not to Vāyu, and though it is loftier in tone and even speaks of Vāta as the soul of the gods, yet is it evident that no consistent mythology has worked upon the purely poetic phraseology, which is occupied merely with describing the rushing of a mighty wind (x. 168). Nevertheless, Vāta is worshipped, as is Vāyu, with oblations.

Hymn to Wind (Vāta).

Now Vāta's chariot's greatness! Breaking goes it,
And thundering is its noise; to heaven it touches,
Goes o'er the earth, cloud[1] making, dust up-rearing;

[1] Compare i. 134. 3.

Then rush together all the forms of Vāta;
To him they come as women to a meeting.
With them conjoint, on the same chariot going,
Is born the god, the king of all creation.
Ne'er sleepeth he when, on his pathway wandering,
He goes through air. The friend is he of waters;
First-born and holy, — where was he created,
And whence arose he? Spirit of gods is Vāta,
Source of creation, goeth where he listeth;
Whose sound is heard, but not his form. This Vāta
Let us with our oblations duly honor.

In times later than the Rig Veda, Vāyu interchanges with Indra as representative of the middle sphere; and in the Rig Veda all the hymns of the family books associate him with Indra (vii. 90–92; iv. 47–48). In the first book he is associated thus in the second hymn; while, *ib.* 134, he has the only remaining complete hymn, though fragments of songs occasionally are found. All of these hymns except the first two simply invite Vāyu to come with Indra to the sacrifice. It is Vāyu who with Indra obtains the first drink of soma (i. 134. 6). He is spoken of as the artificer's, Tvashtar's, son-in-law, but the allusion is unexplained (viii. 26. 22); he in turn begets the storm-gods (i. 134. 4).

With Vāyu is joined Indra, one of the popular gods. These divinities, which are partly of the middle and partly of the lower sphere, may be called the popular gods, yet were the title 'new gods' neither wholly amiss nor quite correct. For, though the popular deities in general, when compared with many for whom a greater antiquity may be claimed, such as the Sun, Varuna, Dyaus, etc., are of more recent growth in dignity, yet there remains a considerable number of divinities, the hymns in whose honor, dating from the latest period, seem to show that the power they celebrate had been but lately admitted into the category of those gods that deserved special worship. Consequently new gods would be a misleading term, as it should be applied to the plainer products of theological speculation and abstraction rather than to Indra and his peers, not to speak of those newest pantheistic gods, as yet unknown. The designation popular must be understood, then, to apply to the gods most frequently, most enthusiastically revered (for in a stricter sense the sun was also a popular god): and reference is had in using this word to the greater power and influence of these gods, which is indicated by the fact that the hymns to Agni and Indra precede all others in the family books, while the Soma-hymns are collected for the most part into one whole book by themselves.

But there is another factor that necessitates a division between the divinities of sun and heaven and the atmospheric and earthly gods which are honored so greatly; and this factor is explanatory of the popularity of these gods. In the case of the older divinities it is the spiritualization of a sole material appearance that is revered; in the case of the popular gods, the material phenomenon is reduced to a minimum, the spirituality behind the phenomenon is exalted, and that spirituality stands not in and for itself, but as a part of a union of spiritualities. Applying this test to the earlier gods the union will be found to be lacking. The sun's spiritual power is united with Indra's, but the sun is as much a physical phenomenon as a spirituality, and always remains so. On the other hand, the equation of Varunic power with Indraic never amalgamated the two; and these are the best instances that can be chosen of the older gods. For in the case of others it is self-evident. Dyaus and Dawn are but material phenomena, slightly spiritualized, but not joined with the spirit-power of others.

Many have been the vain attempts to go behind the returns of Vedic hymnology and reduce Indra, Agni, and Soma to terms of a purely naturalistic religion. It cannot be done. Indra is neither sun, lightning, nor storm; Agni is neither hearth-fire nor celestial fire; Soma is neither planet nor moon.

Each is the transient manifestation of a spirituality lying behind and extending beyond this manifestation. Here alone is the latch-key of the newer, more popular religion. Not merely because Indra was a 'warrior god,' but because Indra and Fire were one; because of the mystery, not because of the appearance, was he made great at the hands of the priests. It is true, as has been said above, that the idol of the warriors was magnified because he was such; but the true cause of the greatness ascribed to him in the hymns lay in the secret of his nature, as it was lauded by the priest, not in his form, as it was seen by the multitude. Neither came first, both worked together; but had it not been for the esoteric wisdom held by the priests in connection with his nature, Indra would have gone the way of other meteorological gods; whereas he became chiefest of the gods, and, as lord of strength, for a time came nearest to the supreme power.

INDRA.

Indra has been identified with 'storm,' with the 'sky,' with the 'year'; also with 'sun' and with 'fire' in general.[1] But if he be taken as he is found in the hymns, it will be noticed at once that he is too stormy to be the sun; too luminous to be the storm; too near to the phenomena of the monsoon to be the year or the sky; too rainy to be fire; too alien from every one thing to be any one thing. He is too celestial to be wholly atmospheric; too atmospheric to be celestial; too earthly to be either. A most tempting solution is that offered by Bergaigne, who sees in Indra sun or lightning. Yet does this explanation not explain all, and it is more satisfactory than others only because it is broader; while it is not yet broad enough. Indra, in Bergaigne's opinion, stands, however, nearer

[1] For the different views, see Perry, JAOS. xi. p. 119; Muir, OST. v. p. 77.

to fire than to sun.[1] But the savant does not rest content with his own explanation: "Indra est peut-être, de tous les dieux védiques, celui qui résiste le plus longtemps à un genre d'analyse qui, appliqué à la plupart des autres, les résout plus ou moins vite en des personnifications des éléments, soit des phénomènes naturels, soit du culte" (*ibid.* p. 167).

Dyaus' son, Indra, who rides upon the storm and hurls the lightnings with his hands; who 'crashes down from heaven' and 'destroys the strongholds' of heaven and earth; whose greatness 'fills heaven and earth'; whose 'steeds are of red and gold'; who 'speaks in thunder,' and 'is born of waters and cloud'; behind whom ride the storm-gods; with whom Agni (fire) is inseparably connected; who 'frees the waters of heaven from the demon,' and 'gives rain-blessings and wealth' to man — such a god, granted the necessity of a naturalistic interpretation, may well be thought to have been lightning itself originally, which the hymns now represent the god as carrying. But in identifying Indra with the sun there is more difficulty. In none of the early hymns is this suggested, and the texts on which Bergaigne relies besides being late are not always conclusive. "Indra clothes himself with the glory of the sun"; he "sees with the eye of the sun" — such texts prove little when one remembers that the sun is the eye of all the gods, and that to clothe ones'self with solar glory is far from being one with the sun. In one other, albeit a late verse, the expression 'Indra, a sun,' is used; and, relying on such texts, Bergaigne claims that Indra is the sun. But it is evident that this is but one of many passages where Indra by implication is compared to the sun; and comparisons do not indicate allotropy. So, in ii. 11. 20, which Bergaigne gives as a parallel, the words say expressly "Indra [did so and so] *like a sun.*"[2] To rest a building so important on a basis so frail is

[1] *La Religion Védique*, ii. pp. 159, 161, 166, 187.

[2] The chief texts are ii. 30. 1; iv. 26. 1; vii. 98. 6; viii. 93. 1, 4; x. 89. 2; x. 112. 3.

fortunately rare with Bergaigne. It happens here because he is arguing from the assumption that Indra primitively was a general luminary. Hence, instead of building up Indra from early texts, he claims a few late phrases as precious confirmation of his theory.[1] What was Indra may be seen by comparing a few citations such as might easily be amplified from every book in the Rig Veda.

According to the varying fancies of the poets, Indra is armed with stones, clubs, arrows, or the thunderbolt (made for him by the artificer, Tvashtar), of brass or of gold, with many edges and points. Upon a golden chariot he rides to battle, driving two or many red or yellow steeds; he is like the sun in brilliancy, and like the dawn in beauty; he is multiform, and cannot really be described; his divine name is secret; in appearance he is vigorous, huge; he is wise and true and kind; all treasures are his, and he is a wealth-holder, vast as four seas; neither his greatness nor his generosity can be comprehended; mightiest of gods is he, filling the universe; the heavens rest upon his head; earth cannot hold him; earth and heaven tremble at his breath; he is king of all; the mountains are to him as valleys; he goes forth a bull, raging, and rushes through the air, whirling up the dust; he breaks open the rain-containing clouds, and lets the rain pour down; as the Açvins restore the light, so he restores the rain; he is (like) fire born in three places; as the giver of rain which feeds, he creates the plants; he restores or begets Sun and Dawn (after the storm has passed);[2] he creates (in the same way) all things, even heaven and earth; he is associated with Vishnu and Pūshan (the sun-gods), with the Açvins, with the Maruts (storm-gods) as his especial followers, and with the artisan Ribhus. With Varuna he is an Adityá, but he is also associated with another

[1] Other citations given by Bergaigne in connection with this point are all of the simile class. Only as All-god is Indra the sun.

[2] i. 51. 4: "After slaying Vritra, thou did'st make the sun climb in the sky."

group of gods, the Vasus (x. 66. 3), as Vasupati, or 'lord of the Vasus.' He goes with many forms (vi. 47. 18).[1]

The luminous character[2] of Indra, which has caused him to be identified with light-gods, can be understood only when one remembers that in India the rainy season is ushered in by such displays of lightning that the heavens are often illuminated in every direction at once; and not with a succession of flashes, but with contemporaneous ubiquitous sheets of light, so that it appears as if on all sides of the sky there was one lining of united dazzling flame. When it is said that Indra 'placed light in light,' one is not to understand, with Bergaigne, that Indra is identical with the sun, but that in day (light) Indra puts lightning (x. 54. 6; Bergaigne ii. p. 187).

Since Indra's lightning[3] is a form of fire, there is found in this union the first mystic dualism of two distinct gods as one. This comes out more in Agni-worship than in Indra-worship, and will be treated below. The snake or dragon killed by Indra is Vritra, the restrainer, who catches and keeps in the clouds the rain that is falling to earth. He often is called simply the snake, and as the Budhnya Snake, or snake of the cloud-depths, is possibly the Python (= Budh-nya).[4] There is here a touch of primitive belief in an old enemy of man — the serpent! But the Budhnya Snake has been developed in opposite ways, and has contradictory functions.[5]

Indra, however, is no more the lightning than he is the sun. One poet says that he is like the sun;[6] another, that he is like the lightning (viii. 93. 9), which he carries in his arms

1 Ādityá, only vii. 85. 4; Vāl. 4. 7. For other references, see Perry (*loc. cit.*).

2 Bergaigne, ii. 160. 187.

3 Indra finds and begets Agni, iii. 31. 15.

4 Unless the Python be, rather, the Demon of Putrefaction, as in Iranian belief.

5 Demons of every sort oppose Indra; Vala, Vritra, the 'holding' snake (*áhi* = ἔχις), Çushna ('drought'), etc.

6 So he finds and directs the sun and causes it to shine, as explained above (viii. 3. 6; iii. 44. 4; i. 56. 4; iii. 30. 12). He is praised with Vishnu (vi. 69) in one hymn, as distinct from him.

(viii. 12. 7); another, that he is like the light of dawn (x. 89. 12). So various are the activities, so many the phenomena, that with him first the seer is obliged to look back of all these phenomena and find in them one person; and thus he is the most anthropomorphized of the Vedic gods. He is born of heaven or born of clouds (iv. 18), but that his mother is Aditi is not certain. As the most powerful god Indra is again regarded as the All-god (viii. 98. 1–2). With this final supremacy, that distinction between battle-gods and gods sovereign, which Bergaigne insists upon — the sovereign gods belonging to *une conception unitaire de l'ordre du monde* (iii. p. 3; ii. p. 167) — fades away. As Varuna became gradually greatest, so did Indra in turn. But Varuna was a philosopher's god, not a warrior's; and Varuna was not double and mystical. So even the priest (Agni) leaves Varuna, and with the warrior takes more pleasure in his twin Indra; of him making an All-god, a greatest god. Varuna is passive; Indra is energetic; but Indra does not struggle for his lordship. Inspired by *soma*, he smites, triumphs, punishes. Victor already, he descends upon his enemies and with a blow destroys them. It is rarely that he feels the effect of battle; he never doubts its issue.

There is evidence that this supremacy was not gained without contradiction, and the novelty of the last extravagant Indra-worship may be deduced, perhaps, from such passages as viii. 96. 15; and 100. 3, where are expressed doubts in regard to the existence of a real Indra. How late is the worship of the popular Indra, and that it is not originality that causes his hymns to be placed early in each collection, may be judged from the fact that only of Indra (and Agni?) are there idols: viii. 1. 5; iv. 24. 10: "Who gives ten cows for my Indra? When he has slain his foe let (the purchaser) give him to me again."[1] Thus it happens that one rarely finds such poems

[1] Bollensen would see an allusion to idols in i. 145. 4–5 (to Agni), but this is very doubtful (ZDMG. xlvii. p. 586). Agni, however, is on a par with Indra, so that the exception would have no significance. See Kaegi, Rig Veda, note 79 a.

to Indra as to Dawn and to other earlier deities, but almost always stereotyped descriptions of prowess, and mechanical invitations to come to the altar and reward the hymn-maker. There are few of Indra's many hymns that do not smack of *soma* and sacrifice. He is a warrior's god exploited by priests; as popularly conceived, a sensual giant, friend, brother, helper of man. One example of poetry, instead of ritualistic verse-making to Indra, has been translated in the introductory chapter. Another, which, if not very inspiring, is at least free from obvious *soma*-worship — which results in Indra being invoked chiefly to come and drink — is as follows (vi. 30):

Great hath he grown, Indra, for deeds heroic;
Ageless is he alone, alone gives riches;
Beyond the heaven and earth hath Indra stretched him,
The half of him against both worlds together!
So high and great I deem his godly nature;
What he hath stablished there is none impairs it.
Day after day a sun is he conspicuous,
And, wisely strong, divides the wide dominions.
To-day and now (thou makest) the work of rivers,
In that, O Indra, thou hast hewn them pathway.
The hills have bowed them down as were they comrades;
By thee, O wisely strong, are spaces fastened.
'Tis true, like thee, O Indra, is no other,
Nor god nor mortal is more venerable.
Thou slew'st the dragon that the flood encompassed,
Thou didst let out the waters to the ocean.
Thou didst the waters free, the doors wide opening,
Thou, Indra, brak'st the stronghold of the mountains,
Becamest king of all that goes and moveth,
Begetting sun and heaven and dawn together.

THE MARUTS.

These gods, the constant followers of Indra, from the present point of view are not of great importance, except as showing an unadulterated type of nature-gods, worshipped without much esoteric wisdom (although there is a certain amount of mystery in connection with their birth). There is something of the same pleasure in singing to them as is discernible in the hymns to Dawn. They are the real storm-gods, following Rudra, their father, and accompanying the great storm-bringer, Indra. Their mother is the variegated cow Priçni, the mother cloud. Their name means the shining, gleaming ones.

HYMN TO THE MARUTS (vii. 56. 1–10).

Who, sooth, are the gleaming related heroes,
the glory of Rudra, on beauteous chargers?
For of them the birthplace no man hath witnessed;
they only know it, their mutual birthplace.
With wings expanded they sweep each other,[1]
and strive together, the wind-loud falcons.
Wise he that knoweth this secret knowledge,
that Priçni the great one to them was mother.[2]
This folk the Maruts shall make heroic,
victorious ever, increased in manhood;
In speed the swiftest, in light the lightest,
with grace united and fierce in power—
Your power fierce is; your strength, enduring;
and hence with the Maruts this folk is mighty.
Your fury fair is, your hearts are wrothful,
like maniacs wild is your band courageous.
From us keep wholly the gleaming lightning;
let not your anger come here to meet us.
Your names of strong ones endeared invoke I,
that these delighted may joy, O Maruts.

What little reflection or moral significance is in the Marut hymns is illustrated by i. 38. 1–9, thus translated by Müller:

What then now? When will ye take us as a dear father takes his son by both hands, O ye gods, for whom the sacred grass has been trimmed?

1 Or 'pluck with beaks,' as Müller translates, SBE. xxxii. p. 373.

2 "Bore them" (gave an udder). In v. 52. 16 Rudra is father and Priçni, mother. Compare viii. 94. 1: "The cow . . . the mother of the Maruts, sends milk (rain)." In x. 78. 6 the Maruts are sons of Sindhu (Indus).

Where now? On what errand of yours are you going, in heaven, not on earth? Where are your cows sporting? Where are your newest favors, O Maruts? Where are blessings? Where all delights? If you, sons of Pṛiçni, were mortals and your praiser an immortal, then never should your praiser be unwelcome, like a deer in pasture grass, nor should he go on the path of Yama.[1] Let not one sin after another, difficult to be conquered, overcome us; may it depart, together with greed. Truly they are terrible and powerful; even to the desert the Rudriyas bring rain that is never dried up. The lightning lows like a cow, it follows as a mother follows after her young, when the shower has been let loose. Even by day the Maruts create darkness with the water-bearing cloud, when they drench the earth, etc.

The number of the Maruts was originally seven, afterwards raised to thrice seven, and then given variously,[2] sometimes as high as thrice sixty. They are the servants, the bulls of Dyaus, the glory of Rudra (or perhaps the 'boys of Rudra'), divine, bright as suns, blameless and pure. They cover themselves with shining adornment, chains of gold, gems, and turbans. On their heads are helmets of gold, and in their hands gleam arrows and daggers. Like heroes rushing to battle, they stream onward. They are fair as deer; their roar is like that of lions. The mountains bow before them, thinking themselves to be valleys, and the hills bow down. Good warriors and good steeds are their gifts. They smite, they kill, they rend the rocks, they strip the trees like caterpillars; they rise together, and, like spokes in a wheel, are united in strength. Their female companion is Rodasī (lightning, from the same root as *rudra*, the 'red'). They are like wild boars, and (like the sun) they have metallic jaws. On their chariots are speckled hides; like birds they spread their wings; they strive in flight with each other. Before them the earth sways like a ship. They dance upon their path. Upon their chests for beauty's sake they bind gold armor. From the heavenly udder

[1] *I.e.*, die.

[2] The number is not twenty-seven, as Muir accidentally states, OST. v. p. 147.

they milk down rain. "Through whose wisdom, through whose design do they come?" cries the poet. They have no real adversary. The kings of the forest they tear asunder, and make tremble even the rocks. Their music is heard on every side.[1]

RUDRA.

The father of the Maruts, Rudra, is 'the ruddy one,' *par excellence*, and so to him is ascribed paternity of the 'ruddy ones.' But while Indra has a plurality of hymns, Rudra has but few, and these it is not of special importance to cite. The features in each case are the same. The Maruts remain as gods whose function causes them to be invoked chiefly that they may spare from the fury of the tempest. This idea is in Rudra's case carried out further, and he is specially called on to avert (not only 'cow-slaying' and 'man-slaying' by lightning,[2] but also) disease, pestilence, etc. Hence is he preëminently, on the one hand, the kindly god who averts disease, and, on the other, of destruction in every form. From him Father Manu got wealth and health, and he is the fairest of beings, but, more, he is the strongest god (ii. 33. 3, 10). From such a prototype comes the later god of healing and woe — Rudra, who becomes Çiva.[3]

RAIN-GODS.

There is one rather mechanical hymn directed to the Waters themselves as goddesses, where Indra is the god who gives them passage. But in the unique hymn to the Rivers it is Varuna who, as general god of water, is represented as their patron. In the first hymn the rain-water is meant.[4] A descrip-

[1] v. 58. 4, 5; i. 88. 1; 88. 5; v. 54. 11; viii. 7. 25; i. 166. 10; i. 39. 1; 64. 2–8; v. 54. 6; i. 85. 8; viii. 7. 34; v. 59. 2.

[2] He carries lightnings and medicines together in vii. 46. 3.

[3] Çiva is later identified with Rudra. For the latter in RV. compare i. 43; 114, 1–5, 10; ii. 33. 2–13.

[4] vii. 47, and x. 75.

tion in somewhat jovial vein of the joy produced by the rain after long drought forms the subject matter of another lyric (less an hymn than a poem), which serves to illustrate the position of the priests at the end of this Vedic collection. The frogs are jocosely compared to priests that have fulfilled their vow of silence; and their quacking is likened to the noise of students learning the Veda. Parjanya is the god that, in distinction from Indra as the first cause, actually pours down the rain-drops.

The Frogs.[1]

As priests that have their vows fulfilled,
  Reposing for a year complete,
The frogs have now begun to talk, —
  Parjanya has their voice aroused.

When down the heavenly waters come upon him,
  Who like a dry bag lay within the river,
Then, like the cows' loud lowing (cows that calves have),
  The vocal sound of frogs comes all together.

When on the longing, thirsty ones it raineth,
  (The rainy season having come upon them),
Then *akkala!*[2] they cry; and one the other
  Greets with his speech, as sons address a father.

The one the other welcomes, and together
  They both rejoice at falling of the waters;
The spotted frog hops when the rain has wet him,
  And with his yellow comrade joins his utterance.

When one of these the other's voice repeateth,
  Just as a student imitates his teacher,
Then like united members with fair voices,
  They all together sing among the waters.

[1] vii. 103.

[2] *Akhkhala* is like Latin *eccere*, a shout of joy and wonder (*Am. J. Phil.* XIV. p. 21).

One like an ox doth bellow, goat-like one bleats;
Spotted is one, and one of them is yellow;
Alike in name, but in appearance different,
In many ways the voice they, speaking, vary.

As priests about th' intoxicating[1] *soma*
Talk as they stand before the well-filled vessel,
So stand ye round about this day once yearly,
On which, O frogs, the time of rain approaches.

(Like) priests who *soma* have, they raise their voices,
And pray the prayer that once a year is uttered;
(Like) heated priests who sweat at sacrifices,
They all come out, concealed of them is no one.

The sacred order of the (year) twelve-membered,
These heroes guard, and never do neglect it;
When every year, the rainy season coming,
The burning heat receiveth its dismission.[2]

In one hymn no less than four gods are especially invoked for rain — Agni, Brihaspati, Indra, and Parjanya. The two first are sacrificially potent; Brihaspati, especially, gives to the priest the song that has power to bring rain; he comes either 'as Mitra-Varuna or Pūshan,' and 'lets Parjanya rain'; while in the same breath Indra is exhorted to send a flood of rain,— rains which are here kept back by the gods,[3] — and Agni is immediately afterwards asked to perform the same favor, apparently as an analogue to the streams of oblation which the priest pours on the fire. Of these gods, the pluvius is Parjanya:

1 Literally, 'that has stood over-night,' *i.e.*, fermented.

2 To this hymn is added, in imitation of the laudations of generous benefactors, which are sometimes suffixed to an older hymn, words ascribing gifts to the frogs. Bergaigne regards the frogs as meteorological phenomena! It is from this hymn as a starting-point proceed the latter-day arguments of Jacobi, who would prove the 'period of the Rig Veda' to have begun about 3500 B.C. One might as well date Homer by an appeal to the Batrachomyomachia.

3 x. 98. 6.

Parjanya loud extol in song,
The fructifying son of heaven;
May he provide us pasturage!
He who the fruitful seed of plants,
Of cows and mares and women forms,
He is the god Parjanya.
For him the melted butter pour
In (Agni's) mouth, — a honeyed sweet, —
And may he constant food bestow![1]

This god is the rain-cloud personified,[2] but he is scarcely to be distinguished, in other places, from Indra; although the latter, as the greater, newer god, is represented rather as causing the rain to flow, while Parjanya pours it down. Like Varuna, Parjanya also upsets a water-barrel, and wets the earth. He is identical with the Slavic Perkuna.

For natural expression, vividness, energy, and beauty, the following hymn is unsurpassed. As a god unjustly driven out of the pantheon, it is, perhaps, only just that he should be exhibited, in contrast to the tone of the sacrificial hymnlet above, in his true light. Occasionally he is paired with Wind; and in the curious tendency of the poets to dualize their divinities, the two become a compound, *Parjanyavātā* ("Parjanya and Vāta"). There is, also, vii. 101, one mystic hymn to Parjanya. The following, v. 83, breathes quite a different spirit:[3]

Greet him, the mighty one, with these laudations,
  Parjanya praise, and call him humbly hither;
With roar and rattle pours the bull his waters,
  And lays his seed in all the plants, a foetus.

He smites the trees, and smites the evil demons, too;
While every creature fears before his mighty blow,
E'en he that hath not sinned, from this strong god retreats,
When smites Parjanya, thundering, those that evil do.

1 vii. 102.

2 Compare Bühler, *Orient and Occident*, i. p. 222.

3 This hymn is another of those that contradict the first assumption of the ritualists. From internal evidence it is not likely that it was made for baksheesh.

As when a charioteer with whip his horses strikes,
So drives he to the fore his messengers of rain;
Afar a lion's roar is raised abroad, whene'er
Parjanya doth create the rain-containing cloud.
Now forward rush the winds, now gleaming lightnings fall;
Up spring the plants, and thick becomes the shining sky.
For every living thing refreshment is begot,
Whene'er Parjanya's seed makes quick the womb of earth.

Beneath whose course the earth hath bent and bowed her,
Beneath whose course the (kine) behoofed bestir them,
Beneath whose course the plants stand multifarious,
He — thou, Parjańya — grant us great protection!
Bestow Dyaus' rain upon us, O ye Maruts!
Make thick the stream that comes from that strong stallion!
With this thy thunder come thou onward, hither,
Thy waters pouring, a spirit and our father.[1]
Roar forth and thunder! Give the seed of increase!
Drive with thy chariot full of water round us;
The water-bag drag forward, loosed, turned downward;
Let hills and valleys equal be before thee!
Up with the mighty keg! then pour it under!
Let all the loosened streams flow swiftly forward;
Wet heaven and earth with this thy holy fluid;[2]
And fair drink may it be for all our cattle!

When thou with rattle and with roar,
Parjanya, thundering, sinners slayest,
Then all before thee do rejoice,
Whatever creatures live on earth.

Rain hast thou rained, and now do thou restrain it;
The desert, too, hast thou made fit for travel;
The plants hast thou begotten for enjoyment;
And wisdom hast thou found for thy descendants.

The different meters may point to a collection of small hymns. It is to be observed that Parjanya is here the father-

1 *Ásuras, pitā́ nas.*

2 Literally, 'with *ghee*'; the rain is like the *ghee*, or sacrificial oil (melted butter).

god (of men); he is the Asura, the Spirit; and rain comes from the Shining Sky (Dyaus). How like Varuna!

The rain, to the poet, descends from the sky, and is liable to be caught by the demon, Vritra, whose rain-swollen belly Indra opens with a stroke, and lets fall the rain; or, in the older view just presented, Parjanya makes the cloud that gives the rain — a view united with the descent of rain from the sky (Dyaus). With Parjanya as an Aryan rain-god may be mentioned Trita, who, apparently, was a water-god, Āptya, in general; and some of whose functions Indra has taken. He appears to be the same with the Persian Thraetaona Āthwya; but in the Rig Veda he is interesting mainly as a dim survival of the past.[1] The washing out of sins, which appears to be the original conception of Varuna's sin-forgiving,[2] finds an analogue in the fact that sins are cast off upon the innocent waters and upon Trita — also a water-god, and once identified with Varuna (viii. 41. 6). But this notion is so unique and late (only in viii. 47) that Bloomfield is perhaps right in imputing it to the [later] moralizing age of the Brāhmanas, with which the third period of the Rig Veda is quite in touch.

1 Some suppose even Indra to be one with the Avestan *Añdra*, a demon, which is possible.

2 Otherwise it is the 'bonds of sin' which are broken or loosed, as in the last verse of the first Varuna hymn, translated above. But the two views may be of equal antiquity (above, p. 65, note). On Trita compare JRAS. 1893, p. 419; PAOS. 1894 (Bloomfield).

CHAPTER V.

THE RIG VEDA (CONTINUED).—THE LOWER GODS.

AGNI.

GREAT are the heavenly gods, but greater is Indra, god of the atmosphere. Greatest are Agni and Soma, the gods of earth.

Agni is the altar-fire. Originally fire, Agni, in distinction from sun and lightning, is the fire of sacrifice; and as such is he great. One reads in v. 3. 1–2, that this Agni is Varuna, Indra; that in him are all the gods. This is, indeed, formally a late view, and can be paralleled only by a few passages of a comparatively recent period. Thus, in the late hymn i. 164. 46: "Indra, Mitra, Varuna, Agni, they say; he is the sun (the bird in the sky); that which is but one they call variously," etc. So x. 114. 5 and the late passage iii. 38. 7, have reference to various forms of Agni.

Indra had a twofold nature in producing the union of lightning and Agni; and this made him mysteriously great. But in Agni is found the first triality, which, philosophically, is interpreted as a trinity. The fire of the altar is one with the lightning, and, again, one with the sun. This is Agni's threefold birth; and all the holy character of three is exhausted in application where he is concerned. It is the highest mystery until the very end of the Vedic age. This Agni it is that is the real Agni of the Rig Veda—the new Agni; for there was probably an Agni cult (as simple fire) long before the *soma* cult. Indra and Agni are one, and both are called the slayers of the demons.[1] They are both united as an indissoluble pair (iii. 12, etc.). Agni, with, perhaps, the

[1] viii. 38. 4; i. 108. 3; Bergaigne, ii. 295.

exception of Soma, is the most important god in the Rig Veda; and it is no chance that gives him the first place in each family hymn-book; for in him are found, only in more fortunate circumstances, exactly the same conditions as obtain in the case of Indra. He appealed to man as the best friend among divine beings; he was not far off, to be wondered at; if terrible, to be propitiated. He was near and kind to friends. And as he seemed to the vulgar so he appealed to the theosophy which permeates the spirit of the poets; for he is mysterious; a mediator between god and man (in carrying to heaven the offerings); a threefold unity, typical of earth, atmosphere, and heaven. From this point of view, as in the case of Indra, so in the case of Agni, only to a greater extent, it becomes impossible to interpret Agni as one element, one phenomenon. There is, when a distinction is made, an *agni* which is single, the altar-fire, separate from other fires; but it is seldom that Agni is not felt as the threefold one.

And now for the interpretation of the modern ritualists. The Hindu ritual had 'the three fires,' which every orthodox believer was taught to keep up. The later literature of the Hindus themselves very correctly took these three fires as types of the three forms of Agni known in the Rig Veda. But to the ritualists the historical precedence is inverted, and they would show that the whole Vedic mythological view of an Agni triad is the result of identifying Agni with the three fires of the ritual. From this crass method of interpretation it would result that all Vedic mythology was the child of the liturgy.[1]

[1] On this point Bergaigne deprecates the application of the ritualistic method, and says in words that cannot be too emphasized: "Mais qui ne voit que de telles explications n'expliquent rien, ou plutôt que le détail du rituel ne peut trouver son explication que dans le mythe, bien loin de pouvoir servir lui-mêmes à expliquer le mythe? . . . Ni le ciel seul ni la terre seule, mais la terre et le ciel étroitement unis et presque confondus, voilà le vrai domaine de la mythologie védique, mythologie dont le rituel n'est que la reproduction" (i. p. 24).

As earthly fire Agni is first ignis:[1] "Driven by the wind, he hastens through the forest with roaring tongues. . . . black is thy path, O bright immortal!" "He mows down, as no herd can do, the green fields; bright his tooth, and golden his beard." "He devours like a steer that one has tied up." This is common fire, divine, but not of the altar. The latter Agni is of every hymn. For instance, the first stanza of the Rig Veda: "Agni, the family priest, I worship; the divine priest of sacrifice; the oblation priest, who bestows riches," where he is invoked under the names of different priests. But Agni is even more than this; he is the fire (heat) that causes production and reproduction, visibly manifest in the sun. This dual Agni, it is to be noticed, is at times the only Agni recognized. The third form is then added, lightning, and therewith Agni is begotten of Indra, and is, therefore, one with Indra: "There is only one fire lighted in many places" (Vāl. 10. 2). As a poetical expression, Agni in the last form is the 'Son of Waters,' an epithet not without significance in philosophical speculation; for water, through all periods, was regarded as the material origin of the universe.

Agni is one with the sun, with lightning (and thunder), and descends into the plants.[2] To man he is house-priest and friend. It is he that has "grouped men in dwelling-places" (iii. 1. 17) like Prometheus, in whose dialectic name, Promantheus, lingers still the fire-creator, the twirling (*math*) sticks which make fire in the wood. He is man's guest and best friend (Mitra, iv. 1. 9; above).

An hymn or two entire will show what was Agni to the Vedic poet. In the following, the Rig Veda's first hymn, he is addressed, in the opening stanza, under the names of house-priest, the chief sacrificial priest, and the priest that pours oblations. In the second stanza he is extolled as the messenger

[1] i. 58. 4; v. 7. 7; vi. 3. 4.

[2] iii. 14. 4; i. 71. 9; vi. 3. 7; 6. 2; iv. 1. 9.

who brings the gods to the sacrifice, himself rising up in sacrificial flames, and forming a link between earth and heaven. In a later stanza he is called the Messenger (Angiras = ἄγγελος?), — one of his ordinary titles:

To Agni (i. 1).

I worship Agni; house-priest, he,
And priest divine of sacrifice,
Th' oblation priest, who giveth wealth.

Agni, by seers of old adored,
To be adored by those to-day —
May he the gods bring here to us.

Through Agni can one wealth acquire,
Prosperity from day to day,
And fame of heroes excellent.

O, Agni! whatsoe'er the rite
That thou surround'st on every side,
That sacrifice attains the gods.

May Agni, who oblation gives —
The wisest, true, most famous priest —
This god with (all) the gods approach!

Thou doest good to every man
That serves thee, Agni; even this
Is thy true virtue, Angiras.

To thee, O Agni, day by day,
Do we with prayer at eve and dawn,
Come, bringing lowly reverence;

To thee, the lord of sacrifice,
And shining guardian of the rite,[1]
In thine own dwelling magnified.

As if a father to his son,
Be easy of access to us,
And lead us onward to our weal.

[1] Or of time or order.

This is mechanical enough to have been made for an established ritual, as doubtless it was. But it is significant that the ritualistic gods are such that to give their true character hymns of this sort must be cited. Such is not the case with the older gods of the pantheon. Ritualistic as it is, however, it is simple. Over against it may be set the following (vi. 8): "Now will I praise the strength of the variegated red bull (Agni), the feasts of the Knower-of-beings[1] (Agni); to Agni, the friend of all men, is poured out a new song, sweet to him as clear *soma.* As soon as he was born in highest heaven, Agni began to protect laws, for he is a guardian of law (or order). Great in strength, he, the friend of all men, measured out the space between heaven and earth, and in greatness touched the zenith; he, the marvellous friend, placed apart heaven and earth; with light removed darkness; separated the two worlds like skins. Friend of all men, he took all might to himself. . . . In the waters' lap the mighty ones (gods) took him, and people established him king. Mātariçvan, messenger of the all-shining one, bore him from afar, friend of all men. Age by age, O Agni, give to poets new glorious wealth for feasts. O ever-youthful king, as if with a ploughshare, rend the sinner; destroy him with thy flame, like a tree! But among our lords bring, O Agni, power unbent, endless strength of heroes; and may we, through thy assistance, conquer wealth an hundredfold, a thousandfold, O Agni, thou friend of all; with thy sure protection protect our royal lords, O helper, thou who hast three habitations; guard for us the host of them that have been generous, and let them live on, friend of all, now that thou art lauded."

Aryan, as Kuhn[2] has shown, is at least the conception if not the particular form of the legend alluded to in this hymn, of fire brought from the sky to earth, which Promethean act is

1 Or 'Finder-of-beings.'

2 *Herabkunft des Feuers und des Göttertrankes.*

attributed elsewhere to the fire-priest.[1] Agni is here Mitra, the friend, as sun-god, and as such takes all the celestials' activities on himself. Like Indra he also gives personal strength: "Fair is thy face, O Agni, to the mortal that desires strength; — they whom thou dost assist overcome their enemies all their lives" (vi. 16. 25, 27). Agni is drawn down to earth by means of the twirling-sticks, one the father, one the mother.[2] "The bountiful wood bore the fair variegated son of waters and plants;[3] the gods united in mind, and payed homage to the glorious mighty child when he was born" (iii. 1. 13). As the son of waters, Agni loves wood but retreats to water, and he is so identified with Indra that he 'thunders' and 'gives rain' (as lightning; ii. 6. 5; iii. 9. 2).

The deeper significance of Agni-worship is found not alone in the fact that he is the god in whom are the other gods, nor in that he is the sun alone, but that "I am Agni, immortality is in my mouth; threefold my light, eternal fire, my name the oblation (fire)," iii. 26. 7. He is felt as a mysterious trinity. As a sun he lights earth; and gives life, sustenance, children, and wealth (iii. 3. 7); as lightning he destroys, as fire he befriends; like Indra he gives victory (iii. 16. 1); like Varuna he releases the bonds of sin; he is Varuna's brother (v. 2. 7; vi. 3. 1; iv. 1. 2); his 'many names' are often alluded to (iii. 20. 3, and above). The ritualistic interpretation of the priest is that the sun is only a sacrificial fire above lighted by the gods as soon as the corresponding fire is lighted on earth by men (vi. 2. 3). He is all threefold; three his tongues, his births, his places; thrice led about the sacrifice given thrice a day (iii. 2. 9; 17. 1; 20. 2; iv. 15. 2;

[1] RV. vi. 16. 13: "Thee, Agni, from out the sky Atharvan twirled," *nir amanthata* (cf. Promantheus). In x. 462 the Bhrigus, φλεγύαι, discover fire.

[2] Compare v. 2. 1. Sometimes Agni is "born with the fingers," which twirl the sticks (iii. 26. 3; iv. 6. 8).

[3] Compare ii. 1: "born in flame from water, cloud, and plants . . . thou art the creator."

1. 7; 12. 1). He is the upholder of the religious order, the guest of mortals, found by the gods in the heavenly waters; he is near and dear; but he also becomes dreadful to the foe (iii. 1. 3–6; 6. 5; vi. 7. 1; 8. 2; iii. 1. 23; 22. 5; vi. 3. 7; iii. 18. 1; iv. 4. 4; 1. 6).

It is easy to see that in such a conception of a triune god, who is fearful yet kind, whose real name is unknown, while his visible manifestations are in earth, air, and heaven, whose being contains all the gods, there is an idea destined to overthrow, as it surpasses, the simpler conceptions of the naturalism that precedes it. Agni as the one divine power of creation is in fact the origin of the human race: "From thee come singers and heroes" (vi. 7. 3). The less weight is, therefore, to be laid on Bergaigne's 'fire origin of man'; it is not as simple fire, but as universal creator that Agni creates man: it is not the 'fire-principle'[1] philosophically elicited from connection of fire and water, but as god-principle, all-creative, that Agni gets this praise.

Several hymns are dedicated to *Indrāgnī*, Indra united with Agni; and the latter even is identified with Dyaus (iv. 1. 10), this obsolescent god reviving merely to be absorbed into Agni. As water purifies from dirt and sin (Varuna), so fire purifies (iv. 12. 4). It has been suggested on account of v. 12. 5: 'Those that were yours have spoken lies and left thee,' that there is a decrease in Agni worship. As this never really happened, and as the words are merely those of a penitent who has lied and seeks forgiveness at the hands of the god of

1 Bergaigne, i. p. 32 ff. The question of priestly names (*loc. cit.* pp. 47–50), should start with Bharata as πυρφόρος, a common title of Agni (ii. 7; vi. 16. 19–21). So Bhrigu is the 'shining' one; and Vasishtha is the 'most shining' (compare Vasus, not good but shining gods). The priests got their names from their god, like Jesuits. Compare Gritsamada in the Bhrigu family (book ii.); Viçvā-mitra, 'friend of all,' in the Bharata family (book iii.); Gautama Vāmadeva belonging to Angirasas (book iv.); Atri 'Eater,' epithet of Agni in RV. (book v.); Bharadvāja 'bearing food' (book vi.); Vasishtha (book vii.); and besides these Jamadagni and Kaçyapa, 'black-toothed (Agni).'

truth, the suggestion is not very acceptable. Agni comprehends not only all naturalistic gods, but such later femininities as Reverence, Mercy, and other abstractions, including Boundlessness.

Of how great importance was the triune god Agni may be seen by comparing his three lights with the later sectarian trinity, where Vishnu, originally the sun, and (Rudra) Çiva, the lightning, are the preserver and destroyer.

We fear the reader may have thought that we were developing rather a system of mythology than a history of religion. With the close of the Vedic period we shall have less to say from a mythological point of view, but we think that it will have become patent now for what purpose was intended the mythological basis of our study. Without this it would have been impossible to trace the gradual growth in the higher metaphysical interpretation of nature which goes hand in hand with the deeper religious sense. With this object we have proceeded from the simpler to the more complex divinities. We have now to take up a side of religion which lies more apart from speculation, but it is concerned very closely with man's religious instincts — the worship of Bacchic character, the reverence for and fear of the death-god, and the eschatological fancies of the poets, together with those first attempts at creating a new theosophy which close the period of the Rig Veda.

SOMA.

Inseparably connected with the worship of Indra and Agni is that of the 'moon-plant,' *soma*, the intoxicating personified drink to whose deification must be assigned a date earlier than that of the Vedas themselves. For the *soma* of the Hindus is etymologically identified with the *haoma* of the Persians (the ὅμωμι of Plutarch),[1] and the cultus at least was begun before

[1] De Isid. et Osir. 46. Compare Windischmann, *Ueber den Somacultus der Arier* (1846), and Muir, *Original Sanskrit Texts*, vol. ii. p. 471. Hillebrandt, *Vedische Mythologie*, i. p. 450, believes *haoma* to mean the moon, as does *soma* in some hymns of the Rig Veda (see below).

the separation of the two nations, since in each the plant is regarded as a god. The inspiring effect of intoxication seemed to be due to the inherent divinity of the plant that produced it; the plant was, therefore, regarded as divine, and the preparation of the draught was looked upon as a sacred ceremony.[1]

This offering of the juice of the *soma*-plant in India was performed thrice daily. It is said in the Rig Veda that *soma* grows upon the mountain Mūjavat, that its or his father is Parjanya, the rain-god, and that the waters are his sisters.[2] From this mountain, or from the sky, accounts differ, *soma* was brought by a hawk.[3] He is himself represented in other places as a bird; and as a divinity he shares in the praise given to Indra, "who helped Indra to slay Vritra," the demon that keeps back the rain. Indra, intoxicated by *soma*, does his great deeds, and indeed all the gods depend on *soma* for immortality. Divine, a weapon-bearing god, he often simply takes the place of Indra and other gods in Vedic eulogy. It is the god Soma himself who slays Vritra, Soma who overthrows cities, Soma who begets the gods, creates the sun, upholds the sky, prolongs life, sees all things, and is the one best friend of god and man, the divine drop (*indu*), the friend of Indra.[4]

As a god he is associated not only with Indra, but also with Agni, Rudra, and Pūshan. A few passages in the later portion of the Rig Veda show that *soma* already was identified with the moon before the end of this period. After this the lunar yellow

1 Compare Kuhn, *Herabkunft des Feuers und des Göttertrankes* (1859); Bergaigne, *La Religion Védique*, i. 148 ff.; Haug's *Āitareya Brāhmana*, Introduction, p. 62; Whitney in *Jour. Am. Or. Soc.* iii. 299; Muir, *Original Sanskrit Texts*, vol. v. p. 258 ff., where other literature is cited.

2 RV. x. 34. 1; ix. 98. 9; 82. 3. The Vedic plant is unknown (not the *sarcostemma viminale*).

3 RV. iii. 43. 7; iv. 26. 6 (other references in Muir, *loc. cit.* p. 262. Perhaps rain as *soma* released by lightning as a hawk (Bloomfield).

4 See the passages cited in Muir, *loc. cit.*

god regularly was regarded as the visible and divine Soma of heaven, represented on earth by the plant.[1]

From the fact that Soma is the moon in later literature, and undoubtedly is recognized as such in a small number of the latest passages of the Rig Veda, the not unnatural inference has been drawn by some Vedic scholars that Soma, in hymns still earlier, means the moon; wherever, in fact, epithets hitherto supposed to refer to the plant may be looked upon as not incompatible with a description of the moon, there these epithets are to be referred directly to Soma as the moon-god, not to *soma*, the mere plant. Thus, with Rig Veda, x. 85 (a late hymn, which speaks of Soma as the moon "in the lap of the stars," and as "the days' banner") is to be compared vi. 39. 3, where it is said that the drop (*soma*) lights up the dark nights, and is the day's banner. Although this expression, at first view, would seem to refer to the moon alone, yet it may possibly be regarded as on a par with the extravagant praise given elsewhere to the *soma*-plant, and not be so significant of the moon as it appears to be. Thus, in another passage of the same book, the *soma*, in similar language, is said to "lay light in the sun," a phrase scarcely compatible with the moon's sphere of activity.[2]

The decision in regard to this question of interpretation is not to be reached so easily as one might suppose, considering that a whole book, the ninth, of the Rig Veda is dedicated to Soma, and that in addition to this there are many hymns addressed to him in the other books. For in the greater number of passages which may be cited for and against this theory the objector may argue that the generally extravagant praise bestowed upon Soma through the Veda is in any one case

1 A complete account of *soma* as given by the Vedic texts will be found in Hillebrandt's *Vedische Mythologie*, vol. i., where are described the different ways of fermenting the juice of the plant.

2 Although so interpreted by Hillebrandt, *loc. cit.* p. 312. The passage is found in RV. vi. 44. 23.

merely particularized, and that it is not incongruous to say of the divine *soma*-plant, "he lights the dark nights," when one reads in general that he creates all things, including the gods. On the other hand, the advocate of the theory may reply that everything which does not apply to the moon-god Soma may be used metaphorically of him. Thus, where it is said, "Soma goes through the purifying sieve," by analogy with the drink of the plant *soma* passing through the sieve the poet may be supposed to imagine the moon passing through the sieve-like clouds; and even when this sieve is expressly called the 'sheep's-tail sieve' and 'wool-sieve,' this may still be, metaphorically, the cloud-sieve (as, without the analogy, one speaks to-day of woolly clouds and the 'mare's tail').

So it happens that, with an hundred hymns addressed to Soma, it remains still a matter of discussion whether the *soma* addressed be the plant or the moon. Alfred Hillebrandt, to whom is due the problem in its present form, declares that everywhere[1] in the Rig Veda Soma means the moon. No better hymn can be found to illustrate the difficulty under which labors the *soma*-exegete than ix. 15, from which Hillebrandt takes the fourth verse as conclusive evidence that by *soma* only the moon is meant. In that case, as will be seen from the 'pails,' it must be supposed that the poet leaps from Soma to *soma* without warning. Hillebrandt does not include the mention of the pails in his citation; but in this, as in other doubtful cases, it seems to us better to give a whole passage than to argue on one or two verses torn from their proper position:

HYMN TO SOMA (ix. 15).

QUERY: Is the hymn addressed to the plant as it is pressed out into the pails, or to the moon?

1. This one, by means of prayer (or intelligence), comes through the fine (sieve), the hero, with swift car, going to the meeting with Indra.

[1] *Loc. cit.* pp. 340, 450.

2. This one thinks much for the sublime assembly of gods, where sit immortals.

3. This one is despatched and led upon a shining path, when the active ones urge (him).[1]

4. This one, shaking his horns, sharpens (them), the bull of the herd, doing heroic deeds forcibly.

5. This one hastens, the strong steed, with bright golden beams, becoming of streams the lord.

6. This one, pressing surely through the knotty (sieve?) to good things, comes down into the vessels.

7. This one, fit to be prepared, the active ones prepare in the pails, as he creates great food.

8. Him, this one, who has good weapons, who is most intoxicating, ten fingers and seven (or many) prayers prepare.

Here, as in ix. 70, Hillebrandt assumes that the poet turns suddenly from the moon to the plant. Against this might be urged the use of the same pronoun throughout the hymn. It must be confessed that at first sight it is almost as difficult to have the plant, undoubtedly meant in verses 7 and 8, represented by the moon in the preceding verses, as it is not to see the moon in the expression 'shaking his horns.' This phrase occurs in another hymn, where Hillebrandt, with the same certainty as he does here, claims it for the moon, though the first part of this hymn as plainly refers to the plant, ix. 70. 1, 4. Here the plant is a steer roaring like the noise of the Maruts (5–6), and then (as above, after the term steer is applied to the plant), it is said that he 'sharpens his horns,' and is 'sightly,' and further, 'he sits down in the fair place . . . on the wooly back,' etc., which bring one to still another hymn where are to be found like expressions, used, evidently, not of the moon, but of the plant, *viz.*, to ix. 37, a hymn not cited by Hillebrandt:

[1] Compare ix. 79. 5, where the same verb is used of striking, urging out the *soma*-juice, *rása*.

This strong (virile) *soma*, pressed for drink, flows into the purifying vessel; this sightly (as above, where Hillebrandt says it is epithet of the moon), yellow, fiery one, is flowing into the purifying vessel; roaring into its own place (as above). This strong one, clear, shining (or purifying itself), runs through the shining places of the sky, slaying evil demons, through the sheep-hair-sieve. On the back of Trita this one shining (or purifying itself) made bright the sun with (his) sisters.[1] This one, slaying Vritra, strong, pressed out, finding good things (as above), uninjured, *soma*, went as if for booty. This god, sent forth by seers, runs into the vessels, the drop (*indu*) for Indra, quickly (or willingly).

So far as we can judge, after comparing these and the other passages that are cited by Hillebrandt as decisive for a lunar interpretation of *soma*, it seems quite as probable that the epithets and expressions used are employed of the plant metaphorically as that tne poet leaps thus lightly from plant to moon. And there is a number of cases which plainly enough are indicative of the plant alone to make it improbable that Hillebrandt is correct in taking Soma as the moon 'everywhere in the Rig Veda.' It may be that the moon-cult is somewhat older than has been supposed, and that the language is consciously veiled in the ninth book to cover the worship of a deity as yet only partly acknowledged as such. But it is almost inconceivable that an hundred hymns should praise the moon; and all the native commentators, bred as they were in the belief of their day that *soma* and the moon were one, should not know that *soma* in the Rig Veda (as well as later) means the lunar deity. It seems, therefore, safer to abide by the belief that *soma* usually means what it was understood to mean, and what the general descriptions in the *soma*-hymns more or less clearly indicate, *viz.*, the intoxicating plant, conceived of as itself divine, stimulating Indra, and, therefore, the *causa movens* of the demon's death, Indra being the *causa efficiens*. Even the allusions to *soma* being in the sky is not

[1] Compare ix. 32. 2, where "Trita's maidens urge on the golden steed with the press-stones, *indu* as a drink for Indra."

incompatible with this. For he is carried thence from the place of sacrifice. Thus too in 83. 1–2: "O lord of prayer,[1] thy purifier (the sieve) is extended. Prevailing thou enterest its limbs on all sides. Raw (*soma*), that has not been cooked (with milk) does not enter into it. Only the cooked (*soma*), going through, enters it. The sieve of the hot drink is extended in the place of the sky. Its gleaming threads extend on all sides. This (*soma's*) swift (streams) preserve the man that purifies them, and wisely ascend to the back of the sky." In this, as in many hymns, the drink *soma* is clearly addressed; yet expressions are used which, if detached, easily might be thought to imply the moon (or the sun, as with Bergaigne) — a fact that should make one employ other expressions of the same sort with great circumspection.

Or, let one compare, with the preparation by the ten fingers, 85. 7: "Ten fingers rub clean (prepare) the steed in the vessels; uprise the songs of the priests. The intoxicating drops, as they purify themselves, meet the song of praise and enter Indra." Exactly the same images as are found above may be noted in ix. 87, where not the moon, but the plant, is conspicuously the subject of the hymn: "Run into the pail, purified by men go unto booty. They lead thee like a swift horse with reins to the sacrificial straw, preparing (or rubbing) thee. With good weapons shines the divine (shining) drop (*indu*), slaying evil-doers, guarding the assembly; the father of the gods, the clever begetter, the support of the sky, the holder of earth. . . . This one, the *soma* (plant) on being pressed out, ran swiftly into the purifier like a stream let out, sharpening his two sharp horns like a buffalo; like a true hero hunting for cows; he is come from the highest press-stone," etc. It is the noise of *soma* dropping that is compared with 'roaring.' The strength given by (him) the drink, makes

[1] On account of the position and content of this hymn, Hillebrandt regards it as addressed to Soma = Brihaspati.

him appear as the 'virile one,' of which force is the activity, and the bull the type. Given, therefore, the image of the bull, the rest follows easily to elaborate the metaphor. If one add that *soma* is luminous (yellow), and that all luminous divinities are 'horned bulls,'[1] then it will be unnecessary to see the crescent moon in *soma*. Moreover, if *soma* be the same with Brihaspati, as thinks Hillebrandt, why are there three horns in v. 43. 13? Again, that the expression 'sharpening his horns' does not refer necessarily to the moon may be concluded from x. 86. 15, where it is stated expressly that the *drink* is a sharp-horned steer: "Like a sharp-horned steer is thy brewed drink, O Indra," probably referring to the taste. The sun, Agni, and Indra are all, to the Vedic poet, 'sharp-horned steers,'[2] and the *soma* plant, being luminous and strong (bull-like), gets the same epithet.

The identity is rather with Indra than with the moon, if one be content to give up brilliant theorizing, and simply follow the poets: "The one that purifies himself yoked the sun's swift steed over man that he might go through the atmosphere, and these ten steeds of the sun he yoked to go, saying Indra is the drop (*indu*)."[3] When had ever the moon the power to start the sun? What part in the pantheon is played by the moon when it is called by its natural name (not by the priestly name, *soma*)? Is *mās* or *candramas* (moon) a power of strength, a great god? The words scarcely occur, except in late hymns, and the moon, by his own folk-name, is hardly praised except in mechanical conjunction with the sun. The floods of which *soma* is lord are explained in ix. 86. 24–25: "The hawk (or eagle) brought thee from the sky, O drop (*indu*), . . . seven milk-streams sing to the yellow one as he purifies himself with the wave in the sieve of sheep's wool. The active strong ones have sent

[1] So the sun in i. 163. 9, 11. 'Sharpening his horns' is used of fire in i. 140. 6; v. 2. 9.

[2] vi. 16. 39; vii. 19. 1; viii. 60. 13.

[3] ix. 63. 8–9; 5. 9. Soma is identified with lightning in ix. 47. 3.

forth the wise seer in the lap of the waters." If one wishes to clear his mind in respect of what the Hindu attributes to the divine drink (expressly drink, and not moon), let him read ix. 104, where he will find that "the twice powerful god-rejoicing intoxicating drink" finds goods, finds a path for his friends, puts away every harmful spirit and every devouring spirit, averts the false godless one and all oppression; and read also ix. 21. 1–4: "These *soma*-drops for Indra flow rejoicing, maddening, light- (or heaven-) finding, averting attackers, finding desirable things for the presser, making life for the singer. Like waves the drops flow into one vessel, playing as they will. These *soma*-drops, let out like steeds (attached) to a car, as they purify themselves, attain all desirable things." According to ix. 97. 41[2] and *ib.* 37. 4 (and other like passages, too lightly explained, p. 387, by Hillebrandt), it is *soma* that "produced the light in the sun" and "makes the sun rise," statements incompatible with the (lunar) Soma's functions, but quite in accordance with the magic power which the poets attribute to the divine drink. Soma is 'king over treasure.' Soma is brought by the eagle that all may "see light" (ix. 48. 3–4). He traverses the sky, and guards order — but not necessarily is he here the moon, for *soma*, the drink, as a "galloping steed," "a brilliant steer," a "stream of pressed *soma*," "a dear sweet," "a helper of gods," is here poured forth; after him "flow great water-floods"; and he "purifies himself in the sieve, he the supporter, holder of the sky"; he "shines with the sun," "roars," and "looks like Mitra"; being here both "the intoxicating draught," and at the same time "the giver of kine, giver of men, giver of horses, giver of strength, the soul of sacrifice" (ix. 2).

Soma is even older than the Vedic Indra as slayer of Vritra and snakes. Several Indo-Iranian epithets survive (of *soma* and *haoma*, respectively), and among those of Iran is the title 'Vritra-slayer,' applied to *haoma*, the others being 'strong' and 'heaven-winning,' just as in the Veda.[1] All three of them are contained in one of the most lunar-like of the hymns to Soma, which, for this reason, and because it is one of the few to this deity that seem to be not entirely mechanical, is given here nearly in full, with the original shift of metre in the middle of the hymn (which may possibly indicate that two hymns have been united).

To Soma (i. 91).

Thou, Soma, wisest art in understanding;
  Thou guidest (us) along the straightest pathway;
'Tis through thy guidance that our pious[2] fathers
  Among the gods got happiness, O Indu.

Thou, Soma, didst become in wisdom wisest;
  In skill[3] most skilful, thou, obtaining all things.
A bull in virile strength, thou, and in greatness;
  In splendor wast thou splendid, man-beholder.

Thine, now, the laws of kingly Varuna;[4]
  Both high and deep the place of thee, O Soma.
Thou brilliant art as Mitra, the belovèd,[5]
  Like Aryaman, deserving service, art thou.

Whate'er thy places be in earth or heaven,
  Whate'er in mountains, or in plants and waters,
In all of these, well-minded, not injurious,
  King Soma, our oblations meeting, take thou.

Thou, Soma, art the real lord,
Thou king and Vritra-slayer, too;
Thou art the strength that gives success.

1 *Hukhratus, verethrajao, hvaresa.* 2 Or: wise.

3 Or: strength. Above, 'shared riches,' perhaps, for 'got happiness.'

4 Or: thine, indeed, are the laws of King Varuna.

5 Or: brilliant and beloved as Mitra (Mitra means friend); Aryaman is translated 'bosom-friend'—both are Ādityas.

And, Soma, let it be thy will
For us to live, nor let us die;[1]
Thou lord of plants,[2] who lovest praise.

Thou, Soma, bliss upon the old,
And on the young and pious man
Ability to live, bestowest.

Do thou, O Soma, on all sides
Protect us, king, from him that sins,
No harm touch friend of such as thou.

Whatever the enjoyments be
Thou hast, to help thy worshipper,
With these our benefactor be.

This sacrifice, this song, do thou,
Well-pleased, accept; come unto us;
Make for our weal, O Soma, thou.

In songs we, conversant with words,
O Soma, thee do magnify;
Be merciful and come to us.

* * * * * * *[3]

All saps unite in thee and all strong powers,
All virile force that overcomes detraction;
Filled full, for immortality, O Soma,
Take to thyself the highest praise in heaven.
The sacrifice shall all embrace — whatever
Places thou hast, revered with poured oblations.
Home-aider, Soma, furtherer with good heroes,
Not hurting heroes, to our houses come thou.
Soma the cow gives; Soma, the swift charger;
Soma, the hero that can much accomplish
(Useful at home, in feast, and in assembly
His father's glory) — gives, to him that worships.

[1] Or: an thou willest for us to live we shall not die.

[2] Or: lordly plant, but not the moon.

[3] Some unessential verses in the above metre are here omitted.

In war unharmed; in battle still a saviour;
  Winner of heaven and waters, town-defender,
Born mid loud joy, and fair of home and glory,
  A conqueror, thou; in thee may we be happy.
Thou hast, O Soma, every plant begotten;
  The waters, thou; and thou, the cows; and thou hast
Woven the wide space 'twixt the earth and heaven;
  Thou hast with light put far away the darkness.
With mind divine, O Soma, thou divine[1] one,
  A share of riches win for us, O hero;
Let none restrain thee, thou art lord of valor;
  Show thyself foremost to both sides in battle.[2]

Of more popular songs, Hillebrandt cites as sung to Soma (!) viii. 69. 8–10:

Sing loud to him, sing loud to him;
Priyamedhas, oh, sing to him,
And sing to him the children, too;
Extol him as a sure defence. . . .
To *Indra* is the prayer up-raised.

The three daily *soma*-oblations are made chiefly to Indra and Vāyu; to Indra at mid-day; to the Ribhus, artisans of the gods, at evening; and to Agni in the morning.

Unmistakable references to Soma as the moon, as, for instance, in x. 85. 3: "No one eats of that *soma* which the priests know," seem rather to indicate that the identification of moon and Soma was something esoteric and new rather than the received belief of pre-Vedic times, as will Hillebrandt. This moon-*soma* is distinguished from the "*soma*-plant which they crush."

The floods of *soma* are likened to, or, rather, identified with, the rain-floods which the lightning frees, and, as it were, brings to earth with him. A whole series of myths depending on this natural phenomenon has been evolved, wherein the lightning-

[1] Or: shining.

[2] The same ideas are prominent in viii. 48, where Soma is invoked as '*soma* that has been drunk,' *i.e.*. the juice of the ('three days fermented') plant.

fire as an eagle brings down *soma* to man, that is, the heavenly drink. Since Agni is threefold and the Gāyatrī metre is threefold, they interchange, and in the legends it is again the metre which brings the *soma*, or an archer, as is stated in one doubtful passage.[1]

What stands out most clearly in *soma*-laudations is that the *soma*-hymns are not only quite mechanical, but that they presuppose a very complete and elaborate ritual, with the employment of a number of priests, of whom the *hotars* (one of the various sets of priests) alone number five in the early and seven in the late books; with a complicated service; with certain divinities honored at certain hours; and other paraphernalia of sacerdotal ceremony; while Indra, most honored with Soma, and Agni, most closely connected with the execution of sacrifice, not only receive the most hymns, but these hymns are, for the most part, palpably made for ritualistic purposes. It is this truth that the ritualists have seized upon and too sweepingly applied. For in every family book, besides this baksheesh verse, occur the older, purer hymns that have been retained after the worship for which they were composed had become changed into a trite making of phrases.

Hillebrandt has failed to show that the Iranian *haoma* is the moon, so that as a starting-point there still is plant and drink-worship, not moon-worship. At what precise time, therefore, the *soma* was referred to the moon is not so important. Since drink-worship stands at one end of the series, and moon-worship at the other, it is antecedently probable that here and there there may be a doubt as to which of the two was intended. Some of the examples cited by Hillebrandt may indeed be referable to the latter end of the series rather than to the former; but that the author, despite the learning and

[1] In the fourth book, iv. 27. 3. On this myth, with its reasonable explanation as deduced from the ritual, see Bloomfield, JAOS. xvi. 1 ff. Compare also Muir and Hillebrandt, *loc. cit.*

ingenuity of his work, has proved his point definitively, we are far from believing. It is just like the later Hindu speculation to think out a subtle connection between moon and *soma*-plant because each was yellow, and swelled, and went through a sieve (cloud), etc. But there is a further connecting link in that the divinity ascribed to the intoxicant led to a supposition that it was brought from the sky, the home of the gods; above all, of the luminous gods, which the yellow *soma* resembled. Such was the Hindu belief, and from this as a starting-point appears to have come the gradual identification of *soma* with the moon, now called Soma. For the moon, even under the name of Gandharva, is not the object of especial worship.

The question so ably discussed by Hillebrandt is, however, one of considerable importance from the point of view of the religious development. If *soma* from the beginning was the moon, then there is only one more god of nature to add to the pantheon. But if, as we believe in the light of the Avesta and Veda itself, *soma*, like *haoma*, was originally the drink-plant (the root *su*, press, from which comes *soma*, implies the plant), then two important facts follow. First, in the identification of yellow *soma*-plant with yellow moon in the latter stage of the Rig Veda (which coincides with the beginning of the Brahmanic period) there is a striking illustration of the gradual mystical elevation of religion at the hands of the priests, to whom it appeared indecent that mere drink should be exalted thus; and secondly, there is the significant fact that in the Indic and Iranian cult there was a direct worship of deified liquor, analogous to Dionysiac rites, a worship which is not unparalleled in other communities. Again, the surprising identity of worship in Avesta and Veda, and the fact that hymns to the earlier deities, Dawn, Parjanya, etc., are frequently devoid of any relation to the *soma*-cult, not only show that Bergaigne's opinion that the whole Rig Veda is but a collection of hymns for *soma*-worship as handed down in different families must be modified; but also that, as we have explained *apropos* of Varuna, the Iranian cult must have branched off from the Vedic cult (whether, as Haug thought, on account of a religious schism or not); that the hymns to the less popular deities (as we have defined the word) make the first period of Vedic cult; and that the special liquor-cult, common to Iran and India, arose after the first period of Vedic worship, when, for example, Wind, Parjanya, and Varuna were at their height, and before the priests had exalted mystically Agni or Soma, and even Indra was as yet undeveloped.

CHAPTER VI.

THE RIG VEDA (CONCLUDED).—YAMA AND OTHER GODS, VEDIC PANTHEISM, ESCHATOLOGY.

In the last chapter we have traced the character of two great gods of earth, the altar-fire and the personified kind of beer which was the Vedic poets' chief drink till the end of this period. With the discovery of *surā*, *humor ex hordeo* (oryzaque; Weber, *Vājapeya*, p. 19), and the difficulty of obtaining the original *soma*-plant (for the plant used later for *soma*, the *asclepias acida*, or *sarcostemma viminale*, does not grow in the Punjāb region, and cannot have been the original *soma*), the status of *soma* became changed. While *surā* became the drink of the people, *soma*, despite the fact that it was not now so agreeable a liquor, became reserved, from its old associations, as the priests' (gods') drink, a sacrosanct beverage, not for the vulgar, and not esteemed by the priest, except as it kept up the rite.

It has been shown that these gods, earthly in habitation, absorbed the powers of the older and physically higher divinities. The ideas that clustered about the latter were transferred to the former. The altar-fire, Agni, is at once earth-fire, lightning, and sun. The drink *soma* is identified with the heavenly drink that refreshes the earth, and from its color is taken at last to be the terrestrial form of its aqueous prototype, the moon, which is not only yellow, but even goes through cloud-meshes just as *soma* goes through the sieve, with all the other points of comparison that priestly ingenuity can devise.

Of different sort altogether from these gods is the ancient Indo-Iranian figure that now claims attention. The older religion had at least one object of devotion very difficult to reduce to terms of a nature-religion.

YAMA.

Exactly as the Hindu had a half-divine ancestor, Manu, who by the later priests is regarded as of solar origin, while more probably he is only the abstract Adam (man), the progenitor of the race; so in Yama the Hindu saw the primitive "first of mortals." While, however, Mitra, Dyaus, and other older nature-gods, pass into a state of negative or almost forgotten activity, Yama, even in the later epic period, still remains a potent sovereign — the king of the dead.

In the Avesta Yima is the son of the 'wide-gleaming' Vivanghvant, the sun, and here it is the sun that first prepares the *soma* (*haoma*) for man. And so, too, in the Rig Veda it is Yama the son of Vivasvant (x. 58. 1; 60. 10) who first "extends the web" of (*soma*) sacrifice (vii. 33. 9, 12). The Vedic poet, not influenced by later methods of interpretation, saw in Yama neither sun nor moon, nor any other natural phenomenon, for thus he sings, differentiating Yama from them all: "I praise with a song Agni, Pūshan, Sun and Moon, Yama in heaven, Trita, Wind, Dawn, the Ray of Light, the Twin Horsemen" (x. 64. 3); and again: "Deserving of laudation are Heaven and Earth, the four-limbed Agni, Yama, Aditi," etc. (x. 92. 11).

Yama is regarded as a god, although in the Rig Veda he is called only 'king' (x. 14. 1, 11); but later he is expressly a god, and this is implied, as Ehni shows, even in the Rig Veda: 'a god found Agni' and 'Yama found Agni' (x. 51. 1 ff.). His primitive nature was that of the 'first mortal that died,' in the words of the Atharva Veda. It is true, indeed, that at a later period even gods are spoken of as originally 'mortal,'[1] but this is a conception alien from the early notions of the Veda, where 'mortal' signifies no more than 'man.' Yama

[1] Compare Tāitt. S. vii. 4. 2. 1. The gods win immortality by means of 'sacrifice' in this later priest-ridden period.

was the first mortal, and he lives in the sky, in the home that "holds heroes," *i.e.*, his abode is where dead heroes congregate (i. 35. 6; x. 64. 3).[1] The fathers that died of old are cared for by him as he sits drinking with the gods beneath a fair tree (x. 135. 1–7). The fire that devours the corpse is invoked to depart thither (x. 16. 9). This place is not very definitely located, but since, according to one prevalent view, the saints guard the sun, and since Yama's abode in the sky is comparable with the sun in one or two passages, it is probable that the general idea was that the departed entered the sun and there Yama received him (i. 105. 9, 'my home is there where are the sun's rays'; x. 154. 4–5, 'the dead shall go, O Yama, to the fathers, the seers that guard the sun'). 'Yama's abode' is the same with 'sky' (x. 123. 6); and when it is said. 'may the fathers hold up the pillar (in the grave), and may Yama build a seat for thee there' (x. 18. 13), this refers, not to the grave, but to heaven. And it is said that 'Yama's seat is what is called the gods' home' (x. 135. 7).[2] But Yama does not remain in the sky. He comes, as do other Powers, to the sacrifice, and is invited to seat himself 'with Angirasas and the fathers' at the feast, where he rejoices with them (x. 14. 3–4; 15. 8). And either because Agni devours corpses for Yama, or because of Agni's part in the sacrifice which Yama so joyfully attends, therefore Agni is especially mentioned as Yama's friend (x. 21. 5), or even his priest (*ib.* 52. 3). Yama stands in his relation to the dead so near to death that 'to go on Yama's path' is to go on the path of death; and battle is called 'Yama's strife.' It is even possible that in one passage Yama is directly identified with death (x. 165. 4, 'to Yama be reverence, to death'; i. 38. 5; *ib.* 116. 2).[3] There is always a close

1 Ludwig (iv. p. 134) wrongly understands a hell here.

2 'Yama's seat' is here what it is in the epic, not a chapel (Pischel), but a home.

3 This may mean 'to Yama (and) to death.' In the Atharva Veda, v. 24. 13–14, it is said that Death is the lord of men; Yama, of the Manes.

connection between Varuna and Yama, and perhaps it is owing to this that parallel to 'Varuna's fetters' is found also 'Yama's fetter,' *i.e.*, death (x. 97. 16).

As Yama was the first to die, so was he the first to teach man the road to immortality, which lies through sacrifice, whereby man attains to heaven and to immortality. Hence the poet says, 'we revere the immortality born of Yama' (i. 83. 5). This, too, is the meaning of the mystic verse which speaks of the sun as the heavenly courser 'given by Yama,' for, in giving the way to immortality, Yama gives also the sun-abode to them that become immortal. In the same hymn the sun is identified with Yama as he is with Trita (i. 163. 3). This particular identification is due, however, rather to the developed pantheistic idea which obtains in the later hymns. A parallel is found in the next hymn: "They speak of Indra, Mitra, Varuna, Agni . . . that which is one, the priests speak of in many ways, and call him Agni, Yama, Fire" (or Wind, i. 164. 46).

Despite the fact that one Vedic poet speaks of Yama's name as 'easy to understand' (x. 12. 6), no little ingenuity has been spent on it, as well as on the primitive conception underlying his personality. Etymologically, his name means Twin, and this is probably the real meaning, for his twin sister Yamī is also a Vedic personage. The later age, regarding Yama as a restrainer and punisher of the wicked, derived the name from *yam*, the restrainer or punisher, but such an idea is quite out of place in the province of Vedic thought. The Iranian Yima also has a sister of like name, although she does not appear till late in the literature.

That Yama's father is the sun, Vivasvant (Savitar, 'the artificer,' Tvashtar, x. 10. 4–5),[1] is clearly enough stated in the

[1] It is here said, also, that the 'Gandharva in the waters and the water-woman' are the ties of consanguinity between Yama and Yamī, which means, apparently, that their parents were Moon and Water; a late idea, as in viii. 48. 13 (unique).

Rik; and that he was the first mortal, in the Atharvan. Men come from Yama, and Yama comes from the sun as 'creator,' just as men elsewhere come from Adam and Adam comes from the Creator. But instead of an Hebraic Adam and Eve there are in India a Yama and Yamī, brother and sister (wife), who, in the one hymn in which the latter is introduced (*loc. cit.*), indulge in a moral conversation on the propriety of wedlock between brother and sister. This hymn is evidently a protest against a union that was unobjectionable to an older generation. In the Yajur Veda Yamī is wife and sister both. But sometimes, in the varying fancies of the Vedic poets, the artificer Tvashtar is differentiated from Vivasvant, the sun; as he is in another passage, where Tvashtar gives to Vivasvant his daughter, and she is the mother of Yama.[1]

That men are the children of Yama is seen in x. 13. 4, where it is said, 'Yama averted death for the gods; he did not avert death for (his) posterity.' In the Brahmanic tradition men derive from the sun (Tāitt. S. vi. 5. 6. 2).[2] So, in the Iranian belief, Yima is looked upon, according to some scholars, as the first man. The funeral hymn to Yama is as follows:

> Him who once went over the great mountains[3] and spied out a path for many, the son of Vivasvant, who collects men, King Yama, revere ye with oblations. Yama the first found us a way . . . There where our old fathers are departed. . . . Yama is magnified with the Angirasas. . . . Sit here, O Yama, with the Angirasas and with the fathers. . . . Rejoice, O king, in this oblation. Come, O Yama, with the venerable Angirasas. I call thy father, Vivasvant, sit down at this sacrifice.

And then, turning to the departed soul:

> Go forth, go forth on the old paths where are gone our old fathers; thou shalt see both joyous kings, Yama and God Varuna. Unite with the

[1] The passage, x. 17. 1–2, is perhaps meant as a riddle, as Bloomfield suggests (JAOS. xv. p. 172). At any rate, it is still a dubious passage. Compare Hillebrandt, *Vedische Mythologie*, i. p. 503.

[2] Cited by Scherman, *Visionslitteratur*, p. 147.

[3] Possibly, 'streams.'

fathers, with Yama, with the satisfaction of desires, in highest heaven. . . . Yama will give a resting place to this spirit. Run past, on a good path, the two dogs of Saramā, the four-eyed, spotted ones; go unto the fathers who rejoice with Yama.

Several things are here noteworthy. In the first place, the Atharva Veda reads, "who first of mortals died,"[1] and this is the meaning of the Rig Veda version, although, as was said above, the mere fact that Varuna is called a god and Yama a king proves nothing.[2] But it is clearly implied here that he who crossed the mountains and 'collected men,' as does Yima in the Iranian legend, is an ancient king, as it is also implied that he led the way to heaven. The dogs of Yama are described in such a way as to remind one of the dogs that guard the path the dead have to pass in the Iranian legend, and of Kerberus, with whose very name the adjective 'spotted' has been compared.[3] The dogs are elsewhere described as white and brown and as barking (vii. 55. 2), and in further verses of the hymn just quoted (x. 14) they are called "thy guardian dogs, O Yama, the four-eyed ones who guard the path, who look on men . . . broad-nosed, dark messengers of Yama, who run among the people."

These dogs are due to the same fantasy that creates a Kerberus, the Iranian dogs,[4] or other guardians of the road that leads to heaven. The description is too minute to make it probable that the Vedic poet understood them to be 'sun and moon,' as the later Brahmanical ingenuity explains them, and as they have been explained by modern scholarship. It is not possible that the poet, had he had in mind any connection

[1] AV. xviii. 3. 13.

[2] Compare AV. vi. 88. 2: "King Varuna and God Brihaspati," where both are gods.

[3] Κέρβερος (= *Çabála*) = *Çárvara*. Saramā is storm or dawn, or something else that means 'runner.'

[4] Here the fiend is expelled by a four-eyed dog or a white one which has yellow ears. See the *Sacred Books of the East*, IV. p. lxxxvii.

between the dogs and the sun and moon (or 'night and day'), would have described them as 'barking' or as 'broad-nosed and dark'; and all interpretation of Yama's dogs must rest on the interpretation of Yama himself.[1]

Yama is not mentioned elsewhere[2] in the Rig Veda, except in the statement that 'metres rest on Yama,' and in the closing verses of the burial hymn: "For Yama press the *soma*, for Yama pour oblation; the sacrifice goes to Yama; he shall extend for us a long life among the gods," where the pun on Yama (*yamad á*), in the sense of 'stretch out,' shows that as yet no thought of 'restrainer' was in the poet's mind, although the sense of 'twin' is lost from the name.

In recent years Hillebrandt argues that because the Manes are connected with Soma (as the moon), and because Yama was the first to die, therefore Yama was the moon. Ehni, on the other hand, together with Bergaigne and some other scholars, takes Yama to be the sun. Müller calls him the 'setting-sun.'[3] The argument from the Manes applies better to the sun than to the moon, but it is not conclusive. The Hindus in the Vedic age, as later, thought of the Manes living in stars, moon, sun, and air; and, if they were not good Manes but dead sinners, in the outer edge of the universe or under ground. In short, they are located in every conceivable place.[4]

The Yama, 'who collects people,' has been rightly compared with the Yima, who 'made a gathering of the people,' but it is doubtful whether one should see in this an Aryan trait; for ῞Αιδης Ἀγησίλαος is not early and popular, but late (Aeschylean),

1 Scherman proposes an easy solution, namely to cut the description in two, and make only part of it refer to the dogs! (*loc. cit.* p. 130).

2 The dogs may be meant in i. 29. 3, but compare ii. 31. 5. Doubtful is i. 66. 8, according to Bergaigne, applied to Yama as fire.

3 *India*, p. 224.

4 Barth, p. 23, cites i. 125. 6; x. 107. 2; 82. 2, to prove that stars are souls of dead men. These passages do not prove the point, but it may be inferred from x. 68. 11. Later on it is a received belief. A moon-heaven is found only in viii. 48.

and the expression may easily have arisen independently in the mind of the Greek poet. From a comparative point of view, in the reconstruction of Yama there is no conclusive evidence which will permit one to identify his original character either with sun or moon. Much rather he appears to be as he is in the Rig Veda, a primitive king, not historically so, but poetically, the first man, fathered of the sun, to whom he returns, and in whose abode he collects his offspring after their inevitable death on earth. In fact, in Yama there is the ideal side of ancestor-worship. He is a poetic image, the first of all fathers, and hence their type and king. Yama's name is unknown outside of the Indo-Iranian circle, and though Ehni seeks to find traces of him in Greece and elsewhere,[1] this scholar's identifications fail, because he fails to note that similar ideas in myths are no proof of their common origin.

It has been suggested that in the paradise of Yama over the mountains there is a companion-piece to the hyperboreans, whose felicity is described by Pindar. The nations that came from the north still kept in legend a recollection of the land from whence they came. This suggestion cannot, of course, be proved, but it is the most probable explanation yet given of the first paradise to which the dead revert. In the late Vedic period, when the souls of the dead were not supposed to linger on earth with such pleasure as in the sky, Yama's abode is raised to heaven. Later still, when to the Hindu the south was the land of death, Yama's hall of judgment is again brought down to earth and transferred to the 'southern district.'

The careful investigation of Scherman[2] leads essentially to the same conception of Yama as that we have advocated. Scherman believes that Yama was first a human figure, and was then elevated to, if not identified with, the sun. Scherman's only error is in disputing the generally-received opinion,

1 Especially with Ymir in Scandinavian mythology.

2 *Visionslitteratur*, 1892.

one that is on the whole correct, that Yama in the early period is a kindly sovereign, and in later times becomes the dread king of horrible hells. Despite some testimony to the contrary, part of which is late interpolation in the epic, this is the antithesis which exists in the works of the respective periods.

The most important gods of the era of the Rig Veda we now have reviewed. But before passing on to the next period it should be noticed that no small number of beings remains who are of the air, devilish, or of the earth, earthy. Like the demons that injure man by restraining the rain in the clouds, so there are *bhūts*, ghosts, spooks, and other lower powers, some malevolent, some good-natured, who inhabit earth; whence demonology. There is, furthermore, a certain chrematheism, as we have elsewhere[1] ventured to call it, which pervades the Rig Veda, the worship of more or less personified things, differing from pantheism in this,[2] that whereas pantheism assumes a like divinity in all things, this kind of theism assumes that everything (or anything) has a separate divinity, usually that which is useful to the worshipper, as, the plough, the furrow, etc. In later hymns these objects are generally of sacrificial nature, and the stones with which *soma* is pressed are divine like the plant. Yet often there is no sacrificial observance to cause this veneration. Hymns are addressed to weapons, to the war-car, as to divine beings. Sorcery and incantation is not looked upon favorably, but nevertheless it is found.

Another class of divinities includes abstractions, generally female, such as Infinity, Piety, Abundance, with the barely-mentioned Gungū, Rākā, etc. (which may be moon-phases). The

[1] *Henotheism in the Rig Veda*, p. 81.

[2] This religious phase is often confounded loosely with pantheism, but the distinction should be observed. Parkman speaks of (American) Indian 'pantheism'; and Barth speaks of ritualistic 'pantheism,' meaning thereby the deification of different objects used in sacrifice (p. 37, note). But chrematheism is as distinct from pantheism as it is from fetishism.

most important of these abstractions[1] is 'the lord of strength,' a priestly interpretation of Indra, interpreted as religious strength or prayer, to whom are accredited all of Indra's special acts. Hillebrandt interprets this god, Brahmanaspati or Brihaspati, as the moon; Müller, somewhat doubtfully, as fire; while Roth will not allow that Brihaspati has anything to do with natural phenomena, but considers him to have been from the beginning 'lord of prayer.' With this view we partly concur, but we would make the important modification that the god was lord of prayer only as priestly abstraction of Indra in his higher development. It is from this god is come probably the head of the later trinity, Brahmā, through personified *brahma*, power, prayer, with its philosophical development into the Absolute. Noteworthy is the fact that some of the Vedic Aryans, despite his high pretensions, do not quite like Brihaspati, and look on him as a suspicious novelty. If one study Brihaspati in the hymns, it will be difficult not to see in him simply a sacerdotal Indra. He breaks the demon's power; crushes the foes of man; consumes the demons with a sharp bolt; disperses darkness; drives forth the 'cows'; gives offspring and riches; helps in battle; discovers Dawn and Agni; has a band (like Maruts) singing about him; he is red and golden, and is identified with fire. Although 'father of gods,' he is begotten of Tvashtar, the artificer.[2]

Weber has suggested (Vājapeya Sacrifice, p. 15), that Brihaspati takes Indra's place, and this seems to be the true solution, Indra as interpreted mystically by priests. In RV. i. 190, Brihaspati is looked upon by 'sinners' as a new god of little value. Other minor deities can be mentioned only briefly, chiefly that the extent of the pantheon may be seen. For the history of

[1] Some seem to be old: thus Aramati, piety, has an Iranian representative, Ārmaiti. As masculine abstractions are to be added Anger, Death, etc.

[2] Compare iv. 50; ii. 23 and 24; v. 43. 12; x. 68. 9; ii. 26. 3; 23. 17; x. 97. 15. For interpretation compare Hillebrandt, *Ved. Myth.* i. 409–420; Bergaigne, *La Rel. Véd.* i. 304; Muir, OST. v. 272 ff. (with previous literature).

religion they are of only collective importance. The All-gods play an important part in the sacrifice, a group of 'all the gods,' a priestly manufacture to the end that no god may be omitted in laudations that would embrace all the gods. The later priests attempt to identify these gods with the clans, 'the All-gods are the clans' (*Çat. Br.* v. 5. 1. 10), on the basis of a theological pun. the clans, *viças*, being equated with the word for all, *viçve*. Some modern scholars follow these later priests, but without reason. Had these been special clan-gods, they would have had special names, and would not have appeared in a group alone.

The later epic has a good deal to say about some lovely nymphs called the Apsarasas, of whom it mentions six as chief (Urvaçī, Menakā. etc.).[1] They fall somewhat in the epic from their Vedic estate, but they are never more than secondary figures, love-goddesses, beloved of the Gandharvas who later are the singing guardians of the moon, and, like the lunar stations, twenty-seven in number. The Rik knows at first but one Gandharva (an inferior genius, mentioned in but one family-book), who guards Soma's path, and, when Soma becomes the moon, is identified with him, ix. 86. 36. As in the Avesta, Gandharva is (the moon as) an evil spirit also; but always as a second-rate power, to whom are ascribed magic (and madness, later). He has virtually no cult except in *soma*-hymns, and shows clearly the first Aryan conception of the moon as a demoniac power, potent over women, and associated with waters.

Mountains, and especially rivers, are holy, and of course are deified. Primitive belief generally deifies rivers. But in the great river-hymn in the Rig Veda there is probably as much pure poetry as prayer. The Vedic poet half believed in the rivers' divinity, and sings how they 'rush forth like armies,' but it will not do to inquire too strictly in regard to his belief.

[1] *Mbhā.* i. 74. 68. Compare Holtzmann, ZDMG. xxxiii. 631 ff.

He was a poet, and did not expect to be catechized. Of female divinities there are several of which the nature is doubtful. As Dawn or Storm have been interpreted Saramā and Saranyū, both meaning 'runner.' The former is Indra's dog, and her litter is the dogs of Yama. One little poem, rather than hymn, celebrates the 'wood-goddess' in pretty verses of playful and descriptive character.

Long before there was any formal recognition of the dogma that all gods are one, various gods had been identified by the Vedic poets. Especially, as most naturally, was this the case when diverse gods having different names were similar in any way, such as Indra and Agni, whose glory is fire; or Varuna and Mitra, whose seat is the sky. From this casual union of like pairs comes the peculiar custom of invoking two gods as one. But even in the case of gods not so radically connected, if their functions were mutually approximate, each in turn became credited with his neighbor's acts. If the traits were similar which characterized each, if the circles of activity overlapped at all, then those divinities that originally were tangent to each other gradually became concentric, and eventually were united. And so the lines between the gods were wiped out, as it were, by their conceptions crowding upon one another. There was another factor, however, in the development of this unconscious, or, at least, unacknowledged, pantheism. Aided by the likeness or identity of attributes in Indra, Savitar, Agni, Mitra, and other gods, many of which were virtually the same under a different designation, the priests, ever prone to extravagance of word, soon began to attribute, regardless of strict propriety, every power to every god. With the exception of some of the older divinities, whose forms, as they are less complex, retain throughout the simplicity of their primitive character, few gods escaped this adoration, which tended to make them all universally supreme, each being endowed with all the attributes of godhead. One might think that no better fate could happen to a god than thus to be magnified. But when each god in the pantheon was equally glorified, the effect on the whole was disastrous. In fact, it was the death of the gods whom it was the intention of the seers to exalt. And the reason is plain. From this universal praise it resulted that the individuality of each god became less distinct; every god was become, so to speak, any god, so far as his peculiar attributes made him a god at all, so that out of the very praise that was given to him and his confreres alike there arose the idea of the abstract godhead, the god who was all the gods, the one god. As a pure abstraction one finds thus Aditi, as equivalent to 'all the gods,'[1] and then the more personal idea of the god that is father of all, which soon becomes the purely personal All-god. It is at this stage where begins conscious premeditated pantheism, which in its first beginnings is more like monotheism, although in India there is no monotheism which does not include devout polytheism, as will be seen in the review of the formal philosophical systems of religion.

It is thus that we have attempted elsewhere[2] to explain that phase of Hindu religion which Müller calls henotheism.

Müller, indeed, would make of henotheism a new religion, but this, the worshipping of each divinity in turn as if it were the greatest and even the only god recognized, is rather the result of the general tendency to exaltation, united with pantheistic beginnings. Granting that pure polytheism is found in a few hymns, one may yet say that this polytheism, with an accompaniment of half-acknowledged chrematheism, passed soon into the belief that several divinities were ultimately and essentially but one, which may be described as homoiotheism; and that the poets of the Rig Veda were unquestionably esoterically

[1] i. 89. 10: "Aditi is all the gods and men; Aditi is whatever has been born; Aditi is whatever will be born."

[2] *Henotheism in the Rig Veda* (Drisler Memorial).

unitarians to a much greater extent and in an earlier period than has generally been acknowledged. Most of the hymns of the Rig Veda were composed under the influence of that unification of deities and tendency to a quasi-monotheism, which eventually results both in philosophical pantheism, and in the recognition at the same time of a personal first cause. To express the difference between Hellenic polytheism and the polytheism of the Rig Veda the latter should be called, if by any new term, rather by a name like pantheistic polytheism, than by the somewhat misleading word henotheism. What is novel in it is that it represents the fading of pure polytheism and the engrafting, upon a polytheistic stock, of a speculative homoiousian tendency soon to bud out as philosophic pantheism.

The admission that other gods exist does not nullify the attitude of tentative monotheism. "Who is like unto thee, O Lord, among the gods?" asks Moses, and his father-in-law, when converted to the new belief, says: "Now I know that the Lord is greater than all gods."[1] But this is not the quasi-monotheism of the Hindu, to whom the other gods were real and potent factors, individually distinct from the one supreme god, who represents the All-god, but is at once abstract and concrete.

Pantheism in the Rig Veda comes out clearly only in one or two passages: "The priests represent in many ways the (sun) bird that is one"; and (cited above) "They speak of him as Indra, Mitra, Varuna, Agni, . . . that which is but one they call variously." So, too, in the Atharvan it is said that Varuna (here a pantheistic god) is "in the little drop of water,"[2] as in the Rik the spark of material fire is identified with the sun.

The new belief is voiced chiefly in that portion of the Rig Veda which appears to be latest and most Brahmanic in tone.

1 Ex. xv. 11; xviii. 11.

2 RV. x. 114. 5; i. 164. 46; AV. iv. 16. 3.

Here a supreme god is described under the name of "Lord of Beings," the "All-maker," "The Golden Germ," the "God over gods, the spirit of their being" (x. 121). The last, a famous hymn, Müller entitles "To the Unknown God." It may have been intended, as has been suggested, for a theological puzzle,[1] but its language evinces that in whatever form it is couched — each verse ends with the refrain, 'To what god shall we offer sacrifice?' till the last verse answers the question, saying, 'the Lord of beings' — it is meant to raise the question of a supreme deity and leave it unanswered in terms of a nature-religion, though the germ is at bottom fire: "In the beginning arose the Golden Germ; as soon as born he became the Lord of All. He established earth and heaven — to what god shall we offer sacrifice? He who gives breath, strength, whose command the shining gods obey; whose shadow is life and death. . . . When the great waters went everywhere holding the germ and generating light, then arose from them the one spirit (breath) of the gods. . . . May he not hurt us, he the begetter of earth, the holy one who begot heaven . . . Lord of beings, thou alone embracest all things . . ."

In this closing period of the Rig Veda — a period which in many ways, the sudden completeness of caste, the recognition of several Vedas, etc., is much farther removed from the beginning of the work than it is from the period of Brahmanic speculation — philosophy is hard at work upon the problems of the origin of gods and of being. As in the last hymn, water is the origin of all things; out of this springs fire, and the wind which is the breath of god. So in the great hymn of creation: "There was then neither not-being nor being; there was no atmosphere, no sky. What hid (it)? Where and in the protection of what? Was it water, deep darkness? There was no death nor immortality. There was no difference between night and day. That One breathed . . . nothing other than this or above it existed.

[1] Bloomfield, JAOS. xv. 184.

Darkness was concealed in darkness in the beginning. Undifferentiated water was all this (universe)." Creation is then declared to have arisen by virtue of desire, which, in the beginning was the origin of mind;[1] and "the gods," it is said further, "were created after this." Whether entity springs from non-entity or *vice versa* is discussed in another hymn of the same book.[2] The most celebrated of the pantheistic hymns is that in which the universe is regarded as portions of the deity conceived as the primal Person: "Purusha (the Male Person) is this all, what has been and will be . . . all created things are a fourth of him; that which is immortal in the sky is three-fourths of him." The hymn is too well known to be quoted entire. All the castes, all gods, all animals, and the three (or four) Vedas are parts of him.[3]

Such is the mental height to which the seers have raised themselves before the end of the Rig Veda. The figure of the Father-god, Prajāpati, 'lord of beings,' begins here; at first an epithet of Savitar, and finally the type of the head of a pantheon, such as one finds him to be in the Brāhmanas. In one hymn only (x. 121) is Prajāpati found as the personal Father-god and All-god. At a time when philosophy created the one Universal Male Person, the popular religion, keeping pace, as far as it could, with philosophy, invented the more anthropomorphized, more human, Father-god — whose name is ultimately interpreted as an interrogation, God Who? This trait lasts from now on through all speculation. The philosopher conceived of a first source. The vulgar made it a personal god.

One of the most remarkable hymns of this epoch is that on Vāc, Speech, or The Word. Weber has sought in this the prototype of the Logos doctrine (below). The Word, Vāc (feminine) is introduced as speaking (x. 125):

1 "Desire, the primal seed of mind," x. 129. 4.

2 x. 72 (contains also the origin of the gods from Aditi).

3 x. 90. Here *chandāṅsi*, carmina, is probably the Atharvan.

I wander with the Rudras, with the Vasus,[1] with the Ādityas, and with all the gods; I support Mitra, Varuna, Indra-Agni, and the twin Açvins. . . . I give wealth to him that gives sacrifice, to him that presses the *soma*. I am the queen, the best of those worthy of sacrifice. . . . The gods have put me in many places. . . . I am that through which one eats, breathes, sees, and hears. . . . Him that I love I make strong, to be a priest, a seer, a wise man. 'Tis I bend Rudra's bow to hit the unbeliever; I prepare war for the people; I am entered into heaven and earth. I beget the father of this (all) on the height; my place is in the waters, the sea; thence I extend myself among all creatures and touch heaven with my crown. Even I blow like the wind, encompassing all creatures. Above heaven and above earth, so great am I grown in majesty.

This is almost Vedantic pantheism with the Vishnuite doctrine of 'special grace' included.

The moral tone of this period — if period it may be called — may best be examined after one has studied the idea which the Vedic Hindu has formed of the life hereafter. The happiness of heaven will be typical of what he regards as best here. Bliss beyond the grave depends in turn upon the existence of the spirit after death, and, that the reader may understand this, we must say a few words in regard to the Manes, or fathers dead. "Father Manu," as he is called,[2] was the first 'Man.' Subsequently he is the secondary parent as a kind of Noah: but Yama, in later tradition his brother, has taken his place as norm of the departed fathers, Pitaras.

These Fathers (Manes), although of different sort than the gods, are yet divine and have many godly powers, granting prayers and lending aid, as may be seen from this invocation: "O Fathers, may the sky-people grant us life; may we follow the course of the living" (x. 57. 5). One whole hymn is addressed to these quasi-divinities (x. 15):

[1] Rudras, Vasus, and Ādityas, the three famous groups of gods. The Vasus are in Indra's train, the 'shining,' or, perhaps, 'good' gods.

[2] ii. 33. 13; x. 100. 5, etc. If the idea of manus = bonus be rejected, the Latin *manes* may be referred to *mānavas*, the children of Manu.

Arise may the lowest, the highest, the middlemost Fathers, those worthy of the *soma*, who without harm have entered into the spirit (-world); may these Fathers, knowing the seasons, aid us at our call. This reverence be to-day to the Fathers, who of old and afterwards departed; those who have settled in an earthly sphere,[1] or among peoples living in fair places (the gods?). I have found the gracious Fathers, the descendant(s) and the wide-step[2] of Vishnu; those who, sitting on the sacrificial straw, willingly partake of the pressed drink, these are most apt to come hither.... Come hither with blessings, O Fathers; may they come hither, hear us, address and bless us.... May ye not injure us for whatever impiety we have as men committed.... With those who are our former Fathers, those worthy of *soma*, who are come to the *soma* drink, the best (fathers), may Yama rejoicing, willingly with them that are willing, eat the oblations as much as is agreeable (to them). Come running, O Agni, with these (fathers), who thirsted among the gods and hastened hither, finding oblations and praised with songs. These gracious ones, the real poets, the Fathers that seat themselves at the sacrificial heat; who are real eaters of oblation; drinkers of oblation; and are set together on one chariot with Indra and the gods. Come, O Agni, with these, a thousand, honored like gods, the ancient, the original Fathers who seat themselves at the sacrificial heat.... Thou, Agni, didst give the oblations to the Fathers, that eat according to their custom; do thou (too) eat, O god, the oblation offered (to thee). Thou knowest, O thou knower (or finder) of beings, how many are the Fathers — those who are here, and who are not here, of whom we know, and of whom we know not. According to custom eat thou the well-made sacrifice. With those who, burned in fire or not burned, (now) enjoy themselves according to custom in the middle of the sky, do thou, being the lord, form (for us) a spirit life, a body according to (our) wishes.[3]

Often the Fathers are invoked in similar language in the hymn to the "All-gods" mentioned above, and occasionally no distinction is to be noticed between the powers and attributes of the Fathers and those of the gods. The Fathers, like the luminous gods, "give light" (x. 107. 1). Exactly like the gods, they are called upon to aid the living, and even 'not to

[1] Or: "in an earthly place, in the atmosphere, or," etc.

[2] That is where the Fathers live. This is the only place where the Fathers are said to be *nápāt* (descendants) of Vishnu, and here the sense may be "I have discovered *Nápāt* (fire?)" But in i. 154. 5 Vishnu's worshippers rejoice in his home.

[3] Or: "form as thou wilt this body (of a corpse) to spirit life."

harm' (iii. 55. 2; x. 15. 6). According to one verse, the Fathers have not attained the greatness of the gods, who impart strength only to the gods.[1]

The Fathers are kept distinct from the gods. When the laudations bestowed upon the former are of unequivocal character there is no confusion between the two.[2]

The good dead, to get to the paradise awaiting them, pass over water (X. 63. 10), and a bridge (ix. 41. 2). Here, by the gift of the gods, not by inherent capacity, they obtain immortality. He that believes on Agni, sings: "Thou puttest the mortal in highest immortality, O Agni"; and, accordingly, there is no suggestion that heavenly joys may cease; nor is there in this age any notion of a *Götterdämmerung*. Immortality is described as "continuing life in the highest sky," another proof that when formulated the doctrine was that the soul of the dead lives in heaven or in the sun.[3]

Other cases of immortality granted by different gods are recorded by Muir and Zimmer. Yet in one passage the words, "two paths I have heard of the Fathers (exist), of the gods and of mortals," may mean that the Fathers go the way of mortals or that of gods, rather than, as is the usual interpretation, that mortals have two paths, one of the Fathers and one of the gods,[4] for the dead may live on earth or in the air as well as in heaven. When a good man dies his breath, it is said, goes to the wind, his eye to the sun, etc.[5] — each part to its appropriate prototype — while the "unborn part" is carried

[1] x. 56. 4; otherwise, Grassmann.

[2] vi. 75. 9 refers to ancestors on earth, not in heaven.

[3] Compare Muir, OST. v. 285, where i. 125. 5 is compared with x. 107. 2: "The gift-giver becomes immortal: the gift-giver lives in the sky; he that gives horses lives in the sun." Compare Zimmer, *Altind. Leben*, p. 409; Geiger, *Ostiran. Cultur*, p. 290.

[4] x. 88. 15, word for word: "two paths heard of the Fathers I, of the gods and of mortals." Cited as a mystery, Brih. Āran. Up. vi. 2. 2.

[5] x. 16. 3: "if thou wilt go to the waters or to the plants," is added after this (in addressing the soul of the dead man). Plant-souls occur again in x. 58. 7.

"to the world of the righteous," after having been burned and heated by the funeral fire. All these parts are restored to the soul, however, and Agni and Soma return to it what has been injured. With this Muir compares a passage in the Atharva Veda where it is said that the Manes in heaven rejoice with all their limbs.[1] We dissent, therefore, wholly from Barth, who declares that the dead are conceived of as "resting forever in the tomb, the narrow house of clay." The only passage cited to prove this is x. 18. 10–13, where are the words (addressed to the dead man at the burial): "Go now to mother earth . . . she shall guard thee from destruction's lap. . . . Open wide, O earth, be easy of access; as a mother her son cover this man, O earth," etc. Ending with the verse quoted above: "May the Fathers hold the pillar and Yama there build thee a seat."[2] The following is also found in the Rig Veda bearing on this point: the prayer that one may meet his parents after death; the statement that a generous man goes to the gods; and a suggestion of the later belief that one wins immortality by means of a son.[3]

The joys of paradise are those of earth; and heaven is thus described, albeit in a late hymn:[4] "Where is light inexhaustible; in the world where is placed the shining sky; set me in this immortal, unending world, O thou that purifiest thyself (Soma); where is king (Yama), the son of Vivasvant, and the paradise of the sky;[5] where are the flowing waters; there make me immortal. Where one can go as he will; in the third heaven, the third vault of the sky; where are worlds full of light, there make me immortal; where are wishes and desires

[1] AV. xviii. 4. 64; Muir, *loc. cit.* p. 298. A passage of the Atharvan suggests that the dead may have been exposed as in Iran, but there is no trace of this in the Rig Veda (Zimmer, *loc. cit.* p. 402).

[2] Barth, *Vedic Religions*, p. 23; *ib.*, the narrow 'house of clay,' RV. vii. 89. 1.

[3] i. 24. 1; i. 125. 6; vii. 56. 24; cited by Müller, *Chips*, i. p. 45.

[4] ix. 113. 7 ff.

[5] *Avaródhanaṁ divás*, 'enclosure of the sky.'

and the red (sun)'s highest place; where one can follow his own habits[1] and have satisfaction; there make me immortal: where exist delight, joy, rejoicing, and joyance: where wishes are obtained, there make me immortal."[2] Here, as above, the saints join the Fathers, 'who guard the sun.'

There is a 'bottomless darkness' occasionally referred to as a place where evil spirits are to be sent by the gods; and a 'deep place' is mentioned as the portion of 'evil, false, untruthful men'; while Soma casts into 'a hole' (abyss) those that are irreligious.[3]

As darkness is hell to the Hindu, and as in all later time the demons are spirits of darkness, it is rather forced not to see in these allusions a misty hell, without torture indeed, but a place for the bad either 'far away,' as it is sometimes said (*parāváti*), or 'deep down,' 'under three earths,' exactly as the Greek has a hell below and one on the edge of the earth. Ordinarily, however, the gods are requested simply to annihilate offenders. It is plain, as Zimmer says, from the office of Yama's dogs, that they kept out of paradise unworthy souls; so that the annihilation cannot have been imagined to be purely corporeal. But heaven is not often described, and hell never, in this period. Yet, when the paradise desired is described, it is a place where earthly joys are prolonged and intensified. Zimmer argues that a race which believes in good for the good hereafter must logically believe in punishment for the wicked, and Scherman, strangely enough, agrees with this pedantic opinion.[4] If either of these scholars had looked away from India to the western Indians he would have seen that, whereas almost all American

[1] Literally, 'where custom' (obtains), *i.e.*, where the old usages still hold.

[2] The last words are to be understood as of sensual pleasures (Muir, *loc. cit.* p. 307, notes 462, 463).

[3] RV. ii. 29. 6; vii. 104. 3, 17; iv. 5. 5; ix. 73. 8. Compare Muir, *loc. cit.* pp. 311–312; and Zimmer, *loc. cit.* pp. 408, 418. Yama's 'hero-holding abode' is not a hell, as Ludwig thinks, but, as usual, the top vault of heaven.

[4] *Loc. cit.* p. 123.

Indians believe in a happy hereafter for good warriors, only a very few tribes have any belief in punishment for the bad. At most a Niflheim awaits the coward. Weber thinks the Aryans already believed in a personal immortality, and we agree with him. Whitney's belief that hell was not known before the Upanishad period (in his translations of the *Katha Upanishad*) is correct only if by hell torture is meant, and if the Atharvan is later than this Upanishad, which is improbable.

The good dead in the Rig Veda return with Yama to the sacrifice to enjoy the *soma* and viands prepared for them by their descendants. Hence the whole belief in the necessity of a son in order to the obtaining of a joyful hereafter. What the rite of burial was to the Greek, a son was to the Hindu, a means of bliss in heaven. Roth apparently thinks that the Rig Veda's heaven is one that can best be described in Dr. Watt's hymn:

> There is a land of pure delight
> Where saints immortal reign,
> Eternal day excludes the night,
> And pleasures banish pain;

and that especial stress should be laid on the word 'pure.' But there is very little teaching of personal purity in the Veda, and the poet who hopes for a heaven where he is to find 'longing women,' 'desire and its fulfillment' has in mind, in all probability, purely impure delights. It is not to be assumed that the earlier morality surpassed that of the later day, when, even in the epic, the hero's really desired heaven is one of drunkenness and women *ad libitum*. Of the 'good man' in the Rig Veda are demanded piety toward gods and manes and liberality to priests; truthfulness and courage; and in the end of the work there is a suggestion of ascetic 'goodness' by means of *tapas*, austerity.[1] Grassman cites one hymn as dedicated to

[1] X. 154. 2; 107. 2. Compare the mad ascetic, *múni*, viii. 17. 14.

'Mercy.' It is really (not a hymn and) not on mercy, but a poem praising generosity. This generosity, however (and in general this is true of the whole people), is not general generosity, but liberality to the priests.[1] The blessings asked for are wealth (cattle, horses, gold, etc.), virile power, male children ('heroic offspring') and immortality, with its accompanying joys. Once there is a tirade against the friend that is false to his friend (truth in act as well as in word);[2] once only, a poem on concord, which seems to partake of the nature of an incantation.

Incantations are rare in the Rig Veda, and appear to be looked upon as objectionable. So in vii. 104 the charge of a 'magician' is furiously repudiated; yet do an incantation against a rival wife, a mocking hymn of exultation after subduing rivals, and a few other hymns of like sort show that magical practices were well known.[3]

The sacrifice occupies a high place in the religion of the Rig Veda, but it is not all-important, as it is later. Nevertheless, the same presumptuous assumption that the gods depend on earthly sacrifice is often made; the result of which, even before the collection was complete (iv. 50), was to teach that gods and men depended on the will of the wise men who knew how properly to conduct a sacrifice, the key-note of religious pride in the Brahmanic period.

Indra depends on the sacrificial *soma* to accomplish his great works. The gods first got power through the sacrificial fire and *soma*.[4] That images of the gods were supposed to be

[1] x. 117. This is clearly seen in the seventh verse, where is praised the 'Brahman who talks,' *i.e.*, can speak in behalf of the giver to the gods (compare verse three).

[2] x. 71. 6.

[3] Compare x. 145; 159. In x. 184 there is a prayer addressed to the goddesses Sinīvālī and Sarasvatī (in conjunction with Vishnu, Tvashtar, the Creator, Prajāpati, and the Horsemen) to make a woman fruitful.

[4] ii. 15. 2; x. 6. 7 (Barth, *loc. cit.* p. 36). The sacrifice of animals, cattle, horses, goats, is customary; that of man, legendary; but it is implied in x. 18. 8 (Hillebrandt, ZDMG. xl. p. 708), and is ritualized in the next period (below).

powerful may be inferred from the late verses, "who buys this Indra," etc. (above), but allusions to idolatry are elsewhere extremely doubtful.[1]

[1] Phallic worship may be alluded to in that of the 'tail-gods,' as Garbe thinks, but it is deprecated. One verse, however, which seems to have crept in by mistake, is apparently due to phallic influence (viii. 1. 34), though such a cult was not openly acknowledged till Çiva-worship began, and is no part of Brahmanism.

CHAPTER VII.

THE RELIGION OF THE ATHARVA VEDA.

THE hymns of the Rig Veda inextricably confused; the deities of an earlier era confounded, and again merged together in a pantheism now complete; the introduction of strange gods; recognition of a hell of torture; instead of many divinities the One that represents all the gods, and nature as well; incantations for evil purposes and charms for a worthy purpose; formulae of malediction to be directed against 'those whom I hate and who hate me'; magical verses to obtain children, to prolong life, to dispel 'evil magic,' to guard against poison and other ills; the paralyzing extreme of ritualistic reverence indicated by the exaltation to godhead of the 'remnant' of sacrifice; hymns to snakes, to diseases, to sleep, time, and the stars; curses on the 'priest-plaguer'—such, in general outline, is the impression produced by a perusal of the Atharvan after that of the Rig Veda. How much of this is new?

The Rig Veda is not lacking in incantations, in witchcraft practices, in hymns to inanimate things, in indications of pantheism. But the general impression is produced, both by the tone of such hymns as these and by their place in the collection, that they are an addition to the original work. On the other hand, in reading the Atharvan hymns the collective impression is decidedly this, that what to the Rig is adventitious is essential to the Atharvan.

It has often been pointed out, however, that not only the practices involved, but the hymns themselves, in the Atharvan, may have existed long before they were collected, and that, while the Atharvan collection, as a whole, takes historical place after the Rig Veda, there yet may be comprised in the former much which is as old as any part of the latter work. It is also customary to assume that such hymns as betoken a lower worship (incantations, magical formulae, etc.) were omitted purposely from the Rig Veda to be collected in the Atharvan. That which eventually can neither be proved nor disproved is, perhaps, best left undiscussed, and it is vain to seek scientific proof where only historic probabilities are obtainable. Yet, if a closer approach to truth be attractive, even a greater probability will be a gain, and it becomes worth while to consider the problem a little with only this hope in view.

Those portions of the Rig Veda which seem to be Atharvan-like are, in general, to be found in the later books (or places) of the collection. But it would be presumptuous to conclude that a work, although almost entirely given up to what in the Rig Veda appears to be late, should itself be late in origin. By analogy, in a nature-religion such as was that of India, the practice of demonology, witchcraft, etc., must have been an early factor. But, while this is true, it is clearly impossible to postulate therefrom that the hymns recording all this array of cursing, deviltry, and witchcraft are themselves early. The further forward one advances into the labyrinth of Hindu religions the more superstitions, the more devils, demons, magic, witchcraft, and uncanny things generally, does he find. Hence, while any one superstitious practice may be antique, there is small probability for assuming a contemporaneous origin of the hymns of the two collections. The many verses cited, apparently pell-mell, from the Rig Veda, might, it is true, revert to a version older than that in which they are found in the Rig Veda, but there is nothing to show that they were not taken from the Rig Veda, and re-dressed in a form that rendered them in many cases more intelligible; so that often what is respectfully spoken of as a 'better varied reading' of the Atharvan may be better, as we have said in the introductory chapter, only in lucidity; and the lucidity be due to tampering with a text old and unintelligible. Classical examples abound in illustrations.

Nevertheless, although an antiquity equal to that of the whole Rig Veda can by no means be claimed for the Atharvan collection (which, at least in its tone, belongs to the Brahmanic period), yet is the mass represented by the latter, if not contemporaneous, at any rate so venerable, that it safely may be assigned to a period as old as that in which were composed the later hymns of the Rik itself. But in distinction from the hymns themselves the weird religion they represent is doubtless as old, if not older, than that of the Rig Veda. For, while the Rig Vedic *soma*-cult is Indo-Iranian, the original Atharvan (fire) cult is even more primitive, and the basis of the work, from this point of view, may have preceded the composition of Rik hymns. This Atharvan religion — if it may be called so — is, therefore, of exceeding importance. It opens wide the door which the Rik puts ajar, and shows a world of religious and mystical ideas which without it could scarcely have been suspected. Here magic eclipses Soma and reigns supreme. The wizard is greater than the gods; his herbs and amulets are sovereign remedies. Religion is seen on its lowest side. It is true that there is 'bad magic' and 'good magic' (the existence of the former is substantiated by the maledictions against it), but what has been received into the collection is apparently the best. To heal the sick and procure desirable things is the object of most of the charms and incantations — but some of the desirable things are disease and death of one's foes. On the higher side of religion, from a metaphysical point of view, the Atharvan is pantheistic. It knows also the importance of the 'breaths,'[1] the vital forces; it puts side by side the different gods and says that each 'is lord.' It does not lack philosophical speculation which, although most of it is puerile,

[1] xv. 15.

sometimes raises questions of wider scope, as when the sage inquires who made the body with its wonderful parts — implying, but not stating the argument, from design, in its oldest form.[1]

Of magical verses there are many, but the content is seldom more than "do thou, O plant, preserve from harm," etc. Harmless enough, if somewhat weak, are also many other hymns calculated to procure blessings:

> Blessings blow to us the wind,
> Blessings glow to us the sun,
> Blessings be to us the day,
> Blest to us the night appear,
> Blest to us the dawn shall shine,

is a fair specimen of this innocuous sort of verse.[2] Another example may be seen in this hymn to a king: "Firm is the sky; firm is the earth; firm, all creation; firm, these hills; firm the king of the people (shall be)," etc.[3] In another hymn there is an incantation to release from possible ill coming from a foe and from inherited ill or sin.[4] A free spirit of doubt and atheism, already foreshadowed in the Rig Veda, is implied in the prayer that the god will be merciful to the cattle of that man "whose creed is 'Gods exist.'"[5] Serpent-worship is not only known, but prevalent.[6] The old gods still hold, as always, their nominal places, albeit the system is pantheistic, so that Varuna is god of waters; and Mitra with Varuna, gods of rain.[7] As a starting-point of philosophy the dictum of the Rig Veda is repeated: 'Desire is the seed of mind,' and 'love, *i.e.*, desire, was born first.' Here Aditi is defined anew as the

[1] x. 2. [2] vii. 69. Compare RV. vii. 35, and the epic (below). [3] x. 173.
[4] v. 30. [5] xi. 2. 28. [6] xi. 9; viii. 6 and 7, with tree-worship.
[7] v. 24. 4–5. On 'the one god' compare x. 8. 28; xiii. 4. 15. Indra as Sūrya, in vii. 11; cf. xiii. 4; xvii. 1. 24. Pantheism in x. 7. 14, 25. Of charms, compare ii. 9, to restore life; iii. 6, a curse against 'whom I hate'; iii. 23, to obtain offspring. On the stars and night, see hymn at xix. 8 and 47. In v. 13, a guard against poison; *ib.* 21, a hymn to a drum; *ib.* 31, a charm to dispel evil magic; vi. 133, magic to produce long life; v. 23, against worms, etc., etc. Aditi, vii. 6. 1–4 (partly Rik).

one in whose lap is the wide atmosphere — she is parent and child, gods and men, all in all — 'may she extend to us a triple shelter.' As an example of curse against curse may be compared ii. 7:

> The sin-hated, god-born plant, that frees from the curse as waters (wash out) the spot, has washed away all curses, the curse of my rival and of my sister; (that) which the Brahman in anger cursed, all this lies under my feet. . . . With this plant protect this (wife), protect my child, protect our property. . . . May the curse return to the curser. . . . We smite even the ribs of the foe with the evil (*mantra*) eye.

A love-charm in the same book (ii. 30) will remind the classical student of Theocritus' second idyl: 'As the wind twirls around grass upon the ground, so I twirl thy mind about, that thou mayst become loving, that thou mayst not depart from me,' etc. In the following verses the Horsemen gods are invoked to unite the lovers. Characteristic among bucolic passages is the cow-song in ii. 26, the whole intent of which is to ensure a safe return to the cows on their wanderings: 'Hither may they come, the cattle that have wandered far away,' etc.

The view that there are different conditions of Manes is clearly taught in xviii. 2. 48–49, where it is said that there are three heavens, in the highest of which reside the Manes; while a distinction is made at the same time between 'fathers' and 'grandfathers,' the fathers' fathers, 'who have entered air, who inhabit earth and heaven.' Here appears nascent the doctrine of 'elevating the Fathers,' which is expressly taught in the next era. The performance of rites in honor of the Manes causes them to ascend from a low state to a higher one In fact, if the offerings are not given at all, the spirits do not go to heaven. In general the older generations of Manes go up highest and are happiest. The personal offering is only to the immediate fathers.

If, as was shown in the introductory chapter, the Atharvan represents a geographical advance on the part of the Vedic Aryans, this fact cannot be ignored in estimating the primitiveness of the collection. Geographical advance, acquaintance with other flora and fauna than those of the Rig Veda, means — although the argument of silence must not be exaggerated — a temporal advance also. And not less significant are the points of view to which one is led in the useful little work of Scherman on the philosophical hymns of the Atharvan. Scherman wishes to show the connection between the Upanishads and Vedas. But the bearing of his collection is toward a closer union of the two bodies of works, and especially of the Atharvan, not to the greater gain in age of the Upanishads so much as to the depreciation in venerableness of the former. If the Atharvan has much more in common with the Brāhmanas and Upanishads than has the Rig Veda, it is because the Atharvan stands, in many respects, midway in time between the era of Vedic hymnology and the thought of the philosophical period. The terminology is that of the Brāhmanas, rather than that of the Rig Veda. The latter knows the great person; the Atharvan, and the former know the original great person, *i.e.*, the *causa movens* under the *causa efficiens*, etc. In the Atharvan appears first the worship of Time, Love, 'Support' (Skambha), and the 'highest *brahma*.' The cult of the holy cow is fully recognized (xii. 4 and 5). The late ritualistic terms, as well as linguistic evidence, confirm the fact indicated by the geographical advance. The country is known from western Balkh to eastern Behār, the latter familiarly.[1] In a word, one may conclude that on its higher side the Atharvan is later than the Rig Veda, while on its lower side of demonology one may recognize the religion of the lower classes as compared with that of the two upper classes — for the latter the Rig Veda, for the superstitious people at large the Atharvan, a collection

[1] Compare Muir, OST. ii. 447 ff.

of which the origin agrees with its application. For, if it at first was devoted to the unholy side of fire-cult, and if the fire-cult is older than the *soma*-cult, then this is the cult that one would expect to see most affected by the conservative vulgar, who in India hold fast to what the cultured have long dropped as superstition, or, at least, pretended to drop; though the house-ritual keeps some magic in its fire-cult.

In that case, it may be asked, why not begin the history of Hindu religion with the Atharvan, rather than with the Rig Veda? Because the Atharvan, as a whole, in its language, social conditions, geography, 'remnant' worship, etc., shows that this literary collection is posterior to the Rik collection. As to individual hymns, especially those imbued with the tone of fetishism and witchcraft, any one of them, either in its present or original form, may outrank the whole Rik in antiquity, as do its superstitions the religion of the Rik — if it is right to make a distinction between superstition and religion, meaning by the former a lower, and by the latter a more elevated form of belief in the supernatural.

The difference between the Rik-worshipper and Atharvan-worshipper is somewhat like that which existed at a later age between the philosophical Çivaite and Durgāite. The former revered Çiva, but did not deny the power of a host of lesser mights, whom he was ashamed to worship too much; the latter granted the all-god-head of Çiva, but paid attention almost exclusively to some demoniac divinity.

Superstition, perhaps, always precedes theology; but as surely does superstition outlive any one form of its protean rival. And the simple reason is that a theology is the real belief of few, and varies with their changing intellectual point of view; while superstition is the belief unacknowledged of the few and acknowledged of the many, nor does it materially change from age to age. The rites employed among the clam-diggers on the New York coast, the witch-charms they use, the incantations, cutting of flesh, fire-oblations, meaningless formulae, united with sacrosanct expressions of the church, are all on a par with the religion of the lower classes as depicted in Theocritus and the Atharvan. If these mummeries and this hocus-pocus were collected into a volume, and set out with elegant extracts from the Bible, there would be a nineteenth century Atharva Veda. What are the necessary equipment of a Long Island witch? First, "a good hot fire," and then formulae such as this:[1]

"If a man is attacked by wicked people and how to banish them:

"Bedgoblin and all ye evil spirits, I, N. N., forbid you my bedstead, my couch; I, N. N., forbid you in the name of God my house and home; I forbid you in the name of the Holy Trinity my blood and flesh, my body and soul; I forbid you all the nail-holes in my house and home, till you have travelled over every hill, waded through every water, have counted all the leaves of every tree, and counted all the stars in the sky, until the day arrives when the mother of God shall bare her second son."

If this formula be repeated three times, with the baptismal name of the person, it will succeed!

"To make one's self invisible:

"Obtain the ear of a black cat, boil it in the milk of a black cow, wear it on the thumb, and no one will see you."

This is the Atharvan, or fire- and witch-craft of to-day — not differing much from the ancient. It is the unchanging foundation of the many lofty buildings of faith that are erected, removed, and rebuilt upon it — the belief in the supernatural at its lowest, a belief which, in its higher stages, is always level with the general intellect of those that abide in it.

The latest book of the Atharvan is especially for the warrior-caste, but the mass of it is for the folk at large. It was

[1] This old charm is still used among the clam-diggers of Canarsie, N. Y.

long before it was recognized as a legitimate Veda. It never stands, in the older period of Brahmanism, on a par with the Sāman and Rik. In the epic period good and bad magic are carefully differentiated, and even to-day the Atharvan is repudiated by southern Brahmans. But there is no doubt that *sub rosa*, the silliest practices inculcated and formulated in the Atharvan were the stronghold of a certain class of priests, or that such priests were feared and employed by the laity, openly by the low classes, secretly by the intelligent.

In respect of the name the magical cult was referred, historically with justice, to the fire-priests, Atharvan and Angiras, though little application to fire, other than in *soma*-worship, is apparent. Yet was this undoubtedly the source of the cult (the fire-cult is still distinctly associated with the Atharva Veda in the epic), and the name is due neither to accident nor to a desire to invoke the names of great seers, as will Weber.[1] The other name of Brahmaveda may have connection with the 'false science of Brihaspati,' alluded to in a Upanishad.[2] This seer is not over-orthodox, and later he is the patron of the unorthodox Cārvākas. It was seen above that the god Brihaspati is also a novelty not altogether relished by the Vedic Aryans.

From an Aryan point of view how much weight is to be placed on comparisons of the formulae in the Atharvan of India with those of other Aryan nations? Kuhn has compared[3] an old German magic formula of healing with one in the Atharvan, and because each says 'limb to limb' he thinks that they are of the same origin, particularly since the formula is found in Russian. The comparison is interesting, but it is far from convincing. Such formulae spring up independently all over the earth.

1 *Ind. Lit.*[2] p. 164.

2 *Māit. Up.* vii. 9. He is 'the gods' Brahmā' (Rik.)

3 *Indische und germanische Segenssprüche*; KZ. xiii. 49.

Finally, it is to be observed that in this Veda first occurs the implication of the story of the flood (xix. 39. 8), and the saving of Father Manu, who, however, is known by this title in the Rik. The supposition that the story of the flood is derived from Babylon, seems, therefore, to be an unnecessary (although a permissible) hypothesis, as the tale is old enough in India to warrant a belief in its indigenous origin.[1]

[1] One long hymn, xii. 1, of the Atharvan is to earth and fire (19-20). In the Rik, *átharvan* is fire-priest and bringer of fire from heaven; while once the word may mean fire itself (viii. 9, 7). The name Brahmaveda is perhaps best referred to *brahma* as fire (whence 'fervor,' 'prayer,' and again 'energy,' 'force'). In distinction from the great *soma*-sacrifices, the fire-cult always remains the chief thing in the domestic ritual. The present Atharvan formulae have for the most part no visible application to fire, but the name still shows the original connection.

CHAPTER VIII.

EARLY HINDU DIVINITIES COMPARED WITH THOSE OF OTHER ARYANS.

NOTHING is more usual than to attempt a reconstruction of Aryan ideas in manners, customs, laws, and religious conceptions, by placing side by side similar traits of individual Aryan nations, and stating or insinuating that the result of the comparison shows that one is handling primitive characteristics of the whole Aryan body. It is of special importance, therefore, to see in how far the views and practices of peoples not Aryan may be found to be identical with those of Aryans. The division of the army into clans, as in the Iliad and the Veda; the love of gambling, as shown by Greeks, Teutons, and Hindus; the separation of captains and princes, as is illustrated by Teuton and Hindu; the belief in a flood, common to Iranian, Greek, and Hindu; in the place of departed spirits, with the journey over a river (Iranian, Hindu, Scandinavian, Greek); in the after-felicity of warriors who die on the field of battle (Scandinavian, Greek, and Hindu); in the reverence paid to the wind-god (Hindu, Iranian, and Teutonic, Vāta-Wotan); these and many other traits at different times, by various writers, have been united and compared to illustrate primitive Aryan belief and religion.

The traits of the Five Nations of the Veda for this reason may be compared very advantageously with the traits of the Five Nations of the Iroquois Indians, the most united and intelligent of American native tribes. Their institutions are not yet extinct, and they have been described by missionaries of the 17th century and by some modern writers, to whom can be imputed no hankering after Aryan primitive ideas.[1] It is but a few years back since the last *avatar* of the Iroquois' incarnate god lived in Onondaga, N. Y.

First, as an illustration of the extraordinary development of memory among rhapsodes, Vedic students, and other Aryans; among the Iroquois "memory was tasked to the utmost, and developed to an extraordinary degree," says Parkman, who adds that they could repeat point by point with precision any address made to them.[2] Murder was compromised for by *Wehrgeld*, as among the Vedic, Iranic, and Teutonic peoples. The Iroquois, like all Indians, was a great gambler, staking all his property[3] (like the Teutons and Hindus). In religion "A mysterious and inexplicable power resides in inanimate things. . . . Lakes, rivers, and waterfalls [as conspicuously in India] are sometimes the dwelling-place of spirits; but more frequently they are themselves living beings, to be propitiated by prayers and offerings."[4] The greatest spirit among the Algonquins is the descendant of the moon, and son of the west-wind (personified). After the deluge (thus the Hindus, etc.) this great spirit (Manabozho, *mana* is Manu?) restored the world; some asserting that he created the world out of water. But others say that the supreme spirit is the sun (Le Jeune, Relation, 1633). The Algonquins, besides a belief in a good spirit (*manitou*), had also a belief in a malignant *manitou*, in whom the missionaries recognized the devil (why not Ormuzd and Ahriman?). One tribe invokes the 'Maker of Heaven,' the 'god of waters,' and also the 'seven spirits of the wind' (so, too, seven is a holy number in the Veda, etc.).

[1] Compare the accounts of Lafitau; of the native Iroquois, baptized as Morgan; and the works of Schoolcraft and Parkman.

[2] *Jesuits in North America*, Introduction, p. lxi.

[3] "Like other Indians, the Hurons were desperate gamblers, staking their all,—ornaments, clothing, canoes, pipes, weapons, and wives," *loc. cit.* p. xxxvi. Compare Palfrey, of Massachusetts Indians. The same is true of all savages.

[4] *Ib.* p. lxvii.

The Iroquois, like the Hindu (later), believe that the earth rests on the back of a turtle or tortoise,[1] and that this is ruled over by the sun and moon, the first being a good spirit: the second, malignant. The good spirit interposes between the malice of the moon and mankind, and it is he who makes rivers; for when the earth was parched, all the water being held back from earth under the armpit of a monster frog, he pierced the armpit and let out the water (exactly as Indra lets out the water held back by the demon). According to some, this great spirit created mankind, but in the third generation a deluge destroyed his posterity.[2] The good spirit among the Iroquois is the one that gives good luck (perhaps Bhaga). These Indians believe in the immortality of the soul. Skillful hunters, brave warriors, go, after death, to the happy hunting-grounds (as in India and Scandinavia); the cowardly and weak are doomed to live in dreary regions of mist and darkness (compare Niflheim and the Iranian eschatology?). To pass over other religious correspondences, the sacrifice of animals, use of amulets, love-charms, magic, and sorcery, which are all like those of Aryans (to compare, also, are the burying or exposing of the dead and the Hurons' funeral games), let one take this as a good illustration of the value of 'comparative Aryan mythology':

According to the Aryan belief the soul of the dead passes over a stream, across a bridge, past a dog or two, which guard the gate of paradise. The Hindu, Iranian, Greek, and Scandinavian, all have the dog, and much emphasis has been laid on the 'Aryan' character of this creed. The native Iroquois Indians believed that "the spirits on their journey (to heaven) were beset with difficulties and perils. There was a swift river

[1] Compare *Çat. Br.* vi. 1. 1, 12; vii. 5. 1, 2 *sq.*, for the Hindu tortoise in its first form. The totem-form of the tortoise is well known in America. (Brinton, *Myths of the New World*, p. 85.)

[2] Charlevoix ap. Parkman.

to be crossed on a log that shook beneath the feet, while a ferocious dog opposed their passage."[1] Here is the Persians' narrow bridge, and even Kerberos himself!

It is also interesting to note that, as the Hindus identify with the sun so many of their great gods, so the Iroquois "sacrifices to some superior spirit, or to the sun, with which the superior spirits were constantly confounded by the primitive Indian."[2]

Weber holds that because Greek and Hindu gave the name 'bear' to a constellation, therefore this is the "primitive Indo-Germanic name of the star."[3] But the Massachusetts Indians "gave their own name for bear to the Ursa major" (Williams' 'Key,' cited Palfrey, I. p. 36; so Lafitau, further west).

Again, three, seven, and even 'thrice-seven,' are holy not only in India but in America.

In this new world are found, to go further, the analogues of Varuna in the monotheistic god Viracocha of the Peruvians, to whom is addressed this prayer: "Cause of all things! ever present, helper, creator, ever near, ever fortunate one! Thou incorporeal one above the sun, infinite, and beneficent";[4] of the Vedic Snake of the Deep, in the Mexican Cloud-serpent; of the Vedic Lightning-bird, who brings fire from heaven, in the Indian Thunder-bird, who brings fire from heaven;[5] of the preservation of one individual from a flood (in the epic, Manu's 'Seven Seers') in the same American myth, even including the holy mountain, which is still shown;[6] of the belief that the sun is the home of departed spirits, in the same belief all over

1 Parkman, *loc. cit.* p. lxxxii; Brinton, *Myths of the New World*, p. 248. A good instance of bad comparison in eschatology will be found in Geiger, *Ostir. Cult.* pp. 274–275.

2 Parkman, *loc. cit.* p. lxxxvi.

3 *Sitz. Berl. Akad.* 1891, p. 15.

4 Brinton, *American Hero Myths*, p. 174. The first worship was Sun-worship, then Viracocha-worship arose, which kept Sun-worship while it predicated a 'power beyond.'

5 Brinton, *Myths of the New World*, pp. 85, 205.

6 *Ib.* pp. 86, 202.

America;[1] of the belief that stars are the souls of the dead, in the same belief held by the Pampas;[2] and even of the late Brahmanic custom of sacrificing the widow (suttee), in the practice of the Natchez Indians, and in Guatemala, of burning the widow on the pyre of the dead husband.[3] The storm wind (Odin) as highest god is found among the Choctaws; while 'Master of Breath' is the Creeks' name for this divinity. Huraka (hurricane, ouragon, ourage) is the chief god in Hayti.[4] An exact parallel to the vague idea of hell at the close of the Vedic period, with the gradual increase of the idea, alternating with a theory of reincarnation, may be found in the fact that, in general, there is no notion of punishment after death among the Indians of the New World; but that, while the good are assisted and cared for after death by the 'Master of Breath,' the Creeks believe that the liar, the coward, and the niggard (Vedic sinners *par excellence!*) are left to shift for themselves in darkness; whereas the Aztecs believed in a hell surrounded by the water called 'Nine Rivers,' guarded by a dog and a dragon; and the great Eastern American tribes believe that after the soul has been for a while in heaven it can, if it chooses, return to earth and be born again as a man, utilizing its old bones (which are, therefore, carefully preserved by the surviving members of the family) as a basis for a new body.[5]

To turn to another foreign religion, how tempting would it be to see in Nutar the 'abstract power' of the Egyptian, an analogue of *brahma* and the other 'power' abstractions of India; to recognize Brahmā in El; and in Nu, sky, and expanse of waters, to see Varuna; especially when one compares the boat-journey of the Vedic seer with Rā's boat in Egypt. Or, again, in the twin children of Rā to see the Açvins; and to associate

1 Brinton, *Myths of the New World*, p. 243. The American Indians "uniformly regard the sun as heaven, the soul goes to the sun."

2 *Ib.* p. 245. 3 *Ib.* p. 239–40. 4 *Ib.* p. 50, 51.

5 *Ib.* pp. 242, 248, 255; Schoolcraft, iii. 229.

the mundane egg of the Egyptians with that of the Brahmans.[1] Certainly, had the Egyptians been one of the Aryan families, all these conceptions had been referred long ago to the category of 'primitive Aryan ideas.' But how primitive is a certain religious idea will not be shown by simple comparison of Aryan parallels. It will appear more often that it is not 'primitive,' but, so to speak, per-primitive, aboriginal with no one race, but with the race of man. When we come to describe the religions of the wild tribes of India it will be seen that among them also are found traits common, on the one hand, to the Hindu, and on the other to the wild tribes of America. With this warning in mind one may inquire at last in how far a conservative judgment can find among the Aryans themselves an identity of original conception in the different forms of divinities and religious rites. Foremost stand the universal chrematheism, worship of inanimate objects regarded as usefully divine, and the cult of the departed dead. This latter is almost universal, perhaps pan-Aryan, and Weber is probably right in assuming that the primitive Aryans believed in a future life. But Benfey's identification of Tartaras with the Sanskrit Talātala, the name of a special hell in very late systems of cosmogony, is decidedly without the bearing he would put upon it. The Sanskrit word may be taken directly from the Greek, but of an Aryan source for both there is not the remotest historical probability.

When, however, one comes to the Lord of the Dead he finds himself already in a narrower circle. Yama is the Persian Yima, and the name of Kerberos may have been once an adjective applied to the dog that guarded the path to paradise; but other particular conceptions that gather about each god point only to a period of Indo-Iranian unity.

Of the great nature-gods the sun is more than Aryan, but doubtless was Aryan, for Sūrya is Helios, but Savitar is a

[1] Renouf, *Religion of Ancient Egypt*, pp. 103, 113 ff.

development especially Indian. Dyāús-pitar is Zeús-pater, Jupiter.[1] Trita, scarcely Triton, is the Persian Thraetaona who conquers Vritra, as does Indra in India. The last, on the other hand, is to be referred only hesitatingly to the demon Añdra of the Avesta. Varuna, despite phonetic difficulties, probably is Ouranos; but Asura (Asen?) is a title of many gods in India's first period, while the corresponding Ahura is restricted to the good spirit, κατ' ἐξοχήν. The seven Ādityas are reflected in the *Amesha Çpentas* of Zoroastrian Puritanism, but these are mere imitations, spiritualized and moralized into abstractions. Bhaga is Slavic Bogu and Persian Bagha; Mitra is Persian Mithra. The Açvins are all but in name the Greek gods Dioskouroi, and correspond closely in detail (riding on horses, healing and helping, originally twins of twilight). Tacitus gives a parallel Teutonic pair (Germ. 43). Ushas, on the other hand, while etymologically corresponding to Aurora, Eos, is a specially Indian development, as Eos has no cult. Vāta, Wind, is an aboriginal god, and may perhaps be Wotan, Odin.[2] Parjanya, the rain-god, as Bühler has shown, is one with Lithuanian Perkúna, and with the northern Fiögyu. The 'fashioner,' Tvashtar (sun) is only Indo-Iranian; Thwāsha probably being the same word.

Of lesser mights, Angiras, name of fire, may be Persian *angaros*, 'fire-messenger' (compare ἄγγελος), perhaps originally one with Sk. *angāra*, 'coal.'[3] Hebe has been identified with *yavyā*, young woman, but this word is enough to show that Hebe has naught to do with the Indian pantheon. The Gandharva, moon, is certainly one with the Persian Gandarewa, but can hardly be identical with the Centaur. Saramā seems to have, together with Sārameya, a Grecian parallel development in

1 Teutonic Tuisco is doubtful, as the identity with Dyaus has lately been contested on phonetic grounds.

2 Vāta, ventus, does not agree very well with Wotan.

3 *Ait. Br.* iii. 34. ἄγγαρον πῦρ is really tautological, but beacon fires gave way to couriers and ἄγγαρος lost the sense of fire, as did ἄγγελος.

Helena (a goddess in Sparta), Selene, Hermes; and Saranyū may be the same with Erinnys, but these are not Aryan figures in the form of their respective developments, though they appear to be so in origin. It is scarcely possible that Earth is an Aryan deity with a cult, though different Aryan (and un-Aryan) nations regarded her as divine. The Maruts are especially Indian and have no primitive identity as gods with Mars, though the names may be radically connected. The fire-priests, Bhrigus, are supposed to be one with the Φλεγύαι. The fact that the fate of each in later myth is to visit hell would presuppose, however, an Aryan notion of a torture-hell, of which the Rig Veda has no conception. The Aryan identity of the two myths is thereby made uncertain, if not implausible. The special development in India of the fire-priest that brings down fire from heaven, when compared with the personification of the 'twirler' (Promantheus) in Greece, shows that no detailed myth was current in primitive times.[1] The name of the fire-priest, *brahman* = fla(g)men(?), is an indication of the primitive fire-cult in antithesis to the *soma*-cult, which latter belongs to the narrower circle of the Hindus and Persians. Here, however, in the identity of names for sacrifice (*yajña*, *yaçna*) and of *barhis*, the sacrificial straw, of *soma* = *haoma*, together with many other liturgical similarities, as in the case of the metres, one must recognize a fully developed *soma*-cult prior to the separation of the Hindus and Iranians.

Of demigods of evil type the *Yātus* are both Hindu and Iranian, but the priest-names of the one religion are evil names in the other, as the *devas*, gods, of one are the *daevas*, demons, of the other.[2] There are no other identifications that seem at

1 But the general belief that fire (Agni, ignis, Slavic ognl) was first brought to earth from heaven by a half-divine personality is (at least) Aryan, as Kuhn has shown.

2 Compare the *kavis* and *uçijs* (poets and priests) of the Veda with the evil spirits of the same names in the Avesta, like *daeva* = *deva*. Compare, besides, the Indo-Iranian feasts, *medha*, that accompany this Bacchanalian liquor-worship.

all certain in the strict province of religion, although in myth the form of Manus, who is the Hindu Noah, has been associated with Teutonic Mannus, and Greek Minos, noted in Thucydides for his sea-faring. He is to Yama (later regarded as his brother) as is Noah to Adam.

We do not lay stress on lack of equation in proper names, but, as Schrader shows (p. 596 ff.), very few comparisons on this line have a solid phonetic foundation. Minos, Manu; Ouranos, Varuna; Wotan, Vāta, are dubious; and some equate flamen with blôtan, sacrifice.

Other wider or narrower comparisons, such as Neptunus from *nápāt apām*, seem to us too daring to be believed. Apollo (*sapary*), Aphrodite (Apsaras), Artamis (non-existent *ṛtamā!*), Pān (*pavana*), have been cleverly compared, but the identity of forms has scarcely been proved. Nor is it important for the comparative mythologist that Okeanus is 'lying around' (*āçáyāna*). More than that is necessary to connect Ocean mythologically with the demon that surrounds (swallows) the waters of the sky. The Vedic parallel is rather Rasā, the far-off great 'stream.' It is rarely that one finds Aryan equivalents in the land of fairies and fays. Yet are the Hindu clever artizan Ribhus[1] our 'elves,' who, even to this day, are distinct from fairies in their dexterity and cleverness, as every wise child knows.

But animism, as simple spiritism, fetishism, perhaps ancestor-worship, and polytheism, with the polydaemonism that may be called chrematheism, exists from the beginning of the religious history, undisturbed by the proximity of theism, pantheism, or atheism; exactly as to-day in the Occident, beside theism and atheism, exist spiritism and fetishism (with their inherent magic), and even ancestor-worship, as implied by the reputed after-effect of parental curses.

[1] Ludwig interprets the three Ribhus as the three seasons personified. Etymologically connected is Orpheus, perhaps.

When the circle is narrowed to that of the Indo-Iranian connection the similarity in religion between the Veda and Avesta becomes much more striking than in any other group, as has been shown. It is here that the greatest discrepancy in opinion obtains among modern scholars. Some are inclined to refer all that smacks of Persia to a remote period of Indo-Iranian unity, and, in consequence, to connect all tokens of contact with the west with far-away regions out of India. It is scarcely possible that such can be the case. But, on the other hand, it is unhistorical to connect, as do some scholars, the worship of *soma* and Varuna with a remote period of unity, and then with a jump to admit a close connection between Veda and Avesta in the Vedic period. The Vedic Aryans appear to have lived, so to speak, hand in glove with the Iranians for a period long enough for the latter to share in that advance of Varuna-worship from polytheism to quasi-monotheism which is seen in the Rig Veda. This worship of Varuna as a superior god, with his former equals ranged under him in a group, chiefly obtains in that family (be it of priest or tribe, or be the two essentially one from a religious point of view) which has least to do with pure *soma*-worship, the inherited Indo-Iranian cult; and the Persian Ahura, with the six spiritualized equivalents of the old Vedic Adityas, can have come into existence only as a direct transformation of the latter cult, which in turn is later than the cult that developed in one direction as chief of gods a Zeus; in another, a Bhaga; in a third, an Odin. On the other hand, in the gradual change in India of Iranic gods to devils, *asuras*, there is an exact counterpart to the Iranian change of meaning from *deva* to *daeva*. But if this be the connection, it is impossible to assume a long break between India and the west, and then such a sudden tie as is indicated by the allusions in the Rig Veda to the Persians and other western lands. The most reasonable view, therefore, appears to be that the Vedic and Iranian Aryans were for a long time in contact, that the contact began to cease as the two peoples separated to east and west, but that after the two peoples separated communication was sporadically kept up between them by individuals in the way of trade or otherwise. This explains the still surviving relationship as it is found in later hymns and in thank-offerings apparently involving Iranian personages.

They that believe in a monotheistic Varuna-cult preceding the Vedic polytheism must then ignore the following facts: The Slavic equivalent of Bhaga and the Teutonic equivalent of Vāta are to these respective peoples their highest gods. They had no Varuna. Moreover, there is not the slightest proof that Ouranos in Greece[1] was ever a god worshipped as a great god before Zeus, nor is there any probability that to the Hindu Dyaus Pitar was ever a great god, in the sense that he ever had a special cult as supreme deity. He is physically great, and physically he is father, as is Earth mother, but he is religiously great only in the Hellenic-Italic circle, where exists no Uranos-cult.[2] Rather is it apparent that the Greek raised Zeus, as did the Slav Bhaga, to his first head of the pantheon. Now when one sees that in the Vedic period Varuna is the type of Ādityas, to which belong Bhaga and Mitra as distinctly less important personages, it is plain that this can mean only that Varuna has gradually been exalted to his position at the expense of the other gods. Nor is there perfect uniformity between Persian and Hindu conceptions. Asura in the Veda is not applied to Varuna alone. But in the Avesta, Ahura is the one great spirit, and his six spirits are plainly a protestant copy and modification of Varuna and his six underlings. This, then, can mean — which stands in concordance with the other

[1] ὁ δὲ χάλκεος ἀσφαλὲς αἰὲν ἕδος μένει οὐρανός, Pind. N. vi. 5; compare Preller[4], p. 40.

[2] Wahrscheinlich sind Uranos und Kronos erst aus dem Culte des Zeus abstrahirt worden. Preller[4], p. 43.

parallels between the two religions—only that Zarathustra borrows the Ahura idea from the Vedic Aryans at a time when Varuna was become superior to the other gods, and when the Vedic cult is established in its second phase.[1] To this fact points also the evidence that shows how near together geographically were once the Hindus and Persians. Whether one puts the place of separation at the Kabul or further to the north-west is a matter of indifference. The Persians borrow the idea of Varuna Asura, whose eye is the sun. They spiritualize this, and create an Asura unknown to other nations.

Of von Bradke's attempt to prove an original Dyaus Asura we have said nothing, because the attempt has failed signally. He imagines that the epithet Asura was given to Dyaus in the Indo-Iranian period, and that from a Dyaus Pitar Asura the Iranians made an abstract Asura, while the Hindus raised the other gods and depressed Dyaus Pitar Asura; whereas it is quite certain that Varuna (Asura) grew up, out, and over the other Asuras, his former equals.

And yet it is almost a pity to spend time to demonstrate that Varuna-worship was not monotheistic originally. We gladly admit that, even if not a primitive monotheistic deity, Varuna yet is a god that belongs to a very old period of Hindu literature. And, for a worship so antique, how noble is the idea, how exalted is the completed conception of him! Truly, the Hindus and Persians alone of Aryans mount nearest to the high level of Hebraic thought. For Varuna beside the loftiest figure in the Hellenic pantheon stands like a god beside a man. The Greeks had, indeed, a surpassing aesthetic taste, but in grandeur of religious ideas even the daring of Aeschylus becomes but hesitating bravado when compared with the serene boldness of the Vedic seers, who, first of their race, out of many gods imagined God.

[1] When Aryan deities are decadent, Trita, Mitra, etc.

In regard to eschatology, as in regard to myths, it has been shown that the utmost caution in identification is called for. It may be surmised that such or such a belief or legend is in origin one with a like faith or tale of other peoples. But the question whether it be one in historical origin or in universal mythopoetic fancy, and this latter be the only common origin, must remain in almost every case unanswered.[1] This is by far not so entertaining, nor so picturesque a solution as is the explanation of a common historical basis for any two legends, with its inspiring 'open sesame' to the door of the locked past. But which is truer? Which accords more with the facts as they are collected from a wider field? As man in the process of development, in whatever quarter of earth he be located, makes for himself independently clothes, language, and gods, so he makes myths that are more or less like those of other peoples, and it is only when names coincide and traits that are unknown elsewhere are strikingly similar in any two mythologies that one has a right to argue a probable community of origin.

But even if the legend of the flood were Babylonian, and the Asuras as devils were due to Iranian influence — which can neither be proved nor disproved — the fact remains that the Indian religion in its main features is of a purely native character.

As the most prominent features of the Vedic religion must be regarded the worship of *soma*, of nature-gods that are in part already more than this, of spirits, and of the Manes; the acknowledgment of a moral law and a belief in a life hereafter. There is also a vaguer nascent belief in a creator apart from

[1] Spiegel holds that the whole idea of future punishment is derived from Persia (*Eranische Alterthumskunde*, i. p. 458), but his point of view is naturally prejudiced. The allusion to the supposed Babylonian coin, *manā*, in RV. viii. 78. 2, would indicate that the relation with Babylon is one of trade, as with Aegypt. The account of the flood may be drawn thence, so may the story of Deucalion, but both Hindu and Hellenic versions may be as native as is that of the American redskins.

any natural phenomenon, but the creed for the most part is poetically, indefinitely, stated: 'Most wonder-working of the wonder-working gods, who made heaven and earth' (as above). The corresponding Power is Cerus in Cerus-Creator (Kronos?), although when a name is given, the Maker, Dhātar, is employed; while Tvashtar, the artificer, is more an epithet of the sun than of the unknown creator. The personification of Dhātar as creator of the sun, etc., belongs to later Vedic times, and foreruns the Father-god of the last Vedic period. Not till the classical age (below) is found a formal identification of the Vedic nature-gods with the departed Fathers (Manes). Indra, for example, is invoked in the Rig Veda to 'be a friend, be a father, be more fatherly than the fathers';[1] but this implies no patristic side in Indra, who is called in the same hymn (vs. 4) the son of Dyaus (his father); and Dyaus Pitar no more implies, as say some sciolists, that Dyaus was regarded as a human ancestor than does 'Mother Earth' imply a belief that Earth is the ghost of a dead woman.

In the Veda there is a nature-religion and an ancestor-religion. These approach, but do not unite; they are felt as sundered beliefs. Sun-myths, though by some denied *in toto*, appear plainly in the Vedic hymns. Dead heroes may be gods, but gods, too, are natural phenomena, and, again, they are abstractions. He that denies any one of these sources of godhead is ignorant of India.

Müller, in his *Ancient Sanskrit Literature*, has divided Vedic literature into four periods, that of *chandas*, songs; *mantras*, texts; *brāhmanas;* and *sūtras.* The *mantras* are in distinction from *chandas*, the later hymns to the earlier gods.[2] The latter distinction can, however, be established only on subjective grounds, and, though generally unimpeachable, is sometimes liable to reversion. Thus, Müller looks upon RV. viii. 30 as 'simple and primitive,' while others see in this

[1] iv. 17. 17.

[2] *Loc. cit.* pp. 70, 480.

hymn a late *mantra*. Between the Rig Veda and the Brāhmanas, which are in prose, lies a period filled out in part by the present form of the Atharva Veda, which, as has been shown, is a Veda of the low cult that is almost ignored by the Rig Veda, while it contains at the same time much that is later than the Rig Veda, and consists of old and new together in a manner entirely conformable to the state of every other Hindu work of early times. After this epoch there is found in the liturgical period, into which extend the later portions of the Rig Veda (noticeably parts of the first, fourth, eighth, and tenth books), a religion which, in spiritual tone, in metaphysical speculation, and even in the interpretation of some of the natural divinities, differs not more from the bulk of the Rig Veda than does the social status of the time from that of the earlier text. Religion has become. in so far as the gods are concerned, a ritual. But, except in the building up of a Father-god, theology is at bottom not much altered, and the eschatological conceptions remain about as they were, despite a preliminary sign of the doctrine of metempsychosis. In the Atharva Veda, for the first time, hell is known by its later name (xii. 4. 36), and perhaps its tortures; but the idea of future punishment appears plainly first in the Brahmanic period. Both the doctrine of re-birth and that of hell appear in the earliest Sūtras, and consequently the assumption that these dogmas come from Buddhism does not appear to be well founded; for it is to be presumed whatever religious belief is established in legal literature will have preceded that literature by a considerable period, certainly by a greater length of time than that which divides the first Brahmanic law from Buddhism.

CHAPTER IX.

BRAHMANISM.

BESIDES the Rig Veda and the Atharva Veda there are two others, called respectively the Sāma Veda and the Yajur Veda.[1] The former consists of a small collection of verses, which are taken chiefly from the eighth and ninth books of the Rig Veda, and are arranged for singing. It has a few more verses than are contained in the corresponding parts of the Rik, but the whole is of no added importance from the present point of view. It is of course made entirely for the ritual. Also made for the ritual is the Yajur Veda, the Veda of sacrificial formulae. But this Veda is far more important. With it one is brought into a new land, and into a world of ideas that are strange to the Rik. The period represented by it is a sort of bridge between the Rik and the Brāhmanas. The Yajus is later than Rik or Atharvan, belonging in its entirety more to the age of the liturgy than to the older Vedic era. With the Brāhmanas not only is the tone changed from that of the Rig Veda; the whole moral atmosphere is now surcharged with hocus-pocus, mysticism, religiosity, instead of the cheerful, real religion which, however formal, is the soul of the Rik. In the Brāhmanas there is no freshness, no poetry. There is in some regards a more scrupulous outward morality, but for the rest there is only cynicism, bigotry, and dullness. It is true that each of these traits may be found in certain parts of the Rig

[1] In *Ait. Br.* i. 22, there is an unexplained antithesis of Rik, Yajus, Sāman, Veda. and Brahma; where the commentator takes Veda to be Atharva Veda. The priests, belonging respectively to the first three Vedas, are for the Rig Veda, the Hotar priest, who recites; for the Sāman, the Udgātar, 'the singer': for the Yājus. the Adhvaryu, who attends to the erection of the altar, etc. Compare Müller, ASL. p. 468.

Veda, but it is not true that they represent there the spirit of the age, as they do in the Brahmanic period. Of this Brahmanic stoa, to which we now turn, the Yajur Veda forms the fitting entrance. Here the priest is as much lord as he is in the Brāhmanas. Here the sacrifice is only the act, the sacrificial forms (*yajus*), without the spirit.

In distinction from the verse-Veda (the Rik), the Yajur Veda contains the special formulae which the priest that attends to the erection of the altar has to speak, with explanatory remarks added thereto. This of course stamps the collection as mechanical; but the wonder is that this collection, with the similar Brāhmana scriptures that follow it, should be the only new literature which centuries have to show.[1] As explanatory of the sacrifice there is found, indeed, a good deal of legendary stuff, which sometimes has a literary character. But nothing is for itself; everything is for the correct performance of the sacrifice.[2]

The geographical centre is now changed, and instead of the Punjāb, the 'middle district' becomes the seat of culture. Nor is there much difference between the district to which can be referred the rise of the Yajur Veda and that of the Brāhmanas. No less altered is the religion. All is now symbolical, and the gods, though in general they are the gods of the Rig Veda, are not the same as of old. The priests have become gods. The old appellation of 'spirit,' *asura*, is confined to evil spirits. There is no longer any such 'henotheism' as that of the Rig Veda. The Father-god, 'lord of beings,' or simply 'the father,' is the chief god. The last thought of the Rig

[1] It is the only literature of its time except (an important exception) those forerunners of later Sūtra and epic which one may suppose to be in process of formation long before they come to the front.

[2] There are several schools of this Veda, of which the chief are the Vājasaneyi, or 'White Yajus,' collection; the Tāittirīya collection; and the Māitrāyaṇī collection; the first named being the latest though the most popular, the last two being the foremost representatives of the 'Black Yajus.'

Veda is the first thought of the Yajur Veda. Other changes have taken place. The demigods of the older period, the water-nymphs of the Rik, here become seductive goddesses, whose increase of power in this art agrees with the decline of the warrior spirit that is shown too in the whole mode of thinking. Most important is the gradual rise of Vishnu and the first appearance of Çiva. Here *brahma*, which in the Rik has the meaning 'prayer' alone, is no longer mere prayer, but, as in later literature, holiness. In short, before the Brāhmanas are reached they are perceptible in the near distance, in the Veda of Formulae, the Yajus:[1] for between the Yajur Veda and the Brāhmanas there is no essential difference. The latter consist of explanations of the sacrificial liturgy, interspersed with legends, bits of history, philosophical explanations, and other matter more or less related to the subject. They are completed by the Forest Books, Āranyakas, which contain the speculations of the later theosophy, the Upanishads (below). It is with the Yajur Veda and its nearly related literature, the Brāhmanas, that Brahmanism really begins. Of these latter the most important in age and content are the Brāhmanas (of the Rig Veda and Yajur Veda), called Āitareya and Çata-patha, the former representing the western district, the latter, in great part, a more eastern region.

Although the 'Northerners' are still respectfully referred to, yet, as we have just said, the people among whom arose the Brāhmanas are not settled in the Punjāb, but in the country called the 'middle district,' round about the modern Delhi. For the most part the Punjāb is abandoned; or rather, the literature of this period does not emanate from the Aryans that remained in the Punjāb, but from the still emigrating descendants of the old Vedic people that used to live there. Some stay behind and keep the older practices, not in all

1 The different traits here recorded are given with many illustrative examples by Schroeder, in his *Literatur und Cultur*, p. 90 ff.

regards looked upon as orthodox by their more advanced brethren, who have pushed east and now live in the country called the land of the Kurus and Pañcālas.[1] They are spread farther east, along the banks of the Jumna and Ganges, south of Nepāl; while some are still about and south of the holy Kurukshetra or 'plain of Kurus.' East of the middle district the Kosalas and Videhas form, in opposition to the Kurus and Pañcālas, the second great tribe (Tirhūt). There are now two sets of 'Seven Rivers,' and the holiness of the western group is perceptibly lessened. Here for the first time are found the *Vrātya*-hymns, intended to initiate into the Brahmanic order Aryans who have not conformed to it, and speak a dialectic language.[2] From the point of view of language and geography, no less than from that of the social and spiritual conditions, it is evident that quite a period has elapsed since the body of the Rig Veda was composed. The revealed texts are now ancient storehouses of wisdom. Religion has apparently become a form; in some regards it is a farce.

"There are two kinds of gods; for the gods are gods, and priests that are learned in the Veda and teach it are human gods." This sentence, from one of the most important Hindu prose works,[3] is the key to the religion of the period which it represents; and it is fitly followed by the further statement, that like sacrifice to the gods are the fees paid to the human gods the priests.[4] Yet with this dictum, so important for the

1 Compare Weber, *Ind. Streifen*, ii. 197. 2 Weber, *Lit.* p. 73.

3 The *Çata-patha Brāhmana* (or "Brāhmana of the hundred paths") ii. 2. 2. 6; 4. 3. 14.

4 The chief family priest, it is said in the *Çat. Br.* ii. 4. 4. 5, is a man of great influence. Sometimes one priest becomes religious head of two clans (an extraordinary event, however; only one name is reported) and then how exalted is his position. Probably, as in the later age of the drama, the chief priest was often at the same time practically prime minister. It is said in another part of the same book that although the whole earth is divine, yet it is the priest that makes holy the place of sacrifice (iii. 1. 1. 4). In this period murder is defined as killing a priest; other cases are not called murder. Weber, *IS.* x. 66.

understanding of the religion of the age, must be joined another, if one would do that age full justice: 'The sacrifice is like a ship sailing heavenward; if there be a sinful priest in it, that one priest would make it sink' (*Çat. Br.* iv. 2. 5. 10). For although the time is one in which ritualism had, indeed, become more important than religion, and the priest more important than the gods, yet is there no lack of reverential feeling, nor is morality regarded as unimportant. The first impression, however, which is gained from the literature of this period is that the sacrifice is all in all; that the endless details of its course, and the petty questions in regard to its arrangement, are not only the principal objects of care and of chief moment, but even of so cardinal importance that the whole religious spirit swings upon them. But such is not altogether the case. It is the truth, yet is it not the whole truth, that in these Brāhmanas religion is an appearance, not a reality. The sacrifice is indeed represented to be the only door to prosperity on earth and to future bliss; but there is a quiet yet persistent belief that at bottom a moral and religious life is quite as essential as are the ritualistic observances with which worship is accompanied.

To describe Brahmanism as implying a religion that is purely one of ceremonies, one composed entirely of observances, is therefore not altogether correct. In reading a liturgical work it must not be forgotten for what the work was intended. If its object be simply to inculcate a special rite, one cannot demand that it should show breadth of view or elevation of sentiment. Composed of observances every work must be of which the aim is to explain observances. In point of fact, religion (faith and moral behavior) is here assumed, and so entirely is it taken for granted that a statement emphasizing the necessity of godliness is seldom found.

Nevertheless, having called attention to the religious spirit that lies latent in the pedantic Brāhmanas, we are willing to admit that the age is overcast, not only with a thick cloud of ritualism, but also with an unpleasant mask of phariseeism. There cannot have been quite so much attention paid to the outside of the platter without neglect of the inside. And it is true that the priests of this period strive more for the completion of their rites than for the perfection of themselves. It is true, also, that occasionally there is a revolting contempt for those people who are not of especial service to the priest. There are now two godlike aristocrats, the priest and the noble. The 'people' are regarded as only fit to be the "food of the nobility." In the symbolical language of the time the bricks of the altar, which are consecrated, are the warrior caste; the fillings, in the space between the bricks, are not consecrated; and these "fillers of space" are "the people" (*Çat. Br.* vi. 1. 2. 25).

Yet is religion in these books not dead, but sleeping; to wake again in the Upanishads with a fuller spiritual life than is found in any other pre-Christian system. Although the subject matter of the Brāhmanas is the cult, yet are there found in them numerous legends, moral teachings, philosophical fancies, historical items, etymologies and other adventitious matter, all of which are helpful in giving a better understanding of the intelligence of the people to whom is due all the extant literature of the period. Long citations from these ritualistic productions would have a certain value, in showing in native form the character of the works, but they would make unendurable reading; and we have thought it better to arrange the multifarious contents of the chief Brāhmanas in a sort of order, although it is difficult always to decide where theology ends and moral teachings begin, the two are here so interwoven.

BRAHMANIC THEOLOGY AND THE SACRIFICE.

While in general the pantheon of the Rig Veda and Atharva Veda is that of the Brāhmanas, some of the older gods are now reduced in importance, and, on the other hand, as in the Yajur Veda, some gods are seen to be growing in importance. 'Time,' deified in the Atharvan, is a great god, but beside him still stand the old rustic divinities; and chrematheism, which antedates even the Rig Veda, is still recognized. To the 'ploughshare' and the 'plough' the Rig Veda has an hymn (iv. 57. 5–8), and so the ritual gives them a cake at the sacrifice (*Çunāçīrya*, *Çat. Br.* ii. 6. 3. 5). The number of the gods, in the Rig Veda estimated as thirty-three, or, at the end of this period, as thousands, remains as doubtful as ever; but, in general, all groups of deities become greater in number. Thus, in TS. i. 4. 11. 1, the Rudras alone are counted as thirty-three instead of eleven; and, *ib.* v. 5. 2. 5, the eight Vasus become three hundred and thirty-three; but it is elsewhere hinted that the number of the gods stands in the same relation to that of men as that in which men stand to the beasts; that is, there are not quite so many gods as men (*Çat. Br.* ii. 3. 2. 18).

Of more importance than the addition of new deities is the subdivision of the old. As one finds in Greece a Ζεὺς καταχθόνιος beside a Ζεὺς ξένιος, so in the Yajur Veda and Brāhmanas are found (an extreme instance) hail 'to Kāya,' and hail 'to Kasmāi,' that is, the god Ka is differentiated into two divinities, according as he is declined as a noun or as a pronoun; for this is the god "Who?" as the dull Brāhmanas interpreted that verse of the Rig Veda which asks 'to whom (which, as) god shall we offer sacrifice?' (Māit. S. iii. 12. 5.) But ordinarily one divinity like Agni is subdivided, according to his functions, as 'lord of food,' 'lord of prayer,' etc.[1]

In the Brāhmanas different names are given to the chief god, but he is most often called the Father-god (Prajāpati, 'lord of creatures,' or the Father, *pitā*). His earlier Vedic type is Brihaspati, the lord of strength, and, from another point of

[1] Barth, *loc. cit.* p. 42.

view, the All-god.[1] The other gods fall into various groups, the most significant being the triad of Fire, Wind, and Sun.[2] Not much weight is to be laid on the theological speculations of the time as indicative of primitive conceptions, although they may occasionally hit true. For out of the number of inane fancies it is reasonable to suppose that some might coincide with historic facts. Thus the All-gods of the Rig Veda, by implication, are of later origin than the other gods, and this, very likely, was the case; but it is a mere guess on the part of the priest. The *Çatapatha*, iii. 6. 1. 28, speaks of the All-gods as gods that gained immortality on a certain occasion, *i.e.*, became immortal like other gods. So the Ādityas go to heaven before the Angirasas (*Āit. Br.* iv. 17), but this has no such historical importance as some scholars are inclined to think. The lesser gods are in part carefully grouped and numbered, in a manner somewhat contradictory to what must have been the earlier belief. Thus the 'three kinds of gods' are now Vasus, of earth, Rudras, of air, and Ādityas, of sky, and the daily offerings are divided between them; the morning offering belonging only to the Vasus, the mid-day one only to (Indra and) the Rudras, the third to the Ādityas with the Vasus and Rudras together.[3] Again, the morning and mid-day pressing belong to the gods alone, and strict rule is observed in distinguishing their portion from that of the Manes (*Çat. Br.* iv. 4. 22). The difference of sex is quite ignored, so that the 'universal Agni' is identified with (mother) earth; as is also, once or twice, Pūshan (*ib.* iii. 8. 5. 4; 2. 4. 19; ii. 5. 4. 7). As the 'progenitor,' Agni facilitates connubial union, and is called "the head god, the progenitor among gods, the lord of beings" (*ib.* iii. 4. 3. 4; iii. 9. 1. 6). Pūshan is interpreted to mean

[1] He has analogy with Agni in being made of 'seven persons (males),' *Çat. Br.* x. 2. 2. 1.

[2] Compare Māit. S. iv. 2. 12, 'sons of Prajāpati, Agni, Vāyu, Sūrya.'

[3] *Çat. Br.* i. 3. 4. 12; iv. 3. 5. 1.

cattle, and Brihaspati is the priestly caste (*ib.* iii. 9. 1. 10 ff.). The base of comparison is usually easy to find. 'The earth nourishes,' and 'Pūshan nourishes,' hence Pūshan is the earth; or 'the earth belongs to all' and Agni is called 'belonging to all' (universal), hence the two are identified. The All-gods, merely on account of their name, are now the All; Aditi is the 'unbounded' earth (*ib.* iii. 9. 1. 13; iv. 1. 1. 23; i. 1. 4. 5; iii. 2. 3. 6). Agni represents all the gods, and he is the dearest, the closest, and the surest of all the gods (*ib.* i. 6. 2. 8 ff.). It is said that man on earth fathers the fire (that is, protects it), and when he dies the fire that he has made his son on earth becomes his father, causing him to be reborn in heaven (*ib.* ii. 3. 3. 3–5; vi. 1. 2. 26).

The wives of the gods (*devānām patnīr yajati*), occasionally mentioned in the Rig Veda, have now an established place and cult apart from that of the gods (*ib.* i. 9. 2. 11). The fire on the hearth is god Agni in person, and is not a divine or mystic type; but he is prayed to as a heavenly friend. Some of these traits are old, but they are exaggerated as compared with the more ancient theology. When one goes on a journey or returns from one, 'even if a king were in his house' he should not greet him till he makes homage to his hearth-fires, either with spoken words or with silent obeisance. For Agni and Prajāpati are one, they are son and father (*ib.* ii. 4. 1. 3, 10; vi. 1. 2. 26). The gods have mystic names, and these 'who will dare to speak?' Thus, Indra's mystic name is Arjuna (*ib.* ii. 1. 2. 11). In the early period of the Rig Veda the priest dares to speak. The pantheism of the end of the Rig Veda is here decided and plain-spoken, as it is in the Atharvan. As it burns brightly or not the fire is in turn identified with different gods, Rudra, Varuna, Indra, and Mitra (*ib.* ii. 3. 2. 9 ff.). Agni is all the gods and the gods are in men (*ib.* iii. 1. 3. 1; 4. 1. 19; ii. 3. 2. 1: Indra and King Yama dwell in men). And, again, the Father (Prajāpati) is the All; he is the year of twelve months and five seasons (*ib.* i. 3. 5. 10). Then follows a characteristic bit. Seventeen verses are to be recited to correspond to the 'seventeenfold' Prajāpati. But 'some say' twenty-one verses; and he may recite twenty-one, for if 'the three worlds' are added to the above seventeen one gets twenty, and the sun (*ya eṣa tapati*) makes the twenty-first! As to the number of worlds, it is said (*ib.* i. 2. 4. 11, 20–21) that there are three worlds, and possibly a fourth.

Soma is now the moon, but as being one half of Vritra, the evil demon. The other half became the belly of creatures (*ib.* i. 6. 3. 17). Slightly different is the statement that Soma was Vritra, iv. 2. 5. 15. In *Āit. Br.* i. 27, King Soma is bought of the Gandharvas by Vāc, 'speech,' as a cow.[1] With phases of the moon Indra and Agni are identified. One is the deity of the new: the other, of the full moon; while Mitra is the waning, and Varuna the waxing moon (*Çat. Br.* ii. 4. 4. 17–18). This opposition of deities is more fully expressed in the attempt to make antithetic the relations of the gods and the Manes, thus: 'The gods are represented by spring, summer, and rains; the Fathers, by autumn, winter, and the dewy season; the gods, by the waxing; the Fathers, by the waning moon; the gods, by day; the Fathers, by night; the gods, by morning; the Fathers, by afternoon' (*Çat. Br.* ii. 1. 31; *ib.* ii. 4. 2. 1 ff.: 'The sun is the light of the gods; the moon, of the Fathers; fire, of men'). Between morning and afternoon, as representative of gods and Manes respectively, stands midday, which, according to the same authority (ii. 4. 2. 8), represents men. The passage first cited continues thus: 'The seasons are gods and Fathers; gods are immortal; the Fathers

[1] Interesting is the fact that only priests may eat sacrificial food and drink *soma* at this period. When even the king should drink *soma*, he is made to drink some transubstantiated liquor which, the priests inform him, has been 'made into *soma*' for him by magic, for the latter is too holy for any warrior really to drink (vii. 19; viii. 20). But in the more popular feasts there are indications that this rule is often broken. Compare Weber, *Rājasūya* p. 98.

are mortal.' In regard to the relation between spring and the other seasons, the fifth section of this passage may be compared: 'Spring is the priesthood; summer, the warrior-caste; the rains are the (*viç*) people.'[1]

Among the conspicuous divine forms of this period is the Queen of Serpents, whose verses are chanted over fire; but she is the earth, according to some passages (*Āit. Br.* v. 23; *Çat. Br.* ii. 1. 4. 30; iv. 6. 9. 17). In their divine origin there is, indeed, according to the theology now current, no difference between the powers of light and of darkness, between the gods and the 'spirits,' *asuras, i.e.*, evil spirits. Many tales begin with the formula: 'The gods and evil spirits, both born of the Father-god' (*Çat. Br.* i. 2. 4. 8). Weber thinks that this implies close acquaintance with Persian worship, a sort of tit-for-tat; for the Hindu would in that case call the holy spirit, *ahura*, of the Persian a devil, just as the Persian makes an evil spirit, *daeva*, out of the Hindu god, *deva*. But the relations between Hindu and Persian in this period are still very uncertain. It is interesting to follow out some of the Brahmanic legends, if only to see what was the conception of the evil spirits. In one such theological legend the gods and the (evil) spirits, both being sons of the Father-god, inherited from him, respectively, mind and speech; hence the gods got the sacrifice and heaven, while the evil spirits got this earth. Again, the two entered on the inheritance of their father in time, and so the gods have the waxing moon, and the evil spirits, the waning moon (*ib.* iii. 2. 1. 18; i. 7. 2. 22).

But what these Asuras or (evil) spirits really are may be read easily from the texts. The gods are the spirits of light; the Asuras are the spirits of darkness. Therewith is indissolubly connected the idea that sin and darkness are of the same nature. So one reads that when the sun rises it frees

[1] For the relations of the different castes at this period, see Weber, in the tenth volume of the *Indische Studien*.

itself 'from darkness, from sin,' as a snake from its slough (*ib.* ii. 3. 1. 6). And in another passage it is said that darkness and illusion were given to the Asuras as their portion by the Father-god (*ib.* ii. 4. 2. 5). With this may be compared also the frequent grouping of the Asuras or Rakshas with darkness (*e.g.*, *ib.* iii. 8. 2. 15; iv. 3. 4. 21). As to the nature of the gods the evidence is contradictory. Both gods and evil spirits were originally soulless and mortal. Agni (Fire) alone was immortal, and it was only through him that the others continued to live. They became immortal by putting in their inmost being the holy (immortal) fire (*ib.* ii. 2. 2. 8). On the other hand, it is said that Agni was originally without brightness; and Indra, identified with the sun, was originally dark (*ib.* iv. 5. 4. 3; iii. 4. 2. 15). The belief in an originally human condition of the gods (even the Father-god was originally mortal) is exemplified in a further passage, where it is said that the gods used to live on earth, but they grew tired of man's endless petitions and fled; also in another place, where it is stated that the gods used to drink together with men visibly, but now they do so invisibly (*ib.* ii. 3. 4. 4; iii. 6. 2. 26). How did such gods obtain their supremacy? The answer is simple, 'by sacrifice' (*Çat. Br.* iii. 1. 4. 3; *Āit. Br.* ii. 1. 1). So now they live by sacrifice: 'The sun would not rise if the priest did not make sacrifice' (*Çat. Br.* ii. 3. 1. 5). Even the order of things would change if the order of ceremonial were varied: Night would be eternal if the priests did so and so; the months would not pass, one following the other, if the priests walked out or entered together, etc. (*ib.* iv. 3. 1. 9–10). It is by a knowledge of the Vedas that one conquers all things, and the sacrifice is part and application of this knowledge, which in one passage is thus reconditely subdivided: 'Threefold is knowledge, the Rig Veda, the Yajur Veda, and the Sāma Veda.[1] The Rig Veda, *i.e.*, the verses sung, are the earth; the Yajus is air; the

[1] The Atharvan is not yet recognized as a Veda.

Sāman is the sky. He conquers earth, air, and sky respectively by these three Vedas. The Rik and Sāman are Indra and are speech; the Yajus is Vishnu and mind' (*ib.* iv. 6. 7. 1 ff.). An item follows that touches on a modern philosophical question. Apropos of speech and mind: 'Where speech (alone) existed everything was accomplished and known; but where mind (alone) existed nothing was accomplished or known' (*ib.* i. 4. 4. 3–4, 7). Mind and speech are male and female, and as yoke-fellows bear sacrifice to the gods; to be compared is the interesting dispute between mind and speech (*ib.* 5. 8). As dependent as is man on what is given by the gods, so dependent are the gods on what is offered to them by men (*Tāitt. Br.* ii. 2. 7. 3; *Çat. Br.* i. 2. 5. 24). Even the gods are now not native to heaven. They win heaven by sacrifice, by metres, etc. (*Çat. Br.* iv. 3. 2. 5).

What, then, is the sacrifice? A means to enter into the godhead of the gods, and even to control the gods; a ceremony where every word was pregnant with consequences;[1] every movement momentous. There are indications, however, that the priests themselves understood that much in the ceremonial was pure hocus-pocus, and not of such importance as it was reputed to be. But such faint traces as survive of a freer spirit objecting to ceremonial absurdities only mark more clearly the level plain of unintelligent superstition which was the feeding-ground of the ordinary priests.

Some of the cases of revolted common-sense are worth citing. Conspicuous as an authority on the sacrifice, and at the same time as a somewhat recalcitrant priest, is Yājñavalkya, author and critic, one of the greatest names in Hindu ecclesiastical history. It was he who, apropos of the new rule in

[1] And even the pronunciation of a word or the accent is fateful. The famous godly example of this is where Tvashtar, the artificer, in anger mispronounced *indraçátru* as *índraçatru*, whereby the meaning was changed from 'conqueror of Indra' to 'Indra-conquered,' with unexpected result (*Çat. Br.* i. 6. 3. 8; *Tāitt. S.* ii. 4. 12. 1).

ethics, so strongly insisted upon after the Vedic age and already beginning to obtain, the rule that no one should eat the flesh of the (sacred) cow ('Let no one eat beef. . . . Whoever eats it would be reborn (on earth) as a man of ill fame') said bluntly: 'As for me I eat (beef) if it is good (firm).'[1] It certainly required courage to say this, with the especial warning against beef, the meat of an animal peculiarly holy (*Çat. Br.* iii. 1. 2. 21). It was, again, Yājñavalkya (*Çat. Br.* i. 3. 1. 26), who protested against the priests' new demand that the benefit of the sacrifice should accrue in part to the priest; whereas it had previously been understood that not the sacrificial priest but the sacrificer (the worshipper, the man who hired the priest and paid the expenses) got all the benefit of the ceremony. Against the priests' novel and unjustifiable claim Yājñavalkya exclaims: 'How can people have faith in this? Whatever be the blessing for which the priests pray, this blessing is for the worshipper (sacrificer) alone.'[2] It was Yājñavalkya, too, who rebutted some new superstition involving the sacrificer's wife, with the sneer, 'who cares whether the wife,' etc. (*kas tad ādriyeta, ib.* 21). These protestations are naïvely recorded, though it is once suggested that in some of his utterances Yājñavalkya was not in earnest (*ib.* iv. 2. 1. 7). The high mind of this great priest is contrasted with the mundane views of his contemporaries in the prayers of himself and of another priest; for it is recorded that whereas Yājñavalkya's prayer to the Sun was 'give me light' (or 'glory,' *varco me dehi*), that of Āupoditeya was 'give me cows' (*ib.* i. 9. 3. 16). The chronicler adds, after citing these prayers, that one obtains

[1] The word is *aṅsala*, strong, or 'from the shoulder' (?). In iii. 4. 1. 2 one cooks an ox or a goat for a very distinguished guest, as a sort of guest-sacrifice. So the guest is called 'cow-killer' (Weber, *Ved. Beiträge*, p. 36).

[2] Compare *ib.* i. 9. 1. 21, "let the priest not say 'guard' me (or us).' but 'guard this worshipper (sacrificer),' for if he says 'me' he induces no blessing at all; the blessing is not for the priest, but for the sacrificer." In both passages, most emphatically, *yajamānasyāiva*, 'for the sacrificer alone.'

whatever he prays for, either illumination or wealth.[1] Yājña-valkya, however, is not the only protestant. In another passage, *ib.* ii. 6. 3. 14–17, the sacrificer is told to shave his head all around, so as to be like the sun; this will ensure his being able to 'consume (his foes) on all sides like the sun,' and it is added: But Āsuri said, 'What on earth has it to do with his head? Let him not shave.'[2]

'Eternal holiness' is won by him that offers the sacrifice of the seasons. Characteristic is the explanation, 'for such an one wins the year, and a year is a complete whole, and a complete whole is indestructible (eternal); hence his holiness is indestructible, and he thereby becomes a part of a year and goes to the gods; but as there is no destruction in the gods, his holiness is therefore indestructible' (*ib.* ii. 6. 3. 1).

Not only a man's self but also his Manes are benefited by means of sacrifice.[3] He gives the Manes pleasure with his offering, but he also raises their estate, and sends them up to live in a higher world.[4] The cosmological position of the Manes are the *avāntaradiças*, that is, between the four quarters; though, according to some, there are three kinds of them, *soma*-Manes, sacrifice-Manes (Manes of the sacrificial straw), and the burnt, *i.e.*, the spirits of those that have been consumed in fire. They are, again, identified with the seasons, and are expressly mentioned as the guardians of houses, so that the Brahmanic Manes are at once Penates, Lares, and Manes.[5]

1 *Yaṁ kāmaṁ kāmayate so 'smāi kāmaḥ samṛdhyate.*

2 Āsuri's name as a theologian is important, since the Sāṅkhya philosophy is intimately connected with him; if this Āsuri be not another man with the same name (compare Weber, *Lit.* p. 152).

3 The regular sacrifices to the Manes are daily and monthly; funerals and 'faith-feasts,' *çrāddha*, are occasional additions.

4 Each generation of Manes rises to a better (higher) state if the offerings continue. As a matter of ceremonial this means that the remoter generations of fathers are put indefinitely far off, while the immediate predecessors of a man are the real beneficiaries; they climb up to the sky on the offering.

5 Compare *Çat. Br.* i. 8. 1. 40; ii. 6. 1. 3, 7, 10, 42; ii. 4. 2. 24; v. 5. 4. 28.

The sacrifice is by no means meant as an aid to the acquirement of heavenly bliss alone. Many of the great sacrifices are for the gaining of good things on earth. In one passage there is described a ceremony, the result of which is to be that the warrior, who is the sacrificer, may say to a man of the people "fetch out and give me your store" (*ib.* i. 3. 2. 15; iv. 3. 3. 10). Everybody sacrifices, even the beasts erect altars and fires![1] That one should sacrifice without the ulterior motive of gain is unknown. Brahmanic India knows no thank-offering. Ordinarily the gain is represented as a compensating gift from the divinity, whom the sacrificer pleases with his sacrifice. Very plainly is this expressed. "He offers the sacrifice to the god with this text: 'Do thou give to me (and) I (will) give to thee; do thou bestow on me (and) I (will) bestow on thee'" (*Vāj. S.* iii. 50; *Çat. Br.* ii. 5. 3. 19). But other ends are accomplished. By the sacrifice he may injure his enemy, but in offering it, if he leaves too much over, that part accrues to the good of his foe (*Çat. Br.* i. 2. 1. 7; 9. 1. 18).

The sacrifice is throughout symbolical. The sacrificial straw represents the world; the metre used represents all living creatures, etc., — a symbolism frequently suggested by a mere pun, but often as ridiculously expounded without such aid. The altar's measure is the measure of metres. The cord of regeneration (badge of the twice-born, the holy cord of the high castes) is triple, because food is threefold, or because the father and mother with the child make three (*Çat. Br.* iii. 5. 1. 7 ff.; 2. 1. 12); the *jagati* metre contains the living world, because this is called *jagat* (*ib.* i. 8. 2. 11).

Out of the varied mass of rules, speculations, and fancies, a few of general character may find place here, that the reader

[1] This passage (*ib.* ii. 1. 2. 7) is preceded by a typical argument for setting up the fires under the Pleiades, the wives of the Great Bear stars. He may do or he may not do so — the reasons contradict each other, and all of them are incredibly silly.

may gain a collective impression of the religious literature of the time.

The fee for the sacrifice is mentioned in one place as one thousand cows. These must be presented in groups of three hundred and thirty-three each, three times, with an odd one of three colors. This is on account of the holy character of the numeral three. 'But Āsuri (apparently fearful that this rule would limit the fee) said "he may give more"' (*Çat. Br.* iv. 5. 8. 14). As to the fee, the rules are precise and their propounders are unblushing. The priest performs the sacrifice for the fee alone, and it must consist of valuable garments, kine, horses,[1] or gold — when each is to be given is carefully stated. Gold is coveted most, for this is 'immortality,' 'the seed of Agni,' and therefore peculiarly agreeable to the pious priest.[2] For his greed, which goes so far that he proclaims that he who gives a thousand kine obtains all things of heaven (*ib.* iv. 5. 1. 11), the priest has good precept to cite, for the gods of heaven, in all the tales told of them, ever demand a reward from each other when they help their neighbor-gods. Nay, even the gods require a witness and a vow, lest they injure each other. Discord arose among them when once they performed the guest-offering; they divided into different parties, Agni with the Vasus, Soma with the Rudras, Varuna with the Ādityas, and Indra with the Maruts. But with discord came weakness, and the evil spirits got the better of them. So they made a covenant with each other, and took Wind as witness that they would not deceive each other. This famous covenant of the gods is the prototype of that significant covenant made by the priest, that he would not, while pretending to beseech

[1] This last fee is not so common. For an oblation to Sūrya the fee is a white horse or a white bull; either of them representing the proper form of the sun (*Çat. Br.* ii. 6. 3. 9); but another authority specifies twelve oxen and a plough (Taitt. S. i. 8. 7).

[2] *Çat. Br.* ii. 1. 1. 5; 2. 3. 28; iv. 3. 4. 14; 5. 1. 15; four kinds of fees, *ib.* iv. 3. 4. 6, 7, 24 ff. (Milk is also 'Agni's seed,' *ib.* ii. 2. 4. 15).

good for the sacrificer,[1] secretly do him harm (as he could by altering the ceremonial).[2] The theory of the fee, in so far as it affects the sacrifices, is that the gods, the Manes, and men all exist by what is sacrificed. Even the gods seek rewards: hence the priests do the same.[3] The sacrificer sacrifices to get a place in *devaloka* (the world of the gods). The sacrifice goes up to the world of gods, and after it goes the fee which the sacrificer (the patron) gives; the sacrificer follows by catching hold of the fee given to the priests (*ib.* i. 9. 3. 1). It is to be noted, moreover, that sacrificing for a fee is recognized as a profession. The work (sacrifice is work, 'work is sacrifice,' it is somewhere said) is regarded as a matter of business. There are three means of livelihood occasionally referred to, telling stories, singing songs, and reciting the Veda at a sacrifice (*Çat. Br.* iii. 2. 4. 16).

As an example of the absurdities given as 'the ways of knowledge' (absurdities which are necessary to know in order to a full understanding of the mental state under consideration) may be cited *Çat. Br.* iv. 5. 8. 11, where it is said that if the sacrificial cow goes east the sacrificer wins a good world hereafter; if north, he becomes more glorious on earth; if west, rich in people and crops; if south, he dies; 'such are the ways of knowledge.' In the same spirit it is said that the sun rises east because the priest repeats certain verses (*Āit. Br.* i. 7. 4). No little stress is laid on geographical position. The east is the quarter of the gods; the north, of men; the south, of the dead (Manes; *Çat. Br.* i. 2. 5. 17); while the west is the region of snakes, according to *ib.* iii. 1. 1. 7. On account of the godly nature of the east ("from the east came the gods

[1] Yet in *Āit. Br.* iii. 19, the priest is coolly informed how he may be able to slay his patron by making a little change in the invocations. Elsewhere such conduct is reprobated.

[2] For other covenants, see the epic (chapter on Hinduism).

[3] *Çat. Br.* iii. 4. 2. 1 ff.; iii. 6. 2. 25; iv. 3. 5. 5; iv. 4. 1. 17; 6. 6. 5; 7. 6, etc.; iii. 8. 2. 27; 3. 26; *Āit. Br.* i. 24.

westward to men," *ib.* ii. 6. 1. 11) the sacrificial building, like occidental churches, is built east and west, not north and south. The cardinal points are elsewhere given to certain gods; thus the north is Rudra's.[1]

It has been said that the theological ideas are not clear. This was inevitable, owing to the tendency to identify various divinities. Especially noticeable is the identification of new or local gods with others better accredited, Rudra and Agni, etc. Rudra is the god of cattle, and when the other gods went to heaven by means of sacrifice he remained on earth; his local names are Çarva, Bhava, 'Beast-lord,' Rudra, Agni (*Çat. Br.* i. 7. 3. 8; Māit. S. i. 6. 6). Indra is the Vasu of the gods. The gods are occasionally thirty-four in number, eight Vasus, eleven Rudras, twelve Ādityas, heaven and earth, and Prajāpati as the thirty-fourth; but this Prajāpati is the All and Everything (*Çat. Br.* i. 6. 4. 2; iv. 5. 7. 2 ff.). Of these gods, who at first were all alike and good, three became superior, Agni, Indra, and Sūrya. But, again, the Sun is death, and Agni is head of all the gods. Moreover, the Sun is now Indra; the Manes are the seasons, and Varuna, too, is the seasons, as being the year (*Çat. Br.* iv. 5. 4. 1; i. 6. 4. 18; iv. 4. 5. 18). Aditi, as we have said, is the Earth; the fee for an offering to her is a cow. Why? Because Earth is a cow and Aditi is Earth; Earth is a mother and a cow is a mother. Hence the fee is a cow.[2]

The tales of the gods, for the most part, are foolish. But they show well what conception the priests had of their divini-

[1] *Ib.* ii. 6. 2. 5. Here Rudra (compare Çiva and Hekate of the cross-roads) is said to go upon 'cross-roads'; so that his sacrifice is on cross-roads—one of the new teachings since the time of the Rig Veda. Rudra's sister, Ambikā, *ib.* 9, is another new creation, the genius of autumnal sickness.

[2] *Çat. Br.* ii. 2. 1. 21. How much non-serious fancy there may be here it is difficult to determine. It seems impossible that such as follows can have been meant in earnest: "The sacrifice, *prayāja*, is victory, *jaya*, because *yaja* = *jaya*. With this knowledge one gets the victory over his rivals" (*ib.* i. 5. 3. 3, 10).

ties. Man's original skin was put by the gods upon the cow; hence a cow runs away from a man because she thinks he is trying to get back his skin. The gods cluster about at an oblation, each crying out 'My name,' *i.e.*, each is anxious to get it. The gods, with the evil spirits—'both sons of the Father'—attract to themselves the plants; Varuna gets the barley by a pun. They build castles to defend themselves from the evil spirits. Five gods are picked out as worthy of offerings: Aditi, Speech, Agni, Soma, the Sun (five, because the seasons are five and the regions are five). Indra and Wind have a dispute of possession; Prajāpati, the Father, decides it. The heavenly singers, called the Gandharvas, recited the Veda to entice (the divine female) Speech to come to them; while the gods, for the same purpose, created the lute, and sang and played to her. She came to the gods; hence the weakness of women in regard to such things. Indra is the god of sacrifice; the stake of the sacrifice is Vishnu's; Vāyu (Wind) is the leader of beasts; Bhaga is blind;[1] Pūshan (because he eats mush) is toothless. The gods run a race to see who shall get first to the sacrifice, and Indra and Agni win: they are the warrior-caste among the gods, and the All-gods are the people (*viçve, viç.*). Yet, again, the Maruts are the people, and Varuna is the warrior-caste; and, again, Soma is the warrior-caste. The Father-god first created birds, then reptiles and snakes. As these all died he created mammalia; these survived because they had food in themselves; hence the Vedic poet says 'three generations have passed away.'[2]

[1] Although Bhaga is here (*Çat. Br.* i. 7. 4. 6–7, *andho bhagas*) interpreted as the Sun, he is evidently the same with Good Luck ("τυφλὸς γὰρ ὁ Πλοῦτος") or wealth.

[2] *Çat. Br.* iii. 1. 2. 13 ff.; i. 1. 2. 18; iii. 6. 1. 8 ff.; ii. 5. 2. 1; iv. 2. 1. 11; iii. 4. 4. 3 ff.; 2. 3. 6–12, 13–14; iv. 5. 5. 12; 1. 3. 13 ff.; iii. 2. 4. 5–6; 3. 2. 8; 7. 1. 17; iv. 2. 5. 17; 4. 1. 15; i. 7. 4. 6–7; ii. 4. 3. 4 ff.; ii. 5. 2. 34; 5. 1. 12; 5. 1. 1 ff.: RV. viii. 101. 14. The reader must distinguish, in the name of Brahmā, the god from the priest, and this from *brahmă*, prayer. The first step is *brahma*—force, power, prayer; then this is, as a masculine Brahmā, the one who prays, that is, pray-er, the Brahman

Varuna is now quite the god of night and god of purification, as a water-god. Water is the 'essence (sap) of immortality,' and the bath of purification at the end of the sacrifice (*avabhṛtha*) stands in direct relation to Varuna. The formula to be repeated is: "With the gods' help may I wash out sin against the gods; with the help of men the sin against men" (*Çat. Br.* iv. 4. 3. 15; ii. 5. 2. 47). Mitra and Varuna are, respectively, intelligence and will, priest and warrior; and while the former may exist without the latter, the latter cannot live without the former, 'but they are perfect only when they coöperate' (*ib.* iv. 1. 4. 1).

Of the divine legends some are old, some new. One speaks of the sacrifice as having been at first human, subsequently changing to beast sacrifice, eventually to a rice offering, which last now represents the original sacrificial animal, man.[1] Famous, too, is the legend of the flood and Father Manu's escape from it (*Çat. Br.* i. 8. 1. 1 ff.). Again, the Vedic myth is retold, recounting the rape of *soma* by the metrical equivalent of fire (*Tāitt. Br.* i. 1. 3. 10; *Çat. Br.* i. 8. 2. 10). Another tale takes up anew the old story of Cupid and Psyche (Purūravas and Urvaçī); and another that of the Hindu Prometheus story, wherein Mātariçvan fetches fire from heaven, and gives it to mortals (*Tāitt. Br.* iii. 2. 3. 2; *Çat. Br.* xi. 5. 1. 1; i. 7. 1. 11).[2]

Interesting, also, is the tale of Vishnu having been a dwarf, and the tortoise *avatar*, not of Vishnu, but of Prajāpati; also the attempt of the evil spirits to climb to heaven, and the trick with which Indra outwitted them.[3] For it is noticeable that

priest, as, in the Rig Veda, x. 141. 3, Brihaspati is the 'Brahmā of gods.' The next (Brahmanic) step is deified *brahma*, the personal Brahmā as god, called also Father-god (Prajāpati) or simply The Father (*pitā*).

[1] Compare *Māit. S.* iii. 10. 2; *Ait. Br.* ii. 8; *Çat. Br.* i. 2. 3. 5; vi. 2. 1. 39; 3. 1. 24; ii. 5. 2. 16, a ram and ewe 'made of barley.' On human sacrifices, compare Müller, ASL. p. 419; Weber, ZDMG. xviii. 262 (see the Bibliography); *Streifen*, i. 54.

[2] Weber has translated some of these legends, *Ind. Streifen*, i. 9 ff.

[3] *Tāitt. Br.* iii. 2. 9. 7; *Çat. Br.* i. 2. 5. 5; ii. 1. 2. 13 ff.; vii. 5. 1. 6.

the evil spirits are as strong by nature as are the gods, and it is only by craft that the latter prevail.[1]

Seldom are the tales of the gods indecent. The story of Prajāpati's incest with his daughter is a remnant of nature worship which survives, in more or less anthropomorphic form, from the time of the Rig Veda (x. 61.) to that of mediaeval literature,[2] and is found in full in the epic, as in the Brahmanic period; but the story always ends with the horror of the gods at the act.[3]

Old legends are varied. The victory over Vritra is now expounded thus: Indra, who slays Vritra, is the sun. Vritra is the moon, who swims into the sun's mouth on the night of the new moon. The sun rises after swallowing him, and the moon is invisible because he is swallowed ("he who knows this swallows his foes"). The sun vomits out the moon, and the latter is then seen in the west, and increases again, to serve the sun as food. In another passage it is said that when the moon is invisible he is hiding in plants and waters (*Çat. Br.* i. 6. 3. 17; 4. 18–20).

BRAHMANIC RELIGION.

When the sacrifice is completed the priest returns, as it were, to earth, and becomes human. He formally puts off his sacrificial vow, and rehabilitates himself with humanity, saying, "I am even he that I am."[4] As such a man, through service to the gods become a divine offering, and no longer human, was doubtless considered the creature that first served as the

1 Compare *Māit. S.* i. 9. 8; *Çat. Br.* i. 6. 1. 1 ff. The seasons desert the gods, and the demons thrive. In *Çat. Br.* i. 5. 4. 6–11, the Asuras and Indra contend with numbers.

2 Müller, ASL. p. 529.

3 *Māit. S.* iv. 2. 12; *Çat. Br.* i. 7. 4. 1; ii. 1. 2. 9; vi. 1. 3. 8; *Ait. Br.* iii. 33. Compare Muir, OST. iv. p. 45. At a later period there are frequently found indecent tales of the gods, and the Brāhmanas themselves are vulgar enough, but they exhibit no special lubricity on the part of the priests.

4 *Idam aham ya evā'smi so asmi*, *Çat. Br.* i. 1. 1. 6; 9. 3. 23.

sacrificial animal. Despite protestant legends such as that just recorded, despite formal disclaimers, human sacrifice existed long after the period of the Rig Veda, where it is alluded to; a period when even old men are exposed to die.[1] The *anaddhāpurusha* is not a fiction; for that, on certain occasions, instead of this 'man of straw' a real victim was offered, is shown by the ritual manuals and by Brahmanic texts.[2] Thus, in *Çat. Br.* vi. 2. 1. 18: "He kills a man first. . . . The cord that holds the man is the longest." It is noteworthy that also among the American Indians the death of a human victim by fire was regarded as a religious ceremony, and that, just as in India the man to be sacrificed was allowed almost all his desires for a year, so the victim of the Indian was first greeted as brother and presented with gifts, even with a wife.[3]

But this, the terrible barbaric side of religious worship, is now distinctly yielding to a more humane religion. The 'barley ewe'[4] is taking the place of a bloodier offering. It has been urged that the humanity[5] and the accompanying silliness of the Brahmanic period as compared with the more robust character of the earlier age are due to the weakening and softening effects of the climate. But we doubt whether the climate of the Punjāb differs as much from that of Delhi and Patna as does the character of the Rig Veda from that of the Brāhmanas. We shall protest again when we come to the subject of

[1] RV. viii. 51. 2; Zimmer, *loc. cit.* p. 328.

[2] Compare Weber, *Episch. in Vedisch. Ritual*, p. 777 (and above). The man who is slaughtered must be neither a priest nor a slave, but a warrior or a man of the third caste (Weber, *loc. cit.* above).

[3] *Le Mercier*, 1637, ap. Parkman, *loc. cit.* p. 80. The current notion that the American Indian burns his victims at the stake merely for pleasure is not incorrect. He frequently did so, as he does so to-day, but in the seventeenth century this act often is part of a religious ceremony. He probably would have burned his captive, anyway, but he gladly utilized his pleasure as a means of propitiating his gods. In India it was just the other way.

[4] Substitutes of metal or of earthen victims are also mentioned.

[5] That the Vedic rite of killing the sacrificial beast (by beating and smothering) was very cruel may be seen in the description, *Ait. Br.* ii. 6.

Buddhism against the too great influence which has been claimed for climate. Politics and society, in our opinion, had more to do with altering the religions of India than had a higher temperature and miasma. As a result of ease and sloth —for the Brahmans are now the divine pampered servants of established kings, not the energetic peers of a changing population of warriors—the priests had lost the inspiration that came from action; they now made no new hymns; they only formulated new rules of sacrifice. They became intellectually debauched and altogether weakened in character. Synchronous with this universal degradation and lack of fibre, is found the occasional substitution of barley and rice sacrifices for those of blood; and it may be that a sort of selfish charity was at work here, and the priest saved the beast to spare himself. But there is no very early evidence of a humane view of sacrifice influencing the priests.

The Brahman is no Jain. One must read far to hear a note of the approaching *ahimsā* doctrine of 'non-injury.' At most one finds a contemptuous allusion, as in a pitying strain, to the poor plants and animals that follow after man in reaping some sacrificial benefit from a ceremony.[1] It does not seem to us that a recognized respect for animal life or kindness to dumb creatures lies at the root of proxy sacrifice, though it doubtless came in play. But still less does it appear probable that, as is often said, aversion to beast-sacrifice is due to the doctrine of *karma*, and re-birth in animal form. The *karma* notion begins to appear in the Brahmanas, but not in the *samsāra* shape of transmigration. It was surely not because the Hindu was afraid of eating his deceased grandmother that he first abstained from meat. For, long after the doctrine of *karma* and *samsāra*[2] is established, animal sacrifices are not only permitted but

[1] *Çat. Br.* i. 5. 2. 4.

[2] *Samsāra* is transmigration; *karma*, 'act,' implies that the change of abode is conditioned by the acts of a former life. Each may exclude the other; but in common parlance each implies the other.

enjoined; and the epic characters shoot deer and even eat cows. We think, in short, that the change began as a sumptuary measure only. In the case of human sacrifice there is doubtless a civilized repugnance to the act, which is clearly seen in many passages where the slaughter of man is made purely symbolical. The only wonder is that it should have obtained so long after the age of the Rig Veda. But like the stone knife of sacrifice among the Romans it is received custom, and hard to do away with, for priests are conservative. Human sacrifice must have been peculiarly horrible from the fact that the sacrificer not only had to kill the man but to eat him, as is attested by the formal statement of the liturgical works.[1] But in the case of other animals (there are five sacrificial animals, of which man is first) we think it was a question of expense on the part of the laity. When the *soma* became rare and expensive, substitutes were permitted and enjoined. So with the great sacrifices. The priests had built up a great complex of forms, where at every turn fees were demanded. The whole expense, falling on the one individual to whose benefit accrued the sacrifice, must have been enormous; in the case of ordinary people impossible. But the priests then permitted the sacrifice of substitutes, for their fees still remained; and even in the case of human sacrifice some such caution may have worked, for ordinarily it cost 'one thousand cattle' to buy a man to be sacrificed. A proof of this lies in the fact that animal sacrifices were not forbidden at any time, only smaller (cheaper) animals took the place of cattle. In the completed Brahmanic code the rule is that animals ought not to be killed except at sacrifice, and practically the smaller creatures were substituted for cattle, just as the latter had gradually taken the place of the old horse (and man) sacrifice.

If advancing civilization results in an agreeable change of morality in many regards, it is yet accompanied with wretched

[1] Weber, *Indische Streifen*, i. p. 72.

traits in others. The whole silliness of superstition exceeds belief. Because Bhāllabheya once broke his arm on changing the metre of certain formulae, it is evident to the priest that it is wrong to trifle with received metres, and hence "let no one do this hereafter." There is a compensation on reading such trash in the thought that all this superstition has kept for us a carefully preserved text, but that is an accident of priestly foolishness, and the priest can be credited only with the folly. Why is 'horse-grass' used in the sacrifice? Because the sacrifice once ran away and "became a horse." Again one is thankful for the historical side-light on the horse-sacrifice; but the witlessness of the unconscious historian can but bring him into contempt.[1] Charms that are said against one are of course cast out by other charms. If one is not prosperous with one name he takes another. If the cart creaks at the sacrifice it is the voice of evil spirits; and a formula must avert the omen. *Soma*-husks are liable to turn into snakes; a formula must avert this catastrophe. Everything done at the sacrifice is godly; *ergo*, everything human is to be done in an inhuman manner, and, since in human practice one cuts his left finger-nails first and combs the left side of the beard first, at the sacrifice he must cut nails and beard first on the other side, for "whatever is human at a sacrifice is useless" (*vyṛddham vāi tad yajñasya yad mānuṣam*). Of religious puns we have given instances already. Agni says: "prop me on the propper for that is proper" (*hita*), etc., etc.[2] One of these examples of depraved superstition is of a more dangerous nature. The effect of the sacrifice is covert as well as overt.

[1] *Çat. Br.* i. 7. 3. 19: iii. 4. 1. 17.

[2] *Çat. Br.* iii. 5. 4. 10; 6. 2. 24; 5. 3. 17 (compare 6. 4. 23–24; 3. 4. 11; 2. 1. 12); iii. 1. 2. 4; 3. 14; i. 7. 2. 9; vi. 1. 2. 14. The change of name is interesting. There is a remark in another part of the same work to the effect that when a man prospers in life they give his name also to his son, grandson, *and to his father and grandfather* (vi. 1. 2. 13). On the other hand, it was the custom of the Indian kings in later ages to assume the names of their prosperous grandfathers (JRAS. iv. 85).

The word is as potent as the act. Consequently if the sacrificer during the sacrifice merely mutter the words "let such an one die," he must die; for the sacrifice is holy, godly: the words are divine, and cannot be frustrated (*Çat. Br.* iii. 1. 4. 1; iv. 1. 1. 26).

All this superstition would be pardonable if it were primitive. But that it comes long after the Vedic poets have sung reveals a continuance of stupidity which is marvellous. Doubtless those same poets were just as superstitious, but one would think that with all the great literature behind them, and the thoughts of the philosophers just rising among them, these later priests might show a higher level of intelligence. But in this regard they are to India what were the monks of mediaeval times to Europe.

We turn now to the ethical side of religion. But, before leaving the sacrifice, one point should be explained clearly. The Hindu sacrifice can be performed only by the priest, and he must be of the highest caste. No other might or could perform it. For he alone understood the ancient texts, which to the laity were already only half intelligible. Again, as Barth has pointed out, the Hindu sacrifice is performed only for one individual or his family. It was an expensive rite (for the gaining of one object), addressed to many gods for the benefit of one man. To offset this, however, one must remember that there were popular fêtes and sacrifices of a more general nature, to which many were invited and in which even the lower castes took part; and these were also of remote antiquity.

Already current in the Brāhmanas is the phrase 'man's debts.' Either three or four of such moral obligations were recognized, debts to the gods, to the seers, to the Manes, and to men. Whoever pays these debts, it is said, has discharged all his duties, and by him all is obtained, all is won. And what are these duties? To the gods he owes sacrifices; to the seers, study of the Vedas; to the Manes, offspring; to man, hospitality (*Çat. Br.* i. 7. 2. 1 ff.; in *Taitt. Br.* vi. 3. 10. 5, the last fails). Translated into modern equivalents this means that man must have faith and good works. But more really is demanded than is stated here. First and foremost is the duty of truthfulness. Agni is the lord of vows among the gods (RV. viii. 11. 1; *Çat. Br.* iii. 2. 2. 24), and speech is a divinity (Sarasvatī is personified speech, *Çat. Br.* iii. 1. 4. 9, etc.). Truth is a religious as well as moral duty. "This (All) is two-fold, there is no third; all is either truth or untruth; now truth alone is the gods (*satyam eva devās*) and untruth is man."[1] Moreover, "one law the gods observe, truth" (*Çat. Br.* i. 1. 1. 4; iii. 3. 2. 2; 4. 2. 8). There is another passage upon this subject: "To serve the sacred fire means truth; he who speaks truth feeds the fire; he who speaks lies pours water on it; in the one case he strengthens his vital (spiritual) energy, and becomes better; in the other he weakens it and becomes worse" (*ib.* ii. 2. 2. 19). The second sin, expressly named and reprobated as such, is adultery. This is a sin against Varuna.[2] In connection with this there is an interesting passage implying a priestly confessional. At the sacrifice the sacrificer's wife is formally asked by the priest whether she is faithful to her husband. She is asked this that she may not sacrifice with guilt on her soul, for "when confessed the guilt becomes less."[3] If it is asked what other moral virtues are especially inculcated besides truth and purity the answer is that the acts commonly cited as self-evidently sins are murder, theft, and abortion; incidentally, gluttony, anger, and procras-

[1] Were it not for the first clause it would be more natural to render the original 'The gods are truth alone, and men are untruth.'

[2] In *Çat. Br.* ii. 4. 2. 5–6 it is said that the Father-god gives certain rules of eating to gods, Manes, men, and beasts: "Neither gods, Manes, nor beasts transgress the Father's law, only some men do."

[3] *Çat. Br.* ii. 5. 2. 20. Varuna seizes on her paramour, when she confesses. *Taitt. Br.* i. 6. 5. 2. The guilt confessed becomes less "because it thereby becomes truth" (right).

tination.[1] As to the moral virtue of observing days, certain times are allowed and certain times are not allowed for worldly acts. But every day is in part a holy-day to the Hindu. The list of virtues is about the same, therefore, as that of the decalogue — the worship of the right divinity; the observance of certain seasons for prayer and sacrifice; honor to the parents; abstinence from theft, murder, adultery. Envy alone is omitted.[2]

What eschatological conceptions are strewn through the literature of this era are vague and often contradictory. The souls of the departed are at one time spoken of as the stars (*Tāitt. S.* v. 4. 1. 3); at another, as uniting with gods and living in the world of the gods (*Çat. Br.* ii. 6. 4. 8).

The principle of *karma*, if not the theory, is already known, but the very thing that the completed philosopher abhors is looked upon as a blessing, viz., rebirth, body and all, even on earth.[3] Thus in one passage, as a reward for knowing some divine mystery (as often happens, this mystery is of little importance, only that 'spring is born again out of winter'), the savant is to be 'born again in this world' (*punar ha vā 'asmin loke bhavati, Çat. Br.* i. 5. 3. 14). The esoteric wisdom is here the transfer of the doctrine of metempsychosis to spring. Man has no hope of immortal life (on earth);[4] but, by estab-

[1] See *Çat. Br.* ii. 4. 2. 6; 4. 1. 14; 1. 3. 9; 3. 1. 28: "Who knows man's morrow? Then let one not procrastinate." "Today is self, this alone is certain, uncertain is the morrow."

[2] Some little rules are interesting. The Pythagorean abstinence from *māṣās*, beans, for instance, is enjoined; though this rule is opposed by Barku Vārshna, *Çat. Br.* i. 1. 1. 10, on the ground that no offering to the gods is made of beans; "hence he said 'cook beans for me.'"

[3] Animals may represent gods. "The bull is a form of Indra," and so if the bull can be made to roar (*Çat. Br.* ii. 5. 3. 18), then one may know that Indra is come to the sacrifice. "Man is born into (whatever) world is made (by his acts in a previous existence)," is a short formula (*Çat. Br.* vi. 2. 2. 27), which represents the *karma* doctrine in its essential principle, though the 'world' is here not this world, but the next. Compare Weber, ZDMG. ix. 237 ff.; Muir, OST. v. 314 ff.

[4] Though youth may be restored to him by the Açvins, *Çat. Br.* iv. 1. 5. 1 ff. Here the Horsemen are identified with Heaven and Earth (16).

lishing the holy fires, and especially by establishing in his inmost soul the immortal element of fire, he lives the full desirable length of life (*ib.* ii. 2. 2. 14. To the later sage, length of life is undesirable). But in yonder world, where the sun itself is death, the soul dies again and again. All those on the other side of the sun, the gods, are immortal; but all those on this side are exposed to this death. When the sun wishes, he draws out the vitality of any one, and then that one dies; not once, but, being drawn up by the sun, which is death, into the very realm of death (how different to the conception of the sun in the Rig Veda!) he dies over and over again.[1] But in another passage it is said that when the sacrificer is consecrated he 'becomes one of the deities'; and one even finds the doctrine that one obtains 'union with Brahmă,' which is quite in the strain of the Upanishads; but here such a saying can refer only to the upper castes, for "the gods talk only to the upper castes" (*Çat. Br.* xi. 4. 4. 1; iii. 1. 1. 8–10). The dead man is elsewhere represented as going to heaven 'with his whole body,' and, according to one passage, when he gets to the next world his good and evil are weighed in a balance. There are, then, quite diverse views in regard to the fate of a man after death, and not less various are the opinions in regard to his reward and punishment. According to the common belief the dead, on leaving this world, pass between two fires, *agniçikhe*, raging on either side of his path. These fires burn the one that ought to be burned (the wicked), and let the good pass by. Then the spirit (or the man him-

[1] *Cat. Br.* ii. 3. 3. 7. Apropos of the Brahmanic sun it may be mentioned that, according to *Ait. Br.* iii. 44. the sun never really sets. "People think that he sets, but in truth he only turns round after reaching the end of the day, and makes night below, day above; and when they think he rises in the morning, he, having come to the end of the night, turns round, and makes day below, night above. He never really sets. Whoever knows this of him, that he never sets, obtains union and likeness of form with the sun, and the same abode as the sun's." Compare Muir, OST. v. 321. This may be the real reason why the Rig Veda speaks of a dark and light sun.

self in body) is represented as going up on one of two paths. Either he goes to the Manes on a path which, according to later teaching, passes southeast through the moon, or he goes northeast (the gods' direction) to the sun, which is his 'course and stay.' In the same chapter one is informed that the rays of the sun are the good (dead), and that every brightest light is the Father-god. The general conception here is that the sun or the stars are the destination of the pious. On the other hand it is said that one will enjoy the fruit of his acts here on earth, in a new birth; or that he will 'go to the next world'; or that he will suffer for his sins in hell. The last is told in legendary form, and appears to us to be not an early view retained in folk-lore, but a late modification of an old legend. Varuna sends his son Bhrigu to hell to find out what happens after death, and he finds people suffering torture, and, again, avenging themselves on those that have wronged them. But, despite the resemblance between this and Grecian myth, the fact that in the whole compass of the Rik (in the Atharvan perhaps in v. 19) there is not the slightest allusion to torture in hell, precludes, to our mind, the possibility of this phase having been an ancient inherited belief.[1]

Annihilation or a life in under darkness is the first (Rik) hell. The general antithesis of light (as good) and darkness (as bad) is here plainly revealed again. Sometimes a little variation occurs. Thus, according to *Çat. Br.* vi. 5. 4. 8, the stars are women-souls, perhaps, as elsewhere, men also. The

[1] *Çat. Br.* i. 4. 3. 11–22 ('The sinner shall suffer and go quickly to yonder world'); xi. 6. 1 (compare Weber, *loc. cit.* p. 20 ff.; ZDMG. ix. 237), the Bhrigu story, of which a more modern form is found in the Upanishad period. For the course of the sun, the fires on either side of the way, the departure to heaven 'with the whole body,' compare *Çat. Br.* i. 9. 3. 2–15; iv. 5. 1. 1; vi. 6. 2. 4; xi. 2. 7. 33; Weber. *loc. cit.*: Muir, *loc. cit.* v. p. 314. Not to have all one's bones in the next world is a disgrace, as Muir says, and for that reason they are collected at burial. Compare the custom as described by the French missionaries here. The American Indian has to have all his bones for future use, and the burying of the skeleton is an annual religious ceremony.

converse notion that darkness is the abode of evil appears at a very early date: "Indra brought down the heathen, *dasyus*, into the lowest darkness," it is said in the Atharva Veda (ix. 2. 17).[1]

In the later part of the great 'Brāhmana of the hundred paths' there seems to be a more modern view inculcated in regard to the fate of the dead. Thus, in vi. 1. 2. 36, the opinion of 'some,' that the fire on the altar is to bear the worshipper to the sky, is objected to, and it is explained that he becomes immortal; which antithesis is in purely Upanishadic style, as will be seen below.

BRAHMANIC THEORIES OF CREATION.

In Vedic polytheism, with its strain of pantheism, the act of creating the world[2] is variously attributed to different gods. At the end of this period theosophy invented the god of the golden germ, the great Person (known also by other titles), who is the one (pantheistic) god, in whom all things are contained, and who himself is contained in even the smallest thing. The Atharvan transfers the same idea in its delineation of the pantheistic image to Varuna, that Varuna who is the seas and yet is contained "in the drop of water" (iv. 16), a Varuna as different to the Varuna of the Rik as is the

[1] Compare RV. iv. 28. 4: 'Thou Indra madest lowest the heathen.' Weber has shown, *loc. cit.*, that the general notion of the Brāhmanas is that all are born again in the next world, where they are rewarded or punished according as they are good or bad; whereas in the Rig Veda the good rejoice in heaven, and the bad are annihilated. This general view is to be modified, however, by such side-theories as those just mentioned, that the good (or wise) may be reborn on earth, or be united with gods, or become sunlight or stars (the latter are 'watery' to the Hindu, and this may explain the statement that the soul is 'in the midst of waters').

[2] There is in this age no notion of the repeated creations found in later literature. On the contrary, it is expressly said in the Rig Veda, vi. 48. 22, that heaven and earth are created but once: "Only once was heaven created, only once was earth created," Zimmer, AIL. 408.

Atharvan Indra to his older prototype. Philosophically the Rik, at its close, declares that "desire is the seed of mind," and that "being arises from not-being."

In the Brāhmanas the creator is the All-god in more anthropomorphic form. The Father-god, Prajāpati, or Brahmā (personal equivalent of *brahma*) is not only the father of gods, men, and devils, but he is the All. This Father-god of universal sovereignty, Brahmā, remains to the end the personal creator. It is he who will serve as creator for the Puranic Sānkhya philosophy, and even after the rise of the Hindu sects he will still be regarded in this light, although his activity will be conditioned by the will of Vishnu or Çiva. In pure philosophy there will be an abstract First Cause; but as there is no religion in the acknowledgment of a First Cause, this too will soon be anthropomorphized.

The Brāhmanas themselves present no clear picture of creation. All the accounts of a personal creator are based merely on anthropomorphized versions of the text 'desire is the seed.' Prajāpati wishes offspring, and creates. There is, on the other hand, a philosophy of creation which reverts to the tale of the 'golden germ.'[1] The world was at first water; thereon floated a cosmic golden egg (the principle of fire). Out of this came Spirit that desired; and by desire he begat the worlds and all things. It is improbable that in this somewhat Orphic mystery there lies any pre-Vedic myth. The notion comes up first in the golden germ and egg-born bird (sun) of the Rik. It is not specially Aryan, and is found even among the American Indians.[2] It is this Spirit with which the Father-god is identified. But guess-work philosophy then asks what

[1] When the principle of life is explained it is in terms of sun or fire. Thus Prajāpati, Lord of beings, or Father-god, is first an epithet of Savitar, RV. iv. 53. 2; and the golden germ must be fire.

[2] Schoolcraft, *Historical and Statistical Information*, i. 32. As examples of the many passages where 'water is the beginning' may be cited *Çat. Br.* vi. 7. 1. 17; xi. 1. 6. 1. The sun, born as Aditi's eighth son, is the bird, 'egg-born,' RV. x. 72. 8.

upheld this god, and answers that a support upheld all things. So Support becomes a god in his turn, and, since he must reach through time and space, this Support, Skambha, becomes the All-god also; and to him as to a great divinity the Atharvan sings some of its wildest strains. When once speculation is set going in the Brāhmanas, the result of its travel is to land its followers in intellectual chaos.[1] The gods create the Father-god in one passage, and in another the Father-god creates the gods. The Father creates the waters, whence rises the golden egg. But, again, the waters create the egg, and out of the egg is born the Father. A farrago of contradictions is all that these tales amount to, nor are they redeemed even by a poetical garb.[2]

In the period immediately following the Brāhmanas, or toward the end of the Brahmanic period, as one will, there is a famous distinction made between the gods. Some gods, it is said, are spirit-gods; some are work-gods. They are born of spirit and of works, respectively. The difference, however, is not essential, but functional; so that one may conclude from this authority, the Nirukta (a grammatical and epexigetical work), that all the gods have a like nature; and that the spirit-gods, who are the older, differ only in lack of specific functions from the work-gods. A not uninteresting debate follows this passage in regard to the true nature of the gods. Some people say they are anthropomorphic; others deny this. "And certainly what is seen of the gods is not anthropomorphic; for example, the sun, the earth, etc."[3] In such a period of theological advance it is matter of indifference to which of a group of gods, all essentially one, is laid the task of creation. And, indeed, from the Vedic period until the completed systems of philosophy, all creation to the philosopher is but emanation; and stories of specific acts of creation are not regarded by him

[1] Among the new creators of Atharvan origin are, for instance, the sun under the name of Rohita, Desire (Love), etc., etc.

[2] Illustrations of these contradictions may be found in plenty *apud* Muir iv. p. 20 ff.

[3] Nirukta, vii. 4; Muir, *loc. cit.* p. 131 and v. 17.

as detracting from the creative faculty of the First Cause. The actual creator is for him the factor and agent of the real god. On the other hand, the vulgar worshipper of every era believed only in reproduction on the part of an anthropomorphic god; and that god's own origin he satisfactorily explained by the myth of the golden egg. The view depended in each case not on the age but on the man.

If in these many pages devoted to the Brāhmanas we have produced the impression that the religious literature of this period is a confused jumble, where unite descriptions of ceremonies, formulae, mysticism, superstitions, and all the output of active bigotry; an *olla podrida* which contains, indeed, odds and ends of sound morality, while it presents, on the whole, a sad view of the latter-day saints, who devoted their lives to making it what it is; we have offered a fairly correct view of the age and its priests, and the rather dreary series of illustrations will not have been collected in vain. We have given, however, no notion at all of the chief object of this class of writings, the liturgical details of the sacrifices themselves. Even a résumé of one comparatively short ceremony would be so long and tedious that the explication of the intricate formalities would scarcely be a sufficient reward. With Hillebrandt's patient analysis of the New- and Full-Moon sacrifice,[1] of which a sketch is given by von Schroeder in his *Literatur und Cultur*, the curious reader will be able to satisfy himself that a minute description of these ceremonies would do little to further his knowledge of the religion, when once he grasps the fact that the sacrifice is but show. Symbolism without folk-lore, only with the imbecile imaginings of a daft mysticism, is the soul of it; and its outer form is a certain number of formulae, mechanical movements, oblations, and slaughterings.

[1] *Neu- und Vollmonds Opfer*, 1880. The *Dīkshā*, or initiation, has been described by Lindner; the *Rājasūya* and *Vajapeya*, by Weber.

But we ought not to close the account of the era without giving counter-illustrations of the legendary aspect of this religion; for which purpose we select two of the best-known tales, one from the end of the Brāhmana that is called the Āitareya: the other from the beginning of the Çatapatha; the former in abstract, the latter in full.

THE SACRIFICE OF DOGSTAIL (*Āit. Br.* vii. 13).

Hariçcandra, a king born in the great race of Ikshvāku, had no son. A sage told him what blessings are his who has a son: 'He that has no son has no place in the world: in the person of a son a man is reborn, a second self is begotten.' Then the king desired a son, and the sage instructed him to pray to Varuna for one, and to offer to sacrifice him to the god. This he did, and a son, Rohita, at last was born to him. God Varuna demanded the sacrifice. But the king said: 'He is not fit to be sacrificed, so young as he is; wait till he is ten days old.' The god waited ten days, and demanded the sacrifice. But the king said: 'Wait till his teeth come.' The god waited, and then demanded the sacrifice. But the king said: 'Wait till his teeth fall out'; and when the god had waited, and again demanded the sacrifice, the father said: 'Wait till his new teeth come.' But, when his teeth were come and he was demanded, the father said: 'A warrior is not fit to be sacrificed till he has received his armor' (*i.e.*, until he is knighted). So the god waited till the boy had received his armor, and then he demanded the sacrifice. Thereupon, the king called his son, and said unto him: 'I will sacrifice thee to the god who gave thee to me.' But the son said, 'No, no,' and took his bow and fled into the desert. Then Varuna caused the king to be afflicted with dropsy.[1] When Rohita heard of this he

[1] The water-sickness already imputed to this god in the Rig Veda. This tale and that of Bhrigu (referred to above) show an ancient trait in the position of Varuna, as chief god.

was about to return, but Indra, disguised as a priest, met him, and said: 'Wander on, for the foot of a wanderer is like a flower; his spirit grows, and reaps fruit, and all his sins are forgiven in the fatigue of wandering.'[1] So Rohita, thinking that a priest had commanded him, wandered; and every year, as he would return, Indra met him, and told him still to wander. On one of these occasions Indra inspires him to continue on his journey by telling him that the *krita* was now auspicious; using the names of dice afterwards applied to the four ages.[2] Finally, after six years, Rohita resolved to purchase a substitute for sacrifice. He meets a starving seer, and offers to buy one of his sons (to serve as sacrifice), the price to be one hundred cows. The seer has three sons, and agrees to the bargain; but "the father said, 'Do not take the oldest,' and the mother said, 'Do not take the youngest,' so Rohita took the middle son, Dogstail." Varuna immediately agrees to this substitution of Dogstail for Rohita, "since a priest is of more value than a warrior."

The sacrifice is made ready, and Viçvāmitra (the Vedic seer) is the officiating priest. But no one would bind the boy to the post. 'If thou wilt give me another hundred cows I will bind him,' says the father of Dogstail. But then no one would kill the boy. 'If thou wilt give me another hundred cows I will kill him,' says the father. The Āprī verses[3] are said, and the fire is carried around the boy. He is about to be slain. Then Dogstail prays to 'the first of gods,' the Father-god, for protection. But the Father-god tells him to pray to Agni, 'the nearest of the gods.' Agni sends him to another, and he to another, till at last, when the boy has prayed to all the gods, including the All-gods, his fetters drop

[1] This is the germ of the pilgrimage-doctrine (see below).

[2] Perhaps (M. ix. 301) interpolated; or the first allusion to the Four Ages.

[3] These (compare *āfri*, 'blessing,' in the Avesta) are verses in the Rig Veda introducing the sacrifice. They are meant as propitiations, and appear to be an ancient part of the ritual.

off; Hariçcandra's dropsy ceases, and all ends well.[1] Only, when the avaricious father demands his son back, he is refused, and Viçvāmitra adopts the boy, even dispossessing his own protesting sons. For fifty of the latter agree to the exaltation of Dogstail: but fifty revolt, and are cursed by Viçvāmitra, that their sons' sons should become barbarians, the Andhras, Pundras, Çabaras, Pulindas, and Mūtibas, savage races (of this time), one of which can be located on the southeast coast. The conclusion, and the matter that follows close on this tale, is significant of the time, and of the priest's authority. For it is said that 'if a king hears this story he is made free of sin,' but he can hear it only from a priest, who is to be rewarded for telling it by a gift of one thousand cows, and other rich goods.

The matter following, to which we have alluded, is the use of sacrificial formulae to defeat the king's foes, the description of a royal inauguration, and, at this ceremony, the oath which the king has to swear ere the priest will anoint him (he is anointed with milk, honey, butter, and water, 'for water is immortality'): "I swear that thou mayst take from me whatever good works I do to the day of my death, together with my life and children, if ever I should do thee harm."[2]

When the priest is secretly told how he may ruin the king by a false invocation at the sacrifice, and the king is made to swear that if ever he hurts the priest the latter may rob him of earthly and heavenly felicity, the respective positions of the two, and the contrast between this era and that of the early hymns, become strikingly evident. It is not from such an age as this that one can explain the spirit of the Rig Veda.

[1] A group of hymns in the first book of the Rig Veda are attributed to Dogstail. At any rate, they do allude to him, and so prove a moderate antiquity (probably the middle period of the Rik) for the tale. The name, in Sanskrit Çunasçepa, has been ingeniously starred by Weber as Cynosoura; the last part of each compound having the same meaning, and the first part being even phonetically the same (*çunas*, *κυνός*).

[2] *Ait. Br.* viii. 10, 15, 20.

The next selection is the famous story of the flood, which we translate literally in its older form.[1] The object of the legend in the Brāhmana is to explain the importance of the Idā (or Ilā) ceremony, which is identified with Idā, Manu's daughter.

"In the morning they brought water to Manu to wash with, even as they bring it to-day to wash hands with. While he was washing a fish came into his hands. The fish said, 'Keep me, and I will save thee.' 'What wilt thou save me from?' 'A flood will sweep away all creatures on earth. I will save thee from that.' 'How am I to keep thee?' 'As long as we are small,' said he (the fish), 'we are subject to much destruction; fish eats fish. Thou shalt keep me first in a jar. When I outgrow that, thou shalt dig a hole, and keep me in it. When I outgrow that, thou shalt take me down to the sea, for there I shall be beyond destruction.'

"It soon became a (great horned fish called a) *jhasha*, for this grows the largest, and then it said: 'The flood will come this summer (or in such a year). Look out for (or worship) me, and build a ship. When the flood rises, enter into the ship, and I will save thee.' After he had kept it he took it down to the sea. And the same summer (year) as the fish had told him he looked out for (or worshipped) the fish; and built a ship. And when the flood rose he entered into the ship. Then up swam the fish, and Manu tied the ship's rope to the horn of the fish; and thus he sailed swiftly up toward the mountain of the north. 'I have saved thee' said he (the fish). 'Fasten the ship to a tree. But let not the water leave thee stranded while thou art on the mountain (top). Descend slowly as the water goes down.' So he descended slowly, and that descent of the mountain of the north is called the

[1] The epic has a later version. This earlier form is found in *Çat. Br.* i. 8. 1. For the story of the flood among the American Indians compare Schoolcraft (*Historical and Statistical Information*), i. 17.

'Descent of Manu.' The flood then swept off all the creatures of the earth, and Manu here remained alone. Desirous of posterity, he worshipped and performed austerities. While he was performing a sacrifice, he offered up in the waters clarified butter, sour milk, whey and curds. Out of these in a year was produced a woman. She arose when she was solid, and clarified butter collected where she trod. Mitra and Varuna met her, and said: 'Who art thou?' 'Manu's daughter,' said she. 'Say ours,' said they. 'No,' said she; 'I am my father's.' They wanted part in her. She agreed to this, and she did not agree; but she went by them and came to Manu. Said Manu: 'Who art thou?' 'Thy daughter,' said she. 'How my daughter, glorious woman?' She said: 'Thou hast begotten me of the offering, which thou madest in the water, clarified butter, sour milk, whey, and curds. I am a blessing; use me at the sacrifice. If thou usest me at the sacrifice, thou shalt become rich in children and cattle. Whatever blessing thou invokest through me, all shall be granted to thee.' So he used her as the blessing in the middle of the sacrifice. For what is between the introductory and final offerings is the middle of the sacrifice. With her he went on worshipping and performing austerities, wishing for offspring. Through her he begot the race of men on earth, the race of Manu; and whatever the blessing he invoked through her, all was granted unto him.

"Now she is the same with the Idā ceremony; and whoever, knowing this, performs sacrifice with the Idā, he begets the race that Manu generated; and whatever blessing he invokes through her, all is granted unto him."

There is one of the earliest *avatar* stories in this tale. Later writers, of course, identify the fish with Brahmā and with Vishnu. In other early Brāhmanas the *avatars* of a god as a tortoise and a boar were known long before they were appropriated by the Vishnuites.

CHAPTER X.

BRAHMANIC PANTHEISM.—THE UPANISHADS.

In the Vedic hymns man fears the gods, and imagines God. In the Brāhmanas man subdues the gods, and fears God. In the Upanishads man ignores the gods, and becomes God.[1]

Such in a word is the theosophic relations between the three periods represented by the first Vedic Collection, the ritualistic Brāhmanas, and the philosophical treatises called Upanishads. Yet if one took these three strata of thought to be quite independent of each other he would go amiss. Rather is it true that the Brāhmanas logically continue what the hymns begin; that the Upanishads logically carry on the thought of the Brāhmanas. And more, for in the oldest Upanishads are traits that connect this class of writings (if they were written) directly, and even closely with the Vedic hymns themselves; so that one may safely assume that the time of the first Upanishads is not much posterior to that of the latest additions made to the Vedic collections, though this indicates only that these additions were composed at a much later period than is generally supposed.[2] In India no literary period subsides with the rise of its eventually 'succeeding' period. All the works overlap. Parts of the Brāhmanas succeed, sometimes with the addition of whole books, their proper

[1] Compare *Çat. Br.* ii. 4. 2. 1–6. where the Father-god gives laws of conduct; and Kaushītaki Brāhmana Upanishad, 3. 8: "This spirit (breath) is guardian of the world, the lord of the world; he is my spirit" (or, myself), *sa ma atma*. The Brahmanic priest teaches that he is a god like other gods, and goes so far as to say that he may be united with a god after death. The Upanishad philosopher says 'I am God.'

[2] Compare Scherman, *Philosophische Hymnen*, p. 93; above, p. 156.

literary successors, the Upanishads. Vedic hymns are composed in the Brahmanic period.[1] The prose Sūtras, which, in general, are earlier, sometimes post-date metrical Çāstra-rules. Thus it is highly probable that, whereas the Upanishads began before the time of Buddha, the Çatapatha Brāhmana (if not others of this class) continued to within two or three centuries of our era; that the legal Sūtras were, therefore, contemporary with part of the Brāhmanic period;[2] and that, in short, the end of the Vedic period is so knit with the beginning of the Brāhmanic, while the Brāhmanic period is so knit with the rise of the Upanishads, Sūtras, epics, and Buddhism, that one cannot say of any one: 'this is later,' 'this is earlier'; but each must be taken only for a phase of indefinitely dated thought, exhibited on certain lines. It must also be remembered that by the same class of works a wide geographical area may be represented; by the Brāhmanas, west and east; by the Sūtras, north and south; by the Vedic poems, northwest and east to Benares (AV.); by the epics, all India, centred about the holy middle land near Delhi.

The meaning of Upanishad as used in the compositions themselves, is either, as it is used to-day, the title of a philosophical work; that of knowledge derived from esoteric teaching; or the esoteric teaching itself. Thus *brahma upanishad* is the secret doctrine of *brahma*, and 'whoever follows this *upanishad*' means whoever follows this doctrine. This seems, however, to be a meaning derived from the nature of the Upanishads themselves, and we are almost inclined to think that the true significance of the word was originally that in which alone occurs, in the early period, the combination *upa-ni-ṣad*, and this is purely external: "he makes

[1] Or, in other words, the thought of the Brahmanic period (not necessarily of extant Brāhmanas) is synchronous with part of the Vedic collection.

[2] The last additions to this class of literature would, of course, conform in language to their models, just as the late Vedic Mantras conform as well as their composers can make them to the older song or *chandas* style.

the common people *upa-ni-ṣādin*," *i.e.*, 'sitting below' or 'subject,' it is said in *Çat. Br.* ix. 4. 3. 3 (from the literal meaning of 'sitting below').[1] Instead, therefore, of seeing in *upaniṣad*, Upanishad, the idea of a session, of pupils sitting down to hear instruction (the prepositions and verb are never used in this sense), it may be that the Upanishads were at first *subsidiary* works of the ritualistic Brāhmanas contained in the Āranyakas or Forest Books, that is, appendices to the Brāhmana, ostensibly intended for the use of pious forest-hermits (who had passed beyond the need of sacrifice): and this, in point of fact, is just what they were; till their growth resulted in their becoming an independent branch of literature. The usual explanation of 'Upanishad,' however, is that it represents the instruction given to the pupil 'sitting under' the teacher.

Although at present between two and three hundred Upanishads are known, at least by name, to exist, yet scarcely a dozen appear to be of great antiquity. Some of these are integral parts of Brāhmanas, and apparently were added to the ritualistic works at an early period.[2]

While man's chief effort in the Brahmanic period seems to be by sacrifice and penance to attain happiness hereafter, and to get the upper hand of divine powers; while he recognizes a God, who, though supreme, has yet, like the priest himself, attained his supremacy by sacrifice and penance; while he dreams of a life hereafter in heavenly worlds, in the realm of light, though hardly seeking to avoid a continuation of earthly re-births; nevertheless he frees himself at times from ritualistic observances sufficiently to continue the questioning asked by his Vedic ancestors, and to wonder whither his immortal part is definitively going, and whether that spirit of his will live independently, or be united with some higher power, such as the sun or Brahmā.

1 Cited by Müller in SBE. i. *Introd.* p. lxxxii.

2 Compare Weber, *Ind. Lit.* p. 171; Müller, *loc. cit.* p. lxviii.

The philosophical writings called Upanishads[1] take up this question in earnest, but the answer is already assured, and the philosophers, or poets, of this period seek less to prove the truth than to expound it. The soul of man will not only join a heavenly Power. It is part of that Power. Man's spirit (self) is the world-spirit. And what is this? While all the Upanishads are at one in answering the first question, they are not at one in the method by which they arrive at the same result. There is no systematic philosophy; but a tentative, and more or less dogmatic, logic. In regard to the second question they are still less at one; but in general their answer is that the world-spirit is All, and everything is a part of It or Him. Yet, whether that All is personal or impersonal, and what is the relation between spirit and matter, this is still an unsettled point.

The methods and results of this half-philosophical literature will most easily be understood by a few examples. But, before these are given, it will be necessary to emphasize the colloquial and scrappy nature of the teaching. Legend, parable, ritualistic absurdities, belief in gods, denial of gods, belief in heaven, denial of heaven, are all mingled, and for a purpose. For some men are able, and some are unable, to receive the true light of knowledge. But man's fate depends on his knowledge. The wise man becomes hereafter what his knowledge has prepared him to be. Not every spirit is fitted for immortality, but only the spirit of them that have wisely desired it, or, rather,

[1] The relation between the Brāhmanas (ritual works discussed in the last chapter) and the early Upanishads will be seen better with the help of a concrete example. As has been explained before, Rig Veda means to the Hindu not only the 'Collection' of hymns, but all the library connected with this collection; for instance, the two Brāhmanas (of the Rig Veda), namely, the Àitareya and the Kāushītaki (or Çānkhāyana). Now, each of these Brāhmanas concludes with an Àranyaka, that is, a Forest-Book (*aranya*, forest, solitude); and in each Forest Book is an Upanishad. For example, the third book of the Kāushītaki Àranyaka is the Kāushītaki Upanishad. So the Chāndogya and Brihad Àranyaka belong respectively to the Sāman and Yajus.

not desired it; for every desire must have been extinguished before one is fitted for this end. Hence, with advancing belief in absorption and pantheism, there still lingers, and not as a mere superfluity, the use of sacrifice and penance. Rites and the paraphernalia of religion are essential till one learns that they are unessential. Desire will be gratified till one learns that the most desirable thing is lack of desire. But so long as one desires even the lack of desire he is still in the fetters of desire. The way is long to the extinction of emotion, but its attainment results in happiness that is greater than delight; in peace that surpasses joy.

In the exposition of this doctrine the old gods are retained as figures. They are not real gods. But they are existent forms of God. They are portions of the absolute, a form of the Eternal, even as man is a form of the same. Absolute being, again, is described as anthropomorphic. 'This is that' under a certain form. Incessantly made is the attempt to explain the identity of the absolute with phenomena. The power (*brahma*), which is originally applied to prayer, is now taken as absolute being, and this, again, must be equated with the personal spirit (ego, self, *ātmā*). One finds himself back in the age of Vedic speculation when he reads of prayer (or penance) and power as one. For, as was shown above, the Rig Veda already recognizes that prayer is power. There the word for power, *brahma*, is used only as equivalent of prayer, and Brihaspati or Brahmanaspati is literally the 'god of power,' as he is interpreted by the priests. The significance of the other great word of this period, namely *ātmā*, is not at all uncertain, but to translate it is difficult. It is breath, spirit, self, soul. Yet, since in its original sense it corresponds to spiritus (comparable, to athmen), the word spirit, which also signifies the real person, perhaps represents it best. We shall then render *brahma* and *ātmā* by the absolute and the ego or spirit, respectively; or leave them, which is perhaps the best way, in their native form. The physical breath, *prāṇa*, is occasionally used just like *ātmā*. Thus it is said that all the gods are one god, and this is *prāṇa*, identical with *brahma* (Brihad Āranyaka Upanishad, 3. 9. 9); or *prāṇa* is so used as to be the same with spirit, though, on the other hand, 'breath is born of spirit' (Praçna Up. 3. 3), just as in the Rig Veda (above) it is said that all comes from the breath of God.

One of the most instructive of the older Upanishads is the Chāndogya. A sketch of its doctrines will give a clearer idea of Upanishad philosophy than a chapter of disconnected excerpts:

All this (universe) is *brahma*. Man has intelligent force (or will). He, after death, will exist in accordance with his will in life. This spirit in (my) heart is that mind-making, breath-bodied, light-formed, truth-thoughted, ether-spirited One, of whom are all works, all desires, all smells, and all tastes; who comprehends the universe, who speaks not and is not moved; smaller than a rice-corn, smaller than a mustard-seed. . . . greater than earth, greater than heaven. This (universal being) is my ego, spirit, and is *brahma*, force (absolute being). After death I shall enter into him (3. 14).[1] This all is breath (=spirit in 3. 15. 4).

After this epitome of pantheism follows a ritualistic bit:

Man is sacrifice. Four and twenty years are the morning libation; the next four and forty, the mid-day libation; the next eight and forty, the evening libation. The son of Itarā, knowing this, lived one hundred and sixteen years. He who knows this lives one hundred and sixteen years (3. 16).

Then, for the abolition of all sacrifice, follows a chapter which explains that man may sacrifice symbolically, so that,

[1] This teaching is ascribed to Çāndilya, to whose heresy, as opposed to the pure Vedantic doctrine of Çankara, we shall have to revert in a later chapter. The heresy consists, in a word, in regarding the individual spirit as at any time distinct from the Supreme Spirit, though Çāndilya teaches that it is ultimately absorbed into the latter.

for example, gifts to the priests (a necessary adjunct of a real sacrifice) here become penance, liberality, rectitude, non-injury, truth-speaking (*ib.* 17. 4). There follows then the identification of *brahma* with mind, sun, breath, cardinal points, ether, etc., even puns being brought into requisition, *Ka* is *Kha* and *Kha* is *Ka* (4. 10. 5);[1] earth, fire, food, sun, water, stars, man, are *brahma*, and *brahma* is the man seen in the moon (4. 12. 1). And now comes the identity of the impersonal *brahma* with the personal spirit. The man seen in the eye is the spirit; this is the immortal, unfearing *brahma* (4. 15. 1 = S. 7. 4). He that knows this goes after death to light, thence to day, thence to the light moon, thence to the season, thence to the year, thence to the sun, thence to the moon, thence to lightning; thus he becomes divine, and enters *brahma*. They that go on this path of the gods that conducts to *brahma* do not return to human conditions (*ib.* 15. 6).

But the Father-god of the Brāhmanas is still a temporary creator, and thus he appears now (*ib.* 17): The Father-god brooded over[2] the worlds, and from them extracted essences, fire from earth, wind from air, sun from sky. These three divinities (the triad, fire, wind, and sun) he brooded over, and from them extracted essences, the Rig Veda from fire, the Yajur Veda from wind, the Sāma Veda from sun. In the preceding the northern path of them that know the absolute (*brahma*) has been described, and it was said that they return no more to earth. Now follows the southern path of them that only partly know *brahma*:

"He that knows the oldest, *jyeṣṭham*, and the best, *çreṣṭham*, becomes the oldest and the best. Now breath is oldest and best" (then follows the famous parable of the senses and breath, 5. 1. 1). This (found elsewhere) is evidently regarded

[1] "God 'Who' is air, air (space) is God 'Who,'" as if one said 'either is aether.'

[2] 'Did penance over,' as one doing penance remains in meditation. 'Brooded' is Müller's apt word for this *abhi-tap*.

as a new doctrine, for, after the deduction has been made that, because a creature can live without senses, and even without mind, but cannot live without breath, therefore the breath is the 'oldest and best,' the text continues, 'if one told this to a dry stick, branches would be produced and leaves put forth' (5. 2. 3).[1] The path of him that partly knows the *brahma* which is expressed in breath, etc., is as follows: He goes to the moon, and, when his good works are used up, he (ultimately mist) rains down, becoming seed, and begins life over again on earth, to become like the people who eat him (5. 10. 6); they that are good become priests, warriors, or members of the third estate; while the bad become dogs, hogs, or members of the low castes.[2] A story is now told, instructive as illustrating the time. Five great doctors of the law came together to discuss what is Spirit, what is *brahma*. In the end they are taught by a king that the universal Spirit is one's own spirit (5. 18. 1).

It is interesting to see that, although the Rig Veda distinctly says that 'being was born of not-being' (*ásatas sád ajāyata*, x. 72. 3),[3] yet not-being is here derived quite as emphatically from being. For in the philosophical explanation of the universe given in 6. 2. 1 ff. one reads: "Being alone existed in the beginning, one, and without a second. Others say 'not-being alone' . . . but how could being be born of not-being? Being alone existed in the beginning."[4] This being is then represented as sentient. "It saw (and desired), 'may I be many,' and sent forth fire (or heat): fire (or heat) desired and produced water; water, food (earth): with the living spirit the

[1] Compare *Brihad Āran. Up.* 6. 3. 7.

[2] This is the *karma* or *samsāra* doctrine.

[3] In J. U. B. alone have we noticed the formula asserting that 'both being and not-being existed in the beginning' (1. 53. 1; JAOS. xvi. 130).

[4] Opposed is 3. 19. 1 and *Tāitt. Up.* 2. 7. 1 (*Br.* ii. 2. 9. 1, 10): "Not-being was here in the beginning. From it arose being." And so *Çat. Br.* vi. 1. 1. 1 (though in word only, for here not-being is the seven spirits of God!)

divinity entered fire, water, and earth" (6. 3). As mind comes from food, breath from water, and speech from fire, all that makes a man is thus derived from the (true) being (6. 7. 6); and when one dies his speech is absorbed into mind, his mind into breath, his breath into fire (heat), and heat into the highest godhead (6. 8. 7). This is the subtile spirit, that is the Spirit, that is the True, and this is the spirit of man. Now comes the grand conclusion of the Chāndogya. He who knows the ego escapes grief. What is the ego? The Vedas are names, and he that sees *brahma* in the Vedas is indeed (partly) wise; but speech is better than a name; mind is better than speech; will is better than mind; meditation, better than will; reflection, than meditation; understanding, than reflection; power, than understanding; food, than power; water, than food; heat (fire), than water; ether, than heat; memory, than ether; hope, than memory; breath (= spirit), than hope. In each let one see *brahma;* ego in All. Who knows this is supreme in knowledge; but more supreme in knowledge is he that knows that in true (being) is the highest being. True being is happiness; true being is ego; ego is all; ego is the absolute.[1]

The relativity of divinity is the discovery of the Upanishads. And the relativity of happiness hereafter is the key-note of their religious philosophy. Pious men are of three classes, according to the completed system. Some are good men, but they do not know enough to appreciate. intellectually or spiritually, the highest. Let this class meditate on the Vedas. They desire wealth, not freedom. The second class wish, indeed, to emancipate themselves; but to do so step by step; not to reach absolute *brahma*, but to live in bliss hereafter. Let these worship the Spirit as physical life. They will attain to the

[1] As the Vedic notion of not-being existing before being is refuted. so the Atharvan homage to Time as Lord is also derided (*Çvet.* 6) in the Upanishads. The supreme being is above time, as he is without parts (*ib.*). In this later Upanishad wisdom, penance, and the grace of God are requisite to know *brahma*.

bliss of the realm of light, the realm of the personal creator. But the highest class, they that wish to emancipate themselves at once, know that physical life is but a form of spiritual life: that the personal creator is but a form of the Spirit; that the Spirit is absolute *brahma;* and that in reaching this they attain to immortality. These, then, are to meditate on spirit as the highest Spirit, that is, the absolute. To fear heaven as much as hell, to know that knowledge is, after all, the key to *brahma;* that *brahma* is knowledge; this is the way to emancipation. The gods are; but they are forms of the ego, and their heaven is mortal. It is false to deny the gods. Indra and the Father-god exist, just as men exist, as transient forms of *brahma.* Therefore, according to the weakness or strength of a man's mind and heart (desire) is he fitted to ignore gods and sacrifice. To obtain *brahma* his desires must be weak, his knowledge strong; but sacrifice is not to be put away as useless. The disciplinary teaching of the sacrifice is a necessary preparation for highest wisdom. It is here that the Upanishads, which otherwise are to a great extent on the highway to Buddhism, practically contrast with it. Buddhism ignores the sacrifice and the stadia in a priest's life. The Upanishads retain them, but only to throw them over at the end when one has learned not to need them. Philosophically there is no place for the ritual in the Upanishad doctrine; but their teachers stood too much under the dominion of the Brāhmanas to ignore the ritual. They kept it as a means of perfecting the knowledge of what was essential.

So 'by wisdom' it is said 'one gets immortality.' The Spirit develops gradually in man; by means of the mortal he desires the immortal; whereas other animals have only hunger and thirst as a kind of understanding, and they are reborn according to their knowledge as beasts again. Such is the teaching of another of the Upanishads, the Aitareya Āranyaka.

This Upanishad contains some rather striking passages: "Whatever man attains, he desires to go beyond it; if he should reach heaven itself he would desire to go beyond it" (2. 3. 3. 1). "*Brahma* is the A, thither goes the ego" (2. 3. 8. 7). "A is the whole of Speech, and Speech is Truth, and Truth is Spirit" (2. 3. 6. 5–14).[1] "The Spirit brooded over the water, and form (matter) was born" (2. 4. 3. 1 ff.); so physically water is the origin of all things" (2. 1. 8. 1).[2] "Whatever belongs to the father belongs to the son, whatever belongs to the son belongs to the father" (*ib.*). "Man has three births: he is born of his mother, reborn in the person of his son, and finds his highest birth in death" (2. 5).

In the exposition of these two Upanishads one gets at once the sum of them all. The methods, the illustrations, even the doctrines, differ in detail; but in the chief end and object of the Upanishads, and in the principle of knowledge as a means of attaining *brahma*, they are united. This it is that causes the refutation of the Vedic 'being from not-being.' It is even said in the Āitareya that the gods worshipped breath (the spirit) as being and so became gods (great); while devils worshipped spirit as not-being, and hence became (inferior) devils (2. 1. 8. 6).

It was noticed above that a king instructed priests. This interchange of the rôles of the two castes is not unique. In the Kāushitaki Upanishad (4. 19), occurs another instance of a warrior teaching a Brahman. This, with the familiar illustration of a Gandhāra (Kandahar) man, the song of the Kurus, and the absence of Brahmanic literature as such in the list of

1 This Vedic λόγος doctrine is conspicuous in the Brāhmana. Compare *Çat. Br.* vii. 5. 2. 21: "Vāc (λόγος) is the Unborn one: from Vāc the all-maker made creatures." See Weber, *Ind. Stud.* ix. 477 ff.

2 Compare J. U. B. 1. 56. 1, 'Water (alone) existed in the beginning.' This is the oldest and latest Hindu explanation of the matter of the physical universe. From the time of the Vedas to mediaeval times, as is recorded by the Greek travellers, water is regarded as the original element.

works, cited vii. 1, would indicate that the Chāndogya was at least as old as the Brāhmana literature.[1]

In their present form several differences remain to be pointed out between the Vedic period and that of the Upanishads. The goal of the soul, the two paths of gods and of *brahma*, have been indicated. As already explained, the road to the absolute *brahma* lies beyond the path to the conditioned *brahma*. Opposed to this is the path that leads to the world of heaven, whence, when good works have been exhausted, the spirit descends to a new birth on earth. The course of this second path is conceived to be the dark half of the moon, and so back to man. Both roads lead first to the moon, then one goes on to *brahma*, the other returns to earth. It will be seen that good works are regarded as buoying a man up for a time, till, like gas in a balloon, they lose their force, and he sinks down again. What then becomes of the virtue of a man who enters the absolute *brahma*, and descends no more? He himself goes to the world where there is "no sorrow and no snow," where he lives forever (*Brihad Āran.* 5. 10); but "his beloved relations get his virtue, and the relations he does not love get his evil" (*Kaushīt. Up.* 1. 4). In this Upanishad fire, sun, moon, and lightning die out, and reappear as *brahma*. This is the doctrine of the *Götterdämmerung*, and succession of aeons with their divinities (2. 12). Here again is it distinctly stated that *prāṇa*, breath, is *brahma*; that is, spirit is the absolute (2. 13).

What becomes of them that die ignorant of the ego? They go either to the worlds of evil spirits, which are covered with darkness—the same antithesis of light and darkness, as good and evil, that was seen in the Brāhmanas—or are reborn on earth again like the wicked (*Īçā*, 3).

It is to be noted that at times all the parts of a man are

[1] The Gandhāra might indicate a late geographical expansion as well as an early heritage, so that this is not conclusive.

said to become immortal. For just as different rivers enter the ocean and their names and forms are lost in it, so the sixteen parts of a man sink into the godhead and he becomes without parts and immortal (*Praçna Up.* 6. 5); a purely pantheistic view of absorption, in distinction from the Vedic view of heaven, which latter, in the form of immortal joy hereafter, still lingers in the earlier Upanishads.

It is further to be observed as the crowning point of these speculations that, just as the bliss of emancipation must not be desired, although it is desirable, so too, though knowledge is the fundamental condition of emancipation, yet is delight in the true a fatal error: "They that revere what is not knowledge enter into blind darkness; they that delight in knowledge come as it were into still greater darkness" (*Içā*, 9). Here, what is not real knowledge means good works, sacrifice, etc. But the sacrifice is not discarded. To those people capable only of attaining to rectitude, sacrifices, and belief in gods there is given some bliss hereafter; but to him that is risen above this, who knows the ego (Spirit) and real being, such bliss is no bliss. His bliss is union with the Spirit.

This is the completion of Upanishad philosophy. Before it is a stage where bliss alone, not absorption, is taught.[1] But what is the ego, spirit or self (*ātmā*)? First of all it is conscious; next it is not the Person, for the Person is produced by the *ātmā*. Since this Person is the type of the personal god, it is evident that the ego is regarded as lying back of personality. Nevertheless, the teachers sometimes stop with the latter. The developed view is that the immortality of the personal creator is commensurate only with that of the world which he creates. It is for this reason that in the Mundaka (1. 2. 10) it is said that fools regard fulfillment of desire in

[1] Gough, *Philosophy of the Upanishads*, has sought to show that the pure Vedantism of Çankara is the only belief taught in the Upanishads, ignoring the weight of those passages that oppose his (in our view) too sweeping assertion.

heavenly happiness as the best thing; for although they have their reward in the top of heaven, yet, when the elevation caused by their good works ends, as it will end, when the buoyant power of good works is exhausted, then they drop down to earth again. Hence, to worship the creator as the *ātmā* is indeed productive of temporary pleasure, but no more. "If a man worship another divinity, *devatā*, with the idea that he and the god are different, he does not know" (*Brihad Āran. Up.* 1. 4. 10). "Without passion and without parts" is the *brahma* (*Mund.* 2. 2. 9). The further doctrine, therefore, that all except *brahma* is delusion is implied here, and the "extinction of gods in *brahma*" is once or twice formulated.[1] The fatal error of judgment is to imagine that there is in absolute being anything separate from man's being. When personified, this being appears as the supreme Person, identical with the ego, who is lord of what has been and what will be. By perceiving this controlling spirit in one's own spirit (or self) one obtains eternal bliss; "when desires cease, the mortal becomes immortal; he attains *brahma* here" in life (*Katha Up.* 2. 5. 12; 6. 14; *Br. Āran. Up.* 4. 4. 7).

How inconsistent are the teachings of the Upanishads in regard to cosmogonic and eschatological matters will be evident if one contrast the statements of the different tracts not only with those of other writings of the same sort, but even with other statements in the same Upanishads. Thus the Mundaka teaches first that Brahmā, the personal creator, made the world and explained *brahma* (1. 1. 1). It then defines *brahma* as the Imperishable, which, like a spider, sends out a web of being and draws it in again (*ib.* 6, 7). It states with all distinctness that the (neuter) *brahma* comes from The (masculine)

[1] See the Parimara described, *Āit. Br.* viii. 28. Here *brahma* is wind, around which die five divinities — lightning in rain, rain in moon, moon in sun, sun in fire, fire in wind — and they are reborn in reverse order. The 'dying' is used as a curse. The king shall say, 'When fire dies in wind then may my foe die,' and he will die; so when any of the other gods dies around *brahma*.

One who is all-wise, all-knowing (*ib.* 9). This heavenly Person is the imperishable ego; it is without form; higher than the imperishable (1. 2. 10 ff.; 2. 1. 2); greater than the great (3. 2. 8). Against this is then set (2. 2. 9) the great being *brahma*, without passions or parts, *i.e.*, without intelligence such as was predicated of the *ātmā*; and (3. 1. 3) then follows the doctrine of the personal 'Lord, who is the maker, the Person, who has his birth in *brahma*' (*purusho brahmayonis*). That this Upanishad is pantheistic is plain from 3. 2. 6, where Vedānta and Yoga are named. According to this tract the wise go to *brahma* or to ego (3. 2. 9 and 1. 2. 11), while fools go to heaven and return again.

On the same plane stands the Īçā, where *ātmā*, ego, Spirit, is the True, the Lord, and is in the sun. Opposed to each other here are 'darkness' and 'immortality,' as fruit, respectively, of ignorance and wisdom.

In the Kāushītaki Upanishad, taken with the meaning put into it by the commentators, the wise man goes to a very different sort of *brahma* — one where he is met by nymphs, and rejoices in a kind of heaven. This *brahma* is of two sorts, absolute and conditioned; but it is ultimately defined as 'breath.' Whenever it is convenient, 'breath' is regarded by the commentators as ego, 'spirit'; but one can scarcely escape the conviction that in many passages 'breath' was meant by the speaker to be taken at its face value. It is the vital power. With this vital power (breath or spirit) one in dreamless sleep unites. Indra has nothing higher to say than that he is breath (spirit), conscious and immortal. Eventually the soul after death comes to Indra, or gains the bright heaven. But here too the doctrine of the dying out of the gods is known (as in *Tāitt.* 3. 10. 4). Cosmogonically all here springs from water (1. 4, 6, 7; 2. 1, 12; 3. 1, 2; 4. 20).

Most striking are the contradictions in the Brihad Āranyaka: "In the beginning there was only nothing; this (world) was covered with death, that is hunger;[1] he desired," etc. (1. 2. 1). "In the beginning there was only ego (*ātmā*)." *Ātmā* articulated "I am," and (finding himself lonely and unhappy) divided himself into male and female,[2] whence arose men, etc. (1. 4. 1). Again: "In the beginning there was only *brahma*; this (neuter) knew *ātmā* . . . *brahma* was the one and only . . . it created" (1. 4. 10–11); followed immediately by "he created" (12). And after this, in 17, one is brought back to "in the beginning there was only *ātmā*; he desired 'let me have a wife.'"

In 2. 3. 1 ff. the explicitness of the differences in *brahma* makes the account of unusual value. It appears that there are two forms of *brahma*, one is mortal, with form; the other is immortal, without form. Whatever is other than air and the space between (heaven and earth) is mortal and with form. This is being, its essence is in the sun. On the other hand, the essence of the immortal is the person in the circle (of the sun). In man's body breath and ether are the immortal, the essence of which is the person in the eye. There is a visible and invisible *brahma* (*ātmā*); the real *brahma* is incomprehensible and is described only by negations (3. 4. 1; 9. 26). The highest is the Imperishable (*neuter*), but this sees, hears, and knows. It is in this that ether (as above) is woven (3. 8. 11). After death the wise man goes to the world of the gods (1. 5. 16); he becomes the *ātmā* of all beings, just like that deity (1. 5. 20); he becomes identical ('how can one know the knower?' *vijñātar*) in 2. 4. 12–13; and, according to 3. 2. 13, the doctrine of *samsāra* is extolled ("they talked of *karma*, extolled *karma*, secretly"), as something too secret to be divulged easily, even to priests.

That different views are recognized is evident from *Tāitt.* 2. 6: "If one knows *brahma* as *asat* he becomes only *asat*

[1] Compare sterben, starve.

[2] The androgynous creator of the Brāhmanas.

(non-existence); if he knows that '*brahma* is' (*i.e.*, a *sad brahma*), people know him as thence existing." Personal *ātmā* is here insisted on ("He wished 'may I be many'"); and from *ātmā*, the conscious *brahma*, in highest heaven, came the ether (2. 1, 6). Yet, immediately afterwards: "In the beginning was the non-existent; thence arose the existent; and That made for himself an ego (spirit, conscious life, *ātmā; tad ātmānaṁ svayam akuruta*, 2. 7). In man *brahma* is the sun-*brahma*. Here too one finds the *brahmaṇaḥ parimaras* (3. 10. 4 = Kāushit. 2. 12, *dāiva*), or extinction of gods in *brahma*. But what that *brahma* is, except that it is bliss, and that man after death reaches 'the bliss-making *ātmā*,' it is impossible to say (3. 6; 2. 8). Especially as the departed soul 'eats and sits down singing' in heaven (3. 10. 5).

The greatest discrepancies in eschatology occur perhaps in the Āitareya Āranyaka. After death one either "gets *brahma*" (i. 3. 1. 2), "comes near to the immortal spirit" (1. 3. 8. 14), or goes to the "heavenly world." Knowledge here expressly conditions the hereafter; so much so that it is represented not (as above) that fools go to heaven and return, but that all, save the very highest, are to recognize a personal creator (Prajāpati) in breath (= ego = *brahma*), and then they will "go to the heavenly world" (2. 3. 8. 5), "become the sun" (2. 1. 8. 14), or "go to gods" (2. 2. 4. 6). Moreover after the highest wisdom has been revealed, and the second class of men has been disposed of, the author still returns to the 'shining sky,' *svarga*, as the best promise (3). Sinners are born again (2. 1. 1. 5) on earth, although hell is mentioned (2. 3. 2. 5). The origin of world is water, as usual (2. 1. 8. 1). The highest teaching is that all was *ātmā*, who sent forth worlds (*lokān asṛjata*), and formed the Person (as guardian of worlds), taking him from waters. Hence *ātmā*, Prajāpati (of the second-class thinkers), and *brahma* are the same. Knowledge is *brahma* (2. 4. 1. 1; 6. 1. 5–7).

In the Kena, where the best that can be said in regard to *brahma* is that he is *tadvana*, the one that 'likes this' (or, perhaps, is 'like·this'), there is no absorption into a world-spirit. The wise 'become immortal'; 'by knowledge one gets immortality'; 'who knows this stands in heaven' (1. 2; 2. 4; 4. 9). The general results are about those formulated by Whitney in regard to the Katha: knowledge gives continuation of happiness in heaven; the punishment of the unworthy is to continue *samsāra*, the round of rebirths. Hell is not mentioned in the Āitareya Upanishad itself but in the Āranyaka[1] (2. 3. 2. 5). That, however, a union with the universal *ātmā* (as well as heaven) is desired, would seem to be the case from several of the passages cited above, notably Brihad Āran., i. 5. 20 (*sa evamvit sarveṣām bhūtānām ātmā bhavati, yathāiṣā devatāivam sa*); 'he that knows this becomes the *ātmā* of all creatures, as is that divinity so is he'; though this is doubtless the *ānanda-maya ātmā*, or joy-making Spirit (Tāitt. 2. 8).

Again two forms of *brahma* are explained (Māit. Up. 6. 15 ff.): There are two forms of *brahma*, time and not-time. That which was before the sun is not-time and has no parts. Time and parts begin with the sun. Time is the Father-god, the Spirit. Time makes and dissolves all in the Spirit. He knows the Veda who knows into what Time itself is dissolved. This manifest time is the ocean of creatures. But *brahma* exists before and after time.[2]

As an example of the best style of the Upanishads we will cite a favorite passage (given no less than four times in various versions) where the doctrine of absorption is most distinctly taught under the form of a tale. It is the famous

[1] We cannot, however, quite agree with Whitney who, *loc. cit.* p. 92, and Journal, xiii, p. cliii ff., implies that belief in hell comes later than this period. This is not so late a teaching. Hell is Vedic and Brahmanic.

[2] This, in pantheistic style, is expressed thus (Çvet. 4): "When the light has arisen there is no day no night, neither being nor not-being; the Blessed One alone exists there. There is no likeness of him whose name is Great Glory."

DIALOGUE OF YĀJÑAVALKYA AND MĀITREYĪ.[1]

Yājñavalkya had two wives, Māitreyī and Kātyāyanī. Now Māitreyī was versed in holy knowledge (*brahma*), but Kātyāyanī had only such knowledge as women have. But when Yājñavalkya was about to go away into the forest (to become a hermit), he said: 'Māitreyī, I am going away from this place. Behold, I will make a settlement between thee and that Kātyāyanī.' Then said Māitreyī: 'Lord, if this whole earth filled with wealth were mine, how then? should I be immortal by reason of this wealth?' 'Nay,' said Yājñavalkya. 'Even as is the life of the rich would be thy life; by reason of wealth one has no hope of immortality.' Then said Māitreyī: 'With what I cannot be immortal, what can I do with that? whatever my Lord knows even that tell me.' And Yājñavalkya said: 'Dear to me thou art, indeed, and fondly speakest. Therefore I will explain to thee and do thou regard me as I explain.' And he said: 'Not for the husband's sake is a husband dear, but for the ego's sake is the husband dear. Not for the wife's sake is a wife dear; but for the ego's sake is a wife dear; not for the son's sake are sons dear, but for the ego's sake are sons dear; not for wealth's sake is wealth dear, but for the ego's sake is wealth dear; not for the sake of the Brahman caste is the Brahman caste dear, but for the sake of the ego is the Brahman caste dear; not for the sake of the Warrior caste is the Warrior caste dear, but for love of the ego is the Warrior caste dear; not for the sake of the worlds are worlds dear, but for the sake of the ego are worlds dear; not for the sake of gods are gods dear, but for the ego's sake are gods dear; not for the sake of *bhūts* (spirits) are *bhūts* dear, but for the ego's sake are *bhūts* dear; not for the sake of anything is anything dear, but for love of one's self (ego) is anything (everything) dear; the ego (self) must be seen,

[1] Brihad Āranyaka Upanishad, 2. 4; 4. 5.

heard, apprehended, regarded, Māitreyī, for with the seeing, hearing, apprehending, and regarding of the ego the All is known. . . . Even as smoke pours out of a fire lighted with damp kindling wood, even so out of the Great Being is blown out all that which is, Rig Veda, Yajur Veda, Sāma Veda, Atharva (-Angiras) Veda, Stories, Tales, Sciences, Upanishads, food, drink, sacrifices; all creatures that exist are blown (breathed) out of this one (Great Spirit) alone. As in the ocean all the waters have their meeting-place; as the skin is the meeting-place of all touches; the tongue, of all tastes; the nose, of all smells; the mind, of all precepts; the heart, of all knowledges; . . . as salt cast into water is dissolved so that one cannot seize it, but wherever one tastes it is salty, so this Great Being, endless, limitless, is a mass of knowledge. It arises out of the elements and then disappears in them. After death there is no more consciousness.[1] I have spoken.' Thus said Yājñavalkya. Then said Māitreyī: 'Truly my Lord has bewildered me in saying that after death there is no more consciousness.' And Yājñavalkya said: 'I say nothing bewildering, but what suffices for understanding. For where there is as it were duality (*dvāitam*), there one sees, smells, hears, addresses, notices, knows another; but when all the universe has become mere ego, with what should one smell, see, hear, address, notice, know any one (else)? How can one know him through whom he knows this all, how can he know the knower (as something different)? The ego is to be described by negations alone, the incomprehensible, imperishable, unattached, unfettered; the ego neither suffers nor fails. Thus, Māitreyī, hast thou been instructed. So much for immortality.' And having spoken thus Yājñavalkya went away (into the forest).

Returning to the Upanishad, of which an outline was given in the beginning of this chapter, one finds a state of things

[1] *Na pretya saṁjñā 'sti.*

which, in general, may be said to be characteristic of the whole Upanishad period. The same vague views in regard to cosmogony and eschatology obtain in all save the outspoken sectarian tracts, and the same uncertainty in regard to man's future fate prevails in this whole cycle.[1] A few extracts will show this. According to the Chāndogya (4. 17. 1), a personal creator, the old Father-god of the Brāhmanas, Prajāpati, made the elements proceed from the worlds he had 'brooded' over (or had done penance over, *abhyatapat*). In 3. 19. 1, not-being was first; this became being (with the mundane egg, etc.). In sharp contradiction (6. 2. 1): 'being was the first thing, it willed,' etc., a conscious divinity, as is seen in *ib.* 3. 2, where it is a 'deity,' producing elements as 'deities' (*ib.* 8. 6) which it enters 'with the living *ātmā*,' and so develops names and forms (so *Tāitt.* 2. 7). The latter is the prevailing view of the Upanishad. In 1. 7. 5 ff. the *ātmā* is the same with the universal *ātmā;* in 3. 12. 7, the *brahma* is the same with ether without and within, unchanging; in 3. 13. 7, the 'light above heaven' is identical with the light in man; in 3. 14. 1, all is *brahma* (neuter), and this is an intelligent universal spirit. Like the ether is the *ātmā* in the heart, this is *brahma* (*ib.* 2 ff.); in 4. 3, air and breath are the two ends (so in the argument above, these are immortal as distinguished from all else); in 4. 10. 5 *yad vāvā kaṁ tad eva kham* (*brahma* is ether); in 4. 15. 1, the ego is *brahma;* in 5. 18. 1 the universal ego is identified with the particular ego (*ātmā*); in 6. 8 the ego is the True, with which one unites in dreamless sleep; in 6. 15. 1, into *parā devatā* or 'highest divinity' enters man's spirit, like salt in water (*ib.* 13). In 7. 15–26, a view but half correct is stated to be that 'breath' is all, but it is better to know that *yo bhūmā*

[1] Some of the Upanishads have been tampered with, so that all of the contradictions may not be due to the composers. Nevertheless, as the uncertainty of opinion in regard to cosmogony is quite as great as that in respect of absorption, all the vagueness cannot properly be attributed to the efforts of later systematizers to bring the Upanishads into their more or less orthodox Vedantism.

tad amṛtam, the immortal (all) is infinity, which rests in its own greatness, with a corrective 'but perhaps it doesn't' (*yadi vā na*). This infinity is ego and *ātmā*.[1]

What is the reward for knowing this? One obtains worlds, unchanging happiness, *brahma;* or, with some circumnavigation, one goes to the moon, and eventually reaches *brahma* or obtains the worlds of the blessed (5. 10. 10). The round of existence, *samsāra*, is indicated at 6. 16, and expressly stated in 5. 10. 7 (insects have here a third path). Immortality is forcibly claimed: 'The living one dies not' (6. 11. 3). He who knows the sections 7. 15 to 26 becomes *ātmānanda* and "lord of all worlds"; whereas an incorrect view gives perishable worlds. In one Upanishad there is a verse (*Çvet.* 4. 5) which would indicate a formal duality like that of the Sānkhyas;[2] but in general one may say that the Upanishads are simply pantheistic, only the absorption into a world-soul is as yet scarcely formulated. On the other hand, some of the older Upanishads show traces of an atheistic and materialistic (*asad*) philosophy, which is swallowed up in the growing inclination to personify the creative principle, and ultimately is lost in the erection of a personal Lord, as in the latest Upanishads. This tendency to personify, with the increase of special sectarian gods, will lead again, after centuries, to the rehabilitation of a triad of gods, the *trimūrti*, where unite Vishnu, Çiva, and, with these, who are more powerful, Brahmā, the Prajāpati of the Veda, as the All-god of purely pantheistic systems. In the purer, older form recorded above, the *purusha* (Person) is sprung from the *ātmā*. There is no distinction between matter and spirit. Conscious being (*sat*) wills, and so produces all. Or *ātmā* comes first; and this is conscious

[1] In 4. 10. 5 *kam* is pleasure, one with ether as *brahma*, not as wrongly above, p. 222, the god Ka.

[2] This Upanishad appears to be sectarian, perhaps an early Çivaite tract (dualistic), if the allusion to Rudra Çiva, below, be accepted as original.

sat, and the cause of the worlds; which *ātmā* eventually becomes the Lord. The *ātmā* in man, owing to his environment, cannot see whole, and needs the Yoga discipline of asceticism to enable him to do so. But he is the same ego which is the All.

The relation between the absolute and the ego is through will. "This (neuter) *brahma* willed, 'May I be many,' and created" (*Chānd.*, above). Sometimes the impersonal, and sometimes the personal "spirit willed" (*Tāitt.* 2. 6). And when it is said, in *Brihad Āran.* 1. 4. 1, that "In the beginning ego, spirit, *ātmā*, alone existed," one finds this spirit (self) to be a form of *brahma* (*ib.* 10–11). Personified in a sectarian sense, this spirit becomes the divinity Rudra Çiva, the Blessed One (*Çvetāçvatara*, 3. 5, 11).[1]

In short, the teachers of the Upanishads not only do not declare clearly what they believed in regard to cosmogonic and eschatological matters, but many of them probably did not know clearly what they believed. Their great discovery was that man's spirit was not particular and mortal, but part of the immortal universal. Whether this universal was a being alive and a personal *ātmā*, or whether this personal being was but a transient form of impersonal, imperishable being;[2] and whether the union with being, *brahma*, would result in a survival of individual consciousness,—these are evidently points they were not agreed upon, and, in all probability, no one of the sages was certain in regard to them. Crass identifications of the vital

[1] As is foreshadowed in the doctrine of grace by Vāc in the Rig Veda, in the *Çvet.*, the *Katha*, and the *Mund.* Upanishads (*K.* 2. 23; *M.* 3. 2. 3), but nowhere else, there enters, with the sectarian phase, that radical subversion of the Upanishad doctrine which becomes so powerful at a later date, the teaching that salvation is a gift of God. "This Spirit is not got by wisdom; the Spirit chooses as his own the body of that man whom He chooses."

[2] See above. As descriptive of the immortal conscious Spirit, there is the famous verse: "If the slayer thinks to slay, if the slain thinks he is slain; they both understand not; this one (the Spirit) slays not and is not slain" (*Katha*, 2. 19); loosely rendered by Emerson, 'If the red slayer think he slays,' etc.

principle with breath, as one with ether, which is twice emphasized as one of the two immortal things, were provisionally accepted. Then breath and immortal spirit were made one. Matter had energy from the beginning, *brahma;* or was chaos, *asat*, without being. But when *asat* becomes *sat*, that *sat* becomes *brahma*, energized being, and to *asat* there is no return. In eschatology the real (spirit, or self) part of man (ego) either rejoices forever as a conscious part of the conscious world-self, or exists immortal in *brahma*—imperishable being, conceived as more or less conscious.[1]

The teachers recognize the limitations of understanding: "The gods are in Indra, Indra is in the Father-god, the Father-god (the Spirit) is in *brahma*"—"But in what is *brahma?*" And the answer is, "Ask not too much" (*Brihad. Āran. Up.* 3. 6).

These problems will be those of the future formal philosophy. Even the Upanishads do not furnish a philosophy altogether new. Their doctrine of *karma*, their identification of particular ego and universal ego, is not original. The 'breaths,' the 'nine doors,' the 'three qualities,' the *purusha* as identical with ego, are older even than the Brāhmanas (Scherman, *loc. cit.* p. 62).

It is not a new philosophy, it is a new religion that the Upanishads offer.[2] This is no religion of rites and ceremonies, although the cult is retained as helpful in disciplining and teaching; it is a religion for sorrowing humanity. It is a religion that comforts the afflicted, and gives to the soul 'that peace which the world cannot give.' In the sectarian Upanishads this bliss of religion is ever present. "Through knowing Him who is more subtile than subtile, who is creator of everything,

[1] The fact remarked by Thibaut that radically different systems of philosophy are built upon the Upanishads is enough to show how ambiguous are the declarations of the latter.

[2] Compare Barth, *Religions*, p. 76.

who has many forms, who embraces everything, the Blessed Lord — one attains to peace without end" (*Çvet.* 4. 14–15). These teachers, who enjoin the highest morality ('self-restraint, generosity, and mercy' are God's commandments in *Brihad Āran.* 5. 2) refuse to be satisfied with virtue's reward, and, being able to obtain heaven, 'seek for something beyond.' And this they do not from mere pessimism, but from a conviction that they will find a joy greater than that of heaven, and more enduring, in that world where is "the light beyond the darkness" (*Çvet.* 3. 8); "where shines neither sun, moon, stars, lightning, nor fire, but all shines after Him that shines alone, and through His light the universe is lighted" (*Mund.* 2. 2. 10). This, moreover, is not a future joy. It is one that frees from perturbation in this life, and gives relief from sorrow. In the Chāndogya (7. 1. 3) a man in grief comes seeking this new knowledge of the universal Spirit; "For," says he, "I have heard it said that he who knows the Spirit passes beyond grief." So in the Īçā, though this is a late sectarian work, it is asked, "What sorrow can there be for him to whom Spirit alone has become all things?" (7). Again, "He that knows the joy of *brahma*, whence speech with mind turns away without apprehending it, fears not" (*Tāitt.* 2. 4); for "fear comes only from a second" (*Brihad Āran. Up.* 1. 4. 2), and when one recognizes that all is one he no longer fears death (*ib.* 4. 4. 15).

Such is the religion of these teachers. In the quiet assumption that life is not worth living, they are as pessimistic as was Buddha. But if, as seems to be the case, the Buddhist believed in the eventual extinction of his individuality, their pessimism is of a different sort. For the teacher of the Upanishads believes that he will attain to unending joy; not the rude happiness of 'heaven-seekers,' but the unchanging bliss of immortal peace. For him that wished it, there was heaven and the gods. These were not denied; they were as real as the "fool" that desired them. But for him that conquered passion, and knew the truth, there was existence without the pain of desire, life without end, freedom from rebirth. The spirit of the sage becomes one with the Eternal; man becomes God.

CHAPTER XI.

THE POPULAR BRAHMANIC FAITH.

FOR a long time after the Vedic age there is little that gives one an insight into the views of the people. It may be presumed, since the orthodox systems never dispensed with the established cult, that the form of the old Vedic creed was kept intact. Yet, since the real belief changed, and the cult became more and more the practice of a formality, it becomes necessary to seek, apart from the inherited ritual, the faith which formed the actual religion of the people. Inasmuch as this phase of Hindu belief has scarcely been touched upon elsewhere, it may be well to state more fully the object of the present chapter.

We have shown above that the theology of the Vedic period had resulted, before its close, in a form of pantheism, which was accompanied, as is attested by the Atharva Veda, with a demonology and witch-craft religion, the latter presumably of high antiquity. Immediately after this come the esoteric Brāhmanas, in which the gods are, more or less, figures in the eyes of the priests, and the form of a Father-god rises into chief prominence, being sometimes regarded as the creative force, but at all times as the moral authority in the world. At the end of this period, however, and probably even before this period ended, there is for the first time, in the Upanishads, a new religion, that, in some regards, is esoteric. Hitherto the secrets of religious mysteries had been treated as hidden priestly wisdom, not to be revealed. But, for the most part, this wisdom is really nonsense; and when it is said in the Brāhmanas, at the end of a bit of theological mystery, that it is a secret, or that 'the gods love that which is secret,' one is not persuaded by the examples given that this esoteric knowledge is intellectually valuable. But with the Upanishads there comes the antithesis of inherited belief and right belief. The latter is public property, though it is not taught carelessly. The student is not initiated into the higher wisdom till he is drilled in the lower. The most unexpected characters appear in the rôle of instructors of priests, namely, women, kings, and members of the third caste, whose deeper wisdom is promulgated oftentimes as something quite new, and sometimes is whispered in secret. Pantheism, *samsāra*,[1] and the eternal bliss of the individual spirit when eventually it is freed from further transmigration, — these three fundamental traits of the new religion are discussed in such a way as to show that they had no hold upon the general public, but they were the intellectual wealth of a few. Some of the Upanishads hide behind a veil of mystery; yet many of them, as Windisch has said, are, in a way, popular; that is, they are intended for a general public, not for priests alone. This is especially the case with the pantheistic Upanishads in their more pronounced form. But still it is only the very wise that can accept the teaching. It is not the faith of the people.

Epic literature, which is the next living literature of the Brahmans, after the Upanishads, takes one, in a trice, from the beginnings of a formal pantheism, to a pantheism already disintegrated by the newer worship of sectaries. Here the impersonal *ātmā*, or nameless Lord, is not only an anthropomorphic Çiva, as in the late Upanishads, where the philosophic *brahma* is equated with a long recognized type of divinity, but *ātmā* is identified with the figure of a theomorphic man.

[1] Literally, transmigration, the doctrine of metempsychosis, successive births; first, as in Plato: *μεταβολή τις τυγχάνει οὖσα καὶ μετοίκησις τῇ ψυχῇ τοῦ τόπου τοῦ ἐνθένδε εἰς ἄλλον τόπον*; then *metabole*, from 'the other place,' back to earth; then, with advancing speculation, fresh *metabole* again, and so on; a theory more or less clumsily united with the hell-doctrine.

Is there, then, nothing with which to bridge this gulf?

In our opinion the religion of the law-books, as a legitimate phase of Hindu religion, has been too much ignored. The religion of Upanishad and Vedānta, with its attractive analogies with modern speculation, has been taken as illustrative of the religion of a vast period, to the discrediting of the belief represented in the manuals of law. To these certainly the name of literature can scarcely be applied, but in their rapport with ordinary life they will be found more apt than are the profounder speculations of the philosophers to reflect the religious belief taught to the masses and accepted by them.

The study of these books casts a broad light upon that interval between the Vedic and epic periods wherein it is customary to imagine religion as being, in the main, cult or philosophy. Nor does the interest cease with the yield of necessarily scanty yet very significant facts in regard to eschatological and cosmogonic views. The gods themselves are not what they are in the rites of the cunning priests or in the dogmas of the sages. In the Hindu law there is a reversion to Vedic belief; or rather not a reversion, but here one sees again, through the froth of rites and the murk of philosophy, the under-stream of faith that still flows from the old fount, if somewhat discolored, and waters the heart of the people.

At just what time was elaborated the stupendous system of rites, which are already traditional in the Brāhmanas, can never be known. Some of these rites have to do with special ceremonies, such as the royal inauguration, some are stated *soma*-sacrifices.[1] Opposed to these *soma*-feasts is the simpler and older fire-cult, which persists in the house-rituals. All of these together make up a sightly array of sacrifices.[2] The

[1] Weber has lately published two monographs on the sacrifices, the Rājasūya and the Vājapeya rites, both full of interesting details and popular features.

[2] The traditional sacrifices are twenty-one in number, divided into three classes of seven each. The formal divisions are (1) oblations of butter, milk, corn, etc.; (2) *soma* sacrifices; (3) animal sacrifices, regarded as part of the first two. The

soma-ritual is developed in the Brāhmanas. But with this class of works there must have been from ancient times another which treated of the fire-ritual, and of which the more modern representatives are the extant Sūtras. It is with Sūtras that legal literature begins, but these differ from the ritualistic Sūtras. Yet both are full of religious meat. In these collections, even in the more special, there is no arrangement that corresponds to western ideas of order. In a completed code, for example, there is a rough distribution of subjects under different heads, but the attempt is only tentative, and each work presents the appearance of a heterogeneous mass of regulations and laws, from which one must pick out the law for which he is seeking. The earlier legal works were in prose; the later evolved codes, of which there is a large number, in metre. It is in these two classes of house-ritual and law-ritual, which together constitute what is called Smriti, tradition-ritual (in distinction from the so-called Çruti, revelation-ritual), that one may expect to find the religion of the time; not as inculcated by the promoters of mystery, nor yet as disclosed by the philosopher, but as taught (through the priest) to the people, and as accepted by them for their daily guidance in matters of every-day observance. We glance first at the religious observances, for here, as in the case of the great sacrifices, a detailed examination would be of no more value than a collective impression; unless, indeed, one were hunting for folk-lore superstitions, of which we can treat now only in the mass. It is sufficient to understand that, according to the house-ritual (*gṛhya-sūtra*) and the law-ritual (*dharma-sūtra*, and *dharma-çāstra*),[1] for every change in life there was an appropriate ceremony and a religious observance; for every day, oblations (three at least); for every fortnight and

sacrifice of the new and full moon is to be repeated on each occasion for thirty years. A *sattra*, session, is a long sacrifice which may last a year or more.

1 The latter are the metrical codes, a part of Smriti (smṛti).

season, a sacrifice. Religious formulae were said over the child yet unborn. From the moment of birth he was surrounded with observances.[1] At such and such a time the child's head was shaved; he was taken out to look at the sun; made to eat from a golden spoon; invested with the sacred cord, etc., etc. When grown up, a certain number of years were passed with a Guru, or tutor, who taught the boy his Veda; and to whom he acted as body-servant (a study and office often cut short in the case of Aryans who were not priests). Of the sacraments alone, such as the observances to which we have just alluded, there are no less than forty according to Gautama's laws (the name-rite, eating-rite, etc.). The pious householder who had once set up his own fire, that is, got married, must have spent most of his time, if he followed directions, in attending to some religious ceremony. He had several little rites to attend to even before he might say his prayers in the morning; and since even to-day most of these personal regulations are dutifully observed, one may assume that in the full power of Brahmanhood they were very straitly enforced.[2]

It is, therefore, important to know what these works, so closely in touch with the general public, have to say in regard to religion. What they inculcate will be the popular theology of completed Brahmanism. For these books are intended to give instruction to all the Aryan castes, and, though this instruction filtrates through the hands of the priest, one may be sure that the understanding between king and priest was such as to make the code the real norm of justice and arbiter of religious opinions. For instance, when one reads that the king is a prime

[1] The Five Paramount Sacrifices (Observances) are, according to Manu iii. 70, study of the Veda (or teaching it): sacrifice to the Manes and to the gods; offerings of foods to ghosts (or spirits); and hospitality.

[2] In the report of the Or. Congress for 1880, p. 158 ff., Williams has a very interesting account of the daily rites of the modern orthodox Hindu ('*Rig Veda in Religious Service*').

divinity, and that, *quid pro quo*, the priest may be banished, but never may be punished corporally by the king, because the former is a still greater divinity, it may be taken for granted that such was received opinion. When we come to take up the Hinduism of the epic we shall point out that that work contains a religion more popular even than that of the legal literature, for one knows that this latter phase of religion was at first not taught at all, but grew up in the face of opposition. But for the present, before the rise of epic 'Hinduism,' and before taking up the heretical writings, it is a great gain to be able to scan a side of religion that may be called popular in so far as it evidently is the faith which not only was taught to the masses, but which, as is universally assumed in the law, the masses accept; whereas philosophers alone accept the *ātmā* religion of the Upanishads, and the Brāhmanas are not intended for the public at all, but only for initiated priests.

What, then, is the religious belief and the moral position of the Hindu law-books? In how far has philosophy affected public religion, and in what way has a reconciliation been affected between the contradictory beliefs in regard to the gods; in regard to the value of works on the one hand, and of knowledge on the other; in regard to hell as a means of punishment for sin on the one hand, and reincarnation (*saṁsāra*) on the other; in regard to heaven as a reward of good deeds on the one hand, and absorption into God on the other; in regard to a personal creator on the one hand, and a First Cause without personal attributes on the other?

For the philosophical treatises are known and referred to in the early codes; so that, although the completed systems post-dated the Sūtras, the cosmical and theological speculations of the earlier Upanishads were familiar to the authors of the legal systems.

The first general impression produced by a perusal of the law-books is that the popular religion has remained unaffected by philosophy. And this is correct in so far as that it must be put first in describing the codes, which, in the main, in keeping the ancient observances, reflect the inherited faith. When, therefore, one says that pantheism[1] succeeded polytheism in India, he must qualify the assertion. The philosophers are pantheists, but what of the vulgar? Do they give up polytheism; are they inclined to do so, or are they taught to do so? No. For there is no formal abatement in the rigor of the older creed. Whatever the wise man thought, and whatever in his philosophy was the instruction which he imparted to his peers, when he dealt with the world about him he taught his intellectual inferiors a scarcely modified form of the creed of their fathers. How in his own mind this wise man reconciled the two sets of opinion has been shown above. The works of sacrifice, with all the inherited belief implied by them, were for him preparatory studies. The elasticity of his philosophy admitted the whole world of gods, as a temporary reality, into his pantheistic scheme. It was, therefore, neither the hypocrisy of the Roman augur, nor the fear of results that in his teaching held him to the inheritance he had received. Gods, ghosts, demons, and consequently sacrifices, rites, ordeals, and formulae were not incongruous with his philosophical opinions. He himself believed in these spiritual powers and in the usefulness of serving them. It is true that he believed in their eventual doom, but so far as man was concerned they were practically real. There was, therefore, not only no reason why the sage should not inculcate the old rites, but there was every reason why he should. Especially in the case of pious but ignorant people, whose wisdom was not yet developed to a full appreciation of divine relativity, was it incumbent on him to keep them, the lower castes, to the one religion that they could comprehend.

[1] We ignore here the later distinction between the Vedānta and Sānkhya systems. Properly speaking, the latter is dualistic.

It is thus that the apparent inconsistency in exoteric and esoteric beliefs explains itself. For the two are not contradictory. They do not exclude each other. Hindu pantheism includes polytheism with its attendant patrolatry, demonology, and consequent ritualism.[1]

With rare exceptions it was only the grosser religion that the vulgar could understand; it was only this that they were taught and believed.

Thus the old Vedic gods are revered and worshipped by name. The Sun, Indra, and all the divinities embalmed in ritual, are placated and 'satiated' with offerings, just as they had been satiated from time immemorial. But no hint is given that this is a form; or that the Vedic gods are of less account than they had been. Moreover, it is not in the inherited formulae of the ritual alone that this view is upheld. To be sure, when philosophical speculation is introduced, the Father-god comes to the fore; Brahmā[2] sits aloft, indulgently advising his children, as he does in the intermediate stage of the Brāhmanas; and *ātmā* (*brahma*) too is recognized to be the real being of Brahmā, as in the Upanishads.[3] But none of this touches the practice of the common law, where the ordinary man is admonished to fear Yama's hell and Varuna's bonds, as he would have been admonished before the philosopher grew wiser than the Vedic seers. Only personified Right, Dharma, takes his seat with shadowy Brahmā among the other gods.[4]

[1] At a later date Buddha himself is admitted into the Brahmanic pantheon as an *avatar* of the All-god!

[2] Sometimes regarded as one with Prajāpati, and sometimes treated as distinct from him.

[3] Thus (for the priestly ascetic alone) in M. vi. 79: 'Leaving his good deeds to his loved ones and his evil deeds to his enemies, by force of meditation he goes to the eternal *brahma*.' Here *brahma*; but in Gautama perhaps Brahmā.

[4] That is, when the latter are grouped as in the following list. Our point is that, despite new faith and new gods, Vedic polytheism is taught not as a form but as a reality, and that in this period the people still believe as of old in the old gods, though they also acknowledge new ones (below).

What is the speech which the judge on the bench is ordered to repeat to the witnesses? Thus says the law-giver Manu: "When the witnesses are collected together in the court, in the presence of the plaintiff and defendant, the (Brahman) judge should call upon them to speak, kindly addressing them in the following manner: 'Whatever you know has been done in this affair . . . declare it all. A witness who in testifying speaks the truth reaches the worlds where all is plenty . . . such testimony is honored by Brahmā. One who in testifying speaks an untruth is, all unwilling, bound fast by the cords of Varuna,[1] till an hundred births are passed.' . . . (Then, speaking to one witness): 'Spirit (soul) is the witness for the Spirit, and the Spirit is likewise the refuge of the Spirit. Despise not, therefore, thine own spirit (or soul), the highest witness of man. Verily, the wicked think 'no one sees us,' but the gods are looking at them, and also the person within (conscience). *Dyaus, Earth, the Waters,* (the person in the) heart, *Moon, Sun. Fire, Yama, Wind, Night, the twin Twilights,* and Dharma know the conduct of all corporeal beings. . . . Although, O good man, thou regardest thyself, thinking, 'I am alone,' yet the holy one (saint) who sees the evil and the good, stands ever in thy heart. It is in truth god Yama, the son of Vivasvant, who resideth in thy heart; if thou beest not at variance with him (thou needest) not (to) go to the Ganges and to the (holy land of) the Kurus (to be purified).'"

Here there is no abatement in Vedic polytheism, although it is circled round with a thin mist from later teachings. In the same way the ordinary man is taught that at death his spirit (soul) will pass as a manikin out of his body and go to Yama to be judged; while the feasts to the Manes, of course, imply always the belief in the individual activity of dead ancestors. Such expressions as 'The seven daughters of

[1] Compare Manu, ix. 245: "Varuna is the lord of punishment and holdeth a sceptre (punishment) even over kings."

Varuna' (*sapta vāruṇīr imās*, Āçv. *Grih. S.* 2. 3. 3) show that even in detail the old views are still retained. There is no advance, except in superstitions,[1] on the main features of the old religion. So the same old fear of words is found, resulting in new euphemisms. One must not say 'scull,' *kapāla*, but call it *bhagāla*, 'lucky' (Gaut. 9. 21); a factor in the making of African languages also, according to modern travellers. Images of the gods are now over-recognized by the priest, for they must be revered like the gods themselves (*ib.* 12; Pār. *Grih. S.* 3. 14. 8. etc.). Among the developed objects of the cult serpents now occupy a prominent place. They are mentioned as worshipful in the Brāhmanas. In the Sūtra period offerings are made to snakes of earth, air, and heaven; the serpents are 'satiated' along with gods, plants, demons, etc. (Çāñkh. 4. 9. 3; 15. 4; Āçv. 2. 1. 9; 3. 4. 1; Pārask. 2. 14. 9) and blood is poured out to them (Āçv. 4. 8. 27).[2] But other later divinities than those of the earliest Veda, such as Wealth (Kubera), and Dharma, have crept into the ritual. With the Vedic gods appears as a divinity in Khād. 1. 5. 31 the love-god Kāma, of the Atharvan; while on the other hand Rudra the beast-lord (Paçupati, Lord of Cattle), the 'kindly' Çiva, appears as 'great god,' whose names are Çankara, Prishātaka, Bhava, Çarva, Ugra, Īçāna (Lord); who has all names and greatness, while he yet is described in the words of the older text as 'the god that desires to kill' (Āçv. 2. 2. 2: 4. 8. 9, 19,[3] 29, 32; *Ait. Br.* 3. 34). On the other hand Vishnu is also adored, and that in connection with the λόγος, or Vāc (*ib.* 3. 3. 4). Quite in Upanishad manner — for it is necessary to show that these

[1] In new rites, for instance. Thus in Pārask. *Grih. S.* 3. 7 a silly and dirty rite 'prevents a slave from running away'; and there is an ordeal for girls before becoming engaged (below).

[2] Blood is poured out to the demons in order that they may take this and no other part of the sacrifice. *Ait. Br.* ii. 7. 1.

[3] Here, 4. 8. 19. Çiva's names are Hara, Mrida, Çarva, Çiva, Bhava, Mahādeva, Ugra, Bhīma, Paçupati, Rudra, Çankara, Içāna.

were then really known — is the formula 'thou art a student of *prāṇa* (Breath,) and art given over to Ka' (*ib.* 1. 20. 8.), or '*whom?*' In Āçvalāyana no Upanishads are given in the list of literature, which includes the 'Eulogies of men,' Itihāsas, Purānas, and even the Mahābhārata (3. 3. 1; 4. 4). But in 1. 13. 1, *Upanishad-rites* (and that of a very domestic nature) are recognized, which would corroborate the explanation of Upanishad given above, as being at first a subsidiary work, dealing with minor points.[1] Something of the sciolism of the Upanishads seems to lie in the prayer that of the four paths on which walk the gods the mortal may be led in that which bestows 'freedom from death' (Pār. 3. 1. 2); and many of the teachers famous in the Upanishads are now revered by name like gods (Āçv. 3. 4. 4, etc.).

On turning from these domestic Sūtras to the legal Sūtras it becomes evident that the pantheistic doctrine of the Upanishads, and in part the Upanishads themselves, were already familiar to the law-makers, and that they influenced, in some degree, the doctrines of the law, despite the retention of the older forms. Not only is *samsāra* the accepted doctrine, but the *ātmā*, as if in a veritable Upanishad, is the object of religious devotion. Here, however, this quest is permitted only to the ascetic, who presumably has performed all ritualistic duties and passed through the stadia that legally precede his own.

Of all the legal Sūtra-writers Gautama is oldest, and perhaps is pre-buddhistic. Turning to his work one notices first that the Mīmāmsist is omitted in the list of learned men (28. 49);[2] but since the Upanishads and Vedānta are expressly mentioned, it is evident that the author of even the oldest Sūtra was

[1] These rites are described in 6. 4. 24 of the *Brihad Āranyaka Upanishad* which consists both of metaphysics and of ceremonial rules.

[2] Especially mentioned in the later Vasistha (see below); on *mīmāmsā* a branch of the Vedānta system see below.

acquainted with whatever then corresponded to these works.[1] The opposed teaching of hell versus *samsāra* is found in Gautama. But there is rather an interesting attempt to unite them. Ordinarily it is to hell and heaven that reference is made, *e.g.*, 'the one that knows the law obtains the heavenly world' (28. 52); 'if one speak untruth to a teacher, even in thought, even in respect to little things, he slays seven men after and before him' (seven descendants and seven ancestors, 23. 31). So in the case of witnesses: 'heaven (is the fruit) for speaking the truth; otherwise hell' (13. 7); 'for stealing (land) hell' (is the punishment, *ib.* 17). Now and then comes the philosophical doctrine: 'one does not fall from the world of Brahmā' (9. 74); 'one enters into union and into the same world with Brahmā' (8. 25).

But in 21. 4–6 there occurs the following statement: 'To be an outcast is to be deprived of the works of the twice-born, and hereafter to be deprived of happiness; this some (call) hell.' It is evident here that the expression *asiddhis* (deprivation of success or happiness) is placed optionally beside *naraka* (hell) as the view of one set of theologians compared with that of another; 'lack of obtaining success, *i.e.*, reward' stands parallel to 'hell.' In the same chapter, where Manu says that he who assaults a Brahman "obtains hell for one hundred years" (M. xi. 207), Gautama (21. 20) says "for one hundred years, lack of heaven" (*asvargyam*), which may mean hell or the deprivation of the result of merit, *i.e.*, one hundred years will be deducted from his heavenly life. In this case not a new and better birth but heaven is assumed to be the reward of good acts. Now if one turns to 11. 29–30 he finds both views combined. In the parallel passage in Āpastamba

[1] The commentator here (19. 12, cited by Bühler) defines Vedānta as the part of the Āranyakas which are not Upanishads, that is, apparently as a local 'Veda-end' (*veda-anta*), though this meaning is not admitted by some scholars, who will see in *anta* only the meaning 'goal, aim.'

only better or worse re-births are promised as a reward for good or evil (2. 5. 11. 10–11); but here it is said: "The castes and orders that remain by their duty, having died, having enjoyed the fruits of their acts, with the remnant of their (merit) obtain re-birth, having an excellent country, caste, and family; having long life, learning, good conduct, wealth, happiness, and wisdom. They of different sort are destroyed in various ways." Here, heavenly joys (such as are implied by *niḥçreyasam* in 26) are to be enjoyed first, and a good birth afterwards, and by implication one probably has to interpret the next sentence to mean 'they are sent to hell and then re-born in various low births.' This, too, is Manu's rule (below). At this time the sacred places which purify are in great vogue, and in Gautama a list of them is given (19. 14), viz.: "all mountains, all rivers, holy pools, places of pilgrimage (*i.e.*, river-fords, *tīrthāni*), homes of saints, cow-pens, and altars." Of these the *tīrthas* are particularly interesting, as they later become of great importance, thousands of verses in the epic being devoted to their enumeration and praise.

Gautama says also that ascetics, according to some teachers, need not be householders first (3. 1), and that the Brahman ascetic stays at home during the rainy season, like the heretic monks (*ib.* 13). If one examine the relative importance of the forms and spirit of religion as taught in this, the oldest *dharma-sūtra*,[1] he will be impressed at first with the tremendous weight laid on the former as compared with the latter. But, as was said apropos of the Brahmanic literature, one errs who fails to appreciate the fact that these works are intended not to give a summary of religious conduct, but to inculcate ceremonial rules. Of the more importance, therefore, is the occasional pause which is made to insist, beyond peradventure, on the superiority of moral rules. A very good instance of this is found in Gautama. He has a list of venial sins. Since lying

[1] The Rudra (Çiva) invocation at 26. 12 ff. is interpolated, according to Bühler.

is one of the most heinous offences to a Hindu lawgiver, and the penances are severe, all the treatises state formally that an untruth uttered in fun, or when one is in danger, or an oath of the sort implied by Plato: ἀφροδίσιον ὅρκον οὔ φασιν εἶναι, — all these are venial, and so are lies told to benefit a (holy) cow, or to aid a priest; or told from religious motives of any sort without self-interest. This is almost the only example of looseness in morals as taught in the law. But the following case shows most plainly the importance of morality as opposed to formal righteousness. After all the forty sacraments (to which allusion was made above), have been recounted, there are given 'eight good qualities of the soul,' viz., mercy, forbearance, freedom from envy, purity, calmness, correct behavior, freedom from greed and from covetousness. Then follows: "He that has (performed) the forty sacraments but has not the eight good qualities enters not into union with Brahmā, nor into the heaven of Brahmā.[1] But he that has (performed) only a part of the forty sacraments and has the eight good qualities enters into union with Brahmā, and into the heaven of Brahmā." This is as near to heresy as pre-buddhistic Brahmanism permitted itself to come.

In the later legal Sūtra of the northern Vasistha[2] occurs a rule which, while it distinctly explains what is meant by liberality, viz., gifts to a priest, also recognizes the 'heavenly reward': "If gifts are given to a man that does not know the Veda the divinities are not satisfied" (3. 8). In the same work (6. 1) 'destruction' is the fate of the sinner that lives without ob-

[1] Here there is plainly an allusion to the two states of felicity of the Upanishads. Whether the law-giver believes that the spirit will be united with Brahmā or simply live in his heaven he does not say.

[2] Gautama, too, is probably a Northerner. The Sūtra, it should be observed, are not so individual as would be implied by the name of the teachers to whom they are credited. They were each texts of a school, *caraṇa*, but they are attributed uniformly to a special teacher, who represents the *caraṇa*, as has been shown by Müller. For what is known in regard to the early 'Sūtra-makers' see Bühler's Introductions to volumes ii. and xiv. of the Sacred Books.

servance of good custom; yet is it said in the same chapter (27): "If a twice-born man dies with the food of a Çūdra (lowest caste) in his belly, he would become a village pig, or he is born again in that (Çūdra's) family"; and, in respect to sons begotten when he has in him such food: "Of whom the food, of him are these sons; and he himself would not mount to heaven . . . he does not find the upward path" (29, 28). In *ib.* 8. 17 the Brahman that observes all the rules 'does not fall from *brahmaloka*,' *i.e.*, the locality of Brahmā. Further, in 10. 4: "Let (an ascetic) do away with all (sacrificial) works; but let him not do away with one thing, the Veda; for from doing away with the Veda (one becomes) a Çudra." But, in the same chapter: "Let (the ascetic) live at the end of a village, in a temple ('god's house'), in a deserted house, or at the root of a tree; there in his mind studying the knowledge (of the *ātmā*) . . . so they cite (verses): 'Sure is the freedom from re-birth in the case of one that lives in the wood with passions subdued . . . and meditates on the supreme spirit' . . . Let him not be confined to any custom . . . and in regard to this (freedom from wordly pursuits) they cite these verses: 'There is no salvation (literally 'release') for a philologist (*na çabdaçāstrābhiratasya mokshas*), nor for one that delights in catching (men) in the world, nor for one addicted to food and dress, nor for one pleased with a fine house. By means of prodigies, omens, astrology, palmistry, teaching, and talking let him not seek alms . . . he best knows salvation who (cares for naught)' . . . (such are the verses). Let him neither harm nor do good to anything. . . . Avoidance of disagreeable conduct, jealousy, presumption, selfishness, lack of belief, lack of uprightness, self-praise, blame of others, harm, greed, distraction, wrath, and envy, is a rule that applies to all the stadia of life. The Brahman that is pure, and wears the girdle, and carries the gourd in his hand, and avoids the food of low castes fails not of obtaining the world of Brahmā" (*ib.* 10. 18 ff.). Yama, the Manes, and evil spirits (*asuras*) are referred to in the following chapter (20, 25); and hell in the same chapter is declared to be the portion of such ascetics as will not eat meat when requested to do so at a feast to the Manes or gods (11. 34), — rather an interesting verse, for in Manu's code the corresponding threat is that, instead of going to hell 'for as long, *i.e.*, as many years, as the beast has hairs,' as here, one shall experience 'twenty-one rebirths,' *i.e.*, the hell-doctrine in terms of *samsāra;* while the same image occurs in Manu in the form 'he that slaughters beasts unlawfully obtains as many rebirths as there are hairs on the beast' (v. 35. 38). The passive attitude sometimes ascribed to the Manes is denied; they rejoice over a virtuous descendant (11. 41); a bad one deprives them of the heaven they stand in (16. 36). The authorities on morals are here, as elsewhere, Manu and other seers, the Vedas, and the Father-god, who with Yama gives directions to man in regard to lawful food, etc. (14. 30). The moral side of the code, apart from ritual impurities, is given, as usual, by a list of good and bad qualities (above), while formal laws in regard to theft, murder (especially of a priest), adultery and drunkenness (20. 44; 1. 20), with violation of caste-regulations by intercourse with outcasts, are 'great crimes.' Though older than Āpastamba, who mentions the Pūrva-mīmāṁsā, Vasistha, too, knows the Vedānta (3. 17), and the Mīmāṁsā (*vikalpin* = *tarkin*, 3. 20, M. xii. 111

From the Sūtras of Bāudhāyana's probably southern school something of additional interest is to be gained. Here 'darkness' takes the place of hell (2. 3. 5. 9), which, however, by a citation is explained (in 2. 2. 3. 34) as 'Yama's hall.' A verse is cited to show that the greatest sin is lack of faith (1. 5. 10. 6) and not going to heaven is the reward of folly (*ib.* 7); while the reward of virtue is to live in heaven for long (4. 8. 7). The same freedom in regard to ascetics as occurs in other Sūtra works is to be found in this author, not in the more suspicious final chapters, but in that part of the work which is accepted as oldest,[1] and agrees with the data found in the Brāhmanas, where the pre-buddhistic monk is called Bhikshu, 'beggar,' or Sannyāsin 'he that renounces,' just as these terms are employed in the heretical writings. As among the Jains (and Buddhists), the Brahmanic ascetic carries a few simple utensils, and wanders about from house to house and village to village, begging food. Some authorities (among the Brahmans) say that one may become an ascetic as soon as he has completed his study, though ordinarily this may be done only after passing through the householder stadium. On becoming an ascetic the beggar takes the vow not to injure any living thing (Bāudh. ii. 10. 17. 2. 11, 29), exactly as the Jain ascetic takes the vow of non-injury. More than this, as will be seen below, the details of the Brahman ascetic's vows are almost identical with those of the Jain ascetic. He vows not to injure living beings, not to lie, not to steal, to be continent, to be liberal; with the five minor vows, not to get angry, to obey the Teacher, not to be rash, to be cleanly and pure in eating.[2] To this ascetic order in the Brahman priesthood may be traced the origin of the heretical monks. Even in the Brāhmanas occur the termini technici of the Buddhist priesthood, notably the Çramana or ascetic monk, and the word *buddha*, 'awakened' (*pratibudh*). The 'four orders' are those enumerated as the householder, student, ascetic, and forest-hermit. If one live in all four orders according to rule, and be serene, he will come to peace, that is, salvation (Āpastamba, 2. 9. 21. 1, 2).

According to this later legal writer, who belongs to Southern India,[3] it is only after one has passed through all the preceding

[1] Compare Bühler's Introduction, p. xxxv. SBE. vol. xiv.

[2] Bāudh. ii. 18. 2-3. Compare Jacobi's Introduction, p. xxiii ff. of SBE. vol. xxii.

[3] Bühler (Introduction, p. xxxi) gives as the district of the Āpastambīya school parts of the Bombay Presidency, the greater parts of the Nizām's possessions, and parts of the Madras Presidency. Apastamba himself refers to Northerners as if they were foreigners (*loc. cit.*).

stadia that he may give up works (sacrifice, etc.) and devote himself to seeking the *ātmā*, 'wandering about, without caring for earth or heaven, renouncing truth and falsehood, pleasure and pain' (*ib.* 10, 13). There follows this passage one significant of the opposition between purely Upanishad-ideas and those of the law-givers: 'Acquirement of peace (salvation) depends, it is said, on knowledge; this is opposed by the codes. If on knowledge (depended) acquirement of peace, even here (in this world) one would escape grief' (*ib.* 14–16). Further, in describing the forest-hermit's austerities (*ib.* 23. 4 ff.), verses from a Purāna are cited which are virtually Upanishadic: 'The eight and eighty thousand seers who desired offspring (went) south on Aryaman's path, and obtained (as their reward) graves; (but) the eight and eighty thousand who did not desire offspring (went) north on Aryaman's path and make for themselves immortality,' that is to say 'abandon desire for offspring; and of the two paths (which, as the commentator observes, are mentioned in the Chāndogya Upanishad), that which gives immortality instead of death (graves) will be yours.' It is admitted that such ascetics have miraculous powers; but the law-maker emphatically protests in the following Sūtra against the supposition that a rule which stands opposed to the received rites (marriage, sacrifice, etc.) is of any power, and asserts that for the future life an endless reward ('fruit'), called in revelation 'heavenly,' is appointed (*ib.* 8–11). The next chapter, however, limits, as it were, this dogma, for it is stated that immortality is the re-birth of one's self in the body of one's son, and a verse is cited: 'Thou procreatest progeny, and that's thy immortality, O mortal,' with other verses, which teach that sons that attend to the Vedic rites magnify the fame and heaven of their ancestors, who 'live in heaven until the destruction of creation' (*ā bhūtasaṁplavāt*, 2. 9. 24. 5). But 'according to the Bhavishyat-Purāna' after this destruction of creation 'they exist again in heaven as the cause of seed' (*ib.* 6). And then follows a quotation from the Father-god: 'We live with those people who do these (following) things: (attend to) the three Vedas, live as students, create children, sacrifice to the Manes, do penance, make sacrifice to the gods, practice liberality; he that extols anything else becomes air (or dust) and perishes' (*ib.* 8); and further: 'only they that commit sin perish' (not their ancestors).

The animus of this whole passage is apparent. The law-maker has to contend with them that would reject the necessity of following in order the traditional stadia of a priest's life; that imagine that by becoming ascetics without first having passed through the preliminary stadia they can by knowledge alone attain the bliss that is obtained by union with *brahma* (or Brahmā). In other words the jurist has to contend with a trait eminently anti-brahmanistic, even Buddhistic. He denies this value of knowledge, and therewith shows that what he wishes to have inculcated is a belief in the temporary personal existence of the Manes; in heaven till the end of the world-order; and the annihilation of the wicked; while he has a confused or mixed opinion in regard to one's own personal immortality, believing on the one hand that there is a future existence in heaven with the gods, and on the other (rather a materialistic view) that immortality is nothing but continued existence in the person of one's descendants, who are virtually one's self in another body: *dehatvam evā'nyat*, "only the body is different" (*ib.* 2). As to cosmogony it is stated to be (not the emanation of an *ātmā*) but the "emission (creation) of the Father-god and of the seers" (the latter being visible as stars, *ib.* 13, 14). In this there is plainly a received popular opinion, which reflects the Vedic and Brahmanic stage, and is opposed to the philosophical views of the Upanishads, in other words of the first Vedantic philosophy; while it is mixed up with the late doctrine of the cataclysms, which ruin each succeeding creation. The equal annihilation of the wicked (*dhvamsanti*) and unorthodox (*dhvamsate*) is to be noticed. They are here subject neither to hell nor to rebirth, but they "become dust and perish" (*ib.* 8, 9).

Throughout the whole legal literature one will find this same antithesis of views in regard to the fate of good and bad, although it is seldom that annihilation is predicated of the latter. Usually hell or rebirth are their fate — two views, which no one can really reconcile. They are put side by side; exactly as in priestly discussion in India and Europe it still remains an unsettled question as to when the soul becomes immortal.[1] Occidental experience teaches how easy it is for such views to stand together unattacked, although they are the object of speculation. This passage is perhaps, historically, the most satisfactory (as it is philosophically unsatisfactory) that can be cited in answer to the questions that were posed above. But from other parts of legal literature a few more statements may be culled, to illustrate still further the lack of uniformity not only in popular belief, but in the teaching provided for the public. First from the same work of Āpastamba, in 2. 11. 29. 9–10 it is said that if a witness in court perjure himself he shall be punished by the king, "and further, in passing to the next world, hell" (is his portion); whereas "(the reward) for truth is heaven, and praise on the part of all creatures." Now, let one compare first *ib.* 2. 5. 11. 10–11: "Men of low castes are reborn in higher castes in successive births, and men of high castes in low castes, if they respectively perform and neglect their duties." And then this Vedantic passage of the same author (1. 8. 22 ff.): "Let one (as penance for sin) devote himself to the Yoga (mental discipline) which has to do with the highest *ātmā*. . . . Nothing is known higher than the acquisition of *ātmā*. We shall (now)

[1] In India the latter question is: does the soul immediately at death unite with the *ātmā* or does it travel to it. In Europe: does the soul wait for the Last Day, or get to heaven immediately? Compare Maine, *Early Law and Custom*, p. 71.

cite some *ātmā*-acquisition-verses, viz.: All living creatures (are) the citadel of him that rests in secret, the indestructible one, the immaculate one. Immortal they that devote themselves to the moveless one who has a movable dwelling . . . the great one whose body is light, universal, free . . . the eternal (part) in all creatures, the wise, immortal, unchanging one, limbless, voiceless, formless, touchless, purest, the highest goal. He that everywhere devotes himself to Him (*ātmā* as Lord), and always lives accordingly; that by virtue of Yoga recognizes Him, the subtile one, shall rejoice in the top of heaven. . . . He, *ātmā*, comprehends all, embraces all, more subtile than a lotus-thread and huger than the earth. . . . From him are created all bodies; he is the root, he the Everlasting, the Eternal One."

This discipline it will be observed is enjoined as penance and to get rid of faults, that is, to subdue the passions. As the same chapter contains a list of the faults which are to be overcome before one "arrives at peace" (salvation) they may be cited here: "Anger, joy, wrath, greed, distraction, injury, threats, lying, over-eating, calumny, envy, sexual desire, and hate, lack of studying *ātmā*, lack of Yoga — the destruction of these (faults) is based on Yoga" (mental concentration). On the other hand: "He that devotes himself, in accordance with the law, to avoiding anger, joy, wrath, greed, distraction, injury, threats, lies, over-eating, calumny and envy; and practices liberality, renunciation, uprightness, kindness, subduing (of the passions), self-control; and is at peace with all creatures; and practices Yoga; and acts in an Āryan (noble) way; and does not hurt anything; and has contentment — qualities which, it is agreed, appertain to all the (four) stadia — he becomes *sārvagāmin*" (*ib.* 23. 6), that is 'one belonging to the all-pervading' (All-soul). There appears to be a contradiction between the former passage, where Yoga is enjoined on ascetics alone; and this, where Yoga is part of the discipline of all four stadia. But what was in the author's mind was probably that all these vices and moral virtues are enumerated as such for all; and he slips in mental concentration as a virtue for the ascetic, meaning to include all the virtues he knows.

A few further illustrations from that special code which has won for itself a preëminent name, 'the law-book of Manu,'[1] will give in epitome the popular religion as taught to the masses; withal even better than this is taught in the Sūtras. For Father Manu's law-book, as the Hindus call it, is a popular Çāstra or metrical[2] composite of law and religion, which reflects the opinion of Brahmanism in its geographical stronghold, whereas the Sūtras emanate from various localities, north and south. To Manu there is but one Holy Land, the Kurus' plain and the region round-about it (near Delhi).

The work takes us forward in time beyond even the latest Sūtras, but the content is such as to show that formal Brahmanism in this latest stage still keeps to its old norm and to Brahmanic models.

It deserves therefore to be examined with care from several points of view if one would escape from the belief of the philosopher to the more general teaching. In this popular religion all morality is conditioned by the castes,[3] which is true also to a certain degree of the earlier Sūtras, but the evil fruit of this plant is not there quite so ripe as it is in the later code. The enormity of all crimes depends on who commits them, and against whom they are committed. The three upper castes

[1] Thought by some scholars to have been developed out of the code of the Mānavas; but ascribed by the Hindus to Father Manu, as are many other verses of legal character contained in the epic and elsewhere.

[2] Although Sūtras may be metrical too in part, yet is the complete metrical form, as in the case of still later Çāstra, evidence that the work is intended for the general public.

[3] The priest alone, in the post-Vedic age, has the right to teach the sacred texts; he has immunity from bodily punishment; the right to receive gifts, and other special privileges. The three upper castes have each the right and duty of studying the sacred texts for a number of years.

alone have religious privileges. The lowest caste, outcasts, women, and diseased persons are not allowed to hear the holy texts or take part in ceremonies.[1] As to the rites, they are the inherited ones, sacrifices to gods, offerings to Manes and spirits, and all the ceremonies of house and individual, as explained above; with especial and very minute rules of observance for each of the four stadia of a priest's life.[2] There is no hint in any of this of the importance of the knowledge of the *ātmā*. But in their proper place the rules of morality and the higher philosophical views are taught. The doctrine of re-birth is formally stated, and the attainment of the world of Brahmā (*brahma*) by union of ceremonies and knowledge is inculcated. The ascetic should seek, by meditation, to go to Brahmā (or *brahma*) for when he is utterly indifferent, then, both here and after death, he gains everlasting happiness. Therefore he should study the Vedas, but especially the teachings in regard to the Supreme Spirit, and the Upanishads; studying the Vedānta is a regular part of his final discipline (vi. 74–94). In another part of the work the distinction made in the Upanishads is upheld, that religious acts are of two sorts, one designed to procure bliss, and cause a good man to reach equality with the gods; the other performed without selfish motive; by which latter "even the five elements are overcome," that is, the absorption into *brahma* is effected. For "among all virtuous acts the knowledge of the spirit, *ātmā*, is highest; through this is obtained even immortality. One that sees spirit in all things and all things in spirit sacrifices to spirit and enters Brahmā (or *brahma*)." "The spirit (or self) is all

[1] Weber has shown, *loc. cit.*, that the Çūdras did attend some of the more popular ceremonies, and at first apparently even took a part in them.

[2] The 'four orders' or stadia of a priest's life, student, householder, hermit, ascetic, must not be confused with the 'four (political) orders' (castes), priest, warrior, farmer, slave — to which, from time to time, were added many 'mixed castes' as well as 'outcasts,' and natural pariahs. At the time of Manu's code there were already many of these half-assimilated groups.

divinities; the All is based on spirit." And in Upanishadic vein the Person is then proclaimed as lord of gods, whom "some call fire, some call Manu, some call Indra, some call air, and some call eternal *brahma*." But though this be the view of the closing verses, yet in the beginning of the work is this Person represented as being produced from a First Cause. It would be out of place here to analyse the conflicting philosophical views of the Manu code. Even his commentators are uncertain whether he belonged to the pantheistic Vedānta or dualistic Sānkhya school. For them that believe in no Manu the solution is simpler. Although Manu is usually called a Puranic Sankhyan, yet are both schools represented, and that without regard to incongruous teaching. Manu is no more Sankhyan than Vedantic. Indeed in the main part of the work the teaching is clearly more Vedantic. But it suffices here to point out that the *ātmā*-philosophy and religion is not ignored: it is taught as essential. Nevertheless, it is not taught in such a way as to indicate that it is requisite for the vulgar. On the contrary, it is only when one becomes an ascetic that he is told to devote himself to the pursuit of the knowledge of *ātmā*. In one passage there is evidence that two replies were given to this fundamental question in regard to works and knowledge. For after enumerating a list of good acts, among which are knowledge and Vedic ceremonies, it is asked which among them most tends to deliverance. The answer is vital. Or it should be, but it is given in an ambiguous form (xii. 85–6): "Amid all these acts the knowledge of self, *ātmā*, is the highest, for it produces immortality. Amid all these acts the one most productive of happiness, both after death and in this life, is the Vedic ceremony."

Knowledge gives real immortality; rites give temporary bliss. The Upanishads teach that the latter is lower than the former, but each answers the question. There were two answers, and Manu gives both. That is the secret of many discrepancies in Hindu rules. The law-giver cannot admit absolutely and once for all that the Vedic ceremony is of no abiding use, as it can be of no use to one that accepts the higher teaching. He keeps it as a training and allows only the ascetic to be a philosopher indeed. But at the same time he gives as a sort of peroration to his treatise some 'elegant extracts' from philosophical works, which he believes theoretically, although practically he will not allow them to influence his ritualism. He is a true Brahman priest.

It is this that is always so annoying in Brahmanic philosophy. For the slavery of tradition is everywhere. Not only does the ritualist, while admitting the force of the philosopher's reasons, remain by Vedic tradition, and in consequence refuse to supplant 'revelation' with the higher wisdom and better religion, which he sees while he will not follow it; but even the philosopher must needs be 'orthodox,' and, since the scriptures themselves are self-contradictory, he is obliged to use his energies not in discovering truth, but in reconciling his ancestors' dogmas, in order to the creation of a philosophical system which shall agree with everything that has been said in the Vedas and Upanishads. When one sees what subtlety and logical acumen these philosophers possessed, he is moved to wonder what might have been the outcome had their minds been as free as those of more liberal Hellas. But unfortunately they were bound to argue within limits, and were as much handicapped in the race of thought as were they that had to conform to the teachings of Rome. For though India had no church, it had an inquisitorial priestly caste, and the unbeliever was an outcast. What is said of custom is true of faith: "Let one walk in the path of good men, the path in which his father walked, in which his grandfathers walked; walking in that path one does no wrong" (Manu iv. 178). Real philosophy, unhampered by tradition, is found only among the heretics and in the sects of a later time.

The gods of old are accepted by the orthodox as a matter of course, although theoretically they are born of the All-god, who is without the need of ceremonial rites. To the other castes the active and most terrible deity is represented as being the priest himself. He not only symbolizes the fire-god, to whom is offered the sacrifice, but he actually is the divinity in person. Hence there is no greater merit than in giving gifts to priests. As to eschatology, opinions are not contrasted any more. They are put side by side. In morality truth, purity, and harmlessness are chiefly inculcated. But the last (ascribed by some scholars to Buddhistic influence) is not permitted to interfere with animal sacrifices.

Some of the rules for the life of a householder will show in brief the moral excellence and theoretical uncertainty of Manu's law-code. The following extracts are from the fourth, the Ten Commandments from the sixth, and the description of the hells (twenty-two in all)[1] from the fourth and twelfth books of Manu's code. These rules may be accepted as a true reflexion of what was taught to the people by stringent Brahmanism as yet holding aloof from Hinduism.

A householder must live without giving any pain (to living creatures). He must perform daily the ceremonies ordained in the Veda. In this way he obtains heaven. Let him never neglect the offerings to seers, gods, spirits (sprites), men, and Manes. Some offer sacrifice only in their organs of sense (not in external offerings); some by knowledge alone. Let him not explain law and rites to the Çūdra (slave) caste; if he does so, he sinks into the hell Boundless. Let him not take presents from an avaricious king who disobeys the law-codes; if he does so, he goes to twenty-one hells (called Darkness, Dense-darkness, Frightful, Hell, Thread of Death, Great Hell, Burning, Place of Spikes, Frying-pan, River of Hell, etc., etc., etc.). Let him never despise a warrior, a snake, or a priest. Let

[1] Theoretically, twenty-one; but an extra one has slipped in by mistake.

him never despise himself. Let him say what is true and what is agreeable, but not disagreeable truth or agreeable falsehood. Let him not dispute with anybody, but let him say 'very well.' Let him not insult anybody. Remembering his former births, and studying the Veda again and again, he gets endless happiness. Let him avoid unbelief and censure of the Vedas, reviling of gods, hatred, pride, anger, and cruelty. He that even threatens a priest will go to the hell Darkness for one hundred years; if he strikes him he will be born in twenty-one sinful rebirths (according to another passage in the eleventh book he goes to hell for a thousand years for the latter offence). Priests rule the world of gods. But deceitful, hypocritical priests go to hell. Let the householder give gifts, and he will be rewarded. One that gives a garment gets a place in the moon; a giver of grain gets eternal happiness; a giver of the Veda gets union with Brahmā (*brahma;* these gifts, of course, are all to priests). He that gives respectfully and he that receives respectfully go to heaven; otherwise both go to hell. Let him, without giving pain to any creature, slowly pile up virtue, as does an ant its house, that he may have a companion in the next world. For after death neither father, nor mother, nor son, nor wife, nor relations are his companions; his virtue alone remains with him. The relations leave the dead body, but its virtue follows the spirit: with his virtue as his companion he will traverse the darkness that is hard to cross; and virtue will lead him to the other world with a luminous form and etherial body. A priest that makes low connections is reborn as a slave. The Father-god permits a priest to accept alms even from a bad man. For fifteen years the Manes refuse to accept food from one that despises a free gift. A priest that sins should be punished (that is, mulcted, a priest may not be punished corporally), more than an ordinary man, for the greater the wisdom the greater the offence. They that commit the Five Great Sins live many years in hells, and afterwards obtain vile births; the slayer of a priest becomes in turn a dog, a pig, an ass, a camel, a cow, a goat, a sheep, etc., etc. A priest that drinks intoxicating liquor becomes various insects, one after another. A priest that steals becomes a spider, snake, etc., etc. By repeating sinful acts men are reborn in painful and base births, and are hurled about in hells; where are sword-leaved trees, etc., and where they are eaten, burned, spitted, and boiled; and they receive births in despicable wombs; rebirth to age, sorrow, and unquenchable death. But to secure supreme bliss a priest must study the Veda, practice austerity, seek knowledge, subdue the senses, abstain from injury, and serve his Teacher. Which of these gives highest bliss? The knowledge of the spirit is the highest and foremost, for it gives immortality. The performance of Vedic ceremonies is the most productive of happiness here and hereafter. The Ten Commandments for the twice-born are: Contentment, patience, self-control, not to steal, purity, control of passions, devotion (or wisdom), knowledge, truthfulness, and freedom from anger. These are concisely summarized again in the following: 'Manu declared the condensed rule of duty for (all) the four castes to be: not to injure a living thing: to speak the truth; not to steal; to be pure; to control the passions' (vi. 92; x. 63). The 'non-injury' rule does not apply, of course, to sacrifice (*ib.* iii. 268). In the epic the commandments are given sometimes as ten, sometimes as eight.

In order to give a completed exposition of Brahmanism we have passed beyond the period of the great heresies, to which we must soon revert. But, before leaving the present division of the subject, we select from the mass of Brahmanic domestic rites, the details of which offer in general little that is worth noting, two or three ceremonies which possess a more human interest, the marriage rite, the funeral rite, and those strange trials, known among so many other peoples, the ordeals. We sketch these briefly, wishing merely to illustrate the religious side of each ceremony, as it appears in one or more of its features.

THE MARRIAGE RITE.

Traces of exogamy may be suspected in the bridegroom's driving off with his bride, but no such custom, of course, is recognized in the law. On the contrary, the groom is supposed to belong to the same village, and special rites are enjoined 'if he be from another village.' But again, in the early rule there is no trace of that taint of family which the totem-scholars of to-day cite so loosely from Hindu law. The girl is not precluded because she belongs to the same family within certain degrees. The only restriction in the House-rituals is that she shall have had "on the mother's and father's side" wise, pious, and honorable ancestors for ten generations (Āçvl. i. 5). Then comes the legal restriction, which some scholars call 'primitive,' that the wife must not be too nearly related. The girl has her own ordeal (not generally mentioned among ordeals!): The wooer that thus selects his bride (this he does if one has not been found already either by his parents or by his own inclination) makes eight balls of earth and calls on the girl to choose one ('may she get that to which she is born'). If she select a ball made from the earth of a field that bears two crops, she (or her child) will be rich in grain; if from the cow-stall, rich in cattle; if from the place of sacrifice, godly; if from a pool that does not dry, gifted; if from the gambler's court, devoted to gambling; if from cross-roads, unfaithful; if from a barren field, poor in grain; if from the burying-ground, destructful of her husband. There are several forms of making a choice, but we confine ourselves to the marriage.[1] In village-life the bride-

[1] The girl is given or bought, or may make her own choice among different suitors. Buying a wife is reprehended by the early law-givers (therefore, customary). The rite of marriage presupposes a grown girl, but child-marriages also were known to the early law.

groom is escorted to the girl's house by young women who tease him. The bridegroom presents presents to the bride, and receives a cow. The bridegroom takes the bride's hand, saying 'I take thy hand for weal' (Rig Veda, x. 85. 36), and leads her to a certain stone, on which she steps first with the right foot (toe). Then three times they circumambulate the fire, keeping it to the right, an old Aryan custom for many rites, as in the *deisel* of the Kelts; the bride herself offering grain in the fire, and the groom repeating more Vedic verses. They then take together the seven solemn steps (with verses),[1] and so they are married. The groom, if of another village, now drives away with the bride, and has ready Vedic verses for every stage of the journey. After sun-down the groom points out the north star, and admonishes the bride to be no less constant and faithful. Three or twelve days they remain chaste, some say one night; others say, only if he be from another village. The new husband must now see to the house-fire, which he keeps ever burning, the sign of his being a householder.

THE FUNERAL CEREMONY.

Roth has an article in the Journal of the German Oriental Society (viii. 467) which is at once a description of one of the funeral hymns of the Rig Veda (x. 18) with the later ritual, and a criticism of the bearing of the latter on the former.[2] He shows here that the ritual, so far from having induced the hymn, totally changes it. The hymn was written for a burial ceremony. The later ritual knows only cremation. The ritual,

[1] The groom 'releases her from Varuna's fetter,' by symbolically loosening the hair. They step northeast, and he says: 'One step for sap; two for strength; three for riches: four for luck; five for children; six for the seasons; seven for friendship. Be true to me; may we have many long-lived sons.'

[2] There is another funeral hymn, x. 16, in which the Fire is invoked to burn the dead, and bear him to the fathers; his corporeal parts being distributed 'eye to the sun, breath to the wind,' etc.

therefore, forces the hymn into its service, and makes it a cremation-hymn. This is a very good (though very extreme) example of the difference in age between the early hymns of the Rig Veda and the more modern ritual. Müller, *ib.* ix. p. I (*sic*), has given a thorough account of the later ritual and ritualistic paraphernalia. We confine ourselves here to the older ceremony.

The scene of the Vedic hymn is as follows: The friends and relatives stand about the corpse of a married man. By the side of the corpse sits the widow. The hymn begins: "Depart, O Death, upon some other pathway, upon thy path, which differs from the path of gods . . . harm not our children, nor our heroes. . . . These living ones are separated from the dead; successful to-day was our call to the gods. (This man is dead, but) *we* go back to dancing and to laughter, extending further our still lengthened lives." Then the priest puts a stone between the dead and living: "I set up a wall for the living, may no one of these come to this goal; may they live an hundred full harvests, and hide death with this stone. . . ."

The matrons assembled are now bid to advance without tears, and make their offerings to the fire, while the widow is separated from the corpse of her husband and told to enter again into the world of the living. The priest removes the dead warrior's bow from his hand: "Let the women, not widows, advance with the ointment and holy butter; and without tears, happy, adorned, let them, to begin with, mount to the altar (verse 7, p. 274, below). Raise thyself, woman, to the world of the living; his breath is gone by whom thou liest; come hither; of the taker of thy hand (in marriage), of thy wooer thou art become the wife[1] (verse 8). I take the bow from the hand of the dead for our (own) lordship, glory, and strength." Then he addresses the dead: "Thou art there, and we are here; we will slay every foe and every attacker (with

[1] See below.

the power got from thee). Go thou now to Mother Earth, who is wide opened, favorable, a wool-soft maiden to the good man; may she guard thee from the lap of destruction. Open, O earth, be not oppressive to him; let him enter easily; may he fasten close to thee. Cover him like a mother, who wraps her child in her garment. Roomy and firm be the earth, supported by a thousand pillars; from this time on thou (man) hast thy home and happiness yonder; may a sure place remain to him forever. I make firm the earth about thee; may I not be harmed in laying the clod here; may the fathers hold this pillar for thee, and Yama make thee a home yonder."

In the Atharva Veda mention is made of a coffin, but none is noticed here.

Hillebrandt (*loc. cit.* xl. 711) has made it probable that the eighth verse belongs to a still older ritual, according to which this verse is one for human sacrifice, which is here ignored, though the text is kept.[1] Just so the later ritual keeps all this text, but twists it into a crematory rite. For in the later period only young children are buried. Of burial there was nothing for adults but the collection of bones and ashes. At this time too the ritual consists of three parts, cremation, collection of ashes, expiation. How are these to be reconciled with this hymn? Very simply. The rite is described and verses from the hymn are injected into it without the slightest logical connection. That is the essence of all the Brahmanic ritualism. The later rite is as follows: Three altars are erected, northwest, southwest, and southeast of a mound of earth. In the fourth corner is the corpse; at whose feet, the widow. The brother of the dead man, or an old servant, takes the widow's hand and causes her to rise while the priest says "Raise thyself, woman, to the world of the

[1] Compare Weber, *Streifen*, I. 66; The king's first wife lies with a dead victim. and is bid to come back again to life. Levirate marriage is known to all the codes, but it is reprehended by the same code that enjoins it. (M. ix. 65.)

living." Then follows the removal of the bow; or the breaking of it, in the case of a slave. The body is now burned, while the priest says "These living ones are separated from the dead"; and the mourners depart without looking around, and must at once perform their ablutions of lustration. After a time the collection of bones is made with the verse "Go thou now to Mother Earth" and "Open, O earth." Dust is flung on the bones with the words "Roomy and firm be the earth"; and the skull is laid on top with the verse "I make firm the earth about thee." In other words the original hymn is fitted to the ritual only by displacement of verses from their proper order and by a forced application of the words. After all this comes the ceremony of expiation with the use of the verse "I set up a wall" without application of any sort. Further ceremonies, with further senseless use of other verses, follow in course of time. These are all explained minutely in the essay of Roth, whose clear demonstration of the modernness of the ritual, as compared with the antiquity of the hymn should be read complete.

The seventh verse (above) has a special literature of its own, since the words "let them, to begin with, mount the altar," have been changed by the advocates of *suttee*, widow-burning, to mean 'to the place of fire'; which change, however, is quite recent. The burning of widows begins rather late in India, and probably was confined at first to the pet wife of royal persons. It was then claimed as an honor by the first wife, and eventually without real authority, and in fact against early law, became the rule and sign of a devoted wife. The practice was abolished by the English in 1829; but, considering the widow's present horrible existence, it is questionable whether it would not be a mercy to her and to her family to restore the right of dying and the hope of heaven, in the place of the living death and actual hell on earth in which she is entombed to-day.

ORDEALS.[1]

Fire and water are the means employed in India to test guilt in the earlier period. Then comes the oath with judgment indicated by subsequent misfortune. All other forms of ordeals are first recognized in late law-books. We speak first of the ordeals that have been thought to be primitive Aryan. The Fire-ordeal: (1) Seven fig-leaves are tied seven times upon the hands after rice has been rubbed upon the palms; and the judge then lays a red-hot ball upon them; the accused, or the judge himself, invoking the god (Fire) to indicate the innocence or the guilt of the accused. The latter then walks a certain distance, 'slowly through seven circles, each circle sixteen fingers broad, and the space between the circles being of the same extent,' according to some jurists; but other dimensions, and eight or nine circles are given by other authorities. If the accused drop the ball he must repeat the test. The burning of the hands indicates guilt. The Teutonic laws give a different measurement, and state that the hand is to be sealed for three days (manus sub sigillo triduum tegatur) before inspection. This sealing for three days is paralleled by modern Indic practice, but not by ancient law. In Greece there is the simple *μύδρους αἴρειν χεροῖν* (Ant. 264) to be compared. The German sealing of the hand is not reported till the ninth century.[2]

(2) Walking on Fire: There is no ordeal in India to correspond to the Teutonic walking over six, nine, or twelve hot ploughshares. To lick a hot ploughshare, to sit on or handle

[1] The ordeal is called *divyam* (*pramāṇam*) 'Gottesurtheil.' This means of information is employed especially in a disputed debt and deposit, and according to the formal code is to be applied only in the absence of witnesses. The code also restricts the use of fire, water, and poison to the slaves (Yāj. ii. 98).

[2] Kaegi, *Alter und Herkunft des Germanischen Gottesurtheils*, p. 50. We call especial attention to the fact that the most striking coincidences in details of practice are not early either in India or Germany.

hot iron, and to take a short walk over coals is *late* Indic. The German practice also according to Schlagintweit "war erst in späterer Zeit aufgekommen."[1]

(3) Walking through Fire: This is a Teutonic ordeal, and (like the conflict-ordeal) an Indic custom not formally legalized. The accused walks directly into the fire. So πῦρ διέρπειν (*loc. cit.*).

Water-ordeals: (1) May better be reckoned to fire-ordeals. The innocent plunges his hand into boiling water and fetches out a stone (Anglo-Saxon law) or a coin (Indic law) without injury to his hand. Sometimes (in both practices) the plunge alone is demanded. The depth to which the hand must be inserted is defined by Hindu jurists.

(2) The Floating-ordeal. The victim is cast into water. If he floats he is guilty; if he drowns he is innocent. According to some Indic authorities an arrow is shot off at the moment the accused is dropped into the water, and a 'swift runner' goes after and fetches it back. "If at his return he find the body of the accused still under water, the latter shall be declared to be innocent."[2] According to Kaegi this ordeal would appear to be unknown in Europe before the ninth century. In both countries Water (in India, Varuna) is invoked not to keep the body of a guilty man but to reject it (make it float).

Food-ordeal: Some Hindu law-books prescribe that in the case of suspected theft the accused shall eat consecrated rice. If the gums be not hurt, no blood appear on spitting, and the man do not tremble, he will be innocent. This is also a

[1] Schlagintweit, *Die Gottesurtheile der Indier*, p. 24.

[2] This is the earliest formula. Later law-books describe the length and strength of the bow. and some even give the measure of distance to which the arrow must be shot. Two runners, one to go and one to return, are sometimes allowed. There is another water-ordeal "for religious men." The accused is to drink consecrated water. If in fourteen (or more or less) days no calamity happen to him he will be innocent. The same test is made in the case of the oath and of poison (below).

Teutonic test, but it is to be observed that the older laws in India do not mention it.

On the basis of these examples (not chosen in historical sequence) Kaegi has concluded, while admitting that ordeals with a general similarity to these have arisen quite apart from Aryan influence, that there is here a bit of primitive Aryan law; and that even the minutiae of the various trials described above are *ur*-Aryan. This we do not believe. But before stating our objections we must mention another ordeal.

The Oath: While fire and water are the usual means of testing crime in India, a simple oath is also permitted, which may involve either the accused alone or his whole family. If misfortune within a certain time (at once, in seven days, in a fortnight, or even half a year) happen to the one that has sworn, he will be guilty. This oath-test is also employed in the case of witnesses at court, perjury being indicated by the subsequent misfortune (Manu, viii. 108).[1]

Our objections to seeing primitive Aryan law in the minutiae of ordeals is based on the gradual evolution of these ordeals and of their minutiae in India itself. The earlier law of the Sūtras barely mentions ordeals; the first 'tradition law' of Manu has only fire, water, and the oath. All others, and all special descriptions and restrictions, are mentioned in later books alone. Moreover, the earliest (pre-legal) notice of ordeals in India describes the carrying of hot iron (in the test of theft) as simply "bearing a hot axe," while still earlier there is only walking through fire.[2]

[1] In the case of witnesses Manu gives seven days as the limit. When one adopts the oath as an ordeal the misfortune of the guilty is supposed to come 'quickly.' As an ordeal this is not found in the later law. It is one of the Greek tests (*loc. cit.*). When swearing the Hindu holds water or holy-grass.

[2] AV. ii. 12 is not a certain case of this, but it is at least Brahmanic. The carrying of the axe is alluded to in the Chāndogya Upanishad (Schlagintweit, *Die Gottesurtheile der Indier*, p. 6).

To the tests by oath, fire, and water of the code of Manu are soon added in later law those of consecrated water, poison, and the balance. Restrictions increase and new trials are described as one descends the series of law-books (the consecrated food, the hot-water test, the licking of the ploughshare, and the lot). Some of these later forms have already been described. The further later tests we will now sketch briefly.

Poison: The earliest poison-test, in the code of Yājñavalkya (the next after Manu), is an application of aconite-root, and as the poison is very deadly, the accused is pretty sure to die. Other laws give other poisons and very minute restrictions, tending to ease the severity of the trial.

The Balance-test: This is the opposite of the floating-test. The man[1] stands in one scale and is placed in equilibrium with a weight of stone in the other scale. He then gets out and prays, and gets in again. If the balance sinks, he is guilty; if it rises, he is innocent.

The Lot-ordeal: This consists in drawing out of a vessel one of two lots, equivalent respectively to *dharma* and *adharma*, right and wrong. Although Tacitus mentions the same ordeal among the Germans, it is not early Indic law, not being known to any of the ancient legal codes.

One may claim without proof or disproof that these are all 'primitive Aryan'; but to us it appears most probable that only the idea of the ordeal, or at most its application in the simplest forms of water and fire (and perhaps oath) is primitive Aryan, and that all else (including ordeal by conflict) is of secondary growth among the different nations.

As an offset to the later Indic tendency to lighten the severity of the ordeal may be mentioned the description of the floating-test as seen by a Chinese traveller in India in the

[1] Yājñavalkya (*loc. cit.*) restricts this test to women, children, priests, the old, blind, lame, and sick. On *phāla* for *agni*, *ib.* ii. 99, see ZDMG. ix. 677.

seventh century A.D.:[1] "The accused is put into a sack and a stone is put into another sack. The two sacks are connected by a cord and flung into deep water. If the sack with the man sinks and the sack with the stone floats the accused is declared to be innocent."

[1] Schlagintweit, *loc. cit.* p. 26 (Hiouen Thsang).

CHAPTER XII.

JAINISM.[1]

One cannot read the Upanishads without feeling that he is already facing an intellectual revolt. Not only in the later tracts, which are inspired with devotion to a supreme and universal Lord, but even in the oldest of these works the atmosphere, as compared with that of the earlier Brahmanic period, is essentially different. The close and stifling air of ritualism has been charged with an electrical current of thought that must soon produce a storm.

That storm reached a head in Buddhism, but its premonitory signs appear in the Upanishads, and its first outbreak preceded the advent of Gautama. Were it possible to draw a line of demarcation between the Upanishads that come before and after Buddhism, it would be historically more correct to review the two great schisms, Jainism and Buddhism, before referring to the sectarian Upanishads. For these latter in their present form are posterior to the rise of the two great heresies. But, since such a division is practically uncertain in its application, we have thought it better in our sketch of the Upanishads and legal literature to follow to the end the course of that agitated thought, which, starting with the great identification of *jīva*, the

[1] We retain here and in Buddhism the usual terminology. Strictly speaking, Jainism is to Jina (the reformer's title) as is Bauddhism to Buddha, so that one should say Jinism, Buddhism, or Jainism, Bauddhism. Both titles, Jina and Buddha ('victor' and 'awakened'), were given to each leader; as in general many other mutual titles of honor were applied by each sect to its own head, Jina, Arhat ('venerable'), Mahāvīra ('great hero'), Buddha, etc. One of these titles was used, however, as a title of honor by the Jains, but to designate heretics by the Buddhists, viz., Tīrthakara, 'prophet' (see Jacobi, SBE. xxii. Introd. p. xx).

individual spirit, and *ātmā*, the world-spirit, the All, continues till it loses itself in a multiplication of sectarian dogmas, where the All becomes the god that has been elected by one communion of devotees.[1]

The external characteristics of Upanishad thought are those of a religion that has replaced formal acts by formal introspection. The Yogin devotee, who by mystic communion desires absorption into the world-spirit, replaces the Sannyāsin and Yati ascetics, who would accomplish the same end by renunciation and severe self-mortification. This is a fresh figure on the stage of thought, where before were mad Munis, beggars, and miracle-mongers. On this stage stands beside the ascetic the theoretical theosophist who has succeeded in identifying himself, soberly, not in frenzy, with God.[2] What were the practical results of this teaching has been indicated in part already. The futility of the stereotyped religious offices was recognized. But these offices could not be discarded by the orthodox. With the lame and illogical excuse that they were useful as discipline, though unessential in reality, they were retained by the Brahman priest. Not so by the Jain; still less so by the Buddhist.

In the era in which arose the public revolt against the dogmatic teaching of the Brahman there were more sects than one that have now passed away forgotten. The eastern part of India, to which appertain the later part of the Çatapatha Brāhmana and the schismatic heresies, was full of religious and philosophical controversy. The great heretics were not innovators in heresy. The Brahmans permitted, encouraged, and shared in theoretical controversy. There was nothing in the

[1] It is possible, however, on the other hand, that both Vishnuite and Çivaite sects (or, less anglicized, Vaishnavas, Çaivas, if one will also say Vaidic for Vedic), were formed before the end of the sixth century B.C. Not long after this the divinities Çiva and Vishnu receive especial honor.

[2] The Beggar (Çramana, Bhikshu), the Renunciator (Sannyāsin), the Ascetic (Yati), are Brahmanic terms as well as sectarian.

tenets of Jainism or of Buddhism that from a philosophical point of view need have caused a rupture with the Brahmans.

But the heresies, nevertheless, do not represent the priestly caste, so much as the caste most apt to rival and to disregard the claim of the Brahman, viz., the warrior-caste. They were supported by kings, who gladly stood against priests. To a great extent both Jainism and Buddhism owed their success (amid other rival heresies with no less claim to good protestantism) to the politics of the day. The kings of the East were impatient of the Western church; they were pleased to throw it over. The leaders in the 'reformation' were the younger sons of noble blood. The church received many of these younger sons as priests. Both Buddha and Mahāvīra were, in fact, revolting adherents of the Brahmanic faith, but they were princes and had royalty to back them.

Nor in the Brahmanhood of Benares was Brahmanhood at its strongest. The seat of the Vedic cult lay to the westward, where it arose, in the 'holy land,' which received the Vedic Aryans after they had crossed out of the Punjāb. With the eastward course of conquest the character of the people and the very orthodoxy of the priests were relaxed. The country that gave rise to the first heresies was one not consecrated to the ancient rites. Very slowly had these rites marched thither, and they were, so to speak, far from their religious base of supplies. The West was more conservative than the East. It was the home of the rites it favored. The East was but a foster-father. New tribes, new land, new growth, socially and intellectually,—all these contributed in the new seat of Brahmanhood to weaken the hold of the priests upon their speculative and now recalcitrant laity. So before Buddha there were heretics and even Buddhas, for the title was Buddha's only by adoption. But of most of these earlier sects one knows little. Three or four names of reformers have been handed down; half a dozen opponents or rivals of Buddha existed and vied with him. Most important of these, both on account of his probable priority and because of the lasting character of his school, was the founder or reformer of Jainism, Mahāvīra Jñātriputra,[1] who with his eleven chief disciples may be regarded as the first open seceders from Brahmanism, unless one assign the same date to the revolt of Buddha. The two schisms have so much in common, especially in outward features, that for long it was thought that Jainism was a sub-sect of Buddhism. In their legends, in the localities in which they flourished, and in many minutiae of observances they are alike. Nevertheless, their differences are as great as the resemblance between them, and what Jainism at first appeared to have got of Buddhism seems now to be rather the common loan made by each sect from Brahmanism. It is safest, perhaps, to rest in the assurance that the two heresies were contemporaries of the sixth century B.C., and leave unanswered the question which Master preceded the other, though we incline to the opinion that the founder of Jainism, be he Mahāvīra or his own reputed master, Pārçvanātha, had founded his sect before Gautama became Buddha. But there is one good reason for treating of Jainism before Buddhism,[2] and that is, that the former represents a theological mean between Brahmanism and Buddhism.

Mahāvīra, the reputed founder of his sect, was, like Buddha

[1] The three great reformers of this period are Mahāvīra, Buddha, and Gosāla. The last was first a pupil and then a rival of Mahāvīra. The latter's nephew, Jamāli, also founded a distinct sect and became his uncle's opponent, the speculative sectarian tendency being as pronounced as it was about the same time in Hellas. Gosāla appears to have had quite a following, and his sect existed for a long time, but now it is utterly perished. An account of this reformer and of Jamāli will be found in Leumann's essay, *Indische Studien*, xvii. p. 98 ff. and in the appendix to Rockhill's *Life of Buddha*.

[2] The Nirgranthas (Jains) are never referred to by the Buddhists as being a new sect, nor is their reputed founder, Nātaputta, spoken of as their founder; whence Jacobi plausibly argues that their real founder was older than Mahāvīra, and that the sect preceded that of Buddha. Lassen and Weber have claimed, on the contrary, that Jainism is a revolt against Buddhism. The identification of Nātaputta (Jñātriputra) with Mahāvīra is due to Bühler and Jacobi (Kalpasūtra, Introd. p. 6).

and perhaps his other rivals, of aristocratic birth. His father is called king, but he was probably hereditary chief of a district incorporated as a suburb of the capital city of Videha, while by marriage he was related to the king of Videha, and to the ruling house of Māgadha. His family name was Jñātriputra, or, in his own Prakrit (Ardhamāgadhī) dialect, Nātaputta; but by his sect he was entitled the Great Hero, Mahāvīra; the Conqueror, Jina; the Great One, Vardahmāna, etc. His sect was that of the Nirgranthas (Nigganthas), *i.e.*, 'without bonds,' perhaps the oldest name of the whole body. Later there are found no less than seven sub-sects, to which come as eighth the Digambaras, in contradistinction to all the seven Çvetāmbara sects. These two names represent the two present bodies of the church, one body being the Çvetāmbaras, or 'white-attire' faction, who are in the north and west; the other, the Digambaras, or 'sky-attire,' *i.e.*, naked devotees of the south. The latter split off from the main body about two hundred years after Mahāvīra's death; as has been thought by some, because the Çvetāmbaras refused to follow the Digambaras in insisting upon nakedness as the rule for ascetics.[1] The earlier writings show that nakedness was recommended, but was not compulsory.[2] Other designations of the main sects, as of the sub-sects, are found. Thus, from the practice of pulling out the hairs of their body, the Jains were derisively termed Luñcitakeças, or 'hair-pluckers.' The naked devotees

1 According to Jacobi, ZDMG. xxxviii. 17, the split in the party arose in this way. About 350 B.C. some Jain monks under the leadership of Bhadrabāhu went south, and they followed stricter rules of asceticism than did their fellows in the north. Both sects are modifications of the original type, and their differences did not result in sectarian separation till about the time of our era, at which epoch arose the differentiating titles of sects that had not previously separated into formal divisions, but had drifted apart geographically.

2 Compare Jacobi, *loc. cit.*, and Leumann's account of the seven sects of the Çvetāmbaras in the essay in the *Indische Studien* referred to above. At the present day the Jains are found to the number of about a million in the northwest (Çvetāmbaras), and south (Digambaras) of India. The original seat of the whole body in its first form was, as we have said, near Benares, where also arose and flourished Buddhism.

of this school are probably the gymnosophists of the Greek historians, although this general term may have been used in describing other sects, as the practice of dispensing with attire is common even to-day with many Hindu devotees.[1]

An account of the Jain absurdities in the way of speculation would indeed give some idea of their intellectual frailty, but, as in the case of the Buddhists, such an account has but little to do with their religion. It will suffice to state that the 'ages' of the Brahmans from whom Jain and Buddhist derived their general conceptions of the ages, are here reckoned quite differently; and that the first Jina of the long series of prehistoric prophets lived more than eight million years and was five hundred bow-lengths in height. Monks and laymen now appear at large in India, a division which originated neither with Jain nor Buddhist,[2] though these orders are more clearly divided among the heretics, from whom, again, was borrowed by the Hindu sects, the monastic institution, in the ninth century (A.D.), in all the older heretical completeness. Although atheistic the Jain worshipped the Teacher, and paid some regard to the Brahmanical divinities, just as he worships the Hindu gods to-day, for the atheistical systems admitted gods as demi-gods or dummy gods, and in point of fact became very superstitious. Yet are both founder-worship and superstition rather the growth of later generations than the original practice. The atheism of the Jain means denial of a divine creative Spirit.[3]

[1] Hemacandra's Yogaçâstra, edited by Windisch, ZDMG. xxviii. 185 ff. (iii. 133). The Jain's hate of women did not prevent his worshipping goddesses as the female energy like the later Hindu sects. The Jains are divided in regard to the possibility of woman's salvation. The Yogaçâstra alludes to women as 'the lamps that burn on the road that leads to the gate of hell,' ii. 87. The Digambaras do not admit women into the order, as do the Çvetãmbaras.

[2] *Die Bharata-sage*, Leumann, ZDMG. xlviii. p. 65. See also above in the Sūtras. With the Jains there is less of the monastic side of religion than with the Buddhists.

[3] Jains are sometimes called Arhats on account of their veneration for the Arhat or chief Jina (whence Jain). Their only real gods are their chiefs or Teachers, whose

Though at times in conflict with the Brahmans the Jains never departed from India as did the Buddhists, and even Brahmanic priests in some parts of India serve to-day in Jain temples.

In metaphysics as in religion the Jain differs radically from the Buddhist. He believes in a dualism not unlike that of the Sānkhyas, whereas Buddhistic philosophy has no close connection with this Brahmanic system. To the Jain eternal matter stands opposed to eternal spirits, for (opposed to pantheism) every material entity (even water) has its own individual spirit. The Jain's Nirvāna, as Barth has said, is escape from the body, not escape from existence.[1] Like the Buddhist the Jain believes in reincarnation, eight births, after one has started on the right road, being necessary to the completion of perfection. Both sects, with the Brahmans, insist on the non-injury doctrine, but in this regard the Jain exceeds his Brahmanical teacher's practice. Both heretical sects claim that their reputed founders were the last of twenty-four or twenty-five prophets who preceded the real founder, each successively having become less monstrous (more human) in form.

The Jain literature left to us is quite large[2] and enough has been published already to make it necessary to revise the old belief in regard to the relation between Jainism and Buddhism.

We have said that Jainism stands nearer to Brahmanism (with which, however, it frequently had quarrels) than does

idols are worshipped in the temples. Thus, like the Buddhist and some Hindu sects of modern times, they have given up God to worship man. Rather have they adopted an idolatry of man and worship of womanhood, for they also revere the female energy. Positivism has ancient models!

[1] The Jain sub-sects did not differ much among themselves in philosophical speculation. Their differences were rather of a practical sort.

[2] See the list of the Berlin MSS.; Weber, *Berlin MSS.* vol. ii. 1892; and the thirty-third volume of the German Oriental Journal, pp. 478, 693. For an account of the literature see also Jacobi's introduction to the SBE. vol. xxii; and Weber, *Ueber die heiligen Schriften der Jaina* in vols. xvi, xvii of the *Indische Studien* (translated by Smyth in the Indian Antiquary); and the Bibliography (below).

Buddhism.[1] The most striking outward sign of this is the weight laid on asceticism, which is common to Brahmanism and Jainism but is repudiated by Buddhism. Twelve years of asceticism are necessary to salvation, as thinks the Jain, and this self-mortification is of the most stringent sort. But it is not in their different conception of a Nirvāna of release rather than of annihilation, nor in the Sānkhya-like[2] duality they affect, nor yet in the prominence given to self-mortification that the Jains differ most from the Buddhists. The contrast will appear more clearly when we come to deal with the latter sect. At present we take up the Jain doctrine for itself.

The 'three gems' which, according to the Jains,[3] result in the spirit's attainment of deliverance are knowledge, faith, and virtue, or literally 'right knowledge, right intuition, and right practices.' Right knowledge is a true knowledge of the relation of spirit and non-spirit (the world consists of two classes, spirit and non-spirit), the latter being immortal like the former. Right intuition is absolute faith in the word of the Master and the declarations of the Āgamas, or sacred texts. Right practices or virtue consists, according to the Yogaçāstra, in the correct fivefold conduct of one that has knowledge and faith: (1) Non-injury, (2) kindness and speaking what is true (in so far as the truth is pleasant to the hearer),[4] (3) honorable conduct, typified by 'not stealing,' (4) chastity in word, thought, and deed, (5) renunciation of earthly interests.

The doctrine of non-injury found but modified approval among the Brahmans. They limited its application in the case of

[1] A case of connection in legends between Buddhist and Jain is mentioned below. Another is the history of king Paêsi, elaborated in Buddhistic literature (Tripitaka) and in the second Jain Upânga alike, as has been shown by Leumann.

[2] The Jain's spirit, however, is not a world-spirit. He does not believe in an All-Spirit, but in a plurality of eternal spirits, fire-spirits, wind-spirits, plant-spirits, etc.

[3] Compare Colebrooke's *Essays*, vol. ii. pp. 404, 444, and the Yogaçāstra cited above.

[4] This is not in the earlier form of the vow (see below).

sacrifice, and for this reason were bitterly taunted by the Jains as 'murderers.' "Viler than unbelievers," says the Yogaçāstra, quoting a law of Manu to the effect that animals may be slain for sacrifice, "are those cruel ones who make the law that teaches killing."[1] For this reason the Jain is far more particular in his respect for life than is the Buddhist. Lest animate things, even plants and animalculae, be destroyed, he sweeps the ground before him as he goes, walks veiled lest he inhale a living organism, strains water, and rejects not only meat but even honey, together with various fruits that are supposed to contain worms; not because of his distaste for worms but because of his regard for life. Other arguments which, logically, should not be allowed to influence him are admitted, however, in order to terrify the hearer. Thus the first argument against the use of honey is that it destroys life; then follows the argument that honey is 'spit out by bees' and therefore it is nasty.[2]

The Jain differs from the Buddhist still more in ascetic practices. He is a forerunner, in fact, of the horrible modern devotee whose practices we shall describe below. The older view of seven hells in opposition to the legal Brahmanic number of thrice seven is found (as it is in the Mārkandeya Purāna), but whether this be the rule we cannot say.[3] It is interesting to see that hell is preserved with metempsychosis exactly as it is among the Brahmans.[4] Reincarnation on

[1] ii. 37 and 41. Although the Brahman ascetic took the vow not to kill, yet is he permitted to do so for sacrifice, and he may eat flesh of animals killed by other animals (Gautama, 3. 31).

[2] *Loc. cit.* iii. 37–38. The evening and night are not times to eat, and for the same reason "The Gods eat in the morning, the Seers at noon, the Fathers in the afternoon, the devils at twilight and night" (*ib.* 58). For at night one might eat a a living thing by mistake.

[3] *Loc. cit.* ii. 27.

[4] The pun *māṁsa*, "*Me eat* will be hereafter whose *meat* I eat in this life" (Lanman), shows that Jain and Brahman believed in a hell where the injured avenged themselves (Manu, v. 55; HYÇ. iii. 26), just as is related in the Bhrigu story (above).

earth and punishment in hells between reincarnation seems to be the usual belief. The salvation which is attained by the practice of knowledge, faith, and five-fold virtue, is not immediate, but it will come after successive reincarnations; and this salvation is the freeing of the eternal spirit from the bonds of eternal matter; in other words, it is much more like the 'release' of the Brahman than it is like the Buddhistic Nirvāna, though, of course, there is no 'absorption,' each spirit remaining single. In the order of the Ratnatraya or 'three gems' Çankara appears to lay the greatest weight on faith, but in Hemacandra's schedule knowledge[1] holds the first place. This is part of that Yoga, asceticism, which is the most important element in attaining salvation.[2]

Another division of right practices is cited by the Yogaçāstra (i. 33 ff.): Some saints say that virtue is divided into five kinds of care and three kinds of control, to wit, proper care in walking, talking, begging for food, sitting, and performing natural functions of the body — these constitute the five kinds of care, and the kinds of control are those of thought, speech, and act. This teaching it is stated, is for the monks. The practice of the laity is to accord with the custom of their country.

The chief general rules for the laity consist in vows of obedience to the true god, to the law, and to the (present) Teacher; which are somewhat like the vows of the Buddhist. God here is the Arhat, the 'venerable' founder of the sect. The laic has also five lesser vows: not to kill, not to lie, not to steal, not to commit adultery or fornication, to be content with little.

According to the Çāstra already cited the laic must rise early in the morning, worship the god's idol at home, go to the temple and circumambulate the Jina idol three times, strewing flowers, and singing hymns, and then read the Pratyākhyāna (an old Pūrva, gospel).[3] Further rules of prayer and practice

[1] By intuition or instruction. [2] *Loc. cit.* i. 15 ff.

[3] *Loc. cit.* iii. 121 ff. Wilson, *Essays*, I. 319, gives a description of the simple Jain ritual.

guide him through his day. And by following this rule he expects to obtain spiritual 'freedom' hereafter; but for his life on earth he is "without praise or blame for this world or the next, for life or for death, having meditation as his one pure wife" (iii. 150). He will become a god in heaven, be reborn again on earth, and so, after eight successive existences (the Buddhistic number), at last obtain salvation, release (from bodies) for his eternal soul (153).

As in the Upanishads, the gods, like men, are a part of the system of the universe. The wise man goes to them (becomes a god) only to return to earth again. All systems thus unite hell and heaven with the *karma* doctrine. But in this Jain work, as in so many of the orthodox writings, the weight is laid more on hell as a punishment than on rebirth. Probably the first Jains did not acknowledge gods at all, for it is an early rule with them not to say 'God rains,' or use any such expression, but to say 'the cloud rains'; and in other ways they avoid to employ a terminology which admits even implicitly the existence of divinities. Yet do they use a god not infrequently as an agent of glorification of Mahāvīra, saying in later writings that Indra transformed himself, to do the Teacher honor; and often they speak of the gods and goddesses as if these were regarded as spirits. Demons and inferior beings are also utilized in the same way, as when it is said that at the Teacher's birth the demons (spirits) showered gold upon the town.

The religious orders of the Çvetāmbara sect contained nuns as well as monks, although, as we have said, women are not esteemed very favorably: "The world is greatly troubled by women. People say that women are vessels of pleasure. But this leads them to pain, to delusion, to death, to hell, to birth as hell-beings or brute-beasts." Such is the decision in the Ācārānga Sūtra, or book of usages for the Jain monk and nun. From the same work we extract a few rules to illustrate the practices of the Jains. This literature is the most tedious in the world, and to give the gist of the heretic law-maker's manual will suffice.

Asceticism should be practiced by monk and nun, if possible. But if one finds that he cannot resist his passions, or is disabled and cannot endure austerities, he may commit suicide; although this release is sometimes reprehended, and is not allowable till one has striven against yielding to such a means. But when the twelve years of asceticism are passed one has assurance of reaching Nirvāna, and so may kill himself. Of Nirvāna there is no description. It is release, salvation, but it is of such sort that in regard to it 'speculation has no place,' and 'the mind cannot conceive of it' (copied from the Upanishads). In other regards, in contrast to the nihilistic Buddhist, the Jain assumes a doubtful attitude, so that he is termed the 'may-be philosopher,' *syādvādin*,[1] in opposition to the Buddhist, the philosopher of 'the void.'

But if the Jain may kill himself, he may not kill or injure anything else. Not even food prepared over a fire is acceptable, lest he hurt the 'fire-beings,' for as he believes in water-beings, so he believes in fire-beings, wind-beings, etc. Every plant and seed is holy with the sacredness of life. He may not hurt or drive away the insects that torment his naked flesh. 'Patience is the highest good,' he declares, and the rules for sitting and lying conclude with the statement that not to move at all, not to stir, is the best rule. To lie naked, bitten by vermin, and not to disturb them, is religion. Like a true Puritan, the Jain regards pleasure in itself as sinful. "What is discontent, and what is pleasure? One should live subject to neither. Giving up all gaiety, circumspect, restrained, one should lead a religious life. Man! Thou art thine own friend; why longest thou for a friend beyond thyself? . . . First troubles, then pleasures; first pleasures, then troubles.

[1] Who says "may be."

These are the cause of quarrels." And again, "Let one think, 'I am I,'" *i.e.*, let one be dependent on himself alone. When a Jain monk or nun hears that there is to be a festival (perhaps to the gods, to Indra, Skanda, Rudra, Vishnu,[1] or the demons, as in Ācārānga Sūtra, ii. 1. 2) he must not go thither; he must keep himself from all frivolities and entertainments. During the four months of the rainy season he is to remain in one place,[2] but at other times, either naked or attired in a few garments, he is to wander about begging. In going on his begging tour he is not to answer questions, nor to retort if reviled. He is to speak politely (the formulae for polite address and rude address are given), beg modestly, and not render himself liable to suspicion on account of his behavior when in the house of one of the faithful. Whatever be the quality of the food he must eat it, if it be not a wrong sort. Rice and beans are especially recommended to him. The great Teacher Jñātriputra (Mahāvīra), it is said, never went to shows, pantomines, boxing-matches, and the like; but, remaining in his parents' house till their death, that he might not grieve his mother, at the age of twenty-eight renounced the world with the consent of the government, and betook himself to asceticism; travelling naked (after a year of clothes) into barbarous lands, but always converting and enduring the reproach of the wicked. He was beaten and set upon by sinful men, yet was he never moved to anger. Thus it was that he became the Arhat, the Jina, the Kevalin (perfect sage).[3] It

[1] Mukunda.

[2] This 'keeping *vasso*' is also a Brahmanic custom, as Bühler has pointed out. But it is said somewhere that at that season the roads are impassible, so that there is not so much a conscious copying as a physical necessity in keeping *vasso;* perhaps also a moral touch, owing to the increase of life and danger of killing.

[3] In the lives of the Jinas it is said that Jñātriputra's (Nātaputta's) parents worshipped the 'people's favorite,' Pārçva, and were followers of the Çramanas (ascetics). In the same work (which contains nothing further for our purpose) it is said that Arhats, Cakravarts, Baladevas, and Vasudevas, present, past, and future, are aristocrats, born in noble families. The heresies and sectaries certainly claim as much.

is sad to have to add, however, that Mahāvīra is traditionally said to have died in a fit of apoplectic rage.

The equipment of a monk are his clothes (or, better, none), his alms-bowl, broom, and veil. He is 'unfettered,' in being without desires and without injury to others. 'Some say that all sorts of living beings may be slain, or abused, or tormented, or driven away — the doctrine of the unworthy. The righteous man does not kill nor cause others to kill. He should not cause the same punishment for himself.'

The last clause is significant. What he does to another living being will be done to him. He will suffer as he has caused others to suffer. The chain from emotion to hell — the avoidance of the former is on account of the fear of the latter — is thus connected: He who knows wrath knows pride; he who knows pride knows deceit; he who knows deceit knows greed (and so on; thus one advances) from greed to love, from love to hate, from hate to delusion, from delusion to conception, from conception to birth, from birth to death, from death to hell, from hell to animal existence, 'and he who knows animal existence knows pain.'

The five great vows, which have been thought by some scholars to be copies of the Buddhistic rules, whereas they are really modifications of the old Brahmanic rules for ascetics as explained in pre-Buddhistic literature, are in detail as follows:[1]

The First vow: I renounce all killing of living beings, whether subtile or gross, whether movable or immovable. Nor shall I myself kill living beings nor cause others to do it, nor consent to it. As long as I live I confess and blame, repent and exempt myself of these sins in the thrice threefold way,[2] in mind, speech, and body.

1 Ācārānga S. ii. 15. We give Jacobi's translation, as in the verses already cited from this work.

2 Acting, commanding, consenting, past, present, or future (Jacobi).

The five 'clauses' that explain this vow are: (1) the Nigganatha (Jain) is careful in walking; (2) he does not allow his mind to act in a way to suggest injury of living beings; (3) he does not allow his speech to incite to injury; (4) he is careful in laying down his utensils; (5) he inspects his food and drink lest he hurt living beings.

The Second Vow: I renounce all vices of lying speech arising from anger, or greed, or fear, or mirth. I confess (etc., as in the first vow).

The five clauses here explain that the Niggantha speaks only after deliberation; does not get angry; renounces greed; renounces fear; renounces mirth—lest through any of these he be moved to lie.

The Third Vow: I renounce all taking of anything not given, either in a village, or a town, or a wood, either of little or much, or small or great, of living or lifeless things. I shall neither take myself what is not given nor cause others to take it, nor consent to their taking it. As long as I live I confess (etc., as in the first vow).

The clauses here explain that the Niggantha must avoid different possibilities of stealing, such as taking food without permission of his superior. One clause states that he may take only a limited ground for a limited time, *i.e.*, he may not settle down indefinitely on a wide area, for he may not hold land absolutely. Another clause insists on his having his grant to the land renewed frequently.

The Fourth Vow: I renounce all sexual pleasures, either with gods, or men, or animals. I shall not give way to sensuality (etc.).

The clauses here forbid the Niggantha to discuss topics relating to women, to contemplate the forms of women, to recall the pleasures and amusements he used to have with women, to eat and drink too highly seasoned viands, to lie near women.

The Fifth Vow: I renounce all attachments, whether little or much, small or great, living or lifeless; neither shall I myself form such attachments, nor cause others to do so, nor consent to their doing so (etc.).

The five clauses particularize the dangerous attachments formed by ears, eyes, smell, taste, touch.

It has been shown above (following Jacobi's telling comparison of the heretical vows with those of the early Brahman ascetic) that these vows are taken not from Buddhism but from Brahmanism. Jacobi opines that the Jains took the four first and that the reformer Mahāvīra added the fifth as an offset to the Brahmanical vow of liberality.[1] The same writer shows that certain minor rules of the Jain sect are derived from the same Brahmanical source.

The main differences between the two Jain sects have been catalogued in an interesting sketch by Williams,[2] who mentions as the chief Jain stations of the north Delhi (where there is an annual gathering), Jeypur, and Ājmīr. To these Mathurā on the Jumna should be added.[3] The Çvetāmbaras had forty-five or forty-six Āgamas, eleven or twelve Angas, twelve Upāngas, and other scriptures of the third or fourth century B.C., as they claim. They do not go naked (even their idols are clothed), and they admit women into the order. The Digambaras do not admit women, go naked, and have for sacred texts later works of the fifth century A.D. The latter of course assert that the scriptures of the former sect are spurious.[4]

1 SBE. xxii. Introd. p. xxiv.

2 JRAS. xx. 279.

3 See Bühler, the last volume of the *Epigraphica Indica*, and his other articles in the WZKM. v. 59, 175. Jeypur, according to Williams, is the stronghold of the Digambara Jains. Compare Thomas, JRAS. ix. 155, *Early Faith of Açoka*.

4 The redaction of the Jain canon took place, according to tradition, in 454 or 467 A.D. (possibly 527). "The origin of the extant Jaina literature cannot be placed earlier than about 300 B.C." (Jacobi, Introduction to *Jain Sūtras*, pp. xxxvii, xliii). The present Angas ('divisions') were preceded by Pūrvas, of which there are said to have been at first fourteen. On the number of the scriptures see Weber, *loc. cit.*

In distinction from the Buddhists the Jains of to-day keep up caste. Some of them are Brahmans. They have, of course, a different prayer-formula, and have no Stūpas or Dāgobas (to hold relics); and, besides the metaphysical difference spoken of above, they differ from the Buddhists in assuming that metempsychosis does not stop at animal existence, but includes inanimate things (as these are regarded by others). According to one of their own sect of to-day, *ahiṅsā paramo dharmas*, 'the highest law of duty is not to hurt a living creature.'[1]

The most striking absurdity of the Jain reverence for life has frequently been commented upon. Almost every city of western India, where they are found, has its beast-hospital, where animals are kept and fed. An amusing account of such an hospital, called Piñjra Pol, at Saurarāshtra, Surat, is given in the first number of the *Journal of the Royal Asiatic Society*.[2] Five thousand rats were supported in such a temple-hospital in Kutch.[3]

Of all the great religious sects of India that of Nātaputta is perhaps the least interesting, and has apparently the least excuse for being.[4] The Jains offered to the world but one great moral truth, withal a negative truth, 'not to harm,' nor was this verity invented by them. Indeed, what to the Jain is the great truth is only a grotesque exaggeration of what other sects recognized in a reasonable form. Of all the sects the Jains are the most colorless, the most insipid. They have

1 Williams, *loc. cit.* The prayer-formula is: 'Reverence to Arhats, saints, teachers, sub-teachers, and all good men.'

2 'A place which is appropriated for the reception of old, worn-out, lame, or disabled animals. At that time (1823) they chiefly consisted of buffaloes and cows, but there were also goats and sheep, and even cocks and hens,' and also 'hosts of vermin.'

3 JRAS. 1834, p. 96. The town was taxed to provide the food for the rats.

4 Because the Jains have reverted to idolatry, demonology, and man-worship. But at the outset they appear to have had two great principles, one, that there is no divine power higher than man; the other, that all life is sacred. One of these is now practically given up, and the other was always taken too seriously.

no literature worthy of the name. They were not original enough to give up many orthodox features, so that they seem like a weakened rill of Brahmanism, cut off from the source, yet devoid of all independent character. A religion in which the chief points insisted upon are that one should deny God, worship man, and nourish vermin, has indeed no right to exist; nor has it had as a system much influence on the history of thought. As in the case of Buddhism, the refined Jain metaphysics are probably a late growth. Historically these sectaries served a purpose as early protestants against ritualistic and polytheistic Brahmanism; but their real affinity with the latter faith is so great that at heart they soon became Brahmanic again. Their position geographically would make it seem probable that they, and not the Buddhists, had a hand in the making of the ethics of the later epic.

CHAPTER XIII.

BUDDHISM.

WHILE the pantheistic believer proceeded to anthropomorphize in a still greater degree the *ātmā* of his fathers, and eventually landed in heretical sectarianism; while the orthodox Brahman simply added to his pantheon (in Manu and other law-codes) the Brahmanic figure of the Creator, Brahmā; the truth-seeker that followed the lines of the earlier philosophical thought arrived at atheism, and in consequence became either stoic or hedonist. The latter school, the Cārvākas, the so-called disciples of Brihaspati, have, indeed, a philosophy without religion. They simply say that the gods do not exist, the priests are hypocrites; the Vedas, humbug; and the only thing worth living for, in view of the fact that there are no gods, no heaven, and no soul, is pleasure: 'While life remains let a man live happily; let him not go without butter (literally *ghee*) even though he run into debt,' etc.[1] Of sterner stuff was the man who invented a new religion as a solace for sorrow and a refuge from the nihilism in which he believed.

Whether Jainism or Buddhism be the older heresy, and it is not probable that any definitive answer to this question will ever be given, one thing has become clear in the light of recent studies, namely, the fact already shown, that to Brahmanism are due some of the most marked traits of both the heretical sects. The founder of Buddhism did not strike out a new system of morals; he was not a democrat; he did not originate a plot to overthrow the Brahmanic priesthood; he

[1] Compare Colebrooke's *Essays*, vol. ii. 460; and Muir, OST. iv. 296

did not invent the order of monks.[1] There is, perhaps, no person in history in regard to whom have arisen so many opinions that are either wholly false or half false.[2]

We shall not canvass in detail views that would be mentioned only to be rejected. Even the brilliant study of Senart,[3] in which the figure of Buddha is resolved into a solar type and the history of the reformer becomes a sun-myth, deserves only to be mentioned and laid aside. Since the publication of the canonical books of the southern Buddhists there is no longer any question in regard to the human reality of the great knight who illumined, albeit with anything but heavenly light, the darkness of Brahmanical belief. Oldenberg[4] has taken Senart seriously, and seriously answered him. But Napoleon and Max Müller have each been treated as sun-myths, and Senart's essay is as convincing as either *jeu d'esprit*.

In Nepāl, far from the site of Vedic culture, and generations after the period of the Vedic hymns, was born a son to the noble family of the Çākyas. A warrior prince, he made at last exclusively his own the lofty title that was craved by many of his peers, Buddha, the truly wise, the 'Awakened.'

The Çākyas' land extended along the southern border of Nepāl and the northeast part of Oude (Oudh), between the Irāvatī (Rapti) river on the west and south, and the Rohinī on the east; the district which lies around the present Gorakhpur, about one hundred miles north-northeast of Benares. The personal history of the later Buddha is interwoven with legend from which it is not always easy to disentangle the threads of truth. In the accounts preserved in regard to the Master, one has first to distinguish the Pāli records of the Southern Buddhists from the Sanskrit tales of the Northerners; and again, it is necessary to discriminate between the earlier and

1 Compare Oldenberg, *Buddha*, p. 155.
2 Especially Köppen views Buddha as a democratic reformer and liberator.
3 Emile Senart, *Essai sur la légende du Buddha*. 1875.
4 *Buddha* (1881), p. 73 ff.

later traditions of the Southerners, who have kept in general the older history as compared with the extravagant tradition preserved in the Lalita Vistara, the Lotus of the Law, and the other works of the North. What little seems to be authentic history is easily told; nor are, for our present purpose, of much value the legends, which mangonize the life of Buddha. They will be found in every book that treats of the subject, and some of the more famous are translated in the article on Buddha in the Encyclopædia Brittanica. We content ourselves with the simplest and oldest account, giving such facts as help to explain the religious significance of Buddha's life and work among his countrymen. Several of these facts, Buddha's place in society, and the geographical centre of Buddhistic activity, are essential to a true understanding of the relations between Buddhism and Brahmanism.

Whether Buddha's father was king or no has rightly been questioned. The oldest texts do not refer to him as a king's son, and this indicates that his father, who governed the Çākya-land, of which the limits have just been specified,[1] was rather a feudal baron or head of a small clan, than an actual king. The Çākya power was overthrown and absorbed into that of the king of Oude (Kosala) either in Buddha's own lifetime or immediately afterwards. It is only the newer tradition that extols the power and wealth which the Master gave up on renouncing worldly ties, a trait characteristic of all the later accounts, on the principle that the greater was the sacrifice the greater was the glory. Whether kings or mere chieftains, the Çākyas were noted as a family that cared little to honor the Brahmanic priests. They themselves claimed descent from Ikshvāku, the ancient seer-king, son of Manu, and traditionally first king of Ayodhā (Oude). They assumed the name of

[1] The exact position of Kapilavastu, the capital of the Çākyas, is not known, although it must have been near to the position assigned to it on Kiepert's map of India (just north of Gorakhpur). The town is unknown in Brahmanic literature.

Gautama, one of the Vedic seers, and it was by the name of 'the Ascetic Gautama' that Buddha was known to his contemporaries; but his personal name was Siddhārtha 'he that succeeds in his aim,' prophetic of his life! His mother's name Māyā (illusion) has furnished Senart with material for his sun-theory of Buddha; but the same name is handed down as that of a city, and perhaps means in this sense 'the wonderful.' She is said to have died when her son was still a boy. The boy Siddhārtha, then, was a warrior *rājput* by birth, and possibly had a very indifferent training in Vedic literature, since he is never spoken of as Veda-wise.[1] The future Buddha was twenty-nine when he resolved to renounce the world. He was already married and had a son (Rāhula, according to later tradition). The legends of later growth here begin to thicken, telling how, when the future Buddha heard of the birth of his son, he simply said 'a new bond has been forged to hold me to the world'; and how his mind was first awakened to appreciation of sorrow by seeing loathy examples of age, sickness, and death presented to him as he drove abroad. Despite his father's tears and protests Siddhārtha, or as one may call him now by his patronymic, the man Gautama, left his home and family, gave up all possessions, and devoted himself to self-mortification and Yoga discipline of concentration of thought, following in this the model set by all previous ascetics. He says himself, according to tradition, that it was a practical pessimism which drove him to take this step. He was not pleased with life, and the pleasures of society had no charm for him. When he saw the old man, the sick man, the dead man, he became disgusted to think that he too would be subject to age, sickness, and death: "I felt disgust at old age; all pleasure then forsook me." In becoming an ascetic Gautama

[1] This is Oldenberg's opinion, for the reason here stated. On the other hand it may be questioned whether this negative evidence be conclusive, and whether it be not more probable that a young nobleman would have been well educated.

simply endeavored to discover some means by which he might avoid a recurrence of life, of which the disagreeable side in his estimation outweighed the joy. He too had already answered negatively the question Is life worth living?

We must pause here to point out that this oldest and simplest account of Gautama's resolve shows two things. It makes clear that Gautama at first had no plan for the universal salvation of his race. He was alert to 'save his own soul,' nothing more. We shall show presently that this is confirmed by subsequent events in his career. The next point is that this narration in itself is a complete refutation of the opinion of those scholars who believe that the doctrine of *karma* and reincarnation arose first in Buddhism, and that the Upanishads that preach this doctrine are not of the pre-Buddhistic period. The last part of this statement of opinion is, of course, not touched by the story of Gautama's renunciation, but the first assumption wrecks on it. Why should Gautama have so given himself to Yoga discipline? Did he expect to escape age, sickness, death, in this life by that means? No. The assumption from the beginning is the belief in the doctrine of reincarnation. It was in order to free himself from future returns of these ills that Gautama renounced his home. But nothing whatever is said of his discovering or inventing the doctrine of reincarnation. Both hell and *karma* are taken for granted throughout the whole early Buddhistic literature. Buddha discovered neither of them, any more than he discovered a new system of morality, or a new system of religious life; although more credit accrues to him in regard to the last because his order was opposed to that then prevalent; yet even here he had antique authority for his discipline.

To return to Gautama's[1] life. Legend tells how he fled

[1] Siddhārtha, the boy, Gautama by his family cognomen, the Çākya-son by his clan-name, was known also as the Çākya-sage, the hermit, Samana (Çramaṇa); the

away on his horse Kanthaka, in search of solitude and the means of salvation, far from his home to the abode of ascetics, for he thought: "Whence comes peace? When the fire of desire is extinguished, when the fire of hate is extinguished, when the fire of illusion is extinguished, when all sins and all sorrows are extinguished, then comes peace." And the only means to this end was the renunciation of desire, the discipline of Yoga concentration, where the mind fixed on one point loses all else from its horizon, and feels no drawing aside to worldly things.

What then has Gautama done from the point of view of the Brahman? He has given up his home to become an ascetic. But this was permitted by usage, for, although the strict western code allowed it only to the priest, yet it was customary among the other twice-born castes at an earlier day, and in this part of India it awakened no surprise that one of the military caste should take up the life of a philosopher. For the historian of Indic religions this fact is of great significance, since such practice is the entering wedge which was to split the castes. One step more and not only the military caste but the lower, nay the lowest castes, might become ascetics. But, again, all ascetics were looked upon, in that religious society, as equal to the priests. In fact, where Gautama lived there was rather more respect paid to the ascetic than to the priest as a member of the caste. Gautama was most fortunate in his birth and birth-place. An aristocrat, he became an ascetic in a land where the priests were particularly disregarded. He had no public opinion to contend against when later he declared that Brahman birth and Brahman wisdom had no value. On the contrary, he spoke to

venerable. Arhat (a general title of perfected saints); Tathāgata 'who is arrived like' (the preceding Buddhas, at perfection); and also by many other names common to other sects. Buddha, Jina, The Blessed One (Bhagavat), The Great Hero, etc. The Buddhist disciple may be a layman, *çravaka*: a monk, *bhikshu*; a perfected saint, *arhat*; a saintly doctor of the law, *bodhisattva*; etc.

glad hearers, who heard repeated loudly now as a religious truth what often they had said to themselves despitefully in private.

Gautama journeyed as a *muni*, or silent ascetic sage, till after seven years he abandoned his teachers (for he had become a disciple of professed masters), and discontentedly wandered about in Māgadha (Behār), 'the cradle of Buddhism,' till he came to Uruvelā, Bodhi Gayā.[1] Here, having found that concentration of mind, Yoga-discipline, availed nothing, he undertook another method of asceticism, self-torture. This he practiced for some time. But it succeeded as poorly as his first plan, and he had nearly starved himself to death when it occurred to him that he was no wiser than before. Thereupon he gave up starvation as a means of wisdom and began to eat. Five other ascetics, who had been much impressed by his endurance and were quite ready to declare themselves his disciples, now deserted him, thinking that as he had relaxed his discipline he must be weaker than themselves. But Gautama sat beneath the sacred fig-tree[2] and lo! he became illumined. In a moment he saw the Great Truths. He was now the Awakened. He became Buddha.

The later tradition here records how he was tempted of Satan. For Māra (Death), 'the Evil One' as he is called by the Buddhists, knowing that Buddha had found the way of salvation, tempted him to enter into Nirvāna at once, lest by converting others Buddha should rob Māra of his power and dominion. This and the legend of storms attacking him and his being protected by the king of snakes, Mucalinda, is lacking in the earlier tradition.

Buddha remains under the *bo*-tree fasting, for four times seven days, or seven times seven, as says the later report. At

[1] South of the present Patna. Less correct is the *Buddha* Gayā form.

[2] The famous *bo* or Bodhi-tree, ficus religiosa, *pippala*, at Bodhi Gayā, said to be the most venerable and certainly the most venerated tree in the world.

first he resolves to be a 'Buddha for himself,'[1] that is to save only himself, not to be 'the universal Buddha,' who converts and saves the world. But the God Brahmā comes down from heaven and persuades him out of pity for the world to preach salvation. In this legend stands out clearly the same fact we have animadverted upon already. Buddha had at first no intention of helping his fellows. He found his own road to salvation. That sufficed. But eventually he was moved through pity for his kind to give others the same knowledge with which he had been enlightened.[2]

Here is to be noticed with what suddenness Gautama becomes Buddha. It is an early case of the same absence of study or intellectual preparation for belief that is rampant in the idea of ictic conversion. In a moment Gautama's eyes are opened. In ecstacy he becomes illuminated with the light of knowledge. This idea is totally foreign to Brahmanism. It is not so strange at an earlier stage, for the Vedic poet often 'sees' his hymn,[3] that is, he is inspired or illumined. But no Brahman priest was ever 'enlightened' with sudden wisdom, for his knowledge was his wisdom, and this consisted in learning interminable trifles. But the wisdom of Buddha was this:

I. Birth is sorrow, age is sorrow, sickness is sorrow, death is sorrow, clinging to earthly things is sorrow.

II. Birth and re-birth, the chain of reincarnations, result from the thirst for life together with passion and desire.

III. The only escape from this thirst is the annihilation of desire.

IV. The only way of escape from this thirst is by following the Eightfold Path: Right belief, right resolve, right word,

[1] A *pacceka* Buddha (Oldenberg, *Buddha*, p. 122).

[2] "Then be the door of salvation opened!
He that hath ears to hear let him hear.
I thought of my own sorrow only, and, therefore,
Have not revealed the Word to the world."

[3] He sometimes, however, quite prosaically 'makes' or 'manufactures' it.

right act, right life, right effort, right thinking, right meditation.[1]

But Buddha is said to have seen more than these, the Four Great Truths, and the Eightfold Path, for he was enlightened at the same time (after several days of fasting) in regard to the whole chain of causality which is elaborated in the later tradition.

The general result of this teaching may be formulated thus, that most people are foolishly optimistic and that the great awakening is to become a pessimist. One must believe not only that pain is inseparable from existence, but that the pleasures of life are only a part of its pain. When one has got so far along the path of knowledge he traverses the next stage and gets rid of desire, which is the root of life, — this is a Vedic utterance, — till by casting off desire, ignorance, doubt, and heresy, as add some of the texts,[2] one has removed far away all unkindness and vexation of soul, feeling good-will to all.

Not only in this scheme but also in other less formal declarations of Buddha does one find the key-note of that which makes his method of salvation different alike to that of Jain or Brahman. Knowledge is wisdom to the Brahman; asceticism is wisdom to the Jain; purity and love is the first wisdom to the Buddhist. We do not mean that the Brahman does not reach theoretically a plane that puts him on the same level with Buddhism. We have pointed out above a passage in the work of the old law-giver Gautama which might almost have been

[1] *Dhammacakkappavattana.* Rhys Davids in his introduction to this *sutta* gives and explains the eight as follows (SBE. xi. p. 144): 1, Right views; freedom from superstition or delusion. 2, Right aims, high and worthy of the intelligent, earnest man. 3, Right speech, kindly, open, truthful. 4, Right conduct, peaceful, honest, pure. 5, Right livelihood, bringing hurt to no living thing. 6, Right effort in self-training and in self-control. 7, Right mindfulness, the active watchful mind. 8, Right contemplation, earnest thought on the deep mysteries of life.

[2] Hardy, *Manual*, p. 496.

uttered by Gautama Buddha: "He that has performed all the forty sacraments and has not the eight good qualities enters not into union with Brahmā nor into the heaven of Brahmā; but he that has performed only a part of the forty sacraments and has the eight good qualities, enters into union with Brahmā and into the heaven of Brahmā"; and these eight good qualities are mercy, forbearance, freedom from envy, purity, calmness, correct behavior, freedom from greed and from covetousness. Nevertheless with the Brahman this is adventitious, with the Buddhist it is essential.

These Four Great Truths are given to the world first at Benares, whither Buddha went in order to preach to the five ascetics that had deserted him. His conversation with them shows us another side of Buddhistic ethics. The five monks, when they saw Buddha approaching, jeered, and said: "Here is the one that failed in his austerities." Buddha tells them to acknowledge him as their master, and that he is the Enlightened One. "How," they ask, "if you could not succeed in becoming a Buddha by asceticism, can we suppose that you become one by indulgence?" Buddha tells them that neither voluptuousness nor asceticism is the road that leads to Nirvāna; that he, Buddha, has found the middle path between the two extremes, the note is struck that is neither too high nor too low. The five monks are converted when they hear the Four Great Truths and the Eightfold Path, and there are now six holy ones on earth, Buddha and his five disciples.

Significant also is the social status of Buddha's first conversion. It is 'the rich youth' of Benares that flock about him,[1] of whom sixty soon are counted, and these are sent out into all the lands to preach the gospel, each to speak in his own tongue, for religion was from this time on no longer to be hid behind the veil of an unintelligible language. And it is not

[1] "A decided predilection for the aristocracy appears to have lingered as an heirloom of the past in the older Buddhism," Oldenberg, *Buddha*, p. 157.

only the aristocracy of wealth that attaches itself to the new teacher and embraces his doctrines with enthusiasm. The next converts are a thousand Brahman priests, who constituted a religious body under the leadership of three ascetic Brahmans. It is described in the old writings how these priests were still performing their Vedic rites when Buddha came again to Bodhi Gayā and found them there. They were overcome with astonishment as they saw his power over the King of Snakes that lived among them. The gods — for Buddhism, if not Buddha, has much to do with the gods — descend from heaven to hear him, and other marvels take place. The Brahmans are all converted. The miracles and the numbers may be stripped off, but thus denuded the truth still remains as important as it is plain. Priests of Brahman caste were among the first to adopt Buddhism. The popular effect of the teaching must have been great, for one reads how, when Buddha, after this great conversion, begins his victorious wanderings in Behār (Māgadha), he converted so many of the young nobles that — since conversion led to the immediate result of renunciation — the people murmured, saying that Gautama (Gotama) was robbing them of their youth.[1]

From this time on Buddha's life was spent in wandering about and preaching the new creed mainly to the people of Behār and Oude (Kāçi-Kosala, the realm of Benares-Oude), his course extending from the (Irāvatī) Rapti river in the north to Rājagriha (*gaha*, now Rajgir) south of Behār, while he spent the *vasso* or rainy season in one of the parks, many of which were donated to him by wealthy members of the fraternity.[2]

Wherever he went he was accompanied with a considerable number of followers, and one reads of pilgrims from distant

[1] *Mahāvagga*, i. 24. On the name (Gautama) Gotama, see Weber, *IS.* i. 180.

[2] The parks of Veluvana and Jetavana were especially affected by Buddha. Compare Oldenberg, *Buddha*, p. 145.

places coming to see and converse with him. The number of his followers appears to have been somewhat exaggerated by the later writers, since Buddha himself, when prophesying of the next Buddha, the "Buddha of love" (Maitreya) says that, whereas he himself has hundreds of followers, the next Buddha will lead hundreds of thousands.

Although,. theoretically, all the castes give up their name, and, when united in the Buddhistic brotherhood, become "like rivers that give up their identity and unite in the one ocean," yet were most of the early recruits, as has been said, from influential and powerful families; and it is a tenet of Buddhism in regard to the numerous Buddhas, which have been born[1] and are still to be born on earth, that no Buddha can be born in a low caste.

The reason for this lies as much as anything in the nature of the Buddhistic system which is expressly declared to be "for the wise, not for the foolish." It was not a system based as such on love or on any democratic sentiment. It was a philosophical exposition of the causal nexus of birth and freedom from re-birth. The common man, untrained in logic, might adopt the teaching, but he could not understand it. The "Congregation of the son of the Çākyas"—such was the earliest name for the Buddhistic brotherhood—were required only to renounce their family, put on the yellow robe, assume the tonsure and other outward signs, and be chaste and high-minded. But the teachers were instructed in the subtleties of the 'Path,' and it needed no little training to follow the leader's thought to its logical conclusion.

Of Buddha's life, besides the circumstances already narrated little is known. Of his disciples the best beloved was Ānanda, his own cousin, whose brother was the Judas of Buddhism. The latter, Devadatta by name, conspired to kill Buddha in order that he himself might get the post of honor. But hell

[1] Like the Jains the Buddhists postulate twenty-four (five) precedent Buddhas.

opened and swallowed him up. He appears to have had convictions of Jain tendency, for before his intrigue he preached against Buddha, and formulated reactionary propositions which inculcated a stricter asceticism than that taught by the Master.[1]

It has been denied that the early church contained lay members as well as monks, but Oldenberg appears to have set the matter right (p. 165) in showing that the laity, from the beginning, were a recognized part of the general church. The monk (*bhikshu, bhikku*) was formally enrolled as a disciple, wore the gown and tonsure, etc. The lay brother, 'reverer' (*upāsaka*), was one that assented to the doctrine and treated the monks kindly. There were, at first, only men in the congregation, for Buddhism took a view as unfavorable to woman as did Jainism. But at his foster-mother's request Buddha finally admitted nuns as well as monks into his fold. When Ānanda asks how a monk should act in presence of a woman Buddha says 'avoid to look at her'; but if it be necessary to look, 'do not speak to her'; but if it be necessary to speak, 'then keep wide awake, Ānanda.'[2]

Buddha died in the fifth century. Rhys Davids, who puts the date later than most scholars, gives, as the time of the great Nirvāna, the second decade from the end of the fourth century. On the other hand, Bühler and Müller reckon the year as 477, while Oldenberg says 'about 480.'[3] From Buddha's own words, as reported by tradition, he was eighty

1 Buddha's general discipline as compared with that of the Jains was much more lax, for instance, in the eating of meat. Buddha himself died of dysentery brought on by eating pork. The later Buddhism interprets much more strictly the rule of 'non-injury'; and as we have shown, Buddha entirely renounced austerities, choosing the mean between laxity and asceticism.

2 Or 'take care of yourself'; *Mahāparinibbāna*, v. 23.

3 The chief Buddhistic dates are given by Müller (introduction to *Dhammapada*, SBE. vol. x.) as follows: 557. Buddha's birth; 477. Buddha's death and the First Council at Rājagriha; 377. the Second Council at Vāiçālī: 259, Açoka's coronation; 242, Third Council at Pātaliputta; 222, Açoka's death. These dates are only tenta-

years old at the time of his death, and if one allots him thirty-six years as his age when he became independent of masters, his active life would be one of forty-four years. It was probably less than this, however, for some years must be added to the first seven of ascetic practices before he took the field as a preacher.

The story of Buddha's death is told simply and clearly. He crossed the Ganges, where at that time was building the town of Patna (Pātaliputta, 'Palibothra'), and prophesied its future greatness (it was the chief city of India for centuries after); then, going north from Rājagriha, in Behār, and Vāiçālī, he proceeded to a point east of Gorukhpur (Kasia). Tradition thus makes him wander over the most familiar places till he comes back almost to his own country. There, in the region known to him as a youth, weighed down with years and ill-health, but surrounded by his most faithful disciples, he died. Not unaffecting is the final scene.[1]

'Now the venerable Ānanda (Buddha's beloved disciple) went into the cloister-building, and stood leaning against the lintel of the door and weeping at the thought: "Alas! I remain still but a learner, one who has yet to work out his own perfection. And the Master is about to pass away from me—he who is so kind." Then the Blessed One called the brethren and said: "Where then, brethren, is Ānanda?" "The venerable Ānanda (they replied) has gone into the cloister-building and stands leaning against the lintel of the door, weeping." . . . . And the Blessed One called a certain brother, and said "Go

tive, but they give the time nearly enough to serve as a guide. From the Buddhists (Ceylon account) it is known that the Council at Vāiçālī was held one hundred years after Buddha's death (one hundred and eighteen years before the coronation of Açoka, whose grandfather, Candragupta, was Alexander's contemporary). The interval between Nirvāna and Açoka, two hundred and eighteen years, is the only certain date according to Köppen, p. 208, and despite much argument since he wrote, the remark still holds.

[1] Englished by Rhys Davids, *Mahāparinibbāna-sutta* (SBE. xi. 95 ff.).

now, brother, and call Ānanda in my name and say, 'Brother Ānanda, thy Master calls for thee.'" "Even so, Lord," said that brother, and he went up to where Ānanda was, and said to the venerable Ānanda: "Brother Ānanda, thy Master calls for thee." "It is well, brother," said the venerable Ānanda, and he went to the place where Buddha was. And when he was come thither he bowed down before the Blessed One, and took his seat on one side. Then the Blessed One said to the venerable Ānanda, as he sat there by his side: "Enough, Ānanda, let not thyself be troubled; weep not. Have I not told thee already that we must divide ourselves from all that is nearest and dearest? How can it be possible that a being born to die should not die? For a long time, Ānanda, hast thou been very near to me by acts of love that is kind and good and never varies, and is beyond all measure. (This Buddha repeats three times.) Thou hast done well. Be earnest in effort. Thou, too, shalt soon be free." . . . When he had thus spoken, the venerable Ānanda said to the Blessed One: "Let not the Blessed One die in this little wattle and daub town, a town in the midst of the jungle, in this branch township. For, Lord, there are other great cities such as Benares (and others). Let the Blessed One die in one of them."'

This request is refused by Buddha. Ānanda then goes to the town and tells the citizens that Buddha is dying. 'Now, when they had heard this saying, they, with their young men and maidens and wives were grieved, and sad, and afflicted at heart. And some of them wept, dishevelling their hair, and stretched forth their arms, and wept, fell prostrate on the ground and rolled to and fro, in anguish at the thought "Too soon will the Blessed One die! Too soon will the Happy One pass away! Full soon will the Light of the world vanish away!"' . . . When Buddha is alone again with his disciples, 'then the Blessed One addressed the brethren and said "It may be, brethren, that there may be doubt or misgiving in the mind of some brother as to the Buddha, the truth, the path or the way. Inquire, brethren, freely. Do not have to reproach yourselves afterwards with this thought: 'Our Teacher was face to face with us, and we could not bring ourselves to inquire of the Blessed One when we were face to face with him.'" And when he had thus spoken they sat silent. Then (after repeating these words and receiving no reply) the Blessed One addressed the brethren and said, "It may be that you put no questions out of reverence for the Teacher. Let one friend communicate with another." And when he had thus spoken the brethren sat silent. And the venerable Ānanda said: "How wonderful a thing, Lord, and how marvellous. Verily, in this whole assembly, there is not one brother who has doubt or misgiving as to Buddha, the truth, the path or the way." Then Buddha said: "It is out of the fullness of thy faith that thou hast spoken, Ānanda. But I know it for certain." . . . Then the Blessed One addressed the brethren saying: "Behold, brethren, I exhort you saying, transitory are all component things; toil without ceasing." And these were the last words of Buddha.'

It is necessary here to make pause for a moment and survey the temporal and geographical circumstances of Buddha's life. His lifetime covered the period of greatest intellectual growth in Athens. If, as some think, the great book of doubt[1] was written by the Hebrew in 450, there would be in three lands, at least, about the same time the same earnestly scornful skepticism in regard to the worn-out teachings of the fathers. But at a time when, in Greece, the greatest minds were still veiling infidelity as best they could, in India atheism was already formulated.

It has been questioned, and the question has been answered both affirmatively and negatively, whether the climatic conditions of Buddha's home were in part responsible for the

[1] *Ecclesiastes.*

pessimistic tone of his philosophy. If one compare the geographical relation of Buddhism to Brahmanism and to Vedism respectively with a more familiar geography nearer home, he will be better able to judge in how far these conditions may have influenced the mental and religious tone. Taking Kabul and Kashmeer as the northern limit of the period of the Rig Veda, there are three geographical centres. The latitude of the Vedic poets corresponds to about the southern boundary of Tennessee and North Carolina. The entire tract covered by the southern migration to the time of Buddhism, extending from Kabul to a point that corresponds to Benares (35° is a little north of Kabul and 25° is a little south of Behār), would be represented loosely in the United States by the difference between the northern line of Mississippi and Key West. The extent of Georgia about represents in latitude the Vedic province (35° to 30°), while Florida (30° to 25°) roughly shows the southern progress from the seat of old Brahmanism to the cradle of young Buddhism. These are the extreme limits of Vedism, Brahmanism and proto-Buddhism. South of this the country was known to Brahmanism only to be called savage, and not before the late Sūtras (c. 300 B.C.) is one brought as far south as Bombay in the West. The Āitareya Brāhmana, which represents the old centre of Brahmanism around Delhi, knows of the Āndhras, south of the Godāvarī river in the southeast (about the latitude of Bombay and Hayti), only as outer 'Barbarians.' It is quite conceivable that a race of hardy mountaineers, in shifting their home through generations from the hills of Georgia and Tennessee to the sub-tropical region of Key West (to Cuba), in the course of many centuries might become morally affected. But it seems to us, although the miasmatic plains of Bengal may perhaps present even a sharper contrast to the Vedic region than do Key West and Cuba to Georgia, that the climate in effecting a moral degradation (if pessimism be immoral) must have produced also the effect of mental debility. Now to our mind there is not the slightest proof for the asseveration, which has been repeated so often that it is accepted by many nowadays as a truism, that Buddhism or even post-Buddhistic literature shows any trace of mental decay.[1] There certainly is mental weakness in the Brāhmanas, but these cannot all be accredited to the miasms of Bengal. They are the bones of a religion already dead, kept for instruction in a cabinet; dry, dusty, lifeless, but awful to the beholder and useful to the owner. Again, does Buddhism lose in the comparison from an intellectual point of view when set beside the mazy gropings of the Upanishads? We have shown that dogma was the base of primal pantheism; of real logic there is not a whit. We admire the spirit of the teachers in the Upanishads, but we have very little respect for the logical ability of any early Hindu teachers; that is to say, there is very little of it to admire. The doctors of the Upanishad philosophy were poets, not dialecticians. Poetry indeed waned in the extreme south, and no spirited or powerful literature ever was produced there, unless it was due to foreign influence, such as the religious poetry of Ramaism and the Tamil *Sittars.* But in secondary subtlety and in the marking of distinctions, in classifying and analyzing on dogmatic premises, as well as in the acceptance of hearsay truths as ultimate verities — we do not see any fundamental disparity in these regards between the mind of the Northwest and that of the Southeast; and what superficial difference exists goes to the credit of Buddhism. For if one must have dogma it is something to have system, and while precedent theosophy was based on the former it knew nothing of the latter. Moreover, in Buddhism there is a greater intellectual vigor than in any phase of

[1] The common view is thus expressed by Oldenberg: "In dem schwülen, feuchten, von der Natur mit Reichthümern üppig gesegneten Tropenlande des Ganges hat das Volk, das in frischer Jugendkraft steht, als es vom Norden her eindringt, bald aufgehört jung und stark zu sein. Menschen und Völker reifen in jenem Lande . . . schnell heran, um ebenso schnell an Leib und Seele zu erschlaffen" (*loc. cit.* p. 11).

Brahmanism (as distinct from Vedism). To cast off not only gods but soul, and more, to deny the moral efficacy of asceticism, this was a leap into the void, to appreciate the daring of which one has but to read himself into the priestly literature of Buddha's rivals, both heterodox and orthodox. We see then in Buddhism neither a debauched moral type, nor a weakened intellectuality. The pessimism of Buddhism, so far as it concerns earth, is not only the same pessimism that underlies the religious motive of Brahmanic pantheism, but it is the same pessimism that pervades Christianity and even Hebraism. This world is a sorry place, living is suffering; do thou escape from it. The pleasures of life are vanity; do thou renounce them. "To die is gain," says the apostle; and the Preacher: "I have seen all the works that are done under the sun and behold all is vanity and vexation of spirit. He that increaseth knowledge increaseth sorrow. For what hath man of all his labor and of the vexation of his heart, wherein he hath laboured under the sun? For all his days are sorrows and his travail grief. That which befalleth the sons of men befalleth beasts; even one thing befalleth them: as the one dieth so dieth the other; yea, they have all one breath; so that a man hath no preëminence above a beast: for all is vanity. All go unto one place; all are of the dust, and all turn to dust again. Who knoweth the spirit of man whether it goeth upward? I praised the dead which are already dead more than the living which are yet alive. The dead know not anything, their love and their hatred and their envy is now perished; neither have they any more a portion for ever in any thing that is done under the sun. The wandering of the desire, this also is vanity."

The Preacher is a fairly good Buddhist.

If pessimism be the conviction that life on earth is not worth living, this view is shared alike by the greatest of earth's religions. If pessimism be the view that all beauty ends with life and that beyond it there is nothing for which it is worth while to live, then India has no parallel to this Homeric belief. If, however, pessimism mean that to have done with existence on earth is the best that can happen to a man, but that there is bliss beyond, then this is the opinion of Brahmanism, Jainism, and Christianity. Buddhism alone teaches that to live on earth is weariness, that there is no bliss beyond, and that one should yet be calm, pure, loving, and wise.

How could such a religion inspire enthusiasm? How could it send forth jubilant disciples to preach the gospel of joy? Yet did Buddhism do even this. Not less happy and blissful than were they that received the first comfort of pantheism were the apostles of Buddha. His progress was a triumph of gladness. They that believed in him rejoiced and hastened to their fellows with the good tidings. Was it then a new morality, a new ethical code, that thus inspired them? Let one but look at the vows and commandments respectively taken by and given to the Buddhist monk, and he will see that in Buddhism there is no new morality.

The Ten Vows are as follows:

> I take the vow not to kill; not to steal; to abstain from impurity; not to lie; to abstain from intoxicating drinks which hinder progress and virtue; not to eat at forbidden times; to abstain from dancing, singing, music and stage plays; not to use garlands, scents, unguents, or ornaments; not to use a high or broad bed; not to receive gold or silver.

The Eight Commandments are as follows:

> Do not kill; do not steal; do not lie; do not drink intoxicating drinks; do not commit fornication or adultery; do not eat unseasonable food at night; do not wear garlands or use perfumes; sleep on a mat spread on the ground.

The first five of these commands are given to every Buddhist, monk, or layman; the last three are binding only on the monk.[1]

These laws and rules were, however, as we have indicated in

[1] Rhys Davids, *Buddhism*, pp. 160, 139.

the chapter on Jainism, the common property, with some unimportant variations and exceptions, of the Brahman ascetic, the Jain, and the Buddhist. There was surely nothing here to rouse especial interest. No. But there was one side of Buddhism that was new, not absolutely new, for it formed part of the moral possession of that early band which we may call the congregation of the Spirit. The Brahman theoretically had done away with penance and with prayer, with the Vedic gods and with the Vedic rites. Yet was it impossible for him practically to absolve the folk of these. The priest might admit that he knew a better way to salvation, but he still led the people over the hard old road, and he himself went that way also, because it was the way of the fathers, because it was the only way for them that were unwise, and perhaps, too, because it was the only way in which the priest could keep his place as guide and leader of the people.

Jainism smote down some of the obstacles that the Brahman had built and kept. Mahāvīra made the way to salvation shorter, but he did not make it easier for the masses. Asceticism, self-mortification, starvation, torture, — this was his means of gaining happiness hereafter.

But Buddha cut down all obstacles. He made the lowest equal with the highest. It is true that he was no democrat. It is true that his success depended, in great part, on political influence, on the conversion of kings and nobles, men of his own class. It is true also that Buddha at first, like every other Hindu theosophist, sought no salvation for the world around him, but only for himself. But he was moved with pity for the multitude. And why? The sages among them knew no path to happiness save through life-long torture; the common people knew only a religion of rites in which they took no interest, the very words of which were unintelligible; and its priests in their eyes, if not contemptible, at least were unsympathetic. And at the same time the old caste-system oppressed and insulted them. It is evident that the times were ripe for a more humane religion and a new distribution of social privileges.

Then Buddha arose and said: "He that is pure in heart is the true priest, not he that knows the Veda. Like unto one that standeth where a king hath stood and spoken, and standing and speaking there deems himself for this a king, seems to me the man that repeateth the hymns, which the wise men of old have spoken, and standing in their place and speaking, deems himself for this a sage. The Vedas are nothing, the priests are of no account, save as they be morally of repute. Again, what use to mortify the flesh? Asceticism is of no value. Be pure, be good; this is the foundation of wisdom — to restrain desire, to be satisfied with little. He is a holy man who doeth this. Knowledge follows this."

Here is the essence of Buddhism, here is its power; and when one reflects that Buddha added: "Go into all lands and preach this gospel; tell them that the poor and lowly, the rich and high, are all one, and that all castes unite in this religion, as unite the rivers in the sea" — he will understand what key was used to open the hearts of Buddha's kinsmen and people.

But, it will be said, there is nothing in this of that extreme pessimism, of which mention has just been made. True. And this, again, is an important point to bear in mind, that whereas the logic of his own system led Buddha into a formal and complete pessimism, which denies an after-life to the man that finds no happiness in this, he yet never insists upon this. He not only does not insist, but in his talks with his questioners and disciples he uses all means to evade direct inquiry in regard to the fate of man after death. He believed that Nirvāna (extinction of lust) led to cessation of being; he did not believe in an immortal soul.* But he urged no such negative doctrine as this. What he urged repeatedly was that every one accepting the undisputed doctrine of *karma* or re-birth in its full extent (*i.e.*, that for every sin here, punishment followed in the next existence), should endeavor to escape, if possible, from such an endless course of painful re-births, and that to accomplish this it was necessary first to be sober and good, then to be learned, but not to be an ascetic. On the other hand the doctrine, in its logical fullness, was a teaching only for the wise, not for fools. He imparted it only to the wise. What is one to understand from this? Clearly, that Buddha regarded the mass of his disciples as standing in need merely of the Four Great Truths, the confession of which was the sign of becoming a disciple; while to the strong and wise he reserved the logical pessimism, which resulted from his first denials and the premises of causality on which was erected his complicated system. Only thus can one comprehend the importance of Buddhism to his own time and people, only in this light reconcile the discrepancy between the accounts of a religion which roused multitudes to enthusiasm and joy, while on the other hand it stood on the cold basis of complete nihilism. Formally there was not an esoteric [1] and exoteric Buddhism, but practically what the apostles taught, what Buddha himself taught to the mass of his hearers was a release from the bondage of the law and the freedom of a high moral code as the one thing needful. But he never taught that sacrifice was a bad thing; he never either took the priest's place himself or cast scorn upon the Brahman caste: "Better even than a harmless [2] sacrifice is liberality" he says, "better than liberality is faith and kindness (non-injury) and truth, better than faith, kindness, and truth is renunciation of the world and the search for peace; best of all, the highest sacrifice and greatest good, is when one enters Nirvāna, saying "I shall not return again to earth." This is to be an Arhat (Perfect Sage).

[1] Buddha taught, of course, nothing related to the thaumaturgy of that folly which calls itself to-day 'Esoteric Buddhism.'

[2] That is a sacrifice where no cattle are slain, and no injury is done to living beings.

These are Buddha's own words as he spoke with a Brahman priest,[1] who was converted thereby and replied at once with the Buddhist's confession of faith: "I take refuge in Buddha, in the doctrine, in the church."

A significant conversation! In many ways these words should be corrective of much that is hazarded today in regard to Buddhism. There is here no elaborate system of metaphysics. Wisdom consists in the truth as it is in Buddha; and before truth stand, as antecedently essential, faith and kindness; for so may one render the passive non-injury of the Brahman as taught by the Buddhist. To have faith and good works, to renounce the pomps and vanities of life, to show kindness to every living thing, to seek for salvation, to understand, and so finally to leave no second self behind to suffer again, this is Buddha's doctrine.

We have avoided thus far to define Nirvāna. It has three distinct meanings, eternal blissful repose (such was the Nirvāna of the Jains and in part of Buddhism), extinction and absolute annihilation (such was the Nirvāna of some Buddhists), and the Nirvāna of Buddha himself. Nirvāna meant to Buddha the extinction of lust, anger, and ignorance. He adopted the term, he did not invent it. He was often questioned, but persistently refused to say whether he believed that Nirvāna implied extinction of being or not. We believe that in this refusal to speak on so vital a point lies the evidence that he himself regarded the 'extinction' or 'blowing out' (this is what the word means literally) as resulting in annihilation. Had he believed otherwise we think he would not have hesitated to say so, for it would have strengthened his influence among them to whom annihilation was not a pleasing thought.

But one has no right to 'go behind the returns' as these are given by Buddha. The later church says distinctly that Buddha himself did not teach whether he himself, his ego, was to live

[1] *Kūtadanta-sutta*, Oldenberg, *Buddha*, p. 175.

after death or not; or whether a permanent ego exists. It is useless, therefore, to inquire whether Buddha's Nirvāna be a completion, as Müller defines it, or annihilation. To one Buddhistic party it was the one; to the other, the other; to Buddha himself it was what may be inferred from his refusal to make any declaration in regard to it.

The second point of interest is not more easily disposed of. What to the Buddhist is the spirit, the soul of man? It certainly is not an eternal spirit, such as was the spirit of Brahmanic philosophy, or that of the Jain. But, on the other hand, it is clear that something survived after death till one was reborn for the last time, and then entered Nirvāna. The part that animates the material complex is to the Buddhist an individuality which depends on the nature of its former complex, home, and is destined to project itself upon futurity till the house which it has built ceases to exist, a home rebuilt no more to be its tabernacle. When a man dies the component parts of his material personality fall apart, and a new complex is formed, of which the individuality is the effect of the *karma* of the preceding complex. The new person is one's karmic self, but it is not one's identical ego. There appears, therefore, even in the doctrine of Nirvāna, to lie something of that altruism so conspicuous in the insistence on kindness and conversion of others. It is to save from sorrow this son of one's acts that one should seek to find the end. But there is no soul to save.

We cannot insist too often on the fact that the religion of Buddha was not less practical than human. He practiced, as he taught, that the more one worked for others, was devoted to others, the less he cared for himself, the less was he the victim of desire. Hence he says that a true Nirvāna may come even in one's own lifetime — the utter surrender of one's self is Nirvāna,[1] while the act of dying only draws the curtain after

[1] Sometimes distinguished from *pari-nirvāṇa* as absolute annihilation.

the tragedy has ended. "Except," Buddha says, "for birth, age, and death, there would be no need of Buddha."

A review of Buddha's system of metaphysics is, therefore, doubly unnecessary for our present purpose.[1] In the first place we believe that most of the categories and metaphysical niceties of Buddhism, as handed down, are of secondary origin; and, were this not so, it is still evident that they were but the unimportant, intellectual appendage of a religion that was based on anything but metaphysical subtleties. Buddha, like every other teacher of his time, had to have a 'system,' though whether the system handed down as his reverts to him it is impossible to say. But Buddha's recondite doctrine was only for the wise. "It is hard to learn for an ordinary person," says Buddha himself. But it was the ordinary person that Buddhism took to its bosom. The reason can be only the one we have given. For the last stage before Arhat-ship Buddha had ready a complicate system. But he did not inflict it on the ordinary person.[2] It was not an essential but the completing of his teaching; in his own eyes truth as represented by the Four Great Truths was the real doctrine.

The religion of Buddha, for the mass of people, lies in the Four Great Truths and their practical application to others, which implies kindness and love of humanity. For Buddha, whatever may have been the reluctance with which he

[1] Some scholars think that the doctrine of Buddha resembles closely that of the Sānkhya philosophy (so Barth, p. 116), but Müller, Oldenberg, and others, appear to be right in denying this. The Sankhyan 'spirit' has, for instance, nothing corresponding to it in Buddha's system.

[2] The twelve Nidānas are dogmatic, and withal not very logical. "From ignorance arise forms, from forms arises consciousness, from consciousness arise name and bodiness; from name and bodiness arise the six senses (including understanding as the sixth) and their objects; from these arises contact; from this, feeling; from this, thirst; from this, clinging; from clinging arises becoming; from becoming arises birth; from birth arise age and sorrow." One must gradually free himself from the ten fetters that bind to life, and so do away with the first of these twelve Nidanas, ignorance.

began to preach, shows in all his teachings and dealings with men an enduring patience under their rebuffs, a brotherly sympathy with their weakness, and a divine pity for their sorrows. Something, too, of divine anger with the pettiness and meanness of the unworthy ones among his followers, as when, after preaching with parable and exhortation to the wrangling brothers of the monastery of Kosambī, he left them, saying, "'Truly these fools are infatuate; it is no easy task to administer instruction to them,' and," it is added simply, "he rose from his seat and went away."[1]

The significance of the church organization in the development of Buddhism should not be under-estimated. Contrasted with the lack of an organized ecclesiastical corporation among the Brahmans the Buddhistic synod, or congregation, Sangha, exerted a great influence. In different places there would be a park set apart for the Buddhist monks. Here they had their monastery buildings, here they lived during the rainy season, from this place out as a centre the monks radiated through the country, not as lone mendicants, but as members of a powerful fraternity. To this monastery came gifts, receipts of all kinds that never would have been bestowed upon individuals. Undoubtedly organization did much for the spread of Buddhism. Yet we think its influence has been emphasized almost too much by some scholars, or rather the effect has been represented as too radical. For the monasteries, as represented by tradition, with their immense wealth and political importance as allies of the heretical kings of the East, are plainly of secondary growth. If one limit their national and political importance to a period one or two hundred years after the Master's time, he will not err in attributing to this cause, as does Barth, the reason for the rapid rise and supremacy of Buddhism over India. But the first beginnings of the institution were small, and what is to be sought in the beginning of Buddhism is rather

[1] *Mahāvagga*, x. 3 (SBE. xvii. 306).

the reason why the monasteries became popular, and what was the hold which Buddha had upon the masses, and which induced the formation of this great engine of religious war. And when this first question is raised the answer must still be that the banding together of the monks was not the cause but the effect of the popularity of Buddhism. The first monasteries, as Barth well says, were only assemblies of pious men who formed a spiritual band of religious thinkers, of men who united themselves into one body to the end that they might study righteousness, learning together how to imitate the Master in holiness of living. But the members converted soon became so many that formal assemblies became a necessity to settle the practical disputes and theoretical questions which were raised by the new multitude of believers, some of whom were more factious than devout. Brahmanism had no need of this. The Brahman priest had his law in tradition; his life and conduct were regulated by immemorial law. The corporations of these priests were but temporary organizations for specific purposes. They made no attempt to proselytize. Their members never exceeded the bounds of the caste. The cause, then, of the rapid spread of Buddhism at the beginning of its career lies only in the conditions of its teaching and the influential backing of its founder. It was the individual Buddha that captivated men; it was the teaching that emanated from him that fired enthusiasm; it was his position as an aristocrat that made him acceptable to the aristocracy, his magnetism that made him the idol of the people. From every page stands out the strong, attractive personality of this teacher and winner of hearts. No man ever lived so godless yet so godlike. Arrogating to himself no divinity, despairing of future bliss, but without fear as without hope, leader of thought but despising lovingly the folly of the world, exalted but adored, the universal brother, he wandered among men, simply, serenely; with gentle irony subduing them that opposed him, to congregation after congregation speaking with majestic sweetness, the master to each, the friend of all. His voice was singularly vibrant and eloquent;[1] his very tones convinced the hearer, his looks inspired awe. From the tradition it appears that he must have been one of those whose personality alone suffices to make a man not only a leader but a god to the hearts of his fellows. When such an one speaks he obtains hearers. It matters little what he says, for he influences the emotions, and bends whoever listens to his will. But if added to this personality, if encompassing it, there be the feeling in the minds of others that what this man teaches is not only a verity, but the very hope of their salvation; if for the first time they recognize in his words the truth that makes of slaves free men, of classes a brotherhood, then it is not difficult to see wherein lies the lightning-like speed with which the electric current passes from heart to heart. Such a man was Buddha, such was the essential of his teaching; and such was the inevitable rapidity of Buddhistic expansion, and the profound influence of the shock that was produced by the new faith upon the moral consciousness of Buddha's people.

The literature of early Buddhism consists of a number of historical works embodying the life and teaching of the master, some of more didactic and epigrammatic intent, and, in the writings of the Northern Buddhists, some that have given up the verbose simplicity of the first tracts in favor of tasteless and extravagant recitals more stagey than impressive. The final collection of the sacred books (earlier is the Suttanta division into Nikāyas) is called Tripitaka, 'the three baskets,' one containing the tracts on discipline; one, the talks of Buddha; and one, partly metaphysical; called respectively Vinaya, Sutta, and Abhidhamma. The Southern[2] Pāli

[1] Compare Kern, the *Lotus*, iii. 21, and Fausböll, *Pārāyana-sutta*, 9 (1131), the "deep and lovely voice of Buddha." (SBE. xxi. 64, and x. 210.)

[2] As Southern Buddhists are reckoned those of Ceylon, Burmah, Siam, etc.

redaction — for the writings of the Northern[1] Buddhists are in Sanskrit — was commented upon in the fifth century of this era by Buddha-gosha ('Buddha's glory'), and appears to be older than the Sanskrit version of Nepāl. Some of the writings go back as far as the Second Council, and their content, so far as it concerns Buddha's own words, in many cases is doubtless a tradition that one should accept as authoritative. The works on discipline, instead of being as dull as one might reasonably expect of books that deal with the petty details of a monastery, are of exceeding interest (although whole chapters conform to the reasonable expectation), for they contain fragments of the work and words of Buddha which give a clearer idea of his personality and teaching than do his more extended and perhaps less original discourses. They throw a strong light also on the early church, its recalcitrant as well as its obedient members, the quarrels and schisms that appear to have arisen even before Buddha's death. Thus in the *Mahāvagga* (ch. x) there is found an account of the schism caused by the expulsion of some unworthy members. The brethren are not only schismatic, some taking the side of those expelled, but they are even insolent to Buddha; and when he entreats them for the sake of the effect on the outer world to heal their differences,[2] they tell him to his face that they will take the responsibility, and that he need not concern himself with the matter. It is on this occasion that Buddha says, "Truly, these fools are infatuate," leaves them, and goes into solitude, rejoicing to be free from souls so quarrelsome and contentious. Again these tracts give a picture of how they should live that are truly Buddha's disciples. Buddha finds three disciples living in perfect harmony, and asks them how

1 As Northern Buddhists are reckoned those of Nepāl, Tibet, China, Corea, Japan, Java, Sumatra, Annam, and Cambodia.

2 "Let your light so shine before the world, that you, having embraced the religious life according to so well-taught a doctrine and discipline, may be seen to be forbearing and mild." (SBE. xvii. 305, David's and Oldenberg's translation.)

they live together so peaceably and lovingly. In quaint and yet dignified language they reply, and tell him that they serve each other. He that rises first prepares the meal, he that returns last at night puts the room in order, etc. (*ib.* 4). Occasionally in the account of unruly brothers it is evident that tradition must be anticipating, or that many joined the Buddhist fraternity as an excuse from restraint. The *Cullavagga* opens with the story of two notorious renegades, 'makers of strife, quarrelsome, makers of dispute, given to idle talk, and raisers of legal questions in the congregation.' Such were the infamous followers of Panduka and Lohitaka. Of a different sort, Epicurean or rather frivolous, were the adherents of Assaji and Punabbasu, who, according to another chapter of the *Cullavagga* (i. 13), 'cut flowers, planted cuttings of flowers, used ointment and scents, danced, wore garlands, and revelled wickedly.' A list of the amusements in which indulged these flighty monks includes 'games played with six and ten pieces, tossing up, hopping over diagrams, dice, jackstraws,[1] ball, sketching, racing, marbles, wrestling,' etc.; to which a like list (*Tevijja*, ii) adds chess or checkers ('playing with a board of sixty-four squares or one hundred squares'), ghost stories, and unseemly wrangling in regard to belief ("I am orthodox, you are heterodox"), earning a living by prognostication, by taking omens 'from a mirror' or otherwise, by quack medicines, and by 'pretending to understand the language of beasts.' It is gratifying to learn that the scented offenders described in the first-mentioned work were banished from the order. According to the regular procedure, they were first warned, then reminded, then charged; then the matter was laid before the congregation, and they were obliged to leave the order. Even the detail of Subhadda's insolence is not wanting in these records (*Cull.* xi. 1. and elsewhere). No sooner was Buddha dead than

[1] 'Removing pieces from a pile without moving the remainder' must, we presume, be jackstraws.

the traitor Subhadda cries out: "We are well rid of him; he gave us too many rules. Now we may do as we like." On which the assembly proceeded to declare in force all the rules that Buddha had given, although he had left it to them to discard them when they would. The Confessional (Pātimokkha), out of which have been evolved in narrative form the Vinaya texts that contain it, concerns graded offences, matters of expiation, rules regarding decency, directions concerning robes, rugs, bowls, and other rather uninteresting topics, all discussed in the form of a confession.[1] The church-reader goes over the rules in the presence of the congregation, and asks at the end of each section whether any one is guilty of having broken this rule. If at the third repetition no one responds, he says, 'They are declared innocent by their silence.' This was the first public confessional, although, as we have shown above, the idea of a partial remission of sin by means of confession to the priest is found in Brahmanic literature.[2] The confession extends to very small matters, but one sees from other texts that the early congregation laid a great deal of weight on details, such as dress, as the sign of a sober life. Thus in *Mahāvagga*, v. 2 ff., certain Buddhists dress in a worldly way. At one time one is informed of the color of their heretical slippers, at another of the make of their wicked gowns. All this is monastic, even in the discipline which 'sets back' a badly behaved monk, gives him probation, forces him to be subordinate. In *Cullavagga*, i. 9, there is an account of stupid Seyyasaka, who was dull and indiscreet, and was always getting 'set back' by the brethren. Finally they grow weary of probating him and carry out the *nissaya* against him, obliging him

1 For instance, rules for eating, drinking (liquor), and for bathing. The Buddhist monk, except in summer, bathed once a fortnight only.

2 No one is so holy that sin does not hurt him, according to Buddhistic belief. The Brahman, on the contrary, was liable to become so holy that he could commit any sin and it did not affect his virtue, which he stored up in a heap by cumulative asceticism.

to remain under the superintendence of others. For, according to Buddha's rule, a wise novice was kept under surveillance, or rather under the authority of others, for five years; a stupid uninformed monk, forever. Buddha's relations with society are plainly set forth. One reads how his devoted friend, King Seniya Bimbisāra, four years younger than Buddha, and his protector (for he was King of Māgadha), gives him a park, perhaps the first donation of this sort, the origin of all the monastic foundations: "The King of Māgadha, Bimbisāra, thought 'here is this bamboo forest Veluvana, my pleasure-garden, which is neither too near to the town nor too far from it. . . . What if I were to give it to the fraternity?' . . . And he took a golden vessel (of water) and dedicated the garden to Buddha, saying, 'I give up the park to the fraternity with Buddha at its head.' And the Blessed One accepted the park" (*Mahāvagga*, i. 22).[1] Another such park Buddha accepts from the courtezan, Ambapāli, whose conversation with Buddha and dinner-party to him forms a favorite story with the monks (*Mahāv.* v. 30; *Cull.* ii). The protection offered by Bimbisāra made the order a fine retreat for rogues. In *Mahāv.* I. 41 ff. one reads that King Seniya Bimbisāra made a decree: "No one is to do any harm to those ordained among the Çākya-son's monks.[2] Well taught is their doctrine. Let them lead a holy life for the sake of complete extinction of suffering." But robbers and runaway slaves immediately took advantage of this decree, and by joining the order put the police at defiance. Even debtors escaped, became monks, and mocked their creditors. Buddha, therefore, made it a rule that no robber, runaway slave, or other person liable to arrest should be admitted into the order. He ordained further

[1] The offering and reception of gifts is always accompanied with water, both in Buddhistic and Brahmanic circles. Whether this was a religious act or a legal sign of surrender we have not been able to discover. Perhaps it arose simply from water always being offered as refreshment to a guest (with fruit), as a sign of guest-friendship.

[2] Sakyaputtiya Samanas, *i.e.*, Buddhists.

that no son might join the order without his parents' consent (*ib.* 54). Still another motive of false disciples had to be combated. The parents of Upāli thought to themselves: "What shall we teach Upāli that he may earn his living? If we teach him writing his fingers will be sore; if we teach him arithmetic his mind will be sore; if we teach him money-changing his eyes will be sore. There are those Buddhist monks; they live an easy life; they have enough to eat and shelter from the rain; we will make him a monk." Buddha, hearing of this, ordained that no one should be admitted into the order under twenty (with some exceptions).

The monks' lives were simple. They went out by day to beg, were locked in their cells at night (*Mahāv.* i. 53), were probated for light offences, and expelled for very severe ones.[1] The people are represented as murmuring against the practices of the monks at first, till the latter were brought to more modest behavior. It is perhaps only Buddhist animosity that makes the narrator say: "They did not behave modestly at table. . . . Then the people murmured and said, 'These Buddhist monks make a riot at their meals, *they act just like the Brahman priests.*'" (*Mahāv.* i. 25; cf. i. 70.)

We turn from the Discipline to the Sermons. Here one finds everything, from moral exhortations to a book of Revelations.[2] Buddha sometimes is represented as entering upon a dramatic dialogue with those whom he wishes to reform, and the talk is narrated. With what soft irony he questions, with what apparent simplicity he argues! In the *Tevijja*[3] the scene opens with a young Brahman. He is a pious and religious youth,

[1] In the case of a monk having carnal connection with a nun the penalty was instant expulsion (*ib.* 60). The nuns were subject to the monks and kept strictly in hand, obliged always to greet the monks first, to go to lessons once a fortnight, and so forth.

[2] Mahasudassana, the great King of Glory whose city is described with its four gates, one of gold, one of silver, one of jade and one of crystal, etc. The earlier Buddha had as 'king of glory' 84,000 wives and other comforts quite as remarkable.

[3] Translated by Davids, *Buddhist Suttas* and *Hibbert Lectures.*

and tells Buddha that although he yearns for 'union with Brahmā,'[1] he does not know which of the different paths proposed by Brahman priests lead to Brahmā. Do they all lead to union with Brahmā? Buddha answers: 'Let us see; has any one of these Brahmans ever seen Brahmā?' 'No, indeed, Gautama.' 'Or did any one of their ancestors ever see Brahmā?' 'No, Gautama.' 'Well, did the most ancient seers ever say that they knew where is Brahmā?' 'No, Gautama.' 'Then if neither the present Brahmans know, nor the old Brahmans knew where is Brahmā, the present Brahmans say in point of fact, "We can show the way to union with what we know not and have never seen; this is the straight path, this is the direct way which leads to Brahmā"— and is this foolish talk?' 'It is foolish talk.' 'Then, as to yearning for union with Brahmā, suppose a man should say, "How I long for, how I love the most beautiful woman in this land," and the people should ask, "Do you know whether that beautiful woman is a noble lady, or a Brahman woman, or of the trader class, or a slave?" and he should say, "No"; and the people should say, "What is her name, is she tall or short, in what place does she live?" and he should say, "I know not," and the people should say, "Whom you know not, neither have seen, her you love and long for?" and he should say, "Yes,"—would not that be foolish?' Then, after this is assented to, Buddha suggests another parallel. 'A man builds a staircase, and the people ask, "Do you know where is the mansion to which this staircase leads?" "I do not know." "Are you making a staircase to lead to something, taking it for a mansion, which you know not and have never seen?" "Yes." Would not this be foolish talk? . . . Now what think you, is Brahmā in possession of wives and wealth?' 'He is not.'

[1] What we have several times had to call attention to is shown again by the side light of Buddhism to be the case in Brahmanic circles, namely, that even in Buddha's day while Brahmā is the god of the thinkers Indra is the god of the people (together with Vishnu and Çiva, if the texts are as old as they pretend to be).

'Is his mind full of anger or free from anger? Is his mind full of malice or free from malice?' 'Free from anger and malice.' 'Is his mind depraved or pure?' 'Pure.' 'Has he self-mastery?' 'Yes.' 'Now what think you, are the Brahmans in possession of wives and wealth, do they have anger in their hearts, do they bear malice, are they impure in heart, are they without self-mastery?' 'Yes.' 'Can there then be likeness between the Brahmans and Brahmā?' 'No.' 'Will they then after death become united to Brahmā who is not at all like them?' Then Buddha points out the path of purity and love. Here is no negative 'non-injury,' but something very different to anything that had been preached before in India. When the novice puts away hate, passion, wrong-doing, sinfulness of every kind, then: 'He lets his mind pervade the whole wide world, above, below, around and everywhere, with a heart of love, far-reaching, grown great, and beyond measure. And he lets his mind pervade the whole world with a heart of pity, sympathy, and equanimity, far-reaching, grown great, and beyond measure.' Buddha concludes (adopting for effect the Brahmā of his convert): 'That the monk who is free from anger, free from malice, pure in mind, and master of himself should after death, when the body is dissolved, become united to Brahmā who is the same—such a condition of things is quite possible.' Here is no metaphysics, only a new religion based on morality and intense humanity, yet is the young man moved to say, speaking for himself and the friend with him: 'Lord, excellent are the words of thy mouth. As if one were to bring a lamp into the darkness, just so, Lord, has the truth been made known to us in many a figure by the Blessed One. And we come to Buddha as our refuge, to the doctrine and to the church. May the Blessed One accept us as disciples, as true believers, from this day forth, as long as life endures.'

The god Brahmā of this dialogue is for the time being playfully accepted by Buddha as the All-god. To the Buddhist himself Brahmā and all the Vedic gods are not exactly non-existent, but they are dim figures that are more like demi-gods, fairies, or as some English scholars call them, 'angels.' Whether Buddha himself really believed in them, cannot be asserted or denied. This belief is attributed to him, and his church is very superstitious. Probably Buddha did not think it worth while to discuss the question. He neither knew nor cared whether cloud-beings existed. It was enough to deny a Creator, or to leave no place for him. Thaumaturgical powers are indeed credited to the earliest belief, but there certainly is nothing in harmony with Buddha's usual attitude in the extraordinary discourse called *Ākankheyya*, wherein Buddha is represented as ascribing to monks miraculous powers, only hinted at in a vague 'shaking of the earth' in more sober speech.[1] From the following let the 'Esoteric Buddhists' of to-day take comfort, for it shows at least that they share an ancient folly, although Buddha can scarcely be held responsible for it: "If a monk should desire to become multiform, to become visible or invisible, to go through a wall, a fence, or a mountain as if through air; to penetrate up or down through solid ground as if through water . . . to traverse the sky, to touch the moon . . . let him fulfil all righteousness, let him be devoted to that quietude of heart which springs from within . . . let him look through things, let him be much alone." That is to say, let him aim for the very tricks of the Yogis, which Buddha had discarded. Is there not here perhaps a little irony? Buddha does not say that the monk will be able to do this — he says if the monk wishes to do this, let him be quiet and meditate and learn righteousness, then perhaps — but he will at least have learned righteousness!

The little tract called *Cetokhila* contains a sermon which has not lost entirely its usefulness or application, and it is characteristic of the way in which Buddha treated eschatological

1 *Mahāparinibbana* iii, to which Rhys Davids refers, is scarcely a fair parallel.

conundrums: 'If a brother has adopted the religious life in the hope of belonging to some one of the angel (divine) hosts, thinking to himself, "by this morality or by this observance or by this austerity or by this religious life I shall become an angel," his mind does not incline to zeal, exertion, perseverance and struggle, and he has not succeeded in his religious life' (has not broken through the bonds). And, continuing, Buddha says that just as a hen might sit carefully brooding over her well-watched eggs, and might torment herself with the wish, 'O that this egg would let out the chick,' but all the time there is no need of this torment, for the chicks will hatch if she keeps watch and ward over them, so a man, if he does not think what is to be, but keeps watch and ward of his words, thoughts, and acts, will 'come forth into the light.'[1]

The questions in regard to Buddha's view of soul, immortality, and religion are answered to our mind as clearly in the following passages as Buddha desired they should be. 'Unwisely does one consider: "Have I existed in ages past . . . shall I exist in ages yet to be, do I exist at all, am I, how am I? This is a being, whence is it come, whither will it go?" Consideration such as this is walking in the jungle of delusion. These are the things one should consider: "This is suffering, this is the origin of suffering, this is the cessation of suffering, this is the way that leads to the cessation of suffering." From him that considers thus his fetters fall away' (*Sabbāsava*). In the *Vangīsa-sutta* Buddha is asked directly: "Has this good man's life been vain to him, has he been extinguished, or is he still left with some elements of existence; and how was he liberated?" and he replies: "He has cut off desire for name and form in this world. He has crossed completely the stream of birth and death." In the *Salla-sutta* it is said: "Without cause and unknown is the life of mortals in this world,

[1] The imitation of the original play on words is Rhys Davids', who has translated these Suttas in SBE. vol. xi. For the following see Fausböll, *ib.* vol. x.

troubled, brief, combined with pain. . . . As earthen vessels made by the potter end in being broken, so is the life of mortals." One should compare the still stronger image, which gives the very name of *nir-vāna* ('blowing out') in the *Upasīvamānavapucchā:* "As a flame blown about by wind goes out and cannot be reckoned as existing, so a sage delivered from name and body disappears, and cannot be reckoned as existing." To this Upasīva replies: "But has he only disappeared, or does he not exist, or is he only free from sickness?" To which Buddha: "For him there is no form, and that by which they say he is exists for him no longer." One would think that this were plain enough.

Yet must one always remember that this is the Arhat's death, the death of him that has perfected himself.[1] Buddha, like the Brahmans, taught hell for the bad, and re-birth for them that were not perfected. So in the *Kokāliya-sutta* a list of hells is given, and an estimate is made of the duration of the sinner's suffering in them. Here, as if in a Brahman code, is it taught that 'he who lies goes to hell,' etc. Even the names of the Brahmanic hells are taken over into the Buddhist system, and several of those in Manu's list of hells are found here.

On the other hand, Buddha teaches, if one may trust tradition, that a good man may go to heaven. 'On the dissolution of the body after death the well-doer is re-born in some happy state in heaven' (*Mahāparinibbāna*, i. 24).[2] This, like hell, is a temporary state, of course, before re-birth begins again on earth. In fact, Buddhist and Brahmanic pantheists agree in their attitude toward the respective questions of hell, heaven, and *karma*. It is only the emancipated Arhat that goes to Nirvāna.[3]

[1] After one enters on the stream of holiness there are only seven more possible births on earth, with one in heaven; then he becomes *arhat*, venerable, perfected, and enters Nirvāna.

[2] Compare the fairies and spirits in *ib.* v. 10; and in i. 31, 'give gifts to the gods.'

[3] We agree with Rhys Davids, *Buddhism*, pp. 111, 207, that Buddha himself was an atheist; but to the statement that Nirvāna was "the extinction of that sinful,

When it is said that Buddha preaches to a new convert 'in due course,' it means always that he gave him first a lecture on morality and religion, and then possibly, but not necessarily, on the 'system.' And Buddha has no narrow-minded aversion to Brahmans; he accepts 'Brahman' as he accepts 'Brahmā,' only he wants it to be understood what is a real Brahman: 'A certain Brahman once asked Buddha how one becomes a Brahman, — what are the characteristics that make a man a Brahman. And the Blessed One said: "The Brahman who has removed all sinfulness, who is free from haughtiness, free from impurity, self-restrained, who is an accomplished master of knowledge, who has fulfilled the duties of holiness, — such a Brahman justly calls himself a Brahman."'[1] The *Mahāvagga*, from which this is taken, is full of such sentiments. As here, in i. 2, so in i. 7: "The Blessed One preached to Yasa, the noble youth, 'in due course,'" that is to say, "he talked about the merit obtained by alms-giving, the duties of morality, about heaven, about the evils of vanity and sinfulness of desire," and when the Blessed One saw that the mind of Yasa, the noble youth, was prepared, "then he preached the principal doctrine of the Buddhists, namely, suffering, the cause of suffering, the cessation of suffering, the Path;" and "just as a clean cloth takes the dye, thus Yasa, the noble youth, even while sitting there, obtained the knowledge that whatsoever is subject to birth is also subject to death."[2]

The "spirit and not the letter of the law" is expressed in the formula (*Mahāvagga*, i. 23): "Of all conditions that proceed

grasping condition of mind and heart which would otherwise be the cause of renewed individual existences" should in our opinion be added "and therewith the extinction of individuality." Compare Rhys Davids' *Hibbert Lectures*, p. 253.

[1] Compare the definition of an 'outcast' in the *Vasala-sutta*: "He that gets angry and feels hatred, a wicked man, a hypocrite, he that embraces wrong views and is deceitful, such an one is an outcast, and he that has no compassion for living things."

[2] Compare *ib.* 5. 36: "In due course he spoke, of charity, morality, heaven, pleasure, and the advantage of renunciation."

from a cause, Buddha has explained the cause, and he has explained their cessation." This is the Buddhist's *credo.*

In several of the sermons the whole gist is comprised in the admonition not to meddle with philosophy, nor to have any 'views,' for "philosophy purifies no one; peace alone purifies."[1]

Buddha does not ignore the fact that fools will not desire salvation as explained by him: "What fools call pleasure the noble say is pain; this is a thing difficult to understand; the cessation of the existing body is regarded as pleasure by the noble, but those wise in this world hold the opposite opinion" (*Dvayatānup. sutta*, 38).[2] But to him the truly wise is the truly pure: "Not by birth is one a Brahman, not by birth is one an outcast; by deeds is one a Brahman, by deeds is one an outcast" (*Vasala-sutta*); and not alone in virtue of *karma* of old, for: "The man who knows in this world the destruction of pain, who lays aside the burden and is liberated, him I call a Brahman; whosoever in this world has overcome good and evil, both ties, who is free from grief and defilement, and is pure, — him I call a Brahman; the ignorant say that one is a Brahman by birth, but one is a Brahman by penance, by religious life, by self-restraint, and by temperance" (*Vāsettha-sutta*).

The penance here alluded to is not the vague penance of austerities, but submission to the discipline of the monastery when exercised for a specific fault.

Later Buddhism made of Buddha a god. Even less exaltation than this is met by Buddha thus: Sāriputta says to him, "Such faith have I, Lord, that methinks there never was and never will be either monk or Brahman who is greater and wiser than thou," and Buddha responds: "Grand and bold are the words of thy mouth; behold, thou hast burst forth into ecstatic

[1] See especially the *Nandaman.*, *Paramatthaka*, *Māgandiya*, and *Suddhatthaka Suttas*, translated by Fausböll, SBE. vol. x.

[2] Fausböll, in SBE. vol. x, Suttanipāta.

song. Come, hast thou, then, known all the Buddhas that were?" "No, Lord." "Hast thou known all the Buddhas that will be?" "No, Lord." "But, at least, thou knowest me, my conduct, my mind, my wisdom, my life, my salvation (*i.e.*, thou knowest me as well as I know myself)?" "No, Lord." "Thou seest that thou knowest not the venerable Buddhas of the past and of the future; why, then, are thy words so grand and bold?" (*Mahāparinibbāna.*)

Metaphysically the human ego to the Buddhist is only a collection of five *skandhas* (form, sensations, ideas, faculties of mind, and reason) that vanishes when the collection is dispersed, but the factors of the collection re-form again, and the new ego is the result of their re-formation. The Northern Buddhists, who turn Buddha into a god, make of this an immortal soul, but this is Buddhism in one phase, not Buddha's own belief. The strength of Northern Buddhism lies not, as some say, in its greater religious zeal, but in its grosser animism, the delight of the vulgar.

It will not be necessary, interesting as would be the comparison, to study the Buddhism of the North after this review of the older and simpler chronicles. In Hardy's *Manual of Buddhism* (p. 138 ff.) and Rockhill's *Life of Buddha* will be found the weird and silly legends of Northern Buddhism, together with a full sketch of Buddhistic ethics and ontology (Hardy, pp. 460, 387). The most famous of the Northern books, the Lotus of the Law and the Lalita Vistara, give a good idea of the extravagance and supernaturalism that already have begun to disfigure the purer faith. According to Kern, who has translated the former work again (after Burnouf), the whole intent of the Lotus is to represent Buddha as the supreme, eternal God. The works, treating of piety, philosophy, and philanthropy, contain ancient elements, but in general are of later form. To this age belongs also the whole collection of Jātakas, or 'birth-stories,' of the Buddhas that were before

Gautama, some of the tales of which are historically important, as they have given rise to Western fables.[1] These birth-stories represent Buddha (often as Indra) as some god or mortal, and tell what he did in such or such a form. It is in a future form that, like Vishnu, who is to come in the *avatar* of Kalki, the next Buddha will appear as Maitreya, or the 'Buddha of love.'[2] Some of the stories are very silly; some, again, are beautiful at heart, but ugly in their bizarre appearance. They are all, perhaps, later than our era.[3]

The history of Buddhism after the Master's death has a certain analogy with that of Mohammedanism. That is to say it was largely a political growth. Further than this, of course, the comparison fails. The religion was affected by heretical kings, and by *nouveaux riches*, for it admitted them all into its community on equal terms — no slight privilege to the haughty nabob or proud king who, if a believer and follower of Brahman orthodoxy, would have been obliged to bend the head, yield the path, and fear the slightest frown of any beggar priest that came in his way.

The Māurya monarch Açoka adopted Buddhism as a state religion in the third century B.C., and taught it unto all his people, so that, according to his own account, he changed the creed of the country from Brahmanism to Buddhism.[4] He was king over all northern India, from Kabul to the eastern ocean, from the northern limit of Brahmanic civilization to its southern boundary. Buddhist missionaries were now spread over India

1 The distinction between the Northern and Southern doctrine is indicated by the terms 'Great Vehicle' and 'Little Vehicle' respectively, the former the works of Nāgārjuna's school (see below).

2 As Māitrakanyaka Buddha came once to earth "to redeem the sins of men."

3 Of historic interest is the rapport between Brahmanic, Jain, and Buddhist tales. A case of this sort has been carefully worked out by Leumann, *Die Legende von Citta und Sambhūta*, WZKM. v. 111; vi. 1.

4 "The gods who were worshipped as true divinities in India have been rendered false . . . by my zeal"; inscription cited by Barth, p. 135. But Açoka was a very tolerant prince. Barth's notion of Buddhistic persecution can hardly be correct.

and beyond it. And here again, even in this later age, one sees how little had the people to do with Buddha's metaphysical system. Like the simple confession 'I take refuge in Buddha, in the doctrine, and in the church' was the only credo demanded, that cited above: "Buddha has explained the cause of whatever conditions proceed from a cause, and he has declared their cessation." In this credo, which is engraved all over India, everything is left in confidence to Buddha. However he explained the reason, that creed is to be accepted without inquiry. The convert took the patent facts of life, believing that Buddha had explained all, and based his own belief not on understanding but on faith.

With the council of Patna, 242 B.C., begins at the hands of the missionaries the geographical separation of the church, which results in Southern and Northern Buddhism.[1]

It is at this period that the monastic bodies become influential. The original Sangha, congregation, is defined as consisting of three or more brethren. The later monastery is a business corporation as well as a religious body. The great emperors that now ruled India (not the petty clan-kings of the centuries before) were no longer of pure birth, and some heresy was the only religion that would receive them with due honor. They affected Buddhism, endowed the monasteries, in every way enriched the church, built for it great temples, and in turn were upheld by their thankful co-religionists. Among the six[2] rival heresies that of Buddha was predominant, and chiefly because of royal influence. The Buddhist head of the Ceylon church was Açoka's own son. Still more important for Buddhism was its adoption by the migratory Turanians in the centuries following. Tibet and China were opened up to it through the influence of these foreign kings, who at least pretended to

1 Köppen, *Die Religion des Buddha*, p. 198.

2 Not to be confused with the seventeen heresies and sixty-three different philosophical systems in the church itself.

adopt the faith of Buddha.[1] But as it was adopted by them, and as it extended beyond the limits of India, just so much weaker it became at home, where its strongest antagonists were the sectarian pantheistic parties not so heterodox as itself.

Buddhism lingered in India till the twelfth or thirteenth century, although in the seventh it was already decadent, as appears from the account of Hiouen-Thsang, the Chinese pilgrim. It is found to-day in Tibet, Ceylon, China, Japan, and other outlying regions, but it is quite vanished from its old home. The cause of its extinction is obvious. The Buddhist victorious was not the modest and devout mendicant of the early church. The fire of hate, lighted if at all by Buddhism,[2] smouldered till Brahmanism, in the form of Hinduism, had begotten a religion as popular as Buddhism, or rather far more popular, and for two reasons. Buddhism had no such picturesque tales as those that enveloped with poetry the history of the man-god Krishna. Again, Buddhism in its monastic development had separated itself more and more from the people. Not mendicant monks, urging to a pure life, but opulent churches with fat priests; not simple discourses calculated to awaken the moral and religious consciousness, but subtle arguments on discipline and metaphysics were now what Buddhism represented. This religion was become, indeed, as much a skeleton as was the Brahmanism of the sixth century. As the Brahmanic belief had decomposed into spiritless rites, so Buddhism,

[1] For more details see Barth, *loc. cit.*, p. 130 ff. According to tradition Buddhism was introduced into Tibet in the fourth century, A.D., the first missionaries coming from Nepāl (Rockhill, p. 210).

[2] Barth justly discredits the tale of Buddhism having been persecuted out of India. In this sketch of later Buddhism we can but follow this author's admirable summary of the causes of Buddhistic decline, especially agreeing with him in assigning the first place to the torpidity of the later church in matters of religion. It was become a great machine, its spiritual enthusiasm had been exhausted; it had nothing poetical or beautiful save the legend of Buddha, and this had lost its freshness; for Buddha was now, in fact, only a grinning idol.

changed into dialectic and idolatry (for in lieu of a god the later church worshipped Buddha), had lost now all hold upon the people. The love of man, the spirit of Buddhism, was dead, and Buddhism crumbled into the dust. Vital and energetic was the sectarian 'love of God' alone (Hinduism), and this now became triumphant. Where Buddhism has succeeded is not where the man-gods, objects of love and fear, have entered; but where, without rivalry from more sympathetic beliefs, it has itself evolved a system of idolatry and superstition; where all that was scorned by the Master is regarded as holiest, and all that he insisted upon as vital is disregarded.[1] One speaks of the millions of Buddhists in the world as one speaks of the millions of Christians; but while there are some Christians that have renounced the bigotry and idolatry of the church, and hold to the truth as it is in the words of Christ, there are still fewer Buddhists who know that their Buddhism would have been rebuked scornfully by its founder.

The geographical growth of formal Buddhism is easily sketched. After the first entrance into Kashmeer and Ceylon, in the third century B.C., the progress of the cult, as it now may be called, was steadily away from India proper. In the fifth century A.D., it was adopted in Burmah,[2] and in the seventh in Siam. The Northern school kept in general to the 'void' doctrine of Nāgārjuna, whose chief texts are the Lotus and the Lalita Vistara, standard works of the Great Vehicle.[3] In Tibet Lamaism is the last result of this hierarchical state-church.[4] We have thought it much more important to give a

1 Here are developed fully the stories of hells, angels, and all supernatural paraphernalia, together with theism, idolatry, and the completed monastic system; magic, fable, absurd calculations in regard to nothings, and spiritual emptiness.

2 At the same time the Ceylon canon was fixed by the commentary of Buddhaghosha.

3 Later it follows the mystical school. Both schools have been affected by Brahmanism. The Great Vehicle, founded by Nāgārjuna, was recognized at a fourth council in Kashmeer about the time of the Christian era. Compare Köppen, p. 199.

4 On the Lamaistic hierarchy and system of succession see Mayers, JRAS. iv. 284.

fuller account of early Buddhism, that of Buddha, than a full account of a later growth in regions that, for the most part, are not Indic, in the belief that the Pāli books of Ceylon give a truer picture of the early church than do those of Kashmeer and Nepāl, with their Çivaite and Brahmanic admixture. For in truth the Buddhism of China and Tibet has no place in the history of Indic religions. It may have been introduced by Hindu missionaries, but it has been re-made to suit a foreign people. This does not apply, of course, to the canonical books, the Great Vehicle, of the North, which is essentially native, if not Buddhistic. Yet of the simple narrative and the adulterated mystery-play, if one has to choose, the former must take precedence. From the point of view of history, Northern Buddhism, however old its elements, can be regarded only as an admixture of Buddhistic and Brahmanic ideas. For this reason we take a little more space, not to cite from the Lotus or the grotesque Lalita Vistara,[1] but to illustrate Buddhism at its best. Fausböll, who has translated the dialogue that follows, thinks that in the Suttas of the Sutta-nipāta there is a reminiscence of a stage of Buddhism before the institution of monasteries, while as yet the disciples lived as hermits. The collection is at least very primitive, although we doubt whether the Buddhist disciples ever lived formally as individual hermits. All the Samanas are in groups, little 'congregations,' which afterwards grew into monasteries.

This is a poetical (amœbic) contest between the herdsman Dhaniya and Buddha, with which Fausböll[2] compares St. Luke, xii. 16, but which, on the other hand reminds one of a spiritualized Theocritus, with whom its author was, perhaps, contemporary.

[1] For the same reason we do not enter upon the outer form of Buddhism as expressed in demonology, snake-worship (JRAS. xii. 286) and symbolism (*ib.* OS. xiii. 71, 114).

[2] SBE. vol. x, part ii, p. 3.

I have boiled the rice, I have milked the kine — so said the herdsman Dhaniya — I am living with my comrades near the banks of the (great) Mahī river; the house is roofed, the fire is lit — then rain if thou wilt, O sky!

I am free from anger, free from stubbornness — so said the Blessed One — I am abiding for one night near the banks of the (great) Mahī river; my house has no cover, the fire (of passion) is extinguished — then rain if thou wilt, O sky!

Here are no gad-flies — so said the herdsman Dhaniya — the cows are roaming in meadows full of grass, and they can endure the rain — then rain if thou wilt, O sky!

I have made a well-built raft — so said the Blessed One — I have crossed over, I have reached the further bank, I have overcome the torrent (of passions); I need the raft no more — then rain if thou wilt, O sky!

My wife is obedient, she is not wanton — so said the herdsman Dhaniya — she has lived with me long and is winning; no wickedness have I heard of her — then rain if thou wilt, O sky!

My mind is obedient, delivered (from evil) — so said the Blessed One — it has been cultivated long and is well-subdued; there is no longer anything wicked in me — then rain if thou wilt, O sky!

I support myself by my own earnings — so said the herdsman Dhaniya — and my children are around me and healthy; I hear no wickedness of them — then rain if thou wilt, O sky!

I am the servant of none — so said the Blessed One — with what I have gained I wander about in all the world; I have no need to serve — then rain if thou wilt, O sky!

I have cows, I have calves — so said the herdsman Dhaniya — cows in calf and heifers also; and I have a bull as lord over the cows — then rain if thou wilt, O sky!

I have no cows, I have no calves — so said the Blessed One — no cows in calf, and no heifers; and I have no bull as a lord over the cows — then rain if thou wilt, O sky!

The stakes are driven in and cannot be shaken — so said the herdsman Dhaniya — the ropes are made of holy-grass, new and well-made; the cows will not be able to break them — then rain if thou wilt, O sky!

Like a bull I have rent the bonds — so said the Blessed One — like an elephant I have broken through the ropes, I shall not be born again — then rain if thou wilt, O sky!

Then the rain poured down and filled both sea and land. And hearing the sky raining, Dhaniya said: Not small to us the gain in that we have seen the Blessed Lord; in thee we take refuge, thou endowed with (wisdom's) eye; be thou our master, O great sage! My wife and myself are obedient to thee. If we lead a pure life we shall overcome birth and death, and put an end to pain.

He that has sons has delight in sons—so said the Evil One—he that has cows has delight in cows, for substance is the delight of man, but he that has no substance has no delight.

He that has sons has care with his sons—so said the Blessed One—he that has cows has likewise care with his cows, for substance is (the cause of) care, but he that has no substance has no care.

From Buddha's sermons choice extracts were gathered at an early date, which, as well as the few longer discourses, that have been preserved in their entirety, do more to tell us what was the original Buddha, before he was enwrapped in the scholastic mysticism of a later age, than pages of general critique.

Thus in the *Mahāparinibbāna* casual allusion is made to assemblies of men and of angels (divine beings), of the great thirty-three gods, Death the Evil One and Brahmā (iii. 21). Buddha, as we have said, does not deny the existence of spiritual beings; he denies only their power to affect the perfect man and their controlling part in the universe. In the same sermon the refuge of the disciple is declared to be truth and himself (ii. 33): "Be ye lamps unto yourselves. Betake yourselves to no external refuge. Hold fast to the truth as to a lamp."

And from the famous 'Path of Duty' or 'Collection of truths':[1]

All that we are is the result of what we have thought: it is founded on our thoughts; it is made up of our thoughts. If a man speaks or acts with an evil thought pain follows him as the wheel follows the foot of the ox that draws the carriage, (but) if a man speaks or acts with a pure thought happiness follows him like a shadow that never leaves him.

Earnestness is the path that leads to escape from death, thoughtlessness is the path that leads to death. Those who are in earnest do not die;[2]

[1] Dhammapada (Franke, ZDMG. xlvi. 731). In Sanskrit one has *dharmapatha* with the same sense. The text in the main is as translated by Müller, separately, 1872, and in SBE., vol. x. It was translated by Weber, *Streifen*. i. 112, in 1860.

[2] That is, they die no more; they are free from the chain; they enter Nirvāna.

those who are thoughtless are as if dead already. Long is the night to him who is awake; long is a mile to him who is tired; long is life to the foolish.

There is no suffering for him who has finished his journey and abandoned grief, who has freed himself on all sides and thrown off the fetters.

Some people are born again; evil-doers go to hell; righteous people go to heaven; those who are free from all worldly desires attain Nirvāna.

He who, seeking his own happiness, punishes or kills beings that also long for happiness, will not find happiness after death.

Looking for the maker of this tabernacle I shall have to run through a course of many births, so long as I do not find; and painful is birth again and again. But now, maker of the tabernacle, thou hast been seen; thou shalt not make up this tabernacle again. All thy rafters are broken, thy ridge-pole is sundered; thy mind, approaching Nirvāna, has attained to extinction of all desires.[1]

Better than going to heaven, better than lordship over all worlds, is the reward of entering the stream of holiness.

Not to commit any sin, to do good, and to purify one's mind, that is the teaching of the Buddhas.

Let us live happily, not hating them that hate us. Let us live happily, though we call nothing our own. We shall be like bright gods, feeding on happiness.

From lust comes grief, from lust comes fear; he that is free from lust knows neither grief nor fear.

The best of ways is the eightfold (path); this is the way, there is no other that leads to the purifying of intelligence. Go on this way! Everything else is the deceit of Death. You yourself must make the effort. Buddhas are only preachers. The thoughtful who enter the way are freed from the bondage of Death.[2]

[1] Buddha's words on becoming Buddha.

[2] It is to be observed that transmigration into animal forms is scarcely recognized by Buddha. He assumes only men and superior beings as subjects of *Karma.* Compare Rhys Davids' *Lectures*, pp. 105, 107. To the same scholar is due the statement that he was the first to recognize the true meaning of Nirvāna, 'extinction (not of soul but) of lust, anger, and ignorance.' For divisions of Buddhist literature other than the Tripitaka the same author's *Hibbert Lectures* may be consulted (see also Müller, SBE. x, Introduction, p. i.).

CHAPTER XIV.

EARLY HINDUISM.

WHILE the great heresies that we have been describing were agitating the eastern part of India,[1] the old home of Brahmanism in the West remained true, in name if not in fact, to the ancient faith. But in reality changes almost as great as those of the formal heresies were taking place at the core of Brahmanism itself, which, no longer able to be the religion of a few clans, was now engaged in the gigantic task of remodelling and assimilating the indigenous beliefs and religious practices of its new environment. This was not a conscious act on the part of Brahmanism. At first it was undertaken almost unwittingly, and it was accomplished later not without repugnance. But to perform this task was the condition of continued existence. Brahmanism had to expand, or shrink, wither, and die.

For a thousand years almost the only source of information in regard to this new growth is contained in the epic poetry of the time, with the help of a few additional facts from the law, and some side light from inscriptions. It is here that Vishnuism and Çivaism are found as fully developed sectarian beliefs, accepted by Brahmanism with more or less distrust, and in more or less fulness of faith. It is to the epic that one

[1] The rival heresies seem also to belong to the East. There were thus more than half a dozen heretical bodies of importance agitating the region about Benares at the same time. Subsequently the Jains, who, as we have shown, were less estranged from Brahmanism, drifted westward, while the Buddhist stronghold remained in the East (both, of course, being represented in the South as well), and so, whereas Buddhism eventually retreated to Nepāl and Tibet, the Jains are found in the very centres of old and new (sectarian) Brahmanism, Delhi, Mathurā, Jeypur, Ajmīr.

must turn to study the budding and gradual flowering of the modern religions, which have cast strict orthodoxy into the shade.

Of the two epics, one, the Rāmāyana,[1] has become the Old Testament of the Ramaite Vishnuites of the present day. The Bhārata,[2] on the other hand, is scriptural for all sects, because it is more universal. The former epic, in its present form, is what the Hindus call an 'art-poem,' and in its finish, its exclusively romantic style, and its total lack of nervous dramatic power, it is probably, as the Hindus claim, the work of one man, Vālmīki, who took the ancient legends of Eastern India and moulded them into a stupid sectarian poem. On the other hand, the Bhārata is of no one hand, either in origin or in final redaction; nor is it of one sect; nor has it apparently been thoroughly affected, as has the Rāmāyana, by Buddhistic influences. Moreover, in the huge conglomeration of stirring adventure, legend, myth, history, and superstition which goes to make up the great epic there is contained a far truer picture of the vulgar custom, belief, and religion of the time than the too polished composition of Vālmīki is able to afford, despite the fact that the latter also has many popular elements welded into it. There are, in fact, only two national works in India, only two works which, withal, not in their entirety, but in their nucleus, after one has stripped each of its priestly toggery, reflect dimly the heart of the people, not the cleverness of one man, or the pedantry of schools. For a few Vedic hymns and a few Bhārata scenes make all the literature, with perhaps the exception of some fables, that is not markedly dogmatic, pedantic, or 'artificial.'[3] So true is this that even in the case of the Rāmāyana one never feels

[1] 'The wandering of Rāma,' who is the sectarian representative of Vishnu.

[2] The 'Bhārata (tale)', sometimes called Mahā-Bhārata, or Great Bhārata. The Vishnuite sectarianism here advocated is that of Krishna. But there is as much Çivaism in the poem as there is Vishnuism.

[3] Dramatic and lyric poetry is artificial even in language.

that he is getting from it the genuine belief of the people, but only that form of popular belief which Vālmiki has chosen to let stand in his version of the old tale. The great epic is heroic, Vālmīki's poem is romantic; the former is real, the latter is artificial; and the religious gleaning from each corresponds to this distinction.[1]

The Bhārata, like other Hindu works, is of uncertain date, but it was completed as a 'Great Bhārata' by the end of the sixth century A.D., and the characters of the story are mentioned, as well known, by Pānini, whose work probably belongs to the fourth century B.C. Furthermore, Dio Chrysostomos, probably citing from Megasthenes, refers to it; and the latter authority describes the worship of the chief gods of the epic; while the work is named in one of the domestic Sūtras, and a verse is cited from it in the legal Sūtra of Bāudhāyana.[2] On the other hand, in its latest growth it is on a par with the earlier Purānas, but it is not quite so advanced in sectarianism as even the oldest of these writings. It may, then, be reckoned as tolerably certain that the beginnings of the epic date from the fourth or fifth century before the Christian era, and that it was quite a respectable work by the time that era began; after which it continued to grow for five centuries more.[3] Its religious importance can scarcely be overestimated. In 600 A.D., far away from its native home, in Cambodia, it was encircled with a temple, and an endowment was made by the

[1] Schroeder, p. 453, compares the mutual relation of the Mahābhārata and Rāmāyana to that of the Nibelungenlied and the Parzival of Wolfram von Eschenbach. Jacobi, in his 'Rāmāyana,' has lately claimed a considerable antiquity for the foundation legends of the Rāmāyana, but he does not disprove the late completed form.

[2] i. 78. 10; see Bühler's Introduction.

[3] Jacobi seeks to put the completed nucleus at the time of the Christian era, but it must have been quite a large nucleus in view of the allusions to it in precedent literature. Holtzmann puts the completion at about 1000 A.D.; but in 700 A.D. it was complete, and most scholars will agree with Bühler that the present Mahā-Bhārata was completed by the sixth or seventh century. In 533 A.D. it contained 100,000 distichs, that is, it was about the size it is now.

king providing for the daily recitation of the poem. Its legal verses are authoritative; its religion is to-day that of India as a whole. The latest large additions to it were, as we think, the Book of Laws, the Book of Peace, and the genealogy of Vishnu, which together form a sort of pseudo-epic. But portions of other books, notably the first, fourth, and seventh, are probably almost as recent as are the more palpable interpolations.

The Bhārata (or the epic κατ' ἐξοχήν) gives us our first view of Hinduism in its sectarian developments. But no less does it show us a changing Brahmanism. The most typical change in the Brahmanism of this period, which covers all that time called by Müller the era of the Renaissance, and ends with the pedantically piquant literature of the drama,[1] is the abnormal growth of the ascetic religious exercise. Older Brahmanism, like the sects, admitted Yogis and ascetics of various kinds, but their aim was to attain oneness with God; and 'union' (with God) is the *yoga* (Latin *jugum* has the same origin) which they sought. But it was not long before the starved ascetic, with his wild appearance and great reputation for sanctity, inspired an awe which, in the unscrupulous, was easily turned to advantage. The Yogi became more or less of a charlatan, more or less of a juggler. Nor was this all. Yoga-practices began to take precedence before other religious practices. In the Brāhmanas it is the sacrifice that is god-compelling; but in the epic, although sacrifice has its place, yet when miraculous power is exerted, it is due chiefly to Yoga concentration, or to the equally general use of formulae; not

[1] By the time the drama began the epic was become a religious storehouse, and the actual epic story represented not a fifth of the whole work, so that, with its simple language, it must have seemed, as a literary production, very wearisome to the minds that delighted in the artificial compounds and romantic episodes of the drama and lyric. But even to-day it is recited at great fêtes, and listened to with rapt attention, as the rhapsodes with more or less dramatic power recite its holy verses.

formulae as part of a sacrifice, but as in themselves potent; and mysterious *mantras*, used by priest and warrior alike, serve every end of magic.[1] Apart from acquisition of power, this Yoga-training is, moreover, all that is needful from the point of view of righteousness. Physical prowess here is the one thing admirable. To stand for years on one leg, to be eaten by ants, to be in every way an ascetic of the most stoical sort, is the truest religion. Such an ascetic has no ordinary rules of morality. In fact, his practices are most peculiar, for to seduce young women is one of his commonest occupations; and in his anger to cause an injury to his foes is one of the ends for which he toils. The gods are nothing to him. They are puppets whom he makes shake and tremble at will. As portrayed in the epic, in terms of common sense, the Muni (silent saint) is a morose[2] and very vulgar-minded old man, who seeks to intimidate others by a show of miraculous power. In the matter of penances those of the law are extended beyond all bounds. The caste-restrictions are of the closest, and the most heinous crime is to commit an offence against caste-order. On the other hand, the greatest merit is to give gifts to priests. This had already proceeded far enough, as was indicated by a passage cited above from Manu. But in the epic the greed and rapacity of the priest exceeds all imaginable limits. He takes whatever he can get and asks for more. He has, by his own showing, scarcely one estimable trait. Avarice, cupidity, sensuality, gluttony, love of finery, effeminacy, meanness, and pride — everything charged against him by the Buddhist — are his most marked characteristics. He appears,

1 The later law-books say expressly that women and slaves have a right to use *mantra, mantrādhikāriṇas*. But the later legal Smritis are no more than disguised sectarian Purānas.

2 Compare the visit of the old Muni on the prince in iii. 262. 8. He is *paramakopana*, 'extremely irritable'; calls for food only to reject it; growls at the service, etc. Everything must be done 'quickly' for him. "I am hungry, give me food, *quick*," is his way of speaking, etc. (12). The adjective is one applied to the All-gods, *paramakrodhinas*.

however, to be worse than he always was. For nothing is plainer, from this very epic, than that the priests, although united as a caste, were sharply distinguished in their lives. The ascetic described above represents the fourth period of the priestly life. Below these stood (apart from students)[1] hermits and householders. The householders, or such of them as the epic unfortunately is busied with, the royal priests, seem to be those that are in reality priests only in name. In the king's palace, his constant advisors, his most unscrupulous upholders in wickedness, they gave themselves up to quest of wealth and power. But one would err if he thus dismissed them all. There were others that had no preferment, who lived in quiet content in their own houses, and deserved none of the opprobrium rightly bestowed upon their hypocritical brothers. The hermits, tōō, appear to have been a mild and inoffensive race, not presuming too much on their caste-privileges.

To offset rapaciousness there are tomes of morality of the purest sort. Even in the later additions to the epic one reads: "Away with gifts; receiving gifts is sinful. The silkworm dies of its wealth" (xii. 330. 29). One should compare, again, the exalted verse (Buddhistic in tone) of *ib.* 321. 47: "The red garment, the vow of silence, the three-fold staff, the water-pot — these only lead astray; they do not make for salvation." There were doubtless good and bad priests, but the peculiarity of the epic priest, rapacious and lustful, is that he glories in his sins.

The chief objects of worship (except for the influence of the sectarian religions) were priests, Manes, and, for form's sake, the Vedic gods. These gods, with the addition of the Hindu Plutus (Kubera, the god of riches), are now called the eight 'world-guardians,' viz., Indra, Yama, Varuna, Kubera, Agni,

[1] Each spiritual teacher instructed high-caste boys, in classes of four or five at most. In xii. 328. 41 the four students of a priest go on a strike because the latter wants to take another pupil besides themselves and his own son.

Sūrya, Vāyu, Soma, and are usually simple and shadowy subordinates of the greater new gods.

In the shifting of religious opinion and in the development of theological conceptions what difference can be traced between the same gods as worshipped in the Veda and as worshipped in the epic? Although the Vedic divinities have been twice superseded, once by the Father-god and again by the *ātmā*, Lord, they still remain adorable and adored, active in many ways, though passive before the great All-god. It is, indeed, extremely difficult, owing to the superstruction of sectarian belief, to get down to the foundation-religion of the epic. The best one can do is to see in what way the old gods differ, as represented in the poem, from their older selves of the Rig Veda. From this point of view alone, and entirely irrespective of the sects, manifold changes will be seen to have taken place. Great Soma is no more. Soma is there, the moon, but the glory of the Vedic Soma has departed. His lunar representative is of little importance. Agni, too, is changed. As Fire in the Rig Veda is not only the altar-fire, but also common, every-day fire, so, too, in the epic this god is the material flame, and as such even performs his greatest deeds for his worshippers. He takes on every form, even becoming a priest, and a dove. He remains the priest of the gods, but his day of action in war is over. He no longer wins battles. But he burns down a forest to aid his party. For the Vedic gods are now but weak partizans of the combatants. In the sectarian parts of the epic Agni is only a puppet. His new representative, Skanda, is the chief battle-god, a name almost unknown before. He himself is either the son of Vishnu or a form of Çiva. He is the All-god, the *ātmā*. It is he who burns the world when the time shall have come for the general destruction.

The high and mighty Varuna of the Rig Veda is no longer great. He is no longer serene. He descends and fights on earth. Indra, too, battles with Vritra as of old, but he is quite anthropomorphic, and of no marked value in the contest of heroes. Not only this, but all the gods together are represented as weaker than a good hero, not to speak of a priestly ascetic. In a word, the gods are believed in, but with what a belief! They no longer, as natural powers, inspire special respect. Their nature-origin is for the most part lost. They are thoroughly anthropomorphic. Even Sūrya, the sun, in action if not in laudation, is often more man than god. This gives a strange effect to the epic battle-scenes as compared with those of Homer. Unless Vishnu is active on the field the action is essentially human. No great god or goddess stands ready to save the fainting warrior. He fights and falls alone. Save for the caresses and plaudits of the half-gods, the most that the Vedic gods can do is to wipe away the sweat from the hero's brow.[1] The All-god does not take the place of the band of watchful and helpful gods pictured by Homer. Vishnu fights on the field; he saves only his protégés, and much as a mortal warrior would do it. But the Vedic gods hang like a mist upon the edge of battle, and are all but idle spectators of the scene. Abstractions, as well as the All-god, have routed them, and Dharma or Duty is a greater god than Indra. But there is an older side to this, as we shall presently show. On the moral side the heroes of the epic profess great belief in the power and awfulness of this god Duty. And so far as go rules of chivalry, they are theoretically moral. Practically they are savage, and their religion does not interfere with their brutal barbarity. The tendency to cite divine instances of sin as excuse for committing it is, however, rebuked: "One should neither practice nor blame the (wrong) acts of gods and seers," xii. 292. 17–18.

[1] The saints in the sky praise the combatants (vii. 188. 41; viii. 15. 27); and the gods roar approval of prowess "with roars like a lion's" (viii. 15. 33). Indra and Sūrya and the Apsarasas cool off the heroes with heavenly fans (*ib.* 90. 18). For the last divinities, see Holtzmann's essays, ZDMG. xxxii. 290; xxxiii. 631.

From an eschatological point of view it is most difficult to get back of the statements made by the priestly composers,[1] who, in their various reëditings of the epic, uniformly have given the pantheistic goal as that in which the characters believe. But it is evident that the warriors were not much affected by this doctrine. To them there was one law of righteousness exceeding all others — to die on the field of battle. And for such as did so, over and over again is the assurance given that 'happiness in Indra's heaven' is their reward. And probably a true note is struck in this reiterated promise. To the mass of the vulgar, union with *brahma* would have been no attractive end.

It is interesting to see the remains of the older belief still flourishing in midst of epic pantheism. Although Indra has no such hymn as has Sūrya, yet is he still lauded, and he is a very real person to the knight who seeks his heaven.[2] In fact, so long as natural phenomena were regarded as divine, so long as thunder was godly, it was but a secondary question which name the god bore; whether he was the 'chief and king of gods,' or Vishnu manifesting himself in a special form. This form, at any rate, was to endure as such till the end of the cycle. There are other Indras. Each cycle has its own (i. 197. 29). But sufficient unto the age is the god thereof. If, relinquishing the higher bliss of absorption, the knight sought only Indra's heaven,

1 The original author of the Mahābhārata is reputed to be of low caste, but the writers of the text as it is to-day were sectarian priests. It was written down, it is said, by Ganeça, 'lord of the troops' of Çiva, i. 1. 79, and some historic truth lies in the tale. The priests of Çiva were the last to retouch the poem, as we think.

2 Agni-worship is partly affected by the doctrine that the Samvartaka fire (which destroys the world at the cycle's end) is a form of Vishnu. In Stambamitra's hymn it is said: "Thou, O Agni, art the all, in thee rests the universe . . . Sages know thee as single yet manifold. At the expiration of time thou burnest up the three worlds, after having created them. Thou art the originator and support of all beings" (i. 232. 12). Elsewhere more Vedic epithets are given, such as 'mouth of the gods' (ii. 31. 42), though here 'the Vedas are produced for Agni's sake.' In this same prayer one reads, 'may Agni give me energy; wind, give me breath: earth, give me strength; and water, give me health' (45). Agni, as well as Çiva, is the father of Kumāra Kārtikeya, *i.e.*, Skanda (*ib.* 44).

and believed he was to find it, then his belief practically does not differ much from that of his ancestor, who accepts Indra as an ultimate, natural power. The question arises whether, after all, the Indra-worship of the epic is not rather popular than merely old and preserved. Certainly the reality of the belief seems quite as strong as that of the ever-newly converted sectary. It may be doubted whether the distribution of theological belief is very different in the epic and Vedic ages. Philosophical pantheism is very old in India. The priest believes one thing; the vulgar, another. The priest of the Vedic age, like the philosopher of the next age, and like the later sectarian, has a belief which runs ahead of the popular religion. But the popular religion in its salient features still remains about the same. Arjuna, the epic hero, the pet of Krishna, visits Indra's heaven and stays there five years. It is the old Vedic gods to whom he turns for weapons, till the Çivaite makes Indra send the knight further, to Çiva himself. The old name, king of the Vasus, is still retained for Indra; and though the 'divine weapons,' which are winged with sacred formulae, are said to be more than a match for the gods; though in many a passage the knight and the saint make Indra tremble, yet still appear, through the mists of ascetic and sectarian novelties, Indra's heaven and his grandeur, shining with something of their old glory. Vishnu still shows his solar origin. Of him and of the sun is it said in identical words: "The sun protects and devours all," and "Vishnu protects and devours" (of Vishnu, passim; of the sun, iii. 33. 71). A good deal of old stuff is left in the Forest Book amongst the absurd tales of holy watering places. One finds repeated several times the Vedic account of Indra's fight with Vritra, the former's thunderbolt, however, being now made of a saint's bones (iii. ch. 100–105). Agni is lauded (*ib.* ch. 123). To the Açvins[1] there is one old hymn

[1] But the Açvins are Çūdras in the 'caste-hood of gods' (the caste-order being Angirasas, Ādityas, Maruts and Açvins), xii. 208. 23–25; and Indra in one passage refuses to associate with them, xiii. 157. 17 (cited by Holtzmann, ZDMD. xxxii. 321).

which contains Vedic forms (i. 3). Varuna is still lord of the West, and goes accompanied with the rivers, 'male and female,' with snakes, and demons, and half-gods (*dāityas*, *sādhyas*, *dāivatas*). Later, but earlier than the pseudo-epic, there stands with these gods Kubera, the god of wealth, the 'jewel-giver,' who is the guardian of travellers, the king of those demons called Yakshas, which the later sect makes servants of Çiva. He is variously named;[1] he is a dwarf; he dwells in the North, in Mt. Kāilāsa, and has a demoniac gate-keeper, Macakruka. Another newer god is the one already referred to, Dharma Vāivasvata, or Justice (Virtue, Right), the son of the sun, a title of Yama older than the Vedas. He is also the father of the new love-god, Kāma. It is necessary to indicate the names of the gods and their functions, lest one imagine that with pantheism the Vedic religion expired. Even that old, impious Brahmanic fable crops out again: "The devils were the older brothers of the gods, and were conquered by the gods only with trickery" (iii. 33. 60), an interesting reminiscence of the fact that the later name for evil spirit was originally the one applied to the great and good spirit (Asura the same with Ahura).[2] According to a rather late chapter in the second book each of the great Vedic gods has a special paradise of his own, the most remarkable feature of the account being that Indra's heaven is filled with saints, having only one king in it—a view quite foreign to the teaching that is current elsewhere in the epic. Where the sectarian doctrine would oppose the old belief it set above Indra's heaven another, of Brahmā, and above that a third, of Vishnu (i. 89. 16 ff.). According to one passage Mt. Mandara[3] is a sort of Indian Olympus. Another account speaks of the Himālayas, Himavat, as 'the divine

[1] Manibhadra, in iii. 64, is king of Yaksash; he is the same with Kubera, *ib.* ch. 41 (Vāiçravana).

[2] In the Cosmogony the gods are the sons of the Manes, xii. 312. 9.

[3] When the gods churn the ocean to get ambrosia, an ancient tale of the epic, Mandara is the twirling-stick. It is situated in modern Behār, near Bhagalpur.

mountain, beloved of the gods,' though the knight goes thence to Gandhamādana, and thence to Indrakila, to find the gods' habitat (iii. 37. 41). Personified powers lie all around the religious Hindu. And this is especially true of the epic character. He prays to Mt. Mandara, and to rivers, above all to the Ganges. Mt. Kolāhala is divine, and begets divine offspring on a river (i. 63). The Vindhya range of mountains rivals the fabled Meru (around which course the sun and all the heavenly bodies), and this, too, is the object of devotion and prayer.[1] In one passage it is said that in Behār (Māgadha) there was a peak which was continuously 'worshipped with offerings of flowers and perfumes,' exactly as if it were a god. The reason why flowers are given and worn is that they bring good luck, it is said in the same chapter (ii. 21. 15, 20, 51).

What is, perhaps, the most striking feature of Hindu religious thought, as a whole, is the steadfastness with which survive, even in the epic and in Buddhism, the forms and formulae of the older faith. At a time when pantheism or nihilism is the avowed creed the ancient gods still exist, weak, indeed, yet infused with a true immortality. This is noticeable even more in unnoticeable ways, in the turns of speech, in little comparisons, in the hymns, in short, in the by-play of the epic. 'Withered are the garlands of the gods, and their glory is departed,'[2] but they still receive homage in time of need. And in that homage is to be seen, and from the same cause, the revived or surviving worship of the Veda. Each god in turn is mighty, though Agni is the mightiest of the old divinities. In an epic hymn to him it is said: "Thou art the mouth

[1] iii. 42; 139. 14, where the Ganges and Jumna are invoked together with the Vedic gods. So in iii. 104 (Vindhya); and Damayantī prays to mountains. Mt. Meru is described in iii. 163. 14 (compare i. 17. 5 ff.). In i. 18. 1 ff., is related the churning of the ocean, where Indra (vs. 12) places Mt. Mandara on Vishnu, the tortoise.

[2] Mbh. i. 30. 37, *mamlur mālyāni devānām*, etc. The older belief was that the gods' garlands never withered; for the gods show no mortal signs, cast no shadows, etc.

of the worlds; the poets declare thee to be one and three-fold; as carrier of the sacrifice they arrange thee eight-fold. By thee was all created, say the highest seers. Priests that have made reverence to thee attain the eternal course their acts have won, together with their wives and sons. They call thee the water-giver in the air, together with lightning. On thee first depends water. Thou art the creator and Brihaspati, thou art the two Horsemen, the two Yamas, Mitra, Soma, Wind" (i. 229. 23 ff.).[1] And yet this is in a pantheistic environment! The Rig Veda is directly invoked, though, of course, not directly cited, in the old hymn to the Horsemen, who are, however, elsewhere put with low animals and Guhyakas, demons (i. 66).[2] They are the "physicians of the gods," the "first-born," the golden birds which weave the white and black of time, create the wheel of time with all its seasons, and make the sun and sky (i. 3. 55 ff., "*vāgbhir ṛgbhis*"). Indra himself is extolled in Kadrū's hymn; he is the slayer of Namuci, the lord of Çacī; he is the great cloud, cloud and its thunder, creator and destroyer; he is Vishnu, 'Soma, greatly praised,' as well as fire, air, time in all its divisions, earth and ocean; when lauded he drinks the *soma*, and he is sung in the Vedāngas (i. 25. 7 ff.). Praised with this hymn in time of need of rain, Indra "commanded the clouds, saying, 'rain down the ambrosia'" (26. 2); where there is still the rain as synonymous with ambrosia, and Indra not very differently conceived from his Vedic self. Thus in comparisons: "As Indra standing in heaven brings bliss to the world of the living, so Vidura ever brought bliss to the Pandus" (i. 61. 15). But at the same time what changes! The gods assemble and sing a hymn to Garuda, the epic form of Garutman, the heavenly bird, who here steals the *soma* vainly guarded

1 Compare the four hymnlets to Agni in i. 232. 7 ff.

2 After the mention of the thirty-three gods, and Vishnu 'born after them,' it is said that the Açvins, plants, and animals, are Guhyakas (vs. 40), though in vs. 35: "Tvashtar's daughter, the wife of Savitar, as a mare (*vaḍavā*) bore in air the two Açvins" (see above), in Vedic style. For Çruti compare iii. 207. 47; 208. 6, 11.

by the gods. Garuda, too, is Prajāpati, Indra, and so forth.[1] The gods are no longer divinities distinct from the dead Fathers, for they are "identical in being." So Agni says when the latter is cursed by Bhrigu: "The divinities and the Manes are satisfied by the oblation in fire. The hosts of gods are waters, so, too, are the Manes. The feasts of the new and full moon belong to the gods with the Manes; hence the Manes are divinities and the divinities are Manes. They are of one being (*ekībhūtās*). I (Fire) am the mouth of both, for both eat the oblation poured upon me. The Manes at the new moon, the gods at the full, are fed by my mouth" (i. 7. 7 ff.).[2] Such gods the epic hero fears not (i. 227. 38 ff.). Hymns to them are paralleled by hymns to snakes, as in i. 3. 134 ff., against whom is made the "*sarpasattram* (snake sacrifice) of the Purānas" (i. 51. 6). Divinity is universal. Knights are as divine as the divinest god, the All-god. Arjuna, the god-born man, to whom Krishna reveals the Divine Song, is himself god.[3] In this case whether god becomes human, or *vice versa*, no one knows.

Under the all-embracing cloak of pantheism the heart of the epic conceals many an ancient rite and superstition. Here is the covenant of blood, the covenant of death (represented by the modern 'sitting'[4]), and the covenant of water, which symbolizes both friendship and the solemnity of the curse. The former are illustrated by Bhīma's drinking blood as a sign that he will fulfil his vow,[5] and by Rāma lying by Ocean to die unless Ocean grants his wish. Of the water-rite that of offer-

1 i. 23. 15 ff. His name is explained fancifully in 30. 7.

2 It is at the funeral feasts to the Manes that the Mahābhārata is to be recited (i. 62. 37).

3 Arjuna is an old name of Indra, and in the epic Arjuna is Indra's son.

4 The legal *dharna* or sitting at a debtor's door, which still obtains in India, is, so far as we know, not a very ancient practice. But its application in the case of heralds (who become responsible) is epic.

5 This is the covenant (with friends) of revenge; the covenant of mutual protection in the sacrifice is indicated by the 'protection covenant' of the gods (see the chapter on Brahmanism above, p. 192).

ing water in hospitality and as a form in reception of gifts is general; that of cursing by 'touching water' (*vāry upaspṛçya*), occurs in iii. 10. 32. For this purpose holy-grass and other symbols are known also,[1] and formulae yield only in potency to love-philters and magic drugs. Another covenant besides those just noticed seems to lie concealed in the avoidance of the door when injury is intended. If one goes in by the door he is a guest who has anticipated hospitality, and then he dares not refuse the respect and offering of water, etc, which makes the formal pact of friendship. If, on the contrary, he does not go in by the door he is not obliged to receive the offering, and may remain as a foe in the house (or in the city) of his enemy, with intent to kill, but without moral wrong. This may be implied in the end of the epic, where Açvatthāman, intent on secret murder of his foe, is prevented by god Çiva from entering in at the gate, but going in by stealth, and 'not by the door' of the camp, gets to his foe, who lies asleep, and kills him (x. 8. 10). This might be thought, indeed, to be merely strategic, but it is in accordance with the strict law of all the law-books that one, in ordinary circumstances, shall avoid to enter a town or a house in any other way than through the door (Manu, iv. 73; Gaut. 9. 32, etc.), and we think it has a moral significance, for this *a-dvāra* (non-door) rule occurs again in the epic in just the circumstances we have described. The heroes in this case are not afraid of their foe, who is in his town. They insult every one as they approach, but they find some other way of getting in than by passing through the gate, for the express purpose of being morally able to make the king fight with them after they have entered his city. And they cite the rule 'according to law,' which is that one may enter his foe's house by *a-dvāra*, 'not by door,' but his friend's house only 'by door.' As they have not entered 'by door' they say they may refuse the hospitality which the king urges them

[1] See an essay on the Ruling Caste in the epic, in JAOS. xiii. 232 ff.

to accept, and so they kill him (ii. 21. 14, 53). Stepping in through the door seems, therefore, to be a tacit agreement that one will not injure the resident.[1]

In the epic, again, fetishism is found. The student of the 'science of war,' in order to obtain his teacher's knowledge when the latter is away, makes a clay image of the preceptor and worships this clay idol, practicing arms before it (i. 132. 33). Here too is embalmed the belief that man's life may be bound up with that of some inanimate thing, and the man perishes with the destruction of his psychic prototype (iii. 135). The old ordeals of fire and water are recognized. "Fire does not burn the house of good men." "If (as this man asserts) he is Varuna's son, then let him enter water and let us see if he will drown" (iii. 134. 27 ff.). A human sacrifice is performed (iii. 127); although the priest who performs it is cast into hell (*ib.* 128).[2] The teaching in regard to hells is about the same with that already explained in connection with the law-books, but the more definite physical interpretation of hell as a hole in the ground (*garta*, just as in the Rig Veda) is retained. Agastya sees his ancestors 'in a hole,' which they call 'a hell' (*niraya*). This is evidently the hell known to the law-punsters and epic (i. 74. 39) as *puttra*, 'the *put* hell' from which the son (*putra*) delivers (*tra*). For these ancestors are in the 'hole' because Agastya, their descendant, has not done his duty and begotten sons (i. 45. 13; iii. 96. 15); one son being 'no son' according to law and epic (i. 100. 68), and all the merit of sacrifice being equal to only one-sixteenth of that obtained by having a son. The teaching, again, in regard to

[1] Reverend Doctor H. C. Trumbull has kindly called our attention to Robert's *Oriental Illustrations*, p. 148 ff., where it is said that in India to-day the threshold is sacred. In reference to threshold-offerings, common in the law, Dr. Trumbull's own forthcoming book on Covenants may be compared.

[2] But these are by no means the last examples of human sacrifices. Several of the modern Hindu sects have caused to be performed such sacrifices, even in this century.

the Fathers themselves (the Manes), while not differing materially from the older view, offers novelties which show how little the absorption-theory had taken hold of the religious consciousness. The very fact that the son is still considered to be as necessary as ever (that he may offer food to his ancestors) shows that the believer, whatever his professed faith, expects to depend for bliss hereafter upon his *post mortem* meals, as much as did his fathers upon theirs. In the matter of the burial of the dead, one finds, what is antique, that although according to the formal law only infants are buried, and adults are burned, yet was burial known, as in the Vedic age. And the still older exposure of the body, after the Iranian fashion, is not only hinted at as occurring here and there even before the epic, but in the epic these forms are all recognized as equally approved: "When a man dies he is burned or buried or exposed" (*nikṛṣyate*)[1] it is said in i. 90. 17; and the narrator goes on to explain that the "hell on earth," of which the auditor "has never heard" (vs. 6) is re-birth in low bodies, speaking of it as a new doctrine. "As if in a dream remaining conscious the spirit enters another form"; the bad becoming insects and worms; the good going to heaven by means of the "seven gates," viz., penance, liberality, quietism, self-control, modesty, rectitude, and mercy. This is a union of two views, and it is evidently the popular view, that, namely, the good go to heaven while the bad go to new existence in a low form, as opposed to the more logical conception that both alike enter new forms, one good, the other bad. Then the established stadia, the pupil, the old teaching (*upanishad*) of the householders, and the wood-dwellers are described, with the remark that there is no uniformity of opinion in regard to them; but the ancient view crops out again in the statement

[1] This can hardly mean 'put out on the river' as has been suggested as an explanation of the corpse 'thrown aside' in accordance with the earlier text, AV. xviii. 2. 34 (*paropta*), where the dead are 'buried, thrown aside, burned, or set out.'

that one who dies as a forest-hermit "establishes in bliss" ten ancestors and ten descendants. In this part of the epic the Punjāb is still near the theatre of events, the 'centre region' being between the Ganges and Jumna (i. 87. 5); although the later additions to the poems show acquaintance with all countries, known and unknown, and with peoples from all the world. Significant in xii. 61. 1, 2 is the name of the third order *bhāikshyacaryam* 'beggarhood' (before the forest-hermit and after the householder).

It was said above that the departed Fathers could assume a mortal form. In the formal classification of these demigods seven kinds of Manes are enumerated, the title of one subdivision being 'those embodied.' Brahmā is identified with the Father-god in connection with the Manes: "All the Manes worship Prajāpati Brahmā," in the paradise of Prajāpati, where, by the way, are Çiva and Vishnu (ii. 11. 45, 50, 52; 8. 30). According to this description 'kings and sinners,' together with the Manes, are found in Yama's home, as well as "those that die at the solstice" (ii. 7 ff.; 8. 31). Constantly the reader is impressed with the fact that the characters of the epic are acting and thinking in a way not conformable to the idea one might form of the Hindu from the law. We have animadverted upon this point elsewhere in connection with another matter. It is this factor that makes the study of the epic so invaluable as an offset to the verisimilitude of belief, even as belief is taught (not practiced) in the law. There is a very old rule, for instance, against slaughtering animals and eating meat; while to eat beef is a monstrous crime. Yet is it plain from the epic that meat-eating was customary, and Vedic texts are cited (*iti çrutis*) to prove that this is permissible; while a king is extolled for slaughtering cattle (iii. 208. 6–11). It is said out and out in iii. 313. 86 that 'beef is food,' *gāur annam*. Deer are constantly eaten. There is an amusing protest against this practice, which was felt to be irreconcilable with the *ahimsā* (non-injury) doctrine, in iii. 258, where the remnant of deer left in the forest come in a vision and beg to be spared. A dispute between gods and seers over vegetable sacrifices is recorded, xii. 338. Again, asceticism is not the duty of a warrior, but the epic hero practices asceticism exactly as if he were a priest, or a Jain, although the warning is given that a warrior 'obtains a better lot' (*loka*) by dying in battle than by asceticism. The asceticism is, of course, exaggerated, but an instance or two of what the Hindu expects in this regard may not be without interest. The warrior who becomes an ascetic eats leaves, and is clothed in grass. For one month he eats fruits every third day (night); for another month every sixth day; for another month every fortnight; and for the fourth month he lives on air, standing on tiptoe with arms stretched up. Another account says that the knight eats fruit for one month; water for one month; and for the third month, nothing (iii. 33. 73; 38. 22–26; 167). One may compare with these ascetic practices, which are not so exaggerated, in fact, as might be supposed,[1] the 'one-leg' practice of virtue, consisting in standing on one leg, *ekapādena*, for six months or longer, as one is able (i. 170. 46; iii. 12. 13–16). Since learning the Vedas is a tiresome task, and ascetic practice makes it possible to acquire anything, one is not surprised to find that a devotee undertakes penance with this in view, and is only surprised when Indra, who, to be sure has a personal interest in the Vedas, breaks in on the scene and rebukes the ascetic with the words: "Asceticism cannot teach the Vedas; go and be tutored by a teacher" (iii. 135. 22).

One finds in the epic the old belief that the stars are the souls of the departed,[2] and this occurs so often that it is

[1] It is assumed in xii. 364. 2 that "leaves and air" are food enough for a great saint. Compare below the actual asceticism of modern devotees.

[2] iii. 25. 14: *saptarṣayas . . . divi viprabhānti.* Compare *ib.* 261. 13, and the apocalypse in vii. 192. 52 ff., where Drona's soul ascends to heaven, a burning fire like a

another sign of the comparative newness of the pantheistic doctrine. When the hero, Arjuna, goes to heaven he approaches the stars, "which seen from earth look small on account of their distance," and finds them to be self-luminous refulgent saints, royal seers, and heroes slain in battle, some of them also being nymphs and celestial singers. All of this is in contradiction both to the older and to the newer systems of eschatology; but it is an ancient belief, and therefore it is preserved. Indra's heaven,[1] Amarāvati, lies above these stars.[2] No less than five distinct beliefs are thus enunciated in regard to the fate of good men after death. If they believe in the All-god they unite with him at once. Or they have a higher course, becoming gradually more elevated, as gods, etc., and ultimately 'enter' the All-god. Again they go to the world of Brahmā. Again they go to Indra's heaven. Again they become stars. The two last beliefs are the oldest, the *brahma-loka* belief is the next in order of time, and the first-mentioned are the latest to be adopted. The hero of the epic just walks up to heaven, but his case is exceptional.

While angels and spirits swarm about the world in every shape from mischievous or helpful fairies to Rāhu, whose head still swallows the sun, causing eclipses (i. 19. 9), there are a few that are especially conspicuous. Chief of the good spirits, attendants of Indra, are the Siddhas,[3] 'saints,' who occasionally appear to bless a hero in conjunction with 'beings invis-

sun; in sharp contrast to the older 'thumbkin' soul which Yama receives and carries off in the tale of Satyavant. Compare also Arundhatī in i. 233. 29.

[1] Described, as above, as a place of singers and dancers, where are the Vedic gods and sages, but no sinners or cowards (iii. 42. 34 ff.).

[2] From another point of view the stars are of interest. They are favorable or unfavorable, sentient, kind, or cruel; influential in man's fate. Compare iii. 200. 84, 85, where the sun is included with the *grahas* (planets) which influence men, and *ib.* 209. 21, *tulyanakṣatramangala*.

[3] Other of Indra's spirits are the singers, Gandharvas and Apsarasas; also the horse-headed Kinnaras and Cāranas, who, too, are singers; while later the Vidyādharas belong both to Indra and to Çiva. In modern times the South Indian Sittars, 'saints,' take their name from the Siddhas.

ible' (iii. 37. 21). Their name means literally 'blessed' or 'successful,' and probably, like the seers, Rishis, they are the departed fathers in spiritual form. These latter form various classes. There are not only the 'great seers,' and the still greater '*brahma*-seers,' and the 'god-seers,' but there are even 'devil-seers,' and 'king-seers,' these being spirits of priests of royal lineages.[1] The evil spirits, like the gods, are sometimes grouped in threes. In a blessing one cries out: "Farewell (*svasti gacchahy anāmayam*) ; I entreat the Vasus, Rudras, Ādityas, Marut-hosts and the All-gods to protect thee, together with the Sādhyas ; safety be to thee from all the evil beings that live in air, earth, and heaven, and from all others that dog thy path."[2] In xii. 166. 61 ff. the devils fall to earth, mountains, water, and other places. According to i. 19. 29. it is not long since the Asuras were driven to take refuge in earth and salt water.[3]

These creatures have every kind of miraculous power, whether they be good or bad. Hanuman, famed in both epics, the divine monkey, with whom is associated the divine 'king of bears' Jāmbavan (iii. 280. 23), can grow greater than mortal eye can see (iii. 150. 9). He is still worshipped as a great god in South India. As an illustration of epic spiritism the case of Ilvala may be taken. This devil, *dāiteya*, had a trick of cooking his embodied younger brother, and giving him to saints to eat. One saint, supposing the flesh to be mutton (here is saintly meat-eating !), devours the dainty viand ; upon which the devil 'calls' his brother, who is obliged to come, whether eaten or not, and in coming bursts the saint

[1] In *dānavarṣi* there is apparently the same sort of compound as in *devarṣi* and *brahmarṣi*, all associated with the *siddhas* in iii. 169. 23. But possibly 'demons and seers' may be meant.

[2] iii. 37. 32–35 (*prapadye viçvedevān !*).

[3] Weber finds in the Asuras' artisan, Asura Maya, a reminiscence of Ptolemaios. He is celebrated in i. 228. 39, and ii. 1, and is the general leader of the *dānavas*, demons, perhaps originally a folk-name of enemies.

that has eaten him (iii. 96). This is folk-lore; but what religion does not folk-lore contain! So, personified Fate holds its own as an inscrutable power, mightier than others.[1] There is another touch of primitive religious feeling which reminds one of the usage in Iceland, where, if a stranger knocks at the door and the one within asks 'who is there?' the guest answers, 'God.' So in the epic it is said that 'every guest is god Indra' (*Parjanyo 'nnānusaṁcaran*, iii. 200. 123. In the epic Parjanya, the rain-god, and Indra are the same). Of popular old tales of religious bearing may be mentioned the retention and elaboration of the Brahmanic deluge-story, with Manu as Noah (iii. 187); the Açvins' feats in rejuvenating (iii. 123); the combats of the gods with the demons (Namuci, Çambara, Vala, Vritra, Prahlāda, Naraka), etc. (iii. 168).

Turning now to some of the newer traits in the epic, one notices first that, while the old sacrifices still obtain, especially the horse-sacrifice, the *rājasūya* and the less meritorious *vājapeya*, together with the monthly and seasonal sacrifices, there is in practice a leaning rather to new sacrifices, and a new cult. The *soma* is scarce, and the *pūtika* plant is accepted as its substitute (iii. 35. 33) in a matter-of-course way, as if this substitution, permitted of old by law, were now common. The sacrifice of the widow is recognized, in the case of the wives of kings, as a means of obtaining bliss for a woman,[2] for the religion of the epic is not entirely careless of woman. Somewhat new, however, is the self-immolation of a man upon the pyre of his son. Such a case is recorded in iii. 137. 19, where a father burns his son's body, and then himself enters

[1] See below. The formal division is, *dāiva, haṭha, karma, i.e.*, man's fate depends on gods, Fate, and his own acts; although *haṭha*, Fate, is often implied in *dāiva*, 'the divine power.' But they are separated, for example, in iii. 183. 86.

[2] Compare the tales and xii. 148. 9, *satī* (suttee). In regard to the horse-sacrifice, compare Yama's law as expounded to Gautama: "The acts by which one gains bliss hereafter are austerities, purity, truth, worship of parents, and the horse-sacrifice." xii. 129. 9, 10.

the fire. New also, of course, are the sectarian festivals and sacrifices; and pronounced is the gain in the godhead of priests, king, parents, elder brother, and husband. The priest has long been regarded as a god, but in the epic he is god of gods, although one can trace even here a growth in adulation.[1] The king, too, has been identified before this period with the gods. But in the epic he is to his people an absolute divinity,[2] and so are the parents to the son;[3] while, since the elder brother is the same with a father, when the father is dead the younger brother worships the elder. So also the wife's god is her husband; for higher even than that of the priest is the husband's divinity (iii. 206). The wife's religious service is not concerned with feasts to the Manes, with sacrifice to the gods, nor with studying the Veda. In all these she has no part. Her religion is to serve her husband (iii. 205. 23), and to die, if worthy of the honor, on his funeral pyre. Otherwise the epic woman has religious practices only in visiting the holy watering-places, which now abound, and in reading the epic itself. For it is said of both practices: "Whether man or woman read this book (or 'visit this holy pool') he or she is freed from sin" (so in iii. 82. 33: "Every sin committed since birth by man or woman is absolved by bathing in holy Pushkara"). It may be remarked that as a general thing the deities invoked by women are, by predilection, female divinities, some of them being mere abstractions, while 'the Creator' is

[1] Compare iii. 200. 88, even *prākṛta* priests are divine and terrible (much more in later books). Here *prākṛta*, vulgar, is opposed to *saṁskṛta*, refined, priests.

[2] iii. 185. 26–31.

[3] "My father and mother are my highest idol; I do for them what I do for idols. As the three and thirty gods, with Indra foremost, are revered of all the world, so are my parents revered by me" (iii. 214. 19, 20). The speaker further calls them *paramam brahma*, absolute godhead, and explains his first remark by saying that he offers fruits and flowers to his parents as if they were idols. In iv. 68. 57 a man salutes (*abhivādya*) his father's feet on entering into his presence. For the worship of parents compare xii. 108. 3; 128. 9, 10; 267. 31, xiii. 75. 26: "heroes in obedience to the mother."

often the only god in the woman's list, except, of course, the priests: "Reverence to priests, and to the Creator . . . May Hrī, Çrī (Modesty and Beauty), Fame, Glory, Prosperity, Umā (Çiva's wife), Lakshmī (Vishnu's wife), and also Sarasvatī, (may all these female divinities) guard thy path, because thou reverest thy elder brother," is a woman's prayer (iii. 37. 26–33).[1]

Of the sectarian cults just mentioned the *brahmamaha*, i. 164. 20, elsewhere referred to, is the all-caste[2] feast in honor of Brahmā (or of the Brahmans); as *ib.* 143. 3 one finds a *samāja* in honor of Çiva; and distinctly in honor of the same god of horror is the sacrifice, *i.e.*, immolation, of one hundred kings, who are collected "in the temple of Çiva," to be slaughtered like cattle in Māgadha (ii. 15. 23); an act which the heroes of the epic prevent, and look upon with scorn.[3] As a substitute for the *rājasūya*, which may be connected with the human sacrifice (*Ind. Streifen*, i. 61), but is the best sacrifice because it has the best largesse (iii. 255. 12), the Vaishnava is suggested to Duryodhana. It is a great *sattram* or long sacrifice to Vishnu (*ib.* 15 and 19); longer than a Vishnuprabodha (26 Oct.). There is a Smriti rite described in iii. 198. 13 as a *svastivācanam*, a ceremony to obtain a heavenly chariot which brings prosperity, the priests being invoked for blessings (*svasti*). Quite modern, comparatively speaking, is the cult of holy pools; but it is to be observed that the blessings expected are rarely more than the acquirement of *brahma*-worlds, so that the institution seems to be at least older than the sectarian religions, although naturally among the holy pools is intruded a Vishnu-pool. This religious rite cannot be passed over in silence. The custom is late Brahmanic (as above), and still survives. It

1 The marked Brahmā Creator-worship is a bit of feminine religious conservatism (see below).

2 Weber has shown that men of low caste took a subordinate part even in the *rājasūya* sacrifice.

3 In ii. 18. there is a brand-new festival appointed in honor of a female fiend, etc.

has been an aspect of Hindu religion for centuries, not only in the view taken of the pools, but even occasionally in the place itself. Thus the Ganges, Gayā, Prayāga, and Kuru-Plain are to-day most holy, and they are mentioned as among the holiest in the epic catalogue.[1] Soma is now revamped by a bath in a holy pool (ix. 35. 75). As in every antithesis of act and thought there are not lacking passages in the epic which decry the pools in comparison with holy life as a means of salvation. Thus in iii. 82. 9 ff., the poet says: "The fruit of pilgrimage (to holy pools) — he whose hands, feet, and mind are controlled;[2] he who has knowledge, asceticism, and fame, he gets all the fruit that holy pools can give. If one is averse from receiving gifts, content, freed from egoism, if one injures not, and acts disinterestedly, if one is not gluttonous, or carnal-minded, he is freed from sin. Let one (not bathe in pools but) be without wrath, truthful, firm in his vows, seeing his self in all beings." This is, however, a protest little heeded.[3] Pilgrimage is made to pool and plain, to mountain, tree, and river. Even then, as now, of all pilgrimages that to Ganges was most esteemed: "Originally all were holy; in the second age Pushkara[4] was holy; in the third age the Plain of the Kurus was holy; and in this age Ganges is holy" (iii. 85. 90).[5] Besides Ganges, the Plain of the Kurus and Prayāga, the junction of Ganges and Jumna, get the highest laudation. Other rivers, such as the Gomal and Sarasvatī, are also extolled, and

[1] iii. 84. 83 (87. 11). We see the first idea in the injunction of Indra to 'wander,' as told in the tale of Dogstail in the Brahmana (see above).

[2] The usual formula (also Avestan) is 'pure in thought, speech, and act.' The comparison of the six senses to unrestrained wild horses is familiar (iii. 211. 24).

[3] There is, further, no unanimity in regard to the comparative value of holy places. In xii. 152. 11, Sarasvatī is holier than Kurukshetra, etc.

[4] At Pushkara is Brahmā's only (?) shrine — the account is legendary, but half historical. The modern shrine at Ajmīr seems to be meant.

[5] Ganges, according to epic legend, was a goddess who sacrificed herself for men when the earth was parched and men perished. Then Ganges alone of immortals took pity on men, and flinging herself from heaven became the stream divine. Her name among the gods is Alakanandā, the 'Blessed Damosel.'

the list is very long of places which to see or to bathe in releases from sin. "He who bathes in Ganges purifies seven descendants.[1] As long as the bones of a man touch Ganges-water so long that man is magnified in heaven." Again: "No place of pilgrimage is better than Ganges; no god is better than Vishnu; nothing is better than *brahma* — so said the sire of the gods" (iii. 85. 94-96). The very dust of Kuru-Plain makes one holy, the sight of it purifies; he that lives south of the Sarasvatī, north of the Drishadvatī (*i.e.*, in Kuru-Plain), he lives in the third heaven (iii. 83. 1-3 = 203-205 [2]). This sort of expiation for sin is implied in a more general way by the remark that there are three kinds of purity, one of speech, one of act, and one of water (iii. 200. 82). But in the epic there is still another means of expiating sin, one that is indicated in the Brahmanic rule that if a woman is an adultress she destroys half her sin by confessing it (as above), where, however, repentance is rather implied than commanded. But in the epic Purāna it is distinctly stated as a Çruti, or trite saying, that if one repents he is freed from his sin; *na tat kuryām punar* is the formula he must use, 'I will not do so again,' and then he is released from even the sin that he is going to commit a second time, as if by a ceremony — so is the Çruti in the laws, *dharmas* (iii. 207. 51, 52).[3] Confession to the family priest is enjoined, in xii. 268. 14, to escape punishment.

[1] In iii. 87. 10, "ten descendants and ten ancestors." The epic, i. 170. 19, regards the Sarasvatī and Jumna as parts of the sevenfold Ganges, which descends from the heavens as these three, and also as the Vitasthā (Rathasthā), Sarayū, Gomatī, and Gaṇḍakī; being itself 'Vāitaraṇī among the Manes.' So xii. 322. 32.

[2] According to the commentator the "(northern altar of the Father-god) Kurukshetra-Samantapañcakam, between Tarantuka, Arantuka, Rāmahrada, and Macakruka," mentioned in iii. 83. 208, lies in Benares; but this must be a late addition, as Kurukshetra's position is without doubt. Compare i. 2. 1 ff.; ix. 53. 1, 23-25.

[3] In *ib.* 47, *mahā dṛtir ivā'dhmātaḥ pāpas*, there is an interesting reminiscence of Rig Veda, vii. 89. 2. The rules of virtue are contained in Vedas and law-books, and the practice of instructed men, *ib.* 83 (the 'threefold sign of righteousness'). A Çruti cited from *dharmas* is not uncommon, but the latter word is not properly used in so wide a sense. See note below, p. 378.

Two other religious practices in the epic are noteworthy. The first is the extension of idolatry in pictures. The amiable 'goddess of the house' is represented, to be sure, as a Rākshasī, or demoniac power, whose name is Jarā. But she was created by the Self-existent, and is really very friendly, under certain conditions: "Whoever delineates me with faith in his house, he increases in children; otherwise he would be destroyed." She is worshipped, *i.e.*, her painted image is worshipped, with perfumes, flowers, incense, food, and other enjoyable things (ii. 18).[1] Another practice that is very common is the worship of holy trees. One may compare the banyan at Bodhi Gayā with the 'worshipful' village-tree of ii. 24. 23. Seldom and late is the use of a rosary mentioned (*e.g.*, iii. 112. 5, *akshamālā*, elsewhere *aksha*), although the word is employed to make an epithet of Çiva, Akshamālin.[2]

As has been said already, an extraordinary power is ascribed to the mere repetition of a holy text, *mantra*. These are applied on all occasions without the slightest reference to the subject. By means of *mantra* one exorcises; recovers weapons; calls gods and demons, etc.[3] When misfortune or disease arrives it is invariably ascribed to the malignant action of a devil, although the *karma* teaching should suggest that it was the result of a former misdeed on the victim's part. But the very iteration, the insistence on new explanations of this doctrine, show that the popular mind still clung to the old idea of demoniac interference. Occasionally the naïveté with which the

1 Some scholars see in the use of the verb *piç*, a Vedic picturing of gods; but in all instances where this occurs it may be only the poet's mind-picture of the god 'adorned' with various glories.

2 In vii. 201. 69, Çiva wears an *akshamālā*. In xii. 38. 23, the Cārvāka wears an *aksha*, for he is disguised as a *bhikshu*, beggar.

3 It must be remembered that the person using the *mantra* probably did not understand what the words meant. The epic says, in fact, that the Vedas are unintelligible: *brahma pracuracchalam*, xii. 329. 6. But an older generation thought the same. In Nirukta, i. 15, Kāutsa is cited as saying that the *mantras* are meaningless.

effect of a *mantra* is narrated is somewhat amusing, as, for instance, when the heroine Krishnā faints, and the by-standers "slowly" revive her "by the use of demon-dispelling *mantras*, rubbing, water, and fanning" (iii. 144. 17). All the weapons of the heroes are inspired with and impelled by *mantras*.

Sufficient insight into the formal rules of morality has been given in the extracts above, nor does the epic in this regard differ much from the law-books. Every man's first duty is to act, inactivity is sinful. The man that fails to win a good reputation by his acts, a warrior, for example, that is devoid of fame, a 'man of no account,' is a *bhūmivardhana*, ἄχθος ἀρούρης, a cumberer of earth (iii. 35. 7). A proverb says that man should seek virtue, gain, and pleasure; "virtue in the morning; gain at noon; pleasure at night," or, according to another version, "pleasure when young, gain in middle-age, and virtue in the end of life" (iii. 33. 40, 41). "Virtue is better than immortality and life. Kingdom, sons, glory, wealth, all this does not equal one-sixteenth part of the value of truth" (*ib.* 34. 22).[1] One very strong summing up of a discourse on virtuous behavior ends thus: "Truth, self-control, asceticism, generosity, non-injury, constancy in virtue—these are the means of success, not caste nor family" (*jāti*, *kula*, iii. 181. 42).

A doctrine practiced, if not preached, is that of blood-revenge. "The unavenged shed tears, which are wiped away by the avenger" (iii. 11. 66); and in accordance with this feeling is the statement: "I shall satiate my brother with his murderer's blood, and thus, becoming free of debt in respect of my brother, I shall win the highest place in heaven" (*ib.* 34, 35).

As of old, despite the new faith, as a matter of priestly, formal belief, all depends on the sacrifice: "Law comes from usage; in law are the Vedas established; by means of the Vedas arise sacrifices; by sacrifice are the gods established;

[1] Compare xii. 174. 46: "The joy of earth and heaven obtained by the satisfaction of desire is not worth one-sixteenth of the bliss of dead desire."

according to the rule of Vedas, and usage, sacrifices being performed support the divinities, just as the rules of Brihaspati and Uçanas support men" (iii. 150. 28, 29). The pernicious doctrine of atonement for sin follows as a matter of course: "Whatver sin a king commits in conquering the earth is atoned for by sacrifices, if they are accompanied with large gifts to priests, such as cows and villages." Even gifts to a sacred bull have the same effect (iii. 33. 78, 79; *ib.* 35. 34; iii. 2. 57), the occasion in hand being a king's violation of his oath.[1] Of these sacrifices a great snake-sacrifice forms the occasion for narrating the whole epic, the plot of which turns on the national vice of gambling.[2] For divine snakes are now even grouped with other celestial powers, disputing the victory of earthly combatants as do Indra and Sūrya: "The great snakes were on Arjuna's side; the little snakes were for Karna" (viii. 87. 44, 45).[3] They were (perhaps) the local gods of the Nāgas (Snakes), a tribe living between the Ganges and Jumna.

The religion of the epic is multiform. But it stands, in a certain sense, as one religion, and from two points of view it is worthy of special regard. One may look upon it either as the summing up of Brahmanism in the new Hinduism, as the final expression of a religion which forgets nothing and absorbs everything; or one may study it as a belief composed of historical strata, endeavoring to divide it into its different layers, as they

[1] By generosity the Hindu poet means 'to priests.' In iii. 200, where this is elaborated, sixteen persons are mentioned (vs. 4) to whom to give is not meritorious.

[2] Little is known in regard to the play. The dice are thrown on a board, 'odd and even' determine the contest here (iii. 34. 5), *ayuja* and *yuja*. At times speed in counting is the way to win (Nala). Dicing is a regular part of the *rājasūya* sacrifice (Weber, p. 67), but not, apparently, an ancient trait.

[3] The snakes belong to Varuna and his region, as described in v. 98. It is on the head of the earth-upholding snake Çesha that Vishnu muses, iii. 203. 12. The reverence paid to serpents begins to be ritual in the Atharva Veda. Even in the Rig Veda there is the deification of the cloud-snake. In later times they answered to the Nymphs, being tutelary guardians of streams and rivers (Bühler). In i. 36, Çesha Ananta supports earth, and it is told why he does so.

have been super-imposed one upon another in the course of ages. From the latter point of view the Vedic divinities claim the attention first. There are still traces of the original power of Agni and Sūrya, as we have shown, and Wind still makes with these two a notable triad,[1] whereas Indra, impotent as he is, hymnless as he is,—save in the oldest portions of the work,—still leads the gods, now godkins, of the ancient pantheon, and still, in theory, at least, offers a paradise to the knight that dies nobly on the field.[2] But one sees at once that the preservation of the dignity of these deities is due to different causes. Indra cannot even save a snake that grasps his hand for safety; he wages war against the demons' 'triple town,' and signally fails of his purpose, for the demons are as strong as the gods, and there are Dānavendras as well as Dānavarshis.[3] But Indra is the figure-head of the whole ancient pantheon, and for this reason he plays so constant, if so weak, a rôle, in the epic. The only important thing in connection with him is his heaven. As an individual deity Indra lives, on the whole, only in the tales of old, for example, in that of his cheating Namuci (ix. 43. 32 ff.). Nothing new and clever is told of him which would indicate power, only a new trick or two, as when he steals from Karna. It is quite otherwise with Agni and Sūrya. They are not so vaguely identified with the one god as is 'Indra and the other Vasus.' It is merely because these gods are prominently forms of Vishnu that they are honored with hymns in the epic. This is seen from the nature of the hymns, and also from the fact that it is either as fire or as sun that Vishnu destroys at the end of the aeons. For it is, perhaps, somewhat daring to say, and yet it seems to be the fact, that the solar origin of Vishnu is not lost sight of.

1 These three are the witnesses for the soul at the judgment, xii. 322. 55. Vāyu, Wind, is said to be even mightier than Indra, Yama, Indra and Varuna. *ib.* 155. 9, 10.

2 But (in a later account) not if he dies ignobly; for if one is slain by a man of low caste he goes to hell, xii. 298. 7.

3 Demoniac Indras (*i.e.*, demon-leaders) and seers, xii. 166. 26.

The pantheistic Vishnu is the *ātmā*, and Vishnu, after all, is but a form of fire. Therefore is it that the epic Vishnu is perpetually lapsing into fire; while fire and sun are doubly honored as special forms of the highest. It is, then, not so much on account of a survival of ancient dignity[1] that sun and fire stand so high, but rather because they are the nearest approach to the effulgence of the Supreme. Thus while in one place one is told that after seven suns have appeared the supreme gods become the fire of destruction and complete the ruin, in another he reads that it is the sun alone which, becoming twelvefold, does all the work of the Supreme.[2]

Indra has hymns and sacrifices, but although he has no so exalted hymn as comes to his 'friend Agni,' yet (in an isolated passage) he has a new feast and celebration, the account of which apparently belongs to the first period of the epic, when the worship of Indra still had significance. In i. 63, an *Indra-maha*, or 'glorification of Indra,' is described a festivity extending over two days, and marked by the erection of a pole in honor of the god — a ceremony which 'even to-day,' it is said, is practiced.[3] The old tales of the fire-cult are retold, and new rites are known.[4] Thus in iii. 251. 20 ff., Prince Duryodhana resolves to starve to death (oblivious of the rule that 'a suicide goes to hell'), and since this is a religious ceremony, he clothes himself in old clothes and holy-grass, 'touches water,' and

[1] 'The god of gods,' who rains blood in i. 30. 36, is declared by the commentator to be — Parjanya! The gods are here defending Soma from the heavenly bird, Garuda, and nearly die of fright.

[2] xii. 313. 1–7, with the same watery finale as is usual.

[3] The morning prayer, etc., to the sun is, of course, still observed, *e.g.*, vii. 186. 4. Indra is thanked for victory and invoked for rain (iii. 117. 11; i. 25. 7; Holtzmann, *loc. cit.* p. 326) in an hymn that is less fulsome than those to Agni and Sūrya.

[4] iii. 222, Atharvan's rediscovery of fire. As to Çrutis they are probably no more valuable than Smritis. The one given in iii. 208. 11, *agnayo mānsakāmās*, seems to be adapted (*cf.* Āçv. Gs. iv. 1; the adjective, by the way, is still starred in Pw.). So Āçv. Gs. i. 15. 9. is repeated Mbhā; i. 74. 63, as a "Vedic *mantragrāma*" (*angād angāt sambhavasi*, etc.).

devotes himself with intense application to heaven. Then the devils of Rudra called Dāiteyas and Dānavas, who live underground ever since they were conquered by the gods, aided by priests, make a fire-rite, and with *mantras* "declared by Brihaspati and Uçanas, and proclaimed in the Atharva-Veda," raise a ghost or spirit, who is ordered to fetch Duryodhana to hell, which she immediately does.[1] The frequent connection of Brihaspati with the Atharva-Veda is of interest (above, p. 159). He is quite a venerable, if not wholly orthodox, author in the epic, and his 'rules' are often cited.[2]

That Vedic deity who, alone of pre-Vedic powers, still holds his proud place, Yama, the king of departed spirits, varies in the epic according to the period represented. In old tales he is still quite Vedic in character; he takes the dead man's soul off to his own realm. But, of course, as pantheism prevails, and eschatology becomes confused, Yama passes into a shadow, and at most is a bugbear for the wicked. Even his companions are stolen from another realm, and one hears now of "King Yama with his Rudras" (iii. 237. 11),[3] while it is only the bad[4] that go to Yama (iii. 200. 24), in popular belief, although this view, itself old, relapses occasionally into one still older, in accordance with which (*ib.* 49) all the world is hounded on by Yama's messengers, and comes to his abode. His home[5] in the south is now located as being at a distance of 86,000

1 The devils are on the Prince's side, and wish to keep him from death. The proverb is found *ib.* 252. 2; *ātmatyāgī hy adho yāti.* The holy-grass is used in much the same way when Rāma lies down by Ocean, resolved to die or persuade Ocean to aid him. The rites (vs. 24) are "in the Upanishad."

2 According to xii. 59. 80–84, the 'treatise of Brihaspati' comes from Çiva through Brahmā and Indra.

3 In Buddhism Yama's messengers are Yakkhas. Scherman, *loc. cit.* p. 57.

4 Compare ii. 22. 26: *gaccha yamakṣayam*, 'go to Yama's destruction'; whereas of a good man it is said, 'I will send Indra a guest' (vii. 27. 8).

5 *Yamasya sadana.* iii. 11. 66. He now has hells, and he it is who will destroy the world. He is called 'the beautiful' (iii. 41. 9), so that he must, if one take this Rudrian epithet with the citation above, be loosely (popularly) identified with Çiva, as god of death. See the second note below.

leagues over a terrible road, on which passes a procession of wretched or happy mortals, even as they have behaved during life; for example, if one has generously given an umbrella during life he will have an umbrella on this journey, etc. The river in Yama's abode is called Pushpodaka, and what each drinks out of it is according to what he deserves to drink, cool water or filth (*ib.* 46, 58).[1] In the various descriptions it is not strange to find discordant views even in portions belonging approximately to the same period. Thus in contradistinction to the prevailing view one reads of Indra himself that he is *Yamasya netā Namuceçca hantā*, 'Yama's leader, Namuci's slayer' (iii. 25. 10), *i.e.*, those that die in battle go to Yama.

On the other hand, in the later speculative portions, Yama is not death. "Yama is not death, as some think; he is one that gives bliss to the good, and woe to the bad."[2] Death and life are foolishness and lack of folly, respectively (literally, 'non-folly is non-mortality'), while folly and mortality are counter opposites. In pantheistic teaching there is, of course, no real death, only change. But death is a female power, personified, and sharply distinguished from Yama. Death as a means of change thus remains, while Yama is relegated to the guardianship of hell. The difference in regard to the latter subject, between earlier and later views, has been noted above. One comparatively early passage attempts to arrange the incongruous beliefs in regard to *samsāra* (re-birth) and hell on a sort of

[1] The old story of a mortal's visit to Yama to learn about life hereafter (*Çat. Br.* xi. 6. 1; Katha Up., of Nāciketas) is repeated in xiii. 71.

[2] v. 42. 6: *Çivaḥ çivānām açivo 'çivānām* (compare xii. 187. 27: 'only fools say that the man is dead'). Dharma (Justice) seems at times to be the same with Yama. Māndavya goes to Dharma's *sadana*, home (compare Yama's *sadana*), just as one goes to Yama's, and interviews him on the justice of his judgments. As result of the angry interview the god is reborn on earth as a man of low caste, and the law is established that a child is not morally responsible for his acts till the twelfth year of his age (i. 108. 8 ff.). When Ruru agrees to give half his life in order to the restoration of Pramadvarā, his wife, they go not to Yama but to Dharma to see if the exchange may be made, and he agrees (i. 9. 11 ff., a masculine Sāvitrī!).

sliding scale, thus: "One that does good gets in the next life a good birth; one that does ill gets an ill birth"; more particularly: "By good acts one attains to the state of gods; by 'mixed' acts, to the state of man; by acts due to confusion of mind, to the state of animals and plants (*viyoniṣu*); by sinful acts one goes to hell" (*adhogāmi*, iii. 209. 29–32).[1] Virtue must have been, as the epic often declares it to be, a 'subtile matter,' for often a tale is told to illustrate the fact that one goes to hell for doing what he thinks (mistakenly) to be right. Thus Kāuçika is sent to hell for speaking the truth, whereas he ought to have lied to save life (viii. 69. 53), for he was "ignorant of virtue's subtilty."[2] A passage (i. 74. 27 ff.) that is reflected in Manu (viii. 85–86) says that Yama Vāivasvata takes away the sin of him with whom is satisfied "the one that witnesses the act, that stands in the heart, that knows the ground"; but Yama tortures him with whom this one (personified conscience) is dissatisfied. For "truth is equal to a thousand horse-sacrifices; truth is highest *brahma*" (*ib.* 103, 106).

Following downward the course of religious development, as reflected in the epic, one next finds traces of Brahmanic theology not only in the few passages where (Brahmā) Prajāpati remains untouched by sectarianism, but also in the harking back to old formulae. Thus the insistence on the Brahmanical sacredness of the number seventeen is preserved (xii. 269. 26; iii. 210. 20, etc.); and Upanishadic is the "food is Prajāpati" of iii. 200. 38 (Yama in 40). There is an interesting rehabilitation of the primitive idea of the Açvins in the new ascription of formal divinity to the (personified) Twilights (Sandhyā) in iii. 200. 83, although this whole passage is more Puranic than

[1] The hells are described in xii. 322. 29 ff. The sight of 'golden trees' presages death (*ib.* 44).

[2] The ordinary rule is that "no sin is greater than untruth," xii. 162. 24, modified by "save in love and danger of life" (Laws, *passim*).

epic. From the same source is the doctrine that the fruit of action expires at the end of one hundred thousand *kalpas* (*ib.* vs. 121). One of the oddest religious freaks in the epic is the sudden exaltation of the Ribhus, the Vedic (season-gods) artisans, to the position of highest gods. In that heaven of Brahmā, which is above the Vedic gods' heaven, there are the holy seers and the Ribhus, 'the divinities of the gods'; who do not change with the change of *kalpas* (as do other Vedic gods), iii. 261. 19–23. One might almost imagine that their threefoldness was causative of a trinitarian identification with a supreme triad; but no, for still higher is the 'heaven of Vishnu' (vs. 37). The contrast is marked between this and *Āit. Br.* iii. 30, where the Ribhus with some difficulty obtain the right to drink *soma*.

There is an aspect of the epic religion upon which it is necessary to touch before treating of the sectarian development. In the early philosophical period wise priests meet together to discuss theological and philosophical questions, often aided, and often brought to grief, by the wit of women disputants, who are freely admitted to hear and share in the discussion. When, however, pantheism, nay, even Vishnuism, or still more, Krishnaism, was an accepted fact upon what, then, was the wisdom of the priest expended? Apart from the epic, the best intellects of the day were occupied in researches, codifying laws, and solving, in rather dogmatic fashion, philosophical (theological) problems. The epic presents pictures of scenes which seem to be a reflection from an earlier day. But one sees often that the wisdom is commonplace, or even silly. In dialectics a sophistical subtlety is shown; in codifying moral rules, a tedious triteness; in amoebic passes of wit there are astounding exhibitions, in which the good scholiast sees treasures of wisdom, where a modern is obliged to take them in their literal dulness. Thus in iii. 132. 18, a boy of twelve or ten (133. 16), who is divinely precocious, defeats the wise men in disputation at a sacrifice, and in the following section (134. 7 ff.) silences a disputant who is regarded as one of the cleverest priests. The conversation is recorded in full. In what does it consist? The opponent mentions a number of things which are one; the boy replies with a verse that gives pairs of things; the other mentions triads; the child cites groups of fours, etc., until the opponent, having cited only one half-verse of thirteens, can remember no more and stops, on which the child completes the verse, and is declared winner. The conundrums which precede must have been considered very witty, for they are repeated elsewhere: What is that wheel which has twelve parts and three hundred and sixty spokes, etc.? Year. What does not close its eye when asleep, what does not move when it is born, what has no heart, what increases by moving? These questions form one-half verse. The next half-verse gives the answers in order: fish, egg, stone, river. This wisdom in the form of puzzles and answers, *brahmodya*, is very old, and goes back to the Vedic period. Another good case in the epic is the demon Yaksha and the captured king, who is not freed till he answers certain questions correctly.[1] But although a certain amount of theologic lore may be gleaned from these questions, yet is it of greater interest to see how the priests discussed when left quietly to their own devices. And a very natural description of such a scene is extant. The priests "having some leisure"[2] or vacation from their labors in the king's house, sit down to argue, and the poet calls their discussion *vitaṇḍā*, *i.e.*, tricky sophistical argumentation, the description bearing out the justness of the phrase: "One cried, 'that is so,' and the other, 'it is not so'; one cried, 'and that is so,' and the other, 'it must be so'; and

[1] The same scenes occur in Buddhistic writings, where Yakkhas ask conundrums. For example, in the *Hemavatasutta* and *Ālavakasutta* the Yakkha asks what is the best possession, what brings bliss, and what is sweetest, to which the answer is: faith, law, and truth, respectively.

[2] *Karmāntaram upāsantas, i.e., virāmakālam upagacchantas.*

some by arguments made weak arguments strong, and strong weak; while some wise ones were always swooping down on their opponent's arguments, like hawks on meat."[1] In iii. 2. 15, the type of clever priest is 'skilled in Yoga and Sāñkhya,' who inculcates renunciation. This sage teaches that mental diseases are cured by Yoga; bodily, by medicine; and that desire is the root of ill.

But by far the most interesting theological discussion in the epic, if one except the Divine Song, is the conversation of the hero and heroine in regard to the cause of earthly happiness. This discussion is an old passage of the epic. The very fact that a woman is the disputant gives an archaic effect to the narration, and reminds one of the scenes in the Upanishads, where learned women cope successfully with men in displays of theological acumen. Furthermore, the theological position taken, the absence of Vishnuism, the appeal to the 'Creator' as the highest Power, take one back to a former age. The doctrine of special grace, which crops out in the Upanishads,[2] here receives its exposure by a sudden claim that the converse of the theory must also be true, viz., that to those not saved by grace and election God is as cruel as He is kind to the elect. The situation is as follows: The king and queen have been basely robbed of their kingdom, and are in exile. The queen urges the king to break the vow of exile that has been forced from him, and to take vengeance on their oppressors. The king, in reply, sings a song of forgiveness: "Forgiveness is virtue, sacrifice, Veda; forgiveness is holiness and truth; in the world of Brahmā are the mansions of them that forgive." This song (iii. 29. 36 ff.) only irritates the queen, who at once launches into the following interesting tirade (30. 1 ff.): "Rev-

[1] ii. 36. 3 ff. The phraseology of vs. 5 is exactly that of τὸν ἥττω λόγον κρείττω ποιοῦσι, but the Pundit's arguments are 'based on the law.'

[2] See above. In a later period (see below) the question arises in regard to the part played by Creator and individual in the workings of grace, some claiming that man was passive; some, that he had to strive for grace.

erence to the Creator and Disposer[1] who have confused thy mind! Hast thou not worshipped with salutation and honored the priests, gods, and manes? Hast thou not made horse-sacrifices, the *rājasūya*-sacrifice, sacrifices of every sort (*puṇḍa-rīka*,[2] *gosava*)? Yet art thou in this miserable plight! Verily is it an old story (*itihāsa*) that 'the worlds stand under the Lord's will.' Following the seed God gives good or ill in the case of all beings. Men are all moved by the divinity. Like a wooden doll, moving its limbs in the hands of a man, so do all creatures move in the Creator's hands. Man is like a bird on a string, like a bead on a cord. As a bull is led by the nose, so man follows the will of the Creator; he never is a creature of free will (*ātmādhīna*). Every man goes to heaven or to hell, as he is sent by the Lord's will. God himself, occupied with noble or with wicked acts, moves about among all created things, an unknown power (not known as 'this one'). The blessed God, who is self-created, the great forefather (*prapitāmaha*), plays with his creatures just as a boy plays with toys, putting them together and destroying them as he chooses. Not like a father is God to His creatures; He acts in anger. When I see the good distressed, the ignoble happy, I blame the Creator who permits this inequality. What reward does God get that he sends happiness to this sinful man (thy oppressor)? If it be true that only the individual that does the act is pursued by the fruit of that act (*karma* doctrine) then the Lord who has done this act is defiled by this base act of His. If, on the other hand, the act that one has done does not pursue and overtake the one that has done it, then the only agency on earth is brute force (this is the only power to be respected) — and I grieve for them that are without it!"

1 Perhaps ironical. In v. 175. 32, a woman cries out: "Fie on the Creator for this bad luck," conservative in belief, and outspoken in word.

2 iii. 30. 17. The *gosava* is a 'cow-sacrifice.' The *puṇḍarīka* is not explained (perhaps 'elephant-sacrifice').

To this plea, which in its acknowledgment of the Creator as the highest god, no less than in its doubtful admission of the *karma* doctrine, is of peculiar interest, the king replies with a refutation no less worthy of regard: "Thy argument is good, clear and smooth, but it is heterodox (*nāstikyam*). I have sacrificed and practiced virtue not for the sake of reward, but because it was right. I give what I ought to give, and sacrifice as I should. That is my only idea in connection with religious observances. There is no virtue in trying to milk virtue. Do not doubt. Do not be suspicious of virtue. He that doubts God or duty goes to hell (confusion), but he that does his duty and is free from doubt goes to heaven (becomes immortal). Doubt not scriptural authority. Duty is the saving ship. No other gets to heaven. Blame not the Lord Creator, who is the highest god. Through His grace the faithful gets immortality. If religious observances were without fruit the universe would go to destruction. People would not have been good for so many ages if there had been no reward for it. This is a mystery of the gods. The gods are full of mystery and illusion."

The queen, for all the world like that wise woman in the Upanishads, whose argument, as we showed in a preceding chapter, is cut short not by counter-argument, but by the threat that if she ask too much her head will fall off, recants her errors at this rebuke, and in the following section, which evidently is a later addition, takes back what she has said. Her new expression of belief she cites as the opinion of Brihaspati (32. 61, 62); but this is applicable rather to her first creed of doubt. Perhaps in the original version this authority was cited at the end of the first speech, and with the interpolation the reference is made to apply to this seer. Something like the queen's remarks is the doubtful saying of the king himself, as quoted elsewhere (iii. 273. 6): "Time and fate, and what will be, this is the only Lord. How else could this distress have come upon my wife? For she has been virtuous always."

We turn now to the great sectarian gods, who eventually unite with Brahmā to form a pantheistic trinity, a conception which, as we shall show, is not older than the fifth or sixth century after Christ.

CHAPTER XV.

HINDUISM (CONTINUED).—VISHNU AND ÇIVA.

In the epic the later union of the sectarian gods is still a novelty. The two characters remain distinct enough. Vishnu and Çiva are different gods. But each in turn represents the All-god, and consequently each represents the other. The Vishnu-worship which grew about Krishna, originally a friend of one of the epic characters, was probably at first an attempt to foist upon Vedic believers a sectarian god, by identifying the latter with a Vedic divinity. But, whatever the origin, Krishna as Vishnu is revered as the All-god in the epic. And, on the other hand, Çiva of many names has kept the marks of Rudra. Sometimes one, sometimes another, is taken as the All-god. At times they are compared, and then each sect reduces the god of the other to an inferior position. Again they are united and regarded as one. The Vishnu side has left the best literary representation of this religion, which has permeated the epic. It is pantheism, but not an impersonal pantheism. The Blessed Lord is the All. This is the simple base and crown of its speculation. It is like the personal development of Vedantic philosophy, only it is here degraded by the personality of the man-god, who is made the incarnate All-god. The Krishna of the epic as a man is a sly, unscrupulous fellow, continually suggesting and executing acts that are at variance with the knightly code of honor. He is king of Dvārakā and ally of the epic heroes. But again, he is divine, the highest divinity, the *avatar* of the All-god Vishnu. The sectaries that see in Çiva rather than in Vishnu the one and only god, have no such representative to which to refer. For Çiva, as the historical descendant of the Vedic Rudra,—although even in his case there is an intrusion of local worship upon an older Vedic belief, — represents a terror-god, either the lightning, the fairest of the gods, or, when he appears on earth, a divine horror, or, again, "a very handsome young man."[1] These two religions, of Vishnu as Krishna and of Çiva alone, are not so much united in the epic as they are super-imposed upon the older worship of Brahmā, and, indeed, in such a way that Çiva-worship, in a pantheistic sense, appears to be the latest of the three beliefs that have influenced the story.[2]

The personal pantheism of the older Vishnuism has in its form and teachings so close a resemblance to the Christian religion that it has always had a great attraction for occidental readers; while the real power of its "Divine Song" gives the latter a charm possessed by few of the scriptures of India. This Divine Song (or Song of the Blessed One) is at present a Krishnaite version of an older Vishnuite poem, and this in turn was at first an unsectarian work, perhaps a late Upanishad. It is accepted by Vishnuites as a kind of New Testament; and with the New Testament it has in truth much in common. It must be pointed out at the outset that there is here the closest connection with the later Upanishads. The verse, like that of the Katha Upanishad (quoted above), which stands almost at the beginning of the Song, is typical of the relation of the Song to the Upanishad. It will be noticed how the impersonal 'That,' *i.e.*, absolute being, *brahma*, changes almost at once to the personal He (*ātmā* as Lord). As shows the whole Song, *brahma* throughout is understood to be personal.[3]

[1] He appears in different complete manifestations, while Vishnu appears only in part, as a 'descent,' *avatar*, *i.e.*, Vishnu is incarnate, Çiva appears whole.

[2] The original story perhaps antedates the Brahmanic Brahmā. But, for all one knows, when the poem was first written Brahmā was already decadent as chief god. In that case two strata of religious belief have been formally super-imposed, Vishnuism and Çivaism.

[3] While agreeing with Telang that the original Gītā is an old poem, we cannot subscribe to his argument (SBE. viii. p. 19) that the priority of the Sāman over the Rig Veda is evidence of antiquity; still less to the argument, p. 21, from the castes.

To understand the religion which reaches its culmination in the epic no better course could be pursued than to study the whole of the Divine Song. It is, however, too long a production to be introduced here in its entirety; but the following extracts give the chief features of the work, than which nothing in Hindu literature is more characteristic, in its sublimity as in its puerilities, in its logic as in its want of it. It has shared the fate of most Hindu works in being interpolated injudiciously, so that many of the puzzling anomalies, which astound no less the reader than the hero to whom it was revealed, are probably later additions. It is a medley of beliefs as to the relation of spirit and matter, and other secondary matters; it is uncertain in its tone in regard to the comparative efficacy of action and inaction, and in regard to the practical man's means of salvation; but it is at one with itself in its fundamental thesis, that all things are each a part of One Lord, that men and gods are but manifestations of the One Divine Spirit, which, or rather whom, the Vishnuite re-writer identifies with Krishna, as Vishnu's present form.

The Divine Song, as it is revealed in the epic by Vishnu (-Krishna) to his favorite knight, Arjuna, begins thus: "Know that the 'That' in which is comprised the 'This' is indestructible. These bodies of the indestructible Eternal One have an end: but whoso knows Him as slayer, and whoso thinks Him to be slain, these two have not true wisdom. He slays not and is not slain. He is not born, he does not die at any time; nor will He, having been born, cease to be. Unborn, everlasting, eternal, He, the Ancient One, is not slain when the body is slain. As one puts away an old garment and puts on another that is new, so He, the embodied (Spirit), puts away the old body and assumes one that is new. Everlasting, omnipresent,

The caste-position of the priest in the Gītā is owing to the religious exaltation of the poem; and the precedence of Sāman is not unusual in the latest portions of the epic (see below).

firm, unchanging is He, the Eternal; indiscernible is He called, inconceivable, unchangeable."[1]

The Song now turns into a plea that the warrior who is hearing it should, as one born to be a soldier, be brave and fight, lest his sorrow for the slain be taken for fear; since "nothing is better for a warrior than a just fight," and "loss of fame is worse than death." Then follows (with the usual inconsequential 'heaven') "If thou art slain thou wilt obtain heaven, and if thou art victorious thou shalt enjoy earth; therefore, careless of pleasure and pain, get ready for the fight, and so thou wilt not incur sin. This is the knowledge declared in the Sānkhya; hear now that of the Yoga," and the Divine Lord proceeds:

"Some are pleased with Vedic words and think that there is nothing else; their souls are full of desires; and they think that going to heaven is the chief thing. Yet have the Vedas reference only to the three qualities (of which all things partake). Be free from the three qualities (do not care for rewards). In action, not in fruit, is the chief thing. Do thy work, abiding by serene devotion (Yoga), rejecting every tie; be indifferent to success and failure. Serene devotion is called indifference (to such things). Action is lower than devotion of mind. Devotion is happiness. Do thou, wise in devotion, abandon the fruit that is sprung from action, and, freed from the bonds of birth, attain a perfect state."

Sānkhya here means the philosophy of religion; Yoga is the philosophical state of mind, serene indifference, religious *sang-froid*, the practical result of a belief in the Sānkhya doctrine of the indestructibility of the spirit. In the following there is Vedantic teaching, as well as Sankhyan in the stricter sense.

On the warrior's asking for an explanation of this state of equipoise, the Deity gives illustrations of the balanced mind that is free from all attachments, serene, emancipated from de-

[1] Compare Manu, i. 7: "He the subtile, indiscernible, eternal, inconceivable One, who makes all creatures."

sires, self-controlled, and perfectly tranquil. As the knight is astonished and confused at the contradiction, action and inactivity both being urged upon him, the Deity replies that there is a twofold law, that of Sānkhyas consisting in knowledge-devotion, and that of Yogis in action-devotion. Idleness is not freedom from action. Freedom from attachment must be united with the accomplishment of such acts as should be performed. The deluded think that they themselves perform acts, but acts are not done by the spirit (self); they are done only by nature's qualities (this is Sānkhya doctrine). "One should know the relation between the individual and Supreme Spirit, and with tranquil mind perform good acts. Let the deluded ones be, who are erroneously attached to action. The wise man should not cause those of imperfect knowledge to be unsettled in their faith, but he should himself not be attached to action. Each man should perform his own (caste) duties. One's own duty ill done is better than doing well another man's work."

The knight now asks what causes one to sin. The Deity answers: "Love and hate; for from love is born hate; and from anger, ignorance in regard to right and wrong; whence comes lack of reason, and consequently destruction. The knowledge of a man is enwrapped with desire as is fire with smoke. Great are the senses; greater, the mind; greater still, the understanding; greatest of all is 'That'" (*brahma;* as above in the *Chāndogya*). The Deity begins again:[1] "This system of devotion I declared to Vivasvant (the sun); Vivasvant declared it to Manu, and Manu to kingly seers." (The same origin is claimed for itself in Manu's lawbook.) The knight objects, not yet knowing that Krishna is the All-god: "How did'st thou declare it first? thy birth is later than the sun's." To whom the Deity: "Many are my births, and I know them all; many too are thine, but thou knowest them not; unborn and Lord of all creatures I assume phenomena, and am

[1] Possibly the original opening of another poem.

born by the illusion of the spirit. Whenever there is lack of righteousness, and wrong arises, then I emit (create) myself.[1] I am born age after age for the protection of the good, for the destruction of the wicked, and for the sake of establishing righteousness. Whoso really believes in this my divine birth and work, he, when he has abandoned his body, enters no second birth, but enters Me. Many there are who, from Me arising, on Me relying, purified by the penance of knowledge, with all affections, fear, and anger gone, enter into my being. As they approach Me so I serve them.[2] Men in all ways follow after my path. Some desire the success that is of action, and worship gods; for success that is born of action is speedy in the world of men. Know Me as the maker of the four castes, know Me as the unending one and not the maker. Action stains Me not, for in the fruit of action I have no desire. He that thus knows Me is not bound by acts.[3] So he that has no attachment is not bound by acts. His acts become naught. *Brahma* is the oblation, and with *brahma* is it offered; *brahma* is in the fire, and by *brahma* is the oblation made. Sacrifices are of many kinds, but he that sacrifices with knowledge offers the best sacrifice He that has faith has knowledge; he that has knowledge obtains peace. He that has no knowledge and no faith, whose soul is one of doubt, is destroyed. Action does not destroy him that has renounced action by means of indifference. Of the two, renunciation of action and indifference, though both give bliss, indifference in action is better than renunciation of action. Children, not Pundits, proclaim Sānkhya and Yoga to be distinct. He that is devoted to either alone

1 The *avatars* of Vishnu are meant. The very knight to whom he speaks is later regarded (in South India) as incarnate god, and to-day is worshipped as an *avatar* of Vishnu. The idea of the 'birth-stories' of the Buddhists is thought by some scholars to have been connected historically with the *avatars* of Vishnu.

2 This is one of the notes struck in the later Upanishads, the doctrine of 'special grace,' originating perhaps still earlier in the Vāc hymn (see above).

3 That is, one that also has no desires may act (without desiring the fruit of action.)

finds the reward of both. Renunciation without Yoga is a thing hard to get; united with Yoga the seer enters *brahma*. . . . He is the renouncer and the devotee who does the acts that ought to be done without relying on the reward of action, not he that performs no acts and builds no sacrificial fires. Through his self (spirit) let one raise one's self. Conquer self by self (spirit). He is the best man who is indifferent to external things, who with equal mind sees (his spirit) self in everything and everything in self (God as the Spirit). Such an one obtains the highest bliss, *brahma*. Whoso sees Me in all and all in Me I am not destroyed for him, and he is not destroyed for Me."

The knight now asks how it fares with a good man who is not equal to the discipline of Yoga, and cannot free himself entirely from attachment. Does he go to destruction like a cloud that is rent, failing on the path that leads to *brahma*? The Deity replies: "Neither in this world nor in the beyond is he destroyed. He that acts virtuously does not enter an evil state. He obtains the heaven that belongs to the doers of good, and after living there countless summers is reborn on earth in the family of pure and renowned men, or of pious devotees. There he receives the knowledge he had in a former body, and then strives further for perfection. After many births he reaches perfection and the highest course (union with *brahma*). There are but few that strive for perfection, and of them only one here and there truly knows Me. Earth, water, fire, air, space, mind, understanding, and egoism (self-consciousness) — so is my nature divided into eight parts.[1] But learn now my higher nature, for this is my lower one. My higher nature is alive, and by it this world is supported. I am the creator and destroyer of all the world. Higher than I is nothing. On Me the universe is woven like pearls upon a thread. Taste am I, light am I of moon and sun, the

[1] This is a Sānkhya division.

mystic syllable *Ōm* (*ăŭm*), sound in space, manliness in men; I am smell and radiance; I am life and heat. Know Me as the eternal seed of all beings. I am the understanding of them that have understanding, the radiance of the radiant ones. Of the strong I am the force, devoid of love and passion; and I am love, not opposed to virtue. Know all beings to be from Me alone, whether they have the quality of goodness, of passion, or of darkness (the three 'qualities' or conditions of all things). I am not in them; but they are in Me. Me, the inexhaustible, beyond them, the world knows not, for it is confused by these three qualities (conditions); and hard to overcome is the divine illusion which envelops Me, while it arises from the qualities. Only they pass through this illusion who come to Me alone. Wicked men, whose knowledge is taken away by illusion, relying on a devilish (demoniac) condition, do not come to Me. They that have not the highest knowledge worship various divinities; but whatever be the form that any one worships with faith I make his faith steady. He obtains his desires in worshipping that divinity, although they are really bestowed upon him by Me.[1] But the fruit of these men, in that they have little wisdom, has its end. He that sacrifices to (lesser) gods goes to those gods; but they that worship Me come to Me. I know the things that were, that are, and are to be; but Me no one knoweth, for I am enveloped in illusion. I am the supreme being, the supreme godhead, the supreme sacrifice, the Supreme Spirit, *brahma*."

The knight asks "What is *brahma*, the Supreme Spirit, the supreme being, the supreme sacrifice?" The Deity: "The supreme, the indestructible, is called *brahma*. Its personal existence is Supreme Spirit (self). Destructible existence is

[1] This cleverly contrived or profound universality of Vishnuism is one of the greatest obstacles to missionary effort. The Vishnuite will accept Christ, but as a form of Vishnu, as here explained. Compare below: "Even they that sacrifice to other gods really sacrifice to Me."

supreme being (all except *ātmā*). The Person is the supreme godhead. I myself am the supreme sacrifice in this body."

Then follow statements like those in the Upanishads and in Manu, describing a day of *brahma* as a thousand ages; worlds are renewed; they that go to the gods find an end of their happiness with the end of their world; but they that go to the indestructible *brahma*, the Deity, the entity that is not destroyed when all else is destroyed, never again return. There are two roads (as in the Upanishads above), one, the northern road leading to *brahma;* one, the southern road to the moon, leading back to earth. At the end of a period of time all beings reënter the divine nature (Prakriti[1]), and at the beginning of the next period the Deity emits them again and again (they being without volition) by the volition of his nature. "Through Me, who am the superintendent, nature gives birth to all things, and for that cause the world turns about. They of demoniac nature recognize me not; they of god-like nature, knowing Me as the inexhaustible source, worship Me. I am the universal Father, the Vedas, the goal, the upholder, the Lord, the superintendent, the home, the asylum, the friend. I am the inexhaustible seed. I am immortality and death. I am being and not-being. I am the sacrifice and he that offers it. Even they that, with faith, sacrifice to other gods, even they (really) sacrifice to Me. To them that ever are devout and worship Me with love (faith), I give the attainment of the knowledge by which they come to Me" (again the doctrine of special grace). "I am the beginning, the middle, and the end of all created things. I am Vishnu among sun-gods; the moon among the stars: Indra among the (Vedic) gods; the Sāman among the Vedas; among

[1] Prakriti (*prakṛti*), nature; the term belongs to the Sânkhya philosophy, which recognizes nature as distinct from spirit, a duality, opposed to *advāita*, the non-duality of the Vedânta system, where the Sānkhya 'nature' is represented by *māyā*, 'illusion.' Otherwise the word Prakrit is the 'natural,' vulgar dialect, opposed to Sanskrit, the refined, 'put-together' language.

the senses, mind; among created beings, consciousness; among the Rudras I am Çiva (Çankara); among army-leaders I am Skanda; among the great sages I am Bhrigu (who reveals Manu's code); among the Siddhas[1] I am Kapila the Muni. . . . I am the love that begets; I am the chief (Vāsuki and Ananta) among the serpents; and among them that live in water I am Varuna; among the Manes I am Aryaman; and I am Yama among controllers;[2] among demons I am Prahlāda . . .; I am Rāma; I am the Ganges. I am among all sciences the highest science (that in regard to the Supreme Spirit); I am the word of the speakers; I am the letter A among the letters, and the compound of union among the compounds.[3] I am indestructible time and I am the Creator. I am the death that seizes all and I am the origin of things to be. I am glory, fortune, speech, memory, wisdom, constancy, and mercy. . . . I am the punishment of the punisher and the polity of them that would win victory. I am silence. I am knowledge. There is no end of my divine manifestations."

The knight now asks to see the real form of the deity, which was revealed to him. "If in heaven the glory of a thousand suns should appear at once, such would be his glory."

After this comes the real animus of the Divine Song in its present shape. The believer that has faith in this Vishnu is even better than the devotee who finds *brahma* by knowledge.

The philosophy of knowledge (which here is anything but Vedantic) is now communicated to the knight, in the course of which the distinction between nature and spirit is explained: "Nature, Prakriti, and spirit, Purusha (person), are both without beginning. All changes and qualities spring from nature. Nature is said to be the cause of the body's and the senses' activity. Spirit is the cause of enjoyment (appreciation) of pleasure

1 Saints, literally 'the successful ones.'

2 Alluding to the later derivation of Yama from *yam*, control.

3 "The letter A," as in the Upanishads (see above, p. 226).

and pain; for the Spirit, standing in nature, appreciates the nature-born qualities. The cause of the Spirit's re-birth is its connection with the qualities. (This is Sānkhya doctrine, and the same with that propounded above in regard to activity.) The Supreme Spirit is the Support and great Lord of all, the *ātmā*, while *brahma* (=*prakriti*) is the womb in which I place My seed, and from that is the origin of all things. The great *brahma* is the womb, and I am the seed-giving father of all the forms which come into being. The three 'qualities' (conditions, attributes), goodness, passion, and darkness, are born of nature and bind the inexhaustible incorporate (Spirit) in the body. The quality (or attribute) of goodness binds the soul with pleasure and knowledge; that of passion (activity), with desire and action; that of darkness (dulness), with ignorance. One that has the attribute of goodness chiefly goes after death to the highest heaven; one that has chiefly passion is born again among men of action; one that has chiefly darkness is born among the ignorant. One that sees that these attributes are the only agents, one that knows what is higher than the attributes, enters into my being. The incorporate spirit that has passed above the three attributes (the origin of bodies), being released from birth, death, age, and pain, obtains immortality. To pass above these attributes one must become indifferent to all change, be undisturbed by anything, and worship Me with devotion. . . . I am to be learned from all the Vedas; I made the Vedānta; I alone know the Vedas. There are two persons in the world, one destructible and one indestructible; the destructible one is all created things; the indestructible one is called the Unchanging one. But there is still a third highest person, called the Supreme Spirit, who, pervading the three worlds, supports them, the inexhaustible Lord. Inasmuch as I surpass the destructible and am higher than the indestructible, therefore am I known in the world and in the Veda as the Highest Person."

The references to the Sānkhyas, or Sānkhya-Yogas, are not yet exhausted. There is another in a following chapter (vi. 18. 13) which some scholiasts say refers to the Vedānta-system, though this is in direct contradiction to the text. But the extracts already given suffice to show how vague and uncertain are, on the whole, the philosophical views on which depends the Divine Song. Until the end of these citations one hears only of nature and spirit, the two that have no beginning, but here one finds the Supreme Spirit, which is as distinct from the indestructible one as from the destructible. Moreover, 'nature' is in one place represented as from the beginning distinct from spirit and entirely apart from it, and in another it is only a transient phase. The delusion (illusion) which in one passage is all that exists apart from the Supreme Spirit is itself given up in favor of the Sānkhya Prakriti, with which one must imagine it to be identified, although from the text itself it cannot be identical. In a word, exactly as in Manu, there are different philosophical conceptions, united without any logical basis for their union. The 'system' is in general that of the Sānkhya-Yogas, but there is much which is purely Vedānta. The Sānkhya system is taught elsewhere as a means of salvation, perhaps always as the deistic Yoga (i. 75. 7: "He taught them the Sānkhya-knowledge as salvation"). It is further noticeable that although Krishna (Vishnu) is the ostensible speaker, there is scarcely anything to indicate that the poem was originally composed even for Vishnu. The Divine Song was probably, as we have said, a late Upanishad, which afterwards was expanded and put into Vishnu's mouth. The Sāṇkhya portions have been redressed as far as possible and to the illusion doctrine is given the chief place. But the Song remains, like the Upanishads themselves, and like Manu, an ill-assorted cabinet of primitive philosophical opinions. On the religious side it is a matter of comparative indifference whether that which is not the spirit is a delusive output of the spirit or indestructible matter. In either case the Spirit is the goal of the spirit. In this personal pantheism absorption is taught but not death. Immortality is still the reward that is offered to the believer that is wise, to the wise that believes. Knowledge and faith are the means of obtaining this immortality; but, whereas in the older Upanishads only wisdom is necessary (wisdom that implies morality), here as much stress, if not more, is laid upon faith, the natural mark of all sectarian pantheism.

Despite its occasional power and mystic exaltation, the Divine Song in its present state as a poetical production is unsatisfactory. The same thing is said over and over again, and the contradictions in phraseology and in meaning are as numerous as the repetitions, so that one is not surprised to find it described as "the wonderful song, which causes the hair to stand on end." The different meanings given to the same words are indicative of its patchwork origin, which again would help to explain its philosophical inconsistencies. It was probably composed, as it stands, before there was any formal Vedānta system; and in its original shape without doubt it precedes the formal Sānkhya; though both philosophies existed long before they were systematized or reduced to Sūtra form. One has not to imagine them as systems originally distinct and opposed. They rather grew out of a gradual intensification of the opposition involved in the conception of Prakriti (nature) and Māyā (illusion), some regarding these as identical, others insisting that the latter was not sufficient to explain nature. The first philosophy (and philosophical religion) concerned itself less with the relation of matter to mind (in modern parlance) than with the relation of the individual self (spirit) to the Supreme Spirit. Different explanations of the relation of matter to this Supreme Spirit were long held tentatively by philosophers, who would probably have said that either the Sānkhya or Vedānta might be true, but that this was not the chief question. Later came the differentiation of the schools, based mainly on a question that was at first one of secondary importance. In another part of the epic Krishna himself is represented as the victim of 'illusion' (iii. 21. 30) on the field of battle.

The doctrine of the Bhagavad Gitā, the Divine Song, is by no means isolated. It is found in many other passages of the epic, besides being imitated in the Anugitā of the pseudo-epic. To one of these passages it is worth while to turn, because of the form in which this wisdom is enunciated. The passage immediately following this teaching is also of great interest. Of the few Vedic deities that receive hymnal homage chief is the sun, or, in his other form, Agni. The special form of Agni has been spoken of above. He is identified with the All in some late passages, and gives aid to his followers, although not in battle. It will have been noticed in the Divine Song that Vishnu asserts that the Song was proclaimed to the sun, who in turn delivers it through Manu to the king-seers, the sun being especially the kingly god.[1] In the third book there is an hymn to the sun, in which this god is addressed almost in the terms of the Divine Song, and immediately preceding is the doctrine just alluded to. After the explanation is given that re-birth affects creatures and causes them to be born in earth, air, or water, the changes of metempsychosis here including the vegetable world as well as the animal and divine worlds,[2] the very essence of the Divine Song is given as "Vedic word," viz., *kuru karma tyajeti ca*, "Perform and quit acts," *i.e.*, do what you ought to do, but without regard to the reward of action (iii. 2. 72, 74). There is an eightfold path of duty, as in Buddhism, but here it consists in sacrifice, study, liberality, and penance; truth, mercy, self-control, and lack of greed. As the

[1] Compare a parallel list of diadochoi in xii. 349. 51.

[2] One of the Jaina traits of the epic, *brahmādiṣu tṛṇānteṣu bhūteṣu parivartate*, in distinction from the Buddhistic metempsychosis, which stops short of plants. But perhaps it is rather borrowed from the Brahman by the Jain, for there is a formal acknowledgment that *sthāvarās*, 'stationary things,' have part in metempsychosis, Manu, xii. 42, although in the distribution that follows this is almost ignored (vs. 58).

result of practicing the first four, one goes on the course that leads to the Manes; as the result of practicing the last four, one goes on the course that leads to the gods. But in practicing any virtues one should practice them without expectation of reward (*abhimāna*, arrière pensée). The Yogi, the devotee, who renounces the fruit of everything, is the greatest man; his powers are miraculous.

There follows (with the same light inconsistency to be found in the Divine Song) the appeal for action and the exhortation to pray to the sun for success in what is desired. For it is explained that the sun is the father of all creation. The sun draws up clouds with his heat, and his energy, being transmuted into water, with the help of the moon, is distilled into plants as rain, and in this way the food that man eats is full of solar energy, and man and all that live by food must regard the sun as their father. Preliminary to the hymn to the sun is given a list of his hundred and eight names,[1] among which are to be noticed: Aryaman, Soma, Indra, Yama, Brahmā, Vishnu, Çiva, Death, Time, Creator, the Endless One, Kapila, the Unborn One, the Person (Purusha; with which are to be compared the names of Vishnu in the Divine Song), the All-maker, Varuna, the Grandfather, the Door of Heaven, etc. And then the Hymn to the Sun (iii. 3. 36 ff.):[2] "Thou, O Sun, of creatures art the eye; the spirit of all that have embodied form: thou art the source of all created things; thou art the custom of them that make sacrifice; thou art the goal of the Sānkhyas and the hope of the Yogis; the course of all that seek deliverance . . . Thou art worshipped by all; the three and thirty gods (!) worship thee, etc. . . . I think that in all the seven worlds[3] and all the *brahma*-worlds there is nothing

[1] It is rather difficult to compress the list into this number. Some of the names are perhaps later additions.

[2] In contrast one may note the frequent boast that a king 'fears not even the gods,' *e.g.*, i. 199. 1.

[3] Later there are twenty-one worlds analogous to the twenty-one hells.

which is superior to the sun. Other beings there are, both powerful and great, but they have no such glory as the sun's. Father of light, all beings rest in thee; O Lord of light, all things, all elements are in thee. The disc of Vishnu was fashioned by the All-maker (one of the sun's names!) with thy glory. Over all the earth, with its thirteen islands, thou shinest with thy kine (rays). . . .[1]. Thou art the beginning and the end of a day of Brahmā. . . . They call thee Indra; thou art Rudra, Vishnu, the Father-god, Fire, the subtile mind; thou art the Lord, and thou, eternal *brahma*."

There is here also a very significant admixture of Vedic and Upanishadic religion.

In Krishna, who in the Upanishads is known already by his own and his mother's name, pantheism is made personal according to the teaching of one sect. But while the whole epic is in evidence for the spuriousness of the claim of Krishna to be regarded as incarnate Vishnu (God), there is scarcely a trace in the original epic of the older view in regard to Vishnu himself. Thus in one passage he is called "the younger brother of Indra" (iii. 12. 25). But, since Indra is at no time the chief god of the epic, and the chapter in which occurs this expression is devoted to extolling Krishna-Vishnu as the All-god, the words appear to be intended rather to identify Krishna with Vishnu, who in the Rig Veda is inferior to Indra, than to detract from Vishnu's glory. The passage is cited below.

What now is the relation of Vishnu-Krishna to the other divinities? Vishnuite and Çivaite, each cries out that his god includes the other, but there is no current identity of Brahmā, Vishnu, Çiva as three co-equal representations of one God. For example, in iii. 189. 5, one reads: "I am Vishnu, I am Brahmā, and I am Çiva," but one cannot read into this any trinitarian doctrine whatever, for in context the passage reads as a whole: "I am Nārāyana, I am Creator and Destroyer,

[1] Elsewhere, on the other hand, the islands are four or seven, the earlier view.

I am Vishnu, I am Brahmā, I am Indra, the master-god, I am king Kubera, Yama, Çiva, Soma, Kaçyapa, and also the Father-god." Again, Vishnu says that the Father-god, or grandparent of the gods, is "one-half of my body," and does not mention Çiva (iii. 189. 39). Thus, also, the hymn to Çiva in iii. 39. 76 ff. is addressed "to Çiva having the form of Vishnu, to Vishnu having the form of Çiva, to the three-eyed god, to Çarva, the trident-holder, the sun, Ganeça," but with no mention of Brahmā. The three gods, Brahmā, Vishnu, Çiva, however, are sometimes grouped together (but not as a trinity) in late passages, in contrast to Indra, *e.g.*, ix. 53. 26. There are many hymns to Vishnu and Çiva, where each is without beginning, the God, the uncreated Creator. It is only when the later period, looking back on the respective claims of the sects, identifies each god with the other, and both with their predecessor, that one gets even the notion of a trinity. Even for this later view of the pseudo-epic only one passage will be found (cited below).

The part of Brahmā in the epic is most distinctly in process of subordination to the sectarian gods. He is holy and eternal, but not omniscient, though wise. As was shown above, he works at the will of Vishnu. He is one with Vishnu only in the sense that all is one with the All-god. When Vishnu 'raises the earth' as a boar, Brahmā tells the gods to go to him.[1] He councils the gods. His heaven is above Indra's, but he is really only an intermediary divinity, a passive activity, if the paradox may be allowed. Not like Indra (to whom he is superior) does he fight with All-gods, or do any great act of his own will. He is a shadowy, fatherly, beneficent advisor to the gods, his children; but all his activity is due to Vishnu. This, of course, is from the point of view of the Vishnuite.

[1] iii. 142. The boar-shape of Vishnu is a favorite one, as is the dwarf-incarnation. Compare Vāmana, Vāmanaka, Vishnupada, in the list of holy watering-places (iii. 83). Many of Vishnu's acts are simply transferred from Brahmā, to whom they belonged in older tales. Compare above, p. 215.

But there is no Brahmâite to modify the impression. There existed no strong Brahmā sect as there were Vishnu and Çiva sects. Brahmā is in his place merely because to the preceding age he was the highest god; for the epic regards Creator, Prajāpati, Pitāmaha, Brahmā as synonymous.[1] The abstract *brahma*, which in the Upanishads is the same with the Supreme Spirit, was called personally Brahmā, and this Brahmā is now the Brahmanic Father-god. The sects could never get rid of a god whose being was rooted alike in the preceding philosophy and in the popular conception of a Father-god. Each age of thought takes the most advanced views of the preceding age as its axioms. The Veda taught gods; the Brāhmanas taught a Father-god above the gods; the Upanishads taught a Supreme Godhead of which this Father-god was the active manifestation. The sects taught that their heroes were incarnations of this Supreme, but they carried with them the older pantheon as well, and, with the pantheon, its earlier and later heads, Indra and Brahmā. Consequently each sect admits that Brahmā is greater than the older Vedic gods, but, while naturally it identifies its special incarnation first with its most powerful opponent, and thus, so to speak, absorbs its rival, it identifies this incarnation with Brahmā only as being chief of lesser divinities, not as being a rival. One may represent the attitude of a Krishna-worshipper in the epic somewhat in this way: "Krishna is a modern incarnation of Vishnu, the form which is taken in this age by the Supreme Lord. You who worship Çiva should know that your Çiva is really my Krishna, and

[1] In i. 197, Prajāpati, the Father-god, is the highest god, to whom Indra, as usual, runs for help. Çiva appears as a higher god, and drives Indra into a hole, where he sees five former Indras; and finally Vishnu comes on to the stage as the highest of all, "the infinite, inconceivable, eternal, the All in endless forms." Brahmā is invoked now and then in a perfunctory way, but no one really expects him to do anything. He has done his work, made the castes, the sacrifice, and (occasionally) everything. And he will do this again when the new aeon begins. But for this aeon his work is accomplished.

the chief point is to recognize my Krishna as the Supreme Lord. The man Krishna is the Supreme Lord in human form. Of course, as such, being the One God in whom are all things and beings, he is also all the gods known by names which designate his special functions. Thus he is the head of the gods, the Father-god, as our ancestors called him, Brahmā; and he is all the gods known by still older names, who are the children of the secondary creator, Brahmā, viz., Agni, Indra, Sūrya, etc. All gods are active manifestations of the Supreme God called Vishnu, who is born on earth to-day as Krishna." And the Çivaite says: "Çiva is the manifestation of the All-god," and repeats what the Vishnuite says, substituting Çiva for Vishnu,[1] but with the difference already explained, namely, that the Çiva-sect has no incarnation to which to point, as has the Vishnuite. Çiva is modified Rudra, and both are old god-names. Later, however, the Çivaite has also his incarnate god. As an example of later Çiva-worship may be taken Vishnu's own hymn to this god in vii. 80. 54 ff.: "Reverence to Bhava, Çarva, Rudra (Çiva), the bestower of gifts, the lord of cattle, the terrible, great, fearful, god of three wives;[2] to him who is peace, the Lord, the slayer of sacrifices (*makhaghna*)[3] . . . to the blue-necked god; to the inventor (or author) . . . to truth; to the red god, to the snake, to the unconquerable one, to the blue-haired one, to the trident-holder; . . . to the inconceivable one . . . to him whose sign is the bull; . . . to the creator of all, who pervades all, who is worshipped by all, Lord of all, Çarva, Çankara, Çiva, . . . who has a thousand heads a

1 Thus in xii. 285. 165: "Neither Brahmā nor Vishnu is capable of understanding the greatness of Çiva."

2 Or "three eyes."

3 Compare iii. 39. 77: "The destroyer of Daksha's sacrifice." Compare the same epithet in the hymn to Çiva, x. 7. 3, after which appear the devils who serve Çiva. Such devils, in the following, feast on the dead upon the field of battle, though, when left to themselves, 'midnight is the hour when the demons swarm,' iii. 11. 4 and 33. In x. 18 and xiii. 161 Çiva's act is described in full.

thousand arms, and death, a thousand eyes and legs, whose acts are innumerable." In vii. 201. 71, Çiva is the unborn Lord, inconceivable, the soul of action, the unmoved one; and he that knows Çiva as the self of self, as the unknowable one, goes to *brahma*-bliss. This also is late Çivaism in pantheistic form. In other words, everything said of Vishnu must be repeated for Çiva.[1]

As an example of the position of the lowest member of the later trinity and his very subordinate place, may be cited a passage from the preceding book of the epic. According to the story in vi. 65. 42 ff., the seers were all engaged in worshipping Brahmā, as the highest divinity they knew, when he suddenly began to worship "the Person (Spirit), the highest Lord"; and Brahmā then lauds Vishnu as such: "Thou art the god of the universe, the All-god, Vāsudeva (Krishna). Therefore I worship thee as the divinity; thou, whose soul is devotion. Victory to thee, great god of all; thou takest satisfaction in that which benefits the world. . . . Lord of lords of all, thou out of whose navel springs the lotus, and whose eyes are large; Lord of the things that were, that are, that are to be; O dear one, self-born of the self-born . . . O great snake, O boar,[2] O thou the first one, thou who dwellest in all, endless one, known as *brahma*, everlasting origin of all beings . . . destroyer of the worlds! Thy feet are the earth . . . heaven is thy head . . . I, Brahmā, am thy form . . . Sun and moon are thy eyes . . . Gods and all beings were by me created on earth, but they owe their origin to thy goodness." Then the creation of Vishnu through Pra-

[1] Çiva, called Bhava, Çarva, the trident-holder, the Lord (Īçāna), Çankara, the Great God, etc., generally appears at his best where the epic is at its worst, the interpolations being more flagrant than in the case of Vishnuite eulogies. The most devout worshipper of Vishnu is represented as an adherent of Çiva, as invoking him for help after fighting with him. He is "invincible before the three worlds." He is the sun; his blood is ashes. All the gods, with Brahmā at their head, revere him. He has three heads, three faces, six arms (compare iii. 39. 74 ff.; 83. 125); though other passages give him more.

[2] Çiva has as sign the bull: Vishnu, the boar.

dyumna as a form of the deity is described, "and Vishnu (Aniruddha) created me, Brahmā, the upholder of the worlds; so am I made of Vishnu; I am caused only by thee."

While Brahmā is represented here as identical with Vishnu he is at the same time a distinctly inferior personality, created by Vishnu for the purpose of creating worlds, a factor of inferior godliness to that of the World-Spirit, Krishna-Vishnu.

It had been stated by Holtzmann[1] that Brahmā sometimes appears in the epic as a god superior to Vishnu, and on the strength of this L. von Schroeder has put the date of the early epic between the seventh and fourth centuries B.C., because at that time Brahmā was the chief god.[2] von Schroeder rather exaggerates Holtzmann's results, and asserts that "in the original form of the poem Brahmā appears *throughout* as the highest and most revered god, while the worship of Vishnu and Çiva as great gods is apparently a later intrusion" (*loc. cit.*). This asseveration will have to be taken *cum grano.* Had von Schroeder said 'pantheistic gods' he would have been correct in this regard, but we think that both Vishnu and Çiva were great gods, equal, if not superior to Brahmā, when the epic proper began. And, moreover, when one speaks of the original form of the poem he cannot mean the pseudo-epic or the ancient legends which have been woven into the epic, themselves of earlier date. No one means by the 'early epic' the tales of Agastya, of the creation of Death, of the making of ambrosia, but the story of the war in its earliest shape; for the epic poem must have begun with its own subject-matter. Now it is not true that Brahmā is regarded 'throughout' the early poem as a chief god at all. If one investigate the cases where Vishnu or Çiva appears 'below' Brahmā he will see, in almost every case that Holtzmann has registered, that this condition of affairs is recorded not in the epic proper but in the Brahmanic portions of the pseudo-epic, or in ancient legends alone. Thus

[1] ZDMG. xxxviii. pp. 197, 200.

[2] *Lit. u. Cultur*, p. 461.

in the story of the winning of ambrosia, of Agastya drinking ocean, and of Rāma, Brahmā appears to be above Vishnu, and also in some extracts from the pseudo-epic. For the real epic we know of but two cases that can be put into this category, and neither is sufficient to support the hypothesis built upon it.

For Krishna, when he ingeniously plots to have Bhīma slay Jarāsandha, is said to have renounced killing Jarāsandha himself, 'putting Brahmā's injunction before him' (ii. 22. 36), *i.e.*, recalling Brahmā's admonition that only Bhīma was fated to slay the foe. And when Krishna and Sātyaki salute Krishna's elder brother they do so (for being an elder brother Baladeva is Krishna's *Guru*) respectfully, 'just as Indra and Upendra salute Brahmā the lord of *devas*' (ix. 34. 18). Upendra is Indra's younger brother, *i.e.*, Vishnu (above). But these passages are scanty proof for the statement that Brahmā appears throughout the early epic as the highest god;[1] nor is there even so much evidence as this in the case of Çiva. Here, too, it is in the tale of the churning of ocean, of Sunda and Upasunda, of the creation of the death-power, and in late didactic (Brahmanic) passages, where Brahmā makes Çiva to destroy earth and Çiva is born of Brahmā, and only in such tales, or extracts from the Book of Peace, etc., that Brahmā appears as superior. In all other cases, in the real action of the epic, he is subordinate to Vishnu and Çiva whenever he is compared with them. When he is not compared he appears, of course, as the great old Father-god who creates and foresees, but even here he is not untouched by passion, he is not all-knowing, and his rôle as Creator is one that, with the allotment of duties among the gods, does not make him the highest god. All the old gods are great till greater appear on the scene. There is scarcely a supreme Brahmā in the epic itself, but there is a

[1] Holtzmann now says (in *Neunzehn Bücher*, p. 198) that the whole episode which terminates with Baladeva's visit is an addition to the original. Holtzmann's monograph on Brahmā is in ZDMG. xxxviii. 167.

great Brahmā, and a greater (older) than the sectarian gods in the old Brahmanic legends, while the old Brahmanhood reasserts itself sporadically in the Çānti, etc., and tells how the sectarian gods became supreme, how they quarrelled and laid the strife.

Since the adjustment of the relations between the persons of the later trinity is one of the most important questions in the theology of the completed epic, it will be necessary to go a little further afield and see what the latest books, which hitherto we have refrained as much as possible from citing, have to say on the subject. As it seems to be true that it was felt necessary by the Çivaite to offset the laud of Vishnu by antithetic laud of Çiva,[1] so after the completion of the Book of Peace, itself a late addition to the epic, and one that is markedly Vishnuitic, there was, before the Genealogy of Vishnu, an antithetic Book of Law, which is as markedly Çivaitic. In these books one finds the climax of sectarianism, in so far as it is represented by the epic; although in earlier books isolated passages of late addition are sporadically to be found which have much the same nature. Everywhere in these last additions Brahmā is on a plane which is as much lower than that of the Supreme God as it is higher than that of Indra. Thus in viii. 33. 45, Indra takes refuge with Brahmā, but Brahmā turns for help to Çiva (Bhava, Sthānu, Jishnu, etc.) with a hymn sung by the gods and seers. Then comes a description of Çankara's[2] (Çiva's) war-car, with its metaphorical arms, where Vishnu is the point of Çiva's arrow (which consists of Vishnu, Soma, Agni), and of this war-car Brahmā himself is the charioteer (*ib.* 34. 76). With customary inconsistency, however, when Çiva wishes his son to be exalted he prostrates himself before Brahmā, who then gives this youth (*kumāra*), called Kārtikeya,

[1] A good example is that of the two visions of Arjuna, first the vision of Vishnu, then another vision of Çiva, whom Arjuna and Vishnu visit (vii. 80).

[2] Çankara and Çiva mean almost the same; 'giver of blessings' and 'prospering' (or 'kindly'), respectively.

the 'generalship' over all beings (*sāināpatyam*, ix. 44. 43–49). There is even a 'celebration of Brahmā,' a sort of harvest festival, shared, as the text tells, by all the castes; and it must have been something like the religious games of the Greeks, for it was celebrated by athletic contests.[1] Brahmā, as the old independent creator, sometimes keeps his place, transmitting posterity through his 'seven mind-born sons,' the great seers (iii. 133; xii. 166. 11 ff.). But Brahmā himself is born either in the golden egg, as a secondary growth (as in xii. 312. 1–7). or, as is usually the case, he is born in the lotus which springs from the navel of musing[2] Vishnu (iii. 203. 14). In this passage Brahmā has four faces (Vedas) and four forms, *caturmūrtis* (15), and this epithet in other sections is transferred to Vishnu. Thus in vii. 29. 26, Vishu says *caturmūrtir aham*, "I have four forms," but he never says *trimūrtir aham* ('I have three forms'). There is one passage, however, that makes for a belief in a trinity. It stands in contrast to the various Vishnuite hymns, one of which may well be reviewed as an example of the regular Vishnuite laudation affected by the Krishna sect (iii. 12. 21 ff.): "Krishna is Vishnu, Brahmā, Soma, the Sun, Right, the Creator ('founder'), Yama, Fire, Wind, Çiva, Time, Space, Earth, and the cardinal points. Thou, Krishna, art the Creator ('emitter'); thou, chief of gods, didst worship the highest; thou, Vishnu called, becamest Indra's younger brother, entering into sonship with Aditi; as a child with three steps thou didst fill the sky, space, and earth, and pass in glory. . . . At the end of the age thou returnest all things into thyself. At the beginning of the age Brahmā was born from thy lotus-navel as the venerable preceptor of all things (the same epithet is in vs. 22 applied to Vishnu himself); and Çiva sprang from thy angry

[1] *Brahmaṇas sumahotsavas* (compare the commentator). The *samāja* of Brahmā may be explained by that of Çiva mentioned in the same place and described elsewhere (iv. 13. 14 ff.; i. 164. 20).

[2] Not *sleeping*. Vishnu, despite *svapimi*, does not slumber; he only muses.

forehead when the demons would kill him (Brahmā); both are born of thee, in whom is the universe." The following verses (45 ff.) are like those of the Divine Song: "Thou, Knight Arjuna, art the soul of Krishna; thou art mine alone and thine alone am I; they that are mine are thine; he that hates thee hates Me, and he that is for thee is for Me; thou art Nara ('man') and I am Nārāyana ('whose home is on the waters,' god);[1] we are the same, there is no difference between us." Again, like the Divine Song in the following verses (51–54) is the expression 'the sacrifice and he that sacrifices,' etc., together with the statement that Vishnu plays 'like a boy with playthings,' with the crowds of gods, Brahmā, Çiva, Indra, etc. The passage opposed to this, and to other identifications of Vishnu with many gods, is one of the most flagrant interpolations in the epic. If there be anything that the Supreme God in Çivaite or Vishnuite form does not do it is to extol at length, without obvious reason, his rivals' acts and incarnations. Yet in this clumsy passage just such an extended laudation of Vishnu is put into the mouth of Çiva. In fact, iii. 272, from 30 to 76, is an interpretation of the most naïve sort, and it is here that we find the approach to the later *trimūrti* (trinity): "Having the form of Brahmā he creates; having a human body (as Krishna) he protects, in the nature of Çiva he would destroy — these are the three appearances or conditions (*avasthās*) of the Father-god" (Prajāpati).[2] This comes after an account of the four-faced lotus-born Brahmā, who, seeing the world a void, emitted his sons, the seers, mind-born, like to himself (now nine in number), who in turn begot all beings, including men (vss. 44–47). If, on the other hand, one take the later sectarian account of

1 Man (divine) and god human, but Nārāyana is a new name of Vishnu, and the two are reckoned as two inseparable seers (divinities).

2 This is the only really trinitarian passage in the epic. In i. 1. 32; xiii. 16. 15, the belief may be indicated, but not certainly, as it is in Hariv. 10,662. See on this point Holtzmann, ZDMG. xxxviii. p. 204. In xiv. 54. 14 the form is Vishnu, Brahmā, Indra.

Vishnu (for the above is more in honor of Krishna the man-god than of Vishnu, the form of the Supreme God), he will see that even in the pseudo-epic the summit of the theological conceptions is the emphasis not of trinity or of multifariousness but of unity. According to the text the Pañcakālajñas are the same with the Vishnuite sect called Pāñcarātras, and these are most emphatically *ekāntinas*, *i.e.*, Unitarians (xii. 336; 337. 46; 339. 66–67).[1] In this same passage 341. 106, Vishnu is again *caturmūrtidhṛt*, 'the bearer of four forms,' an entirely different conception of him (below). So that even in this most advanced sectarian literature there is no real threefoldness of the Supreme as one in three. In the following chapter (xii. 335. 1 ff.) there is a passage like the great Ka hymn of the Rig Veda, 'whom as god shall one worship?' The sages say to Vishnu: "All men worship thee; to whom dost thou offer worship?" and he says, 'to the Eternal Spirit.' The conception of the functions of Brahmā and Çiva in relation to Vishnu is plainly shown in xii. 342. 19: "Brahmā and Çiva create and destroy at the will of Vishnu; they are born of his grace and his anger."

In regard to Çiva himself, his nature and place in Vishnuism have been sufficiently explained. The worship of this god is referred to 'Vedic texts' (the *çata-rudriyam*, vii. 202. 120);[2] Vishnu is made to adore the terrible god (*ib.* 201. 69) who appears as a mad ascetic, a wild rover, a monster, a satire on man and gods, though he piously carries a rosary, and has other late traits in his personal appearance.[3] The strength of Çivaism lay in the eumenidean (Çiva is 'prospering,' 'kindly')

1 Compare 339. 114, "thou art *pañcamahākalpa*." The commentator gives the names of five sects, Sāura, Çākta, Gāneça, Çāiva, Vaishnava. The 'five times,' implied in Pañcakāla, he says are day, night, month, seasons, and year (*ib.* 66). In 340. 117 (which chapter is Pancarātric), Brahmā "knows that Vishnu is superior."

2 Vāj. S. xvi. 1–66; Tāitt. S. iv. 5. 1–11.

3 Çiva has no ordinary sacrifice: he is (as above) in general a destroyer of sacrifice, *i.e.*, of Vedic sacrifice; but as Paçupati, "Lord of beasts," he claims the bloody sacrifice of the first beast, man.

euphemism and fear alike, which shrank in speech and mind from the object of fear. But this religion in the epic had a firmer hold than that of fear. It was essentially phallic in its outward form (vii. 201. 93-96), and as such was deeply rooted in the religious conscience of a people to whom one may venture perhaps to ascribe such a form of worship even in the time of the Rig Veda, although the signs thereof in great part have been suppressed. This may be doubted,[1] indeed, for the earlier age; but there is no question that epic Çivaism, like Çivaism to-day, is dependent wholly on phallic worship (xiii. 14. 230 ff.). It is the parallel of Bacchic rites and orgies, as well as of the worship of the demons in distinction from that of good powers. Çiva represents the ascetic, dark, awful, bloody side of religion: Vishnu, the gracious, calm, hopeful, loving side: the former is fearful, mysterious, demoniac; the latter is joyful, erotic, divine. In their later developments it is not surprising to see that Vishnuism, in the form of Krishnaism, becomes more and more erotic, while Çivaism becomes more and more ghastly and ghoulish.

Wild and varied as are the beliefs of the epic, there is space but to show a few more characteristic sides of its theology — a phase that may seem questionable, yet, since the devout Hindu believes the teachings of the epic, they must all to him constitute one theology, although it was gradually amalgamated out of different creeds.

In connection with Çiva stands, closely united, his son, Ganeça, "leader of troops," still worshipped as one of the popular gods, and the battle-god, Skanda, the son first of Agni then of Çiva, the conqueror of the demons, *dānavas*, and later representative of Indra, with whom the epic identifies him. For it is Skanda that is the real battle-god of the later epic;

[1] The usual opinion is that phallic worship was a trait of southern tribes foisted upon northern Çivaism. Philosophically Çivaism is first monotheistic and then pantheistic. To-day it is nominally pantheistic but really it is dualistic.

though in its original form Indra was still the warrior's refuge, as attests the stereotyped phraseology. In iii. 225–232 honor and praise are ascribed to Skaṇda in much the same language with that used to portray his father, Çiva. "The god of a thousand arms, the Lord of all, the creator of gods and demons" are phrases used in his eulogy. He too has a list of names; his nurse is the "maiden of the red (bloody) sea," called Lohitāyanī. His terrible appearance and fearful acts make him the equal of Çiva.[1] His sign is a *kukkuṭa*, cock; *ib.* 229. 33.

Associated, again, with Skanda are the spirits or 'mothers,' which afflict people. The belief in mother-gods is old, but its epic form is new. The exactness and detail in regard to these beautiful monsters show at least a real belief, which, as one on a lower plane besides the higher religion, cannot be passed over without notice. As in other lands, people are 'possessed' by evil spirits, called possessors or seizers (*grahas*). These are Skanda's demons,[2] and are both male and female. Until one reaches the age of sixteen he is liable to be possessed by one group of 'seizers,' who must be worshipped in proper form that their wrath may be averted. Others menace mortals from the age of sixteen to seventy. After that only the fever-demon is to be feared. Imps of this sort are of three kinds. One kind indulge only in mischievous sport: another kind lead one to gluttony; the third kind are devoted to lust. They are known as Piçācas, Yakshas, etc., and when they seize a person he goes mad. They are to be kept at bay by self-restraint and moderation (iii. 230. 43–56). In ix. 46 and iii. 226 the 'mothers' are described. They are witches, and live in cross-

1 There are indications in this passage of some sectarian feeling, and the fear of partisan warfare (229); in regard to which we add from Muir and Holtzmann the passage xii. 343. 121, where is symbolized a peaceful issue of war between Vishnuism and Çivaism.

2 Grahas are also planets, but in this cult they are not astrological, as show their names.

roads, cemeteries, and mountains. They may be of Dravidian origin, and in their epic form, at any rate, are a late intrusion.[1]

Just before the Divine Song begins, the knight who is about to become illuminated or 'disillusioned' offers a prayer to the terrible goddess Durgā, also one of the new, popular, and horrible forms of divine manifestation. In this hymn, vi. 23, Durgā (Umā, Pārvatī, Kālī, etc.) is addressed as "leader of the armies of the blessed, the dweller in Mandara, the youthful woman, Kālī, wife of Çiva, she who is red, black, variegated; the savior, the giver of gifts, Kātyāyanī, the great benefactress, the terrible one, the victorious one, victory itself . . . Umā, the slayer of demons,"[2] and the usual identification and theft of epithets then follows: "O thou who art the Vedas, who art Revelation, who art virtue, Jātavedasi, . . . thou art *brahma* among the sciences, thou art the sleep of incorporate beings, the mother of Skanda, the blessed one, Durgā . . . thou art the mother of the Vedas and Vedānta . . . thou art sleep, illusion, modesty, happiness . . . thou art satisfaction, growth, contentment, light, the increaser of moon and sun."

Turning from these later parasites,[3] which live on their parent gods and yet tend to reduce them, we now revert to that happiness hereafter to which looks forward the epic knight that has not been tempted to 'renounce' desire. In pantheistic passages he is what the later remodeller makes him. But enough of old belief remains to show that the warrior really cared a great

[1] They are possibly old, as Weber thinks, but they seem to have nothing in common with the ancient female divinities.

[2] Compare another hymn to Durgā in iv. 6. 5 ff. (late). Durgā was probably an independent local deity, subsequently regarded as Çiva's female side. She plays a great rôle, under various names, in the 'revived' literature, as do the love-god and Ganeça. In both hymns she is 'Vishnu's sister,' and in iv. 6 a 'pure virgin.'

[3] One comparatively new god deserves a passing mention, Dharma's son, Kāma, the (Grecian?) love-god, 'the mind-shaker,' 'the limbless one,' whose arrows are like those of Cupid (i. 66. 32; 171. 34; iii. 46. 2). He is an adventitious addition to the epic. His later name of Ananga occurs in xii. 59. 91. In i. 71. 41 and 171. 40 he is Manmatha. The Atharvan god also has darts, iii. 25, a mark of this latest Veda.

deal more for heaven than he did for absorption. As to the cause of events, as was said above, it is Fate. Repeatedly is heard the lament, "Fate (impersonal) is the highest thing, fie on vain human effort." The knight confesses with his lips to a belief in the new doctrine of absorption, but at heart he is a fatalist. And his aim is to die on the field of battle, that he may go thence directly to the heaven that awaits the good and the brave.[1] Out of a long description of this heaven a few extracts here selected will show what the good knight anticipates:

> "Upward goes the path that leads to gods; it is inhabited by them that have sacrificed and have done penance. Unbelieving persons and untruthful persons do not enter there; only they that have duteous souls, that have conquered self, and heroes that bear the marks of battle. There sit the seers and gods, there are shining, self-illumined worlds, made of light, resplendent. And in this heaven there is neither hunger, nor thirst, nor weariness, nor cold, nor heat, nor fear; nothing that is terrible is there, nothing unclean; but pleasing sights, and sounds, and smells. There is no care there, nor age, nor work, nor sorrow. Such is the heaven that is the reward of good acts. Above this is Brahmā's world, where sit the seers and the three and thirty gods," etc.

Over against this array of advantages stands the one great "fault of heaven," which is stated almost in the words of "nessun maggior dolore," "the thought (when one lives again on the lower plane) of former happiness in the higher life is terrible grief" (vs. 30), *i.e.*, this heaven will pass away at the end of the world-period, when the Eternal draws all in to himself again (iii. 261); and the thought that one has been in heaven, while now he is (re-born) on earth, is a sorrow greater than the joy given by heaven.[2]

[1] Compare ii. 22. 18: "Great holiness, great glory, penance, death in battle, these are each respectively productive of heaven; the last alone is a sure cause."

[2] This description and the sentiments are quite late. The same sort of heaven (without the philosophical bitterness, with which compare above, p. 229) is, however, found in other passages, somewhat augmented with nymphs and facile goddesses.

One is reminded by the epic description of heaven of that poet of the Upanishads who describes his heavenly bliss as consisting in the fact that in that world "there is neither snow nor sorrow." The later version is only an amplification. Even with the assurance that the "fault of heaven" is the disappointment of being dropped to earth again in a new birth, the ordinary mortal is more averse from the bliss of absorption than from the pleasure of heaven. And in truth, except to one very weary of his lot in life, it must be confessed that the religion here shown in all its bearings is one eminently pleasant to believe. Its gist, in a word, is this: "If you feel able to endure it, the best thing to do is to study the plan of the universe, and then conform to it. By severe mental discipline you can attain to this knowledge, and for reward you will be immortally united with God." To this the sectarian adds: "Or believe in my god and the result will be the same." But both philosopher and sectarian continue: "If, however, you do not want to be united with the Supreme Spirit so soon as this, then be virtuous and devout, or simply be brave if you are a warrior; do whatever the rules of morality and caste-custom bid you do, and you will go to heaven for thousands of ages; at the end of which time you will be re-born in a fine family on earth, and may again decide whether to repeat the process of gaining heaven or to join God and become absorbed into the World-Spirit at once." There were probably many that chose rather to repeat their agreeable earthly experience, with an interlude of heaven after each death, than to make the renunciation of earth and heaven, and be absorbed once for all into the All-god.

The doctrine of the ages[1] is so necessary to a true understanding of the relative immortality offered as a substitute for

[1] This doctrine is supposed by some scholars to be due to outside influence, but the doubt is not substantiated, and even in the Rig Veda one passage appears to refer to it. Doubtless, however, the later expanded view, with its complicated reckonings, may have been touched by foreign influence.

the higher bliss of absorption (that is, genuine immortality), that an account of the teaching in this regard will not be out of place. The somewhat puzzling distinction between the happy life of them that fail to desire absorption, and yet are religious men, and the blissful life of those people that do attain absorption, is at once explained by a clear understanding of the duration of the time of the gods' own life and of the divine heaven. Whereas the Greek notion of four ages includes within the four all time, all the four ages of the Hindu are only a fraction of time. Starting at any one point of eternity, there is, according to the Hindu belief, a preliminary 'dawn' of a new cycle of ages. This dawn lasts four hundred years, and is then followed by the real age (the first of four), which lasts four thousand years, and has again a twilight ending of four hundred years in addition. This first is the Krita age, corresponding to the classical Golden Age. Its characteristics are, that in it everything is perfect; right eternal now exists in full power. In this age there are neither gods nor demons (Dānavas, Gandharvas, Yakshas, Rākshas, Serpents), neither buying nor selling, By a *lucus a non* the derivation of the name Krita is *kṛtam eva na kartavyam*, *i.e.*, with a pun, it is called the '*sacred* age' because there are no *sacrifices* in that age. No Sāma Veda, Rig Veda, or Yajur Veda exist as distinct Vedas.[1] There is no mortal work. Fruit comes by meditation; the only duty is renunciation. Disease, lack of mental power, moral defects (such as pride and hate) do not exist; the highest course of the ascetic Yogis is universally *brahma* (*paramakam*). In this age come into existence the Brahman, Kshatriya, Vāiçya, Çūdra, *i.e.*, the distinct castes of priest, warrior, husbandman, and slave; all with their special marks, and all

[1] *Na āsan sāma-ṛg-yajur-varṇās.* In xii. 342. 8 the order is Rik-Yajus-Atharvan-Sāman. The habit of putting Sāman instead of Rik at the head of the Vedas is still kept in the late litany to Çiva, who is "the Sāman among the Vedas." meaning, of course, the first and best. In the same place, "Çiva is the Itihāsa" epic (xiii. 14. 323; and *ib.* 17. 78, 91), for the epic outweighs all the Vedas in its own estimation.

delighted with their proper occupations. Yet have all the castes like occupations, like refuge, practice, and knowledge. They are joined to the one god (*eka deva*), and have but one *mantra* in their religious rites. Their duties are distinct, but they follow only one Veda and one rule. The four orders (of the time of life) are duly observed; men do not desire the fruit of their action, and so they obtain the highest course, *i.e.*, salvation by absorption into *brahma*. In this age the 'three attributes' (or qualities) are unknown. After this age follows the dawn of the second age, called Tretā, lasting three hundred years, then the real age of Tretā, three thousand years, followed by the twilight of three hundred years. The characteristics of this age are, that men are devout; that great sacrifices begin (*sattram pravartate*); that Virtue decreases by one quarter; that all the various rites are produced, together with the attainment of salvation through working for that end, by means of sacrifice and generosity; that every one does his duty and performs asceticism. The next age, Dvāpara, is introduced by a dawn of two hundred years, being itself two thousand years in duration, and it closes with a twilight of two hundred years. Half of Virtue fails to appear in this age, that is, the general virtue of the world is diminished by a half ('the Bull of Justice stands on two legs'). The Veda is now subdivided into four. Instead of every one having one Veda, four Vedas exist, but some people know only three, or two, or one, or are even Veda-less (*anṛcas*). Ceremonies become manifold, because the treatises on duty are subdivided (!). The attribute of passion influences people, and it is with this that they perform asceticism and are generous (not with disinterestedness). Few (*kaçcit*) are settled in truth; ignorance of the one Veda causes a multiplication of Vedas (*i.e.*, as Veda means 'knowledge,' the Vedas result from ignorance of the essential knowledge). Disease and sin make penance necessary. People sacrifice only to gain heaven. After this age and its twilight are past begins the Kali, last of the four ages, with a dawn of one hundred, a course of one thousand, and a subsequent twilight of one hundred years. This is the present sinful age, when there is no real religion, when the Vedas are ignored, and the castes are confused, when *itis* (distresses of every form) are rife; when Virtue has only one leg left to stand upon. The believer in Krishna as Vishnu, besides this universal description, says that the Supreme Lord in the Krita age is 'white' (pure); in the Tretā age, 'red'; in the Dvāpara age, 'yellow'; in the Kali age, 'black,' *i.e.*, Vishnu is Krishna, which means 'black.'[1] This cycle of ages always repeats itself anew. Now, since the twelve thousand years of these ages, with their dawns and twilights, are but one of countless cycles, when the Kali age and its twilight have brought all things into a miserable state, the universe is re-absorbed into the Supreme Spirit. There is then a universal (apparent) destruction, *pralaya*, of everything, first by fire and then by a general flood. Seven suns appear in heaven, and what they fail to burn is consumed by the great fire called Samvartaka (really a manifestation of Vishnu), which sweeps the world and leaves only ashes; then follows a flood which completes the annihilation. Thereafter follows a period equal to one thousand cycles (of twelve thousand years each), which is called 'Brahmā's night,' for during these twelve million years Brahmā sleeps; and the new Krita age begins again "when Brahmā wakes up" (iii. 188. 29, 69; 189. 42).[2] All the gods are destroyed in the universal destruction, that is, re-absorbed into the All-god, for there is no such thing as annihilation, either of spirit or of matter (which is illusion). Consequently the gods' heaven and the

[1] iii. 149. 14; 188. 22; 189. 32; probably with a recollection of the colors of the four castes, white, red, yellow, black. According to xii. 233. 32, there is no sacrifice in the Krita age, but, beginning with the Tretā age, there is a general diffusion of sacrifice in the Dvāpara age. In another passage of the same book it is said that marriage laws arose in the Dvāpara age (207. 38 ff.).

[2] The teaching varies somewhat in the allotment of years. See Manu, I. 67.

spirits of good men in that heaven are also re-absorbed into that Supreme, to be re-born in the new age. This is what is meant by the constant harping on quasi-immortality. Righteousness, sacrifice, bravery, will bring man to heaven, but, though he joins the gods, with them he is destroyed. They and he, after millions of years, will be re-born in the new heaven and the new earth. To escape this eventual re-birth one must desire absorption into the Supreme, not annihilation, but unity with God, so that one remains untouched by the new order at the end of Brahmā's 'day.' There are, of course, not lacking views of them that, taking the precept grossly, give a less dignified appearance to the teaching, and, in fact, upset its real intent. Thus, in the very same Puranic passage from which is taken the description above (iii. 188), it is said that a seer, who miraculously outlived the universal destruction of one cycle, was kindly swallowed by Vishnu, and that, on entering his stomach (the absorption idea in Puranic coarseness), he saw everything which had been destroyed, mountains, rivers, cities, the four castes engaged in their duties, etc. In other words, only transference of locality has taken place. But this account reads almost like a satire.

One of the most striking features of the Hindu religions, as they have been traced thus far, is the identification of right with light, and wrong with darkness. We have referred to it several times already. In the Vedic age the deities are luminous, while the demons and the abode of the wicked generally are of darkness. This view, usually considered Iranian and Zoroastrian, is as radically, if not so emphatically, Indic. It might be said, indeed, that it is more deeply implanted in the worship of the Hindus than in that of the Iranians, inasmuch as the latter religion enunciates and promulgates the doctrine, while the former assumes it. All deeds of sin are deeds of darkness, *tamas*. The devils live underground in darkness; the hells are below earth and are gloom lighted only by torture-flames. The development of devil-worship (the side-scenes in the theatre of Çivaism) introduces devils of another sort, but the general effect remains. The fire-priest Bhrigu says: "Untruth is a form of darkness, and by darkness one is brought to hell (downwards); veiled in darkness one sees not the light. Light is heaven, they say, and darkness is hell," xii. 190. 2–3. This antithesis of evil as darkness, good as light, is too native to India to admit of the suggestion that it might have been borrowed. But an isolated and curious Puranic chapter of the epic appears to have direct reference to the Persian religion. All Hindu gods have sacrifices, even Çiva the 'destroyer of sacrifice.' Now in iii. 220, after a preliminary account of the *pāñcajanya* fire (vs. 5 ff.) there is given a list of 'gods that destroy sacrifice,' *devās yajñamuṣas*, fifteen in number, who 'stand here' on earth and 'steal' the sacrifice. They extend over the five peoples in three divisions of five each. The first and third group contain names compounded with Bhīma and Sūra respectively; while the third group is that of Sumitra, Mitravan, Mitrajña, Mitravardhana, Mitradharman. There are others without the *mitra* (vs. 10). The appellation *devās* seems to take them out of connection with Çiva's demoniac troops, and the persistency of *mitra* would look as if these 'gods' were of Iranian origin. There may have been (as are possibly the modern Sāuras) believers in the Persian religion already long established among the Hindus.

The question will naturally present itself whether in the religious *olla podrida* known as the Mahābhārata there are distinct allusions to Buddhism, and, if so, in how far the doctrines of this sect may have influenced the orthodox religion. Buddhism does not appear to have attacked or to have attracted the 'holy land,' whence, indeed, according to law, heretics are 'banished.' But its influence of course must have embraced this country, and it is only a question of in how far epic Brahmanism has accepted it. At a later period Hinduism, as has been observed, calmly accepts Buddha as an *avatar* of Vishnu. Holtzmann, who is inclined to attribute a good deal to Buddhism, sees signs of it even in the personal characteristics of the epic heroes, and believes the whole poem to have been more or less affected by anti-Buddhistic feeling. If this were so one would have to give over to Buddhism much also of the humanitarianism to be found in the moral precepts that are so thickly strewn through the various books. In our opinion these signs-manual of Buddhism are not sufficiently evident to support Holtzmann's opinion for the whole poem, and it is to be noted that the most taking evidence is drawn from the latest parts of the work. It is just here that we think it necessary to draw the line, for while much of late date has been added in earlier books, yet in the books which one may call wholly late additions appear the strongest indications of Buddhistic influence.[1] A great deal of the Book of Peace is Puranic, the book as a whole is a Vishnuite addition further enlarged by Çivaite interpolation. The following book is, again, an offset to the Book of Peace, and is as distinctly Çivaite in its conception as is the Book of Peace Vishnuite.[2] It is here, in these latest additions, which scarcely deserve to be ranked with the real epic, that are found the most palpable touches of Buddhism. They stand to the epic proper as stands to them the Genealogy of Vishnu, a further addition which has almost as much claim to be called 'part of the epic' as have the books just mentioned, only that it is more evidently the product of a later age, and represents the Krishna-Vishnu sect in its glory after the epic was completed. Nevertheless, even in these books much that is suspected of being Buddhistic may be Brahmanic; and in any concrete case a decision, one way

[1] Weber thinks, on the other hand, that the parties represent respectively, Çiva and Vishnu worship, *Ind. St.* i. 206.

[2] This book also is closely in touch with the later Purānas. For instance, Citragupta, Yama's secretary, is known only to the books of the pseudo-epic, the Vishnu Purāna, the Padma Purāna, etc.

or the other, is scarcely to be made on objective grounds. Still more is this the case in earlier books. Thus, for instance, Holtzmann is sure that a conversation of a slave and a priest in the third book is Buddhistic because the man of low caste would not venture to instruct a Brahman.[1] But it is a command emphasized throughout the later Brahmanism that one must take refuge in the ship that saves; and in passages not suspected of Buddhistic tendency Bhishma takes up this point, and lays down the rule that, no matter to which caste a man belongs, his teaching if salutary is to be accepted. It is even said in one passage of the Book of Peace that one ought to learn of a slave, and in another that all the four castes ought to hear the Veda read:[2] "Let him get instruction even from a Çūdra if he can thereby attain to salvation"; and again: "Putting the Brahman first, let the four castes hear (the Veda); for this (giving first place to the priest) is (the rule in) reading the Veda."[3] And in many places are found instructions given by low-caste men. It may be claimed that every case which resembles Buddhistic teaching is drawn from Buddhism, but this would be to claim more than could be established. Moreover, just as the non-injury doctrine is prior to Buddhism and yet is a mark of Buddhistic teaching, so between the two religions there are many points of similarity which may be admitted without compromising the genuineness of the Brahmanic teaching. For Buddhism in its morality is anything but original.[4]

[1] *Neunzehn Bücher*, p. 86.

[2] The epic does not care much for castes in some passages. In one such it is said that members of all castes become priests when they go across the Gomal, iii. 84. 48.

[3] xii. 319. 87 ff. (*prāpya jñānam . . . çūdrād api*); xii. 328. 49 (*çrāvayec caturo varṇān*). The epic regards itself as more than equivalent (*adhikam*) to the four Vedas, i. 1. 272.

[4] Some ascribe the *samsāra* doctrine to Buddhistic influence — a thesis supported only by the fact that this occurs in late Brahmanic passages and Upanishads. But the assumption that Upanishads do not precede Buddha is scarcely tenable. The Katha, according to Weber (*Sitz. Berl. Ak.* 1890, p. 930), is late (Christian!): according to Oldenberg and Whitney, early (*Buddha*, p. 56; *Proc. AOS.* May, 1886).

Another bit of instruction from the Book of Peace illustrates the attitude of the slave just referred to. In sharp contrast to what one would expect from a Buddhist, this slave, who is a hunter, claims that he is justified in keeping on with his murderous occupation because it is his caste-occupation; whereas, as a Buddhist he ought to have renounced it if he thought it sinful, without regard to the caste-rule. The Book of Peace lays it down as a rule that the giving up of caste-occupation is meritorious if the occupation in itself is iniquitous, but it hedges on the question to the extent of saying that, no matter whether the occupation be sinful or not, if it is an inherited occupation a man does not do wrong to adhere to it. This is liberal Brahmanism. The rule reads as follows: "Actors, liquor-dealers, butchers, and other such sinners are not justified in following such occupations, *if they are not born to the profession* (*i.e.* if they are born to it they are justified in following their inherited occupation). Yet if one has inherited such a profession it is a noble thing to renounce it."[1]

The marks of Buddhistic influence on which we would lay greater stress are found not in the fact that Mudgala refuses heaven (iii. 261. 43), or other incidents that may be due as well to Brahmanism as to Buddhism, but in such passages of the pseudo-epical Book of Peace as for example the *dharmyas panthās* of xii. 322. 10–13; the conversation of the female beggar, *bhikshukī*, with the king in 321. 7, 168; the *buddha* of 289. 45; the Buddhistic phraseology of 167. 46; the remark of the harlot Pingalā in 174. 60: *pratibuddhā 'smi jāgṛmi* (I am 'awakened' to a sense of sin and knowledge of holiness), and the like phrase in 177. 22: *pratibuddho 'smi.*[2] Of especial importance is the shibboleth Nirvāna which is often used in the epic. There seems, indeed, to be a subtile connection

[1] xii. 295. 5–6.

[2] Noteworthy is the fact that parts of the Çivaite thirteenth book seem to be most Buddhistic (ch. i.; 143. 48, etc.), and monotheistic (16. 12 ff.): though the White Islanders are made Vishnuite in the twelfth. Compare Holtzmann, *ad. loc.*

between Çivaism and Buddhism. Buddhism rejects pantheism, Çivaism is essentially monotheism. Both were really religions of the lower classes. It is true that the latter was affected and practiced by those of high rank, but its strength lay with the masses. Thus while Vishnuism appealed to the contemplative and philosophical (Rāmaism), as well as to the easy-going middle classes (Krishnaism), Çivaism with its dirty asceticism, its orgies and Bacchanalian revels, its devils and horrors generally, although combined with a more ancient philosophy, appealed chiefly to the magic-monger and the vulgar. So it is that one finds, as one of his titles in the thirteenth book, that Çiva is 'the giver of Nirvāna,' (xiii. 16. 15). But if one examines the use of this word in other parts of the epic he will see that it has not the true Buddhistic sense except in its literal physical application as when the *nirvāṇa* (extinguishing) of a lamp, iv. 22. 22, is spoken of; or the *nirvāṇa* of duties (in the Pañcarātra 'Upanishad,' xii. 340. 67). On the other hand, in sections where the context shows that this must be the case, Nirvāna is the equivalent of 'highest bliss' or 'highest *brahma*,' the same with the felicity thus named in older works. This, for instance, is the case in xii. 21. 17; 26. 16, where Nirvāna cannot mean extinction but absorption, *i.e.*, the 'blowing out' of the individual flame (spirit) of life, only that it may become one with the universal spirit. In another passage it is directly equated with *sukham brahma* in the same way (*ib.* 189. 17). If now one turn to the employment of this word in the third book he will find the case to be the same. When the king reproaches his queen for her atheistic opinions in iii. 31. 26 he says that if there were no reward for good deeds hereafter "people would not seek Nirvāna," just as he speaks of heaven ('immortality') and hell, *ib.* 20 and 19, not meaning thereby extinction but absorption. So after a description of that third heaven wherein is Vishnu, when one reads that Mudgala "attained that highest eternal bliss the sign of which is Nirvâna" (iii. 261. 47), he can only suppose that the word means here absorption into *brahma* or union with Vishnu. In fact Nirvāna is already a word of which the sense has been subjected to attrition enough to make it synonymous with 'bliss.' Thus "the gods attained Nirvāna by means of Vishnu's greatness" (iii. 201. 22); and a thirsty man "after drinking water attained Nirvāna," *i.e.*, the drink made him happy (*ib.* 126. 16). One may best compare the Jain Nirvāna of happiness.

While, therefore, Buddhism seems to have left many manifest traces[1] in the later epic the weight of its influence on the early epic may well be questioned. The moral harangues of the earlier books show nothing more than is consistent with that Brahmanism which has made its way unaided through the greater humanitarianism of the earlier Upanishads. At the same time it is right to say that since the poem is composed after Buddha's time there is no historical certainty in regard to the inner connection of belief and morality (as expounded in the epic) with Buddhism. Buddhism, though at a distance, environed epic Brahmanism, and may well have influenced it. The objective proofs for or against this are not, however, decisive.

Whether Christianity has affected the epic is another question that can be answered (and then doubtfully) only by drawing a line between epic and pseudo-epic. And in this regard the Harivança legends of Krishna are to be grouped with the pseudo-epic, of which they are the legitimate if late continuation. Again one must separate teaching from legend. To the Divine Song belong sentiments and phrases that have been ascribed to Christian influence. Definitive assurance in this regard is an impossibility. When Vishnu says (as is said also in the Upanishads) "I am the letter A," one may, and probably will, decide that this is or is not an imitation of "I am

[1] Nirvāna, loosely used; termini technici; possibly the evils of the fourth age; the mention of (Buddhist) temples, etc.

alpha," strictly in accordance with his preconceived opinions. There are absolutely no historical data to go upon. One may say with tolerable certainty that the Divine Song as a whole is antique, prior to Christianity. But it is as unmistakably interpolated and altered. The doctrine of *bhakti*, faithful love as a means of salvation, cannot be much older than the Song, for it is found only in the latest Upanishads (as shown by comparing them with those undoubtedly old). But on the other hand the *prasāda* doctrine (of special grace) belongs to a much earlier literature, and there is no reason why the whole theory with its startling resemblance to the doctrine of grace, and its insistence on personal affection for the Lord should not have been self-evolved. The old omnipotence of inherited knowledge stops with the Upanishads. To their authors the Vedas are but a means. They desired wisdom, not knowledge. They postulated the desire for the Supreme Spirit as the true wisdom. From this it is but a step to yearning and love for the Supreme. That step is made in the Divine Song. It is recognized by early Buddhism as a Brahmanic trait. Is it necessarily imported from Christianity? The proof is certainly lacking. Nor, to one accustomed to the middle literature of Hindu religion, is the phraseology so strikingly unique as would appear to be the case. Taken all in all, the teaching of Christianity certainly may be suspected, but it cannot be shown to exist in the Divine Song.

Quite different is the case with the miraculous matter that grew up about the infant Krishna. But here one is out of the epic and dealing with the latest literature in regard to the man-god. This distinction cannot be too much insisted upon, for to point first to the teaching of the Divine Song and then to the Krishna legends as equally reflecting Christianity is to mix up two periods as distinct as periods can be established in Hindu literature. And the result of the whole investigation shows that the proofs of borrowing are as different as these periods. The inner Christianity thought to be copied by the re-writer of the Divine Song is doubtful in the last degree. The outer Christianity reflected in the Puranic legends of Krishna is as palpable as it is shocking. Shocking, for here not only are miracles treated grotesquely, but everything that is meant spiritually in the Occident is interpreted physically and carnally. The love of the Bridegroom is sensual; the brides of God are drunken dancing girls.

The 'coincidences,' as some scholars marvellously regard them, between the legends of Christ and Krishna are too extraordinary to be accepted as such. They are direct importations, not accidental coincidences. Whatever is most marvellous in the accounts of Christianity finds itself here reproduced in Krishnaism. It is not in the doctrine of *avatars*, which resembles the doctrine of the Incarnation,[1] it is in the totality of legends connected with Krishna that one is forced to see Christian influence. The scenes of the nativity, the adoration of the magi, the miracles during the Saviour's childhood, the transfiguration, and other stories of Christ are reproduced with astonishing similarity. 'One may add to this the Christmas festival, where Krishna is born in a stable, and the use of certain church-utensils in the temple-service. Weber has proved by collecting and explaining these 'coincidences,'[2] that there must be identity of origin. It remains only to ask from which side is the borrowing? Considering how late are these Krishna legends in India[3] there can be no doubt that the

[1] On this point we agree neither with Weber, who regards the *avatars* as an imitation of the Incarnation (*Ind. St.* ii. p. 169), nor with Schroeder, who (*Literatur und Cultur*, p. 330) would derive the notion from the birth-stories of Buddha. In our opinion the *avatar*-theory is older than either and is often only an assimilation of outlying totem-gods to the Brahman's god, or as in the case of the flood-story the necessary belief that the 'fish' must have been the god of the race. Some of these *avatars* are Brahmanic, presumably pre-Buddhistic.

[2] Krishna's Geburtsfest (*janmâṣṭamî*), 1867.

[3] Since they do not appear till after the real epic we date them tentatively as arising after 600 A.D. Most of them are in still later Purânas.

Hindu borrowed the tales, but not the name; for the last assumption is quite improbable because Krishna (=Christ?) is native enough, and Jishnu is as old as the Rig Veda. That these tales are of secondary importance, as they are of late origin, is a matter of course. They are excrescences upon real Vishnuism (Krishnaism) and the result of anthropomorphizing in its fullest extent the image of the man-god, who is represented in the epic as the incarnation of the Supreme Spirit. The doctrine of the incarnation is thoroughly Indic. It is Buddhistic as well as Brahmanic, and precedes Vishnuism as it does Christianity. The legends are another matter. Here one has to assume direct contact with the Occident.[1] But while agreeing with Weber and disagreeing with Barth in the determination of the relation of this secondary matter, we are unable to agree with Weber in his conclusions in regard to the one passage in the pseudo-epic that is supposed by him[2] to refer to a visit to a Christian church in Alexandria. This is the famous episode of the White Island, which, to be sure, occurs in so late a portion of the Book of Peace (xii. 337. 20 ff.) that it might well be what Weber describes it as being. But to us it appears to contain no allusion at all to Christianity. The account in brief is as follows: Three priests with the insignificant names "First, Second, Third,"[3] go to the far North (*diç uttarā*) where, in the "Sea of Milk," they find an Albion called "White Island," perhaps regarded as one of the seven or thirteen 'islands,' of which earth consists; and there Vishnu

1 Incidental rapport with the Greeks has been pointed out in other instances; the *surangā*, a mine, of the late tale in i. 148. 12, etc. (*Ind. St.* ii. p. 395), has been equated with syrinx; Skanda with Alexander, etc. It is needless to say that each of these is only a guess in etymology. But Greek influence is perceptible in the Greek soldiers and names of (Greek) kings that are found in the epic.

2 *Ind. St.* i. 423; ii. 169. Weber believes that little is native to India which resembles Christianity in the way of theology; love of God, special grace, monotheism, all to him are stolen. We regret that we must disagree with him in these instances.

3 Ekata, Dvita, Trita. A Dvita appears as early as the Rig Veda. Ekata is an analogous formation and is old also.

is worshipped as the one god by white men of extraordinary physical characteristics.

The fact that the 'one god' is already a hackneyed phrase of philosophy; that there is no resemblance to a trinitarian god; that the hymn sung to this one god contains no trace of Christian influence, but is on the other hand thoroughly native in tone and phraseology, being as follows: "Victory to thee, thou god with lotus-eyes; Reverence to thee, thou creator of all things; Reverence be to thee, O Vishnu;[1] thou Great Person; first-born one"; all these facts indicate that if the White-islanders are indeed to be regarded as foreigners worshipping a strange god, that god is strictly monotheistic and not trinitarian. Weber lays stress on the expression 'first-born,' which he thinks refers to Christ; but the epithet is old (Vedic), and is common, and means no more than 'primal deity.'

There is much that appears to be foreign in the epic. This passage seems rather to be a recollection of some shrine where monotheism without Christianity was acknowledged. On the other hand, even in the pseudo-epic, there is much apparently borrowed which yet is altogether native to Brahmanic land and sect. It is not in any passage which is proved to be of foreign origin that one reads of the boy of twelve years who entered among the wise men and confuted their reasoning (above, p. 382). It is not of course due to Christian influence that the great 'saint of the stake' is taken by the 'king's men,' is crucified (or literally impaled) among thieves, and lives so long that the guard go and tell the king of the miracle;[2] nor is it necessary to assume that everything elevated is borrowed. "When I revile, I revile not again," sounds indeed like an echo of Christian teaching, but how thoroughly Hindu is the reason. "For I know that self-control is the door of immortality." And in the

[1] Hrishīkeça is 'lord of senses,' a common epithet of Vishnu (Krishna).

[2] i. 107. 1 ff. The spirits of the dead come to him and comfort him in the shape of birds — an old trait, compare Bāudh. Dh. Çāst. ii. 8. 14. 10; Çat. Br. vi. 1. 1. 2.

same breath, with a connection of meaning patent only when one regards the whole not as borrowed but as native, follow the words that we have ventured to put upon the title-page of this volume, as the highest and at the same time the truest expression of a religion that in bringing the gods to men raised man to equality with God—"This is a holy mystery which I declare unto you : There is nothing nobler than humanity."[1]

[1] xii. 300. 20.

CHAPTER XVI.

THE PURĀNAS.—EARLY SECTS, FESTIVALS, THE TRINITY.

ARCHAEOLOGIA, 'ancient lore,' is the meaning of Purāna (*purāṇa*, 'old'). The religious period represented by the extant writings of this class is that which immediately follows the completion of the epic.[1] These works, although they contain no real history, yet reflect history very plainly, and since the advent and initial progress of Puranic Hinduism, with its various cults, is contemporary with important political changes, it will be necessary briefly to consider the circumstances in which arose these new creeds, for they were destined to become in the future the controlling force in the development of Hindu religion.

In speaking of the extension of Buddhism we showed that its growth was influenced in no small degree by the fact that this caste-less and, therefore, democratic religion was adopted by post-Alexandrine rulers in the Graeco-Bactrian period. At this time the Aryans were surrounded with foreigners and pagans. To North and South spread savage or half Hinduized native tribes, while soldiers of Greece and Bactria encamped in the valley of the Ganges. Barbarians had long been active in the

[1] Parts of the epic are called Purānas, as other parts are called Upanishads. These are the forerunners of the extant Purānas. The name, indeed, is even older than the epic, belonging to the late Vedic period, where are grouped together Purānas and Itihāsas, 'Ancient History' and 'Stories'; to which are added 'Eulogies.' Weber has long since pointed out that even when the 'deeds of kings' were sung at a ceremony they were wont to be so embroidered as to be dubbed 'fiction' by the Hindus themselves. India has neither literary history (save what can be gleaned from genealogies of doubtful worth), nor very early inscriptions. The 'archaeology' of the Purānas was probably always what it is in the extant specimens, legendary material of no direct historical value.

North, and some scholars have even claimed that Buddha's own family was of Turanian origin. The Brahmans then as now retained their prestige only as being repositories of ancient wisdom; and outside of their own 'holy land' their influence was reduced to a minimum by the social and political tendencies that accompanied the growth of Buddhism. After the fourth century B.C. the heart of India, the 'middle district,' between the Himālaya and Vindhya mountains from Delhi to Benares,[1] was trampled upon by one Graeco-Bactrian horde after another. The principal effect of this rude dominion was eventually to give political equality to the two great rival religions. The Buddhist and the Brahman lived at last if not harmoniously, at least pacifically, side by side. Members of the same reigning family would profess Buddhism or Brahmanism indifferently. One king would sometimes patronize both religions. And this continued to be the case till Buddhism faded out, replaced by that Hinduism which owed its origin partly to native un-Aryan influence (paganism), partly to this century-long fusion of the two state religions.

To review these events: In the first decades of the fourth century (320 or 315–291 B.C.) Candragupta, Sandrocottos, had built up a monarchy in Behār[2] on the ruins left by the Greek invasion, sharing his power with Seleucus in the Northwest, and had thus prepared the way for his grandson, Açoka, the great patron of Buddhism (264 or 259). This native power fell before the hosts of Northern barbarians, which, after irruptions into India in the second century, got a permanent foothold there in the first century B.C. These Northern barbarians (their nationality is uncertain), whose greatest king was Kanishka, 78 A.D., ruled for centuries the land they had seized; but they were vanquished at last in the sixth century, probably

[1] Strictly speaking to the present Allahābād, where is the Prayāga, or confluence of Yamunā and Gangā (Jumna and Ganges).

[2] Māgadha; called Behār from its many monasteries, *vihāras*, in Açoka's time.

by Vikramāditya,[1] and were driven out. The breathing-space between Northern barbarian and Mohammedan was nominally not a long one, but since the first Moslem conquests had no definitive result the new invaders did not quite overthrow Hindu rule till the end of the tenth century. During this period the native un-Aryan tribes, with their Hinduizing effect, were more destructive as regards the maintenance of the old Brahmanic cult than were outsiders.[2]

When Tamerlane invaded India his was the fourth invasion after the conquest of the Punjāb by the Moslem in 664.[3] In

[1] So, plausibly, Müller, *loc. cit.* below.

[2] The tribes became Hinduized, their chiefs became Rājputs; their religions doubtless affected the ritual and creed of the civilized as much as the religion of the latter colored their own. Some of these un-Aryan peoples were probably part native, part barbaric. There is much doubt in regard to the dates that depend on accepted eras. It is not certain, for instance, that, as Müller claims, Kanishka's inauguration coincides with the Çaka era, 78 A.D. A great Buddhist council was held under him. Some distinguished scholars still think with Bühler that Vikramāditya's inauguration was 57 B.C. (the date that used to be assigned to him). From our present point of view it is of little consequence when this king himself lived. He is renowned as patron of arts and as a conqueror of the barbarians. If he lived in the first century B.C. his conquest amounted to nothing permanent. What is important, however, is that all Vikramāditya stands for in legend must have been in the sixth century A.D. For the drama, of which he is said to have been patron, represents a religion distinctly later than that of the body of the epic (completed in the sixth or seventh century, Bühler, *Indian Studies*, No. ii.). The dramatic and astronomical era was but introductory to Kumārila's reassertion of Brahmanism in the seventh century, when the Northern barbarian was gone, and the Mohammedan was not yet rampant. In the rest of Northern India there were several native dynasties in different quarters, with different eras; one in Surāshtra (Gujarāt), one again in the 'middle district' or 'North Western Provinces,' one in Kutch; overthrown by Northern barbarians (in the fifth century) and by the Mohammedans (in the seventh and eighth centuries), respectively. Of these the Guptas of the 'middle district,' and the Valabhīs of Kutch, had neither of the eras just mentioned. The former dated from 320–321 (perhaps 319), the latter from 190 (A.D.). The word *samvat*, 'year,' indicates that the time is dated from either the Çaka or Vikramāditya era. See IA. xvii. 362; Fergusson, JRAS. xii. 259; Müller, *India, What Can It Teach Us?* p. 282; Kielhorn, IA. xix. 24; xxii. 111. The Northern barbarians are called Scythians, or Huns, or Turanians, according to fancy. No one really knows what they were.

[3] The first host was expelled by the Hindus in 750. After a period of rest Mahmud was crowned in 997, who overran India more than a dozen times. In the fol-

1525 the fifth conqueror, Baber, fifth too in descent from Tamerlane, founded the Mogul empire that lasted till the fall of this dynasty (nominally till 1857). But it must be remembered that each new conqueror from 997 till 1525 merely conquered old Mohammedan dynasties with new invasions. It was all one to the Hindu. He had the Mohammedan with him all this time; only each new rival's success made his lot the harder, But Baber's grandson, the Great Mogul, Akbar (who reigned from 1556 to 1605), gave the land not only peace but kindness; and under him Jew, Christian, Hindu, and Mohammedan at last forgot to fear or fight. After this there is only the overthrow of the Mohammedan power to record; and the rise of the Mahratta native kingdoms. A new faith resulted from the amalgamation of Hinduism with Mohammedism (after 1500), as will be shown hereafter.

In the pauses before the first Mohammedan invasion, and between the first defeat of the Mohammedans and their successful second conquest, the barbarians being now expelled and Buddhism being decadent, Brahmanism rallied. In the sixth century there was toleration for all faiths. In the seventh century Kumārila renewed the strength of Brahmanism on the ritualistic side with attacks on Buddhism, and in the ninth century Çankara placed the philosophy of unsectarian pantheism on a firm basis by his commentary on the Vedānta Sūtra.[1] These two men are the re-makers of ancient Brahmanism, which from this time on continued in its stereotyped form, adopting Hindu

lowing centuries the land was conquered and the people crushed by the second great Mohammedan, Ghori, who died in 1206, leaving his kingdom to a vassal, Kutab, the 'slave sultan' of Delhi. In 1294, this slave dynasty having been recently supplanted, the new successor to the throne was slain by his own nephew, Allah-ud-dîn, who is reckoned as the third Mohammedan conqueror of India. His successor swept even the Dekhan of all its Hindu (temple) wealth; but his empire finally broke down under its own size; preparing the way for Timur (Tamerlane), who entered India in 1398.

[1] Çankara himself was not a pure Brahman. Both Vishnuites and Çivaites lay claim to him.

gods very coyly, and only as spirits of small importance, while relying on the laws as well as the gods of old, on holy *ācāra* or 'custom,' and the now systematized exposition of its old (Upanishad) philosophy.[1] Its creative force was already spent. Buddhism, on the other hand, was dying a natural death. The time was ripe for Hinduism, which had been gathering strength for centuries. After the sixth century, and perhaps even as late as 1500, or later, were written the modern Purānas, which embody the new belief.[2] They cannot, on account of the distinct advance in their cult, have appeared before the end of the epic age. The breathing spell (between barbarian and complete Mohammedan conquest) which gave opportunity to Kumārila to take a high hand with Buddhism, was an opportunity also for the codification of the new creeds. It is, therefore, to this era that one has probably to refer the first of the mod-

[1] Coy as was the Brahman in the adoption of the new gods he was wise enough to give them some place in his pantheon, or he would have offended his laity. Thus he recognizes Kālī as well as Çrī; in fact he prefers to recognize the female divinities of the sects, for they offer less rivalry.

[2] There was a general revival of letters antedating the Brahmanic theological revival. The drama, which reflects equally Hinduism and Brahmanism, is now the favorite light literature of the cultured. In the sixth century the first astronomical works are written (Varāhamihira, who wrote the *Bṛhat Saṁhitā*), and the group of writers called the Nine Gems (reckoned of Vikramāditya's court) are to be referred to this time. The best known among them is Kālidāsa, author of the *Çakuntalā*. An account of this Renaissance, as he calls it, will be found in Müller's *India, What Can It Teach Us?* The learned author is perhaps a little too sweeping in his conclusions. It is, for instance, tolerably certain that the Bhārata was completed by the time the 'Renaissance' began; so that there is no such complete blank as he assumes prior to Vikramāditya. But the general state of affairs is such as is depicted in the ingenious article referred to. The sixth and seventh centuries were eras that introduced modern literature under liberal native princes, who were sometimes not Rājputs at all. Roughly speaking, one may reckon from 500 B.C. to the Christian era as a period of Buddhistic control, Graeco-Bactrian invasion, and Brahmanic decline. The first five centuries after the Christian see the two religions in a state of equilibrium, under Scythian control, and the Mahā-Bhārata, the expanded Bhārata, is written. From 500 to 1000 is an era of native rulers, Brahmanic revival in its pure form, and Hindu growth, with little trouble from the Mohammedans. Then for five centuries the horrors of Moslem conquest.

ern sectarian Purānas, though the ritualistic Tantras and Āgamas of the lower Çivaite sects doubtless belong rather to the end than to the beginning of the period. We are strengthened in this belief by the fact that the oldest of these works do not pretend to antedate Kumārila's century, though the sects mentioned in the epic are known in the first centuries of the Christian era. The time from the first to the seventh centuries one may accordingly suppose to have been the era during which was developing the Brahmanized form of the early Hindu sects, the literature of these and subsequent sects being composed in the centuries succeeding the latter term. These sects again divide into many subdivisions, of which we shall speak below. At present we take up the character of the Purānas and their most important points of difference as compared with the sectarian parts of the earlier pseudo-epic, examining especially the trinitarian doctrine, which they inculcate, and its history.

Save in details, even the special 'faith-scriptures' called Tantras go no further than go the Purānas in advocating the cult of their particular divinities. And to this advocacy of special gods all else in this class of writings is subordinated. The ideal Purāna is divided into five parts, cosmogony, new creations, genealogies of gods and heroes, *manvantaras* (descriptions of periodic 'ages,' past and future), and dynasties of kings. But no extant Purāna is divided thus. In the epic the doctrine of trinitarianism is barely formulated. Even in the Harivança, or Genealogy, *vañça*, of Vishnu, there is no more than an inverted triunity, 'one form, three gods,' where, in reality, all that is insisted upon is the identity of Vishnu and Çiva, Brahmā being, as it were, perfunctorily added.[1] In the Purānas, on the other hand, while the trinity is acknowledged, religion is resolved again into a sort of sectarian monotheism, where the devotee seems to be in the midst of a squabbling horde of temple-priests, each fighting for his own idol. In the calmer aspects of religion,

[1] Har. 10,662. Compare the laudation of 'the two gods' in the same section.

apart from sectarian schism, these writings offer, indeed, much that is of second-rate interest, but little that is of real value. The idle speculations in regard to former divinities are here made cobweb thin. The philosophy is not new, nor is the spirit of religion raised, even in the most inspired passages, to the level which it has reached in the Divine Song. Some of these Purānas, of which eighteen chief are cited, but with an unknown number of subordinate works,[1] may claim a respectable age; many of them are the most wretched stuff imaginable, bearing about the same literary and historical relation to earlier models as do the later legal Smritis. In fact, save for their religious (sectarian) purport, the Purānas for sections together do not differ much in content from legal Smritis, out of which some may have been evolved, though, probably, they were from their inception legendary rather than didactic. It is more probable, therefore, that they appropriated Smriti material just as they did epic material; and though it is now received opinion that legal Smritis are evolved out of Sūtras, this yet can be the case only with the oldest, even if the statement then can be accepted in an unqualified form. In our own opinion it is highly probable that Purānas and later legal Smritis are divergent developments from the same source.[2] One gives an account of creation, and proceeds to tell about the social side; the other sticks to the accounts of creation, goes on to theology, takes up tales of heroes, introduces speculation, is finally wrenched over to and amplified by sectarian writers, and so presents a composite that resembles epic and law, and yet is generally religious and speculative.

[1] As the Jains have Angas and Upāngas, and as the pseudo-epic distinguishes Nishads and Upanishads, so the Brahman has Purānas and Upapurānas (Kūrma Purāna, i. p. 3). Some of the sects acknowledge only six Purānas as orthodox.

[2] As an example of a Puranic Smriti (legal) we may cite the trash published as the Vṛddha-Hārīta-Saṁhitā Here there is polemic against Çiva; one must worship Jagannāth with flowers, and every one must be branded with the Vishnu disc (*cakra*). Even women and slaves are to use *mantras*, etc.

A striking instance of this may be seen in the law-book of 'Vishnu.' Here there is an old base of legal lore, Sūtra, interlarded with Puranic material, and built up with sectarianism. The writer is a Vishnuite, and while recognizing the trinity, does not hesitate to make his law command offerings to Krishna Vāsudeva, and his family (Pradyumna, Aniruddha), along with the regular Brahmanic oblations to older spirits.[1] Brahmanism recognized Hindu deities as subordinate powers at an early date, at least as early as the end of the Sūtra period; while Manu not only recognizes Vishnu and Çiva (Hara), but recommends an oblation to Çrī and Kālī (Bhadrakālī, here, as elsewhere, is Durgā).[2]

In their original form the Purānas were probably Hesiodic in a great extent, and doubtless contained much that was afterwards specially developed in more prolix form in the epic itself. But the works that are come down as Purānas are in general of later sectarian character, and the epic language, phraseology, and descriptions of battles are more likely taken straight from the epic than preserved from ante-epic times. Properly speaking one ought to give first place to the Purānas that are incorporated into the epic. The epic Mārkandeya Purāna, for instance, is probably a good type of one of the earlier works that went by this name. That the present Purānas are imitations of the epic, in so far as they treat of epic topics, may be presumed from the fact that although they often have the formulae intact of the battlefield,[3] yet do they not remain by epic descriptions but add weapons, etc., of more modern date than are employed in the original.[4]

[1] The lateness of this law-book is evident from its advocacy of *suttee* (xxv. 14), its preference for female ancestors (see below), etc.

[2] Manu, iii. 89; xii. 121.

[3] As, for example, in Kūrma Purāna, xvi. p. 186, where is found a common epic verse description of battle.

[4] A good instance of this is found in Brihan Nāradīya Purāna, x., where the *churikā* and *drughaṇa* (24) appear in an imitative scene of this sort; one of these being later, the other earlier, than the epic vocabulary.

The sectarian monotheism of the Purānas never resulted in dispensing with the pantheon. The Hindu monotheist is a pantheist, and whether sectarian or philosophical, he kept and added to his pantheon.[1] Indra is still for warriors, Maruts for husbandmen, although old views shift somewhat. So for example, in the Kūrma Purāna the Gandharvas are added for the Çūdras.[2] The fourfoldness, which we have shown in the epic to be characteristic of Vishnu, is now represented by the military epithet *caturvyūhas* (agmen quadratum), in that the god represents peace, wisdom, support, and renunciation; though, as a matter of fact, he is *avyūha*, *i.e.*, without any of these.[3] Starting with the physical 'god of the four quarters,' one gets even in the epic the 'controller of four,' or perfect person, conceived like ἀνὴρ τετράγωνος. Tennyson's 'four-square to all the winds that blow' is a good connecting link in the thought. The Purānas are a mine of legend, although most of the stories seem to be but epic tales, more or less distorted. Nala 'the great-great-grandson of Rāma' is described after the history of Rāma himself; the installation of Pūru, when his father had passed over his eldest son, and such reminiscences of the epic are the stock in trade of the legendary writers.[4]

The origin of the four castes;[5] the descriptions of hell, some-

[1] Perhaps the most striking distinction between Vedic and Puranic, or, one may say, Indic Aryan and Hindu religions, is the emphasis laid in the former upon Right; in the latter, upon idols. The Vedic religion insists upon the law of right (order), that is, the sacrifice; but it insists also upon right as rectitude, truth, holiness. Puranic Hinduism insists upon its idols; only incidentally does it recommend rectitude, truth, abstract holiness.

[2] KP. i. p. 29.

[3] Kūrma, xii. p. 102. Contrast *ib.* xxii. p. 245, *caturvyūhadharo Vishnur avyūhas procyate* (elsewhere *navavyūha*). Philosophically, in the doctrine of the epic Pāñcarātras (still held by some sectaries), Vishnu is to be revered as Krishna, Balarāma, Pradyumna, Aniruddha (Krishna's brother, son, and grandson), representing, respectively, *ātmā*, *jīva*, supreme and individual spirit, perception, and consciousness. Compare Mbhā. xii. 340. 8, 72.

[4] KP. xxi. p. 236; xxii. p. 238, etc.

[5] *Ib.* 1, p. 23.

what embellished,[1] where the 'sinful are cooked in fire';[2] the exaltation of Vishnu as Krishna or Rāma in one, and that of Çiva in another — these and similar aspects are reflections of epic matter, spirit, tone, and language, only the faith is still fiercer in religious matters, and the stories are fainter in historical references. According to the Purāna last cited: "There is no expiation for one that bows to a phallic emblem," *i.e.*, Çivaite, and "all the Bāuddhas are heretics";[3] and according to the Kūrma Purāna: "Vishnu is the divinity of the gods; Çiva, of the devils," although the preceding verses teach, in the spirit of the Divine Song, that each man's divinity is that which he conceives to be the divinity. Such is the concluding remark made by Vasistha in adjudicating the strife between the Vishnuite and Çivaite sectaries of the epic heroes.[4] The relation that the Puranic literature bears to religion in the minds of its authors is illustrated by the remark of the Nāradīya to the effect that the god is to be honored "by song, by music, by dance, and by recounting the Purānas" (xvii. 9).

Some of the epic religious ceremonies which there are barely alluded to are here described with almost the detail of a technical handbook. So the Nāradīya (xix.) gives an elaborate account of the raising of a *dhvaja* or standard as a religious ceremony.[5] The legal rules affecting morality and especially caste-intercourse[6] show a laxity in regard to the rules as for-

1 Compare Brihan Nāradīya Purāna. xiv. 10, *bahūni kāṣṭhayāntrāṇi* (torture machines) in hell. The old tale of Nāciketas is retold at great length in the Varāha Purāna. The oldest Purāna, the Mārkandeya, has but seven hells, a conception older than Manu's twenty-one (compare on MP. x. 80 ff., Scherman, *loc. cit.* p. 33), or the later lists of thousands. The Padma Purāna, which celebrates Rāma, has also seven hells, and is in part old, for it especially extols Pushkara (Brahmā's lone shrine); but it recommends the *taptamudra*, or branding with hot iron.

2 Nār. xiv. 2.

3 xiv. 54 and 70.

4 KP. xxii. pp. 239–241.

5 As will be shown below, it is possible that this may be a ceremony first taken from the wild tribes. See the 'pole' rite described above in the epic.

6 Compare for instance *ib.* xxviii. 68, on the strange connection of a Çūdrā wife of a Guru.

merly preached. Even the old Puranic form of the epic is reproduced, as when Mārkandeya converses again with Yudhistris, exactly as he does in the epic.[1] The duration of the ages; the fruit of sacrifices, among which are still mentioned the *rājasūya*, *açvamedha*, and other ancient rites;[2] the virtue of holy-places;[3] the admixture of pure pantheism with the idea of a personal creation[4] — these traits are again just those which have been seen already in the epic, nor is the addition of sections on temple-service, or other more minute details of the cult, of particular importance in a history of religious ideas.

The Purānas for our present purpose may all be grouped with the remark that what is ancient in them is a more or less fugitive resemblance to the epic style and matter;[5] what is new is the more pronounced sectarianism with its adventitious growth of subordinate spiritualities and exaggerated miracles. Thus for instance in the Varāha Purāna there are eleven, in the Bhāgavat Purāna twenty (instead of the older ten) *avatars* of Vishnu. So too the god of love — although Kāma and his dart are recognized in the late Atharvan — as a petty spirit receives homage only in the latest Sūtra (as Cupid. Āpastamba, ii. 2. 4. 1), and in late additions to the epic he is a little god; whereas in the drama he is prominent, and in the Purānas his cult is described at length (though to-day he has no temple). The 'mother'-fiend Pūtanā, who suckles babes to slay them,

1 KP. xxxvi. It is of course impossible to say how much epic material is come from the literary epic and how much is drawn from popular poetry, for the vulgar had their own epoidic songs which may have treated of the same topics. Thus even a wild tribe (Gonds) is credited with an 'epic.' But such stuff was probably as worthless as are the popular songs of to-day.

2 KP. xxx. p. 305; xxxvii. p. 352.

3 *Ib.* p. 355.

4 Compare Nāradīya, xi. 23, 27, 31 'the one whom no one knows,' 'he that rests in the heart,' 'he that seems to be far off because we do not know,' 'he whose form is Çiva, lauded by Vishnu,' xiii. 201.

5 Even Vishnu as a part of a part of the Supreme Spirit in VP. is indicated by Vishnu's adoration of *ātmā* in the epic (see above).

is scarcely known to the early epic, but she is a very real personality in the late epic and Purānas.

The addition to the trinity of the peculiar inferior godhead that is advocated in any one Purāna, virtually making four divinities, is characteristic of the period.

In proportion as sectarian ardor is heightened religious tone is lowered. The Puranic votary clinging to his one idea of god curses all them that believe in other aspects of the divinity. Blind bigotry fills the worshipper's soul. Religion becomes mere fanaticism. But there is also tolerance. Sometimes in one and the same Purāna rival forms are honored. The modern Hindu sects are in part the direct development of Puranic doctrine. But most of the sects of to-day are of very recent date, though their principles are often of respectable antiquity, as are too their sectarian signs, as well as the animals of their gods, some of which appear to be totems of the wild tribes, while others are merely objects of reverence among certain tribes. Thus the ram and the elephant are respectively the ancient beasts of Agni and Indra. Çiva has the bull; his spouse, the tiger. Earth and Skanda have appropriated the peacock, Skanda having the cock also. Yama has the buffalo (compare the Khond, wild-tribe, substitution of a buffalo for a man in sacrifice). Love has the parrot, etc.; while the boar and all Vishnu's animals in *avatars* are holy, being his chosen beasts.[1]

EARLY SECTS.

A classification of older sects (the unorthodox) than those of the present remains to us from the works of Çankara's reputed disciple, Ānanda Giri, and of Mādhava Ācārya, the former a writer of the ninth, the latter of the fourteenth century. According to the statements made by these writers there were a great number of sects, regarded as partly heterodox or wholly

1 Compare Williams' *Brahmanism and Hinduism.*

so, and it is interesting in examining the list of these to see that some of the epic sects (their names at least) are still in full force, while on the other hand the most important factions of to-day are not known at all; and that many sects then existed which must have been at that time of great antiquity, although now they have wholly passed away.[1] These last are indeed to the author of the critique of the sects not wholly heterodox. They are only too emphatic, in worshipping their peculiar divinity, to suit the more modern conceptions of the Hindu reviewer. But such sects are of the highest importance, for they show that despite all the bizarre bigotry of the Purānas the old Vedic gods (as in the epic) still continue to hold their own, and had their own idols and temples apart from other newer gods. The Vedic divinities, the later additions in the shape of the god of love, the god of wealth, Kubera,[2] the heavenly bird, Garuda, the world-snake, Çesha, together with countless genii, spirits, ghosts, the Manes, the heavenly bodies, stars, etc., all these were revered, though of less importance than the gods of Vishnuite and Çivaite sects. Among these latter the Çivaite sects are decidedly of less interest than the corresponding Vishnuite heresies, while the votaries of Brahmā (exclusively) are indeed mentioned, but they cannot be compared with those of the other two great gods.[3] To-day there is scarcely any homage paid to Brahmā, and it is not probable that there ever was the same devotion or like popularity in his case as in the case of his rivals. Other interesting sects of this period are the Sun-worshippers, who still exist but in no such numbers as when

[1] Çankara's adherents are chiefly Çivaite, but he himself was not a sectary. Williams says that at the present day few worship Çiva exclusively. but he has more partial adherents than has Vishnu. *Religious Thought and Life*, pp. 59, 62.

[2] The two last are just recognized in Brahmanic legal works.

[3] See Wilson's sketch of Hindu sects. The author says that there were in his day two shrines to Brahmā, one in Ājmīr (compare Pushkara in the epic), and one on the Ganges at Bithur. The Brahma Purāna is known also as Sāura (sun). This is the first in the list; in its present state it is Vishnuite.

Ānanda Giri counted six formal divisions of them. The votaries of these sub-sects worshipped some, the rising sun, some, the setting sun, while some again worshipped the noonday sun, and others, all three as a *tri-mūrti*. Another division worshipped the sun in anthropomorphic shape, while the last awakens the wrath of the orthodox narrator by branding themselves with hot irons.[1]

Ganeça,[2] the lord of Çiva's hosts, had also six classes of worshippers; but he has not now as he then had a special and peculiar cult, though he has many temples in Benares and elsewhere. Of the declared Çivaite sects of that day, six are mentioned, but of these only one survives, the 'wandering' Jangamas of South India, the Çivaite Rāudras, Ugras, Bhāktas, and Pāçupatis having yielded to more modern sectaries.

Some at least among the six sects of the Vishnuite sects, which are described by the old writers, appear to have been more ancient. Here too one finds Bhāktas, and with them the Bhāgavatas, the old Pāñcarātras, the 'hermit' Vāikhānasas, and Karmahīnas, the latter "having no rites." Concerning these sects one gets scanty but direct information. They all worshipped Vishnu under one form or another, the Bhāktas as Vāsudeva, the Bhāgavatas[3] as Bhagavat. The latter resembled the modern disciples of Rāmānuja and revered the holy-stone, appealing for authority to the Upanishads and to the Bhagavad Gītā, the Divine Song. Some too worshipped Vishnu exclu-

1 Sun-worship (Iranian?) is especially pronounced in the Bhavishya(t) Purāna. Of the other Purānas the Linga is especially Çivaite (*linga* is phallus), as are the Matsya and older Vāyu. Sometimes Çiva is androgynous, *ardhanārīçvara*, 'half-female.' But most of the Purānas are Vishnuite.

2 On the Ganeça Purāna see JRAS. 1846, p. 319.

3 The worshippers of Bhagavat were originally distinct from the Pāñcarātras, but what was the difference between them is unknown. The sect of this name in the pseudo-epic is not Çākta in expression but only monotheistic. Probably the names of many sects are retained with altered beliefs and practices. The Vishnu Purāna, i. 11. 54, gives a model prayer which may be taken once for all as the attitude of the Vishnuite: "Glory to Vāsudeva, him of perfected wisdom, whose unrevealed form is (known as) Brahmā, Vishnu, and Çiva" (Hiraṇyagarbha, Purusha, Pradhāna).

sively as Nārāyana, and believed in a heaven of sensual delights. The other sects, now extinct, offer no special forms of worship. What is historically most important is that in this list of sects are found none that particularly worship the popular divinities of to-day, no peculiar cult of Krishna as an infant and no monkey-service.

Infidel sects are numerous in this period, of which sects the worst in the old writers' opinion is the sensual Cārvāka. Then follow the (Buddhist) Çūnyavāds, who believe in 'void,' and Sāugatas, who believe that religion consists only in kindness, the Kshapanakas, and the Jains. The infamous 'left-hand' sectaries are also well known.

To one side of the Puranic religions, from the earlier time of which comes this account of heresies, reference has been made above: the development of the fables in regard to the infant Krishna. That the cult is well known in the later Purānas and is not mentioned in this list of wrong beliefs seems to show that the whole cult is of modern growth, even if one does not follow Weber in all his signs of modification of the older practice.

RELIGIOUS FESTIVALS.

For the history of the cult there is in these works much to interest one in the description and determination of popular festivals in honor of the great sectarian gods. Further details of more specific nature are given in other works which need not here be regarded. By far the most important of these festivals are those that seem to have been absorbed by the sectarian cults, although they were originally more popular. Weber in the paper on the *rājasūya*, to which we have had occasion several times to refer, has shown that a popular element abided long in the formal celebrations of the Brahmanic ritual.[1]

[1] Weber shows for instance, *loc. cit.*, that Indra takes the place of older Varuna; that the house-priest yields to the Brahmā; that in this feast in honor of the king he

Undoubtedly the original celebration was a popular one. To-day the most interesting of these popular fêtes is in all respects the New Year's Festival and the Spring Festival. The latter has been cut up into several parts, and to show the whole intent of the original ceremonial it is necessary to take up the *disjecta membra* and place them side by side, as has been done by Wilson, whose sketch of these two festivals, together with that by Gover of the New Year's Feast called Pongol, we give in abstract, premising that, however close be the comparison with European festivals of like nature, we doubt whether there is any historical connection between them and the Hindu celebrations.

We begin with the more popular New Year's, the Pongol:[1] The interesting feature of this South India festival is that the Hindus have done their best to alter its divinities and failed. They have, indeed, for Indra and Agni got Krishna formally accepted as the god in whose honor it is supposed to be held, but the feast remains a native festival, and no one really thinks of the Puranic gods in connection with it. Europe also has seen such dynamic alterations of divinities in cases where feasts would persist till patrons of an orthodox kind were foisted upon them to give an air of propriety to that which remained heathenish.[2] The Pongol is a New Year's festival lasting for three days. The first day is for Indra; the second, for (Agni) Sūrya;[3] the third (to which is

is soundly beaten; that gaming creeps into the ceremony as a popular aspect; that there was a special ceremony to cure *katzenjammer* caused by over-drinking; and that the whole ceremony was a popular spring festival, such as is found to-day (but without the royal part in the play).

[1] Gover, JRAS. v. 91; IA. xx. 430.

[2] In Hinduism itself there is a striking example of this. The Jagannāth ('Juggernaut') temple was once dedicated to Buddha as *loka-nāth* or *jagan-nāth*, 'saviour of the world.' Name, temple, and idol-car are now all Vishnu's!

[3] That is, Rain and Sun, for all Indra's warlike qualities are forgotten, absorbed into those of Çiva and his son, the battle-god. The sun crosses the equator at noon of the second day, the 'Mahā Pongol.'

added, as a wind-up, a fourth day), for cattle. The whole feast is a harvest-home and celebration of cattle. The chief ceremony is the cooking of rice, which is put to boil with great solemnity, and luck for the next year is argued from its boiling well. If it does so a universal shout arises,[1] all rush about, congratulate, and give presents to each other, and merry-making follows. On the cattle-days the beasts are led about with painted horns and decorated with ribbons, and are then chased and robbed by the boys. The image of Ganeça is the only one seen, and his worship is rather perfunctory. On the evening of the last day the women have a party, paying obeisance to a peacock, and indulging in a family reunion of very simple character. On this occasion the girl-wife may return for a few hours to her mother. It is the only general fête for women during the year.

Not unlike this festival of the extreme south is the New Year's celebration at the mouth of the Ganges. Here there is a grand fair and jewels are cast into the river as propitiation to the river-goddess. Not long ago it was quite customary to fling children also into the river, but this usage has now been abolished.[2] Offerings are made to the Manes, general and particular, and to the All-gods. As with the Pongol, the feast is one of good-fellowship where presents are distributed, and its limit is the end of the third day. After this the festivities

1 "Now every neck is bent, for the surface of the water is disturbed. Then with a heave, a hiss, and a surge of bubbles, the seething milk mounts to the top of the vessel. Before it has had time to run down the blackened sides, the air resounds with the sudden joyous cry of 'Pongol, oh Pongol, Sūrya, Sūrya, oh Pongol.' The word Pongol means "boiling," from the Tamil word *pongu*, to boil; so that the joyous shout is, 'It boils, oh Sūrya, it boils.' In a moment a convulsion of greetings animates the assembly. Every one seizes his neighbor and asks, 'Has it boiled?' Both faces gleam with delight as the answer comes — 'It has boiled.' Then both shout at the top of their voices — 'Oh Pongol, Pongol, oh Sūrya, oh Indra, Pongol, Pongol.'" Gover, *loc. cit.*

2 The crocodile, *makara*, like the parrot, is sacred to Kāmadeva, Love. But as Ganges also is holy it is difficult to say for which divinity the offering was intended. Some, indeed, interpret *makara* as dolphin.

have no religious character. Thousands of pilgrims assemble for this fête. Wilson, who gives an account of this celebration, compares the ancient Roman New Year's, with the *mutui amoris pignora* which were sent at that season. The gifts in India are sweetmeats and other delicacies, ominous of good for the next year.[1]

On the 2d of February occurs a feast to Çrī, or Lakshmī, Vishnu's bride, patroness of all prosperity to her worshippers. At present it is a literary festival on which all books, inkstands, pens, etc., are cleaned and worshipped, as adjuncts to Sarasvatī, the goddess of learning. This is rather significant, for Sarasvatī is properly the wife of Brahmā, but the Vishnuites of Bengal have made her the wife of Vishnu, and identified her with Çrī. It is to be noticed that in this sole celebration of abstract learning and literature there is no recognition of Çiva, but rather of his rival. Çiva and Ganeça are revered because they might impede, not because, as does Sarasvatī, they further literary accomplishment. Sarasvatī is almost the only fair goddess. She is represented not as a horror, but as a beautiful woman sitting on a lotus, graceful in shape, a crescent on her brow.[2] The boys, too, celebrate the day with games, bat and ball, prisoner's base, and others "of a very European character." The admixture of sectarian cults is shown by the transference to this Vishnuite feast of the Çivaite (Durgā) practice

[1] A feast now neglected, though kept up by strict Brahmans, occurs on or about the 20th January. The orthodox adherents of the Çivaite sects and Çāktas also observe it. It is a Çrāddha, or funeral feast to the Manes. Also on the 26th and 30th January there are rites nearly obsolete, the first being signalized by offerings to Yama; the second, a Çivaite feast (to his spouse, as 'giver of bridegrooms'). The last is more celebrated in the South than in the North. It is interesting chiefly as a parallel to St. Valentine's day, or, as Wilson says, the nearer feast of St. Agnes (21st January), on the eve of which divination is practiced to discover future husbands. It is this time also that the Greeks call 'marriage-month' (Gamelion); and the fourth day from the new moon (which gives the name to this Hindu festival, *caturthī*, "fourth day") is the day when Hesiod recommends the bringing home of the bride.

[2] In case any writing has to be done on this day it is done with chalk, not with the pens, "which have a complete holiday" (Wilson).

of casting into the river the images of the goddess.[1] When applied distinctly to Sarasvatī the feast is observed in August–September; when to Lakshmī, in October–November, or in February. There is, however, another feast, celebrated in the North and South, which comes on the exact date fixed by the Romans for the beginning of spring, and as an ending to this there is a feast to Kāma, Cupid, and his bride Rati ('Enjoyment'). This is the Vasanta, or spring festival of prosperity and love, which probably was the first form of the Lakshmī-Sarasvatī feast.

Another traditional feast of this month is the 10th[2] (the eleventh lunar day of the light half of Māgha). The eleventh lunar day is particularly holy with the Vishnuites, as is said in the Brahma Purāna, and this is a Vishnuite festival. It is a day of fasting and prayer, with presents to priests.[3] It appears to be a mixture of Vedic prayers and domestic Vishnu-worship. On the 11th of February the fast is continued, and in both the object is expiation of sin. The latter is called the feast of 'six sesamum acts,' for sesamum is a holy plant, and in each act of this rite it plays a part. Other rites of this month are to the Manes on the 14th, 22d, and 24th of February. Bathing and oblation are requisite, and all are of a lustral and expiatory nature. Wilson remarks on the fact that it is the same time of year in which the Romans gave oblations to the Manes, and

1 The invocations show very well how the worship of Brahmā has been driven out in honor of his more powerful rivals. For Sarasvatī is invoked first as "Thou without whom Brahmā never lives"; but again as "Thou of eight forms, Lakshmī, Medhā, Dhavā, Pushtī, Gāurī, Tushtī, Prabhā, Dhriti, O Sarasvatī." The great festivals, like the great temples, are not very stricty sectarian. Williams says that in Çiva's temple in Benares are kept monkeys (sacred to Vishnu).

2 Between this and the last occur minor holidays, one to avert small-pox; one (February the 4th) sacred to the sun (Sunday, the seventh day of each lunar fortnight, is strictly observed); and one to the Manes.

3 Fasting is not necessarily a part of civilized religion alone. It is found in the Brahmanic and Hindu cults, but it obtains also among the American Indians. Thus the Dacotahs fast for two or three days at the worship of sun and moon. Schoolcraft, *Histor. and Statist.*, iii. 227.

that Februus is the god of purification. "There can be no reasonable doubt that the Feralia of the Romans and the Çrāddha (feast to the Manes) of the Hindus, the worship of the Pitris and of the Manes, have a common character, and had a common origin."[1]

The 27th of February is the greatest Çivaite day in the year. It celebrates Çiva's first manifestation of himself in phallic form. To keep this day holy expiates from all sin, and secures bliss hereafter. The worshipper must fast and revere the Linga. Offerings are made to the Linga. It is, of course, a celebration formed of unmeaning repetitions of syllables and the invocation of female Çaktis, snapping the fingers, gesticulating, and performing all the humbug called for by Çivaite worship. The Linga is bathed in milk, decorated, wrapped in *bilva* leaves, and prayed to; which ceremony is repeated at intervals with slight changes. All castes, even the lowest, join in the exercises. Even women may use the *mantras*.[2] Vigil and fasting are the essentials of this worship.[3]

The next festival closes these great spring celebrations. It bears two names, and originally was a double feast, the first part being the Dolā Yātrā, or 'Swing-procession,' the second part being the execrable Holī. They are still kept distinct in some places, and when this occurs the Dolotsava, or Dolā Yātrā, follows the Holī. They are both spring festivals, and answer roughly to May-day, though in India they come at the full moon of March. We have followed Wilson's enumeration of all the minor spring feasts, that they may be seen in their

1 The last clause (meaning 'common historical origin') were better omitted.

2 Except the mystic syllable *Om*, supposed to represent the trinity (*Ōm* is *a*, *u*, *m*), though probably it was originally only an exclamation.

3 A small Vishnu festival in honor of Vishnu as 'man-lion' (one of his ten *avatars*) is celebrated on the 13th of March; but in Bengal in honor of the same god as a cow-boy. On the 15th of March there is another minor festival in Bengal, but it is to Çiva, or rather to one of his hosts, under the form of a water pot (that is to preserve from disease).

entirety. But in ancient times there was probably one long Vasantotsava (spring-festival), which lasted for weeks, beginning with a joyous celebration (2d of February) and continuing with lustral ceremonies, as indicated by the now detached feast days already referred to. The original cult, in Wilson's opinion, has been changed, and the Dolā Yātrā is now given over to the Krishna-cult, while the Holī divinity is a hobgoblin. The Dolā Yātrā begins with fasting and ends (as Holī) with fire-worship. An image of Krishna is sprinkled with red powder (*abīr*), and after this (religious) ceremony a bonfire[1] is made, and an effigy, Holikā, is put upon it and burned. The figure is carried to the fire in a religious procession headed by Vishnuite or Brahman priests, of course accompanied with music and song. After seven circumambulations of the fire the figure is burned. This is the united observance of the first day. At dawn on the morning of the second day the image of Krishna is placed in a swing, *dolā*, and swung back and forth a few times, which ceremony is repeated at noon and at sunset. During the day, wherever a swing is put up, and in the vicinity, it is the common privilege to sprinkle one's friend with the red powder or red rose-water. Boys and common people run about the streets sprinkling red water or red powder over all passengers, and using abusive (obscene) language. The cow-herd caste is conspicuous at this ceremony. The cow-boys, collecting in parties under a koryphaios, hold, as it were, a komos, leaping, singing, and dancing[2] through the streets, striking together the wands which they carry. These cow-boys not only dress (as do others) in new clothes on this occasion,[3] but they give their cattle new

[1] The bonfire is made of fences, doorposts, furniture, etc. Nothing once seized and devoted to the fire may be reclaimed, but the owner may defend his property if he can. Part of the horse-play at this time consists in leaping over the fire, which is also ritualistic with some of the hill-tribes.

[2] Compare the Nautch dances on Rāmacandra's birthday. Religious dances, generally indecent, are also a prominent feature of the religions of the wild tribes (as among American and African savages, Greeks, etc., etc.).

[3] The 'Easter bonnet' in Indic form.

equipments, and regard the whole frolic as part of a religious rite in honor of Krishna, the cow-herd. But all sects take part in the performance (that is to say, in the Holī portion), both Çivaites and Vishnuites. When the moon is full the celebration is at its height. Holī songs are sung, the crowd throws *abīr*, the chiefs feast, and an all-night orgy ends the long carousal.[1] In the south the Dolā takes place later, and is distinct from the Holī. The burning here is of Kāma, commemorating the love-god's death by the fire of Çiva's eye, when the former pierced the latter's heart, and inflamed him with love. For this reason the bonfire is made before a temple of Çiva. Kāma is gone from the northern cult, and in upper India only a hobgoblin, Holī, a foul she-devil, is associated with the rite. The whole performance is described and prescribed in one of the late Purānas.[2] In some parts of the country the bonfire of the Holī is made about a tree, to which offerings are made, and afterwards the whole is set on fire. For a luminous account of the Holī, which is perhaps the worst open rite of Hinduism, participated in by all sects and classes, we may cite the words of the author of *Ante-Brahmanical Religions*: "It has been termed the Saturnalia or Carnival of the Hindus. Verses the most obscene imaginable are ordered to be read on the occasion. Figures of men and women, in the most indecent and disgusting attitudes, are in many places openly paraded through the streets; the most filthy words are uttered by persons who, on other occasions, would think themselves disgraced by the use of them; bands of men parade the street with their clothes all bespattered with a reddish dye; dirt and filth are

[1] In sober contrast stands the yearly orthodox Çrāddha celebration (August-September), though Brahmans join in sectarian fêtes.

[2] Wilson draws an elaborate parallel between the Holī and the Lupercalia, etc. (Carnival). But the points of contact are obvious. One of the customs of the Holī celebration is an exact reproduction of April-Fool's day. Making "Holī fools" is to send people on useless errands, etc. (Festum Stultorum, at the Vernal Equinox, transferred by the Church to the first of November, "Innocents' Day").

thrown upon all that are seen passing along the road; all business is at a stand, all gives way to license and riot."[1]

Besides these the most brilliant festivals are the Rās Yātrā in Bengal (September–October), commemorating the dance of Krishna with the *gopīs* or milk-maids, and the 'Lamp-festival' (Dīpālā), also an autumnal celebration.

The festivals that we have reviewed cover but a part of the year, but they will suffice to show the nature of such fêtes as are enjoined in the Purānas. There are others, such as the eightfold[2] temple-worship of Krishna as a child, in July or August; the marriage of Krishna's idol to the Tulasī plant; the Awakening of Vishnu, in October, and so forth. But no others compare in importance with the New Year's and Spring festivals, except the Bengal idol-display of Jagannāth, the Rath Yātrā of 'Juggernaut'; and some others of local celebrity, such as the Dūrgā-pūjā.[3] The temples, to which reference has often been made, have this in common with the great Çivaite festivals, that to describe them in detail would be but to translate into words images and wall-paintings, the obscenity of which is better left undescribed. This, of course, is particularly true of the Çiva temples, where the actual Linga is perhaps, as Barth has said, the least objectionable of the sights presented to the eye of the devout worshipper. But the Vishnu temples are as bad. Architecturally admirable, and even wonderful, the interior is but a display of sensual immorality.[4]

1 Stevenson, JRAS. 1841, p. 239; Williams, *loc. cit.;* Wilkins, *Modern Hinduism*, ch. iii.

2 The daily service consists in dressing, bathing, feeding, etc. It is divided into eight ridiculous ceremonies, which prolong the worship through the day.

3 The brilliant displays attracted the notice of the Greeks, who speak of the tame tigers and panthers, the artificial trees carried in wagons, the singing, instrumental music, and noise, which signalized a fête procession. See Williams, *loc. cit.*

4 Such, for instance, is the most holy temple of South India, the great temple of Çrīrangam at Trichinopoly. The idol car, gilded and gaudy, is carved with obscenity; the walls and ceilings are frescoed with bestiality. It represents Vishnu's heaven.

HISTORY OF THE HINDU TRINITY.

In closing the Puranic period (which name we employ loosely to cover such sects as are not clearly modern) we pause for a moment to cast a glance backwards over the long development of the trinity, to the units of which are devoted the individual Purānas. We have shown that the childhood-tales of Krishna are of late (Puranic) origin, and that most of the cow-boy exploits are post-epic. Some are referred to in the story of Çiçupāla in the second book of the Mahābhārata, but this scene has been touched up by a late hand. The Vishnu Purāna, typical of the best of the Purānas, as in many respects it is the most important and interesting, represents Krishnaite Vishnuism as its height. Here is described the birth of the man-god as a black, *kṛṣṇa*, baby, son of Nanda, and his real title is here Govinda, the cow-boy.[1] 'Cow-boy' corresponds to the more poetical, religious shepherd; and the milk-maids, *gopīs*, with whom Govinda dallies as he grows up, may, perhaps, better be rendered shepherdesses for the same reason. The idyllic effect is what is aimed at in these descriptions. Here Krishna plays his rude and rustic tricks, upsetting wagons, overthrowing trees and washermen, occasionally killing them he dislikes, and acting altogether much like a cow-boy of another sort. Here he puts a stop to Indra-worship, overpowers Çiva, rescues Aniruddha, marries sixteen thousand princesses, burns Benares, and finally is killed himself, he the one born of a hair of Vishnu, he that is Vishnu himself, who in 'goodness' creates, in 'darkness' destroys,[2] under the forms of Brahmā and Çiva.[3]

1 From this name or title comes the Gīta Govinda, a mystic erotic poem (in praise of the cow-boy god) as exaltedly religious as it is sensual (twelfth century).

2 VP. i. 2. 63. The 'qualities' or 'conditions' of God's being are referred to by 'goodness' and 'darkness.'

3 All this erotic vulgarity is typical of the common poetry of the people, and is in marked contrast to the chivalrous, but not love-sick, Bhārata.

In Vishnu, as a development of the Vedic Vishnu; in Çiva, as affiliated to Rudra; in Brahmā, as the Brahmanic third to these sectarian developments, the trinity has a real if remote connection with the triune fire of the Rig Veda, a two-thirds connection, filled out with the addition of the later Brahmanic head of the gods.

To ignore the fact that Vishnu and Rudra-Çiva developed inside the Brahmanic circle and increased in glory before the rise of sectaries, and to asseverate, as have some, that the two chief characters of the later trinity are an unmeaning revival of decadent gods, whose names are used craftily to veil the modernness of Krishnaism and Çivaism, — this is to miscalculate the waxing dignity of these gods in earlier Brahmanic literature. To say with Burnouf that the Vishnu of the Veda is not at all the Vishnu of the mythologists, is a statement far too sweeping. The Vishnu of the Veda is not only the same god with the Vishnu of the next era, but in that next era he has become greatly magnified. The Puranic All-god Vishnu stands in as close a relation to his Vedic prototype as does Milton's Satan to the snaky slanderer of an age more primitive.

Çiva-worship appears to have been adapted from a local cult in the mountainous West, and at an early date to have been amalgamated with that of his next resemblance, the Vedic Rudra; while Krishna-worship flourished along the Ganges. These are those Dionysos and Herakles of whom speak the old Greek authorities. One cult is possibly as venerable as the other, but while Çivaism became Brahmanized early, Krishnaism was adopted much later, and it is for this reason, amongst others, that despite its modern iniquities Çiva has appealed more to the Brahman than has Krishna.

Megasthenes tells us a good deal about these Hindu representatives of Herakles and Dionysos. According to him there were Dionysiac festivals in honor of the latter god (Çiva),[1] who

[1] Compare Duncker, iii.[5] p. 327. More doubtful is the identification of Nysian and

belongs where flourishes the wine, in the Açvaka district, north of the Kabul river. From this place Çiva's worship extended into the East, Māgadha (Behār), around Gokarna in the West, and even to the Kalinga country in the extreme Southeast. But it was especially native to the mountainous Northwest, about the 'Gate of Ganges' (north of Delhi, near Saharampur), and still further north in Kashmeer. In the epic, Çiva has his throne on Kāilāsa,[1] the Northern mountain, in the Himālayas, and Ganges descend from the sky upon his head.

On the other hand, Herakles, of the Ganges land, where grows no wine, is plainly Krishna, who carries club, discus, and conch. The Greek cities Methora and Kleisobora are Mathurā and Krishna-pur, 'Krishna-town'; the latter on the Jumna, the former near it on the same river, capital of the clan which venerated Krishna as its chief hero and god, the Yādavas. Megasthenes says, also, that Herakles' daughter is Pandaie, and this agrees with the Pāndya, a southern development of the epic Gangetic Pāndavas, who especially worship Krishna in conjunction with the Yādavas. Their South-Indic town, Mathurā, still attests their origin.

In speaking of the relative antiquity of Vishnuism and Çivaism one must distinguish the pantheistic form of these gods from the single forms. While Çivaism, *per se*, that is, the worship of Çiva as a great and terrible god, preceded the same exaltation of Krishna, as is shown by their respective literary appearance, and even by Megasthenes' remark that the worship of Dionysos preceded that of Herakles by fifteen generations, yet did Krishnaism, as a popular pantheism, come before Çivaism as such. Although in the late Çvetāçvatara Upanishad Çiva is pantheistic, yet is he not so in the epic till some of the

Nishādan, *ib.* note. Compare, also, Schroeder, *loc. cit.* p. 361. Arrian calls (Çiva) Dionysos the *οἴνου δοτῆρα* 'Ινδοῖς (Schwanbeck, Frg. L).

[1] This remains always as Çiva's heaven in distinction from Goloka or Vāikuntha, Vishnu's heaven. Nowadays Benares is the chief seat of Çivaism.

latest passages make him the All, in imitation of Krishna as All-god. Probably Çivaism remained by the first philosophy, Sankhyan dualism, and was forced into Krishna's Vedantic pantheism, as this became popular. At first neither was more than a single great god without any philosophy.[1]

In one of the early exegetical works, which is occupied somewhat with philosophical matter, there is evidence that a triad existed between the Vedic triad of fires and the Puranic triad. Fire, Wind (or Indra), and the Sun (Sūrya), are stated in a famous passage to be the only real gods, all the others being but names of these. But, although in form this triad (Nirukta, vii. 4, 5) is like the Vedic triad,[2] it is essentially a triad in a pantheistic system like that of the epic and Purānas, for it is added that "all the gods are parts of one soul." In explanation it is said: "Fire is the earth-god, Wind, or Indra, is the god of the atmosphere, and the sun is the god of the sky." Now in the Rig Veda Indra is closely united not only with Agni but with Vishnu, albeit in this period Vishnu is his subordinate. The nearest approach of this Vishnu to his classical descendant is in one of the latest hymns of the Rig Veda, where it is said that the seven seeds of creation are Vishnu's, as in later times he comprises seven males. In the philosophy of the Tāittirīya Samhitā the three places of Vishnu are not, as in the Rig Veda, the two points of the horizon (where the sun sets) and the zenith, but 'earth, air, and sky.'[3] That is to say, in the Brahmanic period Vishnu is already a greater god than he had been. Nay, more, he is explicitly declared to be

1 The doctrine of the immaculate conception, common to Vishnuism and Buddhism (above, p. 431), can have no exact parallel in Çivaism, for Çiva is not born as a child; but it seems to be reflected in the laughable ascription of virginity to Umā (Civa's wife), when she is revered as the emblem of motherhood.

2 In RV. v. 41. 4, the Vedic triad is Fire, Wind, and (Trita of the sky) Indra; elsewhere Fire, Wind, and Sun (above, p. 42), distinct from the triune fire.

3 In the Rig Veda the three steps are never thus described, but in the later age this view is common. It is, in fact, only on the 'three steps' that the identity with the sun is established. In RV. i. 156. 4, Vishnu is already above Varuna.

"the best of the gods."[1] That best means greatest may be shown from the same work, where in savage fable it is recited that all the gods, including Indra, ran up to him to get his strength.[2] But especially in the Upanishads is Vishnu the one great god left from the Rig Veda. And it is with the philosophical (not with the ritualistic) Vishnu that Krishna is equated.

Of Çiva, on the other hand, the prototype is Rudra ('red'), his constant sobriquet. In the Rig Veda he is the god of red lightning, who is the father of the Maruts, the storm-gods. His attributes of a fulgurant god are never lost. Even as Çiva the All-god he is still the god of the blue neck, whose three-forked trident and home among the mountains remind us of his physical origin. He is always the fairest of the gods, and both early and late he is terrible, to be averted by prayer, even where his magic 'medicines' are asked for. To him are addressed the most suppliant cries: "O Rudra, spare us, strike not the men, slay not the kine." In the Atharva Veda at every step one finds characteristics which on the one hand are but exaggerations of the type formulated in the Rig Veda, and on the other precursors of the signs of the later god. In Çivaism, in contradistinction to Vishnuism, there is not a trace of the euhemerism which has been suspected in the Krishna-Vishnu cult. The Rudra of the Rig Veda already begins to be identified with the triune fire, for he bears the standing epithet of fire, "he of three mothers."[3] And this name he keeps, whether as Rudra, who is "brilliant as the sun" (RV. i. 43. 5), whose weapon is "the shining one that is emitted from the sky and passes along the earth" (*ib.* vii. 46. 3); or again, as the "red boar of the sky," the "holder of the bolt" (*ib.* ii. 33. 3), and, above all gods, "the terrible" (x. 126. 5).

[1] Çat. Br. xiv. 1. 1. 5.

[2] For other versions see Muir, *Original Sanskrit Texts*, iv. p. 127 ff.

[3] Later interpreted as wives or eyes.

Coming to the Brahmanic period one finds him a dweller in the mountain tops, of a red color, with a blue neck, the especial lord of the mountains, and so of robbers; while he is also the 'incantation-god,' the 'god of low people.' Some of these are Rudra's attributes; but here his name is already Çiva, so that one may trace the changes down the centuries till he finds again in the epic that Çiva is the lord of mountains, the patron of thieves (Hara, robber?), and endowed with the trident, the blue neck,[1] and the three mothers of old. In the middle period he has so many titles that one probably has to accept in the subsequent Çiva not only the lineal descendant of the Vedic Rudra, but also a combination of other local cults, where clan gods, originally diverse, were worshipped as one in consequence of their mutual likeness. One of the god's especial names is here Bhava, while in the earlier period Bhava and Rudra are distinct, but they are invoked as a pair (AV).[2] What gives Çiva his later tremendous popularity, however, is the feature to which we have alluded in the chapter on the epic. In the epic, all the strength of Çiva lies in the Linga.[3] Both Bhava and Rudra, as Çarva, the archer— his local eastern name—are represented as hurling the lightning, and it is simply from identity of attributes that they have become identified in person (AV. x. 1. 23). Rudra's title of Paçupati, or 'lord of cattle'[4] goes back to the Vedic age: "Be kind to the kine of him who believes in the gods" is a prayer of the Atharva Veda (xi. 2. 28). Agni and Rudra, in the Rig-Veda,

[1] For an epic guess at the significance of the title *nīlakaṇṭha*, 'blue-throated,' see Mbhā. i. 18. 43.

[2] AV. iv. 28; viii. 2; xi. 2. Thus even in the Rig Veda pairs of gods are frequently besung as one, as if they were divinities not only homogeneous but even monothelous.

[3] Brahmā's mark in the lotus; Vishnu's, the discus (sun); Çiva's, the Linga, phallic emblem.

[4] The grim interpretation of later times makes the cattle (to be sacrificed) *men*. The theological interpretation is that Çiva is the lord of the spirit, which is bound like a beast.

are both called 'cattle-guarding,' but not for the same reason. Agni represents a fire-stockade, while Rudra in kindness does not strike with his lightning-bolt. The two ideas, with the identification of Rudra and Agni, may have merged together. Then too, Rudra has healing medicines (his magical side), and Agni is kindest to men. All Agni's names are handed over in the Brāhmanas to Rudra-Çiva, just as Rudra previously had taken the epithets of Pūshan (above), true to his robber-name. To ignore the height to which at this period is raised the form of Rudra-Çiva is surely unhistorical; so much so that we deem it doubtful whether Çiva-invocations elsewhere, as in the Sūtra referred to above, should be looked upon as interpolations. In the Māitrāyanī Collection, the Rudrajapas, the invocations to Rudra as the greatest god, the highest spirit, the lord of beings (Bhava), are expressly to Çiva Giriça, the mountain-lord (2. 9; Schroeder, p. 346). In the Āitareya Brāhmana it evidently is Rudra-Çiva, the god of ghastly forms (made by the gods, it is said, as a composite of all the 'most horrible parts' of all the gods), who is deputed to slay the Father-god (when the latter, as a beast, commits incest with his daughter), and chooses as his reward for the act the office of 'lord of cattle.'[1] This is shown clearly by the fact that the fearsome Rudra is changed to the innocuous Rudriya in the next paragraph. As an example of how in the Brāhmanas Rudra-Çiva has taken to himself already the powers of Agni, the great god of the purely sacrificial period, may be cited Çat. Br. vi. 1. 3. 10 and 2. 1. 12. Here Agni is Kumāra, Rudra, Çarva (Sarva[2]), Paçu-

1 The commenter, horrified by the murder of the Father-god, makes Rudra kill 'the sin'; but the original shows that it is the Father-god who was shot by this god, who chose as his reward the lordship over kine; and such exaltation is not improbable (moreover, it is historical!). The hunting of the Father-god by Rudra is pictured in the stars (Orion), Āit. Br. iii. 33.

2 See Weber, *Ind. St.* ii. 37; Muir, iv. 403. Çarva (Çaurva) is Avestan, but at the same time it is his 'eastern' name, while Bhava is his western name. Çat. Br. i. 7. 3. 8.

pati (lord of beasts), Bhāirava (terrible), Açani (lightning), Bhava (lord of beings), Mahādeva (great god), the Lord—his 'thrice three names.' But where the Brāhmana assumes that these are names of Agni it is plain that one has Rudra-Çiva in process of absorbing Agni's honors.

The third element in the Puranic trinity,[1] identified with the Father-god, genealogically deserves his lower position. His rivals are of older lineage. The reason for his inferior position is, practically, that he has little to do with man. Being already created, man takes more interest in the gods that preserve and destroy.[2] Even Brahmā's old exploits are, as we have shown, stolen from him and given over to Vishnu. The famous (totemistic) tortoise legend was originally Brahmā's, and so with others of the ten 'forms' of Vishnu, for instance the boar-shape, in which Vishnu manifests himself, and the fish-shape of Brahmā (epic) in the flood-story. The formal *trimūrti* or *trāipurusha* ('three persons') is a late figure. It would seem that a Harihara (Vishnu and Çiva as one) preceded the trinity, though the dual name is not found till quite late.[3] But, as we showed above, the epic practically identifies Vishnu and Çiva as equals, before it unites with these Brahmā as an equal third.

There arises now the further question whether sectarian Vishnuism be the foisting of Krishnaism upon a dummy Vishnu. We think that, stated in this way, such scarcely can have been the case. Neither of the great sects is professedly of priestly origin, but each, like other sects, claims Vedic

[1] The epic (*loc. cit.* above), the Purānas, and the very late Atharva Çiras Upanishad and Māitr. Up. (much interpolated). Compare Muir, *loc. cit.* pp. 362–3.

[2] According to the epic, men honor gods that kill, Indra, Rudra, and so forth; not gods that are passive, such as Brahmā, the Creator, and Pūshan (xii. 15. 18), *ya eva devā hantāras tāl loko 'rcayate bhṛçaṁ, na Brahmāṇam.*

[3] Barth seems to imply that Harihara (the name) is later than the *trimūrti* (p. 185), but he has to reject the passage in the Hari-vança to prove this. On Ayenār, a southern god said to be Hari-Hara (Vishnu-Çiva), see Williams, *loc. cit.*

authority, and finds Brahmanical support. We have said that Vishnu is raised to his position without ictic suddenness. He is always a god of mystic character, in short, a god for philosophy to work upon. He is recognized as the highest god in one of the oldest Upanishads. And it is with the philosopher's Vishnu that Krishna is identified. Krishna, the real Vāsudeva (for a false Vāsudeva is known also in the epic), is the god of a local cult. How did he originate? The king of serpents is called Krishna, 'the black,' and Vishnu reposes upon Çesha Ananta, the world-snake; but a more historical character than this can be claimed for Krishna. This god-man must be the same with the character mentioned in the Chāndogya Upanishad, 3. 17. 6. One may notice the similarities between this Krishna and him of the epic cult. Krishna, son of Devakī, was taught by his teacher, Ghora Āngirasa, that sacrifice may be performed without objective means; that generosity, kindness, and other moral traits are the real signs of sacrifice; and it is then said: "The priest Ghora Āngirasa having said this to Krishna, the son of Devakī — and the latter was thereby freed from (thirst) desire — said: "When a man is about to die let him resort to this triad: 'the imperishable art thou,' 'the unmoved art thou,' 'breath's firmness art thou'; in regard to which are these two verses in the Rig-Veda:[1] 'till they see the light of the old seed which is kindled in the sky,' and 'perceiving above the darkness the higher light, the sun, god among gods, we come to the highest light.'" Krishna thus learned the abolition of sacrifice, and the worship of the sun, the highest light (Vishnu), as true being — for this is the meaning of the philosophical passage taken with its context. Kings and

[1] RV. viii. 6. 30; i. 50. 10. Weber refers Krishna further back to a priestly Vedic poet of that name, to whom are attributed hymns of the eighth and tenth books of the Rig Veda (*Janmāṣṭamī*, p. 316). He interprets Krishna's mother's name, Devakī, as 'player' (*ib.*). But the chance of name in a Vedic hymn has no special significance. The name Devakī is found applied to other persons, and its etymology is rather *deva*, divine, as Weber now admits (Berl. Ak. 1890, p. 931).

priests discuss philosophy together in this period,[1] and it would conform to later tradition to see in the pupil the son of a king. It is, moreover, significant that the priest, Ghora Āngirasa, is named specially as priest of the sun-god elsewhere (Kāush. Br. 30. 6), as well as that Krishna Āngirasa is also the name of a teacher. It is said in this same Upanishad (3. 1. 1) that the sun is the honey, delight, of the gods; and this chapter is a meditation on the sun,[2] of which the dark (*kṛṣṇa*) form is that which comes from the Itihāsas and Purānas, the fore-runners of the epic (3. 4. 3). This is taught as a *brahma-upanishad*, a teaching of the absolute, and it is interesting to see that it is handed down through Brahmā, Prajāpati, and Manu, exactly as Krishna says in the Divine Song that his own doctrine has been promulgated; while (it is said further) for him that knows the doctrine 'there is day,' his sun never sets (3. 11. 3–4). It is a doctrine to be communicated only to the eldest son or a good student, and to no one else (*ib.* 5), *i.e.*, it was new, esoteric, and of vital importance. Here, too, one finds Sanatkumāra, the 'ever young,' as Skanda,[3] yet as an earthly student also (7. 1 ; 26. 2), just like Krishna.

It cannot be imagined, however, that the cult of the Gangetic Krishna originated with that vague personage whose pupilage is described in the Upanishad. But this account may still be connected with the epic Krishna. The epic describes the overthrow of an old Brahmanic Aryan race at the hands of the Pāndavas, an unknown folk, whose king's

[1] In the epic, also, kings become hermits, and perform great penance just as do the ascetic priests. Compare the heroes themselves, and i. 42. 23 *rājā mahātapās;* also ii. 19, where a king renounces his throne, and with his two wives becomes a hermit in the woods. In i. 41. 31 a king is said to be equal to ten priests!

[2] In fact, the daily repetition of the Sāvitrī is a tacit admission of the sun god as the highest type of the divine; and Vishnu is the most spiritualized form of the sun-god, representing even in the Rig-Veda the goal of the departing spirit.

[3] Skanda (Subrahmanya) and Ganeça are Çiva's two sons, corresponding to Krishna and Rāma. Skanda's own son is Viçākha, a *graha* (above, p. 415).

polyandrous marriage (his wife is the spouse of his four brothers as well as of himself) is an historical trait, connecting the tribe closely with the polyandrous wild tribes located north of the Ganges. This tribe attacked the stronghold of Brahmanism in the holy land about the present Delhi; and their patron god is the Gangetic Krishna. In the course of the narrative a very few tales are told of Krishna's early life, but the simple original view of Krishna is that he is a god, the son of Devakī. The few other tales are late and adventitious additions, but this is a consistent trait. Modern writers are fain to see in the antithesis presented by the god Krishna and by the human hero Krishna, late and early phases. They forget that the lower side of Krishna is one especially Puranic. In short, they read history backwards, for theirs is not the Indic way of dealing with gods. In Krishna's case the tricky, vulgar, human side is a later aspect, which comes to light most prominently in the Genealogy of Vishnu and in the Vishnu Purāna, modern works which in this regard contrast strongly with the older epic, where Krishna, however he tricks, is always first the god. It is not till he becomes a very great, if not the greatest, god that tales about his youthful performances, when he condescended to be born in low life, begin to rise. An exact parallel may be seen in the case of Çiva, who at first is a divine character, assuming a more or less grotesque likeness to a man; but subsequently he becomes anthropomorphized, and is fitted out with a sheaf of legends which describe his earthly acts.[1] And so with Krishna. As the chief god, identified with the All-god, he is later made the object of encomiums which degrade while they are meant to exalt him. He becomes a cow-boy and acts like one, a god in a mask. But in

[1] Çiva at the present day, for instance, is represented now and then as a man, and he is incarnate as Vīrabhadra. But all this is modern, and contrasts with the older conception. It is only in recent times, in the South, that he is provided with an earthly history. Compare Williams, *Thought and Life*, p. 47.

the epic he is the invading tribe's chief god, in process of becoming identified with that god in the Brahmanic pantheon who most resembles him. For this tribe, the (Yadavas) Pāndavas, succeeded in overthrowing the Brahmanic stronghold and became absorbed into the Brahmanic circle. Their god, who, like most of the supreme gods of this region among the wild tribes, was the tribal hero as sun-god, became recognized by the priests as one with Vishnu. In the Upanishad the priest-philosopher identifies Krishna with the sun as the 'dark side' (*kṛṣṇa*, 'dark') of Vishnu, the native name probably being near enough to the Sanskrit word to be represented by it. The statement that this clan-god Krishna once learned the great truth that the sun is the All-god, at the mouth of a Brahman, is what might be expected. 'Krishna, the son of Devaki,' is not only the god, but he is also the progenitor of the clan. the mystic forefather, who as usual is deified as the sun. To the priest he is merely an *avatar* of Vishnu. The identity of Krishna with the Gangetic god described by Megasthenes can scarcely be disputed. The latter as represented by the Greek is too great a god to have passed away without a sign except for a foreigner's account. And there is no figure like his except that of Krishna.

The numerous *avatars*[1] of Vishnu are first given as ten, then as twenty, then as twenty-two,[2] and at last become innumerable. The ten, which are those usually referred to, are as follows: First come the oldest, the beast-*avatars*, viz., as a fish; as a tortoise;[3] as a boar (rescuing earth from a flood); and as a man-lion (slaying a demon). Next comes the dwarf-*avatar*, where Vishnu cheats Bali of earth by asking, as a dwarf, for three steps of it, and then stepping out over all of it

[1] *Ava-tāra*, 'descent,' from *ava*, 'down,' and *tar*, 'pass' (as in Latin in-*trare*).

[2] In the *Bhāgavata Purāna*.

[3] The tortoise *avatar* had a famous temple two centuries ago, where a stone tortoise received prayer. How much totemism lies in these *avatars* it is guess-work to say.

(the 'three strides' of the Rig Veda). Then come the human *avatars*, that of Paraçu-Rāma (Rāma with the axe), Krishna, Rāma[1] (hero of the Rāmāyana epic), Buddha, and Kalki (who is still to come).

The parallels between the latest Krishna cult and the Biblical narrative are found only in the Purānas and other late works, and undoubtedly, as we have said in the last chapter, are borrowed from Christian sources. Krishna is here born in a stable, his father, like Joseph, going with his virgin spouse to pay taxes. His restoring of a believing woman's son is narrated only in the modern Jāimini Bhārata. These tales might have been received through the first distant Christian mission in the South in the sixth century, but it is more likely that they were brought directly to the North in the seventh century; for at that time a Northern king of the Vāiçya caste, Çilāditya (in whose reign the Chinese pilgrim, Hiouen Thsang, visited India), made Syrian Christians welcome to his court (639 A.D.).[2] The date of the annual Krishna festival, which is a reflex of Christmastide, is variously fixed by the Purānas as coming in July or August.[3]

As Krishna is an *avatar* of Vishnu[4] in the Bhārata, and as the axe-Rāma is another *avatar* in legend (here Vishnu in the form of Paraçu-Rāma raises up the priestly caste, and destroys the warrior-caste), so in the Rāmāyana the hero Rāma (not Paraçu-Rāma) is made an *avatar* of Vishnu. He is a mythical prince of Oude (hence a close connection between the Rāmā-

1 Balarāma (or Baladeva), Krishna's elder brother, is to be distinguished from Rāma. The former is a late addition to the Krishna-cult, and belongs with Nanda, his reputed father. Like Krishna, the name is also that of a snake, Nāga, and it is not impossible that Nāga worship may be the foundation of the Krishna-cult, but it would be hard to reconcile this with tradition. In the sixth century Varāhamihira recognizes both the brothers.

2 Edkins, cited by Müller, *India*, p. 286.

3 Weber, *Janmāṣṭamī*, pp. 259, 318. Weber describes in full the cult of the "Madonna with the Child," according to the Purānas.

4 On the subsequent deification of the Pandus themselves see IA. vii. 127.

yana and Buddhism), who is identified with Vishnu. Vishnu wished to rid earth of the giant Rāvana,[1] and to do so took the form of Rāma. As Krishnaism has given rise to a number of sects that worship Krishna as Vishnu, so Ramaism is the modern cult of Rāma as Vishnu. Both of these sects oppose the Vishnuite that is not inclined to be sectarian; all three oppose the Çivaite; and all four of these oppose the orthodox Brahman, who assigns supreme godship to Çiva or Vishnu as little as does the devotee of these gods in unsectarian form to Krishna or Rāma.

Çiva is on all sides opposed to Vishnu. The Greek account of the third century B.C. says that he taught the Hindus to dance the kordax, but at this time there appears to have been no such phallic worship in his honor as is recorded in the pseudo-epic. Çiva is known in early Brahmanic and in Buddhistic writings, and even as the bearer-of-the-moon, Candraçekhara, he contrasts with Vishnu, as his lightning-form and mountain-habitat differ from the sun-form and valley-home of his rival. This dire god is conceived of as ascetic partly because he is gruesome, partly because he is magical in power. Hence he is the true type of the awful magical Yogi, and as such appealed to the Brahman. Originally he is only a fearful magical god, great, and even all-pervading, but, as seen in the Brahmanic Çatarudriya hymn, he is at first in no sense a pantheistic deity. In this hymn there is a significant addition made to the earlier version. In the first form of the hymn it is said that Rudra, who is here Çiva, is the god of bucolic people; but the new version adds 'and of all people.' Here Çiva appears as a wild, diabolical figure, 'the god of incantations,' whose dart is death; and half of the hymn is taken up with entreaties to the god to spare the speaker. He is praised, in conjunction with trees, of which he is the lord, as

[1] Hence the similarity with Herakles, with whom Megasthenes identifies him. The man-lion and hero-forms are taken to rid earth of monsters.

the one 'clad in skins,' the 'lord of cattle,' the 'lord of paths,' the 'cheater,' the 'deceiver.' When he is next clearly seen, in the epic, he is the god to whom are offered human sacrifices, and his special claim to worship is the phallus; while the intermediate literature shows glimpses of him only in his simple Brahmanic form of terror. It has long been known that Çivaite phallic worship was not borrowed from the Southerners, as was once imagined, and we venture with some scholars to believe that it was due rather to late Greek influence than to that of any native wild tribe.[1]

[1] Greek influence is clearly reflected in India's architecture. Hellenic bas-reliefs representing Bacchic scenes and the love-god are occasionally found. Compare the description of Çiva's temple in Orissa, Weber, *Literature*, p. 368; *Berl. Ak.*, 1890, p. 912. Çiva is here associated with the Greek cult of Eros and Aphrodite.

CHAPTER XVII.

MODERN HINDU SECTS.[1]

ALTHOUGH the faith of India seems to have completed a circle, landing at last in a polytheism as gross as was that of the Vedic age, yet is this a delusive aspect, as will appear if one survey the course of the higher intellectual life of the people, ignoring, as is right, the invariable factor introduced by the base imaginings of the vulgar. The greater spirituality has always expressed itself in independent movement, and voiced itself in terms of revolution. But in reality each change has been one of evolution. To trace back to the Vedic period the origin of Hindu sectarianism would, indeed, be a nice task for a fine scholar, but it would not be temerarious to attempt it. We have failed of our purpose if we have not already impressed upon the reader's mind the truth that the progress of Brahmanic theology (in distinction from demonology) has been one journey, made with rests and halts, it is true, and even with digressions from the straight path; but without abatement of intent, and without permanent change of direction. Nor can one judge otherwise even when he stands before so humiliating an exhibition of groundling bigotry as is presented by some of the religious sects of the present day. The world of lower organisms survives the ascent of the higher. There is always undergrowth; but before the fall of a great tree its seeds sprout, withal in the very soil of the weedy thicket below. So out of

[1] In the following we keep to the practice we have adopted in the early part of the work, giving anglicized words without distinction of vowel-length, and anglicizing as far as possible, writing thus Sānkhya but Sankhyan, Vedānta but Vedantist. In modern proper names we have adopted in each case the most familiar form.

the rank garden of Hindu superstitions arise, one after another, lofty trees of an old seed, which is ever renewed, and which cultivation has gradually improved.

We have shown, especially in the chapters on the Atharva Veda and on Hinduism, as revealed in epic poetry, how constant in India is the relation between these two growths. If surprised at the height of early Hindu thought, one is yet more astonished at the permanence of the inferior life which flourishes beneath the shady protection of the superior. Even here one may follow the metaphor, for the humbler life below is often a condition of the grander growth above.

In the Rig Veda there is an hymn of faith and doubt

TO INDRA.[1]

He who, just born, with thought endowed, the foremost,
Himself a god hemmed in the gods with power;
Before whose breath, and at whose manhood's greatness,
The two worlds trembled; he, ye folk, is Indra.

He who the earth made firm as it was shaking,
And made repose the forward tottering mountains;
Who measured wide the inter-space aerial,
And heaven established; he, ye folk, is Indra.

Who slew the dragon, loosed the rivers seven,
And drove from Vala's hiding place the cattle;[2]
Who fire between the two stones[3] hath engendered,
Conqueror in conflicts; he, ye folk, is Indra.

Who all things here, (things) changeable, created;
Who lowered and put to naught the barbarous color,[4]
And, like victorious gambler, took as winnings
His foe's prosperity; he, ye folk, is Indra.

[1] Rig Veda, ii. 12. Compare x. 121. We omit some of the verses.

[2] See note, p. 20, above.

[3] Metaphor from earthly fire-making; cloud and cliff (Ludwig); or, perhaps, heaven and earth.

[4] 'Made low and put in concealment' the Dāsa color, *i.e.*, the black barbarians, the negroes. 'Color' might be translated 'race' (subsequently 'caste').

Whom, awful, they (yet) ask about: 'where is he?'
And speak thus of him, saying, 'he exists not'—
He makes like dice[1] his foe's prosperity vanish;
Believe on him; and he, ye folk, is Indra.

In whose direction horses are and cattle;
In whose, the hosts (of war) and all the chariots;
Who hath both Sūrya and the Dawn engendered,
The Waters' leader; he, ye folk, is Indra.

Both heaven and earth do bow themselves before him,
And at his breath the mountains are affrighted;
Who bolt in arms is seen, the *soma*-drinker,
And bolt in hand; ('tis) he, ye folk, is Indra.

Who helps the *soma*-presser, (*soma*-) cooker,
The praiser (helps), and him that active serveth;
Of whom the increase *brahma* is and *soma*,
And his this offering; he, ye folk, is Indra.

Here *brahma*, which word already in the Yajur Veda has taken to itself the later philosophical signification, is merely prayer, the meaning which in the Rig Veda is universal.

The note struck in this hymn is not unique:

(The Poet.)

Eager for booty proffer your laudation
To Indra; truth (is he),[2] if truth existeth;
'Indra is not,' so speaketh this and that one;
'Who him hath seen? To whom shall we give praises?'

(The God.)

I am, O singer, he; look here upon me;
All creatures born do I surpass in greatness.
Me well-directed sacrifices nourish,
Destructive I destroy existent beings.[3]

1 Dice, *vijas*, literally 'hoppers' (and so sometimes interpreted as birds). The same figure occurs not infrequently. Compare AV. iv. 16. 5, *akṣān iva*. 'Believe,' *çrád-dhatta*, *i.e.*, cred-(d)ite, literally 'put trust.'

2 Sometimes rendered, "a true (laudation) if any is true."

3 viii. 100. 3–4. The penultimate verse is literally 'the direction(s) of the order magnify me,' the order being that of the seasons and of seasonable rites.

These are not pleas in behalf of a new god. It is not the mere god of physical phenomena who is here doubted and defended. It is the god that in the last stage of the Rig Veda is become the Creator and Destroyer, and, in the light of a completed pantheism, is grown too great to retain his personality. With such a protest begins the great revolt that is the sign of an inner evolution extending through the Brāhmanas and Upanishads. Indra, like other gods,[1] is held by the rite; to the vulgar he is still the great god;[2] to the philosopher, a name. The populace respect him, and sacerdotalism conserves him, that same crafty, priestly power, which already at the close of the Rig Vedic period dares to say that only the king who is subject to the priest is sure of himself, and a little later that killing a priest is the only real murder. We have shown above how the real divinity of the gods was diminished even at the hands of the priests that needed them for the rites and baksheesh, which was the goal of their piety. Even Prajāpati, the Father-god, their own creation, is mortal as well as immortal.[3] We have shown, also, how difficult it must have been to release the reason from the formal band of the rite. Socially it was impossible to do so. He that was not initiated was excommunicated, an outcast. But, on the other hand, the great sacrifices gradually fell over from their own weight. Cumbersome and costly, they were replaced by proxy works of piety; *vidhānas* were established that obviated the real rite; just as to-day, 'pocket altars' take the place of real altars.[4] There was a gradual intrusion of the Hindu cult; popular features began to obtain; the sacrifice was made to embrace in its workings the

1 Compare the 'devil-worship of Uçanas,' and the scoffs at Pūshan. The next step in infidelity is denial of a future life and of the worth of the Vedas.

2 In the Buddhistic writings Indra appears as the great popular god of the Brahmans (with Brahmā as the philosophical god).

3 His body is mortal: his breaths immortal, Çat. Br. x. 1. 4. 1; xi. 1. 2. 12.

4 On these curious pocket-altars, double triangles representing the three gods and their wives, with Linga and Yoni, see JRAS. 1851, p. 71.

whole family of the sacrificer (instead of its effect being confined to him alone, as was the earlier form); and finally village celebrations became more general than those of the individual. Slowly Hinduism built itself a ritual,[1] which overpowered the Brahmanic rite. Then, again, behind the geographical advance of Brahmanism [2] lay a people more and more prone to diverge from the true cult (from the Brahmanic point of view). In the latter part of the great Brāhmana [3] there is already a distrust of the Indus tribes, which marks the breaking up of Aryan unity; not that breaking up into political division which is seen even in the Rig Veda, where Aryan fights against Aryan as well as against the barbarian, but the more serious dismemberment caused by the hates of priests, for here there was no reconciliation.

The cynical scepticism of the Brahmanic ritualists, as well as the divergence of opinions in regard to this or that sacrificial pettiness, shows that even where there was overt union there was covert discord, the disagreement of schools, and the difference of faith. But all this does but reflect the greater difference in speculation and theology which was forming above the heads of the ritualistic bigots. For it is not without reason that the Upanishads are more or less awkwardly laid in as the top-stone on the liturgical edifice. They belong to the time but they are of it only in part. Yet to dissociate the mass of Brahmanic priestlings from the Upanishad thinkers, as if the latter were altogether members of a new era, would be to lose the true historical perspective. The vigor of protest against the received belief continues from the Rig Veda to Buddha, from Buddha till to-day.

The Vedic cult absorbed a good deal of Hinduism, for in-

[1] In the Tantras and late Purānas. In the earlier Purānas there is as yet no such formal cult.

[2] Embodied in the tale of Agni's advance, IS. i. 170.

[3] Çat. Br. ix. 3. 1. 18.

stance the worship of Fate,[1] just as Hinduism absorbed a good deal of Vedic cult. Nor were the popular works obnoxious to the priest. In the Chāndogya Upanishad[2] the Itihāsas and Purānas (fore-runners of the epic) are already reckoned as a fifth Veda, being recognized as a Veda almost as soon as was the Atharvan,[3] which even in Manu is still called merely 'texts of Atharvan and Angiras' (where texts of Bhrigu might as well have been added). Just as the latter work is formally recognized, and the use of its magical formulas, if employed for a good purpose, is enjoined in epic[4] and law (*e.g.*, Manu, xi. 33), so the Hinduistic rites crept gradually into the foreground, pushing back the *soma*-cult. Idols are formally recognized as venerable by the law-makers;[5] even before their day the 'holy pool,' which we have shown to be so important to Hinduism, is accepted by Brahmanism.[6] Something, too, of the former's catholicity is apparent in the cult at an early date, only to be suppressed afterwards. Thus in Āit. Br. ii. 19, the slave's son shares the sacrifice; and the slave drinks *soma* in one of the half-Brahmanical, half-popular festivals.[7] Whether human sacrifice, sanctioned by some modern sects, is aught but pure Hinduism, Çivaism, as affected by the cult of the wild-tribes, it is hard to say. At any rate, such sacrifices in the Brahmanic world were obsolete long before one finds them in Hinduism. Of Buddhistic, Brahmanic, and Hinduistic reciprocity

[1] On this *quasi* deity in modern belief compare IA. xviii. 46. It has happened here that a fate-Providence has become supreme. Thus, too, the Mogul Buddha is really nothing more or less than Providence.

[2] 7. 1. 2.

[3] In RV. x. 90. 9, *chandas*, songs, incantations, imply a work of this nature.

[4] Unless it be distinctly *good* magic the epic heroes are ashamed to use magical rites. They insist on the intent being unimpeachable.

[5] Āp. i. 11. 30. 20, etc. Compare Weber, *Omina*, p. 337, and see the Bibliography.

[6] Tāitt. S. vi. 1. 1. 2, 3, *tīrthe snāti*.

[7] Compare Weber's account of the Rājasūya, p. 98; and, apropos of the Daçapeya, *ib.* 78, note; where it is stated that *soma*-drinking for the warrior-caste is still reflected in this (originally independent) ceremony.

we have spoken already, but we may add one curious fact, namely, that the Buddhism of Çivaism is marked by its holy numbers. The Brahmanic Rudra with eight names[1] and eight forms[2] is clearly Çivaite, and the numbers are as clearly Buddhistic.[3] Thus, as Feer has shown, Buddhist hells are eight, sixteen, etc., while the Brahmanic hells are seven, twenty-one, etc. Again, the use of the rosary was originally Çivaite, not Buddhistic;[4] and Buddha in Bali, where they live amicably side by side, is regarded as Çiva's brother.[5]

Two things result from this interlocking of sectarian Brahmanism with other sects. First, it is impossible to say in how far each influenced the other; and, again, the antiquity of special ideas is rendered doubtful. A Brahmanic idea can pretty safely be allotted to its first period, because the literature is large enough to permit the assumption that it will appear in literature not much later than it obtains. But a sectarian idea may go back centuries before it is permanently formulated, as, for example, the doctrine of special grace in a modern sect.

One more point must be noticed before we proceed to review the sects of to-day. Hindu morality, the ethical tone of the modern sects, is older than the special forms of Hindu viciousness which have been received into the cult. A negative altruism (beyond which Brahmanism never got) is characteristic of the

1 The list given above (p. 464) of the 'thrice three names' is made eight by suppressing Kumāra, and the 'eight names' are to-day the usual number.

2 Çānkh. (Kānsh.) Br. vi. 1.

3 The Brahmanic multiple by preference is (three and) seven (7, 21, 28, 35), that of the Buddhist, eight. Feer, JA., 1893, p. 113 ff., holds the Svargaparva of the epic to be Buddhistic on account of the hells. More probably it is a Çivaite addition. The rule does not always hold good, for groups of seven and eight are sometimes Buddhistic and Brahmanic, respectively.

4 Leumann, *Rosaries*.

5 Friederich, JRAS. viii. 157; ix. 59. The only established reference to Buddha on the part of Brahmanism, with the exception of late Purānas of uncertain date, is after Kshemendra (1066 A.D.). Compare Holtzmann, *z. Geschichte*, p. 103.

Hindu sects. But this is already embodied in the golden rule, as it is thus formulated in the epic 'Compendium of Duty':

> Not that to others should one do
> Which he himself objecteth to.
> This is man's duty in one word;
> All other rules may be ignored.[1]

The same is true of the 'Ten Commandments' of one of the modern sects. It is one of the strong proofs that Christian morals did not have much effect upon early Hinduism, that, although the Christian Church of St. Thomas, as is well established, was in Malabar as early as 522,[2] and Christians were in the North in the seventh century, yet no trace of the active Christian benevolence, in place of this abstention from injury, finds its way into the epic or Purānas. But an active altruism permeates Buddhism, and one reads in the birth-stories even of a saviour Buddha, not the Buddha of love, Māitreya, who was to be the next Buddha on earth, but of that Māitrakanyaka, who left heaven and came to earth that he might redeem the sins of others.[3]

Whether there is any special touch between the older sects and those of modern days[4] that have their headquarters in the

[1] *Na tat parasya sandadhyāt pratikūlam yad ātmanas.* This is a favorite stanza in the epic, and is imitated in later literature (Sprüche, 3253, 6578, 6593).

[2] Burnell in the *Indian Antiquary*, second and following volumes; Swanston, JRAS. 1834; 1835; Germann, *Die Kirche der Thomaschristen.*

[3] Above, cited from Hardy.

[4] Some of the multitudinous sub-castes occasionally focus about a religious principle to such an extent as to give them almost the appearance of religious devotees. Thus the Bhāts and Chārans are heralds and bards with the mixed faith of so many low-caste Hindus. But in their office of herald they have a religious pride, and, since in the present day they are less heralds than expressmen, they carry property with religious reverence, and are respected in their office even by robbers; for it is this caste that do not hesitate to commit *traga*, that is, if an agreement which they have caused to be made between two parties is not carried out they will kill themselves and their families, with such religious effect that the guilt lies upon the offending party in the agreement, who expiates it by his own life. They are regarded as a sort of divine representative, and feel themselves to be so. A case reported from India in this year,

same districts is a question which we have endeavored to investigate, but we have found nothing to substantiate such an opinion. Buddhism retired too early to have influence on the sects of to-day, and between Jainism and the same sects there does not seem to be any peculiar rapport even where the sect is seated in a Jain stronghold.[1] The Jains occupy, generally speaking, the Northwest (and South), while the Buddhists were located in the Northeast and South. So Çivaism may be loosely located as popular in the Northeast and South, while Vishnuism has its habitat rather in the Jain centres of the Northwest (and South).

We have mentioned in the preceding chapter the sects of a few centuries ago, as these have been described in Brahmanic literature.[2] The importance, and even the existence of some of the sects, described in the *Conquest of Çankara*, has been questioned, and the opinion has been expressed that, since they are described only to be exposed as heretical, they may have been creations of fancy, imaginary sects; the refutation of their principles being a *tour de force* on the part of the Brahmanic savant, who shows his acumen by imagining a sect and then discountenancing it. It does not, indeed, seem to us very probable that communities were ever formed as 'Agnis' or 'Yamas,' etc., but on the other hand, we think it is more likely that sects have gone to pieces without leaving any trace than that those enumerated, explained, and criticised should have been mere fancies.[3] Moreover, in the case of some of these sects

1894, shows that the feeling still exists. The herald slew his own mother in the presence of the defaulting debtor, who thereupon slew himself as his only expiation.

[1] As, for example, between the Dādū Panthīs and the Jains in Ajmīr and Jeypur. The last was a chief Digambara town, while Mathurā (on the Jumna) was a Çvetāmbara station. For a possible survival of Buddhism, see below, p. 485, note.

[2] The *Sarvadarçaṇasaṅgraha* of Sāyana (fourteenth century) and the *Çaṅkaravijaya*, or 'Conquest of Çankara.'

[3] Thus the Dabistān enumerates as actual sects of the seventeenth century, 'moon-worshippers,' 'star-worshippers,' 'Agni-worshippers,' 'wind-worshippers,' 'water-worshippers,' 'earth-worshippers,' '*tripūjas*' (or worshippers of all the three kingdoms

there are still survivors, so that *a fortiori* one may presume the others to have existed also, if not as sects or communities, yet as bodies professing faith in Indra or Yama, etc. The sects with which we have to deal now are chiefly those of this century, but many of these can claim a definite antiquity of several centuries at least. They have been described by Wilson in his famous *Sketch*, and, in special cases, more recently and more fully by Williams[1] and other writers.

THE ÇIVAITES.

While the Vishnuites have a dualistic, as well as idealistic background, they are at present Vedantic, and may be divided to-day simply into intelligent and unintelligent adherents of pantheism, the former comprising the Rāma sects, and the latter most of the Krishnaites. On the other hand, in Çivaism one must distinguish quite sharply in time between the different sects that go by Çiva's name. If one look at the sects of modern times he will find that the most degraded are dualistic, in so far as they may be said to have any philosophy, and that idealistic Çivaism is a remnant of the past. But he will not find a pronounced sectarianism in any of these old Vedantic aspects of Çivaism. On the contrary, wherever Çivaism is pantheistic it is a Çivaism which obtains only in certain ancient schools of philosophy; where it is monotheistic it is among leaders who have been influenced by the modern teaching of Islam, and regard Çiva merely as a name for the One God. It is necessary, therefore, as it is everywhere in India, to draw as sharp a line as possible between the beliefs of the vulgar and the learned. For from the earliest period the former accepted

of nature), and 'worshippers of man' (*manuṣyabhaktās*), "who recognize the being of God in man, and know nothing more perfect than mankind" (ii. 12), a faith which, as we have shown, is professed in the Mahābhārata.

[1] *Religious Thought and Life.*

perfunctorily the teaching of the latter, but at heart and in cult they remained true to their own lights.

The older Sānkhya form of Çivaism was still found among the Pāçupatas, 'adherents of the Lord' (Paçupati) and Maheçvaras ('adherents of the great Lord'), who are mentioned in the epic and in inscriptions of the fifth century. In the ninth century there was a purely philosophical Çivaism which is Vedantic. But neither in the fact (which is by no means a certainty) that Çankara accepted Çiva as the name of the All-god, nor in the scholastic Çivaite philosophy of Kashmeer, which in the next two centuries was developed into a purely idealistic system at the hands of Ȧbhinavagupta and Somānanda, is there any trace of a popular religion. Çiva is here the pantheistic god, but he is conceived as such only by a coterie of retired schoolmen. On the other hand, the popular religions which spring up in the twelfth century are, if Vedantic, chiefly Vishnuite, or, if Çivaite, only nominally Vedantic. Thus what philosophy the Jangamas professedly have is Vedantic, but in fact they are deistic (not pantheistic) disciples of Çiva's priest, Basava (Sanskrit Vrishabha), who taught Çiva-worship in its grossest form, the adoration of the Linga (phallus); while his adherents, who are spread over all India under the name of Jangamas, 'vagrants,' or Lingāyits, 'phallus-wearers,' are idolatrous deists with but a tinge of Vedantic mysticism. So in the case of the Tridandins, the Daçanāmis, and other sects attributed to Çivaism, as well as the Smārtas (orthodox Brahmans) who professed Çivaism. According to Wilson the Tridandis (whose triple, *tri*, staff, *dandi*, indicates control of word, thought, and deed) are Southern Vishnuites of the Rāmānuja sect, though some of them claim to be Vedantic Çivaites. Nominally Çivaite are also the Southern 'Saints,' Sittars (Sanskrit Siddhas), but these are a modern sect whose religion has been taught them by Islam, or possibly by Christianity.[1] The extreme North and

1 The Kashmeer Çivaites claim Çankara as their teacher. The sect of Basava

South are the districts where Çivaism as a popular religion has, or had, its firmest hold, and it is for this reason that the higher religions which obtain in these districts are given to Çiva. But in reality they simply take Çiva, the great god of the neighborhood, in order to have a name for their monotheistic god, exactly as missionaries among the American Indians pray to the Great Spirit, to adapt themselves to their audience's comprehension. In India, as in this country, they that proselyte would prefer to use their own terminology, but they wisely use that of their hearers.

We find no evidence to prove that there were ever really sectarian Çivaites who did not from the beginning practice brutal rites, or else soon become ascetics of the lowest and most despicable sort. For philosophical Çivaites were never sectaries. They cared little whether the All-god or One they argued about was called Vishnu or Çiva. But whenever one finds a true Çivaite devotee, that is, a man that will not worship Vishnu but holds fast to Çiva as the only manifestation of the supreme divinity, he will notice that such an one quickly becomes obscene, brutal, prone to bloodshed, apt for any disgusting practice, intellectually void, and morally beneath contempt. If the Çivaite be an ascetic his asceticism will be the result either of his lack of intelligence (as in the case of the sects to be described immediately) or of his cunning, for he knows that there are plenty of people who will save him the trouble of earning a living. Now this is not the case with the Vishnuites. To be sure there are Vishnuites that are no better than Çivaites, but there are also strict Vishnuites, exclusively devotees of Vishnu, who are and remain pure, not brutal, haters of bloodshed, apt for no disgusting practices, intellectually admirable, and morally above reproach. In other words, there are to-day great numbers of

started in the south, Mysore. They have some trashy literature (legends, etc.) which they dignify by the name of Purānas. Bühler has given an account of the Kashmeer school. For further details see Barth, pp. 184, 206.

Vishnuites who continue to be really Vishnuites, and yet are really intelligent and moral. This has never been the case with real Çivaites. Again, as Williams[1] has pointed out, Çivaism is a cheap religion; Krishnaism is costly. The Çivaite needs for his cult only a phallus pebble, *bilva* leaves and water. The Krishnaite is expected to pay heavily for *leitourgiai.* But Çivaism is cheap because Çivaites are poor, the dregs of society; it is not adopted because it is cheap.

We think, therefore, that to describe Çivaism as indifferently pantheistic or dualistic, and to argue that it must have been pantheistic a few centuries after the Christian era because Çiva at that time in scholastic philosophy and among certain intellectual sects was regarded as the one god, tends to obscure the historical relation of the sects. Without further argumentation on this point, we shall explain what in our view is necessary to a true understanding of the mutual relations between Çivaites and Vishnuites in the past.

Monotheism[2] and pantheism are respectively the religious expression of the Sānkhya and Vedānta systems of philosophy. Çivaism, Krishnaism, and Rāmaism are all originally deistic. Pure Çivaism has remained so to this day, not only in all its popular sectarian expressions, but also in the Brahmanic Çivaism of the early epic, and in the Çivaism which expresses itself in the adoration-formulae of the literature of the Renaissance. But there is a pseudo-Çivaism which starts up from the ninth to the twelfth centuries, and tries to work Çiva's name into a

[1] *Brahmanism and Hinduism*, p. 62 ff. To this and to the same author's *Thought and Life*, we are indebted for many facts concerning the sects as they appear to-day, though much in these books is said after Wilson or other scholars, whose work is now common property, and calls for no further acknowledgment.

[2] It is, perhaps, necessary to keep repeating that Hindu monotheism does not exclude other gods which, at the hands of the one god, are reduced to sprites, angels, demons, etc. But it ought not to be necessary to insist on this, for an American monotheist that believes in angels and devils is the same sort of monotheist. The Hindu calls the angels 'gods' or 'divinities,' but they are only attendant hosts of the One.

pantheistic system of philosophy. Every such attempt, however, and all of them are the reflex of the growing importance of Vedantic ideas, fails as such to produce a religion. If the movement becomes popular and develops into a religious system for the masses, it at once gives up Çiva and takes up Vishnu, or, keeping Çiva, it drops pantheism and becomes a low form of sectarian ascetism. Çivaism is, therefore, fundamentally non-Vedantic, and Unitarian.[1]

On the other hand, while Krishnaism and Ramaism begin as deistic (tribal) cults, they are soon absorbed into Brahmanic Vishnuism. Now Vishnuism is essentially Brahmanistic, and the only orthodox (Brahmanic) system is that which holds to the completion of Vedic pantheism. The first systematic philosophy, however, was not orthodox. It was the Sānkhya, which peeps out in the dualism of the oldest distinctly philosophical works, and lingers in the Puranic Sānkhya. The marks of this dualism we have shown in the Divine Song of the epic. It is by means of it that Krishnaism as an expression of this heterodox Vishnuism became possible. Vishnuism was soon rescued from the dualists, and became again what it was originally, an expression of pantheism. But Vishnu carried Krishna with him as his *alter ego*, and in the epic the two are finally one All-god. Vedantic philosophy continued to present Vishnu rather than Çiva as its All-god, until to-day Vishnuism is the sectarian aspect of the Vedānta system. But with Vishnu have risen Krishna and Rāma as still further types of the All-god. Thus it is that Vishnuism, whether as Krishnaism or as Ramaism, is to-day a pantheistic religion. But, while Rāma is the god of the philosophical sects,

1 Some of the Çivaite sects are, indeed, Buddhistic in origin, a fact which raises the question whether Buddhism, instead of disappearing from India, was not simply absorbed; much as Unitarianism in New England has spent its vitality in modifying the orthodox creed. Thus the *karma* of Buddhism may still be working in the person of some modern Hindu sects. See the next note below.

and, therefore, is almost entirely a pantheistic god; Krishna, who was always a plebeian, is continually reverting, so to speak, to himself; that is to say, he is more affected by the vulgar, and as the vulgar are more prone, by whatever sectarian name they call themselves, to worship one idol, it happens that Krishna in the eyes of his following is less of a pantheistic god than is Rāma. Here again, therefore, it is necessary to draw the line not so much between names of sects as between intelligent and unintelligent people. For Krishnaism, despite all that has been done for Krishna by the philosophers of his church, in this regard resembles Çivaism, that it represents the religion of unintelligent (though wealthy) classes, who revere Krishna as their one pet god, without much more thought of his being an All-god *avatar* than is spent by the ordinary Çivaite on the purely nominal trinitarianism which has been foisted upon Çiva.

But we must now give an account of the low sectaries, the miracle-mongers, jugglers,[1] and ascetic whimsicalities, which together stand under the phallic standard of Çivaism. Ancient and recent observers enumerate a sad list of them. The devotees of the 'highest bird' are a low set of ascetics, who live on voluntary alms, the result of their affectation of extreme penance. The Ūrdhvabāhus, 'Up-arms,' raise their arms till they are unable to lower them again. The Ākāçamukhas, 'Sky-facers,' hold their faces toward the sky till the muscles stiffen, and they live thus always. The Nakhīs, 'Nail'

[1] Most of the Yogi jugglers are Çivaites (when they are not Buddhistic), and to-day they share with the (Mohammedan) fakirs the honor of being not only ascetics but knaves. The juggler Yogi is, however, a figure of respectable antiquity. The magical tricks practiced on the epic heroes are doubtless a reflex of the current mesmerism, which deceives so cleverly to-day. We have shown above a Buddhistic strain of Mahātmaism in an early Buddhistic tract, and Barth, p. 213, suggests a Buddhistic origin for the Kānaphāts. See also Holtzmann, *loc. cit.* The deistic Yogis of Gorakhnāth's sect are respectable enough (see an account of some of this sort in the Dabistān, ii. 6), but they are of Buddhistic origin. The Kānaphāts of Kutch (Danodhar) were once a celibate brotherhood. JRAS. 1839, p. 268.

ascetics, allow their nails to grow through their clenched hands, which unfits them for work (but they are all too religiously lazy to work), and makes it necessary for the credulous faithful to support them. Some of these, like the Kānaphāts, 'Ear-splitters,' who pierce the ear with heavy rings, have been respectable Yogis in the past, but most of them have lost what sense their philosophic founders attached to the sign, and keep only the latter as their religion. Some, such as the Ūkharas and Sūkharas, appear to have no distinctive features, all of them being the 'refuse of beggars' (Wilson). Others claim virtue on the strength of nudity, and subdue their passions literally with lock and key. The 'Potmen,' the 'Skull-men,' Gūdaras and Kāpālikas, are distinguished, as their names imply, only by their vessels. The former, however, are the remnant of a once thoughtful sect known by name since the sixth century, and Kānaphāts and Kāpālikas both show that very likely others among these wretches are but the residue of ancient Çivaite sects, who began as philosophers (perhaps Buddhists), and became only ascetic and thus degraded; for, Çiva apparently has no power to make his worshippers better than himself, and he is a dirty monster, now and then galvanized into the resemblance of a decent god.

There is a well-known verse, not in Manu, but attributed to him (and for that reason quite a modern forgery),[1] which declares that Çambhu (Çiva) is the god of priests; Vishnu, the god of warriors; Brahmā, the god of the Vāiçyas (farmers and traders); and Ganeça, the god of slaves. It is, on the contrary, Çiva himself, not his son Ganeça, who is the 'god of low people' in the early literature. It is he who 'destroys sacrifice,' and is anything but a god of priests till he is carefully made over by the latter. Nowadays some Brahmans profess the Çivaite faith, but they are Vishnuite if really sectarian.

[1] See JAOS. xi. 272. To ascribe this verse to the 'older Manu' would be a grave slip on the part of a Sanskrit scholar.

No Brahman, for instance, will serve at a Çiva shrine, except possibly at Benares, where among more than an hundred shrines to Çiva and his family, Vishnu has but one; and though he will occasionally perform service even in a heretic Jain temple he will not lower himself to worship the Linga. Nor is it true that Çiva is a patron of literature. Like Ganeça, his son, Çiva may upset everything if he be not properly placated, and consequently there is, at the beginning of every enterprise (among others, literary enterprises) in the Renaissance literature, but never in the works of religion or law or in any but modern profane literature, an invocation to Çiva. But he is no more a patron of literature than is Ganeça, or in other words, Çivaism is not more literary than is Ganeçaism. In a literary country no religion is so illiterate as Çivaism, no writings are so inane as are those in his honor. There is no poem, no religious literary monument, no Purāna even, dedicated to Çiva, that has any literary merit. All that is readable in sectarian literature, the best Purānas, the Divine Song, the sectarian Rāmāyana, come from Vishnuism. Çivaism has nothing to compare with this, except in the works of them that pretend to be Çivaites but are really not sectaries, like the Sittars and the author of the Çvetāçvatara. Çiva as a 'patron of literature' takes just the place taken by Ganeça in the present beginning of the Mahābhārata. Vyāsa has here composed the poem[1] but Ganeça is invoked as Vighneça, 'Lord of difficulties,' to help the poet write it out. Vyāsa does the intellectual work and Ganeça performs the manual labor. Vishnuism, in a word, is the only cultivated (native) sectarian religion of India; and the orthodox cult, in that it is Vedantic, lies nearer to Vishnuism than to Çivaism. Why then does one find Çiva invoked by philosophy? Because monotheism in distinction from pantheism was the belief of the wise in the first centuries after the Christian era, till the genius of Çankara

[1] i. 1. 76.

definitively raised pantheism in alliance with orthodoxy to be the more esteemed; and because Çiva alone, when the choice lay between him and Vishnu, could be selected as the One God. For Vishnuism was now merged with Krishnaism, a new vulgar cult, and Çiva was an old and venerated god, long since a member of the Brahmanic pantheon. The connection between Çivaism and the Sānkhya system gave it a more respectable and archaic appearance in the eyes of the conservative Brahman, while the original asceticism of Çiva undoubtedly appealed much more to Brahmanic feeling than did the sentimentalism of the Vishnuite. In the extreme North, in the ninth century, philosophy and Çivaism are nominally allied, but really sectarian Çivaism was the cult of the lowest, not of the highest classes. Many of the professed Çivaites are to-day tending to Vedantism, which is the proper philosophy of the Vishnuite; and the Çivaite sects are waning before the Vishnuite power, not only in the middle North, where the mass of the population is devoted to Vishnu, but even in Çiva's later provinces in the extreme South. The social distribution of the sectaries in the Middle Ages was such that one may assign older Vishnuism to the middle classes, and Çivaism to the highest on its philosophical and decently ascetic side, but to the lowest on its phallic and magical side.

But none of the Çivaite sects we have mentioned, imbecile as appear to be the impostors that represent them, are equal in despicable traits to the Çāktas. These worshippers of the androgynous Çiva (or of Çakti, the female principle alone), do, indeed, include some Vishnuites among themselves, but they are originally and prevailingly Çivaite.[1] Blood-offerings and human sacrifices are a modern and an ancient trait of Çiva-

[1] The Dabistān, without any animus, reports of the Çāktas of the seventeenth century that "Çiva is, in their opinion, *with little exception*, the highest of the deities" (ii. 7). Williams calls Çāktaism "a mere offshoot of Çivaism," *Religious Thought and Life*, p. 184.

worship;[1] and the hill-tribes of the Vindhya and the classical drama show that the cult of Aghorī is a Çivaite manifestation which is at once old and derived from un-Aryan sources. Aghorī and all female monsters naturally associate with Çiva, who is their intellectual and moral counterpart. The older Aghorīs exacted human sacrifice in honor of Devī, Pārvatī, the wife of Çiva.[2] The adoration of the female side of a god is as old as the Rig Veda, but Çivaism has combined this cult with features probably derived from other independent local cults, such as that of Pārvati, the 'mountain goddess.' They are all united in the person of Çiva's wife of many names, the 'great goddess,' Mahādevī, the 'hard' Durgā, Kāli, Umā, etc.[3] And it is to this ferocious she-monster that the most abject homage of the Çivaites is paid. So great is the terror inspired by Durgā that they that are not Çivaites at all yet join in her festival; for which purpose, apparently, she is dubbed Vishnu's 'sister.' But it is not blood-guiltiness alone which is laid at the door of this cult. The sectarian religions have an exoteric and an esoteric side, the religion of the 'right hand' and of the 'left hand.' It is the latter (to which belong many that deny the fact) wherein centre the abominations of Çivaism; in less degree, those of Vishnuism also. Obscenity is the soul of this cult. Bestiality equalled only by the orgies of the Indic savages among the hill-tribes is the form of this 'religion.'[4] It is

[1] The Dabistān rather assumes as a matter of course that a body of Yogis would kill and eat a boy of the Mohammedan faith (ii. 12); but here the author may be prejudiced.

[2] The present sect of this name consists only of a few miserable mendicants, particularly savage and filthy (Wilson).

[3] All of them now represent Çakti, the female principle. Linga-worship has also its counterpart, Bhaga-worship (here Yoni), perhaps represented by the altar itself. Compare the Dabistān, ii. 7, on the Çivaite interpretation of the Mohammedan altar. To Durgā human beings were always sacrificed. After mentioning a gold idol of Durgā (to whom men were sacrificed yearly), the author adds: "Even now they sacrifice in every village of the Kohistan of Nandapur and the country adjacent, a man of good family" (*ib.*). Durgā (above, p. 416) is Vishnu's sister.

[4] The sexual antithesis, so unimportant in the earliest Aryan nature-hymns, be-

screened by an Orphic philosophy, for is not Nature or Illusion the female side of the Divine Male? It is screened again by religious fervor, for it is pious profligacy that prompts the rites. It is induced practically by an initial carousal and drunkenness; and this is antique, for even the old *soma*-feasts were to a great extent drunken revels, and the gods have got drunk from the time of the Vedas[1] to do their greatest deeds. But in practice, Çakti-worship, when unveiled, amounts to this, that men and women of the same class and family indulge in a Bacchanalian orgy, and that, as they proceed, they give themselves over to every excess which liquor and lust can prompt. A description of the different rites would be to reduplicate an account of indecencies, of which the least vile is too esoteric to sketch faithfully. Vaguely to outline one such religious festival will suffice. A naked woman, the wife of the chief priest, sits in the middle of the 'holy circle.' She represents Durgā, the divine female principle. The Bacchic orgy begins with hard drinking. Çiva as Bhāirava, 'the dreadful,' has his human counterpart also, who must then and there pair with the impersonated Durgā. The worship proper consists in the repetition of meaningless *mantra* syllables and yells; the worship improper, in indulgence in 'wine and women' (particularly enjoined in the rite-books called Tantras). Human sacrifice at these rites is said to be extinct at the present day.[2]

comes more and more pronounced in the liturgical hymns of the Rig Veda, and may be especially a trait of the older fire-cult in opposition to *soma*-cult (compare RV. x. 18. 7). At any rate it is significant that Yoni means the altar itself, and that in the fire-cult the production of fire is represented as resulting from the union of the male and female organs.

1 Nevertheless the Brahmanic, and even the Hinduistic, law-codes condemn all intoxicating liquors except in religious service. To offer such drink to a man of the lower castes, even to a Çūdra, is punishable with a fine; but to offer intoxicating liquor to a priest is punishable with death (Vishnu, v. 100).

2 Formerly performed by the Karāris. "The Çāktas hold the killing of a man to be permitted," Dabistān, ii. 7. "Among them it is a meritorious act to sacrifice a man," *ib.*

But blood-lust is appeased by the hacking of their own bodies. Garments are cast in a heap. Lots are drawn for the women's garments[1] by the men. With her whose clothes he gets each man continues the debauch, inviting incest in addition to all other excess.[2]

The older Vishnuite sects (Pāñcarātras, etc.) may have had some of this filth in their make-up; but mass for mass the practices are characteristic of Çivaism and not of Vishnuism.[3] Especially Çivaite, however, is the 'mother worship,' to which reference was made in the chapter on epic Hinduism. These 'mothers' are guardian goddesses, or fiends of disease, etc. One may not claim that all Çāktas are Çivaites, but how small a part of Vishnuism is occupied with Çakti-worship can be estimated only by surveying the whole body of worshippers of that name.

We cannot leave the lust and murder of modern Çivaism without speaking of still another sect which hangs upon the heels of Kāli, that of the Thugs. It may, indeed, be questioned whether Çiva should be responsible for the doings of his spouse, Kālī. But like seeks like, and there is every historical justification in making out Çiva to be as bad as the company he keeps. Durgā and Kāli are not vainly looked upon as Çiva's female side. So that a sect like the Thugs,[4]

1 Hence the name of Kāñculiyas (*kañculi*, a woman's garment).

2 This has no parallel in Vishnuism except among some of the Rādhā devotees. Among the Rādhā Vallabhīs the vulgarities of the Çivaites are quite equalled; and the assumption of women's attire by the Sakhī Bhāvas of Benares and Bengal ushers in rites as coarse if less bloody than those of the Çivaites.

3 Of course each god of the male trinity has his Çakti. female principle. Thus Brahmā's Çakti is Sāvitrī (in the epic), or Sarasvatī, or Vāc; that of Vishnu is Çrī, or Lakshmī, or Rādhā; that of Çiva is Umā, Durgā, Kālī, etc. Together they make a female trinity (Barth, p. 199). So even the Vedic gods had their (later) wives, who, as in the case of Sūryā, were probably only the female side of a god conceived of as androgynous, like Prajāpati in the Brahmanic period.

4 Historically, Thags, like Panjāb. Santhāls, etc., is the more correct form, but phonetically the forms Thugs, Punjāb, Sunthāls or Sonthāls, are correct, and ă, the indeterminate vowel (like o in London), is generally transcribed by u or o (in

which worshipped Kālī, may, it is true, be taken out of the Çivaite sects, but only if one will split Çivaism in two and reproduce the original condition, wherein Çiva was one monster and Kālī was another; which is scarcely possible after the two have for centuries been looked upon as identical. With this in mind it may be granted that the Thugs payed reverence to Kālī, rather than to her lord. Moreover, many of them were Mohammedans; but, for our purpose, the significant fact is that when the Thugs were Hindus they were Kālī-Çivaites. And we believe that these secret murderers, strange as it seems, originated in a reformatory movement. As is well known, it was a religious principle with them not to spill blood.[1] They always throttled. They were, of course, when they first became known in 1799 (Sherwood's account), nothing but robbers and murderers. But, like the other Çivaite monstrosities, they regarded their work as a religious act, and always invoked Kālī if they were Hindus. We think it probable, therefore, that the sect originated among the Kālī-worshippers as a protest against blood-letting. Admitting that robbery is under Çiva's protection (Çiva is 'god of robbers'), and that Kālī wanted victims, a sect probably claimed that the victims should be throttled, and not bled. Not that this was necessarily a new reform. There is every reason to suppose that most of Çiva's females are aboriginal wild-tribe

Punjāb, Nepāl, the ā is pronounced very like au, and is sometimes written so, Punjaub, etc.).

1 The Jemidar, captain, gives the order to the Buttoat, strangler, who takes the *rumal* (yard of cotton) with a knot tied in the left end, and, holding his right hand a few inches further up, passes it from behind over the victim's head. As the latter falls the strangler's hands are crossed, and if done properly the Thugs say that "the eyes stand out of the head and life becomes extinct, before the body falls to the ground" (Notes on the 'Thags, Thugs, or Thegs,' by Lieutenant Reynolds; of whom Lieutenant-Colonel Smythe says that he knew more than any other European about the Thugs, 1836). The Buttoat received eight annas extra for his share. Each actor in the scene had a title; the victim was called Rosy. For their argot see the Rāmaseeana.

divinities. Now among these savages one sees at times a distinct refusal to bleed human victims. Thuggery may then have been the claim of an old conservative party, who wished to keep up the traditional throttling; though this is pure speculation, for, at the time when the sect became exposed, this means of death was merely the safest way to kill. They insisted always on being called Thugs, and scorned the name of thief. They were suppressed by 1840. Reynolds describes them as "mostly men of mild and unobtrusive manners, possessing a cheerful disposition."[1]

THE VISHNUITE SECTS.

There is a formal idealistic Çivaism, as we have shown, and there was once a dualistic Vishnuism; but in general the Vishnuite is an idealist. To comprehend the quarrels among the sects of this religion, however, it will be necessary to examine the radical philosophical differences of their founders, for one passes, in going from modern Çivaism to Vishnuism, out of ignorant superstition into philosophical religion, of which many even of the weaker traits are but recent Hinduistic effeminacy substituted for an older manly thinking.

[1] Thugs (defined as 'knaves' by Sherwood, more probably 'throttlers') must be distinguished from Decoits. The latter (Elphinstone, i. 384) are irreligious gangs, secretly bound together to sack villages. Peaceable citizens by day, the Decoits rise at night, attack a village, slay, torture, rob, and disappear before morning, 'melting into the population' and resuming honest toil. When the police are weak enough they may remain banded together; otherwise they are ephemerally honest and nocturnally assassins. The Thugs or Phānsīgars (*phānsī*, noose) killed no women, invoked Kālī (as Jayī), and attacked individuals only, whom the decoys, called Tillais, lured very cleverly to destruction. They never robbed without strangling first, and always buried the victim. They used to send a good deal of what they got to Kālī's temple, in a village near Mirzāpur, where the establishment of priests was entirely supported by them. Kālī (or Bhavānī) herself directed that victims should be strangled, not bled (so the Thug legend). Their symbol was a pick, emblem of the goddess, unto whom a religious ceremony was performed before and after the murder was committed. Local small bankers often acted as fence for them.

The complex of Vishnuite sects presents at first rather a confused appearance, but we think that we can make the whole body separate itself clearly enough into its component parts, if the reader will pause at the threshold and before entering the edifice look at the foundation and the outer plan of Vedantic philosophy.

At the beginning of Colebrooke's essays on Hindu philosophy he thus describes four of the recognized systems: "The two Mīmāmsās . . . are emphatically orthodox. The prior one, *pūrva*,[1] which has Jāimini for its founder, teaches the art of reasoning, with the express view of aiding the interpretation of the Vedas. The latter, *uttara*,[2] commonly called Vedānta, and attributed to Vyāsa (or Bādarāyana), deduces from the text of the Indian scriptures a refined psychology, which goes to a denial of a material world. A different philosophical system, partly heterodox, and partly conformable to the established Hindu creed, is the Sānkhya; of which also, as of the preceding, there are two schools; one usually known by that name,[3] the other commonly termed Yoga."[4]

The eldest of these systems, as we have already had occasion to state, is the dualistic Sānkhya. It was still highly esteemed in the ninth century, the time of the great Vedantist, Çankara.[5] A theistic form of this atheistic philosophy is called the Puranic Sānkhya, and Patañjali's Yoga is thoroughly theistic. Radically opposed to the dualistic Sānkhya stands the Vedānta,[6] based on the Upanishads that teach the identity of spirit and matter.

1 This is called either Pūrva-mīmāmsā (Karma-mīmāmsā) or simply Mīmāmsā.

2 Or Çārīraka-mīmāmsā, or Brahma-mīmāmsā (*mīmāṃsā*, reflexion, philosophy).

3 Kapila's system, usually known as the Sānkhya.

4 And attributed to Patañjali. Compare Deussen, *System des Vedānta*, p. 20.

5 Born in 788. But some scholars refer him to the seventh century. See IA. xiii. 95; xvi. 41. His name, a title of Çiva, indicates his nominal sect.

6 For the meaning of Vedānta (whether 'end of Veda,' or 'goal of Veda') compare Deussen, *loc. cit.* p. 3, note (above, p. 253, note).

As representative of the metaphysics of the Sānkhya and Vedānta systems respectively stand in general the two great religions of India. The former, as we have shown, is still potent in the great Song of the epic, and its principles are essentially those of early Çivaism. The latter, especially in its sectarian interpretation, with which we have now to deal, has become the great religion of India. But there are two sectarian interpretations of Vishnu, and two philosophical interpretations of the All-spirit in its relation to the individual soul or spirit.[1] Again the individual spirit of man either enjoys after death immortal happiness, as a being distinct from the All-spirit; or the *jīva*, individual spirit, is absorbed into the All-spirit (losing all individuality, but still conscious of happiness); or the individual spirit is absorbed into an All-spirit that has no happiness or affection of any kind.

Now the strict philosophy of the Vedānta adopts the last view *in toto*. The individual spirit (soul, self) becomes one with the universal Spirit, losing individuality and consciousness, for the universal Spirit itself is not affected by any quality or condition. A creative force without attributes, this is the All-spirit of Çankara and of the strict Vedantist. To Çankara the Creator was but a phase of the All-spirit, and the former's immortality ended with his creation; in other words, there is no immortal Creator, only an immortal creative power.

In the twelfth century arose another great leader of thought, Rāmānuja. He disputed the correctness of Çankara's interpretation of Vedantic principles. It is maintained by some that Çankara's interpretation is really correct, but for our purpose that is neither here nor there.[2] Çankara's *brahma* is the

[1] The Supreme Spirit or All-Spirit is either purely non-dualistic or qualifiedly non-dualistic; in the latter event he is, says the sectary, identical with Vishnu, who may be represented either by Krishna or Rāma (sub-sects). Pure non-duality (unconditioned *ātmā*) was taught by Çankara.

[2] Gough, *Philosophy of the Upanishads*. Compāre Williams, *loc. cit.* In our own view the unsystematic Upanishads teach both doctrines (above, p. 228, note).

one and only being, pure being, or pure thought. Thought is not an attribute of *brahma*, it is *brahma*. Opposed to this pure being (thought) stands *māyā*, illusion, the material cause of the seen world. It is neither being nor not-being; it is the cause of the appearance of things, in that it is associated with *brahma*, and in so far only is *brahma* rightly the Lord. The infinite part of each individual is *brahma;* the finite part is *māyā*. Thus Bādarāyana (author of the Vedānta Sūtras) says that the individual is only illusion.

Rāmānuja,[1] on the other hand, teaches a *brahma* that is not only universal, but is the universal personal Lord, a supreme conscious and willing God. Far from being devoid of attributes, like Çankara's *brahma*, the *brahma* of Rāmānuja has all attributes, chief of which is thought or intelligence. The Lord contains in himself the elements of that plurality which Çankara regards as illusion. As contrasted with the dualistic Sānkhya philosophy both of these systems inculcate monism. But according to Çankara all difference is illusion; while according to Rāmānuja *brahma* is not homogeneous, but in the diversity of the world about us he is truly manifested. Çankara's *māyā* is Rāmānuja's body of (*brahma*) the Lord. Çankara's personal god exists only by collusion with illusion, and hence is illusory. The *brahma* of Rāmānuja is a personal god, the omnipotent, omniscient, Lord of a real world. Moreover, from an eschatological point of view, Çankara explains salvation, the release from re-birth, *samsāra*, as complete union with this unqualified *brahma*, consequently as loss of individuality as well as loss of happiness. But Rāmānuja defines salvation as the departure from earth forever of the individual

1 Before Rāmānuja it was taught by Çāndilya that *brahma* (and the individual spirit) was conditioned, a doctrine supposed to be that of the old Bhāgavatas or Pāñcarātras; but this is quite uncertain. The Çāndilyan chapter of the Chāndogya Upanishad (above, p. 221) may be thus interpreted, *viz.*, that the (conditioned) individual spirit is identical with *brahma*.

spirit, which enters a heaven where it will enjoy perennial bliss.[1]

Rāmānuja's doctrine inspires the sectarian pantheism of the present time. In this there is a metaphysical basis of conduct, a personal god to be loved or feared, the hope of bliss hereafter. In its essential features it is a very old belief, far older than the philosophy which formulates it.[2] Thus, after the hard saying "fools desire heaven," this desire reasserted itself, and under Rāmānuja's genial interpretation of the Vedānta Sūtras the pious man was enabled to build up his cheerful hope again, withal on the basis of a logic as difficult to controvert as was that of Çankara himself.[3]

Thus far the product of Vedantism is deism. But now with two steps one arrives at the inner portal of sectarianism. First, if *brahma* is a personal god, which of the gods is he, this personal All-spirit? As a general thing the Vedantist answers, 'he is Vishnu'; and adds, 'Vishnu, who embraces as their superior those other gods, Çiva, and Brahmā.' But the sectary is not content with making the All-god one with Vishnu. Vishnu was manifested in the flesh, some say as Krishna, some say as Rāma.[4] The relation of sectary to Vishnuite, and to the All-spirit deist, may be illustrated most clearly by comparison with Occidental religions. One may not acknowledge any personal god as the absolute Supreme Power; again, one may say that this Supreme Power is a

[1] Thibaut, *Introduction to the Vedānta Sūtras*, SBE. xxxiv. p. xxxi; Deussen, *System des Vedānta*, p. 469.

[2] Philosophical illusion, *māyā*, appears first in late Upanishads.

[3] The author of the Dabistān (seventeenth century) tells a Berkeleyan story in regard to Çankara's doctrine of illusion. His enemies wished to test his belief in his own philosophy; so they drove an elephant at him, on which the philosopher ran away. "Ho!" they jeered, "Did you not maintain that all was a mere illusion? Then an elephant is illusion. Yet you take to flight before it." "Yes," replied the philosopher, "all is illusion; there was no elephant, and there was no flight" (ii. 4).

[4] The Smārta (orthodox) Brahman believes, on the other hand, that Vishnu, Çiva, and Brahmā are all mere forms of the Supreme Ātmā.

personal god, Jehovah; again, Jehovah may or may not be regarded as one with Christ. The minuter ramifications of the Christian church then correspond to the sub-sects of Krishnaism or Ramaism.[1]

The Occidental and Oriental conceptions of the trinity are, however, not identical. For in India the trinity, from the Vishnuite point of view, is an amalgamation of Çiva and Brahmā with Vishnu, irrespective of the question whether Vishnu be manifest in Krishna or not; while the Christian trinity amalgamates the form that corresponds to Vishnu with the one that corresponds to Krishna.[2] To the orthodox Brahman, on the other hand, as Williams has very well put it, Krishna is an incarnation of Vishnu, who is himself only an incarnation, that is, a form, of God.

Having now explained the two principal divisions of the modern sects, we can lead the reader into the church of Vishnu. It is a church of two great parties, each being variously subdivided. Of these two parties the Krishnaites are intellectually the weaker, and hence numerically the stronger. All Krishnaites, of course, identify the man-god Krishna with Vishnu, and their sub-sects revert to various teachers, of whom the larger number are of comparatively recent date, although as a body the Krishnaites may claim an antiquity as great, if not greater, than that of the Ramaites.

But the latter party, in their various sub-sects, all claim as

[1] If Mohammed were regarded as one with Allah there would be an Occidental parallel to the Krishna and Rāma sects.

[2] Whether the Hindu trinitarianism derives from the Occident or not (the former view being historically probable, but not possible to prove) the importance of the dogma and its place in Hindu theology is very different to the condition of things in the Christian church. In India trinitarianism is merely a convenience in adjusting the claims of two heterodox sects and orthodoxy, each believer being willing to admit that the god of the other is his own god, only with the understanding that the last is a superior manifestation. In late Çivaism both Vishnu and Brahmā are indeed called the 'sons of God' (Çiva), but in the sense that they are distinctly subordinate creatures of Çiva (JAOS. iv. 147).

their founder either Rāmānuja himself or one of his followers; and since, if the claim be granted, the Rāma sects do but continue his work, we shall begin by following out the result of his teaching as it was interpreted by his disciples; especially since the Krishnaites have left to the Ramaites most of the philosophizing of the church, and devoted themselves more exclusively to the moralities and immoralities of their more practical religion. As a matter of fact, the Ramaites to-day are less religious than philosophical, while in the case of the Krishnaites, with some reservations, the contrary may be said to be the case.

THE RAMAITES.

Since the chief characteristic of growth among Hindu sectaries is a sort of segmentation, like that which conditions the development of amœbas and other lower organisms, it is a foregone conclusion that the Ramaites, having formed one body apart from the Krishnaites, will immediately split up again into smaller segments. It is also a foregone conclusion, since one is really dealing here with human types, that these smaller segments will mutually hate and despise each other much more than they hate their common adversaries. Just as, in old times, a Calvinist hated a Lutheran more than he did a Russian Christian (for he understood his quarrel better), so a 'cat-doctrine' Ramaite hates a 'monkey-doctrine' Ramaite far more than he hates a Krishnaite, while with a Çivaite he often has an amicable union; although the Krishnaite belittles the Ramaite's manifestation of Vishnu, and the Çivaite belittles Vishnu himself.[1]

[1] But some Hindus worship both Vishnu and Çiva without insisting that one is higher than the other. Moreover, there is a Mahratta sect of Vishnuites who complacently worship Buddha (Vishnu's ninth *avatar*) as Viṭhṭhala or Pāṇḍuranga. These are simply eclectic, and their god is without or with quality. Buddha is here not a deceiver, but an instructor (JRAS. 1842, p. 66; IA. xi. 56, 149).

The chief point of difference theologically between the Ramaites is the one just mentioned. The adherents of the 'cat-doctrine' teach that God saves man as a cat takes up its kitten, without free-will on the part of the latter. The monkey-doctrinaires teach that man, in order to be saved, must reach out to their God (Rāma, who is Vishnu, who, again, is All-god, that is, *brahma*), and embrace their God as a monkey does its mother.[1] The resemblance to the Occidental sects here becomes still more interesting. But we have given an earlier example of the doctrine of free grace from the epic, and can now only locate the modern sects that still argue the question. The 'monkey' Ramaites are a sect of the North (*vada*), and hence are called Vada-galais;[2] the 'cat' or Calvinistic Ramaites of the South (*ten*) are called Ten-galais. Outwardly these sects differ in having diverse *mantras*, greetings, dress, and especially in the forehead-signs, which show whether the 'mark of Vishnu' shall represent (Vadagal belief) one or (Tengal) two feet of the god (expressed by vertical lines[3] painted fresh daily on the forehead). The Ten-galais, according to a recent account, are the more numerous and the more materialistic.[4]

All the Ramaites, on the other hand, hold that (1) the deity is not devoid of qualities; (2) Vishnu is the deity and should be worshipped with Lakshmi, his wife; (3) Rāma is the human *avatar* of Vishnu; (4) Rāmānuja and all the great teachers since his day are also *avatars* of Vishnu.

In upper India, about the Ganges, Rāmānuja's disciple,

[1] The Çivaites, too, are divided on the questions both of predestination and of free grace. The greater body of them hold to the 'monkey doctrine'; the Pāçupatas, to the 'cat.'

[2] Sanskrit *kalā*, school (*markaṭa-nyāya* and *m rjāra-nyāya*). The Southern school has its own Veda written in Tamil. Williams, JRAS. xiv. 301. According to the same writer the Ten-galais hold that Vishnu's wife is finite, created, and a mediator; the Vada-galais, that she is infinite, and uncreated.

[3] All Vishnuites have the vertical sign; Çivaites have a horizontal sign (on the forehead).

[4] *Proceed. AOS.* 1894, p. lii. The Vada-school may be affected by Çivaism.

Rāmānand (fifth in descent), who lived in the fourteenth century, has more followers than has the founder. His disciples worship the divine ape, Hanuman[1] (conspicuous in both epics), as well as Rāma. They are called 'the liberated,' Avadhūtas, but whether because they are freed from caste-restrictions,[2] or from the strict rules of eating enjoined by Rāmānuja, is doubtful. Rāmānand himself had in turn twelve disciples. Of these the most famous is Kabīr, whose followers, the Kabīr Panthīs (sect), are widely spread, and of whom no less a person than Nānak, the Sikh, claimed to be a successor. But it will be more convenient to describe the Sikhs hereafter. Of Rāmānand's other disciples that founded sects may be mentioned Kil, whose sectaries, the Khākis, of Oude, unite successfully Rāma-worship, Hanuman-worship, and Çivaite fashions (thus presenting a mixture like that of the southern Mādhvas, who unite the images of Çiva and Vishnu). The Rās Dāsa sect, again, owes to its founder the black Çālagrāma pebble, an object of reverent awe, which gives rise to a sort of sub-cult subsequently imitated by others.[3] Another widely-spread sect which claim Rāmānand as their founder's teacher is that of the Dādū Panthis. This branch also of the Ramaites we shall more appropriately discuss under the head of deism (below). Finally, we have to mention, as an outcome of the Rāmānand faith, the modern

1 A divine monkey appears in the Rig Veda, but not as an object of devotion.

2 The teachers of the Ramaites are generally Brahmans, but no disciples are excluded because of their caste. Rāmānuja adopted the monastic system, which Çankara is said to have taken from the Buddhists and to have introduced into Brahmanic priestly life. Both family priests and cenobites are admitted into his order.

3 What the Linga is to Çivaite the Çālagrāma is to the Vishnuite (who also reveres the *tulasī* wood). The Çālagrāma is a black pebble; the Linga is a white pebble or glass (Williams). The Çivaites have appropriated the *dūrvā* grass as sacred to Ganeça. Sesamum seeds and *dūrvā* are, however, Brahmanically holy. Compare Çat. Br. iv. 5. 10, where *dūrvā* grass is even holier than *kuça*-grass. The rosaries used by the sects have been the subject of a paper by Leumann, and are described by Williams. Thirty-two or sixty-four berries of *eleocarpus ganitrus* (*rudrāksha*) make the Çivaite rosary. That of the Vishnuite is made of lotus-seeds or of *tulsī* wood in one hundred and eight pieces.

Rāmāyana, Ramcaritmanas, the new bible of the sect, composed in the sixteenth century by Tulasīdāsa ('slave of Vishnu'), the greatest of modern Hindu poets. What the Divine Song and the Bhāgavata Purāna are to the Krishnaite, the older (epic) Rāmāyana of Vālmīki and Tulasīdāsa's new poem (of the same name) are to the Ramaite.[1]

THE KRISHNAITES.

There are two great sects that worship Vishnu as especially manifested in the human form of Krishna. But, as distinguished from the philosophical Ramaite, the Krishnaite is not satisfied with a declaration of faith in the man-god, and in fact his chief cult is of the child-god Krishna, the Bāla Gopāla or Infant Shepherd. This recalls the older Krishna (of the Harivança), whose sporting with the milk-maids is a favorite topic in later Krishnaite literature. As a formulated cult; consisting for the most part of observances based on the mystic side of affection for the personal saver of man (the *bhakti* principle of 'devotion,' erotically expanded[2]), this worship obtains both among Cāitanyas and Vallabhas, sects that arose in the sixteenth century.[3]

Cāitanya, born in Bengal in 1485, of whom it is fabled that wise

1 For an account and list of the works of Tulasīdāsā (Tulsīdās), compare IA. xxii. 89, 122, 227. Jayadeva (twelfth century), the author of the Gīta Govinda (translated by Jones, Lassen, and Rückert), is sometimes reckoned falsely to the adherents of Rāmānand, but he is really a Krishnaite.

2 The *bhakti* doctrine is that of the extant Çāndilya Sūtras, which make faith and not works or knowledge a condition of salvation. They are modern, as Cowell, in his preface to the work, has shown. Cowell here identifies Kāçyapa with Kaṇāda, the Vāiçeshika philosopher, his school holding that the individual spirits are infinite in number, distinct from the Supreme Spirit.

3 The infant-cult is of course older than these sects. For an account of the ritual, as well as its intrusion into the earlier cult of the Purānas, with the accompanying resemblances to Madonna-cult, and the new features (the massacre of the innocents, the birth in the stable, the three wise men, etc.) that show borrowing from Christianity, compare Weber's exhaustive treatise referred to above, the *Kṛṣṇajanmāṣṭamī, Krishna's Geburtsfest.*

men came and gave homage to him while he was yet a child, was active in Bengal and Orissa, where his sect (named after him) is one of the most important at the present day. Cāitanya preached a practical as well as a theoretical reform. He taught the equality of all worshippers of whatever caste, and the religious virtue of marriage. At the present day caste-feeling and religious profession are somewhat at variance. But a compromise is affected. While in the temple the high-caste Cāitanyas regard their lowly co-religionists as equals; when out of it they become again arrogantly high-caste. Making a virtue of marriage instead of celibacy caused the sect to become popular with the middle and lower classes, but its adherents are usually drawn from the dregs of the populace.[1] The principle of love for God (that is, for Krishna) is especially dwelt upon by Cāitanya. The devotee should feel such affection as is felt by a young man for a girl. To exercise or inspire this rapt and mystic devotion, recourse is had to singing, dancing, and other familiar means of arousing religious fervor. If the dancing devotee swoons it is a sign that God accepts his love. At the present day Cāitanya himself is regarded as the incarnate deity. He and his two chief disciples, who (like all Gosains, religious Teachers) are divine, form a little sub-trinity for the sect.[2] This sect, like so many others, began as a reform, only to become worse than its rivals.

Vallabha or Vallabhācārya, 'Teacher Vallabha,' was also of the sixteenth century, but his sect belongs especially to the Northwest, while the sphere of Cāitanya's influence was in the Northeast. He lived near the Ganges, is said to have been a scholar, and wrote a commentary on the early life of Krishna in the tenth book of the Bhāgavata Purāna, and on the Divine

1 Williams, *loc. cit.*

2 'Gosain' means shepherd, like Gopāla. Some of the sects, like the Kartābhājs, recognize only the Teacher as God. Williams states that in Bengal a fourth member has been added to this sect-trinity. On Dancing-girls see IA. xiii. 165.

Song. In Bombay and Kutch his disciples are most numerous, the Epicureans of Vishnuism. For their precept is 'eat and enjoy.' No mortification of the senses is allowed. Human love typifies divine love.[1] The teachers acquired great renown and power, assuming and maintaining the haughty title of *mahā rājas* ('great kings'). They are as gods, and command absolutely their devotees.[2] Here the worship of the Infant Krishna reaches its greatest height (or depth). The image of the infant god is daily clothed, bathed, anointed, and worshipped. Religious exercises have more or less of an erotic tendency, and here, if anywhere, as one may learn from Wilson, Williams, and other modern writers on this sect, there are almost as great excesses as are committed among the Çivaite sects. As a sect it is an odd combination of sensual worship and theological speculation, for they have considerable sectarian literature. The most renowned festival of the Infant Krishna is the celebration of the stable-birth of Krishna and of the Madonna (bearing him on her breast), but this we have discussed already. Besides this the Jagannāth procession in Bengal and Orissa, and the great autumnal picnic called the Rās Yātra, are famous occasions for displaying Krishnaite, or, indeed, general Vishnuite zeal. At the Rās Yātra assemble musicians, dancers, jugglers, and other joy-creating additions to the religious feast, the ostensible reason for which is the commemoration of Krishna's dances with the milk-maids. The devotees belong chiefly to the wealthy middle classes. These low sects worship Krishna

1 The philosophical tenet of this sect 'pure *advāita*' (non-duality) distinguishes it from the qualified duality taught by Rāmānuja. This is a reversion to Çankara. The Cāitanya sect teaches not absorption but individual existence in a heaven of sensuous (sensual) pleasure.

2 "In the temples where the Mahārājas (priests) do homage to the idols men and women do homage to the Mahārājas. . . . The best mode of propitiating the god Kṛishna is by ministering to the sensual appetites of his vicars upon earth. Body and soul are literally made over to them, and women are taught to deliver up their persons to Krishna's representatives," Williams, *loc. cit.* p. 309.

with Rādhā (his mistress, instead of Lakshmī, Vishnu's wife). Here, too, as Krishnaites rather than as Vishnuites, are found the 'left-hand' worshippers of the female power.[1]

This sensual corruption of Vishnuism, which is really not Vishnuism but simple Krishnaism, led to two prominent reforms within the fold. Among the Vallabhas arose in protest the Caran Dāsis, who have taken from the Mādhvas of the South their Ten Commandments (against lying, reviling, harsh speech, idle talk, theft, adultery, injury to life, imagining evil, hate, and pride); and evolved for themselves the tenet that faith without works is dead. The same protest was made against the Vallabhas by Svāmi Nārāyana. He was born about 1780 near Lucknow, and advocated a return to Vallabha's purer faith, which had been corrupted. Probably most of the older reformers have had much the same career as had Svāmi Nārāyana. Exalted by the people, who were persuaded by his mesmeric eloquence, he soon became a political figure, a martyr of persecution, a triumphant victor, and then an ascetic, living in seclusion; whence he emerged occasionally to go on tours "like a bishop visiting his diocese" (Williams). He is worshipped as a god.[2] The sect numbers to-day a quarter of a million, some being celibate clergy, some householders.

In contrast to Vishnuism the following points are characteristic of orthodox Brahmanism (Çankara's Vedantism): The

1 On these sects see Wilson, Hunter (Statistical Account), Williams, JRAS. xiv. 289. The festival verses in honor of the Madonna are: "Honor to thee, Devakī, who hast borne Krishna; may the goddess who destroys sin be satisfied, revered by me. Mother of God art thou, Aditi, destroying sin. I will honor thee as the gods honor thee," *etc.* (Weber, *Janmāṣṭamī*, p. 286). The birth-day celebration is not confined to Krishnaites; but in the Rāma sect, though they celebrate the birth, they do not represent the man-god as a suckling. In other respects this feast is imitated from that of Krishna (Weber, p. 310, note). The Rāmacandra celebration takes place in the spring. The birth-day of Ganeça is also celebrated by the Çivaites (in August–September).

2 He himself claimed to be an incarnate god. He adopted the qualified non-duality of Rāmānuja. See Williams' account of him and of the two great temples of the sect, *loc. cit.*

orthodox believe that there is one spirit in three forms, co-eternal impersonal essences—being, knowledge, and joy. When it wills it becomes personal, exists in the object, knows, rejoices, associating itself with illusion. In this state it has three corporeal forms, causal, subtile, gross. With the causal body (identified with illusion, ignorance) it becomes the Supreme Lord, that is, the totality of dreamless human spirits. With the subtile form it becomes the golden seed, or thread-spirit (dreaming spirits); with the gross form it becomes Vīrāj, Vāiçvānara, the waking spirit. The lowest state is that of being wide awake. The personal god (Brahmā, Vishnu, Çiva, of the sectaries) is this it as influenced by the three qualities, *rajas, sattva, tamas* (passion, truth, and ignorance), respectively. Three essences, three corporeal forms, and three qualities constitute, therefore, the threefold trinity of the orthodox, who are called Smārtas, they that 'hold to tradition.'[1] What the sectary rejects, namely, the scriptures (Veda and Upanishads, etc.) and the caste system, that the orthodox retains; what the sectary holds, namely, Rāmānuja's qualified non-duality, and absolute godhead in Çiva or Krishna, that the orthodox rejects (although he may receive the sectary's god into his pantheon). Some of the sects still keep respect for caste, excusing their respect on the ground that "it is well enough for God to ignore social distinctions, but not for man." But caste-distinctions are generally ignored, or there is positive hate of the Brahman. In antithesis to the orthodox, the sectaries all hold one other important tenet. From the idea of *bhakti*, faith or devotion, was developed that of love for Krishna, and then (as an indication of devotion) the confession of the name of the Lord as a means of grace. Hence, on the one hand, the meaningless

[1] From Williams, *loc. cit.* p. 291 ff. The three qualities (sometimes interpreted as activity, purity, and indifference) are met with for the first time in the Atharva Veda, where are found the Vedantic 'name' and 'form' also; Muir, v. p. 309. The three qualities that condition the idealist Vedantist's personal Lord in his causal body are identical with those that constitute the 'nature,' *prakṛti*, of the Sānkhya dualist.

repetition of the sect's special *kirttan*, or liturgies, and *mantra*, or religious formula; the devotion, demanded by the priest, of *man*, *tan*, *dhan* (mind, body,[1] and property); and finally, the whole theory of death-bed confessions. Sinner or heretic, if one die at last with Krishna's name upon the lips he will be saved.[2]

Of the sub-divisions of the sub-sects that we have described, the numbers often run into scores. But either their differences are based on indifferent matters of detail in the cult and religious practice; or the new sect is distinguished from the old simply by its endeavor to make for greater holiness or purity as sub-reformers of older sects. For all the sects appear to begin as reformers, and later to split up in the process of re-reformation.

Two general classes of devotees, besides these, remain to be spoken of. The Sannyāsin, 'renouncer,' was of old a Brahman ascetic. Nowadays, according to Wilson, he is generally a Çivaite mendicant. But any sect may have its Sannyāsins, as it may have its Vāirāgins, 'passionless ones'; although the latter name generally applies to the Vishnuite ascetics of the South.

Apart from all these sects, and in many ways most remarkable, are the sun-worshippers. All over India the sun was (and is) worshipped, either directly (as to-day by the Sauras),[3] or as an incarnate deity in the form of the priest Nimba-āditya, who is said to have arrested the sun's course at one time and to be the sun's representative on earth. Both Puranic authority and inscriptional evidence attest this more direct[4] continuance

1 Among the Vallabhas (above, p. 505). The Teacher is the chief god of most of the Vallabhas (Barth, p. 235). For the Viṭhṭhal view of caste see IA. xi. 152.

2 It is true of other sectaries also, Ramaites and Çivaites, that the mere repetition of their god's name is a means of salvation.

3 Now chiefly in the South. The Dabistān gives several divisions of sun-worshippers. For more details see Barth, p. 258. Apollonius of Tyana saw a sun-temple at Taxila, JRAS. 1859, p. 77.

4 More direct than in the form of Vishnu, who at first is merely the sun. Of the relation with Iranian sun-worship we have spoken above.

of the old Vedic cult. Some of the finest old temples of India, both North and South, were dedicated to the sun.

DEISTIC REFORMING SECTS.

We have just referred to one or two reforming sects that still hold to the sectarian deity. Among these the Mādhvas, founded by (Madhva) Ānandatīrtha, are less Krishnaite or Rāmaite than Vishnuite,[1] and less Vishnuite than deist in general; so much so that Williams declares they must have got their precepts from Christianity, though this is open to Barth's objection that the reforming deistic sects are so located as to make it more probable that they derive from Mohammedanism. Madhva was born about 1200 on the western coast, and opposed Çankara's pantheistic doctrine of non-duality. He taught that the supreme spirit is essentially different to matter and to the individual spirit.[2] He of course denied absorption, and, though a Vishnuite, clearly belonged in spirit to the older school before Vishnuism became so closely connected with Vedānta doctrines. It is the same Sankhyan Vishnuism that one sees in the Divine Song, that is, duality, and a continuation of Çāndilya's ancient heresy.[3]

Here ends the course of India's native religions. From a thousand years B.C. to as many years after she is practically uninfluenced by foreign doctrine, save in externals.

It is of course permissible to separate the reforming sects of

[1] They brand themselves with the Vishnu-mark, are generally high-caste, live in monasteries, and profess celibacy. They are almost unknown in the North. They are generally known by their founder's name, but are also called Brahma-Sampradāyins, 'Brahma-adherents.'

[2] So the Pāçupata doctrine is that the individual spirit is different to the supreme lord and also to matter (*pāça*, the fetter that binds the individual spirit, *paçu*, and keeps it from its Lord, *paçupati*). The fact is that every sectary is more a monotheist than a pantheist. Especially is this true of the Çivaite. The supreme is to him Çiva.

[3] Wilson gives a full account of this sect in the *Asiatick Researches*, xvi, p. 100.

the last few decades from the older reformers; but since we see both in their aim and in their foreign sources (amalgamation with cis-Indic belief) only a logical if not an historical continuance of the older deists, we prefer to treat of them all as factors of one whole; and, from a broader point of view, as successors to the still older pantheistic and unitarian reformers who first predicated a supreme spirit as *ens realissimum*, when still surrounded by the clouds of primitive polytheism. Kabīr and Dādū, the two most important of the more modern reformers, we have named above as nominal adherents of the Rāmānand sect. But neither was really a sectarian Vishnuite.[1]

Kabīr, probably of the beginning of the fifteenth century, the most famous of Rāmānand's disciples, has as religious descendants the sect of the Kabīr Panthīs. But no less an organization than that of the Sikhs look back to him, pretending to be his followers. The religious tenets of the Kabīr Panthīs may be described as those of unsectarian Unitarians. They conform to no rites or *mantras*. Kabīr assailed all idolatry, ridiculed the authority of all scriptures, broke with Pundit and with Mohammedan, taught that outer form is of no consequence, and that only the 'inner man' is of importance. These Panthīs are found in the South, but are located chiefly in and about Benares, in Bengal in the East, and in Bombay in the West. There are said to be twelve divisions of them. Kabīr assailed idolatry, but alas! Discipline requires subordination. The Guru, Teacher, must be obeyed. It was not long before

[1] Of the Kabīr Panthīs Wilson says: "It is no part of their faith to worship any Hindu deity." A glance at the Dabistān will preclude the possibility of claiming much originality for the modern deism of India. This work was written in 1645, and its Persian author describes, as a matter of every-day occurrence, religious debates between 'Jews, Nazarines, Mussulmen, and Hindus,' who meet more to criticise than to examine, but yet to hear explained in full the doctrines of their opponents, in just such tourneys of argument as we showed to be popular among the priests of the Upanishads and epic. Speaking of the Vedas, the author says that every one derives from them arguments in favor of his own creed, whether it be philosophical, mystical, unitarian, atheistic, Judaic, or Christian. Dabistān, vol. ii, p. 45.

he who rejected idolatry became himself a deity. And in fact, every Teacher, Guru, of the sect was an absolute master of thought, and was revered as a god.[1]

In the fifteenth century, near Lahore, was born Nānak (1469), who is the nominal founder of the Sikhs, a body which, as Nānak claimed, was a sect embodying the religion of Kabir himself, of whom he claimed to be a follower. The Granth, or bible of the Sikhs, was first compiled by the pontiff Arjun, in the sixteenth century. Besides the portions written by Nānak and Arjun himself, there were collected into it extracts from the works of 'twelve and a half' other contributors to the volume, Kabīr, Rāmānand, etc.[2] This Granth was subsequently called the Ādigranth, or First Book, to distinguish it from the later, enlarged, collection of several books, one of which was written by Guru Govind, the tenth Sikh pontiff. The change from a religious body to a church militant and political body was made by this Govind in the eighteenth century.[3] The religious sect settled in the Punjāb, became wealthy, excited the greed of the government, was persecuted, rose in revolt, triumphed, and eventually ruled the province. One of the first to precipitate the uprising was the above-mentioned Arjun (fourth pontiff after Nānak). He played the king, was accused of rebellion, imprisoned, and probably killed by the Mohammedans. The Sikhs flew to arms, and from this time on they were perforce little more than robbers and plunderers. Govind made the final change in organization, and,

[1] Before election the Guru must be examined. If the faithful are not satisfied, they may reject him, but, having elected him, they are bound to obey him implicitly. He can excommunicate, but he may not punish corporally. This deification of the Guru was retained by the Sikhs, and the office was made hereditary among them (by Arjun), till Govind, the tenth pontiff, who left no successor, declared that after his death the Granth (bible) should be the sole authority of the church.

[2] The 'half' contributor was a woman, and hence was not reckoned as a complete unit.

[3] The word Sikh means 'disciple' (of Nānak). The name the Sikhs assumed as a nation was Singhs (*siṁhas*), 'Lions of the Punjāb.'

so to speak, at one blow created a nation, for the church at his hands was converted into the united militant body called Khālsā under the Guru as pontiff-king, with a 'council of chiefs.' They were vowed to hate the Mohammedan and Hindu. All caste-distinctions were abrogated. Govind instituted the worship of Steel and Book (sword and bible). His orders were: "If you meet a Mohammedan, kill him; if you meet a Hindu, beat and plunder him." The Sikhs invoked the 'Creator' as 'highest lord,' either in the form of Vishnu or Rāma. Their founder, Nānak, kept, however, the Hindu traditions in regard to rites. He was a travelled merchant, and is said to have been in Arabia. As an example of the Sikh bible may serve the following extracts, translated from the original dialect by Trumpp and Prinsep respectively:

From Trumpp:

True is the Lord, of a true name,
But the import of (this) language is infinite.
They say and beg, give, give!
The Liberal gives presents.
What may again be put before (him)
By which his court may be seen?
What word may be spoken by the mouth,
Which having heard he may bestow love?
Early reflect on the greatness of the True Name.[1]
From his beneficence comes clothing,
From his look the gate of salvation.
Nānak (says): Thus it is known,
That he himself is altogether truthful.

From Prinsep:

Thou art the Lord, to thee be praise;
All life is with thee.
Thou art my parents; I, thy child.
All happiness is from thy mercy.
No one knows God.

[1] The 'true name,' *sat nām*, is the appellation of God.

Highest Lord among the highest,
Of all that is thou art the regulator,
And all that is from thee obeys thy will,
Thy movements, thy pleasure; thou alone knowest.
Nānak, thy slave is a free-will offering unto thee.[1]

The religious side of this organization remained under the name of Udāsis,[2] or Nirmalas ('spotless ones'). The Ādigranth was extended by other additions, such as that of Govind (above), and now constitutes a large heterogeneous collection of hymns and moral rules. Seven sub-sects of the religious body were developed in course of time. The military body has a well-known history. They were complete masters of the Punjāb in 1764, and remained there as an independent race till that province was occupied by the British in 1848. Both Kabīr and his follower Nānak were essentially reformers. They sought for a religion which should rest on the common truths of Hinduism and Mohammedanism.[3] As a matter of form the political party of Govind, the Govind Singhs, or Simhis, worshipped the Hindu gods, and they showed respect for the Brahman priests for a long while; but they rejected the Vedas and caste — the two most essential features of orthodoxy.[4]

Dādū, the second great reformer, who shows Mohammedan influence quite as plainly as does Kabīr, also claimed Rāmānand as his teacher. The sects that revert to Dādū, Dādū Panthīs, now number more than half an hundred. Some of the votaries are soldiers; some are mendicants. The founder lived about the end of the sixteenth century. The outward

[1] JRAS. 1846, p. 43, Prinsep's compilation (Wilson). Compare Trumpp, *ib.* v. 197 (1871); and Ādigranth, 1877.

[2] This sept was founded by a descendant of Nānak.

[3] It was not till Mohammedan persecution influenced them that the religious Sikhs of Nānak became the political haters and fighters of Govind.

[4] It is said that Govind sacrificed to Durgā the life of one of his own disciples to prepare himself for his ministry. Trumpp, Ādigranth; Barth, p. 204. The lives of the later Gurus will be found in Elphinstone's history and Prinsep's sketch (a *résumé* by Barth, p. 248 ff.).

practices of the sects differ somewhat from those of other sects. Like Persians, they expose their dead. They are found about Ājmīr and other districts of the North, in the seats of the Jains. Their faith and reformatory tendency may be illustrated by the following extract, as translated by Wilson:[1]

"He is my God who maketh all things perfect. O foolish one, God is not far from you. He is near you. God's power is always with you. Whatever is to be is God's will. What will be will be. Therefore, long not for grief or joy, because by seeking the one you may find the other. All things are sweet to them that love God. I am satisfied with this, that happiness is in proportion to devotion. O God, Thou who art truth, grant me contentment, love, devotion, and faith. . . . Sit ye with humility at the feet of God, and rid yourselves of the sickness of your bodies. From the wickedness of the body there is much to fear, because all sins enter into it. Therefore, let your dwelling be with the fearless, and direct yourselves toward the light of God. For there neither sword nor poison have power to destroy, and sin cannot enter. The greatest wisdom is in preventing your minds from being influenced by bad passions, and in meditating upon the One God. Afford help also to the poor stranger. Meditate on Him by whom all things were made."[2]

This tradition of reform is maintained by others without intermission down to the present century, and the Mādhvas and Svāmi Nārāyana, of whom we have spoken above as being more directly connected with sectarian bodies, are, in fact, scarcely more concerned with the tenets of the latter than were Kabīr and Dādū. Thus the seventeenth century sees the rising of the Bābālāls and Sādhus; and the eighteenth, of the Satnāmis, 'worshippers of the true name,' who, with other minor bodies, such as the Nāngi Panthīs, founded by Dedrāj in this century, are really pure deists, although some of them, like the Viṭhṭhals, claim to be followers of Kabīr. And so they are, in spirit at least.

[1] With some small verbal alterations.

[2] The conclusion of this extract shows the narrower polemic spirit: "Pundits and Qāzīs are fools. What avails it to collect a heap of books? Let your minds freely meditate on the spirit of God. Wear not away your lives by studying the Vedas."

THE DEISM OF TO-DAY.[1]

And thus one arrives at modern deism, not as the result of new influences emanating from Christian teaching, but rather as the legitimate successor of that deism which became almost monotheistic in the first centuries after our era, and has ever since varied with various reformers between two beliefs, inclining now to the pantheistic, now to the unitarian conception, as the respective reformers were influenced by Vedānta or Sānkhya (later Mohammedan) doctrine.

The first of the great modern reformers is Rāmmohun Roy, who was born in 1772, the son of a high-caste Krishnaite Brahman. He studied Persian and Arabic literature at Patna, the centre of Indic Mohammedan learning. When a mere boy, he composed a tract against idolatry which caused him to be banished from home. He lived at Benares, the stronghold of Brahmanism, and afterwards in Tibet, the centre of Buddhism. "From his earliest years," says Williams, "he displayed an eagerness to become an unbiassed student of all the religions of the globe." He read the Vedas, the Pāli Buddhist works, the Kurān, and the Old Testament in the original; and in later years even studied Greek that he might properly understand the New Testament. The scholastic philosophy of the Hindus appeared to him, however, as something superior to what he found elsewhere, and his efforts were directed mainly to purifying the national faith, especially from idolatry. It was at his instigation that the practice of widow-burning was abolished (in 1829) by the British. He was finally ostracized from home as a schismatic, and retired to Calcutta, uniting about him a small body of Hindus and Jains, and there estab-

[1] For the data of the following paragraphs on the deistic reformers of to-day we are indebted to an article of Professor Williams, which first appeared in the thirteenth volume of the *Journal of the Royal Asiatic Society*, and has since been published in the same author's *Brahmanism and Hinduism*.

lished a sort of church or sect, the Ātmīya Sabhā, 'spiritual society' (1816), which met at his house, but eventually was crushed by the hostility of the orthodox priests. He finally adopted a kind of Broad-church Christianity or Unitarianism, and in 1820, in his 'Precepts of Jesus' and in one of his later works, admits that the simple moral code of the New Testament and the doctrines of Christ were the best that he knew. He never, however, abjured caste; and his adoption of Christianity, of course, did not include the dogma of the trinity: "Whatever excuse may be pleaded in favor of a plurality of persons of the Deity can be offered with equal propriety in defence of polytheism" (Final Appeal). Founded by him, the first theistic church was organized in 1828 at Calcutta, and formally opened in 1830 as the Brāhma Samāj ('the Congregation of God'). In doing this he wished it to be understood that he was not founding a new sect, but a pure monotheistic worship. The only creed was a confession of faith in the unity of God. For himself, he abandoned pantheism, adopted the belief in a final judgment, in miracles, and in Christ as the 'Founder of true religion.' He died in 1833 in England. His successor, Debendranāth Tāgore,[1] was not appointed leader of the Brāhma Samāj till much later; after he had founded a church of his own ('the Truth-teaching Society'), which lasted for twenty years (1839–1859), before it was united with the Brāhma Samāj. In the meantime Debendranāth had become a member of the latter society (1841). He established the covenant of the Samāj, a vow taken by every member to lead holy lives, to abstain from idolatry, to worship no created object, but only God, the One without a second,[2] the Creator, Preserver, Destroyer, the Giver of Emancipation.

[1] Born in 1818.

[2] *ekamātrādvitīya* (masculine); with this form contrast below, in the Brāhma Dharma (religion) of Debendranāth, the neuter *ekam evādvitīyam*. The only God of the first Samāj is a person; that of the reform is exoterically Nature.

The church was newly organized in 1844 with a regularly appointed president and minister, and with the administration of the oath to each believer. This is the Ādi Brāhma Samāj, the First Congregation, in distinction from the schism which soon took place. The first quarrel in this church was due to a difference of opinion in regard to the authority of the Vedas. Some members rejected them, others maintained their infallibility; while between these extremes lay various other opinions, some members questioning the infallibility of the Vedas but maintaining their authority. By a majority vote it was eventually decided that the Vedas (and Upanishads) were not infallible.

In the meantime in other provinces rival Samājas had been formed, and by 1850 there were several of these broad-minded Congregations, all trammelled by their environment, but doing their best to be liberal.

We pause here in the compilation of the data recorded in this paragraph to assert, independently of Professor Williams, who has given us the historical facts, but would doubtless not wish to have imputed to himself the following judgment which we are led to pass, that the next step of the Samāj placed it upon the only ground where the objects of this church can be attained, and that in the subsequent reform of this reform, which we shall have to record below, a backward step has been taken. For Debendranāth changed the essential character of the Samāj from pantheistic theism to pure deism. The inner circle of the society had a narrower declaration of faith, but in his Brāhma Dharma, published about 1850, Debendranāth formulated four articles of faith, to subscribe to which admitted any one into the Samāj. These articles read as follows: (1) Brahma (neuter) alone existed in the beginning before the universe; naught else existed; It [He] created all the universe. (2) It [He] is eternal, intelligent, infinite, blissful, self-governed (independent), without parts, just one (neuter) without a second, all-pervading, the ruler (masculine noun) of all, refuge of all, omniscient, omnipotent, immovable, perfect, without parallel (all these adjectives are neuter). (3) By worship of this One alone can bliss be obtained in the next world and in this. (4) The worship of this (neuter) One consists in love toward this (One) and in performing works pleasant (to this One).

This deism denies an incarnate God, scriptural authority, and the good of rites and penance; but it teaches the efficacy of prayer and repentance, and the belief in God as a personal Creator and Heavenly Father.[1] Intellectual — anything but emotional — it failed to satisfy many worshippers. And as a church it was conservative in regard to social reforms.

In 1858 Keshub Chunder Sen, a Vishnuite by family, then but twenty, joined the Samāj, and being clever, young, eloquent, and cultivated, he, after the manner of the Hindus, undertook to reform the church he had just entered, first of all by urging the abolition of caste-restrictions. Debendranāth was liberal enough to be willing to dispense with his own thread (the caste-mark), but too wisely conservative to demand of his co-religionists so complete a break with tradition and social condition. For the sacred thread to the Hindu is the sign of social respectability. Without it, he is out of society. It binds him to all that is dearest to him. The leader of the older Samāj never gave up caste; the younger members in

[1] But, as will be noticed in the four articles (which are in part a compilation of phrases from the Upanishads) the personality of Brahmā is not insisted on for the outer church. For this reason, although the inner church doubtless understands It as He, yet this neuter should be preserved in the translation. The articles are so drawn up as to enable any deist to subscribe (without Vedantic belief as a condition of acceptance) to the essential creed of the Congregation. One or two sentences in the original will reveal at a glance the origin of the phraseology: *brahma* (being) *vā ekam idam-agra āsīt; tad idaṁ sarvam asṛjat; tad eva nityam, ekam evādvitīyam; tasmin prītis . . . tadupāsanam.* Compare Chāndogya Upanishad: *sad* (being) *idam-agra āsīd ekam evādvitīyam;* and the Vājasaneyī-Brāhmana Upanishad: *brahma vā idam-agra āsīt*, etc.

doing so mix religion with social etiquette, and so hinder the advance they aim at. Sen urged this and other reforms, all repugnant to the society in which he lived, changes in the rite at the worship of ancestors, alterations in the established ritual at birth-ceremonies and funerals, abolition of polyandry and of child-marriages, and, worst of all, granting permission to marry to those of different castes. His zeal was directed especially against caste-restrictions and child-marriages. Naturally he failed to persuade the old Samāj to join him in these revolutionary views, to insist on which, however sensible they seem, cannot be regarded otherwise than as indiscreet from the point of view of one who considers men and passions. For the Samāj, in the face of tremendous obstacles, had just secured a foothold in India. Sen's headlong reforms would have smashed to pieces the whole congregation, and left India more deeply prejudiced than ever against free thought. Sen failed to reform the old church, so in 1865 he, with some ardent young enthusiasts, reformed themselves into a new church, ceremoniously organized in 1866 as the Brāhma Samāj of India, in distinction from the Calcutta Samāj, or Ādi Samāj. A futile effort was made to get all the other local congregations to join the new Samāj, the last, of course, to be the first and head of the organization.

The new Samāj renounced caste-restrictions and Brahmanism altogether, but it was tainted with the hysterical *bhakti* fervor which Sen inherited from his childhood's religion, and which (if one may credit Williams' words) "brought the latest development of Indian Theism into closer harmony with Christian ideas." The chief leader of this Samāj besides Sen was his cousin Protāp Chunder Mozoomdar, official secretary of the society. Its literary organ is the *Indian Mirror*.

The reform of this reform of course followed before long. The new Samāj was accused of making religion too much a matter of emotion and excitement. Religious fervor, *bhakti*, had led to "rapturous singing of hymns in the streets"; and to the establishment of a kind of love-feasts ('Brahma-feasts' they were called) of prayer and rejoicing; and, on the other hand, to undue asceticism and self-mortification.[1] Sen himself was revered too much. One of the most brilliant, eloquent, and fascinating of men, he was adored by his followers — as a god! He denied that he had accepted divine honors, but there is no doubt, as Williams insists, that his Vishnuite tendency led him to believe himself peculiarly the recipient of divine favors. It was charged against him that he asserted that all he did was at God's command, and that he believed himself perennially inspired.[2] If one add to this that he was not only divinely inspired, but that he had the complete control of his society, it would appear to be easy to foresee where the next reformer might strike. For Sen "was not only bishop, priest, and deacon all in one," says Williams, "he was a Pope, from whose decision there was no appeal." But it was not this that caused the rupture. In 1877 this reformer, "who had denounced early marriages as the curse of India," yielded to natural social ambition and engaged his own young daughter to a Koch (Rājbanshi) prince, who in turn was a mere boy. The Samāj protested with all its might, but the marriage was performed the next year, withal to the accompaniment of idolatrous rites.[3] After this Sen became somewhat theatrical. In

[1] It is interesting to see this fervor, or ecstatic delirium, surviving from the time of the Rig Veda, where already (albeit only in the latest hymns, which are quite Brahmanic) flourishes the mad *muni;* and fervid asceticism ('heat,' *tapas*) begins to appear as a means of salvation. RV. x. 109, 136.

[2] "I regard myself as Christ and Cāitanya," reported by Sen's own missionary as the words of the former. Sen's disciples deny some of these assertions, but they seem to be substantiated, and Sen's own language shows that he claimed miraculous powers. Compare the discussions on this point, JRAS. xiii. 281 ff.

[3] This was afterwards excused on the ground that the marriage would not have been legal without these rites. But Sen presumably was aware of this in advance. From the performance of the rites he had the decency to absent himself. It should be said, however, in Sen's behalf, that the marriage itself had nothing revolting about

1879 he recognized (in a proclamation) God's Motherhood — the old dogma of the female divine. In 1880 he announced, in fervid language, that Christianity was the only true religion: "It is Christ who rules British India, and not the British Government. England has sent out a tremendous moral force in the life and character of that mighty prophet to conquer and hold this vast empire. None but Jesus, none but Jesus, none but Jesus, ever deserved this bright, this precious diadem, India, and Jesus shall have it. . . . Christ is a true Yogi." He accepts Christ, but not as God, only as inspired saint (as says Williams). More recently, Sen proposed an amalgamation of Hinduism, Mohammedanism, and Christianity as the true religion.

Meanwhile the Samāj was rent by discord. Sen's opponents, the new reformers, were unable, however, to oust the brilliant leader from the presidency. Consequently they established a new church, intended to be a General Congregation, the fourth development (1878) of the Brāhma Samāj. And so the fight has gone on ever since. At the present day there are more than a hundred deistic churches, in which the devotional exercises consist in part of readings from the Vedas, Bible, Kurān, and Avesta. The Ārya Samāj is one of the most important of the later churches, some of which endeavor to obtain undefiled religion by uniting into one faith what seems best in all; others, by returning to the Vedas and clearing them of what they think to be later corruptions of those originally pure scriptures. Of the latter sort is the Ārya Samāj. Its leader, Dayānanda, claims that the Vedas are a true revelation. The last reformer of which we have knowledge is a bright young high-caste Hindu of upper India, who is about to found a 'world-

it, and though in consenting to it Sen violated his faith, as is evident from the protest of the Samāj, yet was the marriage not an extreme case of child-marriage, for both the 'children' were sixteen. Sen's own excuse (he thought excuse necessary) was that he was inspired when he consented to the nuptials.

religion,' for which task he is now making preliminary studies. He has visited this country, and recently told us that, if he had time, he could easily convert America. But his first duty lies, of course, in the reformation of India's reformations, especially of the Samājas!

The difficulty with which all these reformers and re-reformers have to contend is pitifully clear. Their broad ideas have no fitting environment. Their leaders and thinkers may continue to preach deism, and among their equals they will be heard and understood. They are, however, not content with this. They must form churches. But a church implies in every case an unnatural and therefore dangerous growth, caused by the union either of inferior minds (attracted by eloquence, but unable to think) with those that are not on the same plane, or of ambitious zealots with reluctant conservatists. Many join the church who are not qualified to appreciate the leader's work. They overload the founder's deism with the sectarian theism from which they have not really freed themselves. On the other hand, younger men, who have been educated in English colleges and are imbued with the spirit of practical reform, enter the church to use it as an instrument for social progress. So the church is divided, theists and reformers both being at odds with the original deists; and the founder is lucky if he escapes being deified by one party and being looked upon by the other as too dull.[1]

[1] The theistic tendency in the Hindu mind is so exaggerated that even now it is with the greatest difficulty that the vulgar can be restrained from new idolatry. Not only priests, but even poets are regarded as gods. Jñāndev and Tukārām, the hymn-makers of the Mahratta Viṭhṭhals, are demi-gods to-day (IA. xi. 56. 149). A few striking examples are almost requisite to make an Occidental reader understand against what odds the deism of India has to contend. In 1830 an impudent boy, who could train snakes, announced that he could also work miracles. The boy was soon accepted as Vishnu's last *avatar*; hymns, *abhangs*, were sung to him, and he was worshipped as a god even after his early demise (from a snake-bite). A weaver came soon after to the temple, where stood the boy's now vacant shrine, and fell asleep there at night. In the morning he was perplexed to find himself a god. The people

India is no more prepared as a whole for the reception of the liberal views of the Samāj than was the negro for the right to vote. Centuries of higher preliminary education are needed before the people at large renounce their ancestral, their natural faith. A few earnest men may preach deism; the people will remain polytheists and pantheists for many generations. Then, again, the Samājas have to contend not only with the national predisposition, but with every heretical sect, and, besides these, with the orthodox church. But thus far their chief foe is, after all, their own heart as opposed to their head. As long as deistic leaders are deified by their followers, and regard themselves as peculiarly inspired, they will preach in vain. Nor can they with impunity favor the substitution of emotion for ideas in a land where religious emotion leads downwards as surely as falls a stone that is thrown.

had accepted him as their snake-conquering god in a new form. The poor weaver denied his divinity, but that made no difference. In 1834 the dead boy-god was still receiving flowers and prayers. Another case: In the eighties some Englishmen on entering a temple were amazed to see revered as an *avatar* of Vishnu the brass castings of the arms of the old India Co. This god was washed and anointed daily. Even a statue of Buddha (with the inscription still upon it) was revered as Vishnu. In 1880 a meteorite fell in Behār. In 1882 its cult was fully established, and it was worshipped as the 'miraculous god.' A Mohammedan inscription has also been found deified and regularly worshipped as a god. JRAS. 1842, p. 109; 1884, pt. iii, pp. l, lix.

CHAPTER XVIII.

RELIGIOUS TRAITS OF THE WILD TRIBES.

BESIDES the phases of pure Aryan and modified Aryan religions which have already been examined, there are represented in India several other aspects of civilized religion; for, apart from Brahmanic and sectarian worships, and apart from Tamil (southern) imitations of these, there are at present in the country believers of the Jewish religion to the number of seventeen thousand; of Zoroastrianism, eighty-seven thousand; of Christianity, two and a quarter millions; of Mohammedanism, more than fifty-seven millions. But none of these faiths, however popular, comes into an historical account of India's religions in a greater extent than we have brought them into it already, that is, as factors of minor influence in the development of native faiths till, within the last few centuries, Mohammedanism, which has been the most important of them all in transfiguring the native theistic sects, draws a broad line across the progress of India's religious thought.

All these religions, however, whether aboriginal or imported, must again be separated from the more general phenomena of superstition which are preserved in the beliefs of the native wild tribes. One descends here to that lowest of rank undergrowth which represents a type of religious life so base that its undifferentiated form can be mated with like growths from all over the world. These secondary religions are, therefore, important from two points of view, that of their universal aspect, and, again, that of their historical connection with the upper Indic growth above them;[1] for it is almost certain that some

[1] The Dasyus, heathen, or pagans, are by no means a wholly uncivilized mass to the poets of the Rig Veda. They have wealth, build forts, and are recognized as

of their features have conditioned the development of the latter.

The native wild tribes of India (excluding the extreme Northern Tibeto-Burman group) fall into two great classes, that of the Kolarians and that of the Dravidians, sometimes distinguished as the Yellow and the Black races respectively. The former, again, are called Indo-Chinese by some writers, and the geographical location of this class seems, indeed, to show that they have generally displaced the earlier blacks, and represent historically a yellow wave of immigration from the Northeast (through Tibet) prior to the Aryan white wave (from the Northwest), which latter eventually treated them just as they had treated the aboriginal black Dravidians.[1] Of the Kolarians the foremost representatives are the Koles, the Koches, the Sunthāls, and the Savāras (Sauras), who are all regarded by Johnston as the yellow Dasyus, barbarians, of the earliest period; while he sees in the Vāiçyas, or third caste of the Hindu political divisions, the result of a union of the Northwest and Northeast conquerors. But, although the Vāiçyas are called 'yellow,' yet, since they make the most important numerical factor of the Aryans, this suggestion can scarcely be accepted, for there is no evidence to show that the yellow Mongoloid barbarians were amalgamated so early with the body politic of the Aryans. The chief representatives of the Dra-

living in towns or forts. We learn little about them in Brahmanic literature, except that they bury their dead and with them their trinkets. Their graves and dolmen grave-stones are still found.

1 Some scholars think that the Dravidians entered from the Northwest later than the Kolarians, and, pushing them to either side of the peninsula, descended through them to the South. The fact that some Kolarian tribes closely related by language are separated (to East and West) by hundreds of miles, and have lost all remembrance of their former union, favors this view of a Dravidian wedge splitting and passing through the Kolarian mass. But all here is guess-work. The Dravidians may have been pushed on by Kolarians that entered later, while the latter may have been split by the Aryan invasion; and this seems to us more probable, because the other theory does not explain why the Kolarians did not go South instead of taking to the hills of the East and West.

vidians, on the other hand, are the Khonds and Gonds of the middle of the peninsula, together with the Orāons and the Todas of the extreme South.[1] All of these tribes are of course sub-divided, and in some degree their religious practices have followed the bent of their political inclinations. We shall examine first the religions of the older tribes, the Dravidians, selecting the chief features or such traits as have peculiar interest.

THE DRAVIDIANS.

Gonds: These savages, mentioned in early literature, are the most numerous and powerful of the wild tribes, and appear to have been less affected by outside belief than were any other, except the related Khonds. Their religion used to consist in adoring a representation of the sun, to which were offered human sacrifices.[2] As among the Orāons, a man of straw (literally) is at the present day substituted for the human victim. Besides the sun, the moon and stars are worshipped by them. They have stones for idols, but no temples.[3] Devils, witchcraft, and the evil eye also are feared. They sacrifice animals,

1 The whole list of these tribes as given by Cust, *Sketch of the Modern Languages of the East Indies*, is as follows: The Kolarians include the Sunthāls, Mundāri Koles (Koches), Khārians, Juangs, Korwas, Kurs, Savāras, Mehtos, Gadabas, Pāhārias; the Dravidians include the tribes called Tamil, Telugu, Kanarese, Mayayālim, Tulu, Kudagu, Toda, Kota, Khond, Gond, Orāon, Rājmahāli, Keikādi, Yerukāla.

2 The sacrifices of the wild tribes all appear to have the object of pleasing or placating the god with food, animal or vegetable; just as the Brahmanic sacrifice is made to please, with the secondary thought that the god will return the favor with interest; then that he is bound to do so. Sin is carried away by the sacrifice, but this seems to be merely an extension of the simpler idea; the god condones a fault after an expression of repentance and good-will. What lies further back is not revealed in the early texts, though it is easy to make them fruitful in "theories of sacrifice."

3 Of course no tribe has what civilization would call a temple, but some have what answer to it, namely, a filthy hut where live the god and his priest. Yet the Gonds used to build roads and irrigate very well.

and, with the exception of the Rāj Gonds,[1] have been so little affected by Hindu respect for that holiest of animals, that they slaughter cows at their wedding-feasts, on which occasion the bacchanalian revels in which they indulge are accompanied with such excess as quite to put them upon the level of Çivaite bestiality. The pure Gonds are junglemen, and have the virtues usually found among the lowest savages, truth, honesty, and courage. Murder is no crime, but lying and stealing are sinful; for cowardice is the greatest crime, and lying and stealing (instead of straightforward and courageous robbery and murder) are regarded as indications of lack of courage. But the 'impure,' that is the mixed Gonds that have been corrupted by mingling with Hindus and other tribes, lie and steal like civilized people. In fact, the mixed Gonds are particularly noted for servility and dishonesty. The uncivilized Gonds of the table-lands are said still to cut up and eat their aged relatives and friends, not to speak of strangers unfortunate enough to fall into their hands. Among the pure Gonds is found the practice of carrying an axe, which is the sign of their religious devotion to the sacrifice-god.[2] The favorite religious practice used to be to take a prisoner alive, force him to bow before the god-stone, and, at the moment when he bent his head, to cut it off. To this and to self-defence against other gods (wild beasts) the hatchet is devoted, while for war are used the bow and knife. One particular celebration of the Gonds deserves special notice. They have an annual feast and worship of the snake. The service is entirely secret, and all that is known

1 The (Rāj) Gonds were first subdued by the Rājputs, and where the Hindus and Gonds have intermarried they are known as Rāj Gonds. Others have become the 'Mohammedan Gonds.' Otherwise, in the case of the pure or 'Āssul' (the greater number), neither Hindu nor Mohammedan has had much influence over them, either socially or religiously. The Gonds whipped the British in 1818; but since then they have become 'pacified.'

2 It is often no more than a small hatchet stuck in the belt, if they wear the latter, which in the jungle is more raiment than they are wont to put on.

of it is that it is of esoteric, perhaps phallic character. Both at the sun-feast and snake-feast[1] licentious and bacchanalian worship are combined, and the latter trait is also the chief feature of wedding and funeral sports. In the former case (the natives of the same tribe intermarry, but with the same pretence of running off with the bride that is found in the Hindu ritual)[2] there is given a wedding feast by the bridegroom's father, and the feast ends with a *causerie de lundi* (the favorite drink of the Gonds is called *lundi*); while on the latter occasion there is a mourning feast, or wake, which also ends in general drunkenness.

The Khonds: Even more striking is the religion of the Khonds. Their chief rite is human sacrifice to the earth-goddess,[3] Tari; but, like the Gonds, they worship the sun as chief divinity. Other gods among them are the river-god, rain-god, spring, wealth, hill-god, and smallpox-god. All their religious feasts are excuses for excess both in drinking and otherwise. One of their beliefs is that there is a river of hell, which flows around a slippery rock, up which climbs the one that would escape torment. Their method of sacrificing a human victim is to put him into the cleft of a tree, where he is squashed, or into fire. They seem to have an odd objection to shedding blood for this purpose, and in this respect may be compared with the Thugs. Another very interesting trait is the religion which is intertwined with business, and its peculiar features. Victims offered either to the sun or to the war-god serve to mark boundary lines. Great is the patience with which

[1] The snake in the tree is common to many tribes, both being tutelary. The Gonds are 'sons of the forest trees,' and of the northern bull.

[2] It seems to us that this feature need not be reckoned as a sign of exogamy. It is often, so far as we have observed, only a stereotyped form to express bashfulness.

[3] Some say earth-*god*. Thus the account given in JRAS. 1842. p. 172, says 'male earth-god as ancestor,' but most modern writers describe the divinity as a female. Some of the Khonds worship only earth (as a peacock). This is the peacock revered at the Pongol?

these victims, called *merias*, are waited for. The sacrificer captures fit specimens when they are young, and treats them with particular kindness till they are almost grown up. Indeed, they are treated thus by the whole village. At the appointed time they are slowly crushed to death or smothered in a mud bath, and bits of their flesh are then cut out and strewn along the boundary lines. Boys are preferred, but either boys or girls may be used. This sacrifice is sometimes made directly to the 'Boundary-god,'[1] an abstraction which is not unique; for, besides the divinities recorded above, mention is made also of a 'Judgment-god.' Over each village and house preside the Manes of good men gone; while the 'father is god on earth' to every one. They used to destroy all their female children, and this, together with their national custom of offering human sacrifices, has been put down with the greatest difficulty by the British, who confess that there is every probability that in reality the crime still obtains among the remoter clans. These Khonds are situate in the Madras presidency, and are aborigines of the Eastern Ghāts. The most extraordinary views about them have been published. Despite their acknowledged barbarity, savageness, and polytheism, they have been soberly credited with a belief in One Supreme God, 'a theism embracing polytheism,' and other notions which have been abstracted from their worship of the sun as 'great god.'

Since these are by far the most original savages of India, a completer sketch than will be necessary in the case of others may not be unwelcome. The chief god is the light- or sun-god. "In the beginning the god of light created a wife, the goddess of earth, the source of evil." On the other hand, the

[1] The Gonds also have a boundary-god. Graves as boundaries are known among the Anglo-Saxons. Possibly Hermes as boundary-god may be connected with the Hermes that conducts souls; or is it simply as thief-god that he guards from theft? The Khond practice would indicate that the corpse (as something sacred) made the boundary, not that the boundary was made by running a line to a barrow, as is the case in the Anglo-Saxon connection between barrow and bound.

sun-god is a good god. Tari, the earth-divinity, tried to prevent Bella[1] Pennu (sun-god) from creating man. But he cast behind him a handful of earth, which became man. The first creation was free of evil; earth gave fruit without labor (the Golden Age); but the dark goddess sowed in man the seed of sin. A few were sinless still, and these became gods, but the corrupt no longer found favor in Bella (or Boora) Pennu's eyes. He guarded them no more. So death came to man. Meanwhile Bella and Tari contended for superiority, with comets, whirlwinds, and mountains, as weapons. According to one belief, Bella won; but others hold that Tari still maintains the struggle. The sun-god created all inferior deities, of rain, fruit, hunt, boundaries, etc., as well as all tutelary local divinities.[2] Men have four kinds of fates. The soul goes to the sun, or remains in the tribe (each child is declared by the priest to be N. N. deceased and returned), or is re-born and suffers punishments, or is annihilated.[3] The god of judgment lives on Grippa Valli, the 'leaping rock,' round which flows a black river, and up the rock climb the souls with great effort. The Judgment-

1 Some may compare Bellerophon!

2 Tutelary deities are of house, village, groves, etc. The 'House-god' is, of course, older than this or than Hinduism. The Rig Veda recognizes Vāstoshpati, the 'Lord of the House,' to whom the law (Manu, iii. 89, etc.) orders oblations to be made. But Hinduism prefers a female house-goddess (see above, p. 374). Windisch connects this Vedic divinity, Vāstos-pati, with Vesta and Hestia. The same scholar compares Keltic *vassus*, *vassallus*, originally 'house-man'; and very ingeniously equates Vassorix with Vedic *vasām rājā* = *viçām rājā*, 'king of the house-men' (clan), like *húskarlar*, 'house-fellows,' in Scandinavian (domesticus, οἰκέτης). Windisch, *Vassus und Vassallus*, in the *Bericht. d. k. Sächs. Gesell.* 1892, p. 174.

3 That is to say, a dead man's spirit goes to heaven, or is re-born whole in the tribe, or is re-born diseased (anywhere, this is penal discipline), or finally is annihilated. Justly may one compare the Brahmanic division of the Manes into several classes, according to their destination as conditioned by their manner of living and exit from life. It is the same idea ramifying a little differently; not a case of borrowing, but the growth of two similar seeds. On the other hand, the un-Aryan doctrine of transmigration may be due to the belief of native wild tribes. It appears first in the Çatapatha, but is hinted at in the 'plant-souls' of the RV. (above, pp. 145, 204, 432), possibly in RV. i. 164. 30, 38; Bötlingk, *loc. cit.*, 1893, p. 88.

god decides the fate of the soul, sending it to the sun (the sun-soul), or annihilating it, etc. The chief sins are, to be inhospitable, to break an oath, to lie except to save a guest, to break an old custom, to commit incest, to contract debts (for which the tribe has to pay), to be a coward, to betray council. The chief virtues are, to kill in battle, to die in battle, to be a priest, to be the victim of a sacrifice. Some of the Khonds worship the sun-god; some the earth-goddess, and ascribe to her all success and power, while they hold particularly to human sacrifice in her honor. They admit (theoretically) that Bella is superior, but they make Tari the chief object of devotion, and in her honor are held great village festivals. They that do not worship Tari do not practice human sacrifice. Thus the Çivaite sacrifice of man to the god's consort is very well paralleled by the usage that obtains among them. The Khond priests may indulge in any occupation except war; but some exercise only their priestcraft and do nothing else. The chief feast to the sun-god is Salo Kallo (the former word means 'cow-pen'; the latter, a liquor), somewhat like a *soma*-feast. It is celebrated at harvest time with dancing, and drinking, "and every kind of licentious enjoyment." Other festivals of less importance celebrate the substitution of a buffalo for human sacrifice (not celebrated, of course, by the Tari worshippers). The invocation at the harvest is quite Brahmanic: "O gods, remember that our increase of rice is your increase of worship; if we get little rice we worship little." Among lesser gods the 'Fountain-god' is especially worshipped, with a sheep or a hog as sacrifice. Female infanticide springs from a feeling that intermarriage in the same tribe is incest (this is the meaning of the incest-law above; it might be rendered 'to marry in the tribe').

Of the Orāons, or Dhangars,[1] we shall mention but one or

[1] This tribe now divides with the Lurka Koles the possession of Chota Nagpur, which the latter tribe used to command entire. The Orāons regard the Lurka Koles

two good parallels to what is found in other religions. These Dravidians live in Bengal, and have two annual festivals, a harvest feast and one celebrating the marriage of heaven and earth. Like the Khonds, they recognize a supreme god in the sun, but, just as we showed was the case with the Hindus, who ignore Brahmā because they do not fear him, so here, the Orāons do not pray to the sun, on the ground that he does them no harm; but they sacrifice to evil spirits because the latter are evil-doers. These savages, like the Burmese Mishmis, have no idea of a future life in heaven; but in the case of people killed in a certain way they believe in a sort of metempsychosis; thus, for instance, a man eaten by a tiger becomes a tiger. In the case of unfortunates they believe that they will live as unhappy ghosts; in the case of other men they assume only annihilation as their fate.[1] It is among this tribe that the mouse-ṭotem is found, which is Çiva's beast and the sign of Ganeça.[2]

THE KOLARIANS.

The Sunthāls: These are immigrants into the West Bengal jungles, and have descended from the North to their present site. They are called the finest specimens of the native savage. The guardian of the tribe is its deceased ancestor, and his ghost is consulted as an oracle. Their race-god is the 'Great Mountain,' but the sun represents the highest spirit; though they

as inferiors. Compare JRAS. 1861, p. 370 ff. They are sometimes erroneously grouped with the Koles, ethnographically as well as geographically. Risley; *Tribes and Castes of Bengal*, p. xxxii.

1 Something like this is recorded by Brinton, *Myths of the New World*, p. 243, as the belief of an American tribe, which holds that the fate of the dead depends on the manner of death, the funeral rites, or "some such arbitrary circumstance" (as in Greece).

2 Compare the epic 'Mouse-people,' Mūshikas, as well as Apollo's mouse. Possibly another Hindu mark of sectarianism may be traced to the wild tribes, the use of vermilion markings. This is the most important element in the Bengal wedding rite (Risley).

worship spirits of every sort, and regard beasts as divine; the men revering the tiger, and the women, elephants. The particularly nasty festival called the *bandana*, which is celebrated annually by this tribe, is exactly like the 'left-hand' cult of the Çaktas, only that in this case it is a preliminary to marriage. All unmarried men and women indulge together in an indescribable orgie, at the end of which each man selects the woman he prefers.[1]

The Koles ('pig-stickers'): Like the last, this tribe worship the sun, but with the moon as his wife, and the stars as their children. Besides these they revere Manes, and countless local and sylvan deities. Like Druids, they sacrifice only in a grove, but without images.[2]

All these tribes worship snakes and trees,[3] and often the only oath binding upon them is taken under a tree.[4] The

[1] Above the Sunthāls, who inhabit the jungle and lower slopes of the Rājmahāl hills, live the Pāhārias, who never tell a lie (it is said), and whose religion in some aspects is worth noticing. They believe in one god (over each village god), who created seven brothers to rule earth. The Pāhārias descend from the eldest of these brothers. They believe in transmigration, a future state, and oracles. But it is questionable whether they have not been exposed to Buddhistic influence, as 'Budo Gosain' is the name of the supreme (sun-)god.

[2] In the ninth century Orissa was formed of the territories of Khonds, Koles, and Savāras. In the old grouping of tribes these, together with the Gonds and Bhils, were the "five children of the soil" between the Vindhya mountains, the east chain of the Ghats, and the mouth of the Godāvarī to the centre of the valley of the Nerbudda. The last mentioned tribe of Bhils (Bheels) is almost devoid of native religion, but is particularly noted for truth, honesty, and fidelity. JRAS. 1844, pp. 181, 189, 192; 1852, p. 216 ff. It is an ancient race, but its origin is not certain.

[3] Trees are revered by the Brahmans also, as by the American Indians. Schoolcraft, i. 368. The tree-spirit is an advance on this (Brahmanic and Hinduistic).

[4] Thus the Bhils' wedding is simply a mutual promise under the *singā* tree. These savages, however, live together only so long as they choose. When the family separates, the father takes the elder children, and the mother takes the younger ones. They are polygamous. It is from this tribe that the worship of Aghorī, the Vindhya fiend, accepted as a form of Kālī, was introduced into Çivaite worship. At present their religion is a mixture of Hindu and native superstition. Thus, like the Gonds, they worship stone images of gods placed in a circle, but they recognize among these gods several of the Hindu divinities.

sun-worship, which is found alike in Kolarian and Dravidian tribes, may be traced through all the ramifications of either. In most of the tribes the only form of worship is sacrifice, but oaths are taken on rice, beasts, ants, water, earth, etc. (among some Pāhāriahs on the arrow). Some have a sort of belief in the divinity of the chief, and among the Lurka Koles this dignity is of so much importance that at a chief's death the divine dignity goes to his eldest son, while the youngest son gets the property. In regard to funeral rites, the Koles first burn and then bury the remains, placing a stone over the grave.

Besides the Orāons' totem of the mouse, the Sunthāls have a goose-totem, and the Garos and Kassos (perhaps not to be included in either of the two groups), together with many other tribes, have totems, some of them *avatars*, as in the case of the tortoise. The Garos, a tribe between Assam and Bengal, are in many respects noteworthy. They believe that their vessels are immortal; and, like the Bhārs, set up the bamboo pole, a religious rite which has crept into Hinduism (above, p. 378). They eat everything but their totem, immolate human victims, and are divided into 'motherhoods,' Māhāris, particular Māhāris intermarrying. A man's sister marries into the family from which comes his wife, and that sister's daughter may marry his son, and, as male heirs do not inherit, the son-in-law succeeds his father-in-law in right of his wife, and gets his wife's mother (that is, his father's sister) as an additional wife.[1] The advances are always made by the girl. She and her party select the groom, go to his house, and carry him off, though he modestly pretends to run away. The sacrifice for the

[1] Rowney, *Wild Tribes*, p. 194. The goose-totem of the Sunthāls is also Brahmā's sign. As Vishnu is carried on an eagle, and Çiva on a bull, so Brahmā rides a goose (or flamingo). The 'ten ancestors' demanded of the Brahman priest were originally on the mother's side as well as on the father's. Weber, *Rājasūya*, p. 78. The matriarchal theory is, however, southern. (Compare the oblations to the ancestresses in Vishnu's law-book, 74.)

wedding is that of a cock and hen, offered to the sun. The god they worship most is a monster (very much like Çiva), but he has no local habitation.

Of the Savāras or Sauras of the Dekhan the most interesting deity is the malevolent female called Thākurānī, wife of Thākur. She was doubtless the first patroness of the throttling Thugs (*thags* are *ṭhaks*, assassins), and the prototype of their Hindu Kālī. Human sacrifices are offered to Thākurānī, while her votaries, as in the case of the Thugs, are noted for the secrecy of their crimes.

Birth-rites, marriage-rites, funeral rites (all of blood), human sacrifice, *tabū* (especially among the Burmese), witchcraft, worship of ancestors, divination, and demonology are almost universal throughout the wild tribes. In most of the rites the holy stone[1] plays an important part, and in many of the tribes dances are a religious exercise.

Descendants of the great Serpent-race that once ruled Māgadha (Behār), the Bhārs, and Chīrus (Cheeroos) are historically of the greatest importance, though now but minor tribes of Bengal. The Bhārs, and Koles, and Chirus may once have formed one body, and, at any rate, like the last, the Bhārs are Kolarian and not Dravidian. This is not the place to argue a thesis which might well be supported at length, but in view of the sudden admixture of foreign elements with the Brahmanism that begins to expand at the end of the Vedic period it is almost imperative to raise the question whether the Bhārs, of all the northern wild tribes the most cultivated, whose habitat

[1] The marriage-stone, as in the Hindu rite, is quite common. Of lesser superstitions the *tabū*, analogous to the avoidance of unlucky names among the Hindus, may be mentioned. Friendship among girls is cemented by a religious ceremony. After this, among the Orāons, the two avoid each other's name, calling each other only 'my flower' or 'my meet-to-smile' (Rowney). In this tribe exogamy is 'more respectable,' but not necessary. The girls are generally bought, and have fixed prices, but we have seen the customary price (twenty-five pigs) cited only for Assam among the Meeris. If one man cannot pay so much, several unite, for polyandry prevails all through the northern tribes (JRAS. xi. 38), and even in the Punjāb.

extended from Oude (Gorakhpur) on both sides of the Ganges over all the district between Benares and Allahābād, and whose name is found in the form Bhārats as well as Bhārs, is not one with that great tribe the history of whose war has been handed down to us in a distorted form under the name of Bhārata (Mahābhārata). The Bhāratas, indeed, claim to be Aryans. But is it likely that a race would have come from the North-east and another from the Northwest, and both have the same name? Carnegy believed, so striking was the coincidence, that the Bhārats were a Rājput (Hindu) tribe that had become barbaric. But against this speaks the type, which is not Aryan but Kolarian.[1] Some influence one may suppose to have come from the more intelligent tribes, and to have worked on Hindu belief. We believe traces of it may still be found in the classics. For instance, the famous Frog-maiden, whose tale is told in the Mahābhārata, reminds one rather forcibly of the fact that in Oude and Nepāl frog-worship (not as totem) was an established cult. The time for this worship to begin is October; it is different to thunder-worship (July, the *nāga*-feast), and the frog is subordinate to the snake. And, again, the snake-worship that grows so rapidly into the Hindu cult can scarcely have been uninfluenced by the fact that there are no less than thirty snake-tribes.[2]

But despite some interesting points of view besides those

[1] Sherring (JRAS. v. 376) says decidedly that Bhārs, or Bhārats, and Chirus cannot be Aryans. This article is one full of interesting details in regard to the high cultivation of the Bhārat tribe. They built large stone forts, immense subterranean caverns, and made enormous bricks for tanks and fortifications (19 × 11 × 2½ inches), the former being built regularly to east and west (*surajbedi*). One of their chief cities lay five miles west of Mirzāpur, and covered several miles, entirely surrounding the Puranic city of Vindhyacal, built in the midst of it. Six or seven hundred years ago the Bhārs held Oude and Benares. Carnegy's opinion is given in his *Races, Tribes, and Castes of the Province of Oude* (Oudh). The Bhārs, says Elliot, *Chronicles of Oonayo*, built all the towns not ending in *pur*, *mow*, or *ābād* (Hindu, Mongol, Mohammedan). Their sacra (totems?) are the bamboo, *bel*-tree, tortoise, and peacock.

[2] JRAS. xii. 229; IA. xxii. 293.

touched upon here, details are of little added value, since it is manifest that, whether Kolarian or Dravidian, or, for the matter of that, American or African, the same rites will obtain with the same superstition, for they belong to every land, to the Aryan ancestor of the Hindu as well as to the Hindu himself. Even totemism as a survival may be suspected in the 'fish' and 'dog' people of the Rig Veda, as has recently been suggested by Oldenberg. In the Northeast of India many tribes worship only mountains, rivers, and Manes, again a trait both Vedic and Hinduistic, but not necessarily borrowed. Some of these tribes, like the Khāsias of Oude, may be of Rājput descent (the Khasas of Manu, x. 22), but it is more likely that more tribes claim this descent than possess it. We omit many of the tribal customs lest one think they are not original; for example, the symbol of the cross among the Ābors, who worship only diseases, and whose symbol is also found among the American Indians; the sun-worship of the Katties, who may have been influenced by Hinduism; together with the cult of Burmese tribes too overspread with Buddhism. But often there is a parallel so surprising as to make it certain that there has been influence. The Niadis (of the South), for example, worship only the female principle. Many other tribes worship *çakti* almost exclusively. The Todas worship stone images, buffaloes, and even cow-bells, but they have a celibate priesthood! We do not hesitate to express our own belief that the *çakti*-worship is native and drawn from similar cults, and that the celibate priesthood, on the other hand, is taken from civilization.

Such a fate appears to have happened in modern times to several deities, now half Brahmanized. For example, Vetāla (worshipped in many places) is said in the Dekhan to be an *avatar*, or, properly speaking, a manifestation of Çiva. What is he in reality? A native wild god, without a temple, worshipped in the open air under the shade of a tree, and in an enclosure of stones. Just such a deity, in other words, as we have shown is worshipped in just such a way by the wild tribes. A monolith[1] in the middle of twelve stones represents this primitive Druidic deity. The stones are painted red in flame-shape for a certain distance from the ground, with the upper portion painted white. Apparently there is here a sun-god of the aborigines. He is worshipped in sickness, as is Çiva, and propitiated with the sacrifice of a cock, without the intervention of any priest. The cock to Aesculapius ("*huic gallinae immolabantur*") may have had the same function originally, for the cock is always the sun-bird. Seldom is Vetāla personified. When he has an image (and in the North he sometimes has temples) it is that of an armless and legless man; but again he is occasionally represented as a giant 'perfect in all his parts.'[2] To the Brahman, Vetāla is still a mere fiend, and presides over fiends; nor will they admit that the red on his stones means aught but blood. In such a god, one has a clue to the gradual intrusion of Çiva himself into Brahmanic worship. At first a mountain lightning fiend, then identified with Rudra, a recognized deity, then made anthropomorphic. There are, especially in the South, a host of minor Hindu deities, half-acknowledged, all more or less of a fiendish nature in the eyes of the orthodox or even of the Çivaite. Seen through such eyes they are no longer recognizable, but doubtless in many instances they represent a crude form of nature-worship or demonology, which has been taken from the cult of the wild

1 Among the southern Koders the dolmen form grave-stones; perhaps the religious employment of them in this wise led to the idea of the god-stone in many cases; but it is difficult to say in monolith-worship whether the stone itself be not a god; not a fetish, for (as has been said by others) a fetish is a god only so long as he is regarded as being useful, and when shown to be useless he is flung away; but a god-stone is always divine, whether it grants prayers or not.

2 Wilson's note to Stevenson's description, JRAS. 1838, p. 197. The epic disease-gods are not unique. The only god known to the Andaman Islanders (Bay of Bengal) was a disease-devil, and this is found as a subordinate deity in many of the wild tribes.

tribes, and is now more or less thoroughly engrafted upon that of their civilized neighbors.[1]

One of the most interesting, though not remarkable, cases of similarity between savage and civilized religions is found in the worship of snakes and trees.[2] In the Nāga or dragon form the latter cult may have been aided by the dragon-worshipping barbarians in the period of the northern conquest. But in essentials not only is the snake and dragon worship of the wild tribes one with that of Hinduism, but, as has been seen, the latter has a root in the cult of Brahmanism also, and this in that of the Rig Veda itself. The poisonous snake is feared, but his beautiful wave-like motion and the water-habitat of many of the species cause him to be associated as a divinity with Varuna, the water-god. Thus in early Hinduism one finds snake-sacrifices of two sorts. One is to cause the extirpation of snakes, one is to propitiate them. Apart from the real snake, there is revered also the Nāga, a beautiful chimerical creature, human, divine, and snake-like all in one. These are worshipped by sectaries and by many wild tribes alike. The Nāga tribe of Chota Nāgpur, for instance, not only had three snakes as its battle-ensign, but built a serpent-temple.[3]

[1] In the current *Indian Antiquary* there is an exceedingly interesting series of papers by the late Judge Burnell on Devil-worship, with illustrations that show well the character of these lower objects of worship.

[2] The standard work on this subject is Fergusson's *Tree and Serpent Worship*, which abounds in interesting facts and dangerously captivating fancies.

[3] JRAS. 1846, p. 407. The ensign here may be totemistic. In Hinduism the epic shows that the standards of battle were often surmounted with signa and effigies of various animals, as was the case, for example, in ancient Germany. We have collected the material on this point in a paper in JAOS. xiii. 244. It appears that on top of the flag-staff images were placed. One of these is the Ape-standard; another, the Bull-standard; another, the Boar-standard. Arjuna's sign was the Ape (with a lion's tail); other heroes had peacocks, elephants, and fabulous monsters like the *çarabha*. The Ape is of course the god Hanuman; the Boar, Vishnu; the Bull, Çiva; so that they have a religious bearing for the most part, and are not totemistic. Some are purely fanciful, a bow, a swan with bells, a lily; or, again, they are signifi-

Tree and plant worship is quite as antique as is snake-worship. For not only is *soma* a divine plant, and not only does Yama sit in heaven under his 'fair tree' (above, p. 129), but 'trees and plants' are the direct object of invocation in the Rig Veda (v. 41. 8); and the Brahmanic law enjoins upon the faithful to fling an offering, *bali*, to the great gods, to the waters, and 'to the trees';[1] as is the case in the house-ritual. We shall seek, therefore, for the origin of tree-worship not in the character of the tree, but in that of the primitive mind which deifies mountains, waters, and trees, irrespective of their nature. It is true, however, that the greater veneration due to some trees and plants has a special reason. Thus *soma* intoxicates: and the *tulasī*, 'holy basil,' has medicinal properties, which make it sacred not only in the Krishna-cult, but in Sicily.[2] This plant is a goddess, and is wed annually to the Çālagrāma stone with a great feast.[3] So the *çamī* plant is herself divine, the goddess Çamī. Again, the mysterious rustle of the *bo* tree, *pipal*, may be the reason for its especial veneration; as its seeming immortality is certainly the cause of the reverence given to the banian. It is not necessary, however, that any mystery should hang about a tree. The palm is tall, (Çiva's) *açoka* is beautiful, and no trees are more revered. But trees are holy *per se*. Every 'village-tree' (above, p. 374, and Mbhā. ii. 5. 100) is sacred to the Hindu. And this is just what is found among the wild tribes, who revere their hut-trees and village-trees as divine, without demanding a special show of divinity. The birth-tree (as in Grecian mythology) is also known, both to Hindu sect and to wild tribe. But here also

cant of the heroe's origin (Drona's 'pot'). Trees and flowers are used as standards just like beasts. Especially is the palm a favorite emblem. These signa are in addition to the battle-flags (one of which is blue, carried with an ensign of five stars). On the plants compare Williams, *Brahmanism and Hinduism*, p. 338.

[1] Āpastamba, 2. 2. 3. 22; Manu. iii. 88.

[2] Yule *apud* Williams.

[3] *ib.* The Rig Veda, X. 81. 4, knows also a 'tree of creation.'

there is no basis of Aryan ideas, but of common human experience. The ancestor-tree (totem) has been noticed above in the case of the Gonds, who claim descent from trees. The Bhārs revere the (Çivaite!) *bilva* or *bel*, but this is a medicinal tree. The marriage-tree is universal in the South (the tree is the male or female ancestor), and even the Brahmanic wedding, among its secondary after-rites, is not without the tree, which is adorned as part of the ceremony.

Two points of view remain to be taken before the wild tribes are dismissed. The first is that Hindu law is primitive. Maine and Leist both cite laws as if any Hindu law were an oracle of primitive Aryan belief. This method is ripe in wrong conclusions. Most of the matter is legal, but enough grazes religion to make the point important. Even with the sketch we have given it becomes evident that Hindu law cannot be unreservedly taken as an exponent of early Brahmanic law, still less of Aryan law: For instance, Maine regards matriarchy as a late Brahmanic intrusion on patriarchy, an inner growth.[1] To prove this, he cites two late books, one being Vishnu, the Hindu law-giver of the South. But it is from the Southern wild tribes that matriarchy has crept into Hinduism, and thence into Brahmanism. Here prevails the matriarchal marriage-rite, with the first espousal to the snake-guarded tree that represents the mother's family. In many cases geographical limitations of this sort preclude the idea that the custom or law of a law-book is Aryan.[2]

1 *Early Law and Custom*, p. 73 ff.

2 Thus it is common Aryan law that, on the birth of a child, the mother becomes impure for ten days, either alone or with the father. But the latter's impurity is only nominal, and is removed by bathing (Manu, v. 62, and others). Bāudhāyana alone states that "according to some" only the father becomes impure (1. 5. 11. 21). This is the custom of a land described by Apollonius Rhodius (ii. 1010), "where, when women bear children, the men groan, go to bed, and tie up the head; but the women care for them." Yet Bāudhāyana is a Southerner and a late writer. The custom is legalized only in this writer's laws. Hence it cannot be cited as Brahmanic or even as Aryan law. It was probably the custom of the Southern half-Hinduized environment.

The second point of view is that of the Akkadists. It is claimed by the late Lacouperie, by Hewitt, and by other well-known writers that a primitive race overran India, China, and the rest of the world, leaving behind it traces of advanced religious ideas and other marks of a higher civilization. Such a cult may have existed, but in so far as this theory rests, as in a marked degree it does rest, on etymology, the results are worthless. These scholars identify Gandharva with Gan-Eden, Kāçi (Benares) with the land of the sons of Kush; Gautama with Chinese ('Akkadian') *gut*, 'a bull,' etc. All this is as fruitful of unwisdom as was the guess-work of European savants two centuries ago. We know that the Dasyus had some religion and some civilization. Of what sort was their barbaric cult, whether Finnish (also 'Akkadian')[1] or aboriginal with themselves, really makes but little difference, so far as the interpretation of Aryanism is concerned; for what the Aryans got from the wild tribes of that day is insignificant if established as existent at all. A few legends, the Deluge and the Cosmic Tree, are claimed as Akkadian, but it is remarkable that one may grant all that the Akkadian scholars claim, and still deny that Aryan belief has been essentially affected by it.[2] The Akkadian theory will please them that cannot reconcile the Rig Veda with their theory of Brahmanic influence, but the fault lies with the theory.

[1] American Indians are also Dravidian, because both have totems!

[2] For the Akkadist theory may be consulted Lacouperie in the *Babylonian and Oriental Record*, i. 1, 25, 58; iii. 62 ff.; v. 44, 97; vi. 1 ff.; Hewitt, in reviewing Risley's *Tribes and Castes of Bengal*, JRAS. 1893, p. 238 ff. See also Sayce's *Hibbert Lectures*. On the Deluge and Tree of Life, compare the *Babylonian and Oriental Record*, iv. 15 and 217.

CHAPTER XIX.

INDIA AND THE WEST.

If in Hinduism, and even in Brahmanism, there are certain traits which, with some verisimilitude, may be referred to the immediate environment of these religions, how stands it in respect of that wider circle of influence which is represented by the peoples of the West? With Egypt and Phoenicia, India had intercourse at an early date, but this appears to have been restricted to mercantile exchange; for India till very late was affected neither by the literature nor by the religion of Egyptians or Syrians.[1] Of a more direct sort seem to have been the relations between India and Babylon, and the former may owe to the latter her later astronomy, but no definitive proof exists (or even any great historical probability) that Babylon gave India even legendary additions to her native wealth of myths.[2] From the Iranians the Hindus parted too early to receive from Zoroastrianism any influence. On the contrary, in our opinion the religion of Zoroaster budded from a branch taken from Indic soil. Even where Persian influence may, with propriety, be suspected, in the later Indic worship of the sun, India took no new religion from Persia; but it is very possible that her own antique and preserved heliolatry was

[1] Lassen interprets *ophir* as Abhīras, at the mouth of the Indus. The biblical *koph* is Sanskrit *kapi*, ape. Other doubtful equivalents are discussed by Weber, *Indische Skizzen*, p. 74.

[2] The legend of the Flood and the fancy of the Four Ages has been attributed to Babylon by some writers. Ecstein claims Chaldean influence in Indic atomic philosophy, *Indische Studien*, ii. 369, which is doubtful; but the Indic alphabet probably derived thence, possibly from Greece. The conquests of Serimamis may have included a part of India, but only Brunnhofer finds trace of this in Vedic literature, and the character of his work we have already described.

aided, and acquired new strength from more modern contact with the sun-worshippers of the West. Of Iranian influence in early times, along the line of Hindu religious development, there is scarcely a trace, although in 509 B.C. Darius's general conquered the land about the Indus.[1] But the most zealous advocate of Persia's prestige can find little to support his claims in pre-Buddhistic Brahmanic literature, though such claims have been made, not only in respect of the position of secondary divinities, but even as regards eschatological conceptions. It is not so easy to refute an improbable historical theory as it is to propound it, but, on the other hand, the *onus probandi* rests upon him that propounds it, and till now all arguments on this point have resulted only in increasing the number of unproved hypotheses, which the historian should mention and may then dismiss.

The Northern dynasty that ruled in India in the sixth century seems to have had a hand in spreading Iranian sun-worship beyond the Indus, but we doubt whether the radical effect of this dominion and its belief (it is described by Kosmas, an Egyptian traveller of the time) is as great as has been claimed.[2]

From Greece, the Hindus received architectural designs, numismatic, and perhaps a few literary hints, but they got thence neither religious myths, nor, with the possible exception of the cult of the later Love-god and fresh encouragement to phallic

[1] Senart attributes to the Achaemenides certain Indic formulae of administration. IA. xx. 256.

[2] Certain Hindu names, like those to which we called attention in the epic, containing Mihira, *i.e.*, Mithra; the Magas, *i.e.*, Magi; and recommendations of sun-worship in the Purānas are the facts on which Weber bases a theory of great influence of Persia at this later period. Weber claims, in fact, that the native sun-worship was quite replaced by this importation (*Indische Skizzen*, p. 104). This we do not believe. Even the great number of Persians who, driven out by Arabians, settled in Gujarāt (the name of Bombay is the same with Pumbadita, a Jewish settlement in Mesopotamia) had no other effect on the Brahmanic world that absorbed them (*ib.*, p. 109) than to intensify the fervor of a native cult.

worship, new rites;[1] though they may have borrowed some fables, and one even hears of a Buddhistic king endeavoring to buy a sophist of Antiochus. But there is no ground for assuming philosophical influence on Brahmanism.

Christianity came late into the religious life of India, and as a doctrine made upon her no deep or lasting impression. Certain details of Christian story have been woven into the legends of Krishna, and some scholars believe that the monotheistic worshippers depicted in the pseudo-epic were Christians. But in respect of the latter point it is enough to say that this account of foreign belief had no new monotheizing effect upon the pantheism of India; the strange (unbrahmanic) god was simply accepted as Vishnu. Nor do we believe that the faith-doctrine of Hindu sectarianism and the trinitarianism of India were derived from Christian sources. But it must be admitted to be historically possible that the creed of the Christians, known to the Hindus of the sixth and seventh centuries, may have suggested to the latter the idea of the trinity as a means of adjusting the claims of Brahmanism, Krishnaism, and Çivaism.[2]

But from the Mohammedan India has taken much, albeit

[1] Weber ascribes to Greek influence the Hindus' first acquaintance with the planets. On a possible dramatic loan see above, p. 2, note. The Greeks were first to get into the heart of India (as far as Patna), and between the court of Antiochus the Great and the king Sâubhagasena there was formal exchange of ambassadors in the third century B.C. The name of Demetrius appears as Dattâmitra in the Hindu epic. He had "extended his rule over the Indus as far as the Hydaspes and perhaps over Mâlava and Gujarat" (about 200 B.C.: Weber, *Skizzen*). In the second century Menandros (the Buddhists' 'Milinda') got as far as the Jumna; but his successors retreated to the Punjâb and eventually to Kabul (*ib.*). Compare also Weber, *Sitz. d. könig̣. Preuss. Akad.*, 1890, p. 901 ff., *Die Griechen in Indien*. The period of Greek influence coincides with that of Buddhist supremacy in its first vigor, and it is for this reason that Brahmanic literature and religion were so untouched by it. There is to our mind no great probability that the Hindu epic owes anything to that of Greece, although Weber has put in a strong plea for this view in his essay *Ueber das Râmâyaṇa*.

[2] The romance of a Russian traveller's late 'discovery,' which Sanskrit scholars estimate at its true value, but which may seem to others worthy of regard, is perhaps, in view of the interest taken in it, one that should be told correctly. Nicholas

only in the last few centuries. When Alexander entered India there were still two bodies of Indic people west of the Indus. But the trend was eastward, as it had been for centuries, and the first inroad of the Mohammedan had little further effect than to seize a land forsaken by Aryans and given over to the hordes of the North. The foundation of the new empire was not laid till the permanent occupation of the Punjāb and annexation of Lahore in 1022–23. In the thirteenth century all Hindustan acknowledged the authority of the slave sultan of Delhi.[1] Akbar died in 1605. By the end of the century the Mogul rule was broken; the Mahratta princes became imperial. It is now just in this period of Mohammedan power when arise the deistic reforming sects, which, as we have shown, were surrounded with deists and trinitarians. Here, then, we draw the line across the inner development of India's religions, with

Notovitch asserts that he discovered seven years ago in the Tibetan monastery of Himis, a work which purports to give a life of Christ from birth to death, including sixteen years spent in India. This life of 'Issa' (Jesus) is declared to have been written in the first century of the Christian era. Unfortunately for the reputation of the finder, he made a mistake in exploiting his discovery, and stated that his manuscript had been translated for him by the monks of Himis 'out of the original Pāli,' a dialect that these monks could not understand if they had specimens of it before them. This settled Notovitch's case, and since of course he did not transcribe a word of the MS. thus freely put at his disposal, but published the forgery in a French 'translation,' he may be added to the list of other imposters of his ilk. The humbug has been exposed for some time, and we know of no one who, having a right to express an opinion, believes Notovitch's tale, though some ignorant people have been hoaxed by it. If the blank sixteen years in Christ's life ever be explained, it may be found that they were passed in a Zoroastrian environment; but until real evidence be brought to show that Christ was in India, the wise will continue to doubt it. As little proof exists, it may be added, of Buddhistic influence in the making of the Gospels. But this point is nowadays scarcely worth discussing, for competent scholars no longer refer vague likenesses to borrowing. Certain features are common to the story of Christ and to the legends of Buddha; but they are common to other divine narratives also. The striking similarities are not found in the earliest texts of the Southern Buddhists. Īça for Jesus is modern, Weber, *loc. cit.*, p. 931.

[1] Elphinstone, i. pp. 140, 508; ii. chap. 1. The 'slave dynasty' of Kutab, 1206–1288. It was the bigoted barbarity of these Mohammedans that drove Brahmanic religion into the South.

Kabīr, Nānak, Dādu, and perhaps even Basava. In the philosophy of the age that succeeds the epic there are but two phases of religion, pantheism for the wise, a more or less deistic polytheism for the vulgar[1] (in isolated cases may be added the monotheism of certain scholastic philosophers); and so Indic religion continued till the advent of Islamism. Nevertheless, though under Mohammedan influence,[2] the most thoughtful spirits of India received monotheism and gave up pantheism, yet was the religious attitude of these thinkers not averse from that taken by the Sankyan philosophers and by the earlier pantheists. From a philosophical point of view one must, indeed, separate the two. But all these, the Unitarian Hariharaist, the real pantheist of the Upanishads, who completed the work of the Vedic quasi-pantheist, and the circle that comprises Kabīr, Nānak, and Dādu, were united in that they stood against encircling polytheism. They were religiously at one in that they gave up the cult of many divinities, which represented respectively nature-worship and fiend-worship (with beast-worship), for the worship of one god. Therefore it is that, while native advance stops with the Mohammedan conquest, one may yet claim an uninterrupted progress for the higher Indic religion, a continual elevation of the thoughts of the wise; although at the same time, beside and below this, there is the circle of lower beliefs that continually revolves upon itself. For in the zoölatry[3] and polytheism that adores monsters to-day

1 Though immediately before it the Harihara cult, survival of Sankhyan dualism, is practically monotheistic. Basava belongs to the twelfth century.

2 The literary exchange in the realm of fable between Arabia and later Sanskrit writers (of the twelfth century) is very evident. Thus in Indic dress appear at this time the story of Troy, of the passage over the Red Sea, of Jonas, etc. On the other hand, the Arabians translated native Hindu fables. See Weber, IS. iii. 327, *Ueber den Zusammenhang griechischer Fabeln mit indischen*, and *Indische Skizzen*, p. 111, and *Die Griechen in Indien*. Arabia further drew on India for philosophical material, and Alberūni himself translated Kapila's work (Weber, *loc. cit.*).

3 Whereby cows, snakes, cats (sacred to one of the Çivaite 'mothers'), crocodiles, monkeys, etc., are worshipped.

it is difficult to see a form of religion higher in any respect than that more simple nature-polytheism which first obtained.[1]

This lower aspect of Indic religions hinges historically on the relation between the accepted cults of Hinduism[2] and those of the wild tribes. We cannot venture to make any statements that will cast upon this question more light than has been thrown by the above account of the latter cults and of their points of contact with Hinduism. It may be taken for granted that with the entrance into the body politic of a class composed of vanquished[3] or vanquishing natives, some of the religion of the latter may have been received also. Such, there is every reason to believe, was the original worship of Çiva as Çarva, Bhava, and of Krishna; in other words, of the first features of modern sectarian Hinduism, though this has been so influenced by Aryan civilization that it has become an integral part of Hindu religion.[4]

But, again, for a further question here presents itself, how much in India to-day is Aryan? We are inclined to answer that very little of blood or of religion is Aryan. Some priestly families keep perhaps a strain of Aryan blood. But Hindu literature is not afraid to state how many of its authors are of low caste, how many of its priests were begotten of mixed marriages, how many formed low connections; while both legendary and prophetic (*ex post facto*) history speak too often

[1] Pantheists in name alone, most of the lower caste-men are practically polytheists, and this means that they are at bottom dualists. They are wont to worship assiduously but one of the gods they recognize.

[2] Where Brahmanism may be said to cease and Hinduism to begin can be defined but vaguely. Krishnaism is rank Hinduism. But Çivaism is half Brahmanic. For the rest, in its essential aspects, Hinduism is as old as the Hindus. Only the form changes (as it intrudes upon Brahmanism).

[3] It is highly probable that the mention of the Northwestern Çūdras in Mbhā. vi. 9. 67 refers to the Afghan Sudroi, and that the slave-caste as a whole, which bears the name Çūdra, received this appellation first as conquered tribes of Afghanistan.

[4] Brahmanism has always been an island in a sea. Even in the Brahmanic age there is evidence to show that it was the isolated belief of a comparatively small group of minds. It did not even control all the Aryan population.

of slave-kings and the evil times when low castes will reign, for any unprejudiced person to doubt that the Hindu population, excluding many pure priests but including many of the priests and the Rājputs ('sons of kings'), represents Aryanhood even less than the belief of the Rig Veda represents the primitive religion; and how little of aboriginal Aryan faith is reflected in that work has been shown already.

As one reviews the post-Vedic religions of civilized India he is impressed with the fact that, heterogeneous as they are, they yet in some regards are so alike as to present, when contrasted with other beliefs, a homogeneous whole. A certain uniqueness of religious style, so to speak, differentiates every expression of India's theosophy from that of her Western neighbors. What is common and world-wide in the forms of Indic faith we have shown in a previous chapter. But on this universal foundation India has erected many individual temples, temples built after designs which are not uniform, but are all self-sketched, and therefore peculiar to herself. In each of these mental houses of God there is revealed the same disposition, and that disposition is necessarily identical with that expressed in her profane artistry,[1] for the form of religion is as much a matter of national taste as is that which is embodied in literature, architecture, and painting. And this taste, as expressed in religion, isolates Brahmanic and Hinduistic India,

[1] We refer partly to literature, that of the drama and novel, for instance; and partly to the fine arts. But in connection with the latter it may be remarked that painting, and the fine arts generally, are expressly reckoned as the pursuit of slaves alone. For instance, even as late a jurist as he that wrote the law-code of 'Vishnu' thus (chap. ii.) parcels out the duties and occupations of the four castes: The duty of a priest is to teach the Veda, his means of livelihood is to sacrifice for others and to receive alms; the duty of the warrior is to fight, his means of livelihood is to receive taxes for protecting the other castes; the duty of the Vāiçya is to tend cattle, his means of livelihood is gain from flocks, farm, trade, or money-lending. The duty of a slave, Çudra, is to serve the three upper castes; his means of livelihood is the fine arts.

placing her apart, both from the gloom of Egypt and the grace of Greece; even as in her earliest records she shows herself individual, as contrasted with her Aryan kinsfolk. Like Egypt, she feels her dead ever around her, and her cult is tinged with darkness; but she is fond of pleasure, and seeks it deliriously. Like Greece, she loves beauty, but she loves more to decorate it; and again, she rejoices in her gods, but she rejoices with fear; fear that overcomes reason, and pictures such horrors as are conjured up by the wild leaps of an uncurbed fancy. For an imagination that knows no let has run away with every form of her intellectual productivity, theosophy as well as art. This is perceptible even in her ritualistic, scientific, and philosophical systems; for though it is an element that at first seems incongruous with such systems, it is yet in reality the factor that has produced them. Complex, varied, minute, exact, as are the details which she loves to elaborate in all her work, they are the result of this same unfettered imagination, which follows out every fancy, pleased with them all, exaggerating every present interest, unconfined by especial regard for what is essential.[1] This is a heavy charge to bring, nor can it be passed over with the usual remark that one must accept India's canon as authoritative for herself, for the taste of cosmopolitan civilization is the only norm of judgment, a norm accepted even by the Hindus of the present day when they have learned what it is. But we do not bring the charge of extravagance for the sake of comparing India unfavorably with the Occident. Confining ourselves to the historical method of treatment which we have endeavored heretofore to maintain, we wish to point out the important bearings which this intellectual trait has had upon the lesser products of India's religious activity.

[1] It is this that has exaggerated, though not produced, that most marked of native beliefs, a faith which intertwines with every system, Brahmanic, Buddhistic, or Hinduistic, a belief in an ecstatic power in man which gives him control over supernatural forces. To-day this Yogism and Mahātmaism, which is visible even in the Rig Veda, is nothing but unbridled fancy playing with mesmerism and lies.

Through the whole extent of religious literature one finds what are apparently rare and valuable bits of historical information. It is these which, from the point of view to which we have just referred, one must learn to estimate at their real worth. In nine cases out of ten, these seeming truths are due only to the light imagination of a subsequent age, playing at will over the records of the past, and seeking by a mental caper to leap over what it fails to understand. To the Oriental of an age still later all the facts deducible from such statements as are embodied in the hoary literature of antiquity appear to be historical data, and, if mystic in tone, these statements are to him an old revelation of profoundest truth. But the Occidental, who recognizes no hidden wisdom in palpable mystification, should hesitate also to accept at their face value such historical notes as have been drafted by the same priestly hand.

Nor would we confine the application of this principle to the output of extant Brahmanic works. The same truth cuts right and left among many utterances of the Vedic seers and all the theories built upon them. To pick out here and there an *ipse dixit* of one of the later fanciful Vedic poets, who lived in a period as Brahmanic (that is, as ritualistic) as is that which is represented by the actual ritual-texts, and attempt to reconstruct the original form of divinities on the basis of such vagaries is useless, for it is an unhistorical method which ignores ancient conditions.

In less degree, because here the conditions are more obvious, does this apply to the religious interpretation of the great body of literature which has conserved for posterity the beginnings of Hinduism. But upon this we have already animadverted, and now need only range this literature in line with its predecessors. Not because the epic pictures Krishna as making obeisance to Çiva is Krishna here the undeveloped man-god, who represents but the beginning of his (later) greatness, and is still subject to the older Çiva. On the contrary, it is the epic's last extravagance in regard to Çiva (who has already bowed before the great image of Krishna-Vishnu) that demands a furious counter-blast against the rival god. It is the Çivaite who says that Krishna-Vishnu bows; and because it is the Çivaite, and because this is the national mode of expression of every sectary, therefore what the Çivaite says is in all probability historically false, and the sober historian will at least not discover 'the earlier Krishna' in the Krishna portrayed by his rival's satellites.

But when one comes to the modern sects, then he has to deplore not so much the lack of historical data as the grotesque form into which this same over-vivid imagination of the Hindu has builded his gods. As the scientific systems grow more and more fancifully detailed, and as the liturgy flowers out into the most extraordinary bloom of weird legend, so the images of the gods, to the eye in their temples, to the mind in the descriptions of them, take to themselves the most uncouth details imagined by a curious fancy. This god is an ascetic; he must be portrayed with the ascetic's hair, the ascetic's wild appearance. He kills; he must be depicted as a monster, every trait exaggerated, every conceivable horror detailed. This god sported with the shepherdesses; he must have love-adventures related in full, and be worshipped as a darling god of love; and in this worship all must be pictured in excess, that weaker mortal power may strive to appreciate the magnitude of the divine in every fine detail.

These traits are those of late Vedism, Brahmanism, and Hinduism. But how marked is the contrast with the earlier Vedic age! The grotesque fancy, the love of minutiae, in a word, the extravagance of imagination and unreason are here absent, or present only in hymns that contrast vividly with those of the older tone. This older tone is Aryan, the later is Hindu, and it is another proof of what we have already emphasized, that the Hinduizing influence was felt in the later Vedic or Brahmanic period. There is, indeed, almost as great a gulf between the Dawn-hymns and the Çatapatha as there is between the latter and the Purānas. One may rest assured that the perverted later taste reproduces the advance of Hindu influence upon the Aryan mind exactly in proportion to the enormity displayed.

On the other hand, from the point of view of morality, Brahmanic religion is not in any way individual. The race, whether Aryan or Hinduistic, had as fragile virtue as have other folks, and shows the same tentative efforts to become purer as those which characterize every national advance. There is, perhaps, a little too much formal insistance on veraciousness, and one is rather inclined to suspect, despite Müller's brave defence of the Hindu in this regard, that lying came very naturally to a people whose law-givers were so continuously harping on the beauty of truth. The vicious caste-system necessarily scheduled immorality in accordance with the caste order, as certain crimes in other countries are estimated according to the race of the sinner rather than according to any abstract standard. In the matter of precept we know no better moral laws than those promulgated by the Brahmans, but they are the laws that every people evolves for itself. Religious immorality, the excess of Çakti worship, is also not peculiar to the Hindu. If one ask how the morality of India as a whole compares with that of other countries, we reply that, including religious excesses, it stands level with the personal morality of Greece in her best days,[1]

[1] The Hindu sectarian cults are often strangely like those of Greece in details, which, as we have already suggested, must revert to a like, though not necessarily mutual, source of primitive superstition. Even the sacred free bulls, which roam at large, look like old familiar friends, *ἀφέτων ὄντων ταύρων ἐν τῷ τοῦ Ποσειδῶνος ἱερῷ* (Plato, *Kritias*, 119); and we have dared to question whether Lang's 'Bull-roarer' might not be sought in the command that the priest should make the bull roar at the sacrifice; and in the verse of the Rig Veda which says that the priests "beget (produce) the Dawn by means of the roar of a bull" (vii. 79. 4); or must the bull be *soma?* For Müller's defence of the Hindu's veraciousness, see his *India, What Can It Teach Us*, p. 34.

and that without the religiously sensual (Hindu) element, it is *nominally* on a par with that of London or New York. There are good and bad men, and these make good and bad coteries, which stand inside the pale of a religious profession. There is not much theoretical difference. Few of the older gods are virtuous, and Right, even in the Rig Veda, is the moral power, that is, Right as Order, correct behavior, the prototype both of ritual and of *ācāra*, custom, which rules the gods. In the law-court the gods are a moral group, and two of them, Varuna and Agni, hate respectively the sins of adultery and untruth. In the law it is, however, Dharma and the Father-god or his diadochos, who, handing down heavenly precepts, gives all moral laws, though it must be confessed that the Father-god is almost the last to care for morality. And pure Brahmanism stops with Brahmā. In modern Hinduism, to kill, lust, steal, drink, so far from offending, may please a god that is amorous, or bloodthirsty, or, like Çiva, is 'the lord of thieves.' Morality here has God himself against it. In the Rig Veda, to sin is merely to displease a god. But even in Brahmanism, as in Buddhism, there is not that intimate connection between goodness and godness that obtains in Christianity. The Brahman, like the Buddhist, was self-controlled, in order to exert control upon the gods and the course of his own future life. He not only, as is perhaps the case elsewhere, was moral with an ulterior motive, but his moral code lacked the divine hand. It was felt as a system which he applied to himself for his own good. He did not assume that he offended a god by not following it, except in two special cases, as in sins against Agni and Varuna. Ulterior motives are deprecated, but because he that seeks absorption into God must quit desires.[1]

[1] Some exception may be taken to this on the ground that moral laws really are referred to the Creator in one form or anotherr. This we acknowledge as a theory of authority, but it so seldom comes into play, and there is so little rapport between gods and moral goodness, that the difference in this regard is greater by far than the resemblance. A Christian sins against God, a Hindu sins against himself. The

We have said that the moral code of the Hindus at its best seems to be on a par with the best as found elsewhere. Not to lie, not to steal, not to injure another illegally,[1] to be brave, to be loyal, to be hospitable, — these are the factors of its early and late law. In certain late cases may be added 'to be self-restrained.' But if these laws be compared with those of the savage races it will be found that most of them are also factors of primitive ethics. Therefore we say that the Hindu code as a whole is savage and antique, and that, excluding religious excess and debauchery, it is on a par with the modern ethical code only nominally. In reality, however, this savage and ancient code is not on a level with that of to-day. And the reason is that the ideal of each is different. In the savage and old-world conception of morality it is the ideal virtue that is represented by the code. It was distinct laudation to say of a man that he did not lie, or steal, and that he was hospitable.[2] But to-day, while these factors remain to formulate the code, they no longer represent ideal virtue. Nay rather, they are but the assumed base of virtue, and so thoroughly is this assumed that to say of a gentleman that he does not lie or steal is not praise, but rather an insult, since the imputation to him of what is but the virtue of children is no longer an encomium when applied to the adult, who is supposed to have passed the point where theft and lying are moral temptations, and to have reached a point where, on the basis of these savage, antique, and now childish virtues, he strives for a higher moral ideal. And this ideal of to-day, which makes fair-mindedness, liberality of thought, and altruism the respective representatives of the savage virtues of manual honesty, truth-speaking, and hospitality, is just what

Christian may be punished by God; the Hindu punishes himself (the *karma*). The latter may say that moral laws are of God, but he means that they are natural laws, the violation of which has the same effect as touching fire.

[1] The *lex talionis* is in full force in Hindu law, even in the codes of Hinduism; for example, 'Vishnu,' v. 19.

[2] Deceit of a foe is no sin in any system. "All is fair in war."

is lacking in the more primitive ideal formulated in the code of savages and of the Brahman alike.[1] It is not found at all among savages, and they may be left on one side. In India all the factors of the modern code are entirely lacking at the time when the old code was first completely formulated. Liberality of thought comes in with the era of the Upanishads, but it is a restricted freedom. Altruism is unknown to pure Brahmanism. But it obtains among the Buddhists, who also have liberality of thought and fair-mindedness. Hence, from the point of view of the higher morality, one must confess that Buddhism offers the best parallel to the best of to-day. On the other hand, Buddhistic altruism exceeds all other.

We have sketched the sphere of influence exerted by the West upon India, and found it on the whole inconsiderable. The Indic religions till the twelfth century assimilated what little they drew from foreign sources, and stand before the world as a peculiar growth, native to the soil in all their essential characteristics.[2]

But to the other side of India's contact with the West we have as yet barely alluded. India has given as she has received. What influence has she had upon Western cults and beliefs?

The worship that substituted idols for ideal forms we have traced back to the end of the Vedic period. It is not, however, a mark of early Brahmanism, nor is it a pronounced feature before the age of Buddhism. But in Buddha's time, or soon after, flourished the worship of images, and with it the respect for relics. The latter feature of the new religion made necessary shrines to keep the holy objects, sacred museums, which soon became the formal *stūpas*, above-ground

[1] This idea may be carried out in other instances. The bravery of civilization is not the bravado that savages call bravery, and modesty is now a virtue where boasting used to be reckoned as the necessary complement of bravery. As for hospitality in the old sense, it is not now a 'virtue' not to kill a guest.

[2] India's relations with Rome were late and wholly of mercantile character.

and under-ground, and these made the first temples of India.[1] Fully developed, they became the great religious buildings affected by Buddhism, with their idol service, prostrations, repetitions of prayers, dim religious light (lamp-service), offerings of flowers, fruits, etc. From this source may have been derived many of the details in the Roman Catholic worship, which appears to have taken from Buddhism the rosary, originally a mark of the Çivaite.[2] By what is, to say the least, an extraordinary coincidence, each of these churches is conspicuous for its use of holy water, choirs, sacred pictures, tonsure, vestments, the bell in religious service, the orders of nuns, monks, and the vows of the monastic system.[3] The most curious loan made by the Roman and Greek churches is, however, the quasi-worship of Gotama Buddha himself (in so far as a Romanist worships his saints), for, under cover of the Barlaam and Josaphat story, Buddha has found a niche as a saint in the row of canonized Catholic worthies, and has his saint-day in the calendar of the Greek and Roman churches.[4] But it is not his mother who is the Virgin of Lamaism, which has made of Buddha the Supreme God.

Besides external phases of the religious cult, India has given

[1] It is interesting, as showing incidentally the close connection between Buddhism and Çivaism in other than philosophical aspects, that the first Indic grotto-temple mentioned by foreigners (in the third century A.D.) was one which contained a statue of an androgynous (Çivaite) deity (Weber, *Indische Skizzen*, p. 86, note).

[2] Rosaries are first mentioned in the AV. Pariçiṣṭa, xliii. 4. 11 (Leumann, Rosaries).

[3] In Lamaism there is also the tiara-crowned pope, and the transubstantiation theory; the reverence to Virgin and Child, confessions, fasts, purgatory, abbots, cardinals, etc. Compare David's *Hibbert Lectures*, p. 193.

[4] The literature on this subject is very extensive (see the Bibliography). On Buddhism and Christianity see Bohlen's *Altes Indien*, i. 334 (Weber, *Indische Skizzen*, p. 92). At a recent meeting of the British Association E. B. Tylor presented a paper in which is made an attempt to show Buddhistic influence on pre-Columbian culture in America. On comparing the Aztec picture-writing account of the journey of the soul after death with Buddhistic eschatology, he is forced to the conclusion that there was direct transmission from Buddhism. We require more proof than Aztec pictures of hell to believe any such theory; and reckon this attempt to those already discussed in the eighth chapter.

to the West a certain class of literary works and certain philosophical ideas. The former consists, of course, in the fable-literature, which spread from India to Eastern Europe (Babrius) and has preserved in many tales of to-day nothing more than Buddhistic Birth-stories or other Indic tales (the Pañcatantra) and legends.[1] Of these we can make only passing mention here, to turn at once to the more important question of philosophical and religious borrowing.

It has been claimed, as we have incidentally stated, that the Logos doctrine was imported from India. Were this so, it would, indeed, be a fact of great historical importance, but, interesting as would be such a loan, we cannot see that the suggestion is based on data of cogent character. The history of the doctrine in India and Greece is simply this: Vāc, Speech or Word, appears in the Rig Veda (in the hymn cited above, p. 143) as an active female divine power, showing grace to mortals. In the Brahmanic period Vāc becomes more and more like the Greek Logos, and it may truthfully be said that in this period "the Word was God." In Greece, on the other hand, the conception of Logos begins with Heraclitus, passes on to the Stoics; is adopted by Philo; becomes a prominent feature of Neo-Platonism; and reappears in the Gospel of St. John. It is certainly legitimate to suppose that Heraclitus might have received the idea indirectly, if not directly, from contemporary Eastern philosophers; but the fact that he did so remains unproved; nor is there any foundation for the assumption of borrowing other than the resemblance between the Grecian and Indic conceptions. But this resemblance is scarcely marked enough in essential features to prejudice one in favor of Weber's theory (amplified by Garbe), as it is not detailed enough to be striking, for Vāc is never more than one of many female abstractions.

[1] It is a mooted question in how far the influence in this line has been reciprocal. See *Indische Studien*, iii. 128.

With the exception of the one case to be mentioned immediately, we are forced to take the same position in regard to the similarity between other forms of early Greek and Hindu philosophy. Both Thales and Parmenides were indeed anticipated by Hindu sages, and the Eleatic school seems to be but a reflexion of the Upanishads. The doctrines of Anaximander and Heraclitus are, perhaps, not known first in Greece, but there is no evidence that they were not original to Greece, or that they were borrowed from India, however much older may be the parallel trains of thought on Indic soil.

Quite as decidedly, however, as we deny all appearance of borrowing on the part of the founders of other early Grecian schools, must we claim the thought of India to be the archetype of Pythagorean philosophy. After a careful review of the points of contact, and weighing as dispassionately as possible the historical evidence for and against the originality of Pythagoras, we are unable to come to any other conclusion than that the Greek philosopher took his whole system indirectly from India. His 'numbers,' indeed, are the Sānkhya only in appearances.[1] But his theory of metempsychosis is the Indic *samsāra*, and Plato is full of Sankhyan thought, worked out by him but taken from Pythagoras. Before the sixth century B.C. all the religious-philosophical ideas of Pythagoras are current in India (L. von Schroeder, *Pythagoras*). If there were but one or two of these cases, they might be set aside as accidental coincidences, but such coincidences are too numerous to be the result of chance. Even in details the transmigration theory of Pythagoras harmonizes with that of India. Further (after Schroeder und Garbe) may be mentioned the curious prohibition against eating beans; the Hesiodic-Pythagorean πρὸς ἥλιον μὴ ὀμιχεῖν; the vow of silence, like that taken by the Hindu *muni*; the doctrine of *five* elements (aether as fifth); above all, the so-called Pythagorean Theorem, developed in the mathematical

[1] The Sānkhya has no systematic connection with the 'numbers' of Pythagoras.

Çulvasūtras[1] of India; the irrational number $\sqrt{2}$; then the whole character of the religious-philosophical fraternity, which is exactly analogous to the Indic orders of the time; and finally the mystic speculation, which is peculiar to the Pythagorean school, and bears a striking resemblance to the fantastical notions affected by the authors of the Brāhmana.[2] Greek legend is full of the Samian's travels to Egypt, Chaldaea, Phoenicia, and India. The fire beneath this smoke is hidden. One knows not how much to believe of such tales. But they only strengthen the inference, drawn from 'the Pythagorean school,' the man's work itself, that the mysticism and numbers with which he is surrounded are taken from that system of numbers and from that mysticism which are so astonishingly like his own. All subsequent philosophies borrowed from Pythagoreanism, and in so far has India helped to form the mind of Europe.[3]

But we cannot omit a yet more important religious influence exerted by India upon the West. As is well known, Neo-Platonism and Christian Gnosticism owe much to India. The Gnostic ideas in regard to a plurality of heavens and spiritual worlds go back directly to Hindu sources. Soul and light are one in the Sānkhya system before they become so in Greece, and when they appear united in Greece it is by means of the thought which is borrowed from India. The famous 'three qualities' of the Sānkhya reappear as the Gnostic 'three classes,' *πνευματικοί, ψυχικοί, ὑλικοί.*[4] In regard to Neo-Platonism, Garbe

[1] Compare on the Çulvasūtras, Thibaut, J. A. Beng. xliv. p. 227; von Schroeder, *Pythagoras und die Inder; Literatur und Cultur*, p. 718 ff., who also cites Cantor, *Geschichte der Mathematik*, p. 540, and refutes the possibility, suggested by the latter, of the loan being from Greece to India on the ground that the Çulvasūtra are too old to belong to the Alexandrine period, and too essential a part of the religious literature to have been borrowed; and also on the ground that they are not an addition to the Çrāutasūtra, but they make an independent portion (p. 721, note).

[2] Compare Garbe (*loc. cit.* below), and his *Sāṅkhya Philosophie*, p. 94.

[3] This view is not one universally accepted by Sanskrit scholars. See, for instance, Weber, *Die Griechen in Indien.* But to us the minute resemblance appears too striking to be accidental.

[4] Lassen, and Weber, *Indische Skizzen*, p. 91.

says: "The views of Plotinus are in perfect agreement with those of the Sānkhya system."[1] Porphyry, the disciple of Plotinus, has the Yoga doctrine of immediate perception of truth leading to union with the deity. As is well known and undisputed, this Porphyry copies directly from the treatise of Bardesanes, which contains an account of the Brahmans;[2] while in many instances he simply repeats the tenets of the Sānkhya philosophy. The means of communication may have been Alexandria, where met the trades of the East and West. Perhaps the philosophers of India as well as of Greece were brought together there. But, if the East and West had a mutual meeting-ground, the ideas common to both occupy no common place in their respective homes. In Greece, Pythagoreanism and Gnosticism are strange, and are felt as such by the natives. In India these traits are founded on ancient beliefs, long current, universal, nationally recognized. The question of giver and receiver, then, admitting the identity of thought, can scarcely be raised. If two men meet, one a Methodist and one a Baptist, and after they have conversed the Methodist be found totally immersed, he will not be credited with having invented independently his new mode of baptism.

India's influence as an intellectual factor in modern European thought has thus far been of the slightest. Her modern deism is borrowed, and her pantheism is not scientific. Sanskrit scholars are rather fond of citing the pathetic words of Schopenhauer, who, speaking of the Upanishads, says that the study of these works "has been the solace of my life; it will be the solace of my death"; but Schopenhauer knew the Upanishads only in a very free form of translation, and it can scarcely have been the loose philosophy so much as the elevated spirit of

[1] Garbe, in a recent number of the *Monist*, where is given a *résumé* of the relations between Greek and Hindu philosophical thought.

[2] Weber, *loc. cit.*

these works that solaced the unphilosophical bitterness of his life This general impression will doubtless continue to be felt by all that study the best works of Brahmanism. The sincerity, the fearless search of the Indic sages for truth, their loftiness of thinking, all these will affect the religious student of every clime and age, though the fancied result of their thinking may pass without effect over a modern mind. For a philosophy that must be orthodox can never be definitive. But, if one turn from the orthodox completed systems to the tentative beginnings of the Vedānta (in the Upanishads), he finds as the basis of this earlier speculation only an *a priori* metaphysical assumption.[1]

Apart from philosophical influence there is at present more or less interest in Europe and America in Indic superstition and spiritualism, and half-educated people will doubtless be influenced for some time to come by Mahātmaism and Yogism, just as they are moved by native séance-spirits and mesmerism. Blavatskyism (which represents no phase of Buddhism) will always find disciples among the ignorant classes, especially in an agnostic or atheistic environment, so that one should attribute the mental attitude of such minds to their lack of culture rather than to India; for if Mahātmaism had not been discovered, they would still profess it under another name. Buddhism, too, apart from Hartmann, may be said to have some influence on popular thought, yet it is a very unreal Buddhism, which amounts only to the adoption of an altruistic creed. But we know of none among the many that profess themselves 'Buddhists' who has really adopted Buddhistic principles, and but few who even understand those principles. A bar to the adoption of Buddhism lies in the implicit neces-

[1] The existence of a soul (spirit) in man is always assumed in the Upanishads. In the pantheistic system (the completed Vedānta) the verity of traditional belief is also assumed. The latter assumption is made, too, though not in so pronounced a manner, in the Upanishads.

sity of renunciation for all who would become perfected, and in the explicit doctrine of *karma* in its native form. The true Buddhist is not satisfied to be a third-class Buddhist, that is, simply a man that seeks to avoid lust, anger, and ignorance. He will become a second-class Buddhist and renounce the world, give up all family ties and earthly affections, and enter the Order. But he will not do this, thinking that he is thereby to become perfect. For, to be a first-class Buddhist, he must get wisdom. He must believe in the impermanence of everything, and in the awful continuation of his own *karma* as a resultant group, which, as such, will continue to exist if, to the purity and peace of the lower classes of Buddhists, he fail to add in his own case the wisdom that understands the truth of this *karma* doctrine.[1] Now no modern mind will believe this hypothesis of *karma*, and no modern will even enter the Order. Nevertheless, while one may not become a true Buddhist in the native sense, it is possible to be a Buddhist in a higher sense, and in its new form this is a religion that will doubtless attract many Occidentals, though it is almost too chaste to win adherents where marriage is not regarded as detrimental to high thinking. But if one substitute for the Buddhistic *karma* the *karma* of to-day, he may well believe that his acts are to have effect hereafter, not as a complex but as individual factors in determining the goodness of his descendants and indirectly of his environment. Then there remains the attainment of purity, kindness,[2] and wisdom, which last may be interpreted, in accordance with the spirit of the Master, as seeing things in their

1 The Upanishad philosopher sought only to save his life, but the Buddhist, to lose it.

2 This is not a negative 'non-injury' kindness. It is a love 'far-reaching, all-pervading' (above, p. 333). The Buddhist is no Stoic save in the stoicism with which he looks forward to his own end. Rhys Davids has suggested that the popularity of Tibet Buddhism in distinction from Southern Buddhism may have been due to the greater weight laid by the former on altruism. For, while the earlier Buddhist strives chiefly for his own perfection, the spiritualist of the North affects greater love

true relations, and the abandonment of whatever prevents such attainment, namely, of lust, anger, and ignorance. But to be a true Buddhist one must renounce, as lust, all desire of evil, of future life, which brings evil; and must live without other hope than that of extinguishing all desire and passion, believing that in so doing he will at death be annihilated, that is, that he will have caused his acts to cease to work for good or ill, and that, since being without a soul he exists only in his acts, he will in their cessation also cease to be.

At least one thing may be learned from Buddhism. It is possible to be religious without being devout. True Buddhism is the only religion which, discarding all animism, consists in character and wisdom. But neither in sacrificial works, nor in kindness alone, nor in wisdom alone, lies the highest. One must renounce all selfish desires and live to build up a character of which the signs are purity, love for all, and that courageous wisdom which is calm insight into truth. The Buddhist worked out his own salvation without fear or trembling. To these characteristics may be added that tolerance and freedom of thought which are so dissimilar to the traits of many other religions.

So much may be learned from Buddhism, and it were much only to know that such a religion existed twenty-four centuries ago. But in what, from a wider point of view, lies the importance of the study of Hindu religions? Not, we venture to think, in their face value for the religious or philosophical life of the Occident, but in the revelation, which is made by this study, of the origin and growth of theistic ideas in one land; in the light these cast by analogy on the origin of such ideas elsewhere; in the prodigious significance of the religious factor

for his kind, and becomes wise to save others. The former is content to be an Arhat; the latter desires to be a Bodhisat. 'teacher of the law' (*Hibbert Lectures*, p. 254). We think, however, that the latter's success with the vulgar was the result rather of his own greater mental vulgarity and animism.

in the development of a race, as exhibited in this instance; in the inspiring review of that development as it is seen through successive ages in the loftiest aspirations of a great people; and finally in the lesson taught by the intellectual and religious fate of them among that people that have substituted, like the Brahman ritualist, form for spirit; like the Vedantist, ideas for ideals; like the sectary, emotion for morality. But greatest, if woeful, is the lesson taught by that phase of Buddhism, which has developed into Lamaism and its kindred cults. For here one learns how few are they that can endure to be wise, how inaccessible to the masses is the height on which sits the sage, how unpalatable to the vulgar is a religion without credulity.

Ever since Cotton Mather took up a collection to convert the Hindus,[1] Americans have felt a great interest in missionary labor in India. Under the just and beneficent rule of the British the Hindus to-day are no longer plundered and murdered in the way they once were; nor is there now so striking a contrast between the invader's precept and example as obtained when India first made the acquaintance of Christians militant.

The slight progress of the missionaries, who for centuries have been working among the Hindus, is, perhaps, justified in view of this painful contrast. In its earlier stages there can be no doubt that all such progress was thereby impeded. But it is cause for encouragement, rather than for dismay, that the slowness of Christian advance is in part historically explicable, sad as is the explanation. For against what odds had not the early missionaries to struggle! Not the heathen, but the Christian, barred the way against Christianity. Four hun-

1 Hurst's *Indika*, chap. xlix, referring to *India Christiana* of 1721, and the correspondence between Mather and Ziegenbalg, who was then a missionary in India. The wealthy 'young men' who contributed were, in Hurst's opinion, Harvard students.

dred years ago the Portuguese descended upon the Hindus, cross and sword in hand. For a whole century these victorious immigrants, with unheard-of cruelty and tyranny, cheated, stripped, and slaughtered the natives. After them came the Dutch, but, Dutch or Portuguese, it was the same. For it was merely another century, during which a new band of Christians hesitated at no crime or outrage, at no meanness or barbarity, which should win them power in India. In 1758 the Dutch were conquered by the English, who, becoming now the chief standard-bearers of the Christian church, committed, under Vansittart, more offences against decency, honor, honesty, and humanity than is pleasant for believer or unbeliever to record; and, when their own theft had brought revolt, knew no better way to impress the Hindu with the power of Christianity than to revive the Mogul horror and slay (in their victims' fearful belief) both soul and body alike by shooting their captives from the cannon's mouth. Such was Christian example. It is no wonder that the Christian precept ('thou shalt love thy neighbor as thyself') was uttered in vain, or that the faith it epitomized was rejected. The hand stole and killed; the mouth said, 'I love you.' The Hindu understood theft and murder, but it took him some time to learn English. One may hope that this is now forgotten, for the Hindu has not the historical mind. But all this must be remembered when the expenditures of Christianity are weighed with its receipts.[1]

[1] The Portuguese landed in Calcutta in 1498. They were driven out by the Dutch, to whom they ceded their mercantile monopoly, in 1640–1644. The Dutch had arrived in 1596, and held their ground till their supremacy was wrested from them by Clive in 1758. The British had followed the Dutch closely (arriving in 1600), and were themselves followed soon after by the Germans and Danes (whose activity soon subsided), and by the French. The German company, under whose protection stood Ziegenbalg, was one of the last to enter India, and first to leave it (1717–1726). The most grotesquely hideous era in India's history is that which was inaugurated by the supremacy of the Christian British. Major Munroe's barbaric punishment of the Sepoys took place, however, in Clive's absence (1760–1765). Marshman, i, p. 305, says of this Munroe only that he was "an officer of undaunted

In coming to the end of the long course of Hindu religious thought, it is almost inevitable that one should ask what is the present effect of missionary effort upon this people, and what, again, will eventually be the direction which the native religious sense, so strongly implanted in this folk, will take, whether aided or not by influence from without.

Although it is no part of our purpose to examine into the workings of that honest zeal which has succeeded in planting so many stations up the Indic coast, there are yet some obvious truths which, in the light of religious history, should be an assistance to all whose work lies in making Hindu converts. To compile these truths from this history will not be otiose. In the first place, Christian dogma was formally introduced into South India in the sixth century; it was known in the North in the seventh, and possibly long before this; it was the topic of debate by educated Hindus in the sixteenth and seventeenth. It has helped to mould the Hindus' own most intellectual sects; and, either through the influence of Christian or native teaching, or that of both, have been created not only the Northern monotheistic schools, but also the strict unitarianism of the later Southern sects, whose scriptures, for at least some centuries, have inculcated the purest morality and simplest monotheistic creed in language of the most elevated character.[1] In the second place, the Hindu sectary has interwoven with

resolution"! Clive himself was acquitted by his own countrymen of theft, robbery, and extortion; but the Hindus have not acquitted him or Hastings; nor will Christianity ever do so.

[1] For specimens of the sacred Kural of Tiruvalluvar Nārāyana, see the examples given by Pope, *Indian Antiquary*, seventh and following volumes. The Sittars, to whom we have referred above, are a more modern sect. Their precept that love is the essential of religion is not, as in the case of the Hindu idolators, of erotic nature. They seem to be the modern representatives of that Buddhistic division (see above) called Sāugatas, whose religion consists in 'kindness to all.' In these sects there is found quietism, a kind of quakerism, pure morality, high teaching, sternest (almost bigoted) monotheism, and the doctrine of positive altruism, strange to the Hindu idolator as to the Brahman. The Prem Sāgar, or 'Ocean of Love,' is a modern

his doctrine of pantheism that of the trinity. In the third place, the orthodox Brahman recognizes in the cult of Christianity, as that cult is expressed, for instance, in Christmas festivities, one that is characteristic, in outward form and inner belief, of a native heterodox sect. In the fourth place, the Hindu sectary believes that the native expression of trinitarian dogma, faith-doctrine, child-god worship, and madonna-worship takes historical precedence over that of Christianity; and the orthodox Hindu believes the same of his completed code of lofty moral teachings. Vishnuism is, again, so catholic that it will accept Christ as an *avatar* of Vishnu, but not as an exclusive manifestation of God. In the fifth place, the Hindu doctors are very well educated, and often very clever, both delighting in debate and acute in argument. It follows, if we may draw the obvious inference, that, to attack orthodox Brahmanism, or even heterodox Hinduism, requires much logical ability as well as learning, and that the best thing a missionary can do in India, if he be not conscious of possessing both these requisites, is to let the native scholars alone.

But native scholars make but a small part of the population, and among the uneducated and 'depressed' classes there is plenty for the missionary to do. Here, too, where caste is hated because these classes suffer from it, there is more effect in preaching equality and the brotherly love of Christianity, doctrines abhorrent to the social aristocrats, and not favored even by the middle classes. But what here opposes Christian efforts is the splendid system of devotion, the magnificent fêtes, the gorgeous shows, and the tickling ritualism, which please and overawe the fancy of the native, who is apt to desire for himself a pageant of religion, not to speak of a visible god in

Hindu work, which illustrates the religious love opposed to that of the Sittars, namely, the mystic love of the Krishnaite for his savior, whose grace is given only to him that has faith. It is this mystic rapt adoration that in expression becomes erotic and sensual.

idol form; while from his religious teacher he demands either an asceticism which is no part of the Christian faith, or a leadership in sensuous and sensual worship.

What will be the result of proselytizing zeal among these variegated masses?[1] Evidently this depends on where and how it is exercised. The orthodox theologian will not give up his inherited faith for one that to him is on a par with a schismatic heresy, or take dogmatic instruction from a level which he regards as intellectually below his own. From the Samājas no present help will come to the missionary; for, while they have already accepted the spirit of Christianity, liberal Hindus reject the Christian creed.[2] At a later day they will join hands with the missionary, perhaps, but not before the latter is prepared to say: There is but one God, and many are his prophets.

There remain such of the higher classes as can be induced to prefer undogmatic Christianity to polytheism, and the lowest class, which may be persuaded by acts of kindness to accept the dogmas with which these are accompanied. It is with this class that the missionary has succeeded best. In other cases his success has been in inverse ratio to the amount of his dogmatic teaching. And this we believe to be the key to the second problem. For, if one examine the maze of India's tangled creeds, he will be surprised to find that, though dogmatic Christianity has its Indic representative, there yet is no indigenous representative of undogmatic Christianity. For a

1 Hinduism itself is unconsciously doing a reforming work among the wild tribes that are not touched by the Christian missionary. These tribes, becoming Hinduized, become civilized, and, in so far as they are thus made approachable, they are put in the way of improvement; though civilization often has a bad effect upon their morals for a season.

2 The substitution of the doctrine of redemption for that of *karma* is intellectually impossible for an educated Hindu. He may renounce the latter, but he cannot accept the former. The nearest approach to such a conception is that of the Buddhistic 'Redeemer' heresy referred to above. In all other regards Samāj and pantheism are too catholic to be affected; in this regard they are both unyielding.

god in human form is worshipped, and a trinity is revered; but this is not Christianity. Love of man is preached; but this is not Christianity. Love of God and faith in his earthly incarnation is taught; but this, again, is not Christianity. No sect has ever formulated as an original doctrine Christ's two indissoluble commandments, on which hang all the law and the prophets.

It would seem, therefore, that to inculcate active kindness, simple morality, and the simplest creed were the most persuasive means of converting the Hindu, if the teacher unite with this a practical affection, without venturing upon ratiocination, and without seeking to attract by display, which at best cannot compete with native pageants.[1] Moreover, on the basis of undogmatic teaching, the missionary even now can unite with the Samāj and Sittar church, neither of which is of indigenous origin, though both are native in their secondary growth. For it is significant that it is the Christian union of morality and altruism which has appealed to each of these religious bodies, and which each of them has made its own. In insisting upon a strict morality the Christian missionary will be supported by the purest creeds of India itself, by Brahmanism, unsectarian Hinduism, the Jain heretics, and many others, all of whom either taught the same morality before Christianity existed, or developed it without Christian aid. The strength of Christian teaching lies in uniting with this the practical altruism which was taught by Christ. In her own religions there is no hope for India, and her best minds have renounced them. The

[1] We question, for instance, the advisability of such means to "fill up the church" as is described in a missionary report delivered at the last meeting of the Missionary Union of the Classis of New York for the current year: "A man is sent to ride on a bicycle as fast as he can through the different streets. This invariably attracts attention. Boys and men follow him to the church, where it is easy to persuade them to enter." But this is an admission of our position in regard to the classes affected. The rabble may be Christianized by this means, but the intelligent will not be attracted.

body of Hinduism is corrupt, its soul is evil. As for Brahmanism — the Brahmanism that produced the Upanishads — the spirit is departed, and the form that remains is dead. But a new spirit. the spirit of progress and of education, will prevail at last. When it rules it will undo the bonds of caste and do away with low superstition. Then India also will be free to accept, as the creed of her new religion, Christ's words, 'Thou shalt love the Lord thy God, and thy neighbor as thyself.' But to educate India up to this point will take many centuries, even more, perhaps, than will be needed to educate in the same degree Europe and America.[1]

[1] After the greater part of our work had passed the final revision, and several months after the whole was gone to press, appeared Oldenberg's *Die Religion des Veda*, which, as the last new book on the subject, deserves a special note. The author here takes a liberal view, and does not hesitate to illustrate Vedic religion with the light cast by other forms of superstition. But this method has its dangers, and there is perhaps a little too much straining after original types. giant-gods as prototypes and totemism in proper names, where Vedic data should be separated from what may have preceded Vedic belief. Oldenberg, as a ritualist, finds in Varuna, Dawn, and the Burial Service the inevitable stumbling-blocks of such scholars as confuse Brahmanism with early Vedism. To remove these obstacles he suggests that Varuna, as the moon, was borrowed from the Semites or Akkadians (though he frankly admits that not even the shadow of this moon lingers in Vedic belief); explains Dawn's non-participation in *soma* by stating that she never participates in it (which explains nothing); and jumps over the Burial Hymn with the inquiry whether, after all, it could not be interpreted as a cremation-hymn (the obvious answer being that the service does imply burial, and does not even hint at cremation). On the other hand, when theoretical barbarism and ritualism are foregone, Oldenberg has a true eye for the estimation of facts, and hence takes an unimpeachable position in several important particulars, notably in rejecting Jacobi's date of the Rig Veda; in rejecting also Hillebrandt's moon-*soma*; in denying an originally supreme Dyāus; in his explanation of henotheism (substantially one with the explanation we gave a year ago); and in his account of the relation of the Rig Veda to the (later) Atharvan. Despite an occasional brilliant suggestion, which makes the work more exciting than reliable, this book will prove of great value to them that are particularly interested in the ritual; though the reader must be on his guard against the substitution of deduction for induction, as manifested in the confusion of epochs, and in the tendency to interpret by analogy rather than in accordance with historical data. The worth of the latter part of the book is impaired by an unsubstantiated theory of sacrifice, but as a whole it presents a clear and valuable view of the cult.

ADDENDA.

Page 154, note 3: Add to (RV.) x. 173, AV. vi. 88.

Page 327, third line from the top: Read Buddhaghosha. According to Chalmers, as quoted by T. W. Rhys Davids in his recent lectures, traces of mysticism are found in some of the early texts (as yet unpublished). The fact that the canonical Pāli books know nothing of the controversy (involving the modification of traditional rules) of the second council gives a terminus to the canon. Senart, on the other hand, thinks that the vague language of the Açoka inscriptions precludes the fixing of the canon at so early a date.

Page 340, note 4: The gods here are priests. The real meaning seems to be that the Brahman priests, who were regarded as gods. have been put to naught in being reduced to their true estate. Compare Senart, (revised) *Inscriptions de Piyadasi*, third chapter. Açoka dismissed the Brahman priests that his father had maintained, and substituted Buddhist monks.

Page 436, note 2: From Bērūnī it would appear that the Gupta and Valabhī eras were identical (319–20 A.D). See Fleet, Indian Antiquary, xvii. 245. Many scholars now assign Kumārila to the eighth century rather than to the end of the seventh.

BIBLIOGRAPHY.[1]

GENERAL WORKS.

Journals: Journal of the Royal Asiatic Society (JRAS.):[2] Journal of the German Oriental Society (Zeitschrift der Deutschen Morgenländischen Gesellschaft, ZDMG.); Journal Asiatique (JA.); Journal of the American Oriental Society (JAOS.); Branch-Journals of the JRAS.; Calcutta Review; Madras Journal: Indian Antiquary (IA.). Some of the articles in the defunct Zeitschrift für die Kunde des Morgenlandes (ZKM.), and in the old Asiatick Researches (AR.) are still worth reading. Besides these, the most important modern journals are the transactions of the royal Austrian, Bavarian, Prussian, and Saxon Academies, the Muséon and the Revue de l'histoire des religions. Occasional articles bearing on India's religions or mythology will be found in the American Journal of Philology (AJP.); the Wiener Zeitschrift für die Kunde des Morgenlandes (WZKM.); the Babylonian and Oriental Record (BOR.); Kühn's Zeitschrift für vergleichende Sprachforschung (KZ.); Bezzenberger's Beiträge (BB.); and the Indogermanische Forschungen (IF.).

Histories, Studies, etc.: Prinsep, Essays (Indian Antiquities); Lassen, Indische Alterthumskunde. Histories of India by Elphinstone (religious material, chapters iv book i. and iv book ii), by

[1] This bibliography is meant only to orient the reader in regard to exegetical literature. It is not complete, nor does it give editions of texts. The order follows in general that of the chapters, but the second and last paragraphs respectively must be consulted for interpretation and geography. Works that cover several fields are placed under the literature of the first. The special studies on Vedic divinities have been arranged alphabetically.

[2] On account of the inconvenient form in which appeared the earlier numbers of the JRAS. we cite the Old Series only by date. All references without date refer to the New Series (vol. i, NS., 1864).

Elliot, by Marshman (complements Elphinstone), and by Wheeler (unreliable); The Rulers of India; Hunter's Indian Empire and Brief History. Mill's excellent History of India is somewhat prejudiced. Dutt's History of Civilization in Ancient India is praiseworthy (1890). Invaluable are the great descriptive Archaeological Surveys by Cunningham, Burgess, and Bühler, and Hunter's Statistical Account of Bengal. **Literary History**:[1] Colebrooke, Essays, reëdited by Cowell, with notes by Whitney; Wilson, Essays; Weber, Indische Studien (IS.); Benfey, Orient and Occident (OO.); Müller, Ancient Sanskrit Literature (ASL.), Science of Religion; Weber, Vorlesungen über Indische Literaturgeschichte (also translated), Indische Streifen, Indische Skizzen; L. von Schroeder, Indiens Literatur und Cultur; Whitney, Oriental and Linguistic Studies, Language and the Study of Language; Duncker, Geschichte des Alterthums (third volume, may be bought separately); Williams, Indian Wisdom (inaccurate but readable).

VEDIC RELIGION.

Literature: Roth, Zur Literatur und Geschichte des Weda;[2] Benfey, Vedica und Verwandtes; Zimmer, Altindisches Leben (AIL.); Rājendralala Mitra, Indo-Aryans (unreliable); Bergaigne, La Religion Védique (also JA. ix, xiii); De Gubernatis, Letture sopra la Mitologia Vedica; Pischel and Geldner, Vedische Studien;[3] Regnaud, Le Rig Veda et les origines de la mythologie indo-européenne, and Les hymnes du Rig Veda, sont-ils prières? (Ann. d. Mus. Guimet, Bibl. d'études, t. i, and special studies). Regnaud's point of view renders nugatory most of what he writes on the Veda.[4] The most useful collection of Vedic and Brahmanic Texts that illustrate Hindu Mythology and Religion is to be found in Muir's Original Sanskrit

[1] On the artistic side Emil Schlagintweit's great work, Indien in Wort und Bild, contains much of interest to the student of religious paraphernalia. See also below under wild tribes.

[2] Roth, Morality of the Veda; Whitney, Result of Vedic Researches (JAOS. iii. 289 and 331); Whitney, History of the Vedic Texts, *ib.* iv. 245.

[3] Under this title Roth has an essay (on the comparison of texts), KZ. xxvi. 45.

[4] See below. Defence of the same by the author, WZKM. vii. 103.

Texts (OST.), especially the fourth and fifth volumes.[1] For the Sacred Books of the East (SBE.) see items below.

Translations of the Rig Veda: Complete, by Grassmann and by Ludwig; partial, by Roth, Benfey, Langlois, Bergaigne; in English chiefly by Wilson, Müller, Muir, Peterson, Griffith. Of these the German translation of Grassmann is often inaccurate;[2] that of Ludwig, often unintelligible. Benfey has translated a number of specimens, OO., BB., i, vii, and in Kleinere Schriften. The incomplete translation of Wilson has been carried on by Cowell; those of Peterson and Griffith are publishing in India; Langlois' is useless. Müller's partial translations will be found in various volumes, Ancient Sanskrit Literature, India: What Can it Teach Us, Chips, Hibbert Lectures, JRAS. ii. 448. iii. 199, etc.; and all the Hymns to the Maruts, SBE. xxxii. Whitney has translated the cosmogonic hymn, PAOS., May, 1882; and Deussen has just published the philosophical hymns, Geschichte der Philosophie, i, 1. A group of Vedic hymns in English dress will be found in Muir, OST. v.; extracts (without connection) are given by Bergaigne, in La Religion Védique, and special essays in JA. (above). In German a capital little collection is the Siebzig Lieder of Geldner and Kaegi. The best general introductory manual for the study of the Rig Veda, accompanied with frequent translations, is Kaegi's Der Rig Veda (translated into English by Arrowsmith).

Translations of the Atharva Veda are all partial. The handiest collection is Grill's Hundert Lieder des Atharva Veda. Specimens will be found translated by Aufrecht, IS. i. 121 (book xv): (Roth) Bruce, JRAS. 1862, p. 321 (book xii. 1); Kuhn, Indische und Germanische Segenssprüche, KZ. xiii. 49, 113; Weber, IS. iv. 393, v. 195, 218, xiii. 129, xvii. 178 (books i–iii, xiv); Grohmann, *ib.* ix. 381; Ludwig, vol. iii, of his translation of the Rig Veda; Zimmer, AIL.;

[1] JRAS. i. 51 ff., and subsequent volumes, Contributions to a Knowledge of the Vedic Theogony and Mythology and Progress of the Vedic Religion toward Abstract Conceptions of the Deity.

[2] It cannot be too much emphasized that Grassmann's translation should never be used for comparative purposes. At the same time, for a general understanding of the contents of the whole Rig Veda it is the only book that can be recommended. Ludwig's translation is so uncouth that without a controlling knowledge of the original it is often meaningless.

Victor Henry, books vii and xiii (Les hymnes Rohitas);[1] Bloomfield, Seven Hymns, and Contributions AJP. vii. 466, xi. 319, xii. 414, JAOS. xv. 143, xvi. 1; ZDMG. xlviii. 541; Florenz, BB. xii. 249 (book vi.). Of **The Sāma Veda**: Stevenson (1842) in English (inaccurate) and Benfey (1848) in German have made translations. On the **Yajur Veda** see Schroeder, Literatur und Cultur, and below.

Vedic Mythology: Windischmann, Ursagen der Arischen Völker, Bay. Ak., 1858; Kuhn, KZ. iv. 88, Herabkunft des Feuers (Prometheus);[2] Roth, Die höchsten Götter der Arischen Völker, ZDMG. vi. 67 (*ib.* vii. 607); Wilson, Preface of Langlois; Cox, Aryan Mythology: Whitney, Oriental and Linguistic Studies, ii. p. 149, JAOS. iii. 291, 331; Müller, Second Series of Science of Language, Biographies of Words.[3] General interpretation of divinities, Müller, Muir, Bergaigne, Kaegi, Pischel-Geldner, *loc. cit.* The last books on the subject are Oldenberg's scholarly volume, Die Religion des Veda (note, p. 571, above), and Phillip's The Teaching of the Vedas (1895), the work of a charlatan.

Special Studies of Vedic Divinities:

Aditi: Roth, IS. xiv. 392; Hillebrandt, Ueber die Göttin Aditi; Müller, SBE. xxxii. 241; Colinet, Étude sur le mot Aditi, Muséon, xii. 81. Ādityas, Roth, ZDMG. vi. 67 (above); Darmesteter, Ormazd et Ahriman.

Agni: L. von Schroeder, Apollon-Agni, KZ. xxix. 193[4] (see epic, below).

Apsaras (see Gandharvas).

Aryaman (Açvins, Mitra, etc.): Bollensen, ZDMG. xli. 494.

Asura as Asen, Schrader, p. 599; P. von Bradke, Dyāus Asura. See Dyāus.

[1] Bloomfield, AJP. xii. 429. Compare also Regnaud, Le Mythe de Rohita. The same author has published various Vedic articles in the Rev. de l'histoire des religions, vols. xv–xxvi. Whitney's complete translation of AV. will soon appear.

[2] Sexual side of fire-cult; whirlwind of fire, Mātariçvan, Schwartz, KZ. xx. 202; compare Hillebrandt, ZDMG. xxxiii. 248.

[3] Neisser's Vorvedisches im Veda, BB. xvii. 244, is not a mythological study.

[4] Apollon here is Saparyeṇya, 'worshipful.' This derivation is attacked by Froehde, Apollon, BB. xix. 230 (compare Fick, *ib.* xviii. 138), who derives Apollon from πέλλων, 'word,' comparing ἀπελλάζειν, 'conciliare,' *pell* being 'spell' (in Gospel, etc.), 'inter-pellare.' Thus Apollo would be 'prophet,' 'wârspello.' On *vahni*, Agni, compare Neisser, Vedica, BB. xviii. 301 (xix. 120, 248).

Açvins: Myriantheus, Die Açvins oder Arischen Dioskuren; *not* Dioskuroi, Pischel, Vedische Studien, Preface, p. xxvii; as constellation, etc., Benfey, OO. ii. 245, iii. 159; Gemini, Weber, last in Rājasūya, p. 100; as Venus, 'span-god,' Bollensen, ZDMG. xli. 496; other literature, Muir, OST. v. 234; Colinet, Vedic Chips, BOR. iii. 193 (nāsatya, Avestan nāonhaithya, nā as 'very').[1]

Brihaspati: Roth, ZDMG. i. 66; Muir, v. 272; Hillebrandt, Vedische Mythologie, i. 404.

Dawn (see Ushas).

Dyāus: P. von Bradke, Dyāus Asura, also Beiträge, ZDMG. xl. 347; not the same with Teutonic Tiu, Bremer, IF. iii. 301; as 'all-father' of primitive Aryans, Müller, Origin of Religion, p. 209; followed by Tiele, Outlines of History of Ancient religions, p. 106; see Hopkins, PAOS. Dec. 1894; form of Word, Collitz. KZ. xxvii. 187; BB. xv. 17.

Earth (see Nritus).

Gandharvas: KZ. i. 513; Meyer, Gandharven-Kentauren (list of Apsarasas); Pischel, VS. i. 78; Hillebrandt, Vedische Mythologie, i. 427.

Haritas (sun's steeds) as Charites, KZ. x. 96: ib. 365; Sonne, *loc. cit. s.* Sūrya; Müller, Science of Language, ii. 388.

Heaven (see Dyāus and Varuna).

Indra (etymology, Benfey, OO. i. 49; PW. sv.; añdra, A.-Sax. 'ent,' 'giant,' BB. i. 342;[2] nar, ἀνδρ-, Jacobi, KZ. xxxi. 316; Indra's bolt, vadha, 'wetter,' Delbrück, KZ. xvi. 266): Perry, Indra in the Rig Veda, JAOS. xi. 117 (see epic, below).

Kama: Weber, ZDMG. xiv. 269, IS. v. 224, xvii. 290; Muir, v. 402.

Manu:[3] Roth, ZDMG. iv. 430; Weber, IS. i. 194 ('man and moon'), ZDMG. iv. 302; Muir, OST. i. 161; Kuhn, KZ. iv. 91; Burnouf, Preface of Bhāg. Purāna, p. iii; Ascoli (mānus, mactus),

1 Oldenberg, *loc. cit.*, interprets Açvins as morning and evening stars! The epithet (of Agni and Açvins) *bhuraṇyu* has been equated with Phorōneus, we forget by whom.

2 Oldenberg's (Die Religion des Veda) Old-Man-of-the-Mountains-Indra thus gets etymological support.

3 For convenience included in this list.

KZ. xvii. 334; Maspiter as 'man,' Corssen, KZ. ii. 32;[1] Manu's wife, Weber, ZDMG. xviii. 286. Compare also KZ. xii. 293, xix. 156, Mannus (see Laws, below).

Maruts (dubious etymology, Grassmann, KZ. xvi. 161; P. von Bradke, *loc. cit. s.* Dyāus): von Bradke, Wunderliche Geburt, Festgruss an Roth, p. 117 (Brahmanic, same point of view in parody, RV. x. 102, ZDMG. xlvi. 445). Hymns to Maruts, translated by Müller, SBE. xxxii.

Mitra: Windischmann, Abh. K. M., 1857; Weber, IS. xvii. 212 (see Varuna).

Namuci: Lanman, JAS. Beng. viii. 1889; Bloomfield, JAOS. xv. 143.

Nritus as Nerthus, Hoffmann; (Roth) Bruce, Vedic Conceptions of the Earth, JRAS. 1862, p. 321; Prithivī, ZDMG. xli. 494.

Parjanya: Bühler, Zur Mythologie des Rig Veda, OO. i. 214; Hirt, IF. i. 481, 'oak-god.'[2]

Purandhi: Pischel, VS. i. 202; Hillebrandt, WZKM. iii. 188, 259; Colinet, BOR. ii. 245, iv. 121 ('abundance'), Congress, 1892.

Priçni (pṛçni) as Frigy, KZ. ii. 478; 'freckles,' KZ. xix. 438.

Pūshan: Muir, OST. v. 171; Bergaigne, La Relig. Véd., ii. 420; Hillebrandt, Ved. Myth., i. 456 (with Soma); Gubernatis, Letture, p. 82 (as Setting Sun); Pischel, VS. i. 11 (Sūryā and Pūshan); Perry, Notes on the Vedic Deity Pūshan, Drisler Memorial, p. 240.

Ribhus (ṛbhavas, etymology, 'alf,' 'Orpheus'; or Orpheus from ṛgh, ὀρχέεται, Kuhn, KZ. iv. 103; Wackernagel, KZ. xxiv. 297); Ludwig, iii. 187, as Seasons. Nève, Études sur les hymnes (1842), and Essai sur le mythe des Ribhavas (1847, misleading, Ribhu as apotheosis).

Rohitas: Henry (above).

Rudra (etymology, Pischel, VS. i. 57[3]): Weber, Vedic Conception of, IS. ii. 19; Pischel, Vedica, ZDMG. xl. 120; Rudra's mouse

[1] Maspiter is Mars-pater.

[2] Hirt equates Parjanya, Perkúnas, Fjörgyn, as originally epithet of Dyāus-Zeus, with Φηγοναῖος, the 'Oak-god.' See also Zimmer, ZDA. vii. (19) 164.

[3] Müller explains Rudra as 'howler'; Leo identifies him with Wuotan; Jones with Apollo, Kuhn, KZ. iii. 335: as A.-Sax., Rodor. *ib.* ii. 478: P. von Bradke. ZDMG. xl. 361. Oldenberg's delineation of Rudra in Die Religion des Veda is based on the Brahmanic Rudra-Çiva (see PAOS. Dec. 1894).

and Smintheus, KZ. iii. 335; Grohmann, Apollo Smintheus und die Bedeutung der Mäuse in der Mythologie der Indogermanen.

Saranyu (saraṇyū): ἐριννύς, ZDA. vi. 117; KZ. i. 439 (storm; riddle, *ib.* 440); Bloomfield, JAOS. xv. 172; as Dawn, Müller, Lectures, Second Series; Saramā, and Sārameyas as Hermeias, *ib.*; Aufrecht, ZDMG. xiii. 493 (RV. x. 108, translated).

Soma: Windischmann, Ueber den Somacultus der Arier, Abh. Münch. Ak., iv; Roth, ZDMG. xxxv. 681, xxxviii. 134; Ehni, *ib.* xxxiii. 166; Hillebrandt, Vedische Mythologie, i; Soma and the eagle, Kuhn, Herabkunft (above); Roth, ZDMG. xxxvi. 353; Bloomfield, JAOS. xvi (p. 1, further literature), Festgruss an Roth, p. 149; Weber, Vedische Beiträge, p. 3 (Sitz. Berl. Ak. 1894, p. 775); and Agni ritual, Knauer, Vedische Fragen, Festgruss an Roth, p. 61.

Sūrya (see Haritas): Sonne, hymn to, KZ. xii–xv; form of word, J. Schmidt, KZ. xxvi. 9. See Pūshan (and Hinduism, below). Sāvitrī, Whitney, Colebrooke's Essays, ii. 111.

Trita: Macdonnell, Mythological Studies, JRAS. 1893, p. 419 (apām napāt, lightning; Trita as Thridhi, name of Odin, 'third' form of fire); form of word, BB. ix. 99; Perry, see Indra (p. 26); Bloomfield, PAOS. 1894, p. cxix. Other literature, Kaegi, *loc. cit.*, note 112 d.

Ushas (uṣas): Muir, v. 181; Bergaigne, i. 241, etc.; Sonne, KZ. x. 416; Müller, Science of Language, ii. 391, etc.

Vāc: logos, Weber, IS. ix. 473.

Varuna (varuṇa): Roth, ZDMG. vi. 71; Weber, IS. xvii. 212; Muir, v. 58; Bergaigne, iii. 110; Hillebrandt, Varuṇa und Mitra; Darmesteter, Ormazd et Ahriman; Sonne, KZ. xii. 364; Pischel, VS. i. 188; Geldner, *ib.* 142; Ludwig, iii. 314; Oldenberg as a borrowed god (PAOS. 1894); as water, Geldner, BB. xi. 329; form of word, Bollensen, ZDMG. xli. 504 (var 'hell sein'); Bohnenberger (Roth), Varuṇa nach den Liedern des Rig Veda (Mitra as appellative becomes a new god, p. 85);[1] as svar, Regnaud, Rev. xix. 79.

Vāstoshpati ('house-lord'): Windisch, Vassus und Vassallus, Bericht. d. k. Säch. Gesell. 1892, p. 174 (vassus for vast).

Vāta, Vayu (vāta is ἀήτης, 'wind'): Stokes, BB. xix. 74, compares

[1] Kerbaker, Varuna e gli Aditya (Naples, Proceedings of the Royal Academy) is known to us only by title.

Irish fath, 'breath,' but gives also fáth, a kind of poem (vates, vôds, English 'wood' as 'mad'). Vāta, Wuotan, Zimmer, ZDA. vii. (19) 179.

Vishnu (viṣṇu like jishnu, jiṣṇu, vi, 'fly,' the heavenly bird?): Muir, iv and v (older texts relative to Vishnu), PAOS. Dec. 1894.

Yama: Roth, ZDMG. ii. 216, iv, 417 (Jemshid), JAOS. iii. 335, IS. xiv. 393; Whitney, Oriental and Linguistic Studies, i. 46; Müller, Science of Language, ii. 528, 534; Westergaard, with Weber's notes, IS. iii. 402; Muir, JRAS. i. 287; OST. v. 284; Bergaigne, i. 86, ii. 96, etc.; Grassmann, KZ. xi. 13, 'binder'; Ehni, Der Vedische Mythus des Yama; Hillebrandt, Vedische Mythologie, i. 489; Bloomfield, JAOS. xv. 163, 172; Hopkins, PAOS. 1891, p. xciv; Scherman, Visionsliteratur; Leumann, KZ. xxxii. 301 (Yamī[1]); L. von Schroeder, Literatur, p. 217 (Ymir, Prajāpati); Bréal, Hercule et Cercus; Benfey, Vedica, 149; Van den Gheyn, Cerbère (1883); Casartelli, Dog of Death, BOR. iv. 265.[2] Yama's sadana, Pischel, VS. i. 242.[3]

Veda and Brahmanism: Oldenberg, Die Hymnen des Rig Veda, and ZDMG. xlii. 199, Ueber die Liedverfasser des Rig Veda (see Hinduism, below); Roth, *ib.* iv. 514, divisions of the Rig Veda; Bergaigne, Recherches sur l'histoire de la Samhitā du Rig Veda, JA.

[1] The author justly remarks that no sociological data can be made of Yama's wife or sister.

[2] Dog sees Death, sharp sight of dog causes myth.

[3] Other less important examples of etymological ingenuity are Scherer, Brahman as flamen (Βράγκος, Bragi, see Kaegi, Rig Veda, note 82); abhraditā as Aphrodite, Sonne, KZ. x. 415; Ahalyā as Achilleus, Weber, Sitz. Berl. Ak., 1887; Idā as Iris (Windischmann), Poseidon, potídas, iḍaspati (Fick, KZ. xxi. 462); but in KZ. i. 459 Poseidon is patye davan. On the form compare BB. viii. 80; x. 287; KZ. xxx. 570. Prellwitz, BB. ix. 327, agrees with Fick and Pott as to iḍas representing οἶδμα and compares προσκλύστιος. Garga is Gorgo, Kern, JRAS. iv. 431; Pājasya is Pegasos, etc., KZ. i. 416, xxix. 222; Parvata is Pelasgos, Burda, KZ. xxi. 470; but compare Stier, *ib.* xi. 229, where Pelasgoi are 'cranes'; and Pischel, *ib.* xx. 369, where they are παῤῥάσιοι. Sabheya is Yaviṣṭha (not Hephaistos, as says Kuhn), Müller, *ib.* xviii. 212; and vṛtrahan is not Bellerophon (as says Pott), *ib.* iv. 416, v. 140 (bellero is varvara). Çarád is Ceres, Müller, *ib.* xviii. 211; svavān is εὔας, Aufrecht, ZDMG. xiii. 499; svar 'sing' in Silenus, Siren; Buddhaguru in Pythagoras, etc. Helena is Saramā, and Hermes is Sārameya, Müller, Chips, ii. 138, note. Compare for further clever guesses Cox's Aryan Mythology, Müller's Lectures, Second Series, and Biographies of Words.

(1886 and following years), also on the liturgy, *ib.* 1888; JA. x. No. 3; Pincott, JRAS. xvi. 381; Hillebrandt, Spuren einer älteren Rig Veda Recension, BB. viii. 195; Lanman, JAOS. x. 580; Brunnhofer, KZ. xxv. 374, BB. x. 234 (Collitz, BB. vii. 183); Roth, on the worth of tradition, ZDMG. xxi. 1; Whitney, on Translation of Veda, OLS.; PAOS. Oct. 1867; Goldstücker on Sāyaṇa, in Preface to Pāṇini. Cult against mantra, Roth, ZDMG. vii. 604; viii. 467; Weber, *ib.* viii. 389; Pischel and Geldner, Preface to Vedische Studien and ZDMG. xlviii. 702; Colinet, Les Principes de l'exégèse védique, Muséon, 1890; Bloomfield, Contributions (above); E. Hardy, Die Vedisch-brahmanische Periode d. Relig. d. Alt. Ind.; Muir, Priests and Interpreters of the Veda, JRAS. ii. 257, 303; Haug, Contribution, 1863, and Interpretation of the Veda, Congress, 1874; Ludwig, Die philosophischen und religiösen Anschauungen des Veda; also Ludwig, Rig-Veda, iii (Mantra-Literatur), pp. 262, 284, 301, and his works. Ueber Methode bei Interpretationen des Rig Veda, and Ueber die neuesten Arbeiten auf dem Gebiet der RV. Forschung. Further (Vedic and later literature), Oldenberg, ZDMG. xxxvii. 54; *ib.* xxxix. 52; Windisch, Verh. d. Geraer Philologen Versammlung, Vedische Wettfahrt, in Festgruss an Roth; Weber, Episches im Vedischen Ritual, Sitz. Berl. Ak., 1891; Schermann, Philosophische Hymnen (also Visionsliteratur).

Vedic and Brahmanic Belief: Pott, Vedic and Orphic Kosmic Egg, Ovidiana, KZ. viii. 179 (Peleus as *Urschlamm!*); von Bradke, Beiträge z. altind. Religions und Sprachgeschichte, ZDMG. xl. 347, 655; Schrader, chapter xiii; Zimmer, AIL.; Roth and Böhtlingk, Vedische Räthsel, ZDMG. xxxvii. 109; (and eschatology) xlvi. 759; Windisch, *ib.* xlviii. 353.[1] **Eschatology**: Weber, Eine Legende, ZDMG. ix. 237 (Bhrigu) and 308; Burnell, a Legend from the Talavakāra, Congress, 1880, IA. xiii. 16, 21; Benfey, Orient und Occident, iii. 169, and Hermes, Minos, Tartaros; Whitney, PAOS., Nov., 1858, May, 1886; Böhtlingk, Bericht d. k. Sächs. Gesell., 23. April, 1893, p. 88; **Henotheism**: Whitney, *loc. cit.*, Oct. 1881, see IA. xi. 146; Hopkins, Drisler Memorial. Social position of priests

[1] Compare Deussen, Geschichte der Philosophie, i. 105. On Vedic and Sanskrit Riddles, *loc. cit.;* also Haug, Vedische Räthselfragen (also Brahma und die Brahmanen); Führer, ZDMG. xxxix. 99.

(castes), Weber,[1] Nachträge, p. 795; Collectanea, IS. x; Muir, JRAS. ii. 257; OST. i; Hopkins, Four Castes, also JAOS. xiii; Schlagintweit (Caste at Present), ZDMG. xxxiii. 549. **Cult**: E. Hardy, *loc. cit.* above; on *Om* see Bloomfield, PAOS. Oct. 1889; Cult of **Manes**, Caland, Altind. Ahnencult, and Ueber Totenverehrung bei Einigen der IE. Völker; Winternitz, WZKM. iv. 199; Whitney, OLS. i. 46; Kaegi, *loc. cit.*, note 265, with literature. **Funeral**: Roth, ZDMG. viii. 467; Müller, *ib.* ix. pp. i and xliii (sic): Wilson, JRAS. 1854, p. 201; Regnaud, Çrāddha védique, Rev. d'hist. d. relig. xxv. 1; Donner, piṇḍapitṛyajña; Lanman, Mortuary Urns, PAOS. May, 1891. **Wedding**: Weber, Hochzeitssprüche, IS. v. 177; Stenzler, Pāraskara, ZDMG. vii. 527; Haas, Heiratsgebräuche d. alten Inder, IS. v. 267; Schröder, Die Hochzeitsbräuche der Esten; Winternitz, Das Ai. Hochzeitsrituell. **Omens, Ordeals**, etc.: Weber, Zwei Vedische Texte über Omina und Portenta, Wurfel-Orakel, Vedische Beiträge;[2] Schlagintweit, Gottesurtheile; Stenzler, ZDMG. ix. 661; Kaegi, Alter und Herkunft der germanischen Gottesurtheile (with further literature); Jolly, Beiträge zur Rechtsgeschichte, ZDMG. xliv. 347. The earliest essay on Ordeals was presented by Warren Hastings, 1784, Asiatick Researches, i. 389. **Star-lore**: Colebrooke; Weber, IS. ii. 236; Haug, Introduction to Ait. Br.; Weber, Die Vedischen Nachrichten von d. Nakshatra; Sitz. Berl. Ak. 1861, p. 267;[3] Müller, Ancient Hindu Astronomy and Chronology; Burgess, JRAS. xxv. 717; Jacobi, Methods and Tables. **Witchcraft, Medicine**: Kuhn, KZ. xiii. 49; Grohmann, IS. ix. 381; Bloomfield, Contributions, AJP. vii, xi, xii; Pictet, KZ. v. 24, 321; Jolly, Knoblauch, Festgruss an Roth, p. 18; medicine and divination, Bower MS.,

[1] There is an essay on this subject by Kern, Ind. Theorieen over de Standenverdeeling, which we have not seen.

[2] Sitz. Berl. Ak. 1858, 1859, and 1894, respectively. The Wurfel-Orakel (and Schiefner) is published also in Ind. Streifen, i. 274. The essay on Omina and Portenta contains translations of parts of the Shaḍviṅça Brāhmaṇa, of the Sāma Veda, and of the Kāuçika (AV.) Sūtra.

[3] (Whitney) Burgess, Sūryasiddhānta, JAOS. vi; JRAS. 1863, p. 345; Whitney, *ib.* i. 316; Lunar Zodiac, Or. Ling. St., ii. 341; Kern, translation of BS., JRAS. iv–vii; IS. x, xiv, xv; Weber, Ueber altirānische Sternnamen, Sitz. Berl. Ak., 1888; see also Whitney, JAOS. viii. 1, 382; Burgess, *ib.* 309; Weber, IS. ix. 424, x. 213; Whitney *vs.* Ludwig, PAOS., 1885. On the twelve intercalated days, 'Twelfth Night,' see Weber, IS. v. 437 (Çabalī-homa), xvii. 224.

JASB. 1891; IA. xxi. 29, 129; WZKM. v. 103. **Blood-money**: Roth, ZDMG. xli. 672; Aryan and Indic, Bühler and Schroeder, Festgruss an Roth; Jolly, *loc. cit.*, p. 339. **Sacrifices**: Hillebrandt. Das altind. Neu- u. Vollmondsopfer, and Nationale Opfer, Festgruss an Böhtlingk; Lindner, Die Dīkskā, and *loc. cit.*, Ernteopfer: Weber, Vājapeya and Rājasūya, Sitz. Berl. Ak., 1892, 1893, and Zur Kenntniss d. Ved. Opferrituals, IS. x. 321, xiii. 217; Schwab, Das Altindische Thieropfer. **Suttee and Human Sacrifices**: Colebrooke, Duties of Faithful Hindu Widow, Asiatick Researches, iv. 209; Wilson, JRAS. 1851, p. 96, 1854, p. 201, 1859, p. 209; Müller, Chips, ii. 34; Hall, JRAS. iii. 183, 193; Rājendralāla Mitra, Indo-Aryans, ii. 114; Weber, ZDMG. vii. 585, xviii. 262 (Manu, Minotaur, *ib.* p. 286), Ind. Streifen, i. 54; Zimmer, AIL. p. 328; Hillebrandt, ZDMG. xl. 711. **Ritual,** etc.: (above and) Müller, ZDMG. ix. p. xliii; Garbe, ZDMG. xxxiv. 319 (Pravargya); Rarity of Ṣoma-sacrifice, Haug, ZDMG. xvi. 273; Hindu Doctrine of Atonement, Stenzler, Congress, 1874, p. 205; Atharva Ritual, Garbe, Vāitāna Sūtra; Magoun, Asurī Kalpa; Agni Sacrifice, Thibaut, Agni Citi, Pandit, JAS. Beng., xliv, 1875, Çulva Sūtra; Koulikovski, Les Trois Feux Sacrés, Rev. xx. 121. **Serpent-worship**: Stier, Sarpedon, KZ. xi. 234; Fergusson, Tree and Serpent Worship; Cuthbert, Serpent Temples, JRAS. 1846, p. 407; compare *ib.* 1891; Winternitz, Sarpabali, Schlangencult, Mit. d. anthrop. Gesell., Wien, xviii; IA. xv. 258; Bühler, *ib.* vi. 270; Snakes and Buddha, Bendall, Meghasūtra, JRAS. xii. 286; Senart, Buddha; Oldham, JRAS. xxiii. 361. **Idols**: Weber, Omina und Portenta, p. 337; Ludwig, Nachrichten; Bollensen, ZDMG. xxii. 587, xlvii. 586; Müller, Chips, i. 37:[1] Muir, OST., v. 453; Kaegi, Rig Veda, note 79a. **Ages and Holy Numbers**:[2] Roth, Ueber den AV., and Ueber den Mythus von den fünf Menschen-Geschlechtern bei Hesiod; Weber, Cycles, IS. ix. 460; ZDMG. xv. 132; Kaegi, Die Neunzahl; Schroeder, seven as holy number, KZ. xxix. 224; Hopkins, Holy Numbers of the Rig Veda.[3] See Star-lore, above.

[1] The statement is here made that the Vedic religion knows nothing of idols; but see the other cited works which seem to disprove this.

[2] The 'Fifteen Puzzle' is Indic (IA. x. 89, xi. 83).

[3] Triton und Euphemos, oder Die Argonauten in Libyen, by Water, in 1849, treats of the holy seven in a ridiculous way. Not less ridiculous is the author's attempt to explain everything by the Moon-Cult, thus anticipating modern vagaries.

Brahmanism: Specimens, Muir, OST. iv; Sāman, Benfey, Griffith; Shaḍviṅça, Weber, Omina (above); Māit. S., Haug, IS. ix. 174; von Schroeder, Literatur, and ZDMG. xxxiii. 177; Çatapatha, partial translation, Eggeling, SBE., xii, xxvi, xli: Muir, JRAS. 1862, p. 31 (OST.); Weber, IS. i. 161 and Ind. Streifen, i. 9; first chapter, ZDMG. iv. 289; Brunnhofer (relation of parts), BB. x. 234; Āit. Br., Haug; Weber, IS. ix. 177; Deluge, etc., Bopp, Sündflüt; Weber, ZDMG. v. 525, Ind. Streifen, i. 9; Roth, ZDMG. vi. 243; Lindner, Ir. Fluthsage, Festgruss an Roth. **Upanishads**:[1] Cowell, Roer, Bib. Ind.; Whitney, Böhtlingk (Kaṭha, Chāndogya, Ait. Kāushītakī, Kena, Bṛhadāraṇyaka); Weber, IS. i, ii, ix; Müller, SBE., i, xv (all the chief works);[2] Oertel, Jāiminīya, PAOS. 1894; list of, Müller, ZDMG. xix. 137; Concordance of Upanishads, Jacob. For a general introduction the best work in English are the translations in the Sacred Books. Gough's Philosophy of the Upanishads has many translations, but the book is otherwise not to be recommended. On ātmā as *ἀϋτμήν*, see KZ. xvii. 145. **Philosophy**: Deussen, Das System des Vedānta, 1883, is now the standard work;[3] to which should be added the same author's Sūtra; Jacob's Vedāntasāra; and Thibaut, Vedānta Sūtra, SBE. xxxiv.[4] For the Sānkhya, Davies, Sānkhya; and Ballantyne, Aphorisms; but the best work is now Garbe, Die Sāṃkhya Philosophie (1894). A good general introduction to Hindu Pantheism has been given by Lanman, Beginnings of Hindu Pantheism. The best general summary[5] of Hindu philosophies is found in the revised edition of Colebrooke's Essays. Other special studies include Roth, Brahma und die Brahmanen,[6]

[1] A curious though useless classic is Anquetil du Perron's Oupnekhat, 1801, the first European version of the Upanishads (through the Persian).

[2] Whitney, AJP. vii. 1, xi. 407; Jacob, IA. xv. 279; Whitney Trans. Phil. Ass. xxi. 88; Böhtlingk, Bericht d. k. Sächs. Gesellschaft, 1890, and separately.

[3] Compare Windischmann, Sancara, 1833; Ecstein, IS. ii. 369; and Bruining-Bijdrage tot de Kennis van den Vedānta, 1871.

[4] Compare two native expositions, JRAS. x. 33 (Vedantic conception of *brahma*), and WZKM. ii. 95 (Çankara's *advaita* philosophy); also Müller, Three Lectures.

[5] Compare Ballantyne's Hindu Philosophy, Williams' Indian Wisdom, Brahmanism and Hinduism, Religious Thought and Life, and also the excellent chapters in Weber's Lectures (above), and in Schroeder's Literatur und Cultur. Of Deussen's Allgemeine Geschichte der Philosophie one half volume has appeared.

[6] Haug has an article on the Māit. Saṁh. with the same title, Brahma und Die Brahmanen.

ZDMG. i. 66 (on *brahma*); Müller, *ib.* vi. 1, 219, vii. 287 (Beiträge zur Kenntniss der Ind. Phil.); Roer, *ib.* xxi. 309, xxii. 383 (Die Lehrsprüche der Vaiçeshika Philosophie); Muir, Theism in Vaiçeshika Philosophy, JRAS. 1862, p. 22; Ballantyne, Nyāyasūtras; Windisch, Ueber das Nyāyabhāshya, 1888, and Sitz der denkenden Seele, Beitr. d. k. Sächs. Gesell., 1891, p. 55; Ballantyne and Cowell, Çāṇḍilya's Aphorisms (text by B., translation by C., Bib. Ind.); Regnaud, Le Pessimisme Brāhmanique, Ann. du Mus. Guimet, i, and Matériaux pour servir à l'histoire de la philosophie d'Inde. The Sarvadarçanasaṅgraha is translated by Cowell and Gough. The Sūtras of the six systems have all been translated (with the texts) in India. On the date of Çankara see Pathak, IA. xi. 174; and Telang and Fleet, *ib.* xiii. 95, xvi. 41; Logan, *ib.* xvi. 160.

House-rules and Law: All the most important manuals of custom and law have been translated by Stenzler, Bühler, Jolly, Oldenberg, Bloomfield and Knauer (SBE. ii, vii, xiv, xxv, xxix, xxx, xxxiii; Stenzler, Pāraskara, Āçvalāyana and Yājñavalkya; Oldenberg, IS. xv. 1, Çāñkhāyana; Knauer, Gobhila, also Vedische Fragen, Festgruss an Roth; Bloomfield, Gobhila, ZDMG. xxxv. 533).[1]

JAINISM.

Colebrooke's Essays (Cowell), ii. 402; Lassen, iv. 763; Wilson, Essays, i. 319; Weber, IS. xv. 263, xvi. 211, xvii. 1,[2] and Berlin MSS., vol. ii, 1892; Klatt, Stotra (MSS.), ZDMG. xxxiii. 445; Leumann, Berichte von den Schismen der Jaina, IS. xvii. 91; Jacobi, Stutayas and Stotra, ZDMG. xxxii. 509, IS. xiv. 359, also origin of sects, ZDMG. xxxviii. 1, Introduction to Kalpa Sūtra (Abh. k. M.,[3] 1879, Mahāvīra is Nātaputta). Compare also Jacobi, ZDMG. xxxiv. 247; Oldenberg, *ib.* 748; Jacobi, *ib.* xxxv. 667, xl. 92; Burnell, IA.

[1] House-ritual: Āçvalāyana, Gobhila, Çāñkhāyana, Pāraskara, Khādira, Hiraṇyakeçin, Āpastamba. Law: Āpastamba, Gāutama, Vasistha, Bāudhāyana, Vājñavalkya, Vishnu, Nārada, Brihaspati, Manu. The last is also translated by Loiseleur, Jones, Burnell and Hopkins (besides Bühler, SBE., above).

[2] Ueber die heiligen Schriften, translated into English by Smyth in the Indian Antiquary, 1893.

[3] Feer, JA. 1888 (xii), p. 209. Leumann has published in the same German series the Aupapātika Sūtra, but as yet only the text (1883) has appeared.

ii. 354; Rice and Bühler, *ib.* iii. 153, vii. 28, 143, etc.; Burgess, *ib.* xiii. 191; Windisch, Hemacandra's Yogaçāstra, ZDMG. xxviii. 185. Jacobi has translated Ācārānga and Kalpa Sūtras for SBE. xxii. Hoernle, Digambara Pattavalis, IA. xx. 341, xxi. 57. A popular essay on Jains by Williams appeared JRAS. xx. 279. On Jain tradition compare Bühler, Sitz. Wien. Ak. 1883, WZKM. i. 165, ii. 141, iii. 233, iv. 313, v. 59, 175 (Mathurā, Congress, 1892, p. 219). On Gosāla compare Hoernle, Bib. Ind., Uvāsaga Dasāo (seventh Anga) with Leumann's review; and Rockhill, Life of Buddha, p. 249. Compare also Jain Bhārata and Rāmāyaṇa of Pampa, Rice, JRAS. xiv. 19; Leumann, Daçavaikalika-Sūtra und Niryukti, Jinabhadra's Jītakalpa, Sitz. Berl. Ak. 1892, Die Legende von Citta und Saṁbhūta, WZKM. v. 111, vi. 1; Thomas, Early Faith of Açoka (to show prior Jainism; a dubious contention) JRAS. ix. 155. On the Jain nurture of vermin see JRAS. 1834, p. 96. On dates compare Jacobi, Kalpasūtra and Oldenberg (above). The Çatruñjaya Māhātmyam (Weber, Abh. k. M., 1858) is probably not an early work (Bühler, Three New Edicts, IA. vi. 154). On Weber's view in regard to Jain-Greek legends see his essay Ahalyā-Achilleus, Sitz. Berl. Ak., 1887. See too Barth, Revue, xix. 292 ff., xx. 332.

BUDDHISM.

Colebrook's Essays; Wilson, Buddha and Buddhism, JRAS., 1856, pp. 229, 357; Bennett, Gaudama, JAOS. ii. 3; R. Spence Hardy, Eastern Monarchism and Manual of Buddhism; E. Hardy, Der Buddhismus nach älteren Pāliwerken; Burnouf, Le Lotus de la Bonne Loi and Introduction à l'histoire du Bouddhisme indien (Nepal); Köppen, Die Religion des Buddha; Weber, Ueber den Buddhismus, Ind. Skizzen, and Streifen, i. 104; Barthélemy Saint-Hilaire, Le Bouddha et sa religion (now antiquated); Oldenberg, Buddha; Kern, Der Buddhismus; T. W. Rhys Davids, Manual of Buddhism, and Hibbert Lectures; Copleston, Buddhism; Monier Williams, Buddhism;[1] Mary Sumner's

[1] Of the many manuals we recommend especially those of Rhys Davids for ontology (also Jātakas. First Part) and Oldenberg (now in second edition). For Northern Buddhism Köppen's Religion is still excellent, although it is vitiated by the point of view taken by the author, who regards Buddha as an emancipator, a political innovator, etc. Davids has two recent articles on Buddhist sects, JRAS. xxiii. 409; xxiv. 1 (see also below).

Histoire (ed. Foucaux); Senart's Essai sur la légende du Buddha, JA. 1873, p. 114; 1874, p. 249; 1875, p. 97, and published separately. Valuable is the same author's article, JA. viii, 1876, Notes, and work (containing) Les Inscriptions de Piyadasi; compare IA. xvii. 188; ZDMG. xl. 127 (Bühler). On Nāgārjuna (second century) see Beal, IA. xv. 353. Of historical interest, if otherwise valueless, are Schoebel, Le Buddha et le Bouddhisme, 1857; and Holmboe, Traces de Buddhisme en Norvège avant l'introduction du christianisme. Lillie, Buddha and Early Buddhism, also Influence of Buddhism on Christianity, and JRAS. xiv. 218, Buddhist Saint Worship, and *ib.* xv. 419, on Ceylon Buddhism; Beal, Schools, IA. ix. 299.

Buddhist Texts: Burnouf, Foucaux, above; Weber, Dhammapada,[1] ZDMG. xiv. 29: Müller, Science of Religion, and SBE. x, with Fausböll's Sutta Nipāta; J. Weber and Huth, Tib. Buddhist Sūtras, ZDMG. xlv. 577; Pischel, Assalāyana Sutta; Childers, Khuddaka Pātha, JRAS. iv. 309; Davids, Buddhist Suttas translated from the Pāli; and Davids and Oldenberg,[2] Vinaya Texts, SBE. xi, xiii, xvii, xx; Kern, Lotus, *ib.* xxi; Davids, Milinda, *ib.* xxxv; Cowell and Müller, Mahāyāna Sūtras, *ib.* xlix; Foucaux, Lalita Vistara, Ann. du MG. vi, xix; Pratimokha, above, and Beal and Gogerly, JRAS. 1862, p. 407; Dickson, *ib.* vii. 1, viii. 62; Childers, *ib.* vii. 49; viii. 219; Rogers (and Müller), Buddhaghosha's Parables; Foulkes, IA. xix. 105; Carus, Gospel of Buddha.

Nirvāṇa: Out of the immense literature we select Müller (Buddhist Nihilism), Science of Religion, p. 141; Oldenberg, Buddha, p. 273; Frankfurter, JRAS. xii. 548; Rhys Davids, Manual, and Hibbert Lectures, tenth Appendix.

Date of Nirvāṇa: Westergaard, Buddha's Totesjahr, Ueber den ältesten Zeitraum der Ind. Geschichte; Cunningham, Bhilsa Topes: Bühler IA. vi. 149 ff., Three New Edicts of Açoka; Kern, Jaartelling; Müller, Acad. March 1, 1884, SBE. x.: Davids, Ancient Coins and Measures of Ceylon, p. 57; Oldenberg, Vinaya Pitaka, SBE. xiii. p. xxii.[3]

[1] L. von Schroeder, Worte der Wahrheit. On the word Dhammapada, Franke ZDMG. xlvi. 734.

[2] Also Oldenberg, Dīpavaṁsa, with text.

[3] For Nirvāna and its date all the manuals may be consulted. See also D'Alwis, Nirvāna (with translation); Edkins, JRAS. xiii. 59, Congress, 1880, p. 295; Chil-

Foreign Buddhism: Stan. Julien, Histoire de la vie de Hiouen Thsang, Mémoires (compare JA. Dec. 1857), Voyages des Pélerins Bouddhistes; Wassiljew, Der Buddhismus; Bigandet, Life of Gaudama; Fergusson, Hiouen Thsang's Journey from Patna, JRAS. vi. 213, 396: Wilson, *ib.* 1859, p. 106 ('Summary Account'); JAS. Beng. i; As. Researches, xx (Csoma, Asiatic Buddhism); Beal, Diamond Sūtras (etc., JRAS.); Gutzlaff (Sykes), Buddhism in China, JRAS. 1854, p. 73; 1856, pp. 316, 357 (Wilson, Notes, Inscriptions); Edkins, Chinese Buddhism; Beal (Chinese), Dhammapada, The Romantic Legend, and Travels of the Buddhist Pilgrim Fah-Hian,[1] Life of Buddha, BOR. *passim;* Müller, Buddhist Pilgrims, Chips, i; Köppen (above); Hodgson, Memoirs; Burnouf (above); Schlagintweit, Buddhistic Idols in Tibet, JRAS. 1863, p. 437, and (Ann. du Musée Guimet, iii) Buddhism in Tibet (Lamaism in the second part); Rockhill, The Life of Buddha, and The Land of the Lamas; Lamaistic succession, Mayers, JRAS. iv. 284; Lamaist extension of Buddhist Confession, IA. xxiii. 73; Lamaism and Catholicism, Davids, Hibbert Lectures; Modern Lamaism, Waddell, Buddhism of Thibet or Lamaism; Schiefner, Tāranātha's Geschichte (and Tibetische Lebensbeschreibung); Tibet texts (above); Bastian, Buddhist Literature of the Burmese, ZDMG. xvii. 697, and Buddhist Psychology, *ib.* xx. 419; Führer, Buddhist Manu, BBRAS. xv. 329; Jardine and Forchhammer, Notes on Buddhist Law (in Burmah); Friederich, Buddhism in Bali, JRAS. viii. 158, ix. 59; dharmaçāstra, IA. xiii. 24; Crawfurd, Hindu Religion in Bali, AR. xiii. 128;[2] in Ceylon, Foulkes, IA. xvii. 100.

Buddhist Legends: Burnouf, Introduction; Davids. Buddhist Birth Stories, and BOR. iv. 9; Beal, JRAS. vi. 377; Fausböll, Two Jātakas, JRAS. v. i., Five and Ten (1872); Feer, JA. 1875 (v,

ders, Dictionary, JRAS. v. 219, 289, vii. 49, etc.; Fergusson, *ib.* iv. 81 (Indic Chronology); Müller, Origin of Religion, p. 139, note, and Introduction to Buddhaghosha, and to Dhammapada (above). We incline to accept 471 to 483 as the extreme limits of the date of Buddha's death (Kern, 380; Davids, 412).

1 On I-tsing (671) see Beal, IA. x. 109, 194; Müller, India. 'Fâ-Hien's' travels are now published by Legge, 'Record of Buddhistic Kingdoms.' There are other editions. See also Sykes, JRAS. 1841, p. 248; Beal, *ib.* xix. 191.

2 On Japanese Buddhism there have been published some texts by Japanese scholars (ed. Müller, Aryan Series of Anecdota Oxoniensia). See JRAS. xii. 153.

vi);[1] Fausböll, Weber, IS. v. 412; Açvaghosha (fifth century); Weber, Streifen, i. 186: Cowell, Açvaghosha: Lévi, JA. 1892, p. 201; Beal, SBE. xix. **Hells:** Feer, Études Bouddhiques, l'Enfer indien, JA. 1892, p. 185, 1893, p. 112;[2] Köppen, p. 239; Senart, Notes, JA. viii. 477. **Symbols:** Cunningham, JRAS. 1851, pp. 71, 114; Hodgson, *ib.* 1861, p. 393; Sewell and Pincott, *ib.* xix. 238 and xxii. 299;[3] IA. vii. 176; *ib.* xv. 61, 89, 217, and following volumes (sacred trees); Lillie, Saints and Trees, JRAS. xiv. 218. **Topes, Temples:** Cunningham, above, p. 108, and Stūpa of Bharhut, Bhilsa Topes (synods, schisms): Fergusson, Rock-cut Temples of India, JRAS. 1844, p. 30, and Topes of Sānchi and Amarāvatī; Beal, JRAS. v. 164; Burgess, Arch. Surv. of Western India, and Cave Temples of India (symbols) with Fergusson; the latter, History of Indian and Eastern Architecture, Tree and Serpent Worship; Simpson, JRAS. xxi. 49 (temples from tombs); Müller, Dagobas from Ceylon, ZDMG. xii. 514[4] (also dates). Women leaders of Buddhist Reformation, Miss Bode, JRAS. xxv. 517.

Brahmanism and Buddhism: Burnouf, Bh. P. Introd. p. 137 (Indra highest god); Williams, JRAS. xviii. 127; Holtzmann, Zur Geschichte, p. 103; (and Jainism) Leumann, Die Legende von Citta und Sambhūta, WZKM (above); Bastian, Brahmanic Inscriptions in Buddhist Temples (of Siam), JAOS. viii. 377.

Buddhist heresies, Dīpavaṁsa (above); doctrines, Wassiljew (above); Le Buddhisme et les Grecs, Lévi, Revue, xxiii. 36.

1 Chalmers, Jātakas (ed. Cowell, vol. I) is announced. Compare JRAS. xxiv. 423. On Barlaam u. Joasaph see now the exhaustive essay of Kuhn, Abh. d. k. Bayerisch. Ak. 1894 (with all literature).

2 By the same, Avadānaçataka, Mus. Guimet, xviii (JA. 1879, xiv). The Daṭhavamça, Melloné, Ann. du MG. vii.

3 Triratna and triçula. The articles following are by Murray-Aynsley (Asiatic Symbolism), on svastika, trees, serpents, evil eye, etc. On the evil eye and the poison-girl, viṣakanyā, see now the interesting essay of Hertz (Abh. d. Bayern. Akad, 1894), who connects the superstition with the religious practice described above, p. 505, note 2.

4 For older essays see also Schönberg, ZDMG. vii. 101 (rock-temples); JAS. Beng. xxv. 222 (Khandgiri temples); Yule, JAS. Beng., 1857, Ancient Buddhistic Remains (on the Irawady): Sykes, Miniature Caityas in Buddhist topes, JRAS. 1854, pp. 37, 227.

HINDUISM.

Epic: Ktesias, IA. x. 296 ff.; McCrindle, Ancient India as described by Ktesias and by Megasthenes and Arrian;[1] date of Bhārata, Bühler, Kirste, Ind. Studies, No. ii; in Cambodia, Barth, Inscriptions Sanskrites du Cambodge; of Rāmāyaṇa, Weber, Rāmāyaṇa, IA., reprint; Jacobi, Ramāyaṇa,[2] Festgruss an Böhtlingk, p. 44, GGA., Nos. 16 of 1892, 1893; epic language, Franke, Was ist Sanskrit? BB. xvii. 54; epos and Veda, Oldenberg, ZDMG. xxxvii. 54, xxxviii. 439, xxxix. 52; Weber, Episches im Vedischen Ritual,[3] Sitz, Berl. Ak. 1891; Ludwig, Ironie, Festgruss an Böhtlingk. Résumé, Wheeler, History (unreliable); Williams, Indian Wisdom. Translations, Wilson, Sabhā, JRAS. 1842, p. 137; Thomson (1855), Davies, Lorinser, and Telang (SBE. viii), Bhagavad Gīta, etc.; Milman, Nala; Muir, IA. vii, viii, Metrical Translations, and OST.; Arnold, Sāvitrī, Idylls, etc. (free); Holtzmann (Sr.), Indische Sagen; Foucaux, 'Kairata Parva'; Sadous, fragments (1858); H. Fauche (several books of Bhārata); Pratapa Chandra Roy (almost all); Griffith, Rāmāyaṇa, Schoebel (Mus. Guimet, xiii), Gorresio, Fauche, *id.* Studies, Holtzmann, Indra, Apsaras, Brahmā,[4] ZDMG. xxxii. 290, xxxiii. 631, xxxviii. 167, Agni, Arjuna (each separately), Zur Geschichte, Neunzehn Bücher (literature); Hopkins, Manu in Epic, JAOS. xi. 239, Ruling Caste, *ib.* xiii, etc.; Sauer, Mahābhārata and Wate (primitive epic, unconvincing); Nève, Morals and Women (antiquated); Weber, Mother-Worship, Zwei Ved. Texte, and West, IA. x. 245; Roussel, Les idées religieuses, Muséon, xii. 263, 295. For Philosophy, see above. **Purāṇas, Modern Sects:** Lassen, i. 481; Wilson, Analysis, 1838–39 (essays); Burnouf, Bhāgavata; Wilson, Vishnu; Rückert, Mārkaṇḍeya, Wortham, JRAS. xiii. 103, 355 (partial); *ib.* xvii. 221; Wolheim, Padma (Latin, partial); Stevenson, Gaṇeça, JRAS. 1846, p. 319; Ante-Brahmanic Religions, and Feudal-

[1] Çiva is here falsely interpreted as Herakles, p. 39. Compare too Weber, IS. ii. 409, and his Ahalyā-Achilleus, Berl. Ak. 1887. The original Greek is edited by Schwanbeck. On Darius' conquest see Marshman, i. p. 10.

[2] Sixth or eighth century, developed with Buddhistic or Greek influence.

[3] An example of the survival of the Hindu cult in the Çrāuta ritual is given by Weber, IS. v. 437, Çabalī-homa.

[4] Weber on Skanda, IS. iii. 478.

ism, *ib.* 1846, pp. 330, 390; in Dekhan, *ib.* 1838, p. 189; Sykes, Traits, *ib.* 1860, p. 223; Gīta-Govinda, Lassen (Latin), Rückert, ZKM. i. 132. Fables: WZKM. vii. 215; Pratapa Chandra Gosha, Durgāpūjā; Tīrtha: Williams, Hinduism (list), IA. v. 209, Cunningham, Survey; Hunter, Indian Empire (sects), Orissa, and Report; Çivaite sects, Senāthi Rāja, Mus. Guim. vii; Krishna, Weber, ZDMG. vi. 92; Berl. Ak., 1867, p. 217, IS. xiii. 354; Nève, Des éléments étrangers, etc.; Phallus, IA. iv. 211, v. 183, Kittel, Ueber d. Ursprung des Linga Cultus (refutes Wurm, Geschichte der Indischen Religion); Stevenson, JRAS. 1846, p. 337; Pāñcarātra, Hall, Vāsavadatta. Cārvāka, Colebrooke, Muir, *loc. cit.* Varāhamihira, see above. Fate: IA. xviii. 46. Sects: Jones, AR. ii. 334; names of week-days, Cunningham, IA. xiv. 1; Grierson, *ib.* 322; Dikshit, *ib.* xvi. 113; Wilson's Sketch of the Religious Sects of the Hindus, AR., Essays; Hunter's Statistical Account of Bengal; Kitt's Compendium of Castes and Tribes; Elphinstone's History; Müller, Chips, iv. 329; Williams, Religious Thought and Life, and Brahmanism and Hinduism; W. J. Wilkins, Modern Hinduism; Wilson, On the Sikhs, JRAS. 1846, p. 43; Prinsep, Origin of Sikh Power; MacGregor, History of Sikhs;[1] Kabīr: Trumpp, Ādigranth, JRAS. v. 197, Congress, 1880, p. 159, and Ādigranth (complete), IA. vi ff.; Die Religion der Sikhs. Vishnuism, Williams, JRAS. xiv. 289. Mohammedanism in Hinduism, Dabistān, vol. ii.[2] Ritual: Bühler, IA. 1883; temples; Hurst, Indika (especially p. 294); Burgess, IA. xii. 315; Williams, Thought and Life, p. 448 (see Buddhism). Thugs: Reynolds, JRAS. 1837, p. 200; Sherwood, AR. xiii. 25, Phānsīgars; Shakespear, *ib.* xiii. 282; also Sleeman, Report, and Ramaseeana (Thugs' Argot and papers on Thugs); Elphinstone, i. 369, 371 (Bhāts and Chārans), 384 (Thugs and Decoits). Cāitanyas, Hunter, Statistical Account, Williams and Wilkins, *loc. cit.;* On 'pocket-altars,' JRAS. 1851, p. 71; Vidhānas, Burnell, Meyer; Kānphātis, Celibates, of Kutch, JRAS. 1839, p. 268; Lingāyits, Kittel, above, and IA. iv, v; Tulsi Dās, Rāmāyaṇa, works of Ramavat sect, Grierson, IA. xxii. 89, 122,

[1] Compare also Malcolm, AR. xi (1812), 197; ZKM. v. 1, Die Religion und der Staat der Sikh.

[2] The Dabistān or School of Manners, translated from the Persian, with notes by Shea and Troyer, 1843.

227; Pandus as gods, IA, vii. 127; their fish-emblems, *ib.* xxii. 61; Bombay Dancing Girls, IA. xiii. 165; Sun-worship, temples, St. Julien, Voy. iii. 172; Burgess, Survey, p. 216; in Taxila, JRAS. 1859, p. 77: in Purāṇas, Lassen, ii. 832, 919; IA. vi. 11, vii. 69, 71, viii. 30 (ādityabhaktas). **Theistic Reformers:** Wilson, Essays; Hunter, Account; Müller, Chips; Williams, JRAS. xiii. 1, 281; Tiru Valluvar, Graul, Kural, and Pope, IA. vii ff.; Nāngi Panthīs, IA. xiii. 1; Tamil Çivaites, Foulkes, Catechism; JAOS. iv. 129: Phāndarpur Vishnuites, Viṭhṭhala Bhaktas (Kabīr), Stevenson, JRAS. 1842 p. 64; especially Mitchell, IA. xi. 56, 149, hymns of Tukā, and celebration, Congress, 1892, p. 282. **Festivals:**[1] above, Vājapeya; Hillebrandt, Sonnwendfeste; JRAS. 1846, p. 60; Gover, *ib.* v. 91; IA. xx. 430; Holi, JRAS. 1838, p. 189; 1841, p. 239; Vetāla, *ib.* 1838, p. 192; Dekhan deities, *ib.* 1842, p. 105.

WILD TRIBES.

Johnston, Yellow Men of India; Hunter, *loc. cit.;* Hewitt, Early History of Northern India (speculative), JRAS. xx. 321, etc.; Oppert, Original Inhabitants, Madras Journal, 1887, 1888; Breeks, Account of Primitive Tribes, etc. (Nilagiris, Todas); Hodgson, Aboriginal Tribes, JAS. Beng., xxv. 31; Samuelis, Native Dress and Religious Dances, *ib.* 295; Neumann, English Realm in India, ii; Latham, Ethnology of India; Macpherson, JRAS. 1842, p. 172, and 1852, p. 216 (Khonds); Briggs, Aboriginal Races, *ib.* 275; Sherring, Hindu (Bengal) Tribes; the Sacred City of the Hindus; also Bhar-tribe by the same, JRAS. v. 376; Risley, Tribes and Castes of Bengal; Rowney, Wild Tribes; Khonds, Koles,[2] Sāuras, Gonds (and Bhīls) JRAS. 1852, p. 216 (1844, p. 181); also *ib.* 1842, p. 172; Marshman, History, iii. p. 108 (Khonds); thirty Snake-tribes, JRAS. xii. 229; *ib.* 1859, p. 1,[3] Frye, Uriya and Khonds, religious dances, p. 16; creed and sacrifice, pp. 20, 36; Marshman ii. p. 164 (infanticide);

[1] Williams' Hinduism and the third chapter of Wilkins' Modern Hinduism contain a list of the modern festivals. Grierson, Peasant Life, describes Behār.

[2] Mōns and Koles, JRAS. x. 234. Lards, Congress, 1874, by Drew; 1880, by Leitner.

[3] Snake-nation in America, Shoshone, Clark, Sign-language, p. 337; snake-symbol of life, Schoolcraft, i. 375.

Kitt, Compendium of Castes and Tribes found in India; Santhāls, JRAS. 1852, p. 285; IA. xxii. 294 (emigration); Avery, Aboriginal Tribes, IA. xiv. 125; Carnegy, Races Tribes and Castes (Oude); Dalton (Bengal), Descriptive Ethnology; Social Customs in Kashmeer and Oude, IA. xviii. 287, 386; Campbell, Santāl folklore (totemistic origin from goose);[1] Korkūs, Kolarian Tribe in middle of (Dravidian) Gonds, JRAS. xvi. 164; Newbold, Chenchwars, wild tribe in forests of eastern Ghauts, JRAS. 1845, p. 271; Cain, Koi, southern tribe of Gonds, JRAS. xiii. 410 (witches, Pandus, etc.); Dunbar, Lurka Koles, JRAS., 1861, p. 370; Dravidians, Kittel, and Caldwell, *loc. cit.;* Polyandry, Thomas, JRAS. xi. 37; Simpson (rites, sacrifices, etc.), Pūjas in the Sutlej valley, JRAS. xvi. 13; Burnell, Devil-worship of Tuluvas, IA. 1894; Waddell, Frog-worship (Nepal), IA. xxii. 293; Steere, Swahili Tales, IA. *passim.*[2] A volume has lately been published on the Chittagong Hill Tribes[3] by Riebeck with superb illustrations; and photographic illustrations of racial types may be studied in Watson's and Kaye's volumes, The People of India. Discussion (biassed) of *rājputs* of Scythian origin, Elphinstone, i. 440. On Dravidian literature, see Elliot, IA. xvi. 158. On Gipsies, Grierson, *ib.* 35; etymology, *ib.* 239.

GEOGRAPHY, INDIA AND THE WEST.

Schmidt, Die Urheimath d. Indog. u. d. europäische Zahlsystem, Sitz. Berl. Akad. 1890, p. 297; Hirt,[4] Die Urheimath d. Indogermanen, IF. i. 464; Schrader, Sprachvergleichung und Urgeschichte, p. 616; Lassen, Indische Alterthumskunde, i. 643; Vivien de Saint

[1] Totemism repudiated, Kennedy, on Nāgas, JRAS. xxiii. 480.

[2] The Indian Antiquary contains a vast fund of folk-lore stories of more or less religious importance. See Barth's note, Rev. xxix. 55, for the Orientalist.

[3] Early accounts of Burmah will be found in Buchanan's Religion and Literature of the Burmas, AR. vi. 163; of the Rājmahal tribes, T. Shaw, *ib.* iv. 45; of the inhabitants of the Garrow Hills, Elliot, *ib.* iii. 17; of the Kookies, MacRae (or McRae), *ib.* vii. 183; of Nepal (temples, etc.), *ib.* ii. 307. An account of the Tibeto-Burman tribes by Damant will be found in JRAS. xii. 228.

[4] Compare a suggestive paper by the same author, IF. iv. p. 36 (1894), on Die Verwandtschaftsverhältnisse der Indogermanen (linguistic, but historically important).

Martin, Études sur la Géographie du Véda; Zimmer, Altindisches Leben, p. 3; Aufrecht, ZDMG. xiii. 498 (Rasā as Milky Way); Ludwig, Nachrichten über Geographie, etc.; Whitney, Language and the Study of Language; Oldenberg, Buddha, p. 399 (we cite from the first edition); Thomas, Rivers of the Rig Veda, JRAS. xv. 357.[1] On the relations of the **Hindus and the West**: Weber (relations with Semites), Indische Skizzen, and Die Griechen in Indien, in Sitz. Berl. Akad. 1890, p. 901; Steinthal, ZDMG. xi. 396; Grill, *ib.* xxvii. 425; Stein, IA. xvii. 89. Leo's view in regard to German-Indian unity (reviewed, ZDMG. viii. 389) is worth citing as a curiosity.[2] Brunnhofer's works have been cited above, p. 15. On the Beziehungen der Indier zum Westen a valuable article has lately been written by Franke (ZDMG. xlvii. 595). Weber, Ueber d. Pārasīprakaça d. Kṛṣṇadāsa, as well as in his Rājasūya, Vājapeya, Vedische Beiträge, etc., has treated of the relations with Persia (Fables, IS. iii. 327). In the works cited above the same author has discussed the relations with all other Western nations, including the Greeks, on which Sykes, Notes on Religious State of India, JRAS. 1841, p. 243, is readable; Bohlen, *Altes Indien*, and Lévi, La Grèce et l'Inde d'après les documents indiens (revue des études grecques, 1891) should be read.[3] The subject of **Early Christianity** in India has been treated by Burnell, IA. iii. 308, iv. 153, etc. (see also above, p. 479); while Priaulx, in JRAS. 1861, 1862, has written a series of interesting articles on **India's Connection with Rome.** The Indian travels of Apollonius of Tyana, JRAS. 1859, p. 70, etc., are of no value beside those of Ktesias and Megasthenes. The origin of the Hindu **Alphabet** and the native system of **Dates** have to do with the originality of parts of Hindu literature, but these outlying subjects, which have a literature of their own, we can only touch upon. A good *résumé* of the discussion in regard to the alphabet will be found in JRAS. xvi. 325, by Cust; a new theory of Franke's, ZDMG. xlvi.

1 Volga as 'Pâ, Ranha, Rasā, Kuhn, KZ. xxviii. 214; the Sarasvatī and the lost river, Oldham, JRAS. xxv. 49.

2 Another curiosity will be found in JRAS., 1854, p. 199, where Curzon claims that the Aryan Hindus are autochthonous.

3 Leitner, Greek Influence on India, Congress, 1880, p. 113. On the Drama see above, pp. 2 and 438.

731. Halévy derives the alphabet from Greece. But see now Bühler, Ind. Studies, iii, 1895 (North Semitic, seventh century, B.C.) The native eras are discussed by Cunningham, Book of Indian Eras; and in Müller's India, What Can It Teach Us? p. 282. On the native date for the beginning of the Kali-yuga, *i.e.* this age (the year 3101 or 3102 B.C.), JRAS. iv. 136, and Thomas, edition of Prinsep's Antiquities, may be read.[1] A general survey of primitive Aryan culture will be found in Schrader, *loc. cit.*, to which may be added on Vedic (Aryan) metres, Westphal, KZ. ix. 437; and Allen, *ib.* xxiv. 556 (style, Heinzel, Stil d. altgerm. Poesie). On the name **Ārya**, besides *loc. cit.* above, p. 25, may be added, Windisch, Beitr. z. Geschichte d. D. Sprache, iv. 211; Pott, Internat. Zt. für allgemeine Sprachwissenschaft, ii. p. 105 ff. Criticism of a too great confidence in the results of the comparative method, AJP. xv. 154; PAOS. 1895.

[1] Further, Westergaard, Ueber den ältesten Zeitraum der Indischen Geschichte; Fergusson, JRAS. xii. 259; Fleet, *samvat* for Çaka-era, JRAS., 1884, p. lxxi; Gupta, IA. xv. 189, and xvi. 141; (Bērūnī), *ib.* xvii. 243, 359; also Kielhorn, Vikrama, IA. xix. 24 ff.; xxii. 111; Bühler, WZKM. v. 215. Methods and Tables for Computing Hindu Dates, Jacobi, IA. xvii. 145; and Epigraphia Ind. I. 430. Last literature on date of Rig Veda, above, p. 5, and add now Oldenberg, ZDMG. xlviii. 629. Further references, above, pp. 436, 571, notes.

INDEX.

A (alpha), 226, 397.
abbots, 557.
abhangs, 522.
abhidhamma, 326.
Abhinavagupta, 482.
Abhīras, 543.
abīr, 454, 455.
absorption, 496.
abstractions, 112, 135.
ācāra, 554.
Achaemenides, 544.
Ādi Brāhma Samāj, 517, 519.
Ādigranth, 511 ff.
Aditi, 55, 73, 139, 142, 154.
Ādityas (see Aditi, Varuṇa, etc), 55 (Añça), 143, 167; ādityabhaktas, see sun and Sāuras.
adultery, 203.
advāita, 396, 496, 505.
Aesculapius, 538.
Afghanistan, 30, 548.
āgamas, 295, 439.
ages, 227, 259, 418 ff., 444, 530.
Aghorī, 490, 533.
Agnes, saint, 451.
Agni, 43, 101, 105 ff., 123, 144, 168, 353, 356, 377, 401, 414, 445, 449, 476, 480, 554.
ahiṁsā, 199, 287, 310, 365.
Ahura Mazdāo, 49, 67, 167, 170.
Ākāçamukhas, 486.
Akbar, 437, 546.
Akkadians, Akkadists, 542, 571.
akṣamāla (see rosary) 374.
Al Bērūnī, 547, Addenda.
Alexander, 431, 546.
Alexandria, 431, 561.
All-god, 139, 141, 496.
All-gods, 137, 144, 450.
Allah ūd dīn, 437.
alphabet, 543, 595.
altars, 475, 490.
altruism, 478, 555, 556, 563, 567.
American Indians, see Indians.
Ānanda, 309, 311; Ānanda Giri, 445, 447; Ānandatīrtha, 509.
Ananta, 397.
ancestors (see female, Manes), ten, 534.
Anaximander, 559.
ancestor-tree, 541.
Andaman gods, 538.
androgynous, 447, 492, 557.
aṅgas, 440.
Aṅgiras, 108, 167, 477.
Aṇīmāṇḍavya, 432.
Aniruddha, 441, 442, 457.
annihilation (see Nirvāṇa), 421, 531, 532.
ant-oath, 534.
Antiochus, 545.
Anugītā, 401.
Aphrodite, 471.
Apollonius, 508.
April-Fool, 455.
Apsaras, 137, 169, 355, 368.

Arabia, 547.
Āraṇyakas, 178, 219.
ardhanārīçvara, 447.
Arhat, 280, 285, 303, 320, 564.
Arjun, 511.
Arjuna, 361.
Arrian, 459.
arrow-oath, 534.
art, artists, 549.
Aryaman, 46, 121, 397.
Aryan, 11, 26, 548.
Ārya Samāj, 521.
açani, 464.
ascetics, 148, 254, 258, 304, 352 ff.; asceticism, 287, 366, 470, 520.
açoka, 540.
Açoka, 311, 340, 341, 435.
astrology, 256, 438, 543.
Asuras, 42, 49, 104, 170 ff., 186 ff., 358.
Asura Maya, 368.
Açvins, 38, 54, 78, 80, 381.
Atharva Veda, 3, 29, 43, 151, 175, 419, 477, 571.
Atharvan, 110, 378, 477.
Ātmā, 42, 47 (soul), 56, 220 ff., 232, 249, 354, 396, 398, 442.
Ātmīya Sabhā, 516.
atonement, 376.
Avadhūtas, 502.
avasthas, 412.
avatar, 162, 196, 215, 340, 389, 393, 404, 424, 430; number of, 444, 468; Vishnu's last avatar, 522.
Avesta (see Īranian), 12, 16, 422.
avyūha 442.
Ayenar, 464.
axe (see Paraçu Rāma), 527.
Aztecs, 557.

Bābālāls, 514.
Baber, 437.
Babrius, 558.
Babylon, 543.
Bacchic rites, 414, 427, 528.
Bactria, 32, 33, 434.
Bādarāyaṇa, 495, 497.
Bāla Gopāla, 503.
Balarāma, 442, 469.
bali, 540.
Bali, 478.
bamboo (see pole-rite), 536.
bandana, 533.
banian, 540.
Bardesanes, 561.
Barlaam, 557.
Basava, 482, 547.
basil, see tulasī.
Baskets, see Tripiṭaka.
Behār, 435.
bel-tree, 453, 536, 541.
bell, 557.
Bella Pennu, 530.
Bellerophon, 530.
Benares, 459.
Bhaga, 41, 50 ff.; bhaga, 490.
Bhagavad Gītā, 389 ff., 399, 400, 401, 447.
Bhagavat, 303, 389.
Bhāgavatas, 447, 497.
Bhāirava, 464, 491.
Bhāktas, 447.
bhakti (see faith), 429, 503, 519.
Bhārata, 349 ff., 438, 457.
Bhārs, 534, 535 ff.
Bhāts, 479.
Bhava, 462, 464, 548.
Bhavānī, 494.
bhikṣu, 258, 281, 303, 310, 374; bhikṣukī, 426.
Bhils, 533.
Bhṛgu, 168, 397, 423.

bicycle, used to make converts, 570.
bigotry, 445.
bila, 12.
bilva, see bel.
bird (of the sky) 45, 49, 113, 124, 140, 164; birds as spirits, 432.
birth-impurity, 541.
Birth-stories, see Jātakas.
birth-tree, 540.
Blavatskyism, 562.
Blessed One, 19, 388 ff.
blood-money, 162.
blood-revenge, 375.
bloodless sacrifice (see ahiṁsā, Thugs), 528.
boar, 404, 407, 445.
Bodhisat, bodhisattva, 303, 564.
Bodhi-tree, bo-tree, Bodhi Gayā, 304, 308, 540.
boundary-god, 529.
brahma, 156, 178, 195, 217, 220 ff., 231 ff., 381, 389, 393, ff., 398, 403, 419, 420, 474, 496, 518.
Brahmā, 195, 218, 332, 346, 372, 403 ff., 407, 412, 421, 446, 451, 458 ff., 464 ff., 487, 492, 499, 518, 534.
Brāhma Dharma, 517.
Brahmaloka, 256.
Brahmamaha, 371, 411.
Brāhmaṇas, 4, 5, 6, 22, 23, 174, 219, 502.
Brahmanism, 24, 176 ff., 548.
Brāhma Samāj, 516; of India, 519.
Brahmasampradāyins, 509.
brahmodya, 383.
branding, 440, 447.
Bṛhaspati, 54 (Lord of Strength), 101, 136, 159, 379, 386.
Bṛhat Saṁhitā, 438.
brothers, 370.
Buddha, 258, 280, 303 ff., 426; precedent Buddhas, 309, 523, 557; avatar of Vishnu, 469, 500; brother of Çiva, 478.
Buddhaghoṣa, 327, 343.
Buddhism, 4, 5, 6, 7, 26, 225, 298 ff., 310, 401, 448; Northern and Southern, 326, 327, 341; esoteric, 320, 334; epic, 423 ff.; Çivaite, 485, 486; morals of, 554, 556; Occidental, 563; lesson of, 564.
Budo Gosain, 533.
buffalo (see cow-bells), 445, 531, 537.
bull, 407, 445, 528, 534.
bull-roarer, 204, 553.
burial, 60, 271, 364, 528, 534, 571.
buttoat, 493.

Calvinism, 501.
Candragupta, 311, 434.
Candraçekhara, 470.
caraṇa, 255.
Cāraṇas, 367.
Caran Dāsīs, 506.
Cardinals, 557.
Carnival, 455.
Cārvāka, 298, 374, 448.
castes, 27, 28, 29, 40, 141, 226, 263, 426, 507, 571; duties and occupations of, 549.
cat, holy, 547.
cat-doctrine, 500.
cataclysms, 259, 260.
cattle (see cow), 50, 462 ff., 450.
caturmūrti, 413.
caturthī, 451.
caturvyūha, 442.
celibates (see monks), 537.
Ceylon, Buddhism of, 341.
Cāitanya, 503.

čhandas, 142, 174, 477.
Chārans, 479.
chief, divinity of, 534.
child-marriages, 519.
children, sacrifice of (see merias), 450.
Chīrus, 535.
choirs, 557.
chrematheism, 135, 166.
Christ, Christianity, 389, 395, 428 ff., 431, 479, 482, 503, 524, 545, 566, 569, 570; and Buddhism, 546, 557.
Christmas, 430, 568.
churikā, 441.
circumambulations, 271, 454.
Citragupta, 424.
Clive, 566.
cock, 415, 535, 538.
commandments (see morals), 267, 317, 401, 479, 506.
confessional, 203, 373, 557.
cosmic tree, see tree.
courage, 527.
covenants, 192, 361 ff.
cow, 156, 189, 527, 547.
cow-bells, worship of buffalo cow-bells, 537.
cow-boys, 454.
creation, 60, 141, 173, 207 ff., 216, 540.
creator, 384, 444.
crocodile, 450, 547.
cross, 537.
Cupid, see Love.
custom, 531, 554.

Dabistān, 480, 510.
Dādū Panthīs, 480, 502, 510, 513, 547.
daevas, 10, 168.
Dakṣa, 406.
Dānavas, see devils.
dance, 443, 454, 456, 504, 535.
Darius, 544.
darkness (as hell and evil), 147, 206, 227, 422.
Daçanāmis, 482.
Daçapeya, 477.
Dasyus, 524, 542.
dates, 3–8, 434 ff., 571, 595, note.
Dattāmitra, 545.
Dawn (see Ushas), hymns, character of, 553, 571.
Dayānanda, 521.
Death (see dogs, Māra), 43, 129, 136.
Debendranāth, 516 ff.
Decoits, 494.
Dedrāj, 514.
deism, 498, 515, 523.
deluge, 160, 162, 214, 369, 421, 542, 543.
demons, see devils.
demonology, 46, 135, 168, 538.
Demetrius, 545.
depressed classes, 568.
devas, 10, 168.
Devadatta, 309.
Devakī, 465, 467.
devils, 368, 414, 423, 475, 526, 539.
Dhammapada, 346.
dhan, 508.
Dhangars, 531.
Dharma, dharma (see Path, Right), 249 ff., 358, 373, 380, 417, 420, 554.
dharna, 361.
Dhavā, 452.
Dhṛti, 452.
dhvaja, 443.
Digambaras, 284 ff., 480.

Dionysos, 458 ff.
Dīpālā, 456.
discus, 440, 462.
disease (see small-pox god), 452 ff., 538.
divination, 535.
dogs of Death, 132, 138, 147, 163.
Dolā Yātrā, dolotsava, 453 ff.
dolmen, 538.
dolphin, 450.
dragon (see Nāga, snake), 42, 48, 165, 539.
drama, 2, 436, 438.
Dravidian religion, 416, 425, 426 ff., 542.
dreams, 42.
drughaṇa, 441.
Druids, 533.
drunkenness, 491.
dualism (see prakṛti, Sāṅkhya), 13, 396, 414.
Durgā, 416, 451, 456, 490, 492, 513.
dūrvā, 502.
Dutch rule in India, 566.
dvāpara, 420.
Dyāus, 9, 19 (heaven), 58, 172, 571.

eagle (see soma), 534.
Earth, 58 ff., 168, 445; earth-worshippers, 480, 531.
Easter, 454.
education, salvation of, 571.
egg, mundane, 166, 208, 411.
Egypt, 543, 550.
ekāntinas, 413; eka deva, 420.
Eleatics, 559.
elements, 1, 559.
elephant, 445, 533.
eleocarpus ganitrus, 502.
emperors, imperialism, 36, 435 ff.
English rule in India, 566.
ensigns, 539.
epic, 2, 25, 348 ff., 425, 444, 496; Greek influence on, 545.
Epicureans, 505.
eras, 436.
Eros, see Love.
eschatology (see Heaven, Hell, Manes), 173, 204, 216, 253, 367, 394, 496, 530.
ethnologists, 11.
euphemism, 251.
Europe and India, 556 ff.
evil eye, 155, 526, 589, note 3.
exogamy (see marriage), 534, 535.

fables, 545, 558.
faith, bhakti, 396, 506, 507, 545.
fakirs, 486.
family, see matriarchy.
fasting, 452, 557.
fate (see karma), 369, 417, 477.
Father-god, see Prajāpati; Fathers, see Manes; father (see parents), 529.
fauna, 35.
fees, 192.
female (see abstractions, infanticide, mothers, çakti), divinities, 51, 138, 184, 416; female ancestors, 441, 534.
Feridun, 11.
festivals, 202, 448.
fetishism, 169, 363; distinction between fetish and god-stone, 538.
fire (see Agni), as germ of life, 141; fire-cult, 158, 378; destroys world, see Saṁvartaka; cult, 454, 460, 491.
flood, see deluge.
flowers, 440, 540, 557.
forest (see wood), 528.

fountain-god, 531.
free-will, 384.
frogs, 14, 100 ff.; frog-maiden, frog-feast, 536.
funeral, see burial.

gambler, 14, 162, 376.
games, 328, 451.
Gandharva, 125, 130, 167, 367, 419, 442, 542.
Gan-eden, 542.
Gaṇeça, 414, 416, 447, 450 ff., 456, 466, 487, 506, 532.
Gāṇeças, 413.
Ganges, 30, 372 ff., 450.
Garos, 534.
Garutman, Garuḍa, 45, 360, 378, 446.
Gāurī, 452.
Gautama, 302 ff.; Gotama, 308, note; 542.
gāyatrī, 46, 124.
generosity, 374.
geography, 28, 29, 177, 193, 314, 342 ff.
Ghori, 437.
ghosts, 532.
giants, 470, 571.
Giriça, 463.
gītā, see Bhagavad.
Gīta Govinda, 457, 503.
Gnosticism, 560.
gods (see devas), 29, 90, 141, 182, 209, 395, 402.
golden age, see ages.
golden germ, 141, 208, 507.
golden rule, 479.
Gonds, 444, 526 ff.
goose-totem, 534.
gopīs, 456.
Gorakhnāth, 486.
gosain, 504.
Gosāla, 283.
gospels, 546.
Gotama, see Gautama.
Govind, 511.
grace of God, 143, 384, 393, 396, 413, 429.
grahas (see planets), 415.
grāmas, 27.
Greece, Greeks, 1, 3, 6, 416, 431, 434 ff., 458 ff., 470, 471, 544 ff., 550.
Grippa Valli, 530.
Gūḍaras, 487.
guest, 369, 531.
guṇas, 507.
Gupta era, 436, Addenda.
guru, 246, 510.

Hanuman (see monkey), 368, 502.
haoma, 16.
Hara, 462.
Harahvati, 31.
Harihara, 464, 547.
Harivañça, 424, 428, 439, 464, 467.
Hārīta, 440.
Hartmann, 562.
Harvard students, 565.
harvest (see festival), 531, 532.
Hastings, 567.
Heathen, 524.
Heaven (see Dyāus, Varuṇa, eschatology), 48, 143, 145 ff., 253, 365, 417, 448.
Helen, 12, 168.
Hell, 147, 165, 206, 232 ff., 253, 267, 336, 363, 381, 402, 443, 478, 528, 557.
henotheism, 139, 177, 571.
Herakles, 458 ff., 470.
Heraklitus, 558.

Hestia, 530.
hills, see mountains and wild tribes.
Hinduism, 24, 348 ff., 434 ff., 548, 568 ff.
Hindukush, 31.
Hiraṇyagarbha (see golden germ), 447.
history, 434.
holiness, 442.
Holī, 453.
holy-days, 204, 248 ff.
holy-places, 444.
holy-stone, see Çālagrāma and stone.
holy-water, 557.
horse-sacrifice, 444.
honesty, 527, 555.
hospitality (see guest), 555, 556.
house-god, 374, 530.
Hṛṣīkeça, 432.
humanitarianism, 428.
humanity, 433.

idealism, see advāita.
idolatry, modern, 522.
idols, 95, 370, 371, 374, 442, 446, 477, 537, 556 ff.
Ilium, 12.
illusion, 395, 396, 401, 421, 497.
immaculate conception, 431, 460.
immortality (see Heaven), 141, 396, 422 ; immortality of pots, 534.
incantation (see magic), 470.
incarnation, see avatar.
incēst (see commandments, left-hand), 531.
Indians, 161 ff., 452, 532, 533, 542.
Indra, 10, 20, 39, 56, 57, 89, 91 ff., 101, 123, 332, 353, 355 ff., 369, 377, 404, 405, 412, 414, 445, 448, 449, 473 ff.
Indramaha, 378, 457, 460.
Indus, 30.
infanticide, 529, 531.
infidelity, 448, 475.
Innocents' day, 455.
inspiration, 305.
Iranians, 6, 15, 26, 32 ff., 67, 132, 168, 170, 186, 422, 543.
Īça, 546.
islands, 431.
Issa, 546.
Itihāsa, 434, 477.

Jagannāth, 440, 449, 456, 505.
Jāimini, 495.
Jainism, 280, 318, 348, 401, 448, 480.
Jamāli, 283.
Jāmbavan, 368.
janas, 26, 27.
Jangamas, 447, 482.
Janmāṣṭamī, 465, 469.
Jātakas, 339 ff., 393, 430, 558.
Jātavedas, 416.
Jayadeva, 503.
Jayī, 494.
Jemidar, 493.
Jemshid, 11.
Jews, 524, 544.
jīva, 442, 496.
Jñāndev, 522.
Jñātriputra, 292.
John, saint, 558.
Jonas, story of, 547.
Josaphat, 557.
Judgment-god (see Dharma), 529, 531.
Juggernaut, see Jagannāth.
jugglers, see Yogi.
Justice, see Dharma.

Ka, 182, 413.
Kabīr (Panthīs), 502, 510, 514, 547.
Kabul, Kabulistan, 30.
kalā, 501.

Kāla, see Time.
kali, 421.
Kālī, 416, 438, 441, 490, 492, 533.
Kālidāsa, 438.
Kalki, 340, 469.
kalpa, see ages.
Kāma, see Love.
Kaṇāda, 503.
Kānaphāts, 486, 487.
Kāñculiyas, 492.
Kaniṣka, 435, 436.
Kāpālikas, 487.
kapi, 543.
Kapila, 397, 402, 495, 547.
Kapilavastu, 300.
karma, 199, 231, 253, 302, 319, 369, 374, 401.
Karmahīnas, 447.
Karmamīmāṅsā, 495.
Kartābhājs, 504.
Kārttikeya, see Skanda.
Kāçyapa, 503.
Kashmeer, 31, 314, 482.
Kassos, 534.
Katties, 537.
Khākis, 502.
Khālsā, 512.
Khasas, Khāsīas, 537.
Khonds, 445, 526, 528 ff.
Kīl, 502.
kindness (see love), 448.
kings, 226, 465.
Kinnaras, 367.
kirttan, kīrtan, 508.
Koches, 525.
Koles, Kolarians, 525, 531, 532 ff.
koph, 543.
Kosmas, 544.
Krishna (kṛṣṇa), 349, 361, 388 ff., 399, 401, 405, 411, 412, 429, 448, 449, 456, 457, 465, 498, 548, 551.
Krishnaism, 427, 464, 484 ff., 548.
Krishnaites, 503 ff.
kṛta, 419.
Kṣapanakas, 448.
Kṣatriya, 419.
Kṣemendra, 478.
Kubera, 251, 353, 358, 446.
kukkuṭa, see cock.
Kumāra Kārttikeya (see Skanda), 356, 463.
Kumārila, 436, 437, 572.
Kural, 567.
Kurus, 32, 179.
Kurukṣetra, 33, 263, 372 ff.
kush, 542.

Lakṣmī, 451, 492, 501, 506.
Lalita Vistara, 343.
Lamaism, 343, 557, 565.
Lamp-festival, 456; service, 557.
Law-books, religion of, 247 ff.; Aryanism of, 541.
Left-hand cult, 490, 506, 533.
lex talionis, 555.
liberality of thought, 556.
light, as right, 422.
liṅga (see phallus), 447, 453, 456, 462, 475, 488, 502.
Liṅgāyits, 482.
liquor, 491, 531.
literature, celebration of, 451.
Logos, Vāc, 142, 195, 251, 492, 558.
Lohitāyanī, 415.
lotus, 411, 451, 462, 502.
Lotus of the Law, 343.
Love, 154; love-charm, 155; love as god, 156, 416, 444, 445, 446, 450, 452, 455, 471, 544.
lundi, 528.
Lupercalia, 455.
Lurka Koles, 531, 534.

Mādhava Ācārya, 445.
Mādhvas, 502, 506, 509, 514.
Madonna-worship, 469, 503, 505, 506, 557.
Māgadha, 435.
Magas, Magi, 544.
magic, witchcraft, 135, 137, 149, 151 ff., 477, 526.
Mahādeva, 464, ; mahādevī, 490.
Mahābhārata, see Bhārata.
Mahārājas, 505.
māhāris, 534.
mahātmaism, 486, 550, 562.
Mahāvīra, 280 ff.
Maheçvaras, 482.
Mahmud, 436.
Mahrattas, 437.
Māitreya, Māitrakanyaka, 340, 479.
makara, 450.
Man, 508, worshippers of, 481.
Manes (see Çrāddha), 10, 11, 132, 143 ff., 155, 173, 190, 250, 361, 364, 365, 446, 450, 452, 529, 530, 532, 533, 537.
Man-lion, 453, 470.
mantra, 174, 374, 440, 453, 491, 508.
Manu, 32, 128, 143, 169, 392; code of, 263 ff., 391, 397, 399, 401; verse attributed to, 487.
manvantara, 439.
Māra, 304, 346.
mārjāra nyāya, 501.
markaṭa nyāya, 501.
marriage-rites, 270, 421, 533.
marriage-tree, 541.
Maruts, 8, 56, 97 ff.
Mather, Cotton, 565.
matriarchy, 441, 541.
matter (see prakṛti), 400.
Māyā, see illusion.
May-day, 453.
meat-eating (see ahiṁsā), 365, 368.
medhā, 452.
Megasthenes, 1, 458 ff.
Menandros, 545.
merias, 529.
metals, 35.
metempsychosis, 175, 199, 204, 286, 302, 347, 364, 401, 532, 533, 559; in the Veda, 145, 432, 530.
methods of interpretation, 8, 12 ff., 22, 551.
Mihira, see Mithra.
Milinda, 545.
Mīmāṁsā, 495.
miracles, 430.
missionaries, 566 ff.
Mitra (see Varuṇa), 41, 44, 57, 60, 71, 138; mitra, mihira, 423, 544.
Mohammedans, 436 ff., 482, 509, 524, 546 ff.
monks (see ascetic, bhikṣu, Sannyāsin), 285, 324; monasticism, 502, 557.
monkey (see Hanuman), 448, 452, 502, 547; monkey-doctrine, 500.
monolith, worship of, 538.
monotheism, 11, 13, 67, 70, 139, 172, 413, 414, 427, 432, 442, 481, 483, 509, 547.
monsoon, 35.
moon (see eschatology, Gandharva, Soma), 185, 470, 480, 526, 533.
morals (see commandments, sin), 14, 143, 180, 203, 353, 375, 401, 443, 553, 570.
mother-divinities, 415, 492; motherhoods, 534.
mountains, divine, 137, 359, 416, 461, 463, 528, 532, 537.
mouse, 532.
Mozoomdar, 519.

muni, 148, 520.
Munroe, Major, 566.
murder, 179, 475, 527.
music, 443.
Mūṣikas, 532.
mysticism (see Yoga), 504.

Nāgas (see dragon, snake), 536, 539.
Nāgārjuna, 340, 343.
Nakhīs, 486.
name of the Lord, call upon, 507.
names, 201.
Nānak, 502, 511 ff., 547.
Nāṅgi Panthis, 514.
Nara, Nārāyaṇa, 412, 448; Svāmi Nārayaṇa, 506, 514.
Nature, 397.
nautch, 454.
Neo-Platonism, 558, 560.
New Year's festival, 449, 456.
Niadis, 537.
nidānas, chain of causality, 323.
Night, 48, 76, 79.
Nikāya, 326.
Nimbāditya, 508.
Nirgrantha, 283.
Nirmalas, 513.
Nirvāṇa, 286, 310, 319, 321 ff., 336, 346, 347, 426 ff.
Niṣads, 440.
non-duality, see advāita.
Notovitch, 546.
numbers, 478.
nuns, 290, 310, 330, 557.
nymphs, in heaven, 417.
Nysian, 458.

oath (see ordeals), of king, 213; may be broken, 255; water in oath, 362; other forms of oath, 533, 534.

observances, 246.
oceans, 34.
offerings, 183.
Om, 395, 453.
Omens (see magic), 256, 328.
ophir, 543.
oracles, 533, 534.
Orāons, 526, 531, 535.
ordeals, 3, 270, 275, 363.
orders, political, priestly stadia, 264, 353, 365.
orthodoxy, 507, 562.

pacceka, 305.
Pāhārias, 533.
pairs of gods, 83, 102, 138, 462.
palm, 540.
palmistry (see omens), 256.
Pāñcajanya fire, 423.
Pañcakāla, Pañcakālajñas, 413.
Pañcamahākalpa, 413.
Pañcatantra, 558.
Pāñcarātra, 413, 427, 442, 447, 492, 497.
Pāṇḍavas, 466, 469.
Pāṇḍurāṅga, 500.
pantheism (see Kṛṣṇa, Rāma, Viṣṇu), 37, 47, 57, 138, 140, 248, 356, 407, 414, 484 ff., 498, 547.
Paradise, see Heaven.
Paraçu Rāma, 469.
parents, 370.
parimara, 227, 229, 232.
Parjanya, 100 ff., 369, 378.
Parmenides, 559.
parrot, 445, 450.
Pārvatī, (goddess) 'of mountains,' 416.
Paçupati, 413, 462, 463.
Pāçupatas, 447, 482, 509
Pātaliputta, 311.

Patañjali, 495.
Path, holy, 305 ff., 401, 426.
peacock, 445, 450, 528, 536.
Persian, see Darius, Iranian.
pessimism, 306, 314, 316 ff.
phallus (see liṅga), 150, 414, 443, 470, 471, 528, 544.
Phānsīgars, 494.
Philo, 558.
philosophy (see Sāṅkhya, Vedānta), 141, 495.
Phoenicia, 543.
picture-worship, 374, 557.
pipal-tree, see bo-tree.
Piçācas (see devils), 415.
planets, 367, 415, 545.
plants, worship of (see trees), 540; plant-souls, see metempsychosis.
Plato, 2, 559.
Plotinus, 561.
pocket-altars, 475.
pole-rite, 378, 443, 534.
political divisions, 26, 27.
polyandry, 467, 535.
polygamy, 533.
polytheism, 11, 13, 529, 547.
Pongol, 449, 528.
pools, 254, 370, 372, 404, 444, 478.
pope, 557.
Porphyry, 561.
Portuguese rule in India, 566.
Prabhā, 452.
Pradyumna, 441, 442.
Prahlāda, 397.
Prajāpati, 142, 182 ff., 196 ff., 404, 412, 475, 492, 554.
prakṛti, 396, 397, 399, 507.
prasāda (see grace) 429.
prayāga, 435.
Prem Sāgar, 567.
priest, 28, 29, 40, 176, 179, 370; privileges of, 263, 549; epic priest, 352.
Prçni, 97.
Prometheus, 107, 168.
Punjāb, 30, 33, 34.
Purāṇas, 2, 3, 424, 430, 434 ff., 476, 503.
Puranic Sānkhya, 495.
purity, 148, 369.
purgatory, 557.
Purusa, 142, 397, 447.
Pūrvamīmāṁsā, 495.
Pūṣan, 5, 41, 47, 50 ff., 80, 101, 463, 464, 475.
Puṣkara, 372.
Puṣṭi, 452.
Pūtanā, 444.
pūtika, 369.
Pythagoras, 209, 559 ff., 580, note 3.

quakerism, 567.
quietism (see Yoga), 567.

Rādhā, Rādhā Vallabhis, 492, 506.
Rāhu, 367.
rain-gods, 99, 528.
rajas, 507.
Rājasūya, 444, 448, 477.
Rākṣas (see devils), 419.
ram, 445.
Rāma, 349, 397, 498.
Rāmacandra, 454, 506.
Ramaism, 315, 349, 427, 485, 500 ff.
Rāmānand, 502, 510, 513.
Rāmānuja, 447, 482, 496 ff., 505, 507.
Rāmāyaṇa, 349 ff.
Ramcaritmanas, 503.
Rāmmohun Roy, 515.
Rasā (Volga, 26), 30, 169.
Rās Dāsas, 502.

Rās Yātrā, 456, 505.
Rath Yātrā, 456.
Rati, 452.
Rāudras, 447.
Rāvaṇa, 470.
redemption, doctrine of, 569.
reformation of sects, 508, 522,
relics, 556.
remnant-worship, 151, 157.
Renaissance, 2, 438.
renunciation (see Yogi, Sannyāsi), 394.
responsibility, moral, 380.
Ribhus (Ṛbhavas), 93, 123, 169, 382.
Right (see Dharma), 249, 422, 442, 554.
Right-hand cult, 490.
Rig Veda (ṛg), 3, 5, 7, 9, 10 ff., 22, 29, 37 ff., 44; in epic, 360, 419.
Rishis (Ṛṣis), see Seers.
ritual, 12 ff., 16 ff., 106, 124, 175.
ritualism, 568.
rivers, divine, 30 ff., 32, 99, 138, 528, 537.
Romans, 6, 556.
rosary, 374, 413, 478, 502, 557.
rosy, 493.
Rudra (see Çatarudriya, Çiva), 50, 54, 97, 99, 379, 388, 406; Rudra-Çiva, 458 ff.; Rudrajapas, 463.
rudrākṣa, 502.

sacraments, forty, 255.
sacrifice, 47, 60, 149, 177 ff., 188, 196, 198, 211, 225, 246, 363, 369, 375, 406, 413, 420, 423, 450, 462, 471, 490 ff., 526, 528, 529, 534, 571.
Sādhus, 514.
Çāivas (see Çivaites), 413.
Çaka era, 436.
Sakhī bhāvas, 492.
Çāktas, 413, 489, 533.
çakti, 489, 490, 537, 553.
Çakuntalā, 438.
Çākya, 300, 302.
çālagrāma, holy stone, 447, 502, 540.
sallo kallo, 531.
Samājas, 516 ff., 569, 570.
Sāma Veda, 176, 389, 396, 419.
Samana, 302, 344.
Çambhu, 487.
Çamī, çamī-plant, 540.
saṁvartaka fire, 421.
saṁsāra, 175, 199, 231, 253, 380, 425.
saṁskṛta, 396.
saṁvat, 436.
Sanatkumāra, 466.
Çāṇḍilya, 221, 497, 509; sūtras, 503.
Sandrocottos, 435.
Saṅgha, 324, 341.
Çaṅkara, 289, 437, 445; vijaya, 480; 482, 495, 505, 506.
Sāṅkhya, 323, 365, 391 ff., 396, 399, 400, 402, 460, 482, 484, 489, 495, 509, 547, 560.
Sannyāsin, 258, 281, 508.
Saraṇyū, 81, 138.
Saramā, Sārameya, 131, 132, 138.
Sarasvatī, 31 ff., 149, 451, 492.
Çārīrakamīmāṁsā, 495.
Çarva, 462, 463, 548.
Sarvadarçaṇasangraha, 480.
Çatarudriya, 413, 470.
Sat nām, 512.
sattra, 371, 420.
sattva, 507.
Saturnalia, 455.
Sāubhagasena, 545.
Sāugatas, 448, 567.

Sāuras, 413, 423, 508.
Savāras, Sauras, 535.
Savitar (see Sun), 41 ff., 46 ff.
Sāvitrī, 46, 466, 492.
Sāyaṇa, 480.
Schopenhauer, 561.
sects, 445.
Seers, 368.
Semiramis, 543.
Semites, 571.
Sen, 518.
sesamum, 452, 502.
Çesa, 446, 465.
seven, 18, 26, 32, 49, 64, 98, 162, 533.
Seypoys, 566.
sex, 43, 59, 183, 490.
Siddhas, 367, 397, 482.
Sikhs (Singhs, Siṁhas), 8, 502, 510–513.
sin (see commandments, vows), 42, 47, 51, 60, 65, 329, 376, 392, 530, 554; venial, 254; sin and sacrifice, 526.
siṅgā-tree, 533.
Çiçupāla, 457.
Sittars, 315, 367, 482, 488, 567, 570.
Çiva, 25, 50, 99, 112, 150, 178, 251, 332, 354, 365, 374, 388 ff., 397, 404, 406, 412 ff., 487, 532, 534.
Çivaism (see Çāivas), 348, 389, 407, 413, 423, 427, 446, 451, 453, 466, 480, 484, 488, 496, 548; sacrifice of, 371, 453, 459, 462, 492.
Çivaites, 481 ff., 483.
Skanda (Kārttikeya), 354, 410, 414, 445, 466.
slaves, 29, 425, 477, 548, 549.
small-pox god, 452, 528.
Smārtas, 482, 507.
Smṛti, 440.
snake (see dragon, Nāga), 20, 94, 154, 164, 186, 344, 361, 376, 397, 419, 446, 469, 527, 533, 536, 539, 547.
sociological data, 27, 60, 524 ff.
solar myths, 11.
Soma, 14, 16, 42, 50, 112 ff., 185, 354, 369, 378, 477, 491, 531, 540, 571.
Somānanda, 482.
son, importance of, 148, 363.
sophistry, 383.
sorcery, see magic.
soul (see ātmā, jīva), 530.
sources, 3.
spirit (see ātmā), 400, 442.
spring, god of, 528.
spring-festival, 449, 452, 456.
Çrāddha (see Manes), 451, 453, 455.
Çramaṇa, 281, 292, 302.
çravaka, 303.
Çrī, 438, 441, 451, 492.
Çrīraṅga, 456.
Çruti, 245 ff., 373, 378.
star-souls, 204, 366, 446.
star-worshippers, 480, 526, 533.
Stoics, 558, 563.
stone, worship of (see çālagrāma), 526, 533, 538; marriage-stone, 271, 535.
straw (victim), 526.
stūpas, 556.
Subrahmaṇya, 466.
Çūdra (see slave), 419; Sūdroi, 548.
suicide, 378.
Sūkharas, 487.
Çulvasūtra, 560.
Sun, 17, 39, 40 ff., 47, 51, 56, 57, 82, 164, 205, 354, 377, 401, 402, 446, 449, 452, 460, 492, 508, 509, 526, 528, 530, 532, 534, 543 ff.

Sunday, 452.
Sunthāls, 532.
Çūnyavāds, 448.
surā, 127.
Sūryā (see Sun), 51, 82, 449, 492.
Sutta, 326.
suttee, 165, 274, 369, 441.
Sūtras, 3, 4, 5, 7, 174, 245 ff.
Svāmi, see Nārāyaṇa.
svastivācanam, 371.
Çvetāmbaras, 284 ff., 480.
swing, see Dōlā.

tabū, 251, 535.
tamas (see darkness), 507.
Tamerlane, 436.
Tamil, poetry, 315; religion, 524.
tan, 508.
Tantras, 2, 439, 476, 491.
tapas (see asceticism), 520.
Tari, 528, 530.
Tathāgata, 303.
temples, 428, 444, 447, 452, 456, 471, 526, 557; snake-temple, 539.
Ten-galais, 501.
ṭhaks, 535.
Ṭhākurāṇī, 535.
Thales, 559.
theft (see commandments, morals), 527, 554.
theosophy, 40, 112, 384.
thieves, god of, 554.
Thomas, church of, 479.
three, 42, 49, 110, 164.
Time, see fate.
Thugs, 492 ff., 528, 535.
thunder-worship, 536.
tiger, 533.
tillais, 494.
tīrtha, see pools.
Tiru-valluvar, 567.
Todas, 526, 537.
tonsure, 557.
tortoise (see avatar), 536.
totem, totemism, 163, 430, 445, 464, 468, 532, 534, 537, 557.
traga, 479.
trāipuruṣa, 464.
transmigration, see metempsychosis.
transubstantiation, 557.
trees, worship of, 35, 154, 470, 528, 533, 540; tree of creation, 540, 542.
tretā, 420.
triad, 42, 46, 183, 377, 404, 460.
tribes, 26 ff.
Tridaṇḍis, 482.
trimūrti (see trinity), 447, 464.
trinity (see triad, trimūrti, trāipuruṣa), 57, 105, 237, 387, 404, 410, 411, 412, 432, 439, 507, 516, 545; four members, 445; prayer to, 447; history of, 457 ff.; female, 492, 499.
Tripiṭaka, 326, 347.
Tripūjas, 480.
Trita, 11, 45, 104, 431.
Troy, story of, 547.
truth, 203, 369, 381, 527, 533, 553.
Tukārām, 522.
tulasī, 456, 502, 540.
Tulasīdāsa, 503.
Turanian, 15, 435.
Tuṣṭi, 452.
tutelary gods, 530.

Udāsis, 513.
Ugras, 447.
Ūkharas, 487.
Umā, 416, 460, 490, 492.
Unitarians, 413, 485, 547.
Upāṅgas, 440.

Upaniṣads, 3, 4, 5, 7, 24, 181, 216 ff., 389, 399, 405, 434, 447, 518.
Upapurāṇas, 440.
upāsaka, 310.
Upendra, 409.
Ūrdhvabāhus, 486.
Uçanas, see Bṛhaspati.
Ushas (Uṣas), Dawn, 9, 10, 19, 73 ff.
Uttaramīmāṁsā, 495.

Vāc, see Logos.
Vada-galais, 501.
Vāikhānasas, 447.
Vāirāgins, 508.
Vāiçeṣika, 503.
Vāiṣṇava, 371, 413.
Vāiçvānara (see Agni), 507.
Vāiçya, 419, 487, 525.
Vala, 20.
Valabhī era, 436, 572.
Valentine, saint, 451.
Vallabhas, 504–508.
Vālmīki, 503.
Varāhamihira, 438.
Varuṇa, 18, 41, 42, 44, 47, 58, 61 ff., 138, 170, 196, 353, 354, 397, 448, 539, 554; as the moon, 571.
vasanta, see spring-festival.
Vāstoṣpati, 530.
vassallus, vassus, 530.
vasso, 292.
Vāsuki, 397.
Vāta, Vāyu, see Wind-god.
Veda, 12, 15 ff., 142, 174, 188, 222, 256, 374, 401, 420, 425, 510.
Vedānta, 143, 228, 264, 365, 396, 398 ff., 416, 460, 484, 495 ff.; sūtra, 437.
'Vehicles,' 340.
vermilion, 532.
Vesta, 530.
Vetāla, 537.
Vidyādharas, 367.
Vighneça, 488.
vihāra, 435.
Vikramāditya, 436.
village-tree, 540.
Vinaya, 326.
Vīrabhadra, 467.
Virāj, 507.
Virgin-worship, 557.
virtue (see commandments, dharma, morals), ideals of, 555.
viças, 27, 194.
Viçākha, 466.
Vishnu (Viṣṇu), 41, 52, 56, 112, 144, 178, 251, 332, 354, 365, 388 ff., 412 ff., 451 ff.; feast of, 456; 460, 487, 492, 498, 508, 534.
Vishnuism, 143, 348, 389, 413, 446, 464, 480, 494 ff.
Vishnu's law-book, 441.
Viçvāmitra, 27.
Viṭhṭhala, 500, 508, 514, 522.
Vivasvant, 81, 128 ff., 146, 392.
void, see Çūnya.
Volga, see Rasā.
vows, 293, 317, 378.
Vṛṣabha, 482.
Vrātya-hymns, 179.
Vritra (Vṛtra), 20, 120, 185, 357, 369.
Vyāsa, 488, 495.

warriors, 28, 29, 419.
water (origin of all things), 48, 107, 141, 330, 362, 378.
waters, 99.
water-pot, 453.
water-worshippers, 480.
wealth (see Bhaga), 528.

White Island, 413, 426 ff., 431, 545.
wife, see woman.
wild-tribes, 471, 490, 493, 524 ff., 569.
wind-god, 87 ff., 123, 165, 354, 460; worshippers, 480.
witchcraft, see magic.
witness (see oath), 250.
women (authors of Rig Veda), 27; burned, see suttee; as nuns, 291, 310; religion of, 370; use mantra, 440, 450, 453; price of wife, 270, 535.
wood, see trees.
wood-goddess, 138, 530.
worlds, number of, 402.
writing, 4, 7, 331, 544, 595.
Yajur Veda, 24, 176 ff., 419.
Yakṣas, 415.
Yama (see Citragupta, Hell), 16, 45, 49, 128 ff., 144, 146, 353, 365, 378 ff., 397, 451, 480, 540.
Yima, 11, 16, 128 ff.
Yoga, yogin or yogi, 262, 281, 304, 351, 391 ff., 399, 402, 470, 486, 495, 550.
yoni, vulva, 475, 490.
yuga, see ages.

Zarathustra, Zoroaster (see Iranian), 10, 72, 524.
Zeus, 9, 66.
Ziegenbalg, 565.
zoölatry, 547.